A Forest Beat

The Police Officer

I have been where you fear to be
I have seen what you fear to see
I have done what you fear to do
All these things have I done for you

I am the one you lean upon
The one you cast your scorn upon
The one you bring your troubles to
All of these I've been to you

The one you ask to stand apart
The one you feel should have no heart
The one you call the one in blue
But I'm a person just like you

And when you watch a person die
And hear a battered baby cry
Then do you think that you could be
All these things you ask of me?

Anon

KILLED IN THE LINE OF DUTY

PS SAMUEL BEARD
17/8/1861. Bludgeoned while checking suspects.

PS WILLIAM MORRIS
10/11/1895. Bludgeoned attempting arrest.

PC ERNEST ALBERT COOPER
8/11/1916. Road Traffic Accident.

SC RONALD W. SMITH
19/8/1940. Shot.

PC PAUL J. PURSEHOUSE
15/3/1967. Road Traffic Accident.

A Forest Beat

THE FOREST OF DEAN POLICE
1839 – 2000

Geoff Sindrey & Ted Heath

Black Dwarf Publications

> Dedicated to all members
> of the Gloucestershire Constabulary
> who have served in the Forest of Dean

*Whilst every effort has been made to check facts and report them accurately,
the authors and publisher disclaim liability for any inaccuracy.*

Copyright: Black Dwarf Publications, Geoff Sindrey and Ted Heath 2000
Designed by Neil Parkhouse

British Library Cataloguing-in-Publication Data. A catlogue
record for this book is available from the British Library
ISBN 0 9533028 7 3

All rights reserved. No part of this publication may be reproduced, stored in a retrieval system or transmitted in any form or by any means, electronic, mechanical, photocopying, recording or otherwise, without the written permission of the publisher.

**Black Dwarf Publications
47 – 49 High Street, Lydney, Gloucestershire GL15 5DD**

*Page make-up by
Artytype, 5 The Marina, Harbour Road, Lydney, Gloucestershire GL15 4ET
Printed by APB Colourprint Bristol*

Contents

About the authors . . . 6
Preface . . . 7

Part One
A Potted History of the Forest of Dean Police

Introduction . . . 9
The Early Days . . . 9
Consolidation and Modernisation . . . 16
Violent Times . . . 17
National Strikes . . . 19
Expansion, Rationalisation and Two World Wars . . . 22
More Modernisation and Rationalisation . . . 30
Conditions of Service . . . 33
Away Days . . . 34
Sport . . . 35
Tales From the River Bank . . 40
Changing Times . . . 42
Summary . . . 48

Part Two
Around the Forest of Dean

Ashleworth . . . 51 Blakeney . . . 53 Bream . . . 57
Churcham . . . 61 Cinderford . . . 62 Clearwell . . . 69
Coleford . . . 70 Drybrook . . . 85 Dymock . . . 88
Hartpury . . . 89 Hewelsfield . . . 90 High Beech . . . 90
Huntley . . . 91 Littledean . . . 93 Longhope . . . 98
Lydbrook . . . 100 Lydney . . . 104 Mile End . . . 115
Minsterworth . . . 115 Mitcheldean . . . 116 Newent . . . 118
Newnham . . . 120 Parkend . . . 124 Redmarley D'Abitot . . . 126
Ruardean . . . 126 Ruspidge . . . 128 St. Briavels . . . 129
Staunton & Corse . . . 134   Tutshill/Tidenham . . . 135
Westbury-on-Severn . . . 139 Woodcroft . . . 140
Woolaston . . . 141 Yorkley . . . 144
The Future of Forest Policing? . . . 146

Appendix A: The Second World War Regulars and Specials . . . 147
Appendix B: Police Details from the 1881 Census . . . 160
Bibliography & Acknowledgements . . . 165
Index – General . . . 166
Index – Names . . . 167

About the authors

Geoff Sindrey was born in 1947 in Cheltenham and attended Cheltenham Grammar School. He joined Gloucestershire Constabulary in 1967 and was posted to Lydney. The following year he married and moved to Cheltenham. From 1972 to 1975 he was a village bobby in the Cotswolds and played Rugby for Stow on the Wold. After ten years service in the City of Gloucester he returned to the Forest where he spent the next seven years as the Inspector at Lydney. While there he was active in the Police Federation and also continued his education, gaining a Master of Arts Degree in 1992. From 1993 to 1995 he served at HQ working on IT projects and spent the last two years of his service in charge at Tewkesbury.

Geoff is married with a grown up son and daughter. He and his wife, Sue, still live in Coleford where they are active members of the community.

Ted Heath was born in 1941 in London. He spent his formative years in Port Talbot before moving to Cheltenham, his adopted home town. He played representative schoolboy and youth football at county level and played for both Bristol City and Newport County before joining the Gloucestershire Constabulary in 1967 and being posted to Lydney. Ted also served at Cheltenham, Tewkesbury and Cirencester, before returning to the Forest in 1977 as village bobby at Drybrook. In 1983 he was posted to Cinderford where he worked for many years as a Community Police Officer.

Health problems forced him to retire from the police in 1995 but he still lives in Cinderford pursuing his many interests, one of which is photography. He has a son and daughter and is very proud of his three grandchildren.

Preface

The Forest of Dean in West Gloucestershire is a beautiful yet rugged place. Much of it was once a Royal Hunting Forest and later a place where iron working and coal mining were carried out on an industrial scale. Lying as it does between the rivers Severn and Wye, the Dean has been insulated from both England and Wales for much of history. Its people are proudly independent with their own dialect and customs.

This book contains a potted history of the Forest of Dean Police from the beginnings of the Gloucestershire Constabulary in 1839 to the start of the 21st century. It is not intended to be a definitive history but we hope we have included the salient facts and the key events. The book also contains a pictorial and oral history of everyday policing around the Forest in times gone by. Current and former police stations are identified by map reference and photograph but we ask readers to respect the privacy of the present occupants of the many former stations mentioned.

Forest police boundaries have changed many times, so we have taken as our definition of the Forest of Dean that area of West Gloucestershire which is administered by the Forest of Dean District Council. We have also included the parish of Ashleworth, the police history of which, is linked with that of nearby Hartpury.

It has not been possible to include all the serious incidents that have ever occurred or to name all the officers who have ever served in the Forest, however, we hope readers will forgive any omissions. Those hoping to read gory details of Forest murders will be disappointed. We have omitted such material out of respect for the families of the victims.

During the course of our research we were constantly aware of change and it is an ever present theme throughout the book. Less expected was the sense of continuity which came through strongly, especially when talking to the many people who were kind enough to contribute their memories. Whatever changes may have taken place over the years there is an unbroken thread which links the first bobbies who patrolled the Dean in 1840 to those men and women who are doing what is essentially the same job today.

Geoff Sindrey & Ted Heath
September 2000

Table 1

DISTRIBUTION OF POLICE STATIONS IN THE FOREST OF DEAN AT INTERVALS SINCE 1840

c1840	c1857	c1902	c1933	c1969	c2000
Hewelsfield	St Briavels	St Briavels	St Briavels	St Briavels	
Newnham	Newnham	Newnham	Newnham	Newnham	Newnham
Mitcheldean	Mitcheldean	Mitcheldean	Mitcheldean	Mitcheldean	
Coleford	Coleford	Coleford	Coleford	Coleford	Coleford
Newent	Newent	Newent	Newent	Newent	Newent
	Lydbrook	Lydbrook	Lydbrook	Lydbrook	
	Littledean	Littledean	Littledean	Littledean	
	Blakeney	Blakeney	Blakeney	Blakeney	
Lydney	Lydney	Lydney	Lydney	Lydney	Lydney
	Tidenham	Tutshill	Tutshill	Tutshill	Tutshill
	Dymock	Dymock	Dymock	Dymock	
		Cinderford	Cinderford	Cinderford	Cinderford
		Drybrook	Drybrook	Drybrook	
		Longhope	Longhope	Longhope	
		Parkend	Parkend	Parkend	
		Ruspidge	Ruspidge	Ruspidge	
		Westbury	Westbury	Westbury	
		Woolaston	Woolaston	Woolaston	
		Yorkley	Yorkley	Yorkley	
	Ashleworth	Hartpury	Hartpury	Hartpury	
	Churcham	Churcham	Huntley	Huntley	
		Staunton (N)	Staunton (N)	Staunton (N)	
			Bream	Bream	
			Ruardean	Ruardean	
			Minsterworth	Mile End	

Part One
A Potted History of The Forest of Dean Police

Introduction

This part of the book is an attempt to give a brief history of policing in the Forest of Dean. It attempts to include the key events, trends, and ideas, and to identify the political, social, economic and technical changes which have shaped policing over time. Times change and the police service has had to change with them. One of the most noticeable indicators of change is the number, distribution and status of police stations. The high water mark of locally based policing in the Forest of Dean was in the late 1960s and early 1970s when there were no fewer than twenty-five police stations (see Table 1) in the area now included in the Forest of Dean District and many more officers than there are today. In most of the stations at that time the officer in charge lived on the premises. There are now only six operational stations in the same geographical area and none of these has a resident officer in charge. There are many factors which have influenced the gradual reduction in the number of police stations since the early 1970s, just as there must have been many considerations behind the choice of location, staffing levels and status of the relatively small number of police stations established in the Forest of Dean in 1840.

In the history of the Gloucestershire Constabulary there have been many reviews and reorganisations and consequently police boundaries have changed several times so, for the purpose of this book, we have taken as our boundary the present-day local government District of the Forest of Dean plus Ashleworth.

The Early Days

The County Police Act 1839 permitted Justices in Quarter Sessions to appoint paid police forces for the counties. Gloucestershire's Bench was one of the first to do so but the only models apart from the French state police system were the Metropolitan Police, founded ten years earlier, and the Irish Police which was a colonial style force run on military lines. Anthony Thomas Lefroy, a veteran of the Irish Constabulary, was appointed Gloucestershire's first Chief Constable. He reported the strength and distribution of the force to Quarter Sessions in 1840. The Forest stations were as follows: Newnham-on-Severn, 1 Superintendent (Supt 1st Class William H. Lander) and 5 Constables; Mitcheldean, 5 Constables; Coleford, 7 Constables; Newent, 4 Constables.

A station diary commenced the same year suggests that there was also a station at Hewelsfield from which officers patrolled on foot as far as Beachley and a hand-

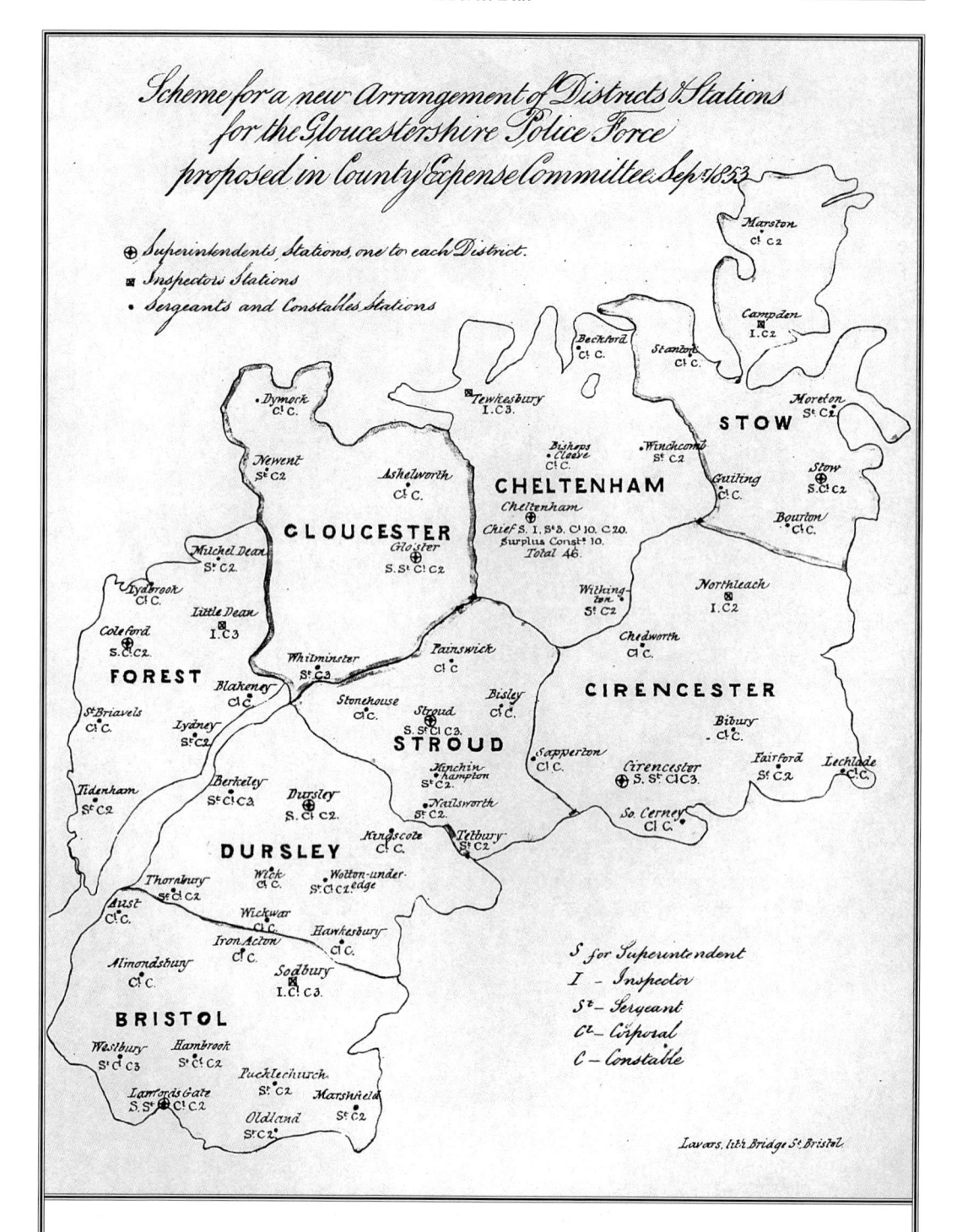

SCHEME FOR PROPOSED ARRANGEMENT OF DISTRICT POLICE STATIONS 1853

(Note the rank of Corporal then in use)
By kind permission of the Chief Constable

written report from this time mentions three officers at Lydney.

Mr Lefroy had organised the force on the Irish model with a group of officers at a station (still called barracks at this time) under the supervision of a sergeant or senior constable. The stations were located near the geographical centre of their area of responsibility and a system of continual patrol was maintained on routes which interlocked with those of neighbouring stations. Patrolling officers were required to make conference points with officers on neighbouring beats or with supervisors. In contrast neighbouring forces posted lone officers to live and work in the rural communities they served. An insight into how the Irish system worked is afforded by the station diary of Hewelsfield Police Station, which survives in Gloucestershire Record Office. Entries made in copperplate handwriting carefully record the daily activities:

Anthony Thomas Lefroy, Gloucestershire's first Chief Constable.
By kind permission of the Chief Constable

Monday 1 March 1841
Constable Daniel Walker, Barrack Guard. Sergeant John Baker and Constable George Beasley left the station at half past 8 am to patrol St Briavels, Bace Common [Bearse?]*, Trowgreen, Bream, Wilsbury, the Dunketts* [Dunkilns?]*, Highgrove and Hewelsfield Met the Coleford patrol at Trowgreen at 10am.*

Saturday 6 March 1841
Constable George Beasley returned from Gloucester Sessions at 1200 and took up Guard. Constables Thomas Box and William Bowels [?] *left this station at 2pm on their way to Coleford. Constable Walker patrolled to the Chase, Woodcroft, Lancote* [sic] *and Bowlash went at 10am returned at 4pm found all correct.*

An entry for Tuesday 23 July 1841 is in Chief Constable Lefroy's own hand:
Visited this station find the house and two regular but one man removed to Lydney not replaced. 23 Feb 1841 Anthony Thomas Lefroy CC

A later entry for the same day reads:
Constable Samuel Kirby left this station for Lydney at 7.06am. Constable George Beasley arrived from Lydney at half past 12pm in place of Constable Kirby.

Chief Constable Lefroy was responsible for introducing the patrol ticket system whereby an officer left a ticket with trusted farmers and others on his beat who would sign and date it. This not only ensured that the officer patrolled where he was instructed but also that key members of the community knew he had done so.

INSTRUCTIONS
FOR THE
CONSTABULARY FORCE
OF THE
COUNTY OF GLOUCESTER.

The following General Instructions for the different ranks of the Constabulary Force are not to be understood as containing Rules of Conduct applicable to every variety of circumstances that may occur in the performance of their duty; something must necessarily be left to the intelligence and discretion of individuals, and according to the degree in which they show themselves possessed of these qualities, and to their zeal, activity, and judgment on all occasions, will be their claims to future promotion and reward.

It should be understood at the outset, that the principal object to be attained is the "Prevention of Crime."

To this great end every effort of the Constabulary Force is to be directed. The Security of Person and Property, the Preservation of the Public Tranquillity, and all the other objects of a Police Establishment, will be better effected than by the detection and punishment of the offender after he has succeeded in committing the crime. This should constantly be kept in mind by every member of the Constabulary Force, as the guide for his own conduct. Superintendents and Constables should endeavour to distinguish themselves by such vigilance and activity as may render it extremely difficult for any one to commit a crime within the portion of the county under their charge.

CONDITIONS.

The Conditions upon which each man is to be admitted into the Constabulary Force are stated here that no complaint may be made hereafter upon their being enforced. The Chief Constable desires it to be understood at the same time that he reserves to himself the power to alter or annul any of these Conditions, and also to make such new Rules as may be found expedient.

No. 1.—Each man shall devote his whole time to the Constabulary Force.

No. 2.—He shall serve and reside wherever he is appointed.

No. 3.—He shall promptly obey all lawful orders which he may receive from the persons placed in authority over him.

No. 4.—He shall conform himself to all the Regulations which may be made from time to time for the good of the service.

No. 5.—He shall not upon any occasion, or under any pretence whatsoever, take money from any person; also, he shall not eat nor drink at the expense or on the invitation of any person, whilst on duty, without the express permission of his superior officer.

No. 6.—He shall at all times appear in his Police Dress, but if it appears necessary for him to put on plain clothes, he will report the same and the cause thereof to his superior officer.

No. 7.—He shall allow a deduction of one shilling per week to be made from his pay when lodgings are found him.

No. 8.—Such debts owing by him as the Chief Constable shall direct to be paid, shall be paid by him forthwith.

No. 9.—He shall receive his pay Monthly, on such day as shall be appointed.

No. 10.—He shall not quit the Constabulary Force without giving a month's previous notice; in case he quit without such notice, all pay then due shall be forfeited. If he be dismissed from the Force, the whole of his pay then due or unpaid is forfeited.

No. 11.—Every man dismissed from the Constabulary Force, or who shall resign his situation, shall, before he quits the service, deliver up every article of dress and appointments which have been supplied to him. If any of such articles have been, in the opinion of the Chief Constable, improperly used or damaged, a deduction from any pay due to the party shall be made, sufficient to make good the damage, or supply a new article.

No. 12.—Every Constable, on his appointment, shall sign the following declaration, viz.—

I, A. B., do hereby promise to fulfil all the duties of a Police Constable with fidelity and sobriety, and to obey all lawful orders that I may receive from my superior officer, and likewise such rules and regulations as may from time to time be made by the Chief Constable, and to submit to whatever fines may be imposed upon me for neglect of duty, and in case I should be dismissed the Constabulary Force, to forfeit such pay as may then be due to me, and to deliver all my clothing and appointments in a fit and proper state.

No. 13.—Each Constable is liable to immediate dismissal for unfitness, negligence, or misconduct, independently of any other punishment to which he may by law be subject. The Chief Constable may also, if he think fit, dismiss him without assigning any reason.

No. 14.—He shall not use, nor allow to be used, the button marked "Police Force," except while he belongs to the service.

No. 15.—Each man is conspicuously marked with the number corresponding with his name in the books, so that he can at all times be known to the public.

No. 16.—The men who are off duty are to consider themselves liable to be called on at all times, and will always prepare themselves, when required, at the shortest notice.

No. 17.—A certain number, when so ordered by their officer, must sleep in their clothes, to be in complete readiness when called on.

ANTHONY THOMAS LEFROY, *Chief Constable.*

Constabulary Office, Cheltenham, February 1, 1840.

Instructions for the Constabulary of the County of Gloucester. Issued by Anthony T. Lefroy, Chief Constable, 1 February 1840.
By kind permission of the Chief Constable

RULES

FOR THE GUIDANCE OF THE

RURAL CONSTABULARY

OF GLOUCESTERSHIRE,

TO BE STRICTLY ATTENDED TO BY ALL ITS MEMBERS.

The Superintendents and Constables in charge of the Stations will be most particular in seeing that they are obeyed, as they will be held responsible.

No. 1.—THE SUPERINTENDENTS OF DISTRICTS will instruct the men under their orders as to the duties of their Office as Constables, and will see that they make themselves acquainted with the contents of the books furnished and approved of by the Marquis of Normanby; they will impress upon the minds of the men that they are not only required to be vigilant in the prevention and detection of crime, but are to endeavour, by a just, temperate, and impartial exercise of their authority, to secure to themselves the confidence of all classes of the community.

No. 2.—They will be held responsible that the Rules, Orders, and Regulations of the Establishment are duly enforced, that the men are regular in their conduct, clean in their person, neat and uniform in their dress, and civil and conciliating in their demeanour towards their fellow subjects.

No. 3.—They will be answerable for the cleanliness of the Station Houses, that all articles of Furniture are kept in good order; all damages must be immediately made good by the individual charged.

No. 4.—There will be a Daily Parade, at Nine o'clock in Summer, and Ten o'clock in Winter, when the Superintendent or Constable in charge will strictly inspect the men of the party, and see that they are clean and properly shaved, and that they never appear out in any other state.

No. 5.—An Orderly is to be named daily for twenty-four hours, and charged with the care of the Station House, which he is not to quit. While thus on duty, he is not to undress during the night, but to be in readiness to answer any call, and rouse his comrades in case of alarm. Whenever the party consists of less than five men, Constable in charge must take his turn of this duty.

No. 6.—The men are not to be permitted to work at trades, nor to engage in private pursuits; their time belongs to the public, and is to be devoted to its service.

No. 7.—The Bedding is to be folded every Morning by Eight o'clock in Summer, and Nine in Winter. No deviation from this rule will be tolerated, excepting in cases of sickness, and where the man has been out all night. The Rooms to be swept out and set in order by the above hours. The Summer Season comprises between the 1st of April and 1st of October. The men are prohibited from using their bedsteads as seats.

No. 8.—The Sheets are to be changed on the first Monday in every Month; the soiled ones are to be washed under the directions of the Constable in charge, on the cheapest terms, and the cost paid by the men.

No. 9.—The Superintendent of the district will minutely inspect the articles of furniture and bedding, at least once a fortnight, and enter in the diary the state he finds the Station House, &c. The women and children of the men are prohibited from using any part of the bedding belonging to the Force.

No. 10.—No pigs, dogs, or birds, are to be kept at any of the Station Houses.

No. 11.—The men, under the direction of the Constable in charge, are to keep every part of the Station House, its approach, the passages and yards, clean and in perfect order, and are to uphold an appearance of regularity and neatness in everything connected with their post.

No. 12.—The Diary Books at each Station to be regularly and neatly kept, and filled up at night, and produced when called for.

No. 13.—The Superintendents and Constables will be held responsible that these Rules are hung up in a conspicuous part of the Station House, that it is kept clean and not defaced, and he will read it aloud from beginning to end to the men on parade every Monday Morning.

No. 14.—The name of the man in charge of the Station House for the twenty-four hours, will be hung up in the most conspicuous place in the Station House every Morning.

No. 15.—The Shirt Collars of the men are never to be seen above their Stocks.

No. 16.—The Superintendent, Serjeant, or Constable in charge of Stations, will be most particular in calling the Roll, and seeing that the men are in their Barracks every Night at Eight o'clock in Winter, and Nine o'clock in Summer, which they are not to quit without permission, unless on duty.

ANTHONY T. LEFROY, Chief Constable.

February 22nd, 1840.

PRINTED BY E. POWER, 6, WESTGATE STREET, GLOUCESTER.

Rules for the guidance of the Rural Constabulary of Gloucestershire. Issued by Anthony T. Lefroy, Chief Constable, 22 February 1840. By kind permission of the Chief Constable

The patrol ticket system was to remain in use in parts of the Forest until the 1940s and conference points continued to be a feature of patrol until rendered obsolete by the personal radio in the 1960s and 70s.

Officers in the early days worked long hours and were on call even when off duty. They were few in number and most were single as accommodation for families was scarce. The pay and conditions were poor and discipline harsh. Many officers left the service or were dismissed, morale was low and the rural police had yet to win public acceptance. The parish of Newland which at that time was rich in rateable businesses and property but had a low incidence of crime was one of many rural parishes which petitioned in October 1840 against a rural police force. The Chief Constable reported that there was *'opposition from the labouring classes'* in the Mitcheldean District and a Vestry Meeting at Abenhall in 1841 resolved to petition the next Quarter Sessions to relieve them of the rate burden of maintaining what they considered was an unnecessary police force in rural areas. In the early period of the Constabulary's life, instructions were issued by the Chief Constable against over-zealous enforcement in order to encourage acceptance by the community.

By 1857 the number of stations in the Forest had doubled. The buildings, some of which might previously have been village lock-ups, had all been rented from private landlords and many were considered unsuitable. In that year the Chief Constable and the County Surveyor carried out a survey of all the stations, considering the suitability of the buildings themselves and their strategic locations, as neighbouring counties had also set up police forces by this time. In 1857 the distribution was as follows:

        Coleford .... 1 Superintendent, 1 Sergeant, 2 Constables
        Lydbrook .... 2 Constables
        Mitcheldean .... 1 Sergeant, 2 Constables
        Littledean .... 1 Sergeant, 2 Constables
        Newnham .... 1 Sergeant, 2 Constables
        Blakeney .... 2 Constables
        Lydney .... 1 Sergeant, 2 Constables
        Tidenham .... 2 Constables
        St Briavels .... 2 Constables
        Newent .... 1 Sergeant, 2 Constables
        Dymock .... 2 Constables
        Churcham .... 2 Constables
        Ashleworth .... 2 Constables

In the seventeen years since 1840 the total number of constables had not increased significantly but an effort had clearly been made to decentralise by basing and housing officers in the smaller communities.

As a result of the 1857 survey, the stations at Lydbrook, Tidenham and Blakeney were declared to be 'unfit' and recommendations were made for the upgrade or relocation of some of the stations.

At that time Lydney's police station was in Church Road, some 200 yards from the Cross. The police moved out in the 1870s but the building was still standing within living memory on the site of the present ambulance station. In Blakeney the station was at the building which is now the post office. It was recommended that it be replaced by a house in The Square, which is now known as 'The Old Police Station'. The first station in Newnham was a house at the bottom of Severn Street (formerly Passage Lane), opposite the Bear Inn. Its cell accommodation was unsuitable so for many years the cells at the Town Hall were used. The first station in Newent was outside the town on the Dymock road. Its exact location has not been ascertained but the best guess of local historian David Bick is that it stood in the area now occupied by the by-pass and Fire Station.

At Coleford a house was rented in Gloucester Road opposite the present station. The landlord, a Mr Butt who lived in Cheltenham, agreed to upgrade the building to meet the Constabulary's needs.

The station house at Lydbrook was considered unsuitable because it was built into the bank of Hangerberry Hill, was overlooked by a quarry and had no room for alterations to be made to the lock-up. It was therefore decided to rent a house a short distance away.

Police records include reference to a police station at High Beech. The building, now called Station House, is believed to date from the 17th century. It is not mentioned in the 1857 Survey, so presumably it had already ceased to be a police station by then.

Mitcheldean's first police station was at 2 Plats Row, in the heart of the old part of the village. The former cell has been converted into a kitchen. Dymock's first station may have been a former village lock-up. It is situated between The Beauchamp Arms and the church, and is now called Church Cottage.

At this time there was a station at Ashleworth Green which also served the Hartpury area. The 1857 survey also mentions a Churcham police station adjacent to the Wesleyan chapel at Birdwood. A cottage situated end-on to the A40 is believed to be the former station.

The situation in the St Briavels and Tidenham area is less clear. There is mention of a station called 'The Chase' in The Police & Constabulary List of 1844. The 1857 survey describes Tidenham's station as facing the main road from St Briavels to Chepstow, two miles distant from Chepstow. The census of 1851 lists a police sergeant, his family and two constables at Woodcroft. It is possible that 'The Chase' of the 1844 list, the Tidenham of the 1857 survey and the Woodcroft of the 1851 census are one and the same. There is, however, a stone in the garden wall of the Woodcroft premises on which is written 'The Old Station House 1852', which hints that the police had moved out by that year, but the census records of succeeding decades suggest that this station continued in use throughout the remainder of the 19th century. The Hewelsfield Police Diary of 1840-43 in Gloucestershire Record Office refers to patrols of St Briavels and as far afield as Beachley. The 1841 census shows officers living in Hewelsfield but does not give the address. We know from the 1844 Police & Constabulary List that there was a station in St Briavels by then. If there was a station at Hewelsfield it probably closed in 1843/44 and its exact whereabouts remains a mystery.

In 1854 prison reform legislation made the former House of Correction at Littledean available for use as a police station and as a short term remand prison. On 15 March of that year Sergeant Edward Birch and two Constables moved in and the police station in Church Street was closed. Newnham Petty Sessional Court moved to the premises in 1874, as the lease on the courtroom at Newnham Town Hall had expired.

One of the earliest surviving photographs of Gloucestershire Police Officers, showing the deliberately non-military 'Peeler' style of uniform worn in the early days. The photograph was actually taken at Northleach around 1860.   By kind permission of the Chief Constable

Consolidation and Modernisation

As the police became more established, Parliament passed numerous Acts which added to their duties and responsibilities. By 1889 the police were not only responsible for the prevention and detection of crime and the maintenance of the Peace, they were also assistant relieving officers (issuing workhouse or lodging house tickets and 8 oz of bread to the poor and homeless who were genuinely seeking work – an early example of the Job Seekers Allowance!), they were Coroner's officers, highway and bridge inspectors, inspectors of weights and measures, diseases of animals inspectors, sergeants at mace, javelin men, and other duties in relation to Quarter Sessions and Assizes. Other legislation such as the Town Police Clauses Act created hundreds of minor offences designed to reduce the annoyance, danger or obstruction caused to the public by the actions of individuals. Thus the police were drawn into disputes between people over matters that would be considered trivial today. This was a period when the police were becoming more involved in people's lives often by giving assistance rather than being coercive and thus became more acceptable to people of all classes. No doubt the fact that police officers lived with their families in the communities they served helped this process.

The last three decades of the 19th century witnessed an extensive public building programme throughout the county. Many imposing Victorian police stations date from this particular period and were either purpose-built or altered to meet the needs of a modern police force, with cells, a general office and living accommodation for the family of the officer in charge and usually for one or more single officers too. Examples in the Forest of Dean include those at:

Hill Street, Lydney
Station Street, Cinderford
High Street, Newnham on Severn
Westbury on Severn,
Kempley Road, Dymock
Nicholson House, Newent.

The stations at Dymock and Westbury are almost mirror images of one another. Stations such as Lydney, Coleford and Newent were built to include the Petty Sessional Court. Some Victorian stations proudly display a date stone giving the date of their commissioning (or re-commissioning) but not necessarily the date of construction of the building, such as Lydney (1876), Newnham (1873), Dymock (1895) and Westbury (1898). By the end of the Victorian period, the number of stations had increased to twenty-two, with the Forest Superintendent being based at Coleford, an Inspector at Lydney and Sergeants in charge at Blakeney, Cinderford, Littledean, Newnham and Newent (then Gloucester District). The first of Staunton & Corse's three stations was opened around this time. It was a stone-built house in Malvern Road. The main stations were not the only ones to have cells; village stations such as those at Westbury, Dymock, Parkend, Ruspidge, Longhope, Drybrook and Mitcheldean also had cells but perhaps this is not surprising. It was a time when mining and heavy industry flourished in the Forest of Dean, and villages had far more pubs and sometimes bigger populations than they do today. Furthermore the police were on foot and could not call for transport or assistance in these often violent times.

Violent Times

Police Officers Killed

The only officers of the Gloucestershire force to have been attacked and killed on duty between 1 January 1840 and 1 January 2000 met their violent ends in the Forest of Dean in the 19th century.

The early days of policing in the Forest took place against the background of tension between the Free Miners, Commoners and organised labour on the one hand, capitalist mine-owners and The Crown (Forestry) Commission on the other. The issue of sheep grazing rights was in dispute and there were many allegations of sheep stealing. It was while watching for sheep thieves near Speech House one night in 1861, that Sgt. Samuel Beard of Littledean was set upon by a gang and was given severe injuries from which he died a few days later.

In the 1890s a gang from the Blakeney Hill area were said to exercise a system of terrorism over the inhabitants of the Forest. Questions were asked in The House of Commons and the Deputy Surveyor of the Forest of Dean at the time thought the situation serious enough to ask for a troop of cavalry. Instead the Chief Constable, Admiral Henry Christian, sent eight additional officers. It was in this context that, in May 1895, PC Newport was attacked in Blakeney by alleged members of the gang and would have been killed but for the timely intervention of his colleagues. In November of the same year, Sgt. William Morris was attacked by a group of young men at Viney Hill and died after being hit on the head with a stone.

Intimidation

In 1871 Supt. Edward Thomas Chipp moved to Coleford to take charge of the Forest of Dean, which he described in his diary as being in a *'most lawless state'*. Cases collapsed because witnesses went in fear of their lives and Supt. Chipp, a man who led from the front, had his own life threatened. On one occasion he was leading a raid on a house in Bream, looking for illicit alcohol, when the occupier grabbed a gun but was quickly disarmed by one of the constables. On another occasion in 1872 he succeeded, with the help of other officers, in capturing three notorious sheep stealers. While locked up they conspired to shoot the Superintendent as he drove about at night in his pony and trap. Chipp changed his habits and walked. One night he was caught in a dreadful thunderstorm while walking near the spot where Sgt. Beard had been killed, which was somewhat unnerving. He later learned that it was only by changing his routine that he had thwarted an assassin acting on behalf of the gang.

Superintendent Edward Thomas Chipp, later to be Deputy Chief Constable.
Courtesy Rosemary Howells (nee Chipp)

In another case, worthy of a Sherlock Holmes story, the writer of an anonymous letter, containing threats to kill a Russian draughtsman at Trafalgar Colliery, was detected when police searched the locker of a miner and found a piece of blotting paper bearing a facsimile of parts of the letter in question.

Riots

Elections in February 1874 provided an excuse for heavy drinking and riotous behaviour in the town of Cinderford, when several shops and houses were completely ruined by a drunken and unruly mob. Order was only restored when reinforcements arrived and officers patrolled the town with cutlasses. A Magistrates' order was issued to close the public houses and a battalion of infantry was held in reserve at Littledean. Over the next few days twenty-five alleged ringleaders were rounded up by

The Grave of Edward Chipp in Horton Road Cemetery, Gloucester.
Photo Ted Heath

police officers armed with cutlasses and led by Supt. Chipp himself.

Strikes

Free-mining for coal and iron ore had been a right of native Foresters for centuries but it had always been a simple, small scale affair, as it still is in the those few free mines that remain in operation today. In the 19th century, however, the Industrial Revolution brought a much greater demand for coal and the Forest attracted capitalist investors, who sank deep mines and employed large numbers of workers in poor conditions and on low pay. In 1877 miners at Lightmoor and Trafalgar Pits went on strike and police rushed to the collieries to head off a procession of striking colliers thought to be bent on mischief. In those days the magistracy included colliery owners and iron masters among their number and the strike weapon was not recognised as legitimate by many, including Superintendent Chipp. Though not used to break the strikes, the police found themselves deployed to protect the mines from sabotage and the strike breakers from assault and intimidation. This was not without good reason. While Joseph Morris of Harry Hill (Harrow Hill) was at work someone blew up his cottage with his wife and children inside!

National Strikes

At the time of the Great War there were about 7,000 miners in the Forest of Dean. Coal was essential to the war effort and although the mines remained in private ownership they came under Government control for the duration. Pay and conditions improved and morale was high. All this changed after the war. Coal prices slumped, the hoped-for nationalisation of the industry didn't happen and miners were asked to accept pay cuts and longer hours. In 1921 there was a strike throughout Britain. The mine owners responded with a lockout and after fourteen weeks, the miners had to accept the new conditions and return to work.

Working miners and police, Flour Mill Colliery, Bream, Coal Strike 1921. Courtesy Ruth Proctor Hirst

In 1926 another national coal strike was called. This time it was supported by the TUC and there was a General Strike. Non-union labour and volunteers were mobilised to keep the country moving and the police were deployed to protect them. After just over a week the General Strike ended but the miners carried on for many more weeks before going back to work, defeated but unbowed. A troop of mounted police was based in the Forest during the strike and made regular patrols. Mobile police on solo motorcycles and motorcycle combinations were also available for rapid deployment and routine patrol. In the event, however, there was very little trouble during either the 1921 or the 1926 strike, and in fact football and rugby matches were played between the striking miners and the Forest of Dean Police. Superintendent Shelswell was in overall command of the police and had at his personal disposal a Chevrolet car and a driver.

A detailed account of the 1926 strike in the Forest of Dean, together with people's own memories, is given in Ralph Anstis's excellent book *Blood on Coal*.

Motorcycle Police, Miners Strike 1926. The officer in the sidecar nearest to the left is Insp. Bent of Coleford.
By kind permission of the Chief Constable

A group of colliers and police officers during the 1926 Miner's Strike. By kind permission of the Chief Constable

PC Fred Taylor of Yorkley with a collier at Flour Mill Colliery, Bream, during the 1926 National Miners' Strike.
Courtesy of Jim Taylor

Mounted police at the Feathers Hotel, Lydney, during the 1926 Miners Strike. The fourth officer from the left is PS Harry Watkins of Littledean and on his right is PC W. Rogers, later to be in charge at Drybrook. The officer in the centre with the white brimmed cap has been tentatively identified as a Superintendent by the name of Meadows. By kind permission of the Chief Constable

Expansion, Rationalisation and Two World Wars

In 1896 the Force purchased its first bicycles. In 1899 Lydney Police Station was connected to the telephone system – the telephone number of the station was 7. In 1902 the strength of the Forest Division (not including Newent and its satellites) was 41 officers serving a population of 45,445.

By the 1930s all stations were connected to the telephone system and there were public call boxes in villages and on the main roads. Conference points were now made at telephone kiosks at fixed times so that the officer could be contacted if necessary. The Force had a small fleet of motor vehicles and police stations had bicycles. The police had become easier to contact and more mobile than had previously been the case. The Forest had its first official Motor Patrol vehicle in 1929 in the form of a motorcycle combination. The motor patrol officer was issued with a stop watch for the detection of offenders against the speed limit. A few years later the Forest had its first Patrol Car. The motor car brought benefits but it had also brought an additional workload. Not only were there now mobile criminals and car thieves but in the 1930s there were as many road deaths per annum as in the 1990s, if not more. The strategic location of police stations along the road network therefore became an important consideration.

Above: *In 1931 Gloucestershire Constabulary bought six motor cars for use as Motor Patrol vehicles. They bought a mixture of Fords and Morrises, in both saloon and tourer versions, presumably to test the suitability of all of them. One of the vehicles, thought to be a Morris tourer, is seen here leaving Force Headquarters at Cheltenham. One of the cars later came down to the Forest – the first Police Patrol Car in Dean – although which particular one is not known.*

Above right: *PC Pole, Motor Patrol 1930. The motorbike is a 968cc, twin cylinder BSA with sidecar combination.*

Right: *PC C. A. ('Cas') Smith, Motorcycle Patrolman, outside Lydney Police Station in 1931 or 1932.*
All by kind permission of the Chief Constable

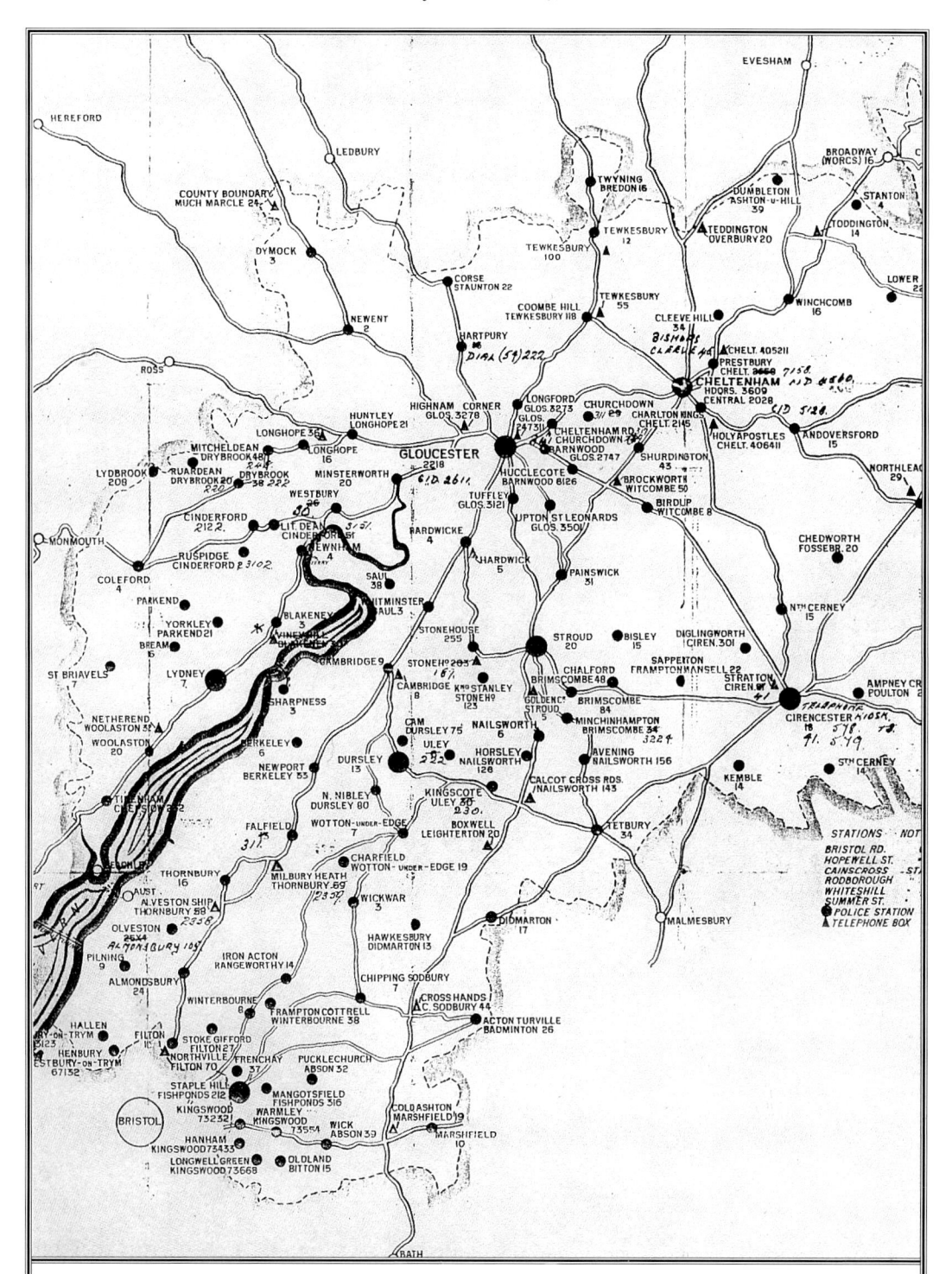

GLOUCESTERSHIRE CONSTABULARY POLICE MAP SEPT. 1933

Shown are the locations of police stations and call boxes with their telephone numbers.
Courtesy Gloucestershire Record Office GRO Ref.Q/Y 5/4/3

A station on the main road at Huntley, at the junction with North Road, replaced the one at Churcham and a station had been opened at Minsterworth, on the bend in the main road near the Apple Tree public house. A station had also been opened at Ruardean to serve that community. At Bream, a house in the High Street, just above the New Inn, served for a while, before the police moved to a building (formerly a shop and now demolished) near the Maypole. Tuthill House at the bottom of Highfield Hill in Lydney, where the Roman Catholic Church now stands, was the Divisional Headquarters and home of the Superintendent, until it was replaced by a house in Church Road in Superintendent Shelswell's time

During The Great War 1914 to 1918, officers on the reserve list were recalled to the colours and many others volunteered. Recruiting to the police came to a standstill as young men joined the Army or Navy, many never to return. The Chief Constable, Lieut. Col. Richard Chester-Master, was a veteran of the South African War. He rejoined his regiment and was killed in action in 1917 and is buried at Lochre-Hospice Military Cemetery near Ypres. It was during this war that the first women police patrols were seen. In Gloucestershire, a few Women Special Constables were recruited at first, then, in 1918, two women were appointed as regular members of the County Force.

Supt. Shelswell commanded the Forest Division from 1923 until 1937, when he was succeeded by Albert Henry Carter, who was later to become Assistant Chief Constable. Mr Carter was the last Superintendent to have an official driver (a post which probably dated from the pony and trap era). The last driver was PC Arthur Woodward. Mr Carter was succeeded during the Second World War by Supt. Charles Large. When war broke out in 1939 the police service was a reserved occupation

Supt. Shelswell with Inspectors and Sergeants of the Forest Division at Lydney Police Station, 1933. **Standing**, *left to right : PS Bull, PS Coldicutt, PS Coates, PS Ferryman;* **Seated**: *PS Freeman, Insp. Green, Supt. Shelswell MBE, Insp. Large, PS Hobday.*   By kind permission of the Chief Constable

Forest Division 1932. **Back row**, left to right: PCs Bailey, Crowther, A.W. Taylor, Lipett, Pagett, Cole, Green, Boughton, Baldwin, Phelps, Barnes, Jeffries and Hale. **Middle row:** PCs Pole, Gay, Batchelor, Blick, Francis, Tuttiett, Minett, Beddis, Williams, Day, Rogers, Cox, James, Randell, Fardon and Smith. **Front row:** PCs Ireland and Weekes, PSs Coldiciutt, Bull and Freeman, Insp. Green, Supt. Shelswell MBE, Insp. Large, PSs Hobday, Coates and Ferryman, PCs F. Taylor and Morris, and WPC Cameron.

Courtesy Mrs Margaret Wyatt

'F' Division Officers at Lydney Police Station, 1937. **Back row**, left to right: PC Chris Beddis (Bream); PC 114 Bert Carter; PC 64 Dick Tibbotts; PC Cliff Dibden; PC 442 George Holmes; PC 172 Tom Antell; unidentified; PC 133 Harold Bayliss (Woolaston); PC 391 Bill Chandler (Westbury); PC A. Taylor; PC Frank Hewinson; PC 78 Len Merriman (Tutshill); PC 281 Cyril Paget (Mitcheldean); PC 411 Joe Reeks (Lydney); PC J. Brown; PC 407 Frank Emerson (Yorkley); PC 530 Fred Minett (Lydney). **Middle row:** PC 154 Ted James (Newnham); PC 51 Jim Houghton (Ruardean); PC 21 Tom Pugsley (Lydbrook); PC 122 Ossie Broad (Lydney Div. Office); PC 141 Vic Bullock (Coleford); PC 419 Edgar Bowring (Newnham); PC 428 Joe McKnight (Lydney); PC C Midwinter; PC Fred Miller (Coleford); PC 211 Cecil Birch (Coleford); PC 40 Frank Nicholls; PC Wilf 'Joe' Fardon (Yorkley); PC 35 Arthur Finch (Lydbrook); PC 191 Ted Wakefield (Blakeney); PC 291 Paul Foice (Lydney); PC 195 Tom Buckland (Coleford). **Front row:** DC Edwin Tuttiett (Lydney); WPC 6 Doris Gould (Lydney); PS 410 Harry Watkins (Littledean); PC 256 Edgar Day (St Briavels); PS 224 Joe Ireland (Blakeney); PS John Coates (Cinderford); Insp. George Dowsell (Coleford); Supt. Albert Carter (Lydney); Insp. A.F. Newman (Lydney); PS 162 Fred Swift (Cinderford); PS Fred Taylor (Coleford); PS Frank Morris (Tutshill); PC 308 Reg Weekes (Parkend); PC B Nicholls.

The Class of '39. The last police recruit intake of peacetime, County Police HQ Sept 1939. Most later joined the armed forces. **Standing**, *left to right: PC Theo Hart, PC George Bliss, PC John Daykin, PC William Betteridge, PS McWilmott (Instructor), PC John Hyett, PC Jim Ludlow, PC Jack Turner, PC Doug Hawkes, PC Fred Hudson, PC Percy Faulconer.* **Sitting:** *PC Noel Drennan, PC John Howkins, PC Arthur Meadows, PC Cyril Woodward, PC Jack Rogers, PC Ben Gwilliam.*   Courtesy Dora Gwilliam

but this status was rescinded after 18 months. Nevertheless, reservists were recalled to the colours and many police officers also volunteered, having their armed service pay made up to police levels by the Standing Joint Committee (the forerunner of the Police Authority). For those remaining, a ban was put on retirement for the duration and very few officers moved from the post they occupied at the start of hostilities. The last peacetime recruit intake, which included Ben Gwilliam and Jim Ludlow, spent much of the first weeks of their police careers filling sandbags at Force HQ in Cheltenham! The police assumed additional duties in relation to Air Raid Precautions and sirens were fitted to the stations. A Police War Reserve and a Women's Auxiliary Police Corps was raised to meet the authorised numbers required. Many additional Special Constables were also recruited and much was asked of them.

The Forest was touched by the war in

Albert H. Carter, who was appointed Assistant Chief Constable in 1946, had been appointed Superintendent in charge of 'F' Division (Forest) in 1937.
Courtesy Pat Hutchings

A wartime parade through Newnham. The officer leading the parade is PC Edward George James. The senior Special Constable on the left is Reg Blanton, owner of Blanton's Garage in the High Street. Mr Blanton joined the Special Constabulary on leaving the Army at the end of the Great War. Courtesy Mrs A. Gould

Digging for victory ceremony at Temple Way, Lydney, early 1940s, with regular police and Special Constables in attendance. Of those identified, to the fore is SC Martyn; centre behind the little girl with the bow in her hair, is SC Thorn; right and behind him is SC Williams; the regular on the right is PS Clarke and behind him, right, is SC Born. The little boy with the wheelbarrow is Brian Russell, today well known as a historian and campaigner for Lydney harbour. Photograph G. Caldwell

many ways. There were, of course, many bereavements, there was bombing, there were crashed aircraft and later there were hundreds of US soldiers (blacks and whites, segregated on and off duty by the US authorities). There were also many prisoners of war, some of whom escaped and had to be recaptured. The Forest was used by both the RAF and the US Army to store bombs and rumours about mustard gas canisters down mine shafts persist to this day.

Crime and road traffic accidents, which are the daily fare of the police in peacetime, did not go away in wartime. Average annual peacetime road death figures were below a hundred for the county but in 1942 there were 167 traffic fatalities, the blackout being a contributory factor. In 1943 only 45 motor vehicles were stolen but a staggering 1,700 bikes were taken! Station Offence Books of the time show people being prosecuted for having no lights on a motor vehicle at night in early

Wartime. PC Fred Hudson (Coleford) and PC Percy F. Falconer at Police HQ, Sept. 1939, wearing their air raid helmets.
Courtesy Fred Hudson

1939 and being booked for displaying lights in 1940. Other typical wartime offences for which people were prosecuted were 'Failing to comply with a direction to plough land' (Fined £3.3.0), 'Being absent from essential work without reasonable excuse' and 'Unlawful use of petrol'.

At a meeting of the Standing Joint Committee on 5 October 1943, Viscount Bledisloe of Lydney Park moved *'That this committee do record their high appreciation of the service rendered by members of the Force during the present emergency'*. The motion was carried.

More Modernisation and Rationalisation

In the 1940s many police houses and rural police stations were still without electricity, piped water or indoor toilets. The post-war years saw a major building programme, including the replacement of a number of the older village stations with a standard pattern of one or two houses, in a distinctive style with an office attached. Examples of these can be seen throughout the county and also what is now called South Gloucestershire (until 1974 part of Gloucestershire) and at Bala in North Wales. Strangely, however, there are no examples to be found in the counties surrounding Gloucestershire. Standardisation of family accommodation was intended to enable police families to take their carpets and curtains with them on transfer. In the Forest the following stations conform to this type:

Bream, Parkend Road
Ruspidge, adjacent to its predecessor in Ruspidge Road
St Briavels, near the cross-roads
Staunton & Corse, on the corner of Boundary Place and Prince Crescent (replacing the second station on the corner opposite The Swan Inn)
Longhope, Church Road, replacing Brook House in The Latchen
Hartpury, by the war memorial
Huntley, on the main road opposite the lay-by
Drybrook, top of High Street
Ruardean, (the fourth station in the village in less than fifty years!)

Police numbers remained low for a few years after the war, as recruiting lagged behind overdue retirements, but soon the Force had new blood in the form of returning servicemen. Former Lydney Inspector Alfred Frederick Newman returned to the Forest in 1946 to take command. He was respected by his men as a hands-on copper and earned the respect of the criminal elements for his fairness.

During the severe winter of 1947 most of the communities in the Forest were isolated for varying periods of time, some for weeks. The thaw brought extensive flooding which again cut off isolated houses and whole communities, bringing widespread damage and distress. The police were kept very busy during this period co-ordinating and carrying out relief operations.

Motor Patrol was modernised in 1948 with a new fleet of wireless-equipped Riley 2.5 litre cars, to replace the seventeen tired Ford V8s which had seen the Force through the War. The following year a central Information Room (control room) was set up at Cheltenham to receive all 999 calls. At about the same time the stiff 'dog collar' uniform jackets were replaced by open-collar jackets, and ties. Later,

'F' Division at Lydney Police station, 1948. Supt. A.F. Newman is in the middle of the front row.
By kind permission of the Chief Constable

One of the new Riley 2.5 patrol cars purchased in 1948 and equipped with radio. The driver pictured with it is PC 237 Ben Gwilliam. Courtesy Dora Gwilliam

PC Ron Savage with his Riley 2.6 patrol car at Lydney police station, 1961.
Courtesy Ron Savage

Motor Patrol Officer, PC Ron Savage with his black Austin patrol car at Soudley, in the particularly severe winter conditions of January 1963.
Courtesy Ron Savage

An 'F' Division Pay Parade at Lydney Police Club, 1949. **Back row**, *left to right: Bill Webb, George Workman, Donald Stephens, Eric Markham, Gordon Saunders, unidentified, Cyril Thomas, Leonard Francis, Stan Cross, Rex Watkins, PC Constable.* **Middle row:** *Ossie Broad, Bob Parker, Edgar Day, Frank Nicholls, Nobby Clarke, Ken Moss, Frank Emerson, Bill Barmby, WPC Elizabeth Millichip, Dickie Bird, Arthur Merrett, Reg Pitman, Ron Stephens, Francis Field, Gilbert Elliott, Alan Smith, Phil Masterson, Ron Smith, Les Perry.* **Front row:** *John Griffin, Cyril Paget, Lewis Watkins, Chas Walkley, Bert Hills, Frank Jayne, Bert Leakey, Fred Glover, Alan Ballinger. Note open necked tunics and ties had replaced the high-necked jackets previously worn by Constables and Sergeants. The chevrons on the lower sleeve denote long service.*

Courtesy Francis Field

Motor Patrol was re-equipped with Riley Pathfinders and in the late 1950s with Riley 2.6 litre cars. In the early 1960s, Austin Westminster patrol cars were phased in and the first white one appeared in 1966. Hitherto, patrol cars had been black.

In 1962 work began on a new police station and magistrates court, adjacent to the old Coleford police station on the junction of Lord's Hill and Gloucester Road. It was opened in 1964 following the demolition of the old building.

In 1966 Supt. Henry Lodge took over command of the Division and took up residence at the Superintendent's house in Church Road, Lydney, where he had his office. The Divisional Admin. Office was also located there. The late 1960s and early 1970s were the heyday of the village police station in the Forest of Dean and many village police officers were active in the community, founding and running youth clubs and sports teams and generally keeping most of their local youths out of mischief. New purpose-built police stations replaced the old ones at:

Townsend, Mitcheldean (opposite its predecessor)
Slade Road, Yorkley (1967),
Fancy Road, Parkend (1967),
Lydbrook, opposite the church (1968),
Beeches Road, Newnham (1972)
Watery Lane, Newent, (1974)

The station at the former House of Correction at Littledean finally closed. The last sergeant was the late Campbell J. Willett. The Littledean Sergeant's post was transferred to the new station at Newnham and the Petty Sessional Court moved to Coleford in the 1980s. Newent Petty Sessional Court moved to Gloucester and Nicholson House, as the former Newent police station and court building is known, is now a museum.

Conditions of Service

The subjects of police pay and conditions are too complex to be dealt with in any depth in this book. A few facts, however, might be of interest, even surprise, to some readers. In the 19th century, police officers had no right to weekly leave (i.e. every week was 7 days duty with no day off) and they were on call for no extra pay when off shift. In 1907, Second Class Constables in Gloucestershire petitioned both the Chief Constable and the Standing Joint Committee for more pay, citing higher pay in other forces and listing current prices of basic necessities which exceeded their weekly pay. A national pay structure was introduced only after police in major cities went on strike in 1918. The Police Federation was founded to represent officers up to the rank of Chief Inspector but strikes and trade union membership were made illegal.

Up until the 1940s police officers' wives were not allowed to work. For four more decades the wife of a PC or Sergeant-in-charge of a police station was still expected to answer the telephone and take reports at the door while her husband was out on

Appendix "A."

N.B.—The following figures must be read as approximating most nearly to the rank of Second Class Constables in this County. Owing to the fact that hardly any two Counties classify their Constabulary in the same way, figures showing the pay to Second Class Constables alone could not properly be compared to those for this County.

POLICE FORCE.	WAGE. £ s. d.	REFERENCE IN BLUE BOOK.
Gloucester County	1 4 11	149
City of Bristol	1 11 0	150
County of Glamorgan	1 10 11	188
County of Monmouth	1 9 9	166
Borough of Newport	1 11 0	167
County of Worcester. (Rent allowance to married Constables, 2s. weekly).	1 6 10	60
City of Worcester	1 10 0	62
Borough of Kidderminster	1 6 10	61
County of Oxford	1 7 3	40
County of Stafford	1 10 4	48
Borough of Shrewsbury	1 8 1	47
County Borough of Reading	1 10 0	138
County of Wilts. (Rent allowance of 2s. a week to married Constables and all special duty paid for in addition).	1 3 8	181
County of Somerset	1 5 8	168
City of Bath	1 8 0	169
City of Oxford	1 10 0	42

2ND CLASS CONSTABLES.

THE GENERAL SUPPLY OF NECESSITIES REDUCED TO ITS LOWEST POSSIBLE SCALE.

PER WEEK—	£ s. d.
RENT, at 5s. 6d. to 5s. 9d. per week	0 5 6
COAL, at 1s. 1d. per cwt. (2 cwt.)	0 2 2
WOOD, for fire-lighting	0 0 3
LIGHT, oil or gas	0 0 10
BREAD	0 3 0
FLOUR	0 0 9
MEAT, Beef at 8d. per lb., Mutton at 10d. per lb.	0 4 0
FISH, at 4d. per lb.	0 1 0
BACON, at 8d. per lb.	0 0 8
CHEESE, at 8d. per lb.	0 0 8
BUTTER, at 1s. 1d. per lb.	0 1 1
JAM	0 0 4
TEA, at 2s. per lb.	0 1 0
SUGAR, at 2½d. per lb.	0 0 10
MILK, at 1½d. per pint	0 1 0
EGGS, at 1d. each (1 per day)	0 0 7
RICE, for puddings, etc.	0 1 0
LARD, at 8d. per lb., for cooking, etc.	0 0 4
SOAP, SODA, BLUE, BLACKING, BLACK-LEAD, etc.	0 1 0
	£1 6 0

Four Weeks at £1 6s. 0d. per week   £5 4s. 0d. per month.

[P.T.O.]

Extracts from a petition for better pay for Second Class Constables, 1907. **Left:** *Appendix A, Comparison of pay with other forces.* **Right:** *Table showing cost of everyday necessities.*   Courtesy Roy Haviland

patrol. The permission of the Chief Constable was required to marry and an officer was directed where to live. This restriction persisted even when officers were granted the right to be owner-occupiers in the 1970s. When police families were required to live in police provided accommodation they were expected to keep the gardens tidy. There was an annual gardening competition with very high standards achieved. Many officers grew vegetables in police station and police house gardens to supplement their poor pay.

As a result of the Sex Discrimination Act 1975, women officers at last enjoyed equal pay and conditions of service with the men, and new career paths were opened up to them as they now did the same work. A police officer would not be permitted to work in an area where any member of his or her family had a business, or a pecuniary interest in a licence (e.g. a pub, betting office etc.). Up until 1960, officers had to muster for a monthly pay parade at which they received their pay in cash. Divisional Conferences were still known as 'pay parade' long after this practice ceased. Unlike their colleagues in the Fire Service, police officers are not permitted to belong to a political party or trade union.

Few people outside the service realise that a serving police officer contributes 11% of gross salary towards the pension, which is therefore, in effect, deferred pay.

Away Days

Forest of Dean police officers did not spend all their working time on their own beat. During the Miner's Strike of 1911 rioting broke out in Tonypandy, in the Rhondda. Two sergeants and twenty-three constables were sent from Gloucestershire to support the Glamorgan force. During the General Strike of 1926, officers were

Postcard of the 23 constables and 2 sergeants sent from Gloucestershire to Tonypandy in South Wales. Other forces also contributed men to help combat the unrest and rioting. Unfortunately, it has not been possible to ascertain which of the policemen pictured here were from the Forest.   Courtesy The Archive Shop

again sent to South Wales and later, during 'the Blitz', Forest officers were often sent to assist in Bristol. The 'Cold War' meant that the Force had to maintain a state of Civil Defence readiness and regular Mobile Column exercises were staged up until the early 1960s. These exercises involved officers going around the country in a convoy of lorries and being self-supporting for several days.

For many years one of the few ways to earn payment for overtime was a 'special occasion' and one of the most special was the National Hunt Festival at Cheltenham. Officers from all over the county would meet up and renew old acquaintances, and place the odd furtive bet. There was a serious side to this duty, however. Members of the Royal Family needed to be protected, the huge influx of traffic needed to be controlled and criminals had to be deterred or caught. The 'Races' always attract professional criminals of all kinds, from pickpockets and tricksters to potential armed robbers and protection racketeers. In recent decades there has also been the potential for terrorist activity. That there are rarely any serious incidents is due to the vigilance of the police officers from all over the county who are largely there on what should be their day off.

Forest officers have also been deployed to aid other forces on occasions such as inner city riots, Summer Solstice problems at Stonehenge and the 1984 Miner's Strike, during which Forest officer PC Neil Thomas was injured. He was on duty in everyday uniform at Gascoigne Wood Colliery in Yorkshire when trouble flared. The police were pelted with stones by a crowd and Neil was hit on the head.

Sport

Sport has always played an important part in Forest police life. Most rugby clubs in the Forest have numbered police officers among their players and over the years many officers born or serving west of the Severn have played rugby, soccer and cricket for the Force. Supt. Shelswell MBE, who commanded the Forest Division in the 1920s and 30s, was Chairman of Lydney RFC where many of his officers played, including Fred Taylor, Frank Morris and Frank Nicholls. In the 1980s and

Forest of Dean Police Football Team 1922. Supt. Shelswell, in long dark overcoat, is standing on the left and the player seated second from left is Frank Morris.
Courtesy of Gloucestershire Record Office. GRO Ref. Q/Y 6/1/14-16

A cartoon depicting the Tug of War Event at the Police Sports Day in 1920. 'F' Division defeated Cheltenham Division in the final.   Courtesy Roy Haviland

Cartoon of the 1921 Police Sports Day Tug of War event. A jubilant Supt. Shelswell mocks the defeated Gloucester team.   Courtesy Roy Haviland

Forest of Dean Police Tug of War Team, 1922. **Back row:** *PS Wilks (Secretary), PC Frank Morris, PC Meadows, PC Coldicutt, PS Hobday, Insp. Gardner.* **Front row:** *PS Beale, PC Hicks, Supt. Shelswell (Capt.), PS Merrett, PC Grayhurst. Courtesy Gloucestershire Record Office. GRO Ref. Q/Y 6/1/14-16*

The Police Rugby Team which played a St Gregory's XV at the Athletic Ground, Cheltenham in 1923 in a Benefit Match for Cheltenham Unemployed. Far right standing is Supt. John Shelswell, fourth from right, Don Anderson, fifth from right, Fred Taylor, and far left seated, Frank Morris. Courtesy Jim Taylor

Lydney RFC 1928/29. There is a long tradition of police representation in the Lydney line up. This picture shows Club Chairman Supt. John Shelswell (far right standing), PC Fred Taylor (2nd player from the right standing) and PC Frank Morris (far left seated). Courtesy of the Taylor Family collection

Forest of Dean Police Cricket Team 1949. **Back row:** *Frank Emerson, Bill Webb, Cyril Thomas, Victor Clarke, Ferdy Moss, Reg Mock, Bob Parker, Ron Smith, Fred Minett.* **Front row:** *Bob Parsons, Gordon Saunders, Supt. A.F. Newman, Dickie Bird, Alan Smith.* Courtesy Bob Parker

Forest of Dean Police Rugby XV, early 1980s.
Standing: *Roy Rumbelow, Vic Kenny, Rod Sarson, Mark Calver, Dave Turner, Ian McNeill, Neil Thomas, Terry Lark, Dave Jones, John Wilcox.* **Kneeling:** *Win Morris, Malcolm Cameron, Pete Sharpe, Roger Miles, Bob Berryman, Mike Jones.*
Courtesy Neil Thomas

Forest of Dean Police Rugby Team, mid 1980s.
Standing: *Bob Berryman, Rod Sarson, Ian McNeill, Dick Berry, Dave Jones, Neil Thomas, Dave Turner, Dave Ballard, Terry Keyse, Steve McCormick, Gordon Sargent.* **Kneeling:** *Keith Phillips(?), Paul Gale, Lee Weaver, Roger Miles, Des Hughes, Russell Berryman.*
Courtesy Bob Berryman

Forest of Dean Police Cricket Team, mid 1980s. **Standing:** *Umpire Eric Moore, Keith Smith, Neil Thomas, Geoff Light, Ted Heath, Terry Keyse, Lee Weaver, Terry Lark, Umpire John Williams.* **Seated:** *Paul Gale, Paul Kerrod, Chief Constable L.A.G. Soper QPM, Shaun Cook, Bob Berryman.*

Courtesy Bob Berryman

Forest of Dean Police Soccer Team c.1990. **Back row:** *Sheila Berryman, Bob Berryman (Manager), K. Bolan, I. Dorothy, I. Houghton, M. Thomas, J. Underwood, I. McNeill, T. Keyse.* **Front row:** *R. Simpson, P. Roderick, S. Mills, A. Halford, C. Reed, D. Thompson, P. Hutchinson.*

Courtesy Bob Berryman

90s, a Forest Police Sunday XV played regular 'friendly' fixtures with pub and works sides fostering better community relations – as well as permitting old scores to be settled on both sides!

Sgt. Bob Berryman managed a very successful Forest Police soccer team in the 1980s and 90s which won promotion year on year in the Sunday League and, during the same period, the Chief Constable's Cup for Cricket had an almost permanent place in the trophy cabinet at Lydney. Other sports which have proved popular with Forest coppers over the years include tennis, bowls, angling and, of course, golf. Well known Gloucester angler Terry Girdlestone was an Inspector at Coleford and later Cinderford in the 1980s. Tug of War was very popular up until the 1950s and the Forest Police team were something to be reckoned with, regularly winning the event at the Constabulary Sports Day.

Tales From The River Bank

The Forest of Dean lies between the Rivers Severn and Wye and the police are responsible for co-ordinating search and rescue upstream of the M48 Severn Bridge. The treacherous tides and currents in the River Severn have claimed many lives over the years. So too have the cliffs of the Wye Valley, and the mines and caves of the Forest. It is the job of the police to co-ordinate emergency services and carry out investigations at the scene of serious incidents. For many years, in addition to the County Fire & Rescue Service and the Ambulance Service, they have been assisted by volunteer groups such as the Severn Auxiliary Rescue Association (SARA), which still operates inshore lifeboats and cliff rescue teams. There was also a volunteer cliff rescue team based at Coleford, until its role was taken over by the Fire Service in the late 1980s and the Forest of Dean can still boast an active volunteer cave rescue team which was started by Gordon Clissold.

Thankfully major incidents in the Forest have been few in number but there is one which stands out in recent history not only for the tragic loss of life but also for the loss of a local landmark. One foggy October night in 1960, two fuel tankers overshot the entrance to Sharpness docks in thick fog and were carried upstream on a strong tide. They collided with

The Severn Bridge Disaster, 25 October 1960. Photograph taken the following morning from the Sharpness side, showing the gap left by the two missing spans. Courtesy Gloucestershire Record Office. GRO Ref. Q/Y 6/3/12

Sgt. Bob Berryman recovering a salmon poacher's net from the River Wye at Bigsweir 1986.
By kind permission of the Chief Constable

the Severn Railway Bridge and exploded, killing five seamen and severely damaging the bridge. The gas supply to much of the Forest of Dean had been piped over this bridge and many people from both sides of the river relied on the rail link to attend school or employment. Although plans were initially drawn up to repair it, the broken bridge was eventually totally dismantled in the late 1960s. The incident echoed a similar one which happened on 4 February 1939, when some Severn barges failed to make the Sharpness harbour entrance on a difficult tide, collided with the Severn Railway Bridge and capsized, killing six seamen. Two others were rescued but four bodies were never recovered. Frank Jayne was the Sergeant at Berkeley who dealt with that incident. He was later to be the Coleford Inspector.

In the 1970s and 1980s, organised poaching of salmon on the River Wye had become a serious problem. Water bailiffs employed by the Welsh Water Authority, which was then the responsible statutory body, made a number of arrests but were in turn regularly assaulted and intimidated. There were large sums of money to be made by the poachers, many of whom were known to the police. In 1980, in response to the growing problem, a number of ordinary village and town police officers stationed in the Forest of Dean volunteered to form a squad, which would turn out at short notice in all weathers, although poorly equipped and with no expectation of overtime payment. This squad was run by PS Tony Berryman and later by his brother PS Bob Berryman. Operations would often involve hours of covert surveillance of an area of the bank where poachers were expected. If no poachers came to that spot the squad would then openly search the banks for miles upstream and down, confiscating any nets they found. The nets themselves were expensive, so this amounted to a summary fine. Better equipment was soon forthcoming in the form of night-sights, camouflage clothing and high powered lamps, and joint operations were held with water bailiffs and police anti-poaching squads which had been set up in the neighbouring divisions of the Gwent and West Mercia Constabularies. In 1984 Forest of Dean Officers made eleven arrests and seized no fewer than twenty two nets, as well as two boats.

Changing Times

Within a few years of being opened, the new (almost identical) stations at Yorkley and Parkend were closed and the houses sold. Many of the other 'Constable-in-charge' village stations suffered the same fate. Over the course of thirty years, the number of police stations in the Forest reduced from twenty-five to six (see Table 1, page 8).

A number of political, social, economic and technological factors may have played a part in the demise of the resident village police officer. In 1965 police officers in Gloucestershire with twenty years service or being forty years of age were permitted to become owner-occupiers in Gloucester, Cheltenham, Stroud and Staple Hill. By 1972 this permission had been extended to all officers throughout the force. Understandably many chose to buy their own homes and consequently several police houses in the towns were sold off, in some cases to police officers. This single change had the effect of gradually reducing the pool of suitable officers available for posting to residential village police stations (see Table 2 below).

A second significant improvement in the conditions of service came a year or so later when officers became entitled to payment for overtime. One of the operational advantages of dispersed, residential stations in rural areas had been that officers would be expected to deal with local problems, whether on or off duty, and could be called out by the Control Room, at night or on their day off, to deal with any type of incident, on their own or neighbouring beats. The right to payment for overtime

Table 2
POLICE HOUSING STATISTICS
GLOUCESTERSHIRE CONSTABULARY

Year	Owner Occupiers	Officers In Police Accommodation
1965	50	673
1980	703	268

meant that this practice would have to cease to be the norm. In financial terms each of the village police stations represented both a capital asset and an ongoing annual cost in maintenance, upgrading, heating and lighting for the office etc., at a time when the Constabulary was embarking on capital projects such as the Motor Patrol Centre at Bamfurlong, on which work began in 1977.

In the early 1970s all village police stations had either a police motorcycle or more likely a small van, which would have been unavailable for use when the officer was off duty. A regional VHF radio scheme had operated during the war and a Gloucestershire Force VHF vehicle radio scheme had been in existence since 1949 but from 1977 many rural police vehicles were equipped with hand-portable repeater radios, enabling the officer to remain in radio contact when away from the vehicle. These were costly and priority was given to vehicles used round the clock at the main rural stations. In the same year, a UHF personal radio scheme was introduced linking Lydney, Coleford and Cinderford. At the same time, a more sophisticated telephone owning public was making increasing demands and expecting a quick response. Closing village police stations and posting the officers to the main stations would have had the attraction of realising capital, making savings on the revenue budget, enabling more effective use to be made of the vehicle fleet, and improving flexibility and capacity to respond to demand but this was to be at the expense of public contact and local knowledge. The process was a gradual one, however. Some village police stations, such as Bream, retained their resident officers into the 1990s; other stations remained in use while the officer responsible for the beat lived elsewhere. In some cases, although the office continued to be used, the adjoining

Forest of Dean Police Cadets at the Annual Cadet Inspection, South Cerney 1962. Escorting the inspecting dignitaries is Insp. Beasant who was in charge at Cinderford. Cadets, right to left: Kevin Burke, Gary Short, Clifford Skinner, Roy Fisher, Neil Thomas and Bernard Giles. Courtesy Neil Thomas

house was either sold, as at St Briavels, or let, as in the cases of Tutshill and Huntley.

For most of the life of the Gloucestershire Constabulary, the area of the Forest of Dean roughly south of the A40 was a separate Division under the command of a Superintendent. In 1967 there was a Detective Inspector in charge of Forest CID and two Traffic Sergeants supervising 24 hour motor patrol car cover, plus two main road motorcyclists equipped with 650cc Triumphs. The Newent Section and the parishes neighbouring the city were then part of Gloucester Division. In 1968 Forest born Ben Gwilliam, a career detective who had served throughout the Force, was promoted to Superintendent in charge of the Forest Division and occupied the Superintendent's house in Church Road. He remained at Lydney until he retired in 1973. During this period he was kept quite busy – there were, for example, three murders in the space of one year. His widow, the well-known soprano Dora Gwilliam, still lives in Coleford.

The year 1968 was to be a year of change. In response to a Home Office Circular,

A career policeman. Left: PC 237 Ben Gwilliam, Sept 1939. Right: Inspector Ben Gwilliam c.1960.
Both courtesy Dora Gwilliam

the Force was reorganised into fewer but larger Divisions. Newent and its satellite station at Staunton became part of Northern Division, with its Div. HQ at Cheltenham. The Forest became a Sub-Division of the newly created Western Division, with its Div. HQ at Gloucester. In 1974 most of Southern Division became part of the new Avon & Somerset Constabulary and Newent, Huntley and Staunton & Corse became part of Western Division. During this period the detachment of Traffic officers, their cars and motorcycles, were withdrawn from Lydney to Barton Street in Gloucester and some of the officers opted to come off Traffic in order to stay in the Forest. In 1978 the Bamfurlong Motor Patrol Centre near Cheltenham was opened and became home to a centralised Traffic Division serving the whole county. In 1982, Newent, Staunton & Corse and Huntley became part of the Forest Sub-Division, as did the parishes of Hartpury, Ashleworth and Minsterworth which had previously been patrolled by the Gloucester Rural Beat Officer. For emergency response purposes the Forest Sub-Division was patrolled by one double-crewed response car based at Lydney. In 1983, a Home Office Circular effectively did away with any relationship between authorised police staffing levels and the size of the population. Approval for increases in establishment now depended on being able to demonstrate effectiveness, efficiency and economy in the use of manpower. This thinking placed little value on the preventive effects of high visibility patrol or the symbolic, reassuring presence of police on the streets, as these were difficult to measure.

Further reorganisation in the late 1980s once again divided the Force into smaller devolved Divisions (or 'Basic Command Units' to use the jargon of the day), of which the Forest of Dean was one. It had its own Divisional Administration office in Lydney Police Station and Traffic cars and motorcycles were once more based in the Forest under the control of the local Superintendent. A Detective Inspector was again based at Lydney, Wayne Murdock being the first. Wayne, now a DCI, is the younger brother of Graham Murdock who was at Lydney as a Chief Inspector in the 1970s and who retired as a Chief Superintendent.

There were many changes in the 1990s. A move towards intelligence-led crime prevention and detection resulted in a Crime Management Unit being set up at Lydney and the formation of a proactive squad under the general banner of Operation Gemini, signifying the twin objectives of burglary and car crime and the partnership between police and public. Helicopter support became available and Armed Response Vehicles went on patrol in the county for the first time. Town centre CCTV surveillance was introduced in Coleford then in Lydney, Cinderford and Newent. A computerised command and control system, together with improved telephony and radio, made it possible to operate a single call-centre and centralised control rooms, thereby removing that function from the Forest stations. Forest folk now find themselves trying to explain their problem (and where they live) to someone in a call-centre at Force HQ in Cheltenham and may be more than a little reluctant to report things. It has to be said, though, that most large organisations now have similar systems. Also in the 1990s, patrol officers received better equipment for their personal safety such as rigid handcuffs, ASP extendible metal batons, CS spray and stab-proof vests. The Special Constabulary, those volunteer citizens who give up their time to assist the regular police, have played an increasing part in recent years. Not only do they augment the strength on Friday and Saturday nights and at special events, they also carry out crime prevention surveys, drive police vehicles and perform many of the tasks normally associated with regular officers.

Another significant change in the 1990s was in how the police were funded. The Police & Magistrates Court Act devolved decisions on staffing levels to the Chief Constable but allowed the Government to set its own limits on its share of police funding, thus applying downward pressure on police numbers. The Home Office police funding formula changed in favour of constabularies with highly urbanised areas. This meant a year-on-year reduction in real terms of the Government's contribution to the funding of the Gloucestershire Constabulary and therefore the Force was being asked each year to do more with less. In early 1998 the Forest had

Helicopters are a vital part of the armoury of the police force today. These two snapshots show a police helicopter changing crews at Corse, May 2000.

Photos Geoff Sindrey

a ratio of one Constable to approximately one thousand of the population (estimated at 77,100). An in-depth scrutiny carried out by the Constabulary led to reorganisation throughout the county and the shedding of many senior and middle management posts. As a result of this reorganisation, the Forest once more became part of a larger Division based on Gloucester. It lost its Superintendent, its Chief Inspector, its Detective Inspector, one of its uniformed Inspectors, its own Admin. Unit plus a significant number of Sergeants and Constables. Since April 1998 the Forest has been divided into two INAs or Inspector Neighbourhood Areas (North and South) with an Inspector in charge of each, stationed at Cinderford and Coleford respectively. Sergeants are stationed at Lydney, Coleford, Cinderford and Newent and these stations are open to the public at certain times of the day. The other two stations are used as base offices by non-resident police officers. The Traffic Section, the Gemini Squad and the Crime Management Unit were centralised at Gloucester, and the Forest CID complement was reduced to a small team of Detectives based at Cinderford. The Traffic Section was restored in 1999 and is now based at Coleford. A proactive Operation Gemini Team was restored in 2000 drawn from existing Forest staff.

Boundary changes also followed the scrutiny, making the police Divisions, as far as possible, coterminous with District Council boundaries, in order to facilitate a partnership approach to the reduction of crime and disorder in accordance with the provisions of the Crime & Disorder Act. Each parish or group of parishes in the Forest was allocated a designated community police officer, to attend parish council meetings and work to resolve problems in the parish (or parishes) for which he or she is responsible. Another innovation is the Police Information Point (PIP). These are being set up at places such as post offices to improve contact between the police and the public. In each Neighbourhood Area there is 24 hour cover from an Incident Response car and a Traffic car also covers the whole Forest.

Superintendent John Horan, who is the commander of the Forest & Gloucester Division, explains the philosophy behind the system of policing in operation in the Forest of Dean, at the start of the new century:

> *"People are at the heart of policing and communication with people will continue to be the life blood of policing in the 21st century in the Forest.*
>
> *The Forest & Gloucester Division of the Gloucestershire Constabulary covers the Local Authority Areas administered by the Forest of Dean District Council and the Gloucester City Council. Within that Division there are six Neighbourhood Areas two of which are in the Forest of Dean – Forest North and Forest South – having responsibility for 30 and 13 parishes respectively. Gone are the days of 'beats'. The police staff now relate to Parish and District Councils, believing that we should be accountable to local people.*
>
> *So what are the benefits of this type of policing? Quite simply, local police officers, under the command of the local Neighbourhood Area Inspector, 'own' everything that is going on in that area. It is they who are responsible for reducing and detecting crime, reducing disorder and helping to make their local communities even more peaceful places in which to live.*
>
> *The police cannot work in isolation and need to work very closely with partners in other statutory agencies like the District and County Councils but, most important of all, with the people who live in the parishes. Local policing and local accountability will make a successful Police Service and to that end, we now have regular Police and Community Consultative Meetings at different places throughout the Forest, to which anybody is welcome. These meetings are chaired by a member of the Police Authority and are designed to discuss local matters of concern to which the police will respond. They are successful and regularly attract 40 or more people. In essence, that is what the Crime & Disorder Act is about.*
>
> *The Act has a simple ambition: 'To help build a safer and more responsible society'. It has three themes:*
>
> ** to reform youth justice to focus efforts on preventing offending by children and other young people.*
>
> ** to build safer communities through new local partnerships and by giving better protection against anti-social behaviour, sex offenders and drugs-misusing offenders.*
>
> ** within the Criminal Justice System, to improve problems, reduce delays and promote public confidence in the system.*
>
> *In the Forest the District and County Councils and the police now work closely together on many issues, including burglary, car crime, disorder, violence, drug abuse and more. There is no doubt that this partnership and the help of the local people has contributed to the downward trend of crime and to more crimes being detected.*
>
> *Policing in the 21st century is not very different from what it has always been. It is about talking, listening and then doing."*

Nobody would deny that the Forest of Dean needs more officers. During 2000 the lack of public confidence in rural policing was brought into sharp focus nationally by the conviction of a Norfolk farmer for shooting a burglar at his home.

A Forest Beat

Only now, at the turn of the century, is the Home Office recognising the cost of the 'sparsity' factor in rural policing. The Gloucestershire Constabulary learned in early 2000 that its bid for additional staff funding under the scheme announced by Jack Straw at the Labour Party Conference in 1999 had been successful. Four of these 'Jack Straw's Bobbies' were allocated to the Forest. In April 2000, Forest Police took delivery of two Skoda Felicia estates, sponsored by Winner Garage of Cinderford, for use by Rural Beat Officers, to visit rural communities on a more regular basis and co-ordinate the Rural Watch Schemes. A Rural Policing Panel was set up in the Forest to involve members of the public and community leaders in the decision making process in relation to the Rural Policing Strategy, which was officially launched on 26 June 2000.

Rural Watch Co-ordinators PC Rob Dix of Forest South (left) and PC Roger Hall, Forest North, taking delivery of two Skoda Felicia estates, sponsored by Winner Garage of Cinderford, in April 2000. Courtesy Citizen Newspapers

Summary

The essential nature of police work has altered little since 1840 but changing conditions, new legislation and technological advances have inevitably led to changes in the way police work is done. The expansion of police stations into the smaller communities of the Forest of Dean was a gradual one which continued until the early 1970s. The process went into reverse over the next two decades, however, as a result of a combination of different factors. The physical and documentary evidence speaks to us of significant changes in circumstances and fundamental shifts in ideas over the past century-and-a-half of policing. Now, at the beginning of the 21st century, the Forest of Dean again has a system of policing which is delivered from a relatively small number of police stations, much as was the case in 1840. It has to be said, however, that despite all the pressures, the Gloucestershire Constabulary has never abandoned the concept of community-based policing and still operates more police stations than other forces of a similar size and profile.

Dave Smith, Inspector Forest North, Cinderford, in early 2000, was appointed Inspector in charge of Forest South, 24 July 2000. By kind permission of the Chief Constable

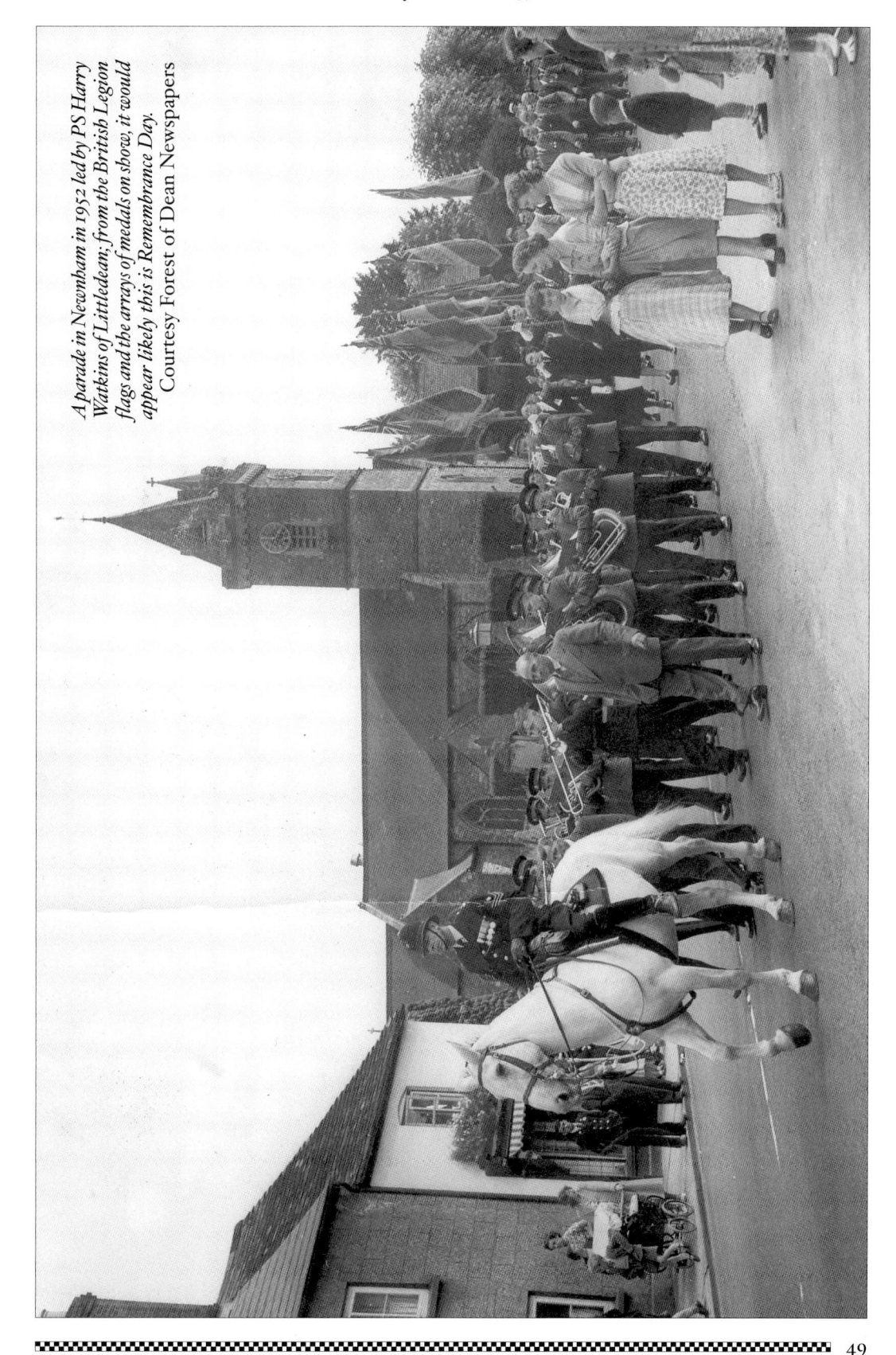

A parade in Newnham in 1952 led by PS Harry Watkins of Littledean; from the British Legion flags and the arrays of medals on show, it would appear likely this is Remembrance Day.
Courtesy Forest of Dean Newspapers

GLOUCESTERSHIRE CONSTABULARY
Map of Police Stations 1839 – 2000
Forest of Dean Division

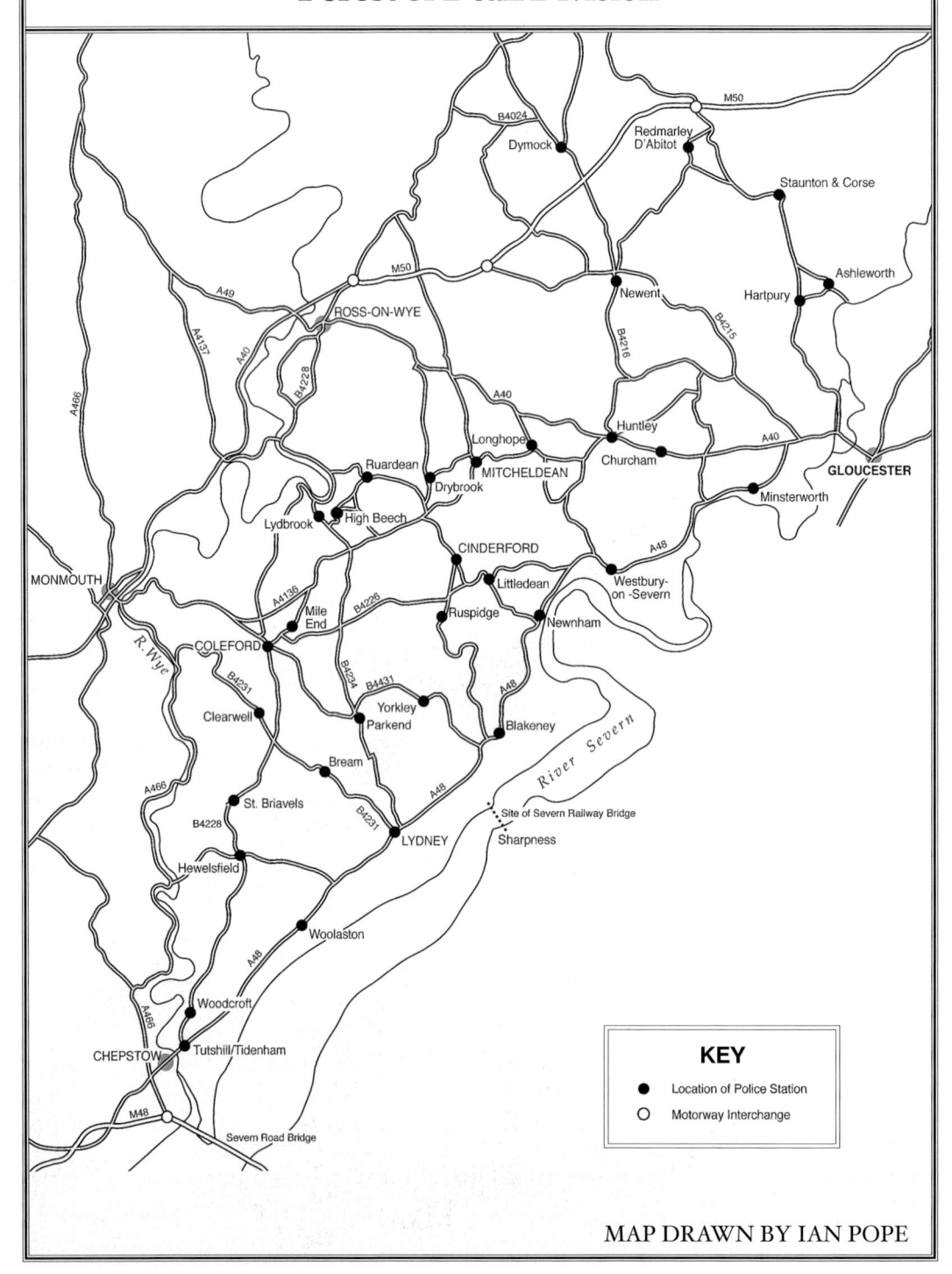

KEY
- Location of Police Station
- ○ Motorway Interchange

MAP DRAWN BY IAN POPE

Part 2
Around The Forest of Dean

It is often said that police officers either love the Forest or they hate it. Most love it. There have been many cases of officers who, having been posted to the Forest of Dean under protest, have been content to spend the rest of their lives there!

This part of the book is about people and places. It visits Forest communities and seeks to tell the story of policing in local terms, using personal accounts where these have been forthcoming. All present and former police stations so far traced by the authors are identified by a photograph and a map reference. Rather than geographically, the stations are covered in alphabetical order.

Ashleworth

Though not in the Forest of Dean District, Ashleworth has been included because its policing history has been shared with neighbouring Hartpury. Over the years there have been five successive police stations covering the area, three in Ashleworth and two in Hartpury. For most of the life of the Gloucestershire Constabulary, Ashleworth was part of Gloucester District/Division but from 1982 it became part of the Forest of Dean Division, before further reorganisation made it part of Cheltenham & Tewkesbury Division in 1998.

'Barksdale' on the Village Green is believed to have been Ashleworth's first police station. In 1851 Irish born PC John Chantry was in charge, assisted by PC Walter Hicks. PC Chantry was possibly one of the experienced Irish officers that Chief Constable Lefroy had brought over as the nucleus for the new force. The station is mentioned in the 1857 survey, in which it is described as being in good repair. It had

Ashleworth
NGR SO 812 254
'Barksdale' on 'The Green' was the village's first police station. Photo Ted Heath

three bedrooms but *'no strong room or cells'*.

In 1881 PC Edmund Wilson lived there with his wife Elizabeth and their son George, aged two. PC William Fletcher lived there as a lodger.

'The Croft', in Longridge Lane, served briefly as the police station according to the 1871 census, perhaps while alterations were being made to 'Barksdale'. In that year the resident Constable, John Gould, and his family, shared with William Roberts, a collector of taxes.

'Goodrich Cottage' was Ashleworth's last police station. It closed around 1950 and was replaced by a new building at Hartpury. PC Jefferies is thought to have been the last officer in charge. He had two sons who joined the Force, Colin Jefferies and John Jefferies, who both became Sergeants.

When the last station closed, the parish became part of the Gloucester Rural Beat and many local people will remember PC Bob Jones and PC Terry Smith who patrolled the area for years. Keen cyclist Gerry McGarr was one of the last of these rural beat officers, because in 1982 a reorganisation of the Force put the parish under the PC at Staunton and the Sergeant at Newent. Further reorganisation in 1998 aligned police boundaries with those of local government. As a result, the people of Ashleworth found themselves in the Cheltenham & Tewkesbury Police Division.

Ashleworth
NGR SO 812 250
'The Croft', Longridge Lane, also served as the police station for a period in the 19th century.   Photo Ted Heath

Ashleworth
NGR SO 812 258
'Goodrich Cottage' was the village's last police station.
Photo Ted Heath

Blakeney

Blakeney's first police station is the building which straddles the brook alongside the main road and now houses the post office. In the 1857 survey it was considered not to be in a good situation. It had no cells and no room for alterations. It was decided to move to more suitable premises in the *'lower part of the town'*.

Blakeney
NGR SO 670 069
This building, now the village Post Office, is Blakeney's first recorded police station.
Photo Ted Heath

The house called the 'Old Police Station' in The Square is probably the building taken into use after the survey. It remained in service until the 1960s and for most of its life it was a Sergeant station. It was also the village police station during a particularly violent period in Blakeney's history. In the 1890s a gang from the Blakeney Hill area were said to exercise a system of terrorism over the inhabitants of the Forest. Questions were asked in The House of Commons and the Deputy Surveyor of the Forest of Dean at the time thought the situation serious enough to ask for a troop of cavalry. Instead the Chief Constable, Admiral Henry Christian, sent eight additional police officers.

Blakeney
NGR 672 070
The second station was this imposing building in The Square. It is now a private residence, although its past use is commemorated in its name – 'The Old Police Station'.
Photo Ted Heath

In May 1895 PC Newport was attacked by a gang in the village and, according to some reports, would have been killed had his colleagues not come to his aid. In November of the same year Sergeant William Morris and PC Cornelius Harding were on duty at Viney Hill, when they encountered a group of men who were on their way home after visiting various public houses in Blakeney. There was a scuffle and both officers were hit by stones. PC Harding was knocked unconscious and PS Morris was killed, having sustained a fractured skull and a broken neck. He left a widow and three small children. Three young men from Whitecroft and Pillowell were arrested and charged with murder and attempted murder, and were convicted of manslaughter. Sergeant Morris is buried in Lydney Churchyard. The inscription on his gravestone reads as follows:

IN THE MIDST OF LIFE WE ARE IN DEATH.
OF WHOM MAY WE SEEK FOR SUCCOUR
BUT THEE O LORD.

Somewhat less nasty is an apocryphal story from the 1920s, which tells how the local lads tied a donkey to the door of the police station, so that when an officer tried to open the door the donkey pulled in the opposite direction and the more the officer pulled the more the donkey pulled! (donkeys are like that).

Jim Ludlow wondered what he had come to when he was posted to Blakeney in 1939. He was out on patrol with his sergeant when they were confronted by a group of local youths barring the way across the bridge over the brook. Jim says that the Sergeant marched through the group pushing them aside. One of the 'yobs' was heard to say

'*Thinks himself something of a policeman*'.

With that the sergeant turned to the young man, pulled him very close and said,

'*Not something of a policeman, all of a policeman!*'

The lad then somehow ended up in the brook!

Jim lived in the station with PS Joe Ireland and his wife. Also stationed there were Tom Pugsley and Bert Carter. Joe's rules were that officers were not allowed to use the local pubs but strangely were permitted to go into the kitchen at the Cock

Blakeney in the early 1930s. An unidentified constable is crossing The Square in front of the police station (on the left, gable front just visible).
Courtesy
The Archive Shop

A superb study, taken outside Lydney Police Station circa 1890. The officer on the left is Sgt. William Morris, who was stoned to death at Viney Hill on 10 November 1895, aged 32. Geoff Sindrey collection

Inn where they could stay all night! Sixty seven shillings a week didn't go very far so off duty evenings were often spent playing whist. Mrs Ireland liked to partner Jim so that she would be playing against her husband. Both were fiercely competitive.

Mr M.F. Carter of Newnham was the local Coroner and Clerk to the Justices. One day he ran short of money to pay witness expenses. Jim remembers that he loaned Mr Carter £5 (a lot of money in those days) and was too frightened to ask this important man for it back. When Mr Carter did his accounts he found himself £5 to the good and asked the sergeant if he had borrowed money from anybody.

The patrol ticket system introduced by the first Chief Constable (see pages 13 and 16) was still in use in Blakeney. Jim recalled where some of the drops were: Mr Box at Viney Hill post office, Capt. Bancroft at Nibley cross-roads, The Hon. Ethel Lopes at Underdean and the Schweppes Cider factory on the main road (where a bottle of cider was left for the copper). Although there were two bicycles allocated to the station (one for the Sergeant and one for the men), all these ticket points had to be made on foot. Jim quickly made friends with the local postman, however, and got his tickets delivered!

In those days trucks going out of control on the hill were common. Early one morning such a lorry crashed into Ludlow House, next to the police station, killing not only the driver but the milk boy who was just delivering milk. The lorry spilled its load of offal into the front room of the house and the lady who lived there suffered a stroke. Edgar Bowring from Newnham was on main road bicycle patrol that night making points at Westbury, Elton Corner, Newnham and Viney Hill cross-roads. He was due to finish early at 4am. to attend court. If he had worked until 6am. as normal he would have been in Blakeney at the time of the accident. As it was he was about half way back to Newnham when it happened and he was completely unaware. Insp. A.F. Newman (who later, as a Superintendent, commanded the Division) attended from Lydney, with PS Phelps and PC Wakefield. Another fatal accident in Blakeney at that time involved a pedestrian killed by a car containing two Royal New Zealand Air Force men. Before the Inquest could be held, the driver himself had been killed in action.

The police station at Blakeney was closed in the 1960s.

Runaways on the hill into the village were quite common. The driver of this lorry had a lucky escape in the early 1950s, his vehicle left hanging precariously over the brook.
Courtesy
The Archive Shop

Bream

Bream does not seem to have had a police station until the late 19th century, when there is evidence of expansion in the village associated with extensive deep coal mining. There was also unrest in the industry at this time. Four successive buildings served the village and soon after the closure of the last one, Bream became the first community in the Forest to have a 'Police Information Point' at the village post office.

The former blacksmith's shop, now a barn, on the property of 'Forest View', New Road, was Bream's police station in 1878. It is said that there were two cells but subsequent conversion has left little evidence of its former use.

Bream
NGR SO 602 058
The village's first police station as it appears today. Previously a blacksmiths shop, this building in New Road was the police station in 1878. By the 1920s it was in residential use and was called 'Forest View Cottage'.
Photo Ted Heath

'Rosehill Cottage', the house just above the New Inn in High Street, is believed to have been Bream's second police station. Although extensively altered, it is still possible to identify the former cell. PC Albert Hull was the officer in charge in 1923.

Bream
NGR SO 603 059
This house in High Street was Bream's second police station.
Photo Ted Heath

A Forest Beat

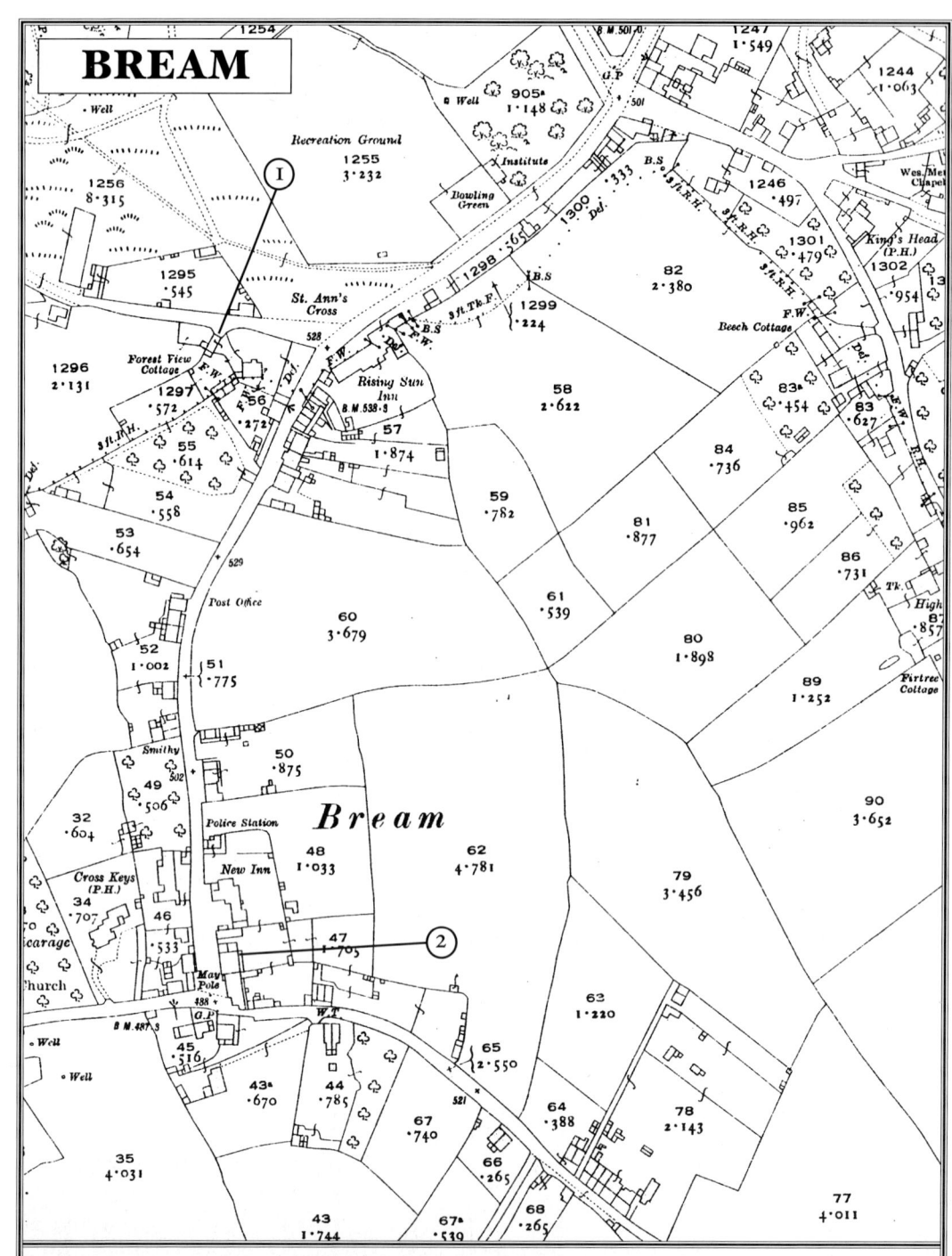

Part of the 1922 edition 25 inch OS which shows the positions of three of the four police stations to have served Bream. The blacksmith's, thought to be the first police station in 1878, is shown 1; by this date it was a dwelling called 'Forest View Cottage'. The second station, in use at the date of this map, is shown just above the New Inn. In the 1930s it moved into the building formerly occupied by Cannock's newsagents, marked 2. The last police station in Bream was a 1950s purpose-built pair of houses and office in Parkend Road, which is shown branching off the High Street to the right in the top right corner.

Courtesy Gloucestershire Record Office. Crown copyright reserved

58

Bream's third station (formerly a shop) was situated in High Street, close to the Maypole which stood at the junction with the Lydney road. The building, like the Maypole itself, has since been demolished. PC Chris Beddis was in charge in the 1930s, with Jack Harding as his second man. In 1949, PCs Reg Weeks and Jock Brown were stationed there.

Bream
NGR SO 603 058
PC Beddis (right) and another officer outside the station (formerly Cannock's shop) which stood in High Street, near the Maypole, in the 1930s. The building has since been demolished.
Courtesy Gloucestershire Record Office.
GRO Ref Q/Y 6/3/14

The station in Parkend Road was built in the 1950s and was still the village police station into the 1990s. In the 1960s PC Bruce Reed was in charge. He retired as a Sergeant at Lydney in the mid-1980s. PC Andy Barrow, a founder of The Gloucestershire Constabulary Male Voice Choir, served that community through three decades and was the last resident officer-in-charge. He took over in 1975, having moved from Yorkley with his wife and family when the station there was closed. He now had responsibility for the general policing of Bream, Parkend, Whitecroft, Pillowell and Yorkley, as a result of a reorganisation of policing in the Forest of Dean which was to be the start of the decline of the village constable. During his tenure at Bream, it was necessary for Andy to spend quite a bit of time away, helping to sort out other problems elsewhere; for example, trouble in Gloucester or Cheltenham, New Age Travellers and the Miners' Strike.

PC Denis Shergold, with his wife. He is well remembered from his time as village bobby at Bream in the 1950s.
Courtesy Ruth Proctor Hirst

Bream   NGR SO 606 065
The 1950s built station in Parkend Road.   Photo Ted Heath

Andy saw this period as a crisis for rural policing. He wrote:

". . . much as the local bobbies tried to contain it they were fighting a losing battle against rising crime, lack of respect by some for authority, lack of parental control, together with senior police officers trying what they thought were new ideas but which had been tried before and failed. It also seemed they were being frustrated in their efforts by some officers furthering their own careers at the expense of the public and their colleagues."

It was taken for granted by the service and by the public that the wife of an officer in charge would be an unpaid assistant. Andy appreciates the support he had from his wife Cherryl, who is a nurse. He writes:

"Although she had her work cut out rearing four fine boys, she was always on hand to deal with all sorts of problems such as miscarriages, epilepsy, convulsions, road accidents, chainsaw accidents, stray animals, lost dogs, cats and pigeons, acting as resident constable when her husband was away and arranging for other officers to attend incidents. This is just a potted version of what actually took place but it was brilliant teamwork which was given without a thought."

Andy also recalls some lighter moments:

"I attended a reported house burglary in which a radio had been stolen. At the attacked premises the occupant proudly showed off his gleaming 'Diamond White' refrigerator. It was only after about ten minutes that it dawned on me that that it was not plugged in. In fact there was no electricity in the house at all!

On another occasion I was interviewing a young fellow at the station on a November evening. It was going to be a lengthy process so I offered the fellow a fag. I was trying to give up smoking at the time, with the support and encouragement of my family but I knew that there was at least one cigarette in a packet in the house so I went to get it. The offer was gratefully accepted, the fag was lit and the interview resumed. I was busy writing down the lad's dictated statement when suddenly there was a loud bang. I looked up and saw the remains of the fag in

Andy Barrow was the village police officer at Bream for many years. His service to the community, beyond the call of duty, was recognised by the award of the Caroline Symes Memorial Bowl. Andy and his wife Cherryl are seen here with HRH The Prince of Wales at the presentation ceremony. By kind permission of the Chief Constable

the fellows lips with shreds of tobacco in all directions. He was pale and sweating. I asked him what had happened and he replied, "Honest Mr Barrow, I didn't do anything. It just exploded in me face". I could hear laughter from inside the house but Cherryl and the boys were quite concerned when they realised their victim had been a member of the public, not me as intended. However the fellow was okay about it and didn't retract his statement on the grounds of duress!"

Andy was highly respected by the public and his colleagues alike. He had this to say about policing today:

"... sadly, all the work at creating good relations over the years seems to have been to no avail. There seems to be little or no contact between police and public nowadays. It isn't the fault of the humble Constable but of the system, of under-funding, of politics and politicians, together with the failure of the courts to apply the appropriate sentences where all the time sufficient power exists ... and a general lack of RESPECT."

Churcham

A cottage on the A40 near the cross-roads at Birdwood is believed to be the old Churcham police station. The station is mentioned in the 1857 Survey, at which time it was in the Gloucester Police District. In the early 20th century it was replaced by a station at Huntley. Now, as we enter the 21st century, 'Robocop' in the form of a speed camera stands watch where once there was a police station.

Churcham   NGR SO 742 188
This cottage near the crossroads at Birdwood is believed to be the old police station.   Photo Ted Heath

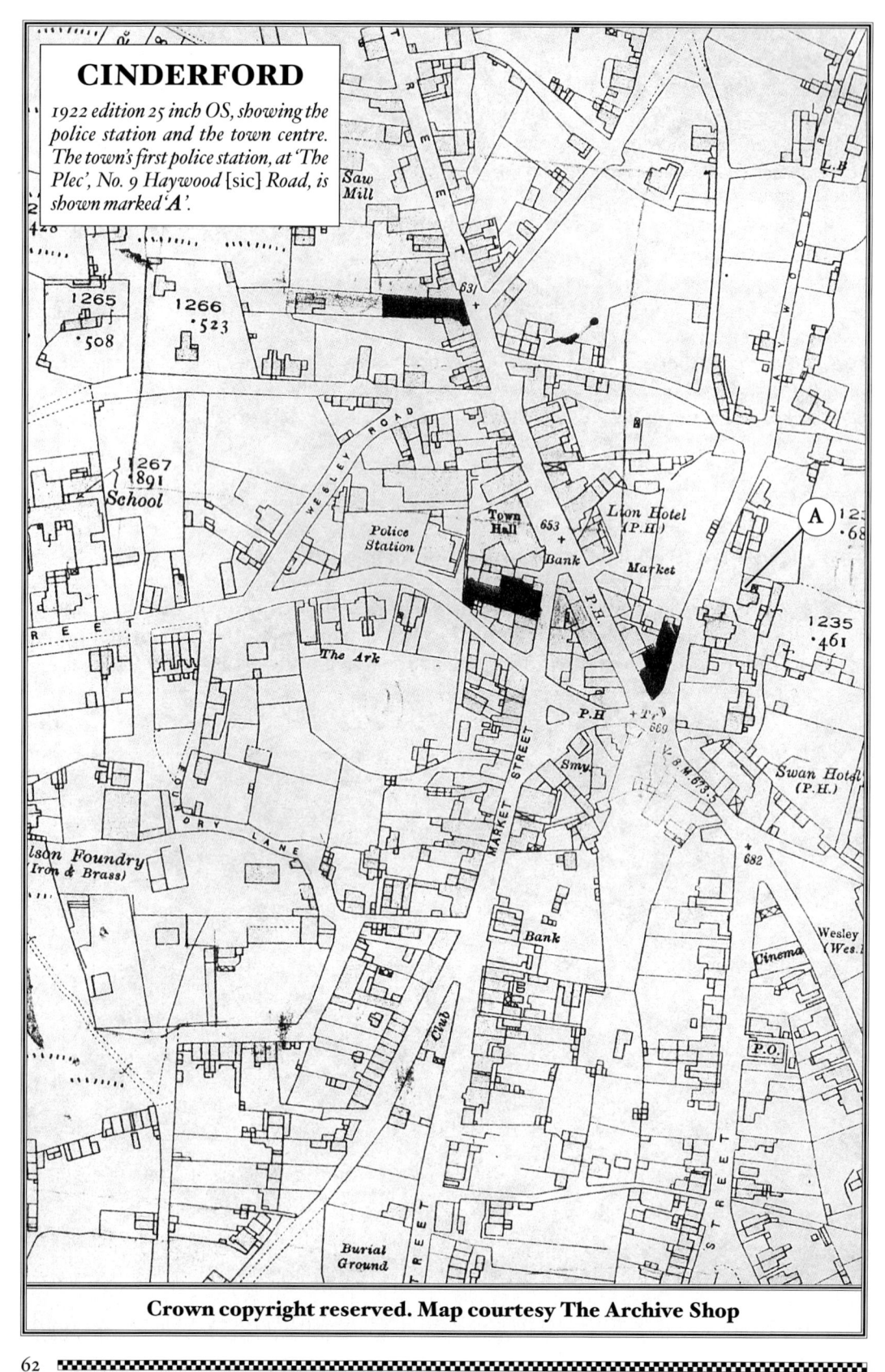

CINDERFORD

1922 edition 25 inch OS, showing the police station and the town centre. The town's first police station, at 'The Plec', No. 9 Haywood [sic] Road, is shown marked 'A'.

Crown copyright reserved. Map courtesy The Archive Shop

Cinderford

A house known as 'The Plec', at No 9 Heywood Road, is the first known police station in Cinderford and was opened in 1865. This building would have been at the centre of dramatic scenes in 1874 when rioting broke out in the town.

Elections in February 1874 passed off quietly throughout the rest of the Forest but in Cinderford they provided an occasion for heavy drinking and riotous behaviour, in a town which at that time probably had more in common with Kimberly or Dawson than with neighbouring Coleford. The town had grown rapidly around the coal and iron industry, and there had been an influx of people from outside the area looking for work. At this time Cinderford police station had a complement of just two Constables.

It was on the Saturday that several people suspected of Conservative sympathies were attacked and injured by a drunken and unruly mob, several shops and houses were completely ruined, and shots were fired by people in fear of their lives and property. Superintendent Edward Chipp (later to be Deputy Chief Constable) went there from Coleford with all the officers available and telegraphed Cheltenham and Gloucester for assistance. He then issued cutlasses to his officers and patrolled the town restoring order.

On the following day, Sunday, tension was still high. The Superintendent obtained an order from two Justices of the Peace, Edwin Crawshay and Captain Gould, to close all the public houses. Fifty six officers made sure the order was enforced. Later on Sunday, the Chief Constable arrived at Littledean, as did the 103rd Regiment of Foot from Newport. Military assistance was not needed, however, and on Monday, the redoubtable Superintendent Chipp led officers on raids of houses in Cinderford and Ruspidge, arresting fifteen alleged ringleaders. Ten more arrests followed in the next two days. The trial began later the same month at Newnham but was adjourned to the club room at The George Inn at Littledean. Mr Chipp remained in Cinderford for several weeks, parted from his beloved wife while she gave birth to their daughter, Lucy, at the police station in Coleford.

Cinderford
NGR SO 659 142
This house in Heywood Road is Cinderford's first police station, so far as is known.
Photo Ted Heath

The police station in Station Street, as seen on a postcard of circa 1910. It was well situated for the town centre – and any potential trouble!
Courtesy The Archive Shop

The police station in Bilson Road (now Station Street), was opened in 1877 and remains in use today, largely unaltered. Cinderford continued to enjoy a rough reputation as can be seen in this extract from *The Gloucester Journal*, April 28 1877, kindly provided by Alec Pope:

> '... Some proceedings have been instituted arising out of an alleged assault upon one of Cinderford's police officers, who came in for rough treatment on Saturday night at the hands of a number of Foresters near the Seven Stars Inn. Warrants were issued on Monday, and the ringleaders are likely to be charged with the offence. The officer's staff was broken to pieces, and a stone struck him upon the head. Rowdyism of this nature is not unknown in Cinderford ...'

So much for the good old days!

Cinderford
NGR SO 656 141
The police station as it is today.
Photo Ted Heath

In the years before the First World War, Cinderford, of all the Forest towns, enjoyed its processions and demonstrations. Temperance groups, Baptists, Methodists, Sports groups and the Co-operative Society, all had their annual march through the town, with the local police often leading the procession as well as keeping a watchful eye. Here the Baptist march of 1910 is seen, with one of the colourful miners' banners to the fore.
Courtesy Ian Pope

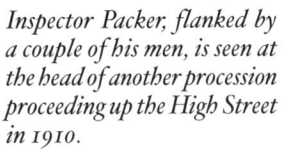

Inspector Packer, flanked by a couple of his men, is seen at the head of another procession proceeding up the High Street in 1910.
Courtesy Ian Pope

With two constables flanking the leaders of the march and two more watching on, the Co-operative Demonstration rounds the corner into the Triangle and Market Street, in front of the store, once again in 1910.
Courtesy
The Archive Shop

Cinderford police in attendance at the aftermath of the fire at the Empire Theatre, in 1906.
Courtesy Ian Pope

The popular Inspector Packer with his trusty police bicycle.
Courtesy Ian Pope

Frederick Voyce, a Cinderford butcher, who was awarded an engraved cane for going to the assistance of an officer in trouble – one Sgt. Bull, not the one in the picture!
Courtesy Lionel Voyce

In gaiters and greatcoat, one of Cinderford's constables was captured on this circa 1930 postcard directing traffic at the junction of Market Street and High Street.
Courtesy
The Archive Shop

In 1923 Mr Frederick Voyce, a Cinderford Butcher, was presented with an ebony cane with a horn handle for going to the assistance of Sgt. Charles Bull, who was on the ground being kicked by a gang. The inscription on the cane's silver handle joint reads: *'Presented to Fredk. Voyce by Forest of Dean Police for assisting a comrade 24. 12. 23.'*

A popular figure during the First World War and after was Inspector Packer, who lost two sons in that horrific conflict. Albert Carter, who later commanded the Division and went on to be Assistant Chief Constable, was an Inspector at Cinderford in the 1930s. Mike Perry, who had been a Sergeant at Lydney, was the Inspector-in-charge for many years, followed by the late Geoff Miles. For a short period the Inspector was Eddy Baud who, as a Sergeant, had been seconded to Rhodesia in 1980 to help supervise the Independence elections. Doug Hunt, later Chairman of Cinderford RFC, was a Sergeant at Cinderford for many years.

Insp. Albert H. Carter, Cinderford, 1930s.
Courtesy Pat Hutchings

Above: *A group of officers outside Cinderford Police Station in the late 1930s. The smart young man on the right of the group is Joe McKnight who went on to be a high ranking detective. The badge on his left sleeve is a First Aid qualification.* Courtesy Gloucestershire Records Office GRO Ref. Q/Y 6/1/59

Right: *PC Alf Reeve, February 1938. He retired as a DS at Lydney in the 1960s.* Courtesy The Archive Shop

Appropriately in keeping with Cinderford's unique character, a public right of way passes through the police station site and police vehicles share an open car park at the rear. Being within the statutory Forest, it is not uncommon for sheep to be seen standing on the low wall of the police station looking in through the window! Graham Murdock recalled how in 1977, as a newly promoted Chief Inspector, he decided to visit Cinderford police station. Dressed in his best uniform and clutching his personal radio, he tried the door and found it locked although there were people inside. He knocked on the door and went to one of the windows and as he did so his feet went from under him and he landed unceremoniously on the ground holding up his radio to prevent it being damaged. On getting up he realised he had slipped on some sheep droppings. Welcome to the Forest, Mr Murdock!

Several Gloucestershire police officers have hailed from Cinderford, among them, Dennis Freeman, Ken Parsons and Frank Coombes QPM, who was head of the County CID.

A group outside Cinderford police station on the last day of Forest Division, 31 March 1998. **Back row**, *left to right: PC Paul Hutchinson, PS Colin Heselton, PS Bob Phelps.* **Front row:** *PC Justin Parnell, PC Dean Morse, Civilian Clerk Mary Parker (appointed Force Welfare Officer in 2000), PC John Cann, PC Annette Gunter, PC Andy Johnson, PC Glen Morse.   By kind permission of the Chief Constable*

Clearwell

A police station at Clearwell is mentioned in the Police & Constabulary Almanac of 1916. It was located in an old stone building in the centre of the village, near the cross. The life of the police station was a short one and the building is now a fine house. Freeminer Dennis Gething remembered being told a story from the days when Clearwell had its own bobby. Apparently, it was common for some of the regulars to stay behind at the Butcher's Arms and play cards upstairs until quite late. The Constable called at the pub one night and the landlord answered the door to him. He borrowed the officer's helmet and walked upstairs, emerging slowly, helmet-first, into the room where the card players were and, it is said, gave them the fright of their lives!

Clearwell NGR SO 572 081
Clearwell police station, behind the cross, on an old postcard, circa 1905. Courtesy Mr & Mrs G. Parker

Coleford

A plan of Coleford dated 1849 shows the police station at No. 3 Gloucester Road. The plan shows no building whatsoever on the site of the present and previous police stations, at the junction of Gloucester Road and Lord's Hill. The 1857 survey describes a house owned by a Mr Butt of Cheltenham, facing the road; *'the entrance road from Mitcheldean and Littledean to Coleford'*.

Coleford
NGR SO 577 108
No. 3 Gloucester Road as it appears today. It was the police station in 1849 and probably remained in use as such until the completion of the new station on the corner of the Lord's Hill junction a short distance away, in 1860.
Photo Ted Heath

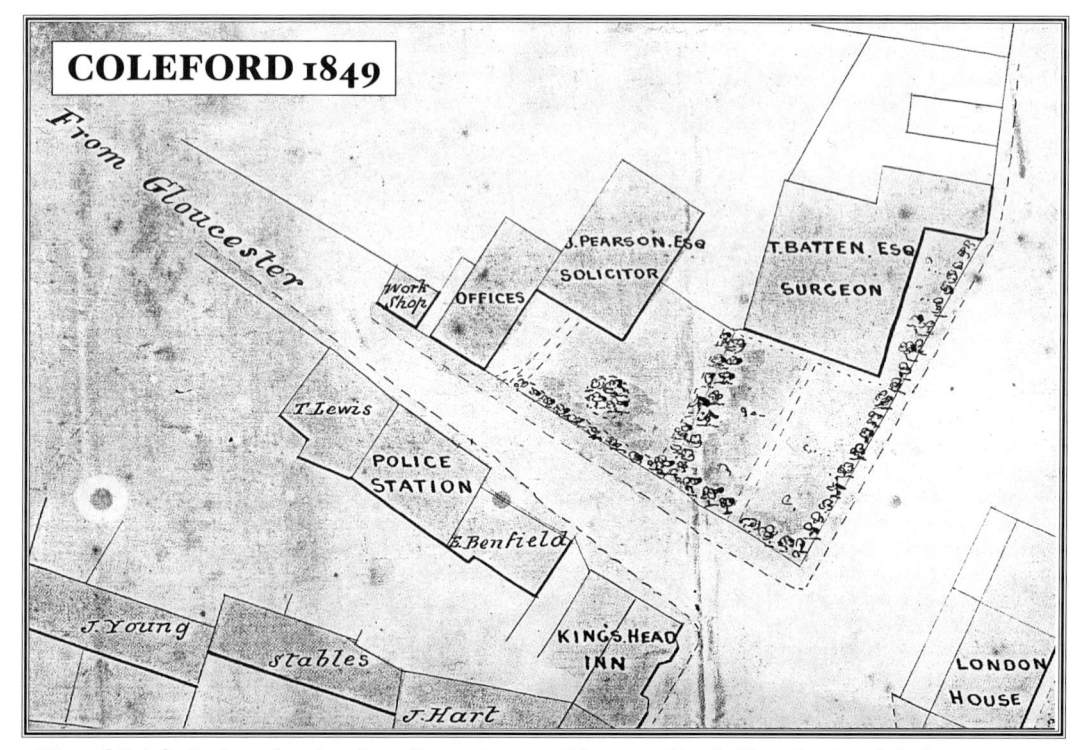

Plan of Coleford, 1849, showing the police station at 3 Gloucester Road. Note the site of the later stations, opposite the King's Head, is undeveloped. Plan drawn up by S. G. Gregg, Land Surveyor of Coleford.
Courtesy Gwen Baker

Coleford
NGR SO 576 108

Top: *Coleford's second police station was purpose-built in 1860, on the corner of Gloucester Road and Lords Hill. It was an imposing structure, built in a commanding situation, projecting an air of authority no doubt purposely intended by its providers. This postcard view dates from around 1905.*
Courtesy The Archive Shop

Right: *A later view, taken a few years before its closure and demolition in 1964.*
Courtesy Photowatch, Cheltenham

Plans for a replacement police station were drawn up in 1860. It was built on the corner of Gloucester Road and Lord's Hill and remained in use until 1964. Supt. Chipp lived there with his family in the 1870s.

Local historian Ray Allen came across the following Coleford tale in his research into Forest pubs. During a police crackdown on licensed premises, the Prince of Wales, which stood at the corner of Bank Street and Sparrow Hill, came in for close police scrutiny. At the annual 'Brewster' Sessions in 1907, Supt. Griffin opposed the renewal of the licence on the grounds that the premises were frequented by the *"lowest of the low"*. He was promptly asked by the Licensing Justices where the 'lowest of the low' would go if the pub were to close.

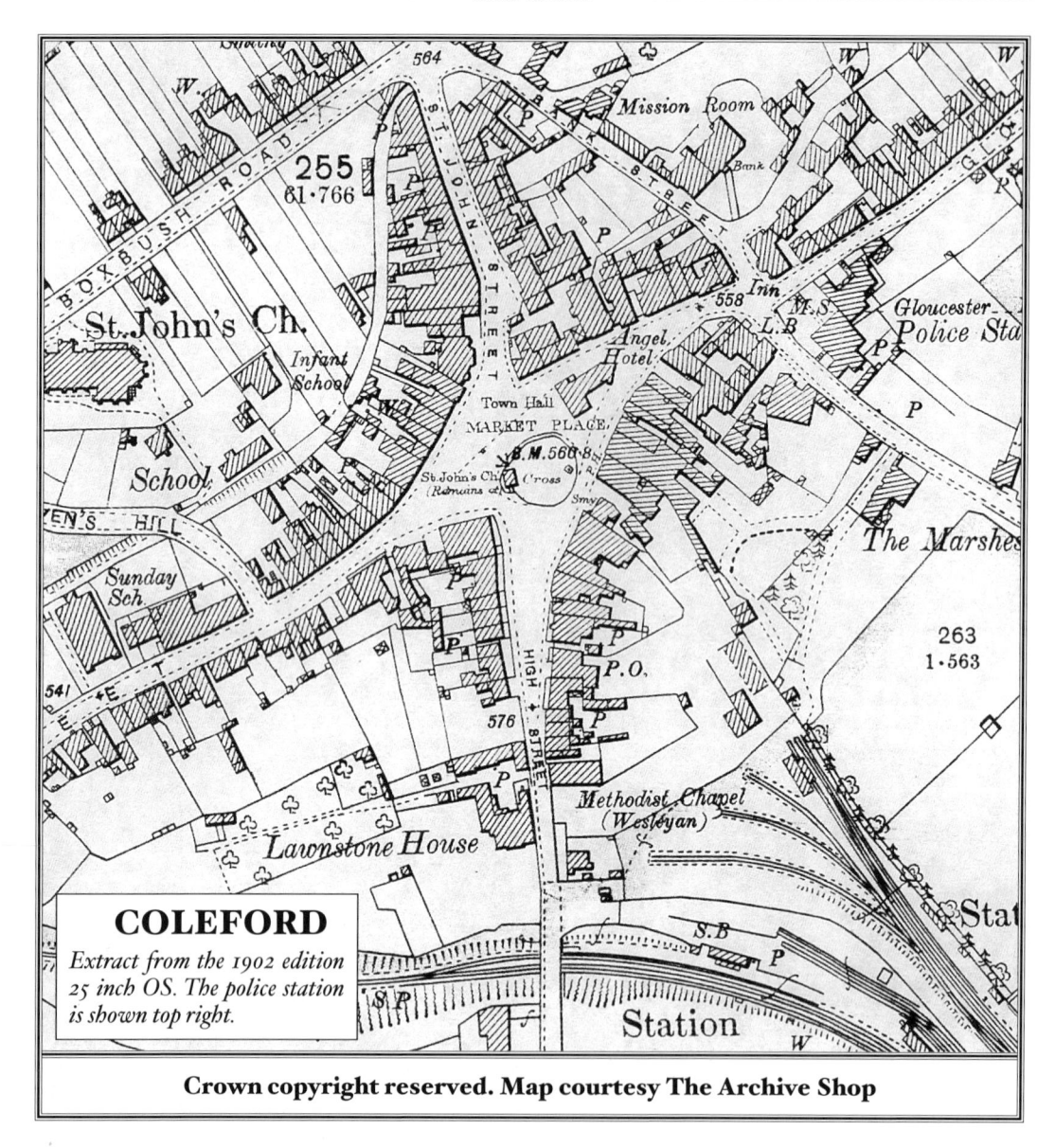

COLEFORD
Extract from the 1902 edition 25 inch OS. The police station is shown top right.

Crown copyright reserved. Map courtesy The Archive Shop

In 1923 Coleford Police Station was fitted with electric lighting. In 1926, during the General Strike, Inspector Bent and Sergeant Hamblin lived at the station. Lionel Voyce remembered that, as a teenager, he delivered their meat while working for his father (Frederick Voyce). Lionel later had a butcher's shop at Coleford Town Hall. Also in that year, Coleford officer PC Albert Henry Bleaken was awarded two bravery medals, one from the RSPCA and one from The Dumb Friends League, for rescuing a dog from a pit. The pit, it is said, was called 'Bleaken's pond' for many years thereafter.

More acts of gallantry took place on 22 October 1939, when a fire broke out at Duncan Cottage, Victoria Road. Four police officers were decorated for their part in the rescue of people trapped in the blaze. They were Sgt. Fred Taylor, PC Vic Bullock, Special Constable W. Williams and Special Constable F. Prisk. They were each presented with silver braids for conspicuous gallantry and bronze medals were

POLICE HEROES HONOURED

March 1940

COL. W. F. HENN, Chief Constable of Gloucestershire, presenting the silver braid for conspicuous gallantry to four members of the Gloucestershire Constabulary who took part in the rescues of the trapped occupants of a blazing house in Coleford. P.C. V. J. Bullock is receiving his braid, and the others are Special Constable W. F. Williams, Special Constable W. E. Pride, and P.S. F. F. Taylor.

The officers involved in the rescue at Duncan Cottage receiving awards from the Chief Constable, Col. Henn. Note SC W.F. Prisk has erroneously become W.E. Pride in the newspaper caption. Frank Prisk was at home off duty on the night of the fire, which occurred at the house of one of his near neighbours. Sadly, one of the family involved died in the fire. Newspaper cutting from the Taylor family collection

awarded by The Society for Protection of Life from Fire. PS Taylor was later promoted Inspector but died suddenly on duty at Dursley police station on 23 May 1942.

Fred Hudson was stationed at Coleford, early in his career before war service. He recalled that one of the Coleford beats involved patrolling on foot to Redbrook and back!

In December 1939 Edgar Bowring, recently married, was transferred from Newnham to Coleford. He was on foot patrol in Gloucester Road one night, soon after being posted there, when he saw a man at the door of a garage business, which was where Farriers Court now stands. A few questions soon ascertained that the man was genuine and was locking up. In fact he was Sam Evans who ran the business with Frank Prisk. Mr Evans revealed that he was a Special Constable and the two men chatted as they walked down Gloucester Road together. Edgar was a big fan of motorcycle racing but it was a while before he realised that he was talking to one of his heroes, S.S. Evans, who raced at Brooklands for the Gloucester-based Cotton team.

Edgar was on early turn on 16 April 1941 and had just returned to the station from a foot patrol of the 'Lane Ends' (Mile End, Broadwell, Coalway etc.), when three German airmen were brought to the station by civilians. One

Police Sergeant Fitzroy Fred. Taylor, Coleford.   Courtesy Jim Taylor

When gaiters were the fashion! Left to right: PS Fred Taylor, PC Fred Hudson, PC Arthur Mynett and Insp. George Dowsell in the garden of Coleford Police Station, c1940.   Courtesy Fred Hudson

of the men had been found by Mr Adams of Clements End sheltering under his lorry. He had given the German a cup of tea before taking him to the police station in the lorry. Edgar Bowring wrote:

> "I took turns as guard the rest of the day. They gave their rank and names as Gefreiter August Heffner, Unteroffizier Czaplinski and Obergefreiter Heinrich Schmidt. I always remember the remark made by Supt. Charlie Large when he heard the last one's name "Oh yes, Henry Smith". Local man Henry Machin was an Inspector in the Special Constabulary and spoke fluent German. He conversed at length with the prisoners."

Margaret Wyatt (nee Taylor) recalled the same incident. She was living at Coleford police station where her father, Fred Taylor, was Sergeant. Margaret remembers that her mother cooked them breakfast (much to the annoyance of the military who arrived to take them away hours later!). Margaret's brother Jim (who later joined the police) was only eight at the time. He remembered getting his toy gun, sloping arms and marching up and down outside the cells. Looking back he often wondered what the Luftwaffe men thought of that! The men are believed to have been the first German airmen to be captured in the county and eyewitnesses testify to a certain amount of celebration. A yellow German parachute was hung in triumph from an upstairs window of the police station!

Edgar Bowring was one of many officers sent to Bristol during the Blitz to help the local police and he spent time guarding unexploded bombs there. Back in the Forest he had to attend and guard parachute mines dropped at Coalway and deal with incendiary bombs dropped near Symonds Yat. He also attended his share of fatal aircraft crashes, all Allied planes:

> "... one at Edenwall, believed a Proctor Trainer, two occupants, one British the other French, both killed. Another at Speech House, a Westland Whirlwind fighter dived into the cricket field close to the road and was completely buried apart from bits of twisted metal. The pilot apparently had no time to bale out. While we were there we could hear the thud thud of rounds exploding under the ground! I was off duty one day walking at the Scowles when I saw a four engine bomber fly over with smoke and vapour coming from the starboard outer engine. It flew out of sight towards Lydbrook and immediately afterwards I heard an explosion and saw a cloud of smoke rising. I later attended the scene with Insp. Dowsell. I learned that a War Reserve Constable permanently stationed at the cable works at Lydbrook had swum the Wye to get to the plane but there were no survivors. The officer was commended."

Despite what he had witnessed, Edgar applied to the RAF in 1943 for flying duties, together with PCs Reg Crouch and Tom Pugsley. They were all accepted and ordered to report for training locally while continuing with their police duties but they were stood down before seeing active service. Edgar remained at Coleford until October 1945, during which time he was commended, together with PS Paget, for making an arrest in connection with an attempted cinema break-in.

Ken Parsons was transferred from Lydney to Coleford in 1941. He wrote:

> "In about July 1941 I arrived at the single men's quarters behind Coleford police station and settled in quickly, having meals at the Lamb Inn. We all worked a six day week with a weekend off after every six weeks. It was necessary to apply through the Superintendent to the Chief Constable for permission to leave the district to visit my home at Cinderford! It was also necessary to apply for permission to marry and the girlfriend and her parents were vetted by the Inspector to ascertain if they were suitable.
> On Aug 26 1942 I joined the Royal Navy and transferred to the Fleet Air Arm. The police made up the difference in my pay. After Basic Training I was told that young police officers were being selected for training as commissioned officers to command landing craft. I didn't fancy being an officer so I opted for trade training as I wanted a trade to fall back on if my police career didn't work out. I applied to be an electrician..."

Ken Parsons was demobbed from the Royal Navy in November 1945 after

Ken Parsons early in his police career.
Courtesy Ken Parsons

service in Europe and the Far East, taking up where he had left off as he recounts:

> "I went back to being a copper in Coleford where nothing much seemed to have changed, but with my RN gratuity I purchased a motorcycle, a Royal Enfield, which proved very useful. I was given a mileage allowance of twopence halfpenny a mile to perform duties, enquiries, attend accidents etc. There were no station cleaners in those days and duty officers did such work as cleaning windows. The night shift had to scrub the oak timber floor and even polish the fire grate before going off duty."

Ron Davis, who retired as an Inspector at Cheltenham, was a young, single PC at Coleford in 1948. He wrote the following:

> "Later in 1948 I was moved to Coleford and took up residence in the Single Men's Quarters at the police station which was then at the junction of Gloucester Road...
>
> There was an Inspector and a Sergeant who both lived with their families in quarters above the police station and the single men's quarters were across the yard, above the garages. There were, if I remember correctly, three single rooms, together with a bathroom (bliss after Tutshill) and also, if you believe, a 'Games Room'!!
>
> Having a bath required some pre-planning, as to get the necessary hot water we had to light a coal-fired boiler, which was underneath the bathroom, and wait for an hour or so for the water to heat up.
>
> The 'Games Room' was a small room in which there was half of a table-tennis table against a wall, with a chalk line on the wall representing the net. One player would play the ball from the end of the table up to the wall over the chalk line to rebound onto the table for the other player to play. Needless to say we did not produce any table tennis champion from Coleford police.
>
> We had our meals at a public house a little way up the Gloucester Road, with the licensee's family in their private room. His wife provided the meat and the fat!
>
> I remember one morning I was on early turn and, having signed on duty in the diary, and being the only one on duty at 6am, I was patrolling around the town when, at about 6.30 am, I had an urgent call of nature and returned to the station. I went across the yard and up the stairs to the single men's bathroom. I was sitting there when I heard the fire siren sounding, and as it was our practice to phone the Fire Brigade to find out what and where the fire was, I went downstairs and across the yard, doing up my tunic on the way, and into the office. As I put the phone down after speaking to the Fire Brigade, the sergeant appeared from his quarters and accused me of being late for duty as he had just seen me coming across the yard from the single men's quarters doing my tunic up. (His kitchen overlooked the yard.) I was unable to convince him that I had signed on at 6am but fortunately he took no further action.
>
> On another occasion I was on night duty (on my own of course), and returned to the station at 1am for a meal break. I was in the office eating my sandwiches when the phone rang and I was given an express message by Divisional HQ at Lydney. I cannot recall the exact details of the message but I think it was something to do with a serious crime in South Wales and descriptions of the suspects were circulated. Anyway, in accordance with previous instructions on the receipt of express messages, I phoned the Inspector's extension, woke him up and told him the message. He then told me to take the message up to his bedroom, which I did, and handed it over to him as he lay in bed with his wife beside him!"

Francis Field had a spell at Coleford. He wrote:

> "In 1954 I moved to Coleford and lived in a County-rented council house in Tufthorn Avenue, vacated by Don Townsend ... I was in Coleford from 1954 until February 1956, when I went to Minsterworth in charge. Those fourteen months at Coleford were absolutely hilarious.
>
> Frank Jayne was Inspector, Jimmy Johnson was Sergeant and we had Lawrence Griffiths, Dennis Emery, Theo Powell, Fred Wood, Eric Sandells, Bob Newman and myself.
>
> How about a cycle patrol today down through Whitecliff to Clearwell, Newland and Redbrook to make a point with the local Special Constable who lived there, then patrol all the way back?
>
> One day someone put two expired batteries into a bucket of slack coal which was used to bank up the fire in the main office. Well, Frank Jayne came in during the afternoon and sat down by the fire. When the batteries exploded it brought soot down the very high chimney all across the office, making poor old Frank look like a sweep! It took a lot of clearing up afterwards. I don't think Frank ever found out who was responsible.
>
> When Frank Jayne went round his Sub-Division, he always took Jimmy Johnson, the Sergeant, to do his driving in an old Morris Series E saloon. Their last call one day was Lydbrook police station, where big PC Frank Nicholls lived. When Frank and Jim got back to Coleford, Jim discovered that he had left his helmet at Lydbrook. "Go back and get it, Sergeant" says Frank. Out goes Jim (increasing Frank's mileage claim, of course) back to Lydbrook, comes back twenty minutes later swinging a helmet in his hand. "Have you got your helmet?" says Frank. "Oh yes, Sir" says Jim and puts on this helmet, which was huge and came down over his ears and eyes. Frank Jayne nearly burst a gut laughing, Jim had brought back Frank Nicholls' helmet. "Go back and get your own," says Frank, so off goes Jim again. He later got it in the neck from his wife for being late for dinner.
>
> Frank Jayne retired in the middle of 1955 and Jimmy Johnson became the Inspector (unusual at the same station). Ken Parsons became Sergeant and things became slightly more sober."

Ken Parsons was a sergeant at Coleford from 1955 to 1958. He wrote as follows:

> "I lived in the upstairs flat of the old police station with a peculiar bathroom; the washbasin was fitted over the bath so that you slid under it to bath. An electric geyser provided hot water. On wash day I had to light a fire in the furnace of a large wash room. There was only one Sergeant at

Jimmy Johnson who was promoted Inspector at Coleford in 1955. Courtesy Graham Murdock

Coleford at that time so I spent most of the time in uniform except Rest Days. There were about eight Constables there then and six police houses were built – two adjacent to the station and four on the Coombs Park estate. I became frustrated as young married Constables moved into them so I informed the Deputy Chief Constable when he visited the station one day and within three weeks I moved from the flat to a new house alongside the station, which provided a much happier home."

Local man, Mike Burns, later a respectable citizen, admitted that in his younger days he was a bit of a tearaway (he is still known as 'Knuckles'). He told an amusing story. One day he was on his way home when he saw some bags of Blue Circle cement left unattended and thought *'I could find a use for that'*, so he helped himself. It wasn't long before there was a knock at the door. It was Ken Parsons and another officer: *"We know you nicked that cement – we've got concrete evidence!"*

The old station and the adjoining Town Club building were demolished in 1964 when the present station had been completed. The new station was officially opened on 29 October 1964 by the Lord Lieutenant of the County, His Grace The Duke of Beaufort. The total cost of the new station and adjoining Magistrates Court was £64,699. The modern station has multiple garages and was originally designed to accommodate the Forest Traffic detachment in addition to the local police. Along the Lord's Hill frontage and at the back of the rear car park are former police houses, two of which were built before the new station. PC Brokenshire and his wife were the last to occupy the flat in the old police station and Mrs Brokenshire claims the distinction that she was the last police officer's wife to conceive there!

Ron Stephens was posted to Coleford in 1960 and worked in both the old and new stations. In addition to his normal duties he was given the job of Court officer. Prior to the move to the new station, he had the task of sorting all the old court records for archiving at HQ. These included some from the 18th century when it was considered appropriate to sentence a female child to three

Photographs from front and rear of the demolition of the old Coleford police station, taken by Joan Kingscott who was then living in the police house at 5 Lord's Hill.
Courtesy Joan Kingscott

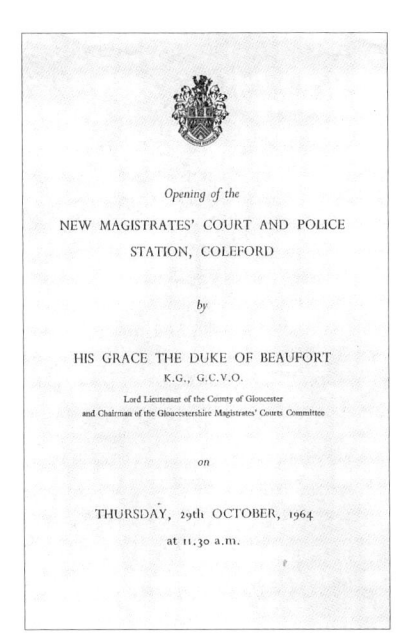

Above: *PS Bert Kingscott and his wife, Joan, at the new Coleford police station.*   Courtesy Joan Kingscott

Left: *Programme of the opening ceremony for the new Magistrates Court and Police Station at Coleford, 1964.* Courtesy Jack Kite

years imprisonment for theft of a chicken. He also recalled seeing a 19th century Station Diary entry for St Briavels, which recorded a three day patrol (on foot) from St Briavels to Bigsweir and on to Redbrook the first day, Redbrook to Mitcheldean on the second day and finally back to St Briavels. En route the officer had booked two people.

At about 10.15pm one night Ron was on station duty when he received a report of an accident at Edge End. The Sergeant and the other PC were on duty at the fair in Mushet Place and couldn't be contacted. Ron stopped a car and got the driver to find the Sergeant and tell him. He then returned to the station where the phone was ringing constantly with reports of the same accident. The casualty count rose with each call. On arrival at the scene it was found that five people had died. Inspector Walter Long was called out and was at the scene most of the night. It was after this accident that changes were made to the road junction.

Young single coppers have always been a source of amusement for the 'old sweats'. Ron Stephens recalled one young man, who shall be nameless, turning up for work one morning scruffy and unshaven. On being questioned he admitted he had not gone back to his digs but had spent the night in his car. His reason for this bizarre behaviour was that he believed his landlady had taken a fancy to him and he was terrified that he would be ravished if he spent another night under her roof! The Sergeant got on the phone and arranged a transfer to another station the very same day. That Sergeant is said to have been Dave Jones, who was later Inspector at Coleford and later still a Chief Superintendent.

Another young man in digs on the top floor of Sunny Bank House had a chronic inability to get up for early turn, much to the annoyance of the night men he was supposed to relieve. His solution was to tie a piece of string round his big toe and hang the other end out of the window so that the night shift could pull it to wake him up at 5am. This left him somewhat vulnerable to practical jokers but it was a dog that first noticed the string and jumped up and swung on it at 2am! Vicky Deakin (nee Gwynn) remembered that, as young girls, she and her sister had a lot of fun at the expense of the young single policemen and cadets who lodged with their family at Sunny Bank House. Apple pie beds were one thing but one poor chap had his false teeth hidden and having searched in vain sat down to breakfast without them!

Ron Stephens told how, towards the end of his service, he made history and set an important precedent. In the early 1970s he suddenly received an order to move to Fairford. His wife was then working at Coleford Post Office and his two daughters were at the local Grammar School so he queried why it was so important that he should be transferred. He was told that it was because the police house he occupied in Coombs Park was surplus to requirements and was going to be sold. Officers had only just been given the general right to become owner occupiers so Ron offered to buy his police house. He was told emphatically by someone at Force HQ that he could not. He then rang Shire Hall and spoke to a senior person in Property Services who came down to Coleford and valued the house. Ron offered him the asking price, which was accepted subject to a written application being at Shire Hall by next morning. He saw the bank manager the same afternoon and secured a mortgage. Then he told how he ruffled a few feathers all the way up the chain of command by insisting that his written application be at Shire Hall the following day!

Many Coleford and Newland folk will remember a bobby from those times, PC Norman Barnes, who took the Ostrich Inn at Newland when he retired and a number of local chaps remember, as youths, being taught judo by PC John Milton.

A frequent visitor to Coleford police station in those days was Jack 'Cromp' Roberts, who had a shop in Gloucester Road. He was the local RSPCA volunteer and cared for, or destroyed, sick and injured animals. He was also responsible for the town's pound which stood near 'The Spout', off Bank Street, behind Gloucester Road.

In 1964 PC Jack Kite was posted to Coleford. He was a veteran of the Russian convoys and had taken part in the action in which the German battlecruiser *Scharnhorst* was sunk. He was allocated a police house at Mile End, one of a group of three that had been purchased two years earlier by the County from a local builder for just over £10,000. Walter Long was the Coleford Inspector at the time though he was soon to be promoted to Chief Inspector at Lydney. The 'F' Division

Jack 'Cromp' Roberts RSPCA in the Guardroom at Coleford police station, 1958.
Courtesy Photowatch, Cheltenham

PC Jack Kite in Market Place, Coleford, c1965. In the background is the Town Hall, demolished in 1968.
By kind permission of Jack Kite and the Chief Constable

Superintendent was Harry Drinkwater, who as a young PC had been involved in the famous Haw Bridge Murder inquiry. When Jack moved to Coleford the old station was still in use and coal had to be hauled up several flights of stairs to light a fire in the court but Jack was present when the new police station and court were officially opened in October 1964. Jack had Bert Kingscott and Peter Blake as his Sergeants, the latter being his next door neighbour. Peter Blake was a giant of a man who didn't stand for any nonsense.

In 1964 foot and cycle patrol still meant making pre-arranged points at telephone boxes etc. Almost as soon as he had arrived Jack had to deal with a fatal road traffic accident at the Lambsquay and on Thursday 9 May 1974 he was first on the scene of a gas explosion at Clements End which had killed three people. Jack recalled the incident:

> *"I was driving the van and I heard and felt the thud of the explosion, then I was called on the radio and directed to Clements End. When I arrived the ground was ablaze and the devastation was obvious. I was taken off the duty roster to complete the report for the Coroner which involved taking fifty statements."*

Jack received a commendation for his work on this case. The Coleford Inspector who also attended the scene was the late Arthur Taylor.

On a lighter note, Jack was able to reveal an ingenious low-tech method of communication employed by the Specials. Symonds Yat was a busy tourist attraction in those days, as it still is today. The narrow road from Yat Rock down to the river is a single track with passing places and without assistance quickly became snarled up on Sundays. A neat method of communication was adopted for convoying traffic up and down the narrow road. The bottom of the hill is in Herefordshire and the top is in Gloucestershire. Special Constables from each force would be at their respective ends and would hand a carved baton to the driver of the last car to be allowed through with the instruction to hand it to the Special at the other end.

Jack also recalled that Leo Tapscott, who was later to command the Forest Sub-Division in the 1980s, was a Sergeant at Coleford in the 1970s, as was the late Graham Holmes. In 1977 a UHF personal radio scheme was introduced at Coleford and officers no longer had to make points. Between coming to Coleford in 1964 and his retirement in 1980 Jack had seen a great deal of change.

By 1964 Ken Parsons had already been an Inspector for two years in Cheltenham (where he had the unfortunate duty to investigate a Road Traffic Accident involving the Chief Constable):

"When I was told of my move from Cheltenham to Coleford, my daughter, who was preparing to take her 'O' level exams, said "You've had your life, Dad, give me a chance." Luckily my neighbour agreed to look after her for the few months she needed.

I worked in the old Coleford station whilst preparing to move into the new station, which went smoothly. The working area was roomy, light and centrally heated. By now there were two Sergeants attached to the station and I was responsible for Tutshill, St Briavels, Woolaston, Lydbrook and Mile End. At this time the first Severn Motorway Bridge was under construction and was eventually opened in 1966. (Security measures had to be undertaken because of threats to the bridge by the self-styled 'Free Wales Army'.)

Three murders occurred during a six month period. The first involved a husband who travelled to Coleford from the Norfolk area, stayed at the Angel Hotel and then went to the home of his ex-wife and stabbed her to death."

Jack Kite recalled the same incident. He was detailed to remain in the room at the Angel where the suspect had left some of his belongings and to arrest him if he returned. In the event, he failed to put in an appearance.

Ken Parsons continued:

"The second murder involved a man being stabbed by his wife and the third was a shooting arising from a dispute between two men. The man's body was discovered in an isolated cottage near Moseley Green and the murder squad spent much time at Coleford station. A man was later arrested in Scotland.

Shortly after the new station was opened a man was brought in having been found acting strangely, standing in the River Wye. He was placed in the new cell-block. A loose drain cover was used by the man to smash up a 4inch thick porcelain toilet pan – not a bad start!

At around the same time a juvenile was placed in a small detention room next to the guard room and when the door was opened to take him into court he dashed across the room and jumped feet first against a large window, smashing it in an attempt to escape. After a struggle he was overpowered."

Ken joined Coleford Bowls Club soon after arriving at Coleford and helped in improving and enlarging the bowling green using stone from the old Town Hall which had just been demolished. He formed a social club which is now thriving and up with the best in the county. He acquired a full size snooker table from Cheltenham

Retirement party for Ken Parsons at the Angel Hotel, Coleford, 1971. Left to right: Supt. Ben Gwilliam, Dora Gwilliam, Insp. Ken Parsons, Pearl Parsons.
Courtesy Dora Gwilliam

Police Club and set it up in a spare room in Coleford Police Station so that off-duty officers could enjoy a game. It wasn't long before a police snooker team was making its presence felt in the Forest of Dean league. Among the players were PC Dave Willetts from St Briavels and PC Arthur Wood from Mile End. The station also boasted a pretty formidable skittles team at that time.

Ken Parsons retired in 1971 having spent fifteen of his thirty years service at Coleford, as a PC, a Sergeant and as the Inspector in charge.

Up until the 1970s there were officers in the Forest who were veterans of the Second World War. Sid Parris, who was a Constable stationed at Coleford during the 1960s, had been a Leading Seaman (while a serving PC) on *HMS Melbreak* on D Day and is mentioned in '*The Longest Day*' by Cornelius Ryan.

Another D Day veteran was Bert Kingscott, a Sergeant at Coleford from 1960, who had joined the Royal Marines at the age of seventeen. His wife Joan, a retired music teacher, wrote the following:

> "Bert and I met near Anstruther harbour on 19 January 1943. I had always been told not to speak to 'these soldiers and sailors' so I would not have stopped when he said "Hello" had he not chanced to call me by my name. We always said it was fate.
>
> We wrote to each other for the four years we were apart. After his demob. he brought back a very old Gurkha knife in a leather sheath. It was kept in a safe place but like Bert's other war time memories, never mentioned.
>
> On leaving the Marines, Bert joined the Gloucestershire Constabulary in 1947 and we married the next March. He served as a policeman for thirty years, retiring with the rank of Inspector. He enjoyed three years of semi-retirement before his sudden death in November 1979."

Bert had been Coxswain on a landing craft at 'Sword Beach' on D Day and went ashore with his comrades. In May 1945 he underwent Commando training and was on embarkation leave prior to being sent to the Far East when Japan surrendered.

There is a view that a Forest posting is a bar to further promotion. One of the many exceptions was Peter Hood, who was a Sergeant at Coleford in the late 1980s

Coleford
NGR SO 576 108
Left: *Coleford's present police station was built next to its predecessor and opened in 1964.* Photo Ted Heath

Below: *PS John Bevan and PC Malcolm Dyer at Coleford Police Station March 2000.* Photo Ted Heath

and has just retired in 2000 with the rank of Superintendent.

Reorganisation of the Constabulary in 1998 saw talented musician and composer Tony Davis become the first Inspector in charge of the new Forest South Neighbourhood Area which included Lydney. At about the same time CCTV cameras brought about a dramatic reduction in alcohol related violence and disorder in the town. Before the cameras were installed, incidents of vandalism were common and one victim, barber and tobacconist Pat Bolter, resorted to a bit of self-help. On Friday nights someone had regularly urinated through the letterbox of his shop so Pat decided to lie in wait just inside the door. Sure enough, a group of young men stopped outside the shop and one of them climbed the steps and opened the flap of the letterbox. Pat was ready and when the offending appendage appeared through the slot he gave it a smart whack with a fish slice! The lad got no sympathy from his mates, one of whom was heard to say *"Where's thee off to in a hurry"*. There was no reply.

PS John Bevan was stationed at Coleford in 2000. He had previously served at Lydney and as the Team Leader of the Forest Operation Gemini Unit.
By kind permission of the Chief Constable

Drybrook

Drybrook's earliest known police station was the house now called 'Oakville' in High Street. It was in use at the time of the now notorious killing of two performing bears and assault on their French owners. The incident happened in April 1889 after unfounded rumours had started that the bears had killed a child in Cinderford. The bears and their owners were followed by a large group of men and boys through Steam Mills, Nailbridge and on towards Ruardean. During this procession, the bears and their handlers were repeatedly attacked and the bears eventually killed. Fourteen local men of previous good character were charged and appeared before Littledean Court in May. The investigating officers were PC Price, PS Hawkins, PC White and PC Jones. It is said that the bears are buried in the garden of the police station.

Drybrook
NGR SO 647 176
'Oakville' in High Street was Drybrook's first police station.
Photo Ted Heath

Mrs Joan Rooum's father, PC 154 Edward George James, was stationed at Mitcheldean and at Newnham during her childhood in the 1930s and she recalled visiting the later police station in Drybrook Road and being shown Charlie Chaplin films in the cell by PC Francis. Mr Francis was followed by Bert Johnson.

Drybrook
NGR SO 645 174
The former police station in Drybrook Road.
Photo Ted Heath

This station was still in use during the Second World War when a terrible accident occurred. In 1940 rumours of German parachutists were rife and tension was high. On 19 August, Special Constable Walter Clement Smith was returning from duty at Lydney in his car in the blackout when he was tragically shot dead by a member of the Home Guard. The Coroner returned a verdict of 'Justifiable Homicide'. The Standing Joint Committee agreed that SC Smith's fatal injury be classified as a 'War Injury' and granted his widow a special pension of £60.13.4d per annum.

On a happier note, a respected local bobby from this era called Jim Crewe, appears in some of the hilarious tales told by John Christian in his book *'Tales from Dunk's Carner'* (sic).

PC Rogers, a member of the Constabulary's mounted section, is believed to have been the last officer at the station in Drybrook Road.

Left: PC Rogers who was the last officer in charge at the Drybrook Road police station. This photograph is believed to have been taken at the Feathers Hotel, Lydney, during the 1926 Miners Strike.
Courtesy of his daughter

Below: Drybrook Road, Drybrook, in the early 1920s. The police station is the nearest house of the second block on the right.
Courtesy
The Archive Shop

Drybrook Carnival, c1905. The tail-end of the procession is seen here at Nailbridge, turning up towards Ruardean Hill, with the local 'bobby' bringing up the rear alongside the horse and cart in the centre background.
Courtesy The Archive Shop

The village's last police station at the top of the High Street was built in the 1950s. Among the officers who served there in charge were big Barry Watkins, Mike Endy (later a Sergeant at Cinderford) and Ted Heath. Terry Lark, who was the last, had the nickname 'Skylark'. He played full-back for the Force Rugby Team in the 1970s and 80s. His high up and under kicks would prompt the war cry '*All aboard the Skylark*' from the marauding police forwards as they followed up the kick.

Drybrook
NGR SO 649 178
The village's last police station which was built in the 1950s.
Photo Ted Heath

Barry Watkins was Constable-in-charge at Drybrook. By kind permission of the Chief Constable

Dymock

Situated between the Beauchamp Arms and the church, 'Church Cottage' was the village's first police station. It was replaced in 1895 by a new building in Kempley Road.

The building in Kempley Road, now called 'Constable's House', is a near mirror image of the station at Westbury on Severn. It was purpose built in 1895, with cells and living quarters, and is located near the former railway and canal wharf. The parish was not part of the Forest of Dean police area until 1974. Prior to that it had been part of Gloucester and Cheltenham Divisions at different times.

Dymock
NGR SO 701 312
Left: 'Church Cottage' was the first police station in the village. Photo Ted Heath

Dymock
NGR SO 699 312
Below: Now appropriately named 'Constable's House', this residence in Kempley Road was purpose-built as a police station in 1895. Photo Ted Heath

Hartpury

The police station for Hartpury and Ashleworth in the late 19th and early 20th centuries was the house now known as 'Woodlynch' in Broad Street. PC Reid was in charge there in 1899. It preceded the use of 'Goodrich Cottage' in Ashleworth, which in turn was replaced by a new purpose built station in Hartpury.

Built in the 1950s, then closed and sold in the 1960s, Hartpury's last police station stands on the corner of the main A417 road and Broad Street, by the War Memorial. The Hartpury sub-section was part of the Gloucester City Sub-Division and when the last station closed the parish became part of the Gloucester Rural Beat. Many local people will remember PC Bob Jones and PC Terry Smith who patrolled the area for years. Keen cyclist Gerry McGarr was one of the last of these rural beat officers, because in 1982 a reorganisation of the Force put the parish under the PC at Staunton and the Sergeant at Newent, as part of the Forest of Dean Sub-Division.

Hartpury
NGR SO 802 252
The former police station now called 'Woodlynch' in Broad Street. Photo Ted Heath

Hartpury
NGR SO 800 249
Purpose-built as a village police station in the 1950s, this house stands on the corner of the main road and Broad Street, by the War Memorial. Photo Ted Heath

Hewelsfield

There was a police station at Hewelsfield from 1840 to 1843. (See St Briavels, page 129). However, its exact location has not yet been pinpointed and further research needs to be carried out.

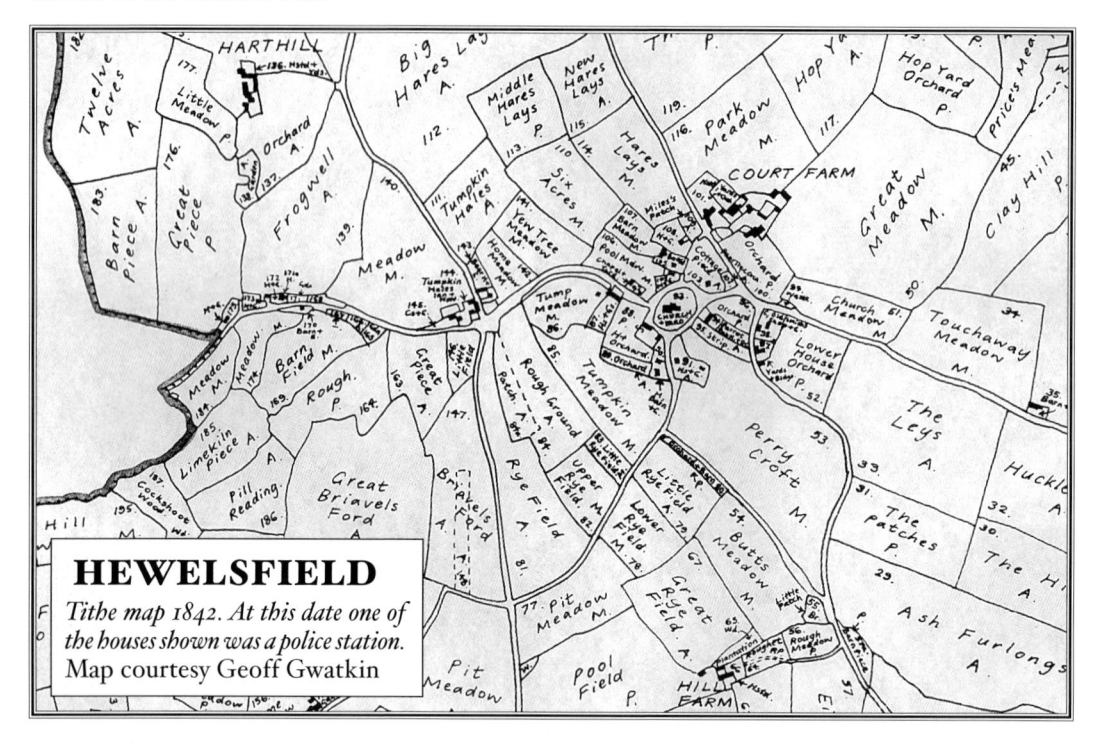

HEWELSFIELD
Tithe map 1842. At this date one of the houses shown was a police station.
Map courtesy Geoff Gwatkin

High Beech

A house believed to date from the 17th century and now called 'The Old Station House' is thought to be the site of the High Beech Police Station mentioned in the 1844 Police & Constabulary List. It is not mentioned in the Chief Constable's report of 1840 nor the 1857 survey, so its life as a police station was a short one. The location might appear somewhat out of the way at first sight but it is central for Lydbrook and Ruardean which at the time had no police stations of their own and it is also on a possible packhorse route. Under the system employed by Mr Lefroy at that time (see page 11), it might have been a base, like the short-lived station at Hewelsfield, from which a group of officers covered a wide area.

High Beech
NGR SO 609 164
'The Old Station House', off the Joys Green to Ruardean road.
Photo Ted Heath

Huntley

The house at the junction of North Street with the main A40 road is believed to have been the first police station in Huntley. It appears to have succeeded the station at Churcham and coincided with the increase in motor transport. It was replaced in the 1950s by a new house and office, of the standard design of the period, about 200 yards west along the main road. This in turn was closed and sold in 2000.

Huntley NGR SO 723 194
The police station at the junction of North Street with the main road, c1930. Courtesy of Ted Heath

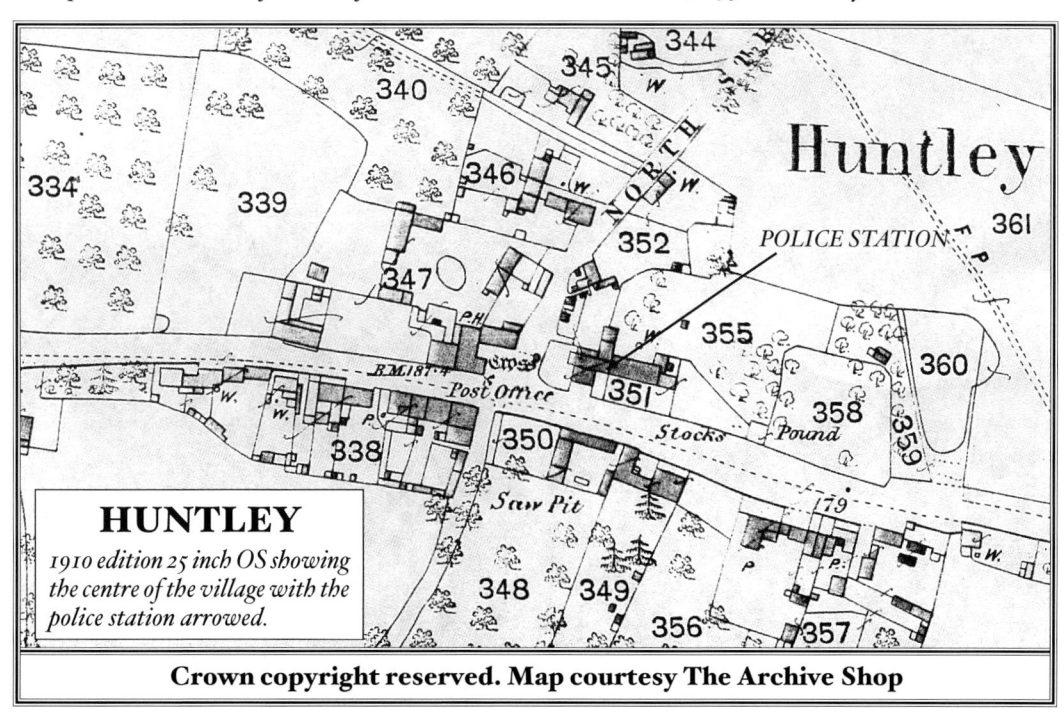

HUNTLEY
1910 edition 25 inch OS showing the centre of the village with the police station arrowed.

Crown copyright reserved. Map courtesy The Archive Shop

The old Huntley police station on the junction of North Street, as it looks today.
Photo Ted Heath

Huntley NGR SO 720 194
This replacement police station on the main A40 road through the village was built in the 1950s. Photo Ted Heath

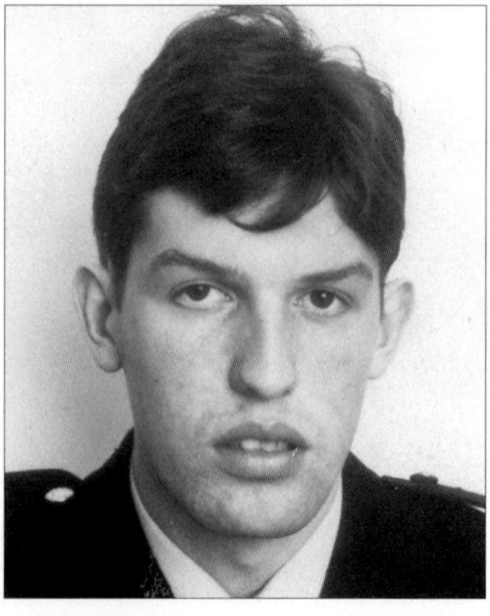

Bob Phelps, who was PC-in-Charge at Huntley 1981-83.
By kind permission of the Chief Constable

Littledean

The village's first police station was in Church Street. In 1854 prison reform made the former House of Correction available for use as a police station and short term remand prison. On 15 March Sgt. Edward Birch and two constables moved in. From that date the Sergeant-in-charge also had the title of Master of the Gaol and his wife was the Matron.

Littledean
NGR SO 671 134
Right: *The village's first police station in Church Street.* Photo Ted Heath

Littledean
NGR SO 673 138
Below: *The former House of Correction on a c1910 postcard. By this date it had been use as the village's police station for over sixty years. It was also used as short term remand prison, so the postcard caption is correct in its description. From 1874 the building had also been used as the petty sessional court for Newnham.*
Courtesy The Archive Shop

LITTLEDEAN

Extract from the 1910 edition 25 inch OS. The village's first police station in Church Street is arrowed. Also shown, top right, is the prison, which housed the police station from 1854.

Crown copyright reserved. Map courtesy The Archive Shop

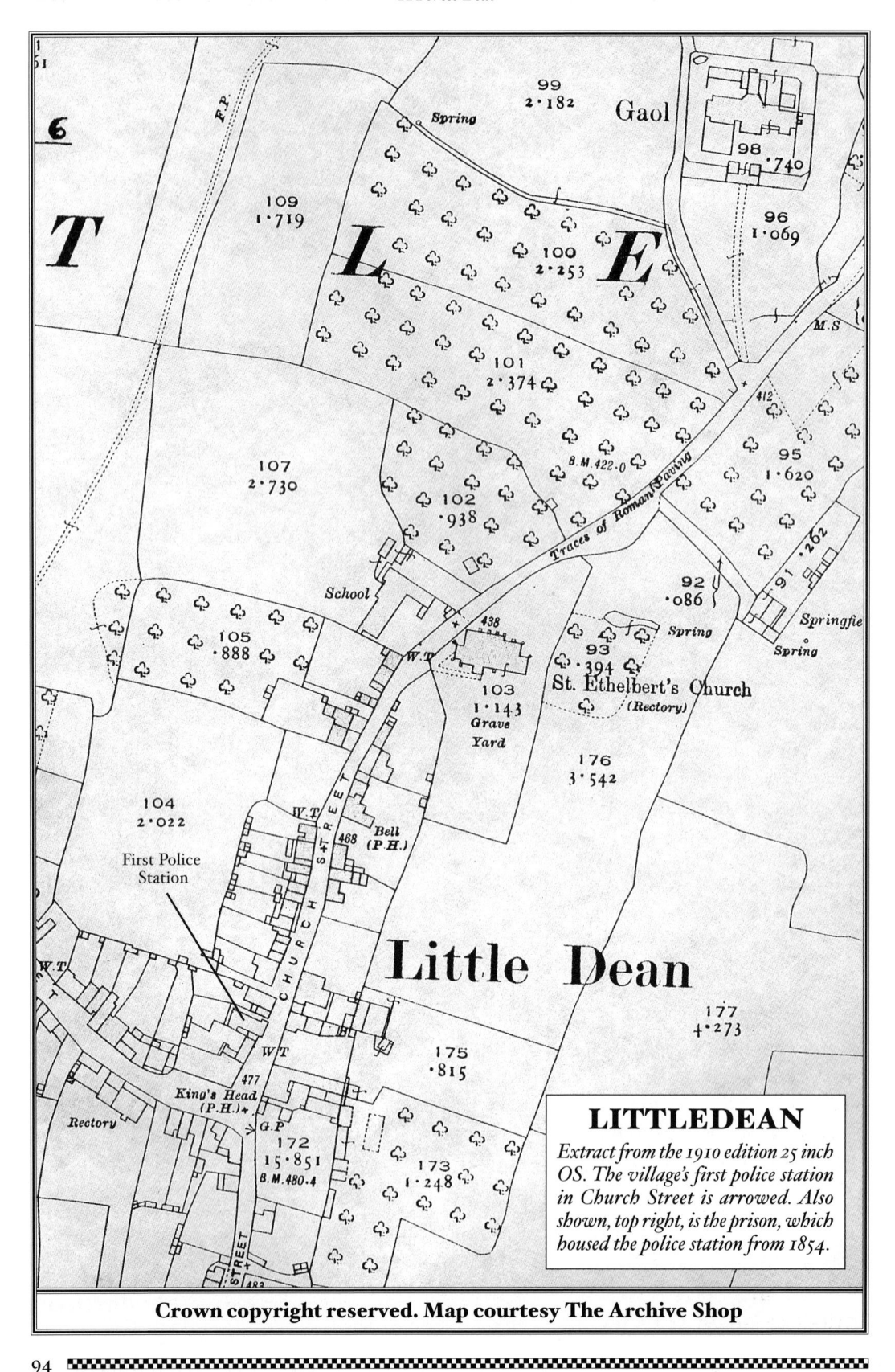

Just seven years later, Littledean's Police Sergeant Samuel Beard was to become the Gloucestershire Constabulary's first officer to be murdered on duty. It was while watching for sheep rustlers near Speech House one night in 1861 that Sgt. Beard was set upon by a gang and was given severe injuries from which he died a few days later. Before his death, however, he was able to identify four men arrested on suspicion and to make a deposition against them. The four men were subsequently sentenced to fifteen years penal servitude. PS Beard is buried in Littledean churchyard.

Len Perry of Mile End was researching his family history when he discovered a Littledean connection with the man who is credited with the introduction of the first 'TARDIS' police box in England. Fred Crawley, who had attended Littledean School and Sir Thomas Rich's, Gloucester, had enjoyed a meteoric police career, being appointed Chief Constable of Lincoln while still a Sergeant in the Metropolitan Police. In 1915 he was appointed Chief Constable of Sunderland and soon had 22 police boxes built on City beats where officers could take their meals, do clerical work and temporarily house prisoners.

On 29 May 1953 Sergeant Harry John Lewis Watkins retired after sixteen years in charge of Littledean police station. A keen horseman, he had joined the Territorials in 1910 and during the Great War had been attached to The Royal Horse Artillery, seeing action at Ypres and on the Somme. In 1926 he was a member of the mounted police unit that was based at Lydney during the General Strike and National Coal Strike and for many years he performed mounted police duties at Cheltenham Races. He was in charge at Littledean during the Second World War when the County Archives were moved there for safety.

Newnham Petty Sessional Court moved to the prison in 1874 when the lease on Newnham Town Hall expired. Former Guardsman, the late Campbell Jack Willett, was the last Sergeant-in-charge of the police station and the last to hold the title of 'Master of the Gaol', for which he was paid the princely sum of 15 shillings per month, whilst his wife received £1.15 shillings as 'Matron'. Littledean remained open as a Constable-in-charge station for a few more years but the Sergeant's post was transferred to the new station built at Newnham in 1972. The Court last sat at Littledean Jail on 24 October

Sgt. Harry Watkins of Littledean. A keen horseman, he is seen here riding out through the entrance portal to the old prison, probably sometime in the late 1940s. Note the 'POLICE' sign on the crossbeam, denoting this unusual building as the police station. By kind permission of the Chief Constable and the Dean Heritage Centre, Soudley

Cam Willett and John Goode (formerly an Inspector at Cinderford) at Littledean on 24 October 1985, on the occasion of the last Court to be held there.
Courtesy
Mrs Edna Willett

1985. The occasion brought back many memories for Mrs Edna Willett who wrote the following:

"Today has been a sad day for us, a misty raw sort of a day when Cam and I attended the opening of the last court held at Littledean Jail. We were accompanied by John Goode, a former Inspector at Cinderford, who, like us, has happy memories of the jail.

We walked into the sadly neglected yard and then into the warm impersonal court room, how strange to sit in the public gallery on the hard benches and survey the court. Memories came flooding back of an old Gypsy man who said "Thank you your Majesty and a Happy Christmas" to the chairman of the bench on receiving his sentence, of policemen choosing seats by the big iron stove on cold days and then regretting it as they got hotter and hotter. I could visualise an old Gypsy woman sitting outside smoking a clay pipe waiting for a case to be heard.

I thought of the problems we had with the electricity supply in the early sixties when my sons, home for half-term, switched on their electric train set and fused all the lights! In the winter we always had stew on Court days, this could be left in the Rayburn oven with jacket potatoes and rice pudding without harm if court went on late and there was no recess for lunch. If things dragged on I used to go into the kitchen and lift the lid of the casserole and waft the smell towards the court! I often had to go out to feed the hens and cockerel at the back of the stables to stop the cockerel crowing and disturbing the court, or scoop up my cat, Susy, who would come into the court and miaow looking for me; sometimes she caused amusement by looking in through the high windows from the roof to attract my attention.

Court days were sometimes three or four times a week for matrimonial and juvenile courts; we also had Inquests and tax tribunals held there. Seven fires had to be lit on each court day and they all had to be burning brightly by the time court started . . . we had fun in those days if smoke blew back!! Court days were unpredictable and seldom without an amusing incident. One of my duties was to feed prisoners if they were kept hanging about. More often it was the juveniles who stayed to lunch; we used to sit round our dining table with them having egg and chips, and peaches and cream. It saddened me that the fact that they were going away from home, sometimes for a short time for reports, didn't seem to upset them. Often it was like a party and they ate every scrap. One case that particularly saddened us was a coloured youth who was being sent to borstal and was completely indifferent, he sat on a chair, folded his arms and promptly went to sleep.

People used to ask me if the jail was haunted, most of them said "I wouldn't sleep there, I'd be afraid of ghosts". I slept there alone with my children then aged eleven and seven for ten weeks. The only time I was afraid was one evening when I felt that someone was watching me and looking towards the window saw a huge tabby cat on the window sill. We had no need to draw curtains there if no policeman was on duty and last thing at night closed the big gates. There were five doors to be locked at night which had some quite substantial keys. The only other time I may have seen a ghost was one Saturday night. My husband and PC Harman had gone out to see the pubs out and I was awaiting their return. I heard something which I thought was probably the small gate and looked out and saw a little old man in an overcoat and flat cap standing under the gate. He was looking to his right and I thought that the men were there and went to unlock the door for them. No one came in and I went outside to see where they were but there was absolutely no one about. When they returned they searched the garden and buildings but could find no one. I don't believe in ghosts but did I see one?

Another strange incident happened in 1963. The office chimney started to smoke, so we decided it would have to be swept before it was used again. When we came home the next day from Gloucester (it was Cam's rest day) we found a huge tawny owl perched on the desk covered in soot. He soon made graceful flight through the sash window when I opened it. Talking of flying things the jail is home to a colony of bats. I have known as many as seven to be flying around our bedroom in summer through the open windows, they never worried me though Cam didn't care for them. I even found one who had hung himself up on the back of our wardrobe to hibernate for the winter. I unhooked him and took him up to the attic to join his family and got nipped for my pains.

During our time at the jail I was able to make quite a bit of money for charity by serving coffee. I never charged for it but everyone knew that they had to buy a raffle ticket for the current charity or put a contribution in the charity box. I also sold poppies that way. I wish I had kept a record of the amounts sent to various charities, it must have been quite a lot. I also wish we had kept a visitors book, we met some very interesting people. One man who had appeared for several weeks on remand, before finally being sent to prison, turned up a couple of years later, said he was passing through and couldn't pass the door without calling in to see if there was any coffee going and say 'hello'. He paid his contribution and got his coffee and also a few words of advice, namely 'Get out of my patch, preferably out of the county', and went on his way

One case that was distressing was the committal proceeding for a local murder. I remember feeling sick when the accused was first brought into the building with a blanket over his head but as the weeks went by and he appeared on remand he became more 'cocky' and unconcerned at the charge hanging over him, in fact at the committal when shown exhibits was quite unmoved. He was one of the two prisoners who didn't have coffee from me, the other was one who had been impersonating a ship's doctor and in my hearing said that a girl he had had an affair with was probably pregnant, that was her problem. He'd used her to get his hands on her cheque book and had he had a spend-up!"

The former House of Correction, which served as Littledean's police station for over a century, is still a fine sight. After closure, there was an attempt to turn it into a hotel which came to nothing, and today it is a records centre for an ecclesiastical insurance company.
Photo Ted Heath

Longhope

Longhope's first police station, from sometime in the second half of the 19th century (certainly after 1857), was 'Brook House', located near the pound in The Latchen. PC Gilbert Pagett was in charge in 1937. In 1945 the tranquillity of the village was shattered by a murder in its midst.

In the late 1940s, 'Brook House' was succeeded by the station which is now a private residence called 'Copseville', in Church Road. Built in brick, it is of the design associated with this period of extensive new building by the Constabulary.

Longhope
NGR SO 688 187
'Brook House', The Latchen, on the left of this recent view, is thought to have been the village's earliest police station.
Photo Ted Heath

Longhope
NGR SO 685 196
The village's most recent police station is the house now called 'Copseville', in Church Road. It was built in 1948 at a cost of £2,424 4s. 7d.
Photo Ted Heath

Three old postcard views of Longhope showing the police station. The first picture, **top**, dates from c1908 and shows the station on the left with Penwarden's Stores on the right. The second view, **middle right**, is looking from The Latchen around the same time, with the police station and shop just left of centre nearest to the camera. Finally, **bottom right**, this is looking down the road in the late 1940s, with the station again prominent on the left, shortly before it was superceded by the new building in Church Road.
All courtesy
The Archive Shop

Lydbrook

On 14 March 1817, just over twenty years before the formation of the Gloucestershire Constabulary, a Parish Constable named Henry Thompson, aged 33, was shot dead at Lydbrook while making an arrest.

'Oaklands Cottage', Hangerberry, was the first station and is the one mentioned in the 1857 survey, when the cell was described by the Chief Constable as being *'only 7ft 6ins by 2ft 9ins'*. This rather cramped former cell is used by the present occupier as a storeroom. In 1851 the officer in charge was PC Samuel Beard who, ten years later as the Sergeant at Littledean, was to meet a most violent end.

Lydbrook's next station, which served the village for a century, is a short distance down Hangerberry on the opposite side of the road. The addition of a lean-to office is easy to spot. In 1923 PC George Edward Jones was in charge and in 1937 it was Joe Ireland with Denis Blick. Frank Nicholls took over from PC Finch in the early 1940s. He was in charge there throughout the remainder of the war and was still

Lydbrook
NGR SO 602 155
'Oaklands Cottage', Hangerberry, was Lydbrook's earliest known police station.
Photo Ted Heath

Lydbrook
NGR SO 603 156
The next police station was only about 50 yards down Hangerberry Hill and on the opposite side of the road from the first one. It served the village for a century.
Photo Ted Heath

A c1930 panorama of Hangerbury Hill from Church Hill. The old Severn & Wye Railway runs across the front of the view and in the left foreground is a gated crossing. Taking a line from the gate straight up the picture to where it crosses the road up Hangerberry, the house facing the camera is Lydbrook's first police station. A little to the right, distinguisable by the lean-to, can be seen the rear of the second and – at the date of this photograph – current station. A third police station was built in the 1960s on the site of Upper Lydbrook railway station, just the other side of the church, extreme right.

Courtesy The Archive Shop

there until the 1950s. He was a big man who had played rugby for Great Britain Police before the war. It is said that he used his stomach rather than his fist to send people flying. He played wicket keeper for a Forest Police XI which beat Parkend CC (no mean feat in those days or now!). PC Nicholls was followed by PC Jacobson, who was followed by Frank Rooum in 1959, with PC Merrett as his second man. Frank recalled that in those days Sunday duty involved pedalling his bike round to Symonds Yat to deal with the tourist traffic. Frank spent nine months clearing and digging the garden to the amusement of the local colliers and had just finished when he was promoted and replaced by Frank Durn. Ralph Wilkins remembered that from 1965 to about 1969 the officer in charge at Lydbrook was PC Bill Green, who in 1966 rescued two people from a burning house.

The last station, which is situated opposite the church on the road to Ruardean, was built in the 1960s on the track-bed of the Severn & Wye Railway, actually on the site of Upper Lydbrook station. The last resident officer in charge was the late PC John Sandells, who succumbed to heart disease in his thirties.

**Lydbrook
NGR SO 604 157**
The village's last station, opposite the church, was built in the 1960s.
Photo Ted Heath

Left:
Malcolm Dyer was Constable-in-charge, Lydbrook, 1980 - 82.
By kind permission of the Chief Constable

Right:
Winston Morris was Constable-in-charge at Lydbrook from 1973 to 1976. He was later a Sergeant at Lydney in the 1980s and 90s. His father, Frank Morris, was Sergeant-in-charge at Tutshill. Winston's son, Simon, also joined the Gloucestershire Force.
By kind permission of the Chief Constable

By coincidence or otherwise, Lydbrook can boast at least four Lydney Rugby stars among its former village bobbies: Frank Nicholls, Terry Keyes (who retired as Chief Inspector at Lydney), Winston Morris and Lee Weaver.

In the year 2000, with the last police station long since closed, Lydbrook's Community Police Officer, PC Denise Meredith, set up a Police Information Point (PIP) at the Post Office. There people can pick up police advice leaflets and leave non-urgent messages for the officer who visits on a regular basis.

Lydbrook Postmaster Stuart Manning and PC Denise Meredith at the opening of the Police Information Point (PIP) in early 2000. By kind permission of the Chief Constable

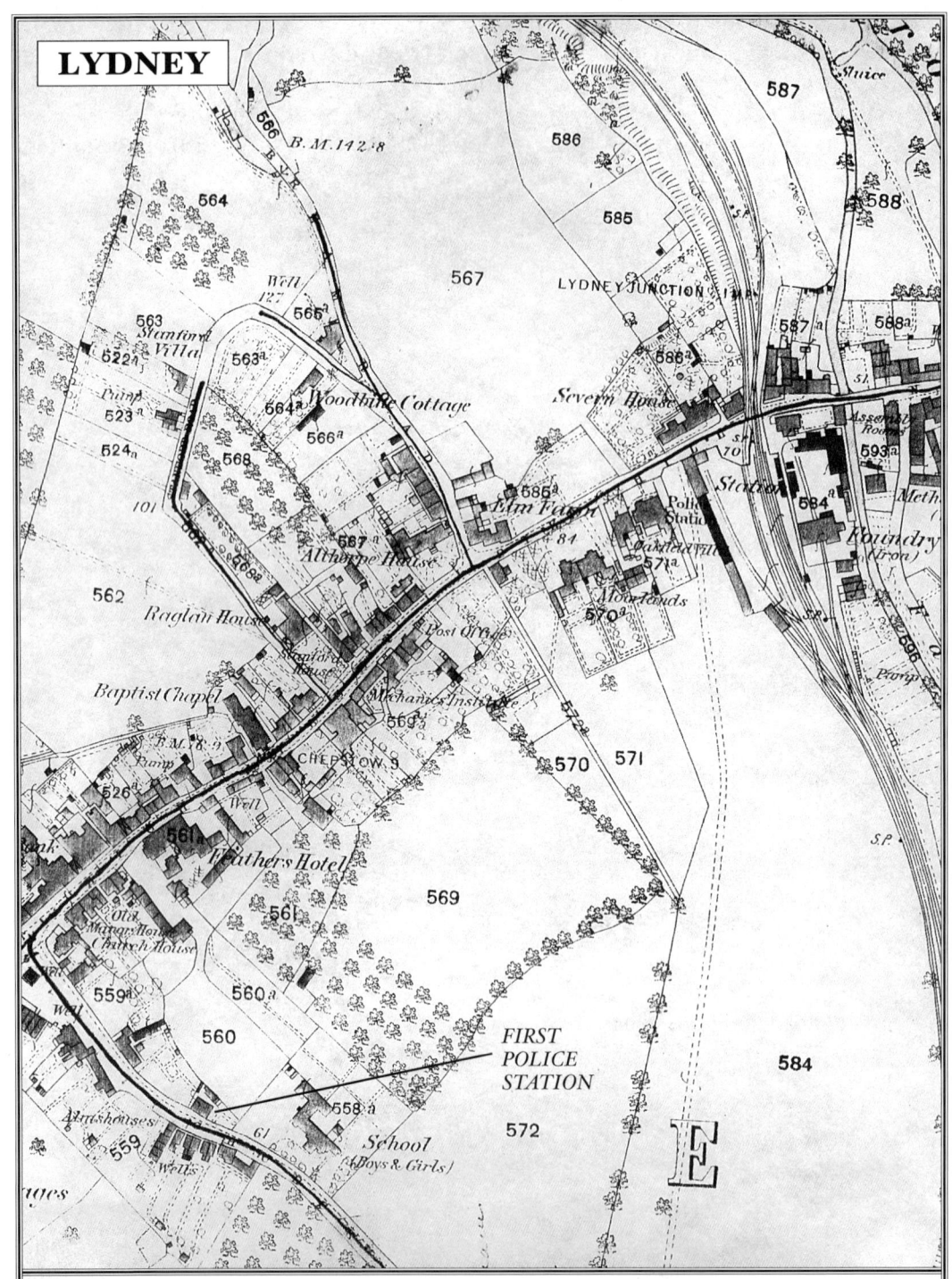

Extract from the 1910 edition 25 inch OS (reduced by 25% to fit the page). The police station is marked centre right, just by Lydney Town railway station. The town's first police station was in the house arrowed, at the top of Church Road. Further down Church Road, the Superintendent's house was built in the 1920s, just past the junction with Whitecross Road, whilst the two pairs of red brick semi-detached houses next to the almshouses were built in the early 1950s as police accommodation.

Crown copyright reserved. Map courtesy The Archive Shop

Aerial view of Lydney c1955. The house thought to have been the first police station is facing the road, centre far right, now the entrance to the ambulance station. Courtesy Welsh Industrial & Maritime Museum

Lydney

The Ambulance Station in Church Road is believed to be the site of Lydney's first police station, which was built for the police by Charles Bathurst Esq. The building was still standing within living memory. Records show that there were three constables at Lydney in 1840 and that Sgt. Charles Tanner was in charge during the 1860s and early 1870s. The Petty Sessional Court was held at the Feathers Hotel in those days.

The imposing Victorian station in Hill Street dates from 1876 and originally incorporated Lydney Magistrates Court, as well as family accommodation, cells and

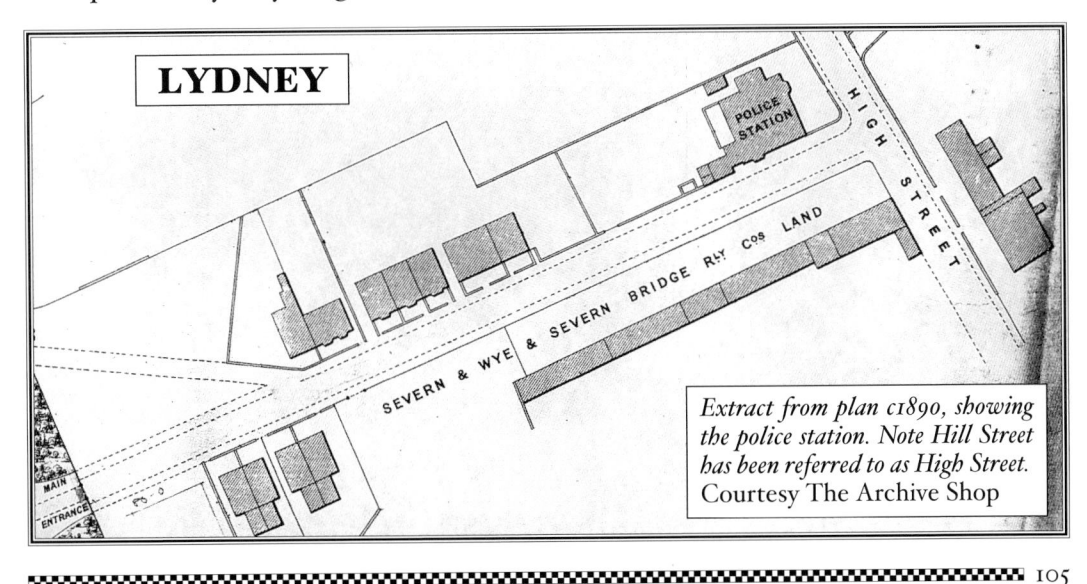

Extract from plan c1890, showing the police station. Note Hill Street has been referred to as High Street. Courtesy The Archive Shop

Lydney   NGR SO 633 031
The imposing Victorian station in Hill Street, a most attractive building constructed of the local red sandstone. It is to be hoped that, if the police do move from here into a new combined emergency services centre at the fire station in the near future, this will not be swept away as already have so many of Lydney's finest 19th century buildings.
                                                                                    Photo Ted Heath

a mortuary. It is an excellent example of a purpose-built police station of the period. Structural alterations inside the building took place in 1900 and again in 1972. Some may remember that in the 1940s and 50s welfare orange juice was dispensed from a counter on the Bathurst Park Road side of the building.

This circa 1910 postcard of Primitive Methodists marching through Lydney also provides a rare glimpse of Tuthill House, centre background between the tree trunks. For many years until the 1930s, when it was replaced by a house in Church Road, it was both Divisional HQ as well as the home for 'F' Division's Superintendent.
Courtesy The Archive Shop

Coronation Day, Lydney, 1911. The crowd, most of whom have dressed for the occasion, has gathered to hear the pronouncements regarding the coronation of King Edward VII, from the steps of the Cross. In the right foreground one of the town's PCs stands with his back to the camera, clutching a pair of white gloves worn for this special day.
Courtesy
The Archive Shop

In 1874 one of the men stationed at Lydney was a PS Swatton, he being recorded in *The Forester* as appearing in court having charged a local man with drunkenness. Charles Albert Clark, another Sergeant at Lydney, died aged 29 on 21 August 1881. The reason for his death is thought to have been natural causes but it is clear from his headstone that he was well respected. His grave is next to that of murdered PS William Morris in Lydney churchyard.

Mary Impett recalled that as a girl she lived at Lydney police station, where her father, Alfred Frederick Newman, was the Inspector from February 1938 to August 1939. The telephone number was still Lydney 7! Prisoners in the cells meant a treat for the family because Mary's mother had to prepare their meals, so it was corned beef all round. Mary's mother also had to clean the courtroom.

Jim Ludlow was posted to Lydney in 1940 where he teamed up with Cliff Dibden, who was to lose his life after being shot down while serving as a Flying Officer in the RAF; he is buried in Italy. Jim recalled some lighter moments from his time with Cliff Dibden:

> *"Cliff had a clumber spaniel called 'Monty' who used to patrol with him at night. When Cliff was on station duty Monty would hide behind Cliff's coat, which was hanging on a peg behind him, and growl invisibly at any callers. The Station Diary and Occurrence Book from that period were completely bereft of any binding, bearing witness to the number of times they had been thrown at Monty!*
>
> *Sergeant Freeman, who lived at Lydney police station, had a parrot which he entrusted to the single men when he went away on leave. Jim and Cliff invested a lot of time and effort trying to teach the parrot to swear but the parrot remained stubbornly silent. PS Freeman returned to claim his parrot but soon let it be known that the parrot had to go. Apparently it wouldn't stop swearing!"*

Jim Ludlow also recalled that two retired Sergeants, Caldicutt and Ferryman rejoined as Reserve Constables during the war and while at Lydney Jim had to take his turn at guarding the exiled Dutch Royal family, who were then staying at Lydney Park.

Ken Parsons joined the police in March 1941 (his 19th birthday!) and recalled how he spent his first three to four months at Lydney:

"No uniform was issued for about 1-2 months so I walked about wearing a trenchcoat and a trilby hat and carrying a gas mask. Training consisted of being told to write out a page a day of Moriarty's Police Law and I learned from the senior constables about demobilising cars and the blackout regulations. One evening I found a Rolls Royce with the door open and shortly afterwards a smartly dressed gent came to the car. I told him that the door had been open and that I could have driven the car away. He replied "Go on then". It turned out to be John Watts, owner of the Red and White Bus Co. etc. etc. who then told me that the steering was locked!"

Ken also recalled the following:

"At this time there was a squad called the Police War Reserve recruited to maintain security at vulnerable points like the Severn (Rail) Bridge, the power station, electricity installations etc. I often did this sort of duty to relieve the PWR officers on Rest days. One day I was on 2-10 at the Severn Bridge and walked across to talk to the PWR on duty on the other side. Whilst there the phone went and the Lydney Sergeant told me I was neglecting my duty and to return at once. I ran the whole length of the bridge, two sleepers at a stride, to receive a good telling off.

The police bicycle was the only transport for PCs. The front light was operated with carbide and water and was shaded to comply with the Blackout Regs.

At this time the police were thin on the ground. There was a Detective Sergeant and one DC providing CID cover for the whole of 'F' Division. The Superintendent prosecuted all the cases in the Magistrates Courts at Lydney, Coleford and Cinderford. One patrol car covered the Forest of Dean, the two traffic officers who crewed it were 'CAS' Smith, who was one of the earliest Motor Patrol officers, and Paul Foice, who went on to command the Forest Division and the Force's Traffic Dept. Split shifts 10am to 1pm and 7pm to 12am were common in those days and beat officers made points at telephone kiosks every half hour so they could be contacted if any incident requiring attention occurred."

Ron Stephens, who joined the police after war service in the Army, was stationed at Lydney for five years from 1949. In the late 1940s the force was very short of officers. Lydney at that time only had one Sergeant and seven Constables.

Ron went to Lydney as a single man but got married and his first daughter was born while he was there. He lived in Albert Road, near the Step Aside Inn, where he was a member of the crib. team. He played cricket for Forest Police and football for Lydney Town, as well as for the Force. One day in 1952 he and other officers were on their way to play soccer for the Force against Dorset Police. They had got as far as Highnam when they heard that the King had died. They turned back and did eight hours duty instead.

Fear of the dark can be a bit of a disadvantage in the police. Ron Stephens told how one night he was ordered by his Sergeant to make a point at midnight at Redhill House, which was unoccupied while Lord Bledisloe was abroad. Ron expected that he would get a visit from the Sergeant so he got there early, checked the house and then waited in the darkness under a Rhododendron bush. The house was up a long unlit drive. Ron could hear footsteps approaching on the gravel and suspected that the Sergeant was afraid of the dark. He waited until the footsteps drew level and leaped out of the bushes to report *"All correct, Sarge!"*. According to Ron, the Sergeant nearly jumped out of his skin.

On another occasion a safe had been stolen during a burglary in Lydney and it was found intact in a quarry. Two officers were detailed to watch the safe and arrest the offenders if they returned. Supt. Newman decided to go out that night to visit the officers who were keeping observation on the safe, only to find them sitting in the car with the lights on! He was none too pleased.

At the rear of the station building at Lydney is the Forest Police Social Club building. Members of the Forest Division had purchased a hut from the wartime camp at nearby Naas Court and worked in their own time to dismantle it, intending to transport it by lorry to the police station and rebuild it as a club. It was on 22 April 1948, during the dismantling operation, that disaster struck. A brick wall, which divided the hut, collapsed killing PC Bruce Alway instantly and seriously injuring PC Clifford Park who died the following day. War Reserve PC Edward Trotman was also seriously injured and PC Andy Weir was hurt too. Superintendent Newman was extremely upset by the tragedy. Ron Stephens remembered that the club was completed by the County Council in 1953 in memory of the officers.

The rear of Lydney police station showing the single storey club building. Photo Ted Heath

Francis Field and Alf Thomas were posted to Lydney to replace PCs Park and Alway. They began courting two daughters of Mary Smith, who kept the Railway Inn just below the level crossing in Hill Street, and had a double wedding on 1 June 1949. Francis recalled his Lydney days:

> *"Early days at Lydney were much different to what they are today. Just after the war there were very few cars about, in fact you knew most of the cars in the town and their owners, mostly businessmen, doctors etc. When Bert Leakey came to Lydney as Inspector in the early 1950s, he boasted a little Austin 10. The only PC I can remember with a car then was PC Clarke, who lived in Bathurst Park Road next to the police garage."*

Officers had to apply for the Chief Constable's permission to marry and were required to submit details of their intended spouse for vetting. Ron Stephens recalled one officer at Lydney, nicknamed 'Fearless' by his mates, who refused to comply with that requirement and effectively tendered his resignation from the force by telling the Superintendent where he could shove his job!

In December 1949, A.E. 'Bert' Leakey was transferred from Staple Hill, Bristol, to become the Inspector at Lydney. A career policeman, Bert Leakey had joined the Force in 1923 and was first stationed in Cheltenham. In 1926, he was posted to the Forest for a short time during the Miners Strike. During the war he was seconded to Queen Mary's staff as an Inspector, travelling thosands of miles in that capacity. Bert is still remembered with affection in Lydney by older folk, as is his daughter Sheila, who instructed St. John's Ambulance classes. Recalled as being always immaculately groomed and turned out, he retired from Lydney and from the police on 30 June 1955.

Also to Lydney in 1949 came PS W. Horton, from Cheltenham, whilst PS Finch was promoted from Lydney to Kingswood as Inspector. Other remembered officers from the 1950s are Supt. A. Hills, Detective Sergeant J.P. Griffin and WPS Millichip.

Edgar Bowring, who retired as a Sergeant at Lydney in 1964, was on duty on the night of the Severn Bridge Disaster in 1960. He recalled that, as with most major incidents, confusion reigned at first but slowly the full facts emerged. Edgar himself went to Awre on that night and searched in vain for survivors. Years later, PS Theo Powell and PC Ted Heath were in attendance when the remaining piers of the bridge were demolished.

Tragedy struck the local force again on 15 March 1967. Motor Patrol officers PC Paul Pursehouse and PC Gerry Wyatt were on patrol in their Austin Westminster patrol car when they were involved in an accident at Peter's Cross on the A48. PC

Insp. A.E. 'Bert' Leakey, c1950.
Courtesy Mrs Sheila Brown (nee Leakey)

Insp. Bert Leakey (centre) photographed at Lydney Docks on the day of his retirement.
Courtesy Mrs Sheila Brown (nee Leakey)

Police Ball, Lydney Town Hall, 1950s. Left, DS Ben Gwilliam, right, DC Peter White.
Courtesy Dora Gwilliam

This group picture was taken at the same event. Standing, left to right: Peter White, Dennis Ryder, Doug Duval. Seated, far right: Dora Gwilliam.
Courtesy Dora Gwilliam

Pursehouse was killed and PC Wyatt was seriously injured. Their motor patrol colleague, PC Peter Stoneham, was first on the scene.

A snapshot of Lydney station life in 1967 reveals the staff and organisation in what was to be the last year and perhaps the high point of 'F' Division. Superintendent Henry Lodge was in command of the Division and had his office and an Admin. Section attached to his house in Church Road. He was assisted there by PC Dave Brunsdon, a skilled all-round sportsman. Chief Insp. Jim Hemming was in charge of the station and there was a Sergeant and three or four Constables on each of four shifts. The station was open to the public 24 hours of the day, with a PC on station duty. One of the Sergeants at that time was Mike Perry, who was later to be Inspector at Cinderford. The other Sergeants were Pip Lawrence, Theo Powell and Dave Bullock. Also stationed there at that time were: PS Graham Watkins (Training), DS Len Cullimore (Crime Prevention), PS Frank Monks and PS Tony Berryman (both Traffic), D/Insp. Alan Wadley (in charge of the Division's CID) and DS Herbie Thomas, who in 1978 as a DI at Stroud was to be Highly Commended for his actions in dealing with a very dangerous man. (Acting DC Roger Turley, a Forester, was also highly commended following the same incident. Roger is now a Detective Chief Inspector).

Remembrance Day parade, Lydney, c1970. Supt. Ben Gwilliam is seen leading the parade past the police station, with C/Insp. Don Witts and Sergeants Graham Watkins and Theo Powell.
Courtesy Dora Gwilliam

PC Neil Thomas performing Traffic Control at the junction of Forest Road and Hill Street, Lydney, c1986.
Courtesy Neil Thomas

In 1968, 'F' Division ceased to exist and the Forest became a Sub-Division of the newly created Western Division, which included Gloucester City. Lydney police station continued to serve as the H.Q. for the Forest of Dean from the 1970s until the 1990s. Born at English Bicknor, Ben Gwilliam finished his distinguished police career as Superintendent at Lydney. Ben had been at Lydney previously as a Detective Sergeant in 1958 and was the Inspector-in-charge at Stonehouse when the Severn Bridge Disaster occurred in 1960. In 1973 Campbell Jack Willett, who had been the last Sergeant at Littledean, retired from the Force with the rank of Inspector and took up a civilian post at Lydney Police Station. Cam Willett died in 1998.

In 1977 Graham Murdock, a DI on the Regional Crime Squad, was promoted to uniform Chief Inspector at Lydney, where he followed Peter Day. Chief Insp. Murdock had not been at Lydney long before he was appointed Temporary Superintendent and seconded to 'Operation Countryman', a major investigation into allegations of police corruption in London. He was, however, in the Forest long enough to be awarded an official 'Fern Ticket'.

There is a story that the officers performing duty as station clerk in those days had made a 'mood meter', which they kept under the counter to record the mood of the Superintendent each morning.

Many people will remember some of the characters from the recent past. Lydney man and sometime County Police scrum-half John Wilcox had an unusual career, in that he specialised in both Motor Patrol and CID. John Bryant and Dick Vaile were well known as main road motorcyclists at Lydney for many years and Traffic officer and wildlife expert Tudor Davies was a popular figure. Other well known personalities include Malcolm Cameron, Neil Thomas, Gerry Best, Dick Perkins, Bob Berryman and the late Derek Underwood. Inspector Peter Mannion was the Lydney Inspector in the late 1970s and early 1980s, at which time he became immortalised in case law (Snook v Mannion). He was active in the Police Federation and became a full-time member of its national council, the Joint Central Committee. He was followed by the late Geoff Miles who had previously been Inspector at Cinderford and who had been a good boxer in his younger days. Bob Gwilliam, who later distinguished himself by disarming a violent man armed with two loaded guns in Gloucester, started his police career at Lydney.

Cyril Bailey, licensee of the Annexe Inn, Newerne Street, with joint author of this book Insp. Geoff Sindrey, at the launch of Lydney Pubwatch Scheme 1990. Geoff Sindrey collection

In August 1990 the Forest's first Pubwatch Scheme was launched at Lydney. Licensees agreed to ban from all pubs in the town anyone convicted of violence on licensed premises. The result was a significant decrease in violence and disorder. In 1999 CCTV cameras became operational in the town, further reducing public disorder and fear of crime.

In 1998 the station ceased to be an HQ and only housed a small complement of local officers plus, from 2000, the officers of the Forest of Dean Operation Gemini Squad. The building is considered too large for the Constabulary's present needs and plans are being made to replace it using part of the Fire Station site. While most people would accept that public money should not be wasted on the upkeep of an unnecessarily large building, it would be very unfortunate indeed if the building were to be demolished. It is an excellent example of a Victorian public building and is part of Lydney's heritage but unfortunately is not listed.

Lydney boy, Dean Walker, became a Chief Inspector at Gloucester and, under the reorganisation of 1998, assumed responsibilities for the Forest. Kevin Lambert, a Lydney PC from the late 1980s, was promoted Superintendent responsible for Community Partnership in 2000.

Left: *Gerry Best was a Sergeant at Lydney in the 1980s and 90s and had previously been a Traffic Motorcyclist.*
By kind permission of the Chief Constable

Right: *Bob Berryman was also a Sergeant at Lydney during the 1980s and 90s.*
By kind permission of the Chief Constable

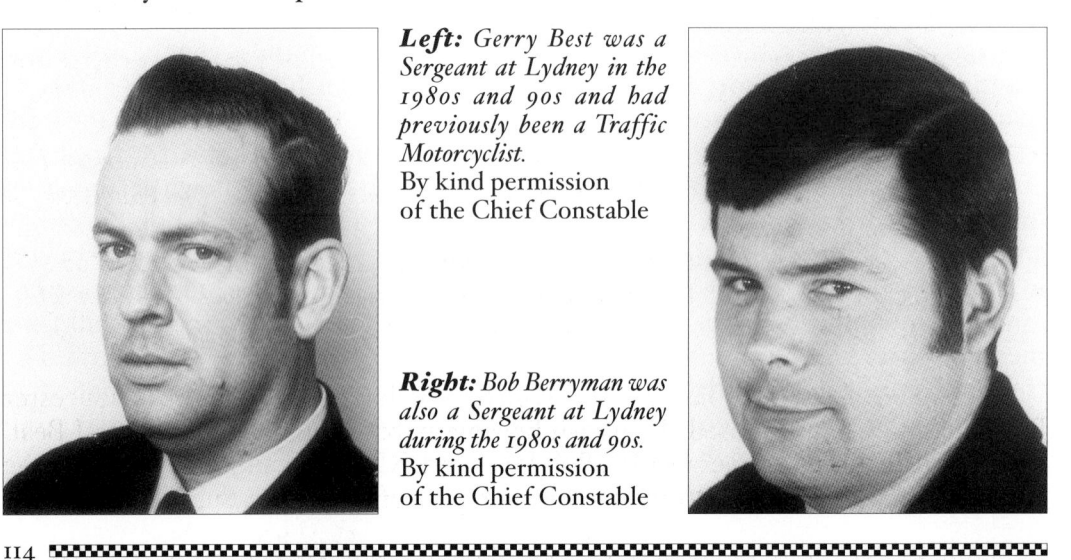

Mile End

One might wonder why it was thought necessary to build a police station just a mile from the main station in the centre of Coleford. The house now called 'The Three Oaks', in Gloucester Road, Mile End, was the last new police station to be opened in a Forest community where none had previously existed. It therefore represents something of a high water mark in community police stations. Thereafter, although some stations were replaced by newer buildings, there was to be no further expansion in the Forest of Dean. The house is in the typical 1950s sub-station style but the layout of the plot and the driveway is evidence of the reported original intention for a district nurse's house to share the site.

The first officer in charge was Tom Prosser. Others included Ken Martin who was there in 1959 and Arthur Wood who was there in the 1960s.

Mile End   NGR SO 587 120
This house, now called 'The Three Oaks', was the village's police station.   Photo Ted Heath

Minsterworth

The right hand house of a pair of semi-detached properties on a bend of the A48 near the Apple Tree Inn served as a police station during the first half of the 20th century. It was probably intended as a link in a chain of stations along the A48, its purpose being as much to provide a quick response to serious road accidents as to serve the immediate community. PC Francis Field was posted to Minsterworth in February 1956. In those days it was part of the Longford Section of Gloucester Division. He wrote the following:

Minsterworth   NGR SO 789 176
The house on the right of this pair is the former police station on the main A48 road.   Photo Ted Heath

> "Minsterworth was a sort of 'No Man's Land' between the Forest and Gloucester. I had three separate Courts which I attended, namely, Littledean, Newent and Gloucester County Magistrates Court.
>
> There were numerous accidents on the two main roads, A48 and A40. I wonder how we managed to deal with them single handed in those days, especially when you hear of the road closures today, following accidents and the number of cars and people attending."

During the life of the police station Minsterworth was always part of Gloucester Division and when it closed the parish became part of the Gloucester Rural Beat. Many local people will remember PC Bob Jones and PC Terry Smith, who patrolled the area for years. In 1982 Minsterworth became part of the Forest Sub-Division.

Mitcheldean

Mitcheldean had a police presence from the outset and there is evidence that it was resented by more than one section of society. The Chief Constable reported in 1840 that there had been opposition from the labouring classes, while the minutes of a Vestry meeting (forerunner of the parish council) at Abenhall in 1841 resolved to petition Quarter Sessions against what they considered to be the unnecessary rate burden for supporting the police. There were five constables allocated to Mitcheldean originally but that number was scaled down as the area became more tranquil.

We know that in 1857 the police station was at No 2 Plats Row and this was probably the town's first police station. In 1851 Joseph Cockings was the senior man and he lived at the station with his wife, their four children and two other constables, William Nash and John Cooke. The house has been in the present occupier's family since the police moved out over a century ago. The former cell is now a kitchen. When the iron bars were removed from the window by the present occupier it was found that they reached at least 12 inches into the stonework!

The town's second police station was in Townsend, next to the court. It was at Mitcheldean on 8 November 1916 that PC Ernest Albert Cooper unfortunately made history, when he became the first member of the Gloucestershire Constabulary to die as a result of a cycling accident on duty.

Mitcheldean NGR SO 664 186
The town's first police station, probably from late 1839, at No. 2 Plats Row, with the present occupier Mr Hyatt. The house has been in his wife's family for over 100 years.   Photo Ted Heath

Mitcheldean NGR SO 664 188
The town's second police station in Townsend, with the old Court House on the left.   Photo Ted Heath

Above: PC 154 Edward George James with his wife and children, Les, Joan and Robin, at Mitcheldean, 1930s.

Right: Every inch the proud country copper! PC 154 Edward George James and his wife at Mitcheldean, 1929.
Both courtesy Les Tuffley

PC Frank Parslow was in charge in 1923 and PC 154 Edward George James was stationed there before moving to Newnham in the 1930s. The cell was at the back and Joan Rooum, PC James's daughter, recalled how one night she was kept awake by a drunk singing *'Carolina Moon'*.

During the Second World War, offences for which people were booked by PC Tom Buckland included 'Being absent from Home Guard Parades' (fined £2.0.0) and 'Black Market' offences such as 'Possession of HM Government Property', 'Possession of US Government Property' and 'Possession of Excessive Amounts of Rationed Goods'.

The modern village police station in Townsend was built in the 1960s when Rank Xerox was bringing new prosperity to the village. One of the early occupants of this house was PC John Hawkins, in 1968. Although the house is of modern design, central heating was not installed until 1980. One of the last resident officers in charge was PC Simon Bailey.

Mitcheldean
NGR SO 665 188
The station in Townsend built in the 1960s.
Photo Ted Heath

A Forest Beat

Newent

Newent's earliest police station was on the Dymock Road according to the 1857 survey. Local historian David Bick's best guess is that it stood where the by-pass or the fire station now are.

'Nicholson House', near the lake, was Newent's police station and court from 1880, until the court moved to Gloucester and a new police station was built in Watery Lane. The late Stan Cross was the last sergeant at Nicholson House which is now a museum. He is fondly remembered by Liz Lloyd-Nash (nee Pritchard) who, as a young girl in Newent, was always up to mischief. Liz is grateful for the timely 'guidance' of the ubiquitous PS Cross, who seemed to be able to anticipate her every mischievous plan.

PS 97 Child who was Sergeant-in-charge at Newent in the 1880s. By coincidence, a Newent Sergeant in the 1980s had the same surname and PC Kevin Ireland, stationed at Newent in 2000, had the same uniform number! This rare early police portrait was photocopied from a since lost glass plate negative. Courtesy Bob Phelps

Newent
NGR SO 723 258
The former police station, now called 'Nicholson House', another well designed and proprotioned building of the Victorian era, which happily survives in use as a museum, albeit with some macabre exhibits!
Photo Ted Heath

The M50 'Ross Spur' Motorway was opened in the 1960s and it passes through three counties, Gloucestershire, Herefordshire and Worcestershire. In the early days, the different police forces took turns to patrol it for eight hours at a time before it was agreed that it would be policed by the West Mercia Constabulary throughout its entire length.

The modern station in Watery Lane was built in 1974. One of the Sergeants from that time, PS Brian Calway, retired from the Force with the rank of Chief Inspector and went on to be a County Councillor and member of the Police Authority!

Dave Peake, an Inspector at the time of writing, was a PC at Newent in 1977. He told how one Sunday he was called to the United Reform Church in Broad Street, where a drunk was making a nuisance of himself during a service. On entering the church, Dave saw a big, strongly built man whom he recognised as a well known character around Gloucester. The man was drunk, swearing and generally disturbing the service. Dave felt sure that an obscure piece of legislation covered these very circumstances but in order to get the man out with the minimum of fuss he told him that he was wanted on the telephone! Amazingly this improvised bit of policemanship worked and the man left the church quietly but as Dave invited him to sit in his police car to discuss the matter the man punched him in the head. The man swung at Dave a second time but this time he ducked. The man staggered off with Dave in pursuit and was arrested. He was not only charged with assault on police but, with the benefit of Stone's Justices Manual back at the station, he was also charged with an offence contrary to Section 2 of the Ecclesiastical Courts Jurisdiction Act 1860!

Newent NGR SO 721 259
Below: *The present station in Watery Lane.*
Right: *Newent Police Officers, March 2000. Left to right PC 1450 Deena Smith, PC 848 Gary Eagger and PC 1331 Sam Williams.* Both photos Ted Heath

In the 1980s, Newent could boast the Force's first female Sergeant to be in charge of a police station, the late Liz Child, who sadly succumbed to cancer. There is a seat dedicated to her memory in Westbury-on-Severn churchyard.

A reorganisation of the Force in 1982 saw Newent incorporated into an enlarged Forest of Dean Sub-Division, which was later to become a separate Division again for a decade. However, in 1998, Newent became part of the newly formed Forest North Inspector Neighbourhood Area (INA).

Inspector David Peake, who was a PC at Newent in the 1970s. Courtesy D. Peake

Newnham

In 1840 the Forest's police commander, Superintendent William H. Lander, was based at Newnham. In the year 1857 a survey carried out by Chief Constable Lefroy describes the police station (which was also home to the Sergeant-in-charge) as being *'situate nearly opposite the Bear Inn in the lower part of the town... The premises are very old and the rooms very small'*. The Bear Inn was in Passage Lane, now called Severn Street. The cell accommodation was deemed unsuitable so, for many years, the cells at the Town Hall (now The Club) were used. When PS Hugh Brown, and PCs William Godfrey and Henry Gleed were stationed there in the 1850s, the Petty Sessional Court was held at The Bear. By 1856 there had been a change of Sergeant, PS John Hernamann having taken over as officer in charge.

Newnham NGR SO 692 117
Severn Street, opposite the Bear Inn, was the site of Newnham's first police station. Photo Ted Heath

Right: Looking down Severn Street towards the river, c1910. The police station was at the bottom on the left.
Courtesy The Archive Shop

The old Newnham Town Hall, c1930, with First World War artillery piece outside. The cells here were used for prisoners for many years because of the unsuitability of the ones in the station in Severn Street. After it ceased to be used as the Town Hall, the building was the offices of the Conservative & Unionist party up until WW1 and became the Comrades Hall, as seen here, after. It is now a social hall called The Club.
Courtesy
The Archive Shop

In 1873 a new purpose built station with cells was built on a plot in High Street, near the junction with Severn Street. Records show that, in 1923, William Strawford was in charge assisted by Gilbert Pagett. The Severn at Newnham features in Gloucestershire police folklore thanks to PC Hector Evans, who is reputed to have cycled across the frozen river! Joan Rooum's father, PC 154 Edward George James was in charge there throughout the Second World War. Edgar Bowring, then a young, single officer, lodged and worked there with him from 1937 to December 1939.

Edgar was born in 1913 at Forest Green, Nailsworth. He was accepted for the Gloucestershire Constabulary in 1933 and was called up in 1934. After serving at Cheltenham and Gloucester, he was posted to Newnham. While there he dealt with numerous accidents and reports of petty crime on the A48. He remembers that one day he and PC James, assisted by the ferryman, recovered a body from the middle of the River Severn. It turned out to be a tramp who had days earlier been seen trying to ford the river at low tide. During his spell at Newnham, Edgar was commended for the detection of a series of shop break-ins.

Newnham NGR SO 691 117
The purpose built Victorian station in the High Street.   Photo Ted Heath

Newnham High Street c1905. The police station is just to the right of the baker's cart, the only traffic on the road – such a difference to the often busy section of the A48 this is today.   Courtesy The Archive Shop

A Forest Beat

In 1958 Jim Ludlow succeeded Harry Pennington at Newnham. The late Fred 'Trumpeter' Evans from Fairford was there as second man. Mr M.F. Carter, HM Coroner and Clerk to the Justices, used to hold a court there in the front room of the house. Mrs Ludlow would light a fire and Mr Carter would pay her £5 for the use.

The latest station, with a row of police houses attached, was built in Beeches Road in 1974. It was established as a Sergeant station but has since been a two PC and one PC station. In the early 1990s the Forest of Dean Traffic Section was based there. Locals will remember Nigel Gulliford, Kevin Burke, Pete Davies, Nigel Isaacs, Dave Jones and others from recent years.

PC James clearing snow outside Newnham Police Station 1947, a couple of years before his retirement from the Force. Note the mixture of uniform clothing and civilian cloth cap. Courtesy Mrs A. Gould

Top: *PC Edward George James c1930, wearing his WW1 medals. He transferred from Mitcheldean to Newnham in the early 1930s.* Courtesy Joan Rooum (nee James)

Newnham NGR SO 693 119
The station in Beeches Road, with attached row of police houses, was built in 1974. Photo Ted Heath

FORM C 12.

GLOUCESTERSHIRE CONSTABULARY

Certificate of Service.

THIS IS TO CERTIFY THAT Edward George James.

born at Leckhampton, Cheltenham in the County of Gloucester joined this Force on 1st May 1919 and was pensioned on completion of service as a Constable on 31st January 1949

Length of service Twenty Nine years Two hundred and Seventy six days

His conduct was **EXEMPLARY.**

DESCRIPTION OF ABOVE-NAMED.

Date of birth 22nd October 1892 Height 5 feet 10¾ inches
Eyes Brown Hair Dark, turning grey
Complexion Fresh Marks —

Chief Constable of Gloucester.

Headquarters Office,
Cheltenham 31st January 1949.

Certificate of Service of Edward George James. He retired from Newnham station in January 1949 after nearly 30 years of exemplary service, much of it as a village bobby in the Forest. The description speaks volumes – Hair: 'Dark, turning grey'! Courtesy Joan Rooum (nee James)

Parkend

A house now called 'Hazeldene' is believed to have been Parkend's first station. It is quite large and had a cell. Its location was convenient for the centre of the village, with its industry, railway and pubs. In fact the railway went right past the front door to Marsh Sidings. In 1937 PC Reg Weekes was in charge.

Parkend
NGR 616 079
'Hazeldene' was Parkend's police station up until the 1960s; it is believed to have been the first station in the village. However, the station mentioned in the 1881 Census – West Dean, somewhere near Russels Lodge – is probably Parkend (see page 161). If so, it would seem to indicate there may well be an earlier station to locate.   Photo Ted Heath

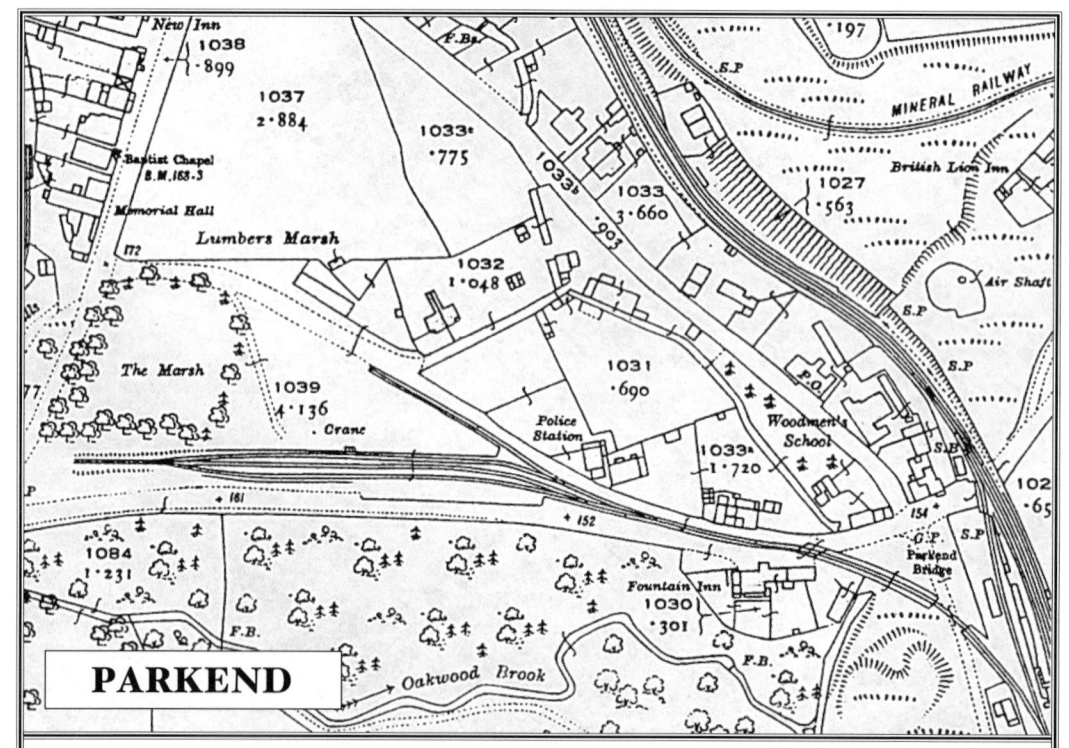

Extract from the 1922 edition 25 inch OS. The police station is in the centre, facing Marsh Sidings. The 1859 Survey of West Dean by F.W. Dibben shows the house, even then called 'Hazeldene', as being owned by Henry Kear and occupied by Ellen Wintle, so it would seem unlikely it was in use by the police at that date. The 1878 edition 25 inch OS also shows it – interestingly called 'Ivy Cottage' at this time – but does not mark it as a police station, most likely indicating its use by the constabulary dates from sometime after that.

Map courtesy Gloucestershire Record Office, Crown copyright reserved

Throughout the Second World War the officer in charge was PC George Carter, a keen gardener and a respected village policeman. He was secretary of Parkend Football Club and ran a weekly whist drive in the Memorial Hall. Geoff Waygood was a student at the Forestry Training School at the time. He recalled that dances at the Memorial Hall would be attended not only by the local lads but also by forestry students and US servicemen. This was a volatile mix, especially as they would have first called at the New Inn (now the Woodman) to get 'tanked up'. Fights inevitably broke out on the dance floor and PC Carter would nip in, pull the combatants out and invite them to settle their differences on the village green before being allowed back in.

When Geoff returned to Parkend to live in 1961, the officer in charge was PC Tony Philpott who was very much involved in village life, being church treasurer and youth club leader. He was followed by PC Malcolm Bricknell, who was followed by keen hiker Ron Evans.

'Woodlands' in Fancy Road was a brand new police station in 1967. It was built by the same builder and to the same design as the one at Yorkley. It has a pull-in at the front for customers but vehicular access to the garage is from a road at the rear, because the bend in Fancy Road severely reduces visibility. The last resident Parkend police officer was Phil Hopson, who played cricket and football for the village and who is said by Geoff Waygood to have patrolled the village at night with his own Alsatian dog. After Phil Hopson, Parkend was policed by Andy Barrow, who was stationed at Yorkley until it closed and then at Bream.

Parkend has itself produced a number of police officers: David Price (founder member of Gloucestershire Police Band), Cyril Thomas (Glos), Reg Preest (Glos), Roger Gwynne (Met), John Gwynne (Met) and Roger Meek (Met), whilst Harry Thomas QPM, the author of *The History of the Gloucestershire Constabulary 1839-1985*, hailed from Whitecroft. Mr Thomas joined the Gloucestershire Constabulary after service in the Welsh Guards and retired with the rank of Chief Superintendent.

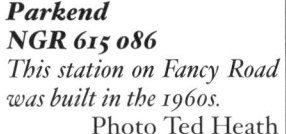

Parkend
NGR 615 086
This station on Fancy Road was built in the 1960s.
Photo Ted Heath

Redmarley D'Abitot

There is a house in Pendock Road called 'The Old Police Station', which was once a Worcestershire Police station before boundary changes in 1931 brought the parish within Gloucestershire. A stout stone built out-house is believed to have been the cell. The present occupier found a Worcestershire Police helmet badge there.

Redmarley
NGR SO 765 319
'The Old Police Station', Pendock Road, dates from when this community was in Worcestershire.
Photo Ted Heath

Ruardean

Ruardean is one of the oldest settlements in the Forest and is one of the few to be mentioned in the Domesday Book (Ruuirdin) Yet according to available records it did not have a police station until after 1902. Since then no fewer than four different buildings have served as the village police station.

'Varnister House' in Varnister Road, which stands proudly in its own grounds overlooking the Wye Valley, is thought to have been Ruardean's first station.

Ruardean
NGR SO 628 178
'Varnister House' is thought to have been Ruardean's first station.
Photo Ted Heath

'The Lawns' in Ruardean's main street is another fine house which was, for a time, the village police station and it was followed by 'The Laurels', also in the main street. At the time of writing there is still a man in the village who admits to having been locked up there for the night! In 1937 Jim Boughton was the officer in charge.

The former station on the corner of St John's (*sic*) was built in the 1950s, in the distinctive style used for sub-stations throughout the county in that period. It was the last of Ruardean's four police stations. Jim Hemming, who was later to be Chief Inspector at Lydney, went to Ruardean in 1954 from Hanham and many will recall Jock Hart and Gordon Saunders, who were there for a time.

Ruardean   NGR SO 619 176
'The Lawns' was the next house to serve as the police station.   Photo Ted Heath

Ruardean   NGR SO 622 177
'The Laurels' was also once the village police station.
                           Photo Geoff Sindrey

Ruardean High Street, c1930. The police station now called 'The Lawns' was on the corner on the right, behind the stone wall.
Courtesy
The Archive Shop

Ruardean
NGR SO 623 178
The former station on the corner of St John's was built in the style typical of the 1950s.
Photo Ted Heath

Ruspidge

The site of the earlier police station in Ruspidge Road is a large stone house that once had a cell where drunks were held to sober up. One of the last officers to live in this station was PC Alec Taylor.

Ruspidge
NGR SO 653 123
The earlier police station in Ruspidge Road.
Photo Ted Heath

The more recent police station building in Ruspidge Road is just a few yards up the street from its predecessor. Former parish councillor Derrick Adams remembered that his uncle, Tom Sladen, worked as a bricklayer on this station in about 1950, although it was not until 1979 that central heating was installed. The first officer to occupy it was Jack Rogers, followed by Jack Hyett and later footballer Bob Twyford, who will still be remembered by many. Neil Thomas was there in the early 1970s and the last resident village coppers at Ruspidge included Rod Sarson and Simon Bannister.

Ruspidge NGR SO 653 123

Above left: *Ruspidge's second police station was still operational when this picture was taken, c1972.*
Courtesy Neil Thomas

Left: *Another view of the 1950s-built station in Ruspidge Road, as it looks today.* Photo Ted Heath

Above: *Ruspidge Police Station with Officer-in-charge PC Neil Thomas, c1972.* Courtesy Neil Thomas

Above right: *Lydney Old Grammarian Neil Thomas was Officer-in-charge at Ruspidge and later the Community Officer for Woolaston.*
By kind permission of the Chief Constable

Right: *Rod Sarson was the Officer-in-charge at Ruspidge before serving as a DC at Coleford for many years in the 1980s and 1990s.*
By kind permission of the Chief Constable

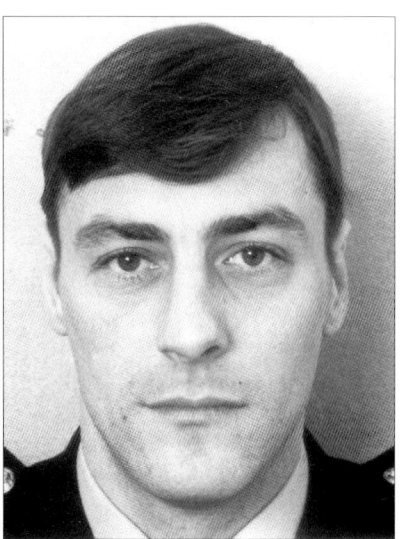

St Briavels

A Police Station Diary, dated 1840 to 1843, relates to a station at Hewelsfield. This is confirmed by the 1841 Census, which lists three Police Constables, John Sherlls, George Beasley and William Bailey in Hewelsfield but gives no clue as to the whereabouts of the building. A search of available records and extensive enquiries in the village have so far failed to trace its location. The diary records foot patrols as far as Beachley and Woolaston, as well as Bream, the village of St Briavels and the maze of lanes and settlements down to Brockweir Quay, which was then a busy wharf. A vast area to patrol on foot!

The diary meticulously records that on Sunday 25 April 1841, Constables George Beasley and Daniel Walker were dispatched to Tidenham where they took into custody two men accused of the theft of three ducks. They brought them back to Hewelsfield to be detained. The following day the two men were taken before a local magistrate who committed them to Gloucester Gaol. The men then had to be escorted to Lydney where they were handed over for onward escort to Gloucester. All accomplished on foot and all for three ducks.

The Police & Constabulary List for 1844 does not mention Hewelsfield but refers to a 'Chase' police station, which could have been at Hewelsfield, Tidenham or even Tutshill (see page 135).

There is a building called the 'Old Police House' in the High Street, which is believed to have been St Briavels first police station. According to the census, Sergeant John Bunning, aged 39, and his wife Elizabeth, aged 21, lived there in 1851. Both had been born in Stow on the Wold.

St Briavels
NGR SO 558 044
'The Old Police House' in High Street.
Photo Ted Heath

St Briavels NGR SO 558 045
'Siebert House' was also the village police station for a time.
Photo G Sindrey

John Dougan once lived in a small cottage now called 'Siebert House' in the High Street. He was sure that this house also served as the village police station for a time and that he converted the old cell into a bathroom. John was able to recall the names of the St Briavels officers over a long period: PC Garston (probably the last in 'Siebert House'), PC Pickering, PC Holder, PC Holmes, PC Coates, PC Day, PC Henderson, PC Parker, PC Drennan, PC Cottle, PC Sands, PC Checkley, PC Endy, PC Willets, PC Farmer, PC Isaacs, PC Ollie Turner.

St Anne's Way, a new development off the High Street, is the site of the police station which served the area for many years prior to the early 1950s. It stood next to Williams & Cotton's shop which has also been demolished.

In 1949 PC Edgar Day was in charge and was probably the last to occupy this station and the first to occupy its successor. His son John joined the Force and retired with the rank of Chief Inspector.

Bob Parker, who also retired as a Chief Inspector, was posted to St Briavels in the late 1940s and recalled those times:

> "I served at St. Briavels police station in 1949 and the early part of 1950 as 'Second Man' to P.C. No 256 Edgar Day, who served there for well over 15 years and later moved, on promotion to Sergeant, to Coalpit Heath. With him were his wife Lilian and his son John, who later joined the Gloucestershire Force.
>
> The police station was then a 300 year old, double-fronted stone cottage in which one of the front-facing rooms was known as the 'guard room' but was, in fact, the station office. The building had no electricity, gas or main sewer and was one of only six houses in the village with a cold water tap in the kitchen (most households collected their water from the village tap). Behind the house was a long garden, the landscape fell away to reveal a breathtaking view of the Wye Valley at Bigsweir. In fact such was the attraction of the view that when the then Chief Constable paid an occasional visit to the station, he spent most of the time admiring the view and very little time in the station.
>
> The station adjoined the village shop run by a well-known Forest of Dean company, Williams & Cotton, and it became a regular task for us to obtain biscuit tin lids, cut them to a required size and nail them to the floors of the Police Station to cover the holes gnawed by invading rats!! Some off-duty time was also spent in trying to stem the damage caused by woodworm which ravaged not only the building but many pieces of furniture.
>
> Although I was in lodgings at 'The Manse' (no longer there) in the village, life at the police station was not easy for residents. Lighting was by oil lamp or candles, most week-day cooking was done on a Primus stove but on Sundays, the range in the living room was lit and used for cooking and when it had cooled was lovingly cleaned and polished with black lead to an incredible shine. Bath-time involved filling the large 'copper' boiler in the kitchen, lighting the solid fuel fire beneath it and when the water was hot the galvanised tin bath would be brought from its place, hanging on a wall outside, to be placed in front of the range, if lit, and then the hot water ladled from the 'copper' into it.
>
> The village centre had its impressive castle (then, as now, a Youth Hostel), the church, shops and two public houses. It was in relation to policing the latter that I have fond memories which could easily be described as involving the early use of Police Dogs!!!

Left to right: John Day, Lilian Day and PC Edgar Day, Officer-in-charge at St Briavels for many years, with Sally the Alsatian. Courtesy Bob Parker

St Briavels NGR SO 558 045
The pre-1950 station in High Street, next to Williams & Cotton's shop. Photographed on the day it was demolished in 1973.
Courtesy John Dougan

Edgar Day had a very handsome Alsatian bitch called 'Sally', well-known to all the villagers and when Edgar and I patrolled the village at night we would walk around the castle, past the rectory, (where the incumbent, Rev. Harold Heal was always to be seen at his desk in his study and who, without looking up, would call out into the darkness "Goodnight Mr Day, Goodnight Mr Parker") and thence to the 'George' and on to 'The Crown' to 'see the pubs out'. It was rarely necessary for us to enter the pubs because 'Sally' would wander in, whereupon the general conversation emanating from the bars would cease and one could hear voices saying "Hello Sally" and then "Goodnight Fred, Goodnight Charlie, etc . . ."

Tony Cresick, who still lives in the village, was a young pub-goer in those days and appreciated this tactful approach to law enforcement. Bob continued:

"Prior to being posted to St. Briavels from Gloucester, I had never been through the Forest of Dean and the journey was something of an adventure for me. In fact, travelling to my home, in Cheltenham, and back on my first 'rest-day' was even more fascinating. The journey involved a bus from Cheltenham to Gloucester, a short walk from Kings Square to Westgate Street in Gloucester, another bus to Blakeney where I changed to yet another bus to St. Briavels. It was on this first journey that, upon reaching Whitecroft, the bus was boarded by a number of women, each carrying a suitcase. I was intrigued and wondered whether this was a different way of taking home the weeks shopping but I later learned that they were all employed at the Pin Factory and took home quantities of pins and hairgrips to be 'carded up' at home. Similarly fascinating were the incessant conversations carried on by these lady passengers not just with those sitting near them but with those sitting anywhere and, of course, to me they were speaking in some foreign tongue!!! I have to say that I quickly became used to the 'Forest' accent.

My posting to St. Briavels was accompanied by the issue of a police motor cycle, an Ariel 350cc Reg. No. GDF 16 and this, in a way, revolutionised policing what was a very large district, bounded on one side by the county boundary with Monmouthshire, viz: the River Wye. The motor cycle enabled me to arrive at different parts of the area quite quickly and sometimes from the direction of Monmouthshire – quite a surprise for the local lads at Brockweir!!!

Because of my mobility, I was occasionally required to perform duties at either Tutshill or Coleford and I well remember being sent to the site of a pit rescue at 'The Pludds' where as the result of a pit flood a wooden tripod and steel bucket on a hand operated hawser had been erected over a pit air shaft to enable one man to descend in the bucket and bring up the trapped miners (more often known as 'colliers' in the Forest) one at a time. I recall that the first man up was aged 74 years and together with his work-mates had walked approximately five miles underground, often chest high in water, to reach the air shaft. Operating the winch was tough demanding work done by a giant of a man with the well-known 'Forest' name of Teague. Everyone was brought to safety.

On a lighter note, it must be said that 'Forest' humour was memorable. A lad from the village was walking two puppies, owned by a spinster lady when he was met by another villager who looked at the puppies and said, "... 'ere, Godfrey, yunt they two buggers alike" whereupon Godfrey replied "Aye – specially thic 'un on the left".

Policing at that time was very much at 'grass roots' level, where most people admired and respected the local 'bobby' and saw him as someone to whom they could turn in a crisis and also someone who was revered and liked by the children.

At St. Briavels, even the local doctor would attend any road accident and treat the injured long before an ambulance could arrive – all part of the community spirit."

The most recent police station in Coleford Road was built around 1950 but by September 1951 it still could not be occupied because despite a 30-foot well having been sunk there was still no water! Approval had to be given for a storage tank on the roof and piping so that it could receive a water supply from the District Council. In 1964 Dave Willetts was in charge, whilst Bill Tracy occupied the other house and travelled to work at Coleford. One of the resident officers, PC Trevor Crocker, emigrated to Canada and joined the Vancouver Police. During the 1980s one of the houses was sold off while the village Constable occupied the other. PC Leanne Schofield, Gloucestershire's first female Constable to be given charge of a station, lived there in the late 1980s.

In the 1990s the station was closed and the other house sold. PC Keith Bucknell was to be the last resident officer-in-charge.

St Briavels
NGR SO 563 045
The station in Coleford Road built in the 1950s is now private houses.
Photo Ted Heath

Staunton & Corse

A stone-built house first on the left in Malvern Road and now called 'The Cottage' is believed to have been the village's first police station.

**Staunton & Corse
NGR SO 793 295**
'The Cottage' in Malvern Road is thought to have housed Staunton's first police station.
Photo Ted Heath

In 1847, soon after the formation of the Gloucestershire Constabulary, the National Land Company, part of the Chartist movement, purchased 268 acres of land in Staunton and Corse for the settlement of ex-industrial workers. It was a bold social and political experiment which ultimately failed but not before some 85 single storey cottages had been built, each with 3 to 4 acres of land. There was also a schoolhouse, with communal rooms and offices, designed like a larger version of the cottages. By 1870 the school had become a public house, 'The Prince of Wales', which is still there today. Visitors to the village can see many of the Chartist cottages on either side of the main A417 at Snigg's End, and also in Moat Lane and at Lowbands.

'Old Police House' at Staunton Cross overlooks the junction of the A417 Ledbury Road and the minor roads to Malvern and Eldersfield. It was the village's second police station and was strategically placed near 'The Swan' public house. Tony Fardon, whose son runs the local garage, remembered his childhood in that house when his father 'Joe' Fardon was the village policeman in the 1950s. PC Harold Eley was a later incumbent.

The most recent police station, which consists of two houses adjoining an office, stands in Prince Crescent. The officer in charge for many years was popular PC Bob Lloyd. When he left to become a Crime Prevention Officer the station was closed.

Staunton did not become part of the Forest of Dean Sub-Division until 1982.

Staunton & Corse   NGR SO 792 294
'Old Police House', Staunton Cross. Photo Ted Heath

Above: *Postcard view of Staunton Cross c1910. The police station (now 'Old Police House') just features on the extreme right, by the signpost.*
Courtesy The Archive Shop

Staunton
NGR SO 786 290
The most recent police station in Prince Crescent. Photo Ted Heath

Tutshill/Tidenham (see also Woodcroft)

The census of 1841 shows P.C. Maden, P.C. Thomas Beard and P.C. Paul Townsend in Tutshill but the exact location of the station is unclear. In 1844 there was a station called 'The Chase' mentioned in the Police Almanac. Its location is also unknown. By 1851 there was a station at Woodcroft which continued to cover the parish until the early 20th century.

The station which stands on the Junction of Beachley Road and the old Gloucester Road was commissioned in 1903 and for most of the time since that date it has been staffed by a Sergeant and a small number of Constables, who covered an area from the Beachley peninsula to Tidenham Chase, and eastwards to Stroat, including the villages and hamlets of Sedbury, Tutshill, Woodcroft and Tidenham. The guardroom at the station was designated as an occasional courtroom. In the 19th and early 20th century many local people made their living from fishing in the Severn Estuary or

Crossways, Tutshill, with Gloucester Road ahead. The Cross Keys, the first pub in England for Welshmen when it used to be 'dry Sundays', is on the left. The police station is on the right, behind the brick wall. This c1905 postcard is by well-known Chepstow photographer William Call. Courtesy The Archive Shop

working on the Severn trows (sailing barges). A car ferry operated between Beachley and Aust from the early 1930s, until the first Severn road bridge opened in 1966.

During the First World War, a shipyard opened on the Chepstow side of the River Wye and a camp of wooden huts was constructed on the Beachley Peninsula to house the workers (one of the original huts can be seen on the side of Beachley Road just past Loop Road). In the 1920s this camp was taken over by the Army Apprentices College. The college closed in the 1990s and the site became an Infantry barracks. The present police station is only a mile from the centre of Chepstow and stands opposite the first pub in England. This was of particular significance in the days when all pubs were closed on Sundays in Wales!

Jim Ludlow replaced Andy Weir at Tutshill in 1941, where he joined Len Merriman. PS Frank Morris greeted Jim by saying *"Do you drink?"* to which Jim replied *"A little, Sergeant"*. *"Well you'll have to drink more than a little if you're stopping here,"* was the reply. Frank Morris was a tough man who had played rugby for Lydney and had been a regular member of the respected Forest Police Tug of War team. Both Jim and Len had 'digs' in the Sergeant's house, which was attached to the station. They were issued with a bucket for those night-time calls of nature.

Split shifts were common then and evenings often consisted of a pint or two in the Cross Keys, a meal in the 'digs', then back to work to see the pubs out. Jim was courting in Cheltenham and in those days bus travel on John Watts' Red & White service was free to police officers on production of a warrant card. Jim married Marj. while waiting for call up to flying duties in 1942. In May of that year Jim went into the RAF and underwent flying training in Rhodesia, before converting to heavy aircraft. He skippered a Lancaster on a full tour of thirty raids over Germany and occupied Europe, leaving the RAF with the rank of Flight Lieutenant and returning to police duties.

Another pre- First World War postcard view of Gloucester Road, Tutshill, showing the police station more clearly on the right. Completed in 1903, it is solidly built of red brick, with a stone plaque on the front announcing 'Gloucestershire Constabulary'. Courtesy The Archive Shop

When Ron Davis was posted to Tutshill in the early Summer of 1948 the complement was a Sergeant and three Constables. He wrote as follows:

> "The Sergeant and his family lived in the station and there was an office and two cells. I was not then married and, together with another single man, I shared a bedroom in the Sergeant's quarters. It was a small room at the top of the stairs, and on my arrival, I opened the door from the office to the Sergeant's hallway, only to be greeted by the Sergeant's wife calling out from somewhere out of sight that I was to take my boots off before coming through the door and up the stairs. This is what we had to do every time we went through that door!
>
> We could not share the Sergeant's bathroom, of course, so we had to wash and shave in the cells. We collected water in a bucket from a pump in the garden and heated it up on a gas ring in a cell.
>
> We had our meals at an old lady's house down the Beachley Road. She cooked for us and we shared her table. In some stations in those days single men provided their own meat and groceries, which were then cooked by the wife of the officer in charge, and whilst at Tutshill I discovered, amongst some old papers, a General Order issued by the Chief Constable a year or two before, the gist of which was as follows: when meat is handed over by single men for the wife of the officer in charge to cook on their behalf, all fat resulting from the cooking must be handed back to the single men".

Born in Somerset Road, Cinderford, Dennis Freeman joined the Gloucestershire Constabulary in July 1946 on demob. from the RAF Regiment. From 1956 to 1961 he was at Tutshill where he had a succession of Sergeants – Fred Glover, Bill Webb and Ron Robinson. He lived in one of a pair of police houses in Sedbury Lane near the railway halt and describes the two biggest sources of police work at Tutshill at that time as the absconders from Sedbury Park Approved School and the many road accidents on the A48 in the days before the first Severn road bridge.

There were other memorable incidents too. One day the skeleton of a man was found at Lancaut. Papers in his clothing suggested he had been a patient at St. Lawrence Hospital in Chepstow. He was subsequently identified by dental records although he had been dead for two years. On the night of the Severn Bridge Disaster in 1960, a patrol car crew called at Dennis Freeman's house in the middle of the night to tell him of the incident and call him out. He was directed to go to the pier at Beachley and watch for bodies or survivors but it was a very foggy night.

Dennis also recalled a successful operation with an amusing ending:

"Wooden wedges that went into the clamps that held railway lines to the sleeper were being stolen. I went out to Tidenham Halt by TS Thomas' Dayhouse quarry with a British Rail policeman to keep observation. We had noticed a motorcycle lying in the hedge. Knowing the explosive store was a hazard I asked the other chap to go round the back of the quarry, which was on higher ground where he could look down into the quarry. I went to the entrance, could hear a banging and could see a chap banging a shovel against a shed. I went to him and at the same time a second chap appeared carrying a can which contained petrol. I called to the BR officer and we then had to walk back to the road with two prisoners to get to Tutshill. I had taken possession of the can and as I walked along could feel my trousers getting wet. There was a small hole in the can and we were losing our evidence! Result I walked back until we got a lift holding the can with one finger over the hole".

Above: *Cinderford born Dennis R. Freeman, photographed when he was stationed at Tutshill.*

Tutshill
NGR ST 539 946
The station is still in use today and shows few changes from when it was first built; even the railings have survived. Photo Ted Heath

When the first Severn Motorway crossing was opened in 1966 it was agreed that, although one end of the bridge was in Monmouthshire, it would be policed for its entire length by Gloucestershire Police from their new Motorway Station at Almondsbury. Boundary changes in 1974 put Almondsbury and the bridge under the control of the newly formed Avon & Somerset Constabulary, even though several piers stand on Beachley peninsula which is in the Forest of Dean.

Until recently the only bridge across the Wye at Chepstow was the old Castleford Bridge, which is narrow and so hump-backed that drivers cannot see the opposite end. Traffic lights were installed but when they failed it was necessary to control the busy A48 traffic using police officers from Tutshill and Chepstow on their respective sides. With no compatible radio communication, they used a beautifully spliced rope-end which was handed to the last driver to be allowed across from one side with instructions that it be given to the police officer on the other bank, in order to let him know that he could release traffic from his side.

In 1989 the Sergeant's post at Tutshill was transferred to the Prosecutions Dept at Gloucester. The last Sergeant at Tutshill was Terry Davies.

Westbury-on-Severn

Purpose-built in 1898, the police station on the main street is virtually a mirror image of the one at Dymock. Its high garden wall might have something to do with its location on the main road, about half way between Lydney and Gloucester. Prisoners committed to Gloucester Gaol would once have been escorted on foot by a police officer and a secure exercise yard would have been a humane provision at an overnight stop.

During World War One many Gloucestershire police officers joined or rejoined the colours. Among them was the Chief Constable, Lt. Col. Richard Chester-Master. He was mentioned in despatches and awarded the DSO and Bar. During his absence the Force was run by the Deputy Chief Constable and the Chairman of the Standing

A view of the main road through Westbury, looking towards the Forest, c1910. The police station is the building with the two tall chimneys in the centre distance. Courtesy The Archive Shop

Joint Committee, Mr M.W. Colchester-Wemyss of Westbury Court, as Acting Chief Constable. On 30 August 1917 Col. Chester-Master was killed in action.

During World War Two another member of the Colchester-Wemyss family played an important part in the life of the Force. Lt. Col. J.M. Colchester-Wemyss OBE, JP, served as Special Superintendent for the Forest of Dean and was responsible for the greatly enlarged Forest of Dean Special Constabulary.

Officers-in-charge at Westbury over the years included PC Bill Chandler, there in 1937, and later incumbents such as Ferdy Moss and John Gardner, who was followed by 'Taff' Williams. Both the latter had large families. PC Gardner was badly injured when struck by a car whilst dealing with an accident at the bottom of Wintles Hill.

Westbury
NGR SO 715 144
Another handsome, purpose-built Victorian police station, situated on the main road through the village.
Photo Ted Heath

Woodcroft

A cottage on the main road near the Rising Sun Inn was an early police station. The garden wall of this cottage contains a stone inscribed 'Old Station House 1852'. According to the census, this station was occupied in 1851 by PS George Cooke and his family, plus PCs James Shipton and Joseph Sealbright. It must have been rather cramped! The same station was occupied in 1891 by P.C. William Thomas and it almost certainly continued to serve the Parish of Tidenham until 1903, when a new police station was built at Tutshill crossroads.

Woodcroft
NGR ST 543 957
The garden wall of this cottage contains a stone inscribed 'Old Station House 1852'.
Both photos Ted Heath

Woolaston NGR SO 596 000
PC Beddis outside the station on the main road at Woolaston, sometime in the 1930s.
Courtesy Gloucestershire Record Office.GRO Ref. Q/Y 6/3/14

Woolaston

The house and office on the A48 at Woolaston was taken into use in about 1885, when the first resident officer, PC 232 Eagles, was transferred from Littledean. The building is believed to have been a blacksmith's shop prior to being a police station and it has a rather unusual dry cellar. As well as serving the communities of Alvington, the Woolastons and Netherend, the station was a vital link in the chain of main road stations up until the 1970s. In the early 1930s PC Beddis was in charge, whilst in 1937 it was PC Harold Bayliss, who was later to be Chief Inspector at Lydney. PC Bayliss allegedly held the County record for the most arrests for bicycle theft. This was a common offence in those days and it is said that he could tell from a mile off if the rider didn't belong with the bike. It is even said that he and his wife would watch the A48 while off duty on the lookout for stolen bikes! Mr Bayliss was succeeded by Les Perry, who was in turn succeeded in 1950 by Jim Ludlow.

In Jim's time charabancs galore would come across from 'dry' Wales on Sunday nights to visit pubs. One night a coach stopped right outside the police station in Woolaston for the occupants to get out and urinate against the wall. This made Jim rather angry and he ordered the driver to move. The driver said he wouldn't go without the passengers so Jim told him to get them aboard quickly and

The 'Old Police Station', as it is today. Photo Ted Heath

PC Beddis with his dog outside Higgs general stores in the village on a postcard view of the 1930s. This was still the era of stiff collars and gaiters.   Courtesy The Archive Shop

to make his point Jim picked on a young man who was sauntering along with his hands in his pockets and booted him up the backside. The man's hands shot out of his pockets and with them went a load of coins. Jim didn't give him chance to retrieve his cash and the bus drove off. On the next morning a young lad who lived a few doors away was on his way to school when he struck it rich!

While at Woolaston Jim was a member of the very successful Forest Police Tug-of-War team, which went all over the country and were County champions several years running. Despite the children's illnesses, Marj. Ludlow says her eight years at Woolaston were the happiest of her life. She did, however, have a brush with authority. In those days the wife was expected to be at the station if the husband was out. Frank Jayne, who, as Sergeant at Whitminster, had taken charge at the first Severn Bridge Disaster in 1939, was now the Coleford Inspector and was responsible for Woolaston. He visited Woolaston station one day and innocently left a note

The Forest Police Tug of War Team, 1950. Jim Ludlow is the fifth from right.   Courtesy Jim Ludlow

that he had found it unmanned. When poor Supt. Bert Hills visited later in the week he got the backlash, as Mrs Ludlow firmly pointed out that her children were not going to be expected to cross the A48 to and from school unescorted, whether that meant leaving the station unattended or not!

When Jim left in 1958, he was asked by his successor to leave a list of reliable informants. Jim left him the entire electoral roll!

Later came PC Bill Scudamore, then PC Jim Taylor, who was there in the 1960s and who retired from the force as Inspector at Tewkesbury. Jim's father, Fred Taylor, had been a Sergeant at Coleford during the Second World War. Like his father, Jim enjoyed rugby and fitted in well with the community. At first he played for the Watts works side and was recruited by Bream where he played with local character, 'German' Green. He also played for Whitecroft RFC where 'Demon' Davies nicknamed him 'Blakeney Red' after the local perry pear. The high point was representing Lydney in the Forest Combination Cup, a competition with a reputation for particularly robust play.

The last resident officer in charge at Woolaston was another Rugby player, genial Welshman Glyn Radcliffe, who sadly died from cancer while serving as a Sergeant.

Jim Taylor, standing, photographed at Gloucester shortly after being promoted from Woolaston. Also pictured, in the panda car, is Brian Farmer.
Courtesy Jim Taylor

PC Neil Thomas, Community Officer for Woolaston and Aylburton, seen at the latter village with a Special Constable in 1986. Courtesy Neil Thomas

Yorkley

The house called 'The Oakes', on Bailey Hill, opposite the Institute, was a police station until the 1960s. Fitzroy 'Fred' Taylor was in charge there, prior to being promoted in 1933 to Sergeant at Coleford. Fred Taylor had been a Royal Marine gunner during the First World War on board *HMS Marlborough*, a Dreadnought class battleship. In 1919 he took part in a mission to the Black Sea to rescue members of the Romanov family, during the Russian Civil War which followed the Bolshevik Revolution. Fred was a keen and respected rugby player and a regular member of the Lydney RFC sides of that period. In 1928 he represented Great Britain Police at rugby and was the only Englishman in the side, the rest being Welsh!

Yorkley
NGR SO 639 070
'The Oakes', opposite the Institute, was the police station until the 1960s.
Photo Ted Heath

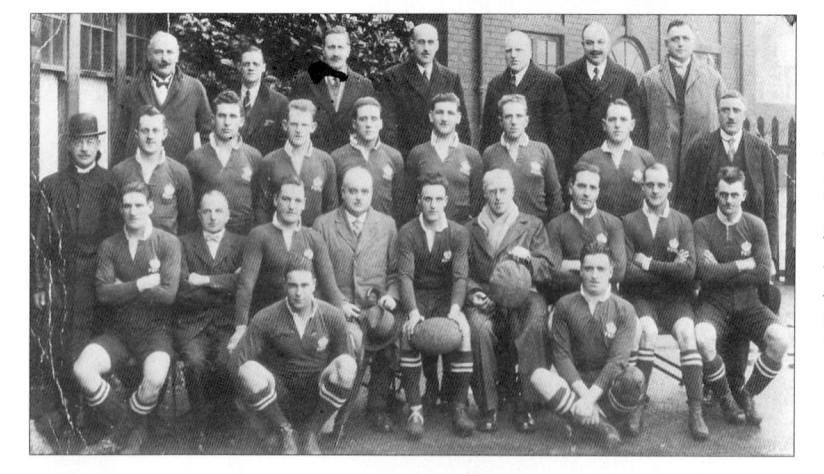

The Great Britain Police XV that beat the Army 13-9 in 1928. PC Fred Taylor (3rd from right seated) was the only Englishman in the side. All the rest were Welsh!
Courtesy of the Taylor Family Collection

Tony Fardon remembered his childhood at Yorkley, when his father Wilf 'Joe' Fardon was in charge during World War Two with PC Frank Emerson. Tony recalled that the sound of German aircraft going overhead led to an alert for enemy parachutists and understandably Special Constables from the community would report for duty with their own firearms. Later, the officer in charge was PC Albert Henry Bleaken who, together with Soldier/Poet F.W. Harvey, helped to resurrect the Yorkley branch of the Royal British Legion. PC Bleaken retired from the police service in 1949, Yorkley being his last posting.

In 1955 PCs Edgar Bowring and the late Alan Drew were involved in an incident which made the pages of *The Lydney Observer*. It concerned the rescue of a dog which had fallen down a disused pit shaft. Miss Jennifer Jones had been walking past the old shaft when she heard sounds and telephoned Yorkley police. Both officers attended and en route they recruited two Cinderford Town footballers who had been out for a walk. They were Terry Truman, Cinderford and County centre forward, and Ted Winters, the Cinderford centre half. They also called on the RSPCA Inspector W.J. Adams. Being the lightest, Terry Truman volunteered to go down the shaft on a rope. He tucked the dog under his arm and the others pulled him up. After a tricky ascent Terry and dog reached the surface. The dog was cleaned up at Yorkley police station but its owner remained unknown so Miss Jones adopted it and called it 'Terry'.

Whenever an ex-collier or quarryman died, the matter was reported to the police and to HM Coroner and a Post Mortem carried out. Compensation was payable under the Industrial Diseases legislation if Silicosis or Pneumoconiosis could be shown to be a contributory factor. The police officer in the case was required to attend the P.M. and take custody of the lungs, heart etc. and deliver them to the surgeon appointed by the Ministry at Bristol Hospital. This task involved catching a train from Lydney Town railway station at 9am, crossing the Severn Bridge, changing at Berkeley Road for Temple Meads, then walking some distance through the centre of Bristol carrying the heavy container. After examination, the container, its contents and any paperwork had to be collected for the return journey, arriving at Lydney at about 5pm. It was a grim and solemn job but it was a day out. Edgar remembered that he and Alan Drew took it in turns to deal with such cases from start to finish, i.e. from the first report through to the inquest.

While at Yorkley, Edgar Bowring discovered an amazing coincidence. In the early 1920s, Albert Hills of Biggleswade joined the Gloucestershire Constabulary and in the 1950s was Superintendent at Lydney. Also in the 1920s, Richard Morgan of Yorkley Wood joined the Bedfordshire Force and became Superintendent at Biggleswade. Edgar recalled the following ironic incident:

"I had occasion to contact Supt. Morgan when he was on leave at Yorkley Wood and while I was in conversation with him one of the local residents of long standing came by and greeted us with 'Good morning Mr Bowring, good morning Richard'..."

Far left: *Never off duty. Bert Kingscott digging his spuds at Yorkley, in uniform*
Courtesy Joan Kingscott

Left: *PC Bert Kingscott, Officer-in-charge, Yorkley 1959.*
Courtesy Joan Kingscott

Yorkley
NGR SO 640 071
This station in Slade Road was built in the 1960s.   Photo Ted Heath

In 1959 PC Bert Kingscott was in charge for a short time before being promoted to Sergeant and transferred to Coleford. While at Yorkley, he and his wife, Joan, started a youth club to try to keep the local teenagers out of trouble. The couple continued to be involved with the club long after moving and, together with the late Joe Norris, held fundraising events and even got three members of the Coronation Street cast to open a fete.

The modern police station in Slade Road opened in 1967 and was built by the same builder and to the same design as its near neighbour in Fancy Road, Parkend. Within a few years of being opened it was closed and sold. Many will remember Dave Tredgett who was there in the 1960s. The last resident Officer-in-charge was Andy Barrow, who moved to Bream when the station closed in 1975. The former station is now a private house called 'Winhro'.

Following the closure of the station, Yorkley and Parkend became part of a much larger beat under the officer at Bream.

The Future of Forest Policing?

Technology continues to offer new opportunities to do things better. The Internet poses threats of cyber-crime but it also presents opportunities, as yet difficult to imagine, for access to and dissemination of information. The Government's Public Safety Radio Communications Project (PSRCP) will provide police forces with state of the art, secure digital radio. Among its many advantages, it will allow person-to-person communication and will also facilitate communications with other emergency services. Gloucestershire will be one of the first Constabularies to benefit from the roll-out of this new radio system, which also offers the possibility of a combined emergency services control room which would be in line with the Government's requirement that Local Authorities provide 'Best Value' services. The Best Value doctrine might also result in more examples of shared premises, such as is being proposed for Lydney Police and Fire Service.

Devolution of power to Scotland and Wales and the regionalisation of England could mean a reduction in the number of separate police forces within the next few years and the real possibility that Gloucestershire could become part of a South West Regional Police Force. If that were to be the case, the Forest would be right on the edge, having a common boundary with two other regions.

Finally, widespread public concern in the year 2000 about the perceived under-resourcing of rural policing (in stark contrast to the petitions of the 1840s against any rural policing) could give rise to a number of interesting new initiatives in the near future.

Appendix A
THE SECOND WORLD WAR 1939-45
REGULARS and SPECIALS in the FOREST of DEAN
COMMANDERS

ALBERT HARRY CARTER
Superintendent 'F' Division 1937-41
Born 12 Aug 1895. Served Gloucestershire Regiment 1914-19. Joined Force 5 Jan 1920. Promoted Sergeant 13 April 1927. Promoted Inspector 'F' Divison, 19 Sept 1934. Promoted Superintendent 21 Dec 1937, Lydney. Transferred Staple Hill 7 Jan 1941. Transferred to HQ as Asst. Chief Constable 1 Jan 1946.

CHARLES FREDERICK LARGE
Superintendent 'F' Division 1941-46
Born 15 Oct 1892. Joined Force 1 July 1912. Served Machine Gun Corps 1918-19. Promoted Sergeant Clerk 22 Oct 1921, Gloucester. Promoted Inspector 1 Sept 1932, Coleford. Transferred Tewkesbury 6 Feb 1936. Promoted Superintendent 8 Jan 1941, Lydney.

LT. COL. J.M. COLCHESTER-WEMYSS, OBE, JP,
Ex-Special Superintendent, 'F' Division.
Scottish Rifles 1899. Served South African War, including at Ladysmith, Spion Kop and Tugela Heights. Wounded, awarded Queen's Medal. West African Frontier Force 1906-8. Staff Captain 1914-18, served Tanganyika. Awarded OBE for military service. Resigned as Special Superintendent for other important duties, 1943.

THE FOREST SECTIONS

Note: Not all of the Sections were photographed and, of those that were, not all of them included everyone who had served (for various reasons) or the names of those in the picture. Most of the details included here have been taken from *The War Record of the Gloucestershire Special Constabulary* but some of the names have been filled in from local knowledge and memories. It is entirely possible that errors exist, either perpetuated from the original book or due to faulty memories over the passage of time, but, hopefully, these are at a minimum. Finally, where they exist, photographs for all of the stations covered in this book are included, although some were not in the Forest Division at that time.

Abbreviations: SC – Special Constable; HSC – Higher Special Constable; SS – Special Sergeant; SI – Special Inspector; PWR – Police War Reserve

ASHLEWORTH SECTION
Back row: SCs Jelf, Franklin, Finch, Bartlett, Hiam, Price, Blace, Marmon, Corn, Hale, Cole.
Front row: SC Chamberlain, HSCs Driver, Ballard, SS L.N. Gay, SI Gillespy, PC Davies, HSC Watts, SCs Powell, Woodward.

BLAKENEY SECTION
Back row: SCs Miles, Penn, Lane, Turner, Porter, Saint, Turley.
Front row: SCs R. Biddington, Hammond, Screen, SS Wayman, PC Large, SCs Gosling, H. Biddington, Bleaken.

**BREAM
SUB-SECTION**
Back row:
SCs F. Morse, W. Ellway,
J. Windsor, H. Haddock, A. Parr,
J. Reader, W. Robinson.
Middle row:
SCs W. Lewis, G. Cooper,
G. Meek, B. Lewis, A. Edmunds,
W. Hill, J. Hancocks.
Front row:
SCs H. Horsley, A. Thomas,
HS W. Burdess, PC Weekes,
PC Brown, SCs C. James,
E. Edmunds.

**CINDERFORD
SECTION**
No names given.
Courtesy Ian Pope

**CORSE
SUB-SECTION**
No names given.

COLEFORD SUB-SECTION
Back row: SCs Smart, Jeffries, S.L.H. Smith, Joseph, Holbrook, E.W. Smith, Brain, Baldwin.
Third row: SCs Hart, Collett, J.E. Williams, Phipps, Morgan, Higgs, Miller, Pritchard, R.L. Jones, Gwilliam, Baldwin. **Second row:** SCs Saunders, Barnett, Hooper, Baynham, Burbrough, Bucknell, F.W. Jones, James, H.H. Smith, Trotter, W.F. Williams, Dangerfield. **Front row:** SCs Green, Powell, Homer, HS Ashworth, SI Machen, SSupt. Colchester-Wemyss, SS Pudsey, HS Horton, SCs Dovey, Hoare.

DRYBROOK SECTION
Back row:
SCs P.G. Terrett, G. Cinderey, E.C. Morman, F. Shirley, H. Blears, G. Roberts, M.T. Roberts, B. Greening
Front row:
SC R.T. Collier, HC T.D. Morman, PC W.T. Rogers, SCs P.W. Annetts, H. Hunt.

DYMOCK SUB-SECTION
Back row:
HSs W. Gibson, L. Smith, SCs W. Williams, R. Hyett, G. Hyett.
Middle row:
HSC. Carless, SCs E. Gibson, J. Maile, F. Preece, T. Sayer, J. Burlow.
Seated:
HS A. Bayliss, SI A.W. Mann, SS R. Chew, PC H. Widdows, SS C. Hobbs, PWR R. Hegarty, SC J. Barnfield.

**HUNTLEY
SUB-SECTION**
No names given

**HUNTLEY
MOBILE SECTION**
No names given

**LONGHOPE
SUB-SECTION**
Back row:
SCs W. Bowkett, F. Hill,
D. Warren, S.G. Constance,
R.V. Little, E. Bullock.
Front row:
SCs J.E. Morris,
J.R. Adams,
HS A.H. Jones,
PC L.S. James,
SCs A.W. Lord,
H.P.M. Williams,
E.J. Poole.

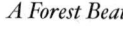

LYDNEY SECTION
Back row: SCs Windsor, Davis, Goddard, R. Hadley, H. Hadley, Imm, Martyn, Bayliss, Garland.
Middle row: SCs Ball, Gibson, Hancock, Waters, Bailey, Wright, Seaborne, Miell, Born.
Front row: SCs Dunn, Williams, Nelmes, SS Wild, Supt. C.F. Large, PS Clarke, SCs Morris, Thorn.

MINSTERWORTH SUB-SECTION
No names given

MITCHELDEAN SUB-SECTION
Standing:
SCs J. Betteridge, C. Jackson, R. Hale, H. Baldwin, S. Newman, H. Clarke, E. Smith.
Seated:
SCs A. Vincent, H. Little, HSC W. Bullock, PC Tom Buckland, SCs V. Ellis, F. Cottrell.
Courtesy Les Tuffley

NEWENT SECTION
No names given

NEWNHAM SECTION
Back row:
SCs Ferris, Rymer, James, Hooper, Cox, Hodgson, Grimmett, Lloyd.
Front row:
SCs Lowes, Harrison, PC James, HSC Blanton, SC Atkins, PWR Rawlins
   Courtesy Mrs A. Gould

PARKEND SECTION
Back row: *SCs E. James, Dawe, Cawley, Hook, Edmunds, Sheward, Turley.* **Middle row:** *SCs Brown, Morgan, S. James, Bethell, Davis, H. Turley, Goldsworthy, Jessop.* **Front row:** *SC Turley, HSC Rossiter, SS Pudsey, SI Machen, Supt. C.F. Large, Insp. Dowsell, PS Paget, PC Carter, SC Thomas.*

RUARDEAN SECTION
Back row:
SCs E.J. Knight,
H.J. Marfell, R. Vaughan.
Front row:
SC A.L. Dunkley,
HSC S.A. Scott,
PC Boughton,
SC W.G. Beard.

RUSPIDGE SECTION
Back row:
SCs W. Shermer,
C. Warren, O. Edwards,
T. Middlecote,
F. Pritchard, W. Bowdler.
Front row:
HSC W. Walkley,
PC A.W. Taylor,
SI R. James, SS W. Ellis,
SC D. Godwin.

ST BRIAVELS SECTION
Back row:
SCs Scrivens, Lewis,
Davies, James, Davis.
Middle row:
SCs Voyce, Keedwell,
Price, Burley,
Whittington.
Front row:
HSC Morgan, PC Day,
Insp. Dowsell,
SC Rivers,
PWR Henderson.

TUTSHILL SECTION
Back row: SCs Williams, Tandy, Reeks, King, Foster, Riley, Flowers. **Second row:** SCs Randle, Simmonds, Orgee, Grier, Clark, Corne, Lewis. **Seated:** PWR King, PS Morris, SSgt. Shirley, HS Ball, PWR Verrier. **In front:** SCs Wood, Manson, Blandford, Beddoe, Jones.

WESTBURY-ON-SEVERN SECTION
Back row:
SCs Leaper, F.J. Wyman, Smart, Heaven, S. Jennings, Gleed, Price.
Front row:
SCs Littleton, J. Jennings, Selwyn, PC Cook, HSC Boughton, SCs L. Wyman, Middlecote.

WOOLASTON SECTION
Back row:
SCs Beal, McLaren, Bucknell.
Front row:
HSC Bollen, PC Bayliss, SC Williams

YORKLEY SECTION
Back row: SCs Roy Gunter, Foster Robbins, Frank Brown, Bert Beddis,
Third row: SCs Sid Jones, Harry Craddock, Jack Morse, Rowley Beddis, Bert Jones
Second row: SCs Albert Wilce, Frank Fletcher, Charlie Gunter, Ossie Ames, Tom Price
Front row: PC Frank Emerson, SC Eddie Lewis, SC Harry Jones, PC Wilf 'Joe' Fardon, SC Sid Lewis.
Picture taken c1942. Courtesy Tony Fardon

MEMBERS OF THE FOREST OF DEAN COMMUNITY
WHO SERVED IN 'F' DIVISION SPECIAL CONSTABULARY
1939 to 1945

Source: The War Record of the Gloucestershire Special Constabulary
Copy courtesy Mrs P. Hutchings and by kind permission of The Chief Constable

Adams G.G.	Beddis R.J.	Bucknell J.	Cooper D.W.	Dymond W.R.
Adams J.R.	Beddis T.R.	Bucknell R.J.	Cooper G.	
Adams J.T.	Beddis W.A.	Bullock E.F.	Cooper I.	Eagle A.S.
Adams S.H.	Beddoe H.I.	Bullock F.	Corne J.E.	Edmunds A.
Addis W.J.	Bell R.A.	Bullock F.T.	Cotterell F.	Edmunds A.E.
Alden J.	Berrow B.J.	Bullock W.	Cox J.H.	Edmunds E.
Allan S.R.	Berthon H.P.	Burbrough W.	Craddock G.H.	Edmunds P.J.
Allford W.H.	Bethell W.T.	Burdess W.J.	Craze L.	Edwards J.
Ames O.A.	Betteridge J.	Burke J.	Cresswell E.F.	Edwards L.E.
Annetts P.W.	Biddington H.	Burley H.	Cullis W.T.	Edwards O.H.
Ansell C.A.	Biddington R.	Burridge A.A.		Ellis T.L.
Arkell B.	Bishop A.E.	Burris C.	Dalley C.A.	Ellis V.A.
Arkell J.	Blanch F.R.	Butcher F.W.	Dance W.H.	Ellis W.
Ashley-Towell F.	Blandford J.		Dangerfield H.	Ellway A.H.
Ashworth S.	Blanton R.W.	Cadogan I.C.	Darters L.R.	Ellway W.H.
Atkins R.S.	Bleaken F.W.	Cadogan T.W.	Davey T.	Endy H.H.
	Blears H.	Cadogan W.V.	Davies H.S.	Evans E.R.
Babb H.G.	Blower F.	Cannock H.	Davies P.G.	Evans J.T.
Baber F.	Body I.S.	Carter A.	Davies W.H.	Evans S.S.
Bailey C.	Bollen V.A.	Carter A.	Davis A.H.	
Baker E.R.	Born C.J.	Carter R.E.	Davis E.A.	Fairweather W.
Baker S.	Boughton C.J.	Carter W.L.	Davis F.H.	Farmer R.M.
Baldwin A.W.	Boughton H.	Cawley S.C.	Davis F.J.	Farr A.E.
Baldwin H.H.	Bowdler W.T.	Chadd F.H.	Davis J.E.	Fear R.F.
Baldwin L.	Bowen A.G.	Charles W.H.	Davis S.	Fellowes G.
Baldwin P.E.	Bowen F.V.	Chilton P.	Davis T.H.	Ferris A.H.
Baldwin R.A.	Bowen J.	Chivers A.G.	Davis W.H.	Fewings N.
Baldwin R.G.	Bowkett J.S.	Cinderby W.J.	Dawe W.H.	Field W.J.
Ball E.C.	Bowkett P.	Cinderey W.F.	Day W.G.	Fisher A.J.
Barnard C.	Bowkett W.C.	Clark L.	Deakin T.C.	Fletcher F.
Barnes D.E.	Boyes W.	Clarke W.H.	Deans G.K.	Fletcher H.R.
Barnett A.V.	Bradley J.E.	Colchester-	Donnal F.J.	Flewelling E.
Barrett W.H.	Bragington G.	Wemyss J.M.	Dorrington R.	Flewelling G.H.
Bartlett G.	Brain C.J.	Coldrick T.E.	Dovey M.J.	Flowers W.R.
Bass G.W.	Brain J.	Cole W.A.	Downing B.	Foster L.C.
Bate J.S.	Brain J.J.	Collett C.E.	Drennen A.L.	Franklin W.H.
Bayliss R.G.	Brain M.	Collier J.H.	Drew P.J.	French A.T.
Bayliss S.H.	Brain T.J.	Collier R.T.	Drew P.V.	
Baynham A.L.	Brinkworth W.	Constable H.R.	Driscol D.	Gabbett D.H.
Beal F.C.	Briscoe T.W.	Constance S.G.	Dufty J.	Gale F.O.
Beard W.G.	Brown F.W.	Cook H.	Dunkley A.L.	Games G.D.
Beattie A.A.	Brown L.V.	Cooke E.	Dunn C.H.	Gardham G.
Beddis A.B.	Brown W.T.	Coombs F.	Dykins P.	Garland T.F.
Beddis H.	Buckle A.H.	Cooper A.	Dymond S.G.	Gibb J.H.

Gibson A.J.	Hatton S.W.	James F.	Kirkby R.	Meredith S.C.
Gibson W.B.	Hawkins F.L.	James G.H.	Knight C.A.	Merrett D.H.
Giles F.	Head A.A.	James H.C.	Knight E.J.	Middlecote T.
Giles H.V.	Heaven C.J.	James H.H.	Knight P.H.	Miell J.W.
Gleed E.W.	Hellier J.I.	James J.	Kyte C.E.	Miles A.A.
Goddard R.V.	Henderson A.	James R.O.		Miles C.
Godwin D.	Hewlett E.A.	James S.J.	Lane A.G.	Miles H.
Goffey A.	Hewlett W.E.	James S.M.	Lane C.	Miles S.
Goldsworthy F.	Heyes B.V.	James W.I.	Lang G.F.	Miller A.W.
Goode E.G.	Hicks J.C.	James W.T.	Large H.	Milton W.
Goode G.A.	Higgs C.J.	James W.T.	Lark M.V.	Moore A.
Goode G.R.	Higgins H.I.	Jaynes F.J.	Larner F.T.	Morgan E.C.
Goode L.A.	Hill E.W.	Jefferies E.	Lauder T.J.	Morgan F.H.
Gosling W.H.	Hill F.A.	Jeffs R.	Leaper R.B.	Morgan F.J.
Goulder R.L.	Hill T.	Jennings A.J.	Legg J.H.	Morgan G.C.
Grail E.	Hinton T.	Jennings S.	Leighton F.G.	Morgan L.
Green W.W.	Hirst F.	Jessop T.E.	Lenagan J.	Morgan R.
Greening B.J.	Hirst N.	Johnson E.	Leverick W.	Morgan R.A.
Greenway T.E.	Hoare W.A.	Jones A.E.	Lewis A.W.	Morgan T.H.
Grier J.T.	Hodges A.	Jones A.H.	Lewis B.G.	Morgan V.J.
Griffin A.D.	Hodges R.A.	Jones A.J.	Lewis E.	Morgan W.G.
Griffiths G.I.	Hodgson A.	Jones C.	Lewis G.	Morman E.C.
Grimmett A.	Holbrook S.V.	Jones E.B.	Lewis S.T.	Morman T.D.
Grindle P.	Holder K.	Jones F.W.	Lewis W.G.	Morris E.P.
Grindon B.N.	Homer O.D.	Jones G.H.	Lewis W.H.	Morris G.L.
Guest E.E.	Hook W.A.	Jones H.	Lewis W.W.	Morris J.E.
Guest R.	Hooper C.H.	Jones H.S.	Little H.C.	Morris S.G.
Gunter C.A.	Hooper G.	Jones J.	Little R.V.	Morris S.H.
Gunter H.R.	Hopes F.G.	Jones J.L.	Littleton J.	Morse F.
Gwilliam T.S.	Horsley H.	Jones R.	Lloyd C.E.	Morse F.
	Horton S.	Jones R.L.	Lloyd G.E.	Morse H.R.
Haddock H.S.	Howell H.R.	Jones R.N.	Lloyd L.	Morse W.J.
Hadley H.W.	Howell O.	Jones R.W.	Lord A.W.	
Hadley R.A.	Howell W.H.	Jones S.D.	Lowes J.H.	Nash F.
Haile L.L.	Hubbard J.	Jones T.E.	Lucas F.J.	Nash H.J.
Hale H.	Hughes C.J.	Jordan A.C.	Lythaby W.A.	Neale J.
Hale R.R.	Hughes G.F.	Joseph T.A.		Nelmes A.
Hammond G.F.	Hullett L.P.		Machen H.A.	Nelmes F.
Hancock E.G.	Hunt C.H.	Kear A.I.	Mann H.J.	Nelmes H.G.
Hancocks C.	Hunt F.W.	Kear S.J.	Manson J.W.	Newman S.J.
Hancocks J.H.	Hurd E.D.	Keedwell H.T.	Marfell H.J.	Newman W.
Harper R.G.	Hurst P.R.	Kerley W.F.	Marshall A.T.	
Harris A.R.		Keyse F.J.	Martin C.H.	Onions O.G.
Harris F.V.	Imm F.I.	Keyse R.T.	Martin J.G.	Orgee A.
Harris H.	Ireland A.W.	Kibble H.F.	Martyn E.H.	
Harrison R.T.		King A.E.	Martyn E.S.	Parr A.M.
Hart H.	Jackson C.W.	King C.C.	Matthews B.	Parrish F.A.
Hart R.	Jackson I.	King E.C.	McCullagh A.K.	Parry J.
Hart S.G.	James A.A.	King J.A.	McLaren A.W.	Parry W.
Harvey H.S.	James A.D.	King W.H.	Meek E.	Parsons E.
Hathaway F.	James C.A.	Kingman E.	Meek G.W.	Parsons E.J.
Hatter A.F.	James E.J.	Kirby J.W.	Meredith A.	Parsons L.W.

Pateman J.
Pattle P.W.
Pearce A.
Pearce H.
Penn H.
Penn R.
Penn R.A.
Phelps A.A.
Phelps S.J.
Phillips B.D.
Phillips J.
Phillips P.
Phillips W.G.
Philp A.
Phipps C.W.
Phipps S.H.
Poole E.J.
Porter A.
Porter A.J.
Porter H.A.
Porter L.
Porter T.
Povah M.
Powell B.
Powell H.K.
Powell P.M.
Preece T.
Preest J.H.
Preest J.R.
Price E.
Price G.G.
Price L.T.
Price T.M.
Prisk W.F.
Pritchard E.
Pritchard F.
Pritchard S.
Procter R.
Pudsey E.H.
Pugh P.W.

Randle L.B.
Rawlings H.A.
Rawlings V.
Read G.
Reader J.
Reeks T.
Ricks N.V.
Riley A.G.
Rivers W.C.
Roberts A.J.
Roberts M.T.

Roberts R.
Roberts R.G.
Robins F.A.
Robins W.G.
Robinson R.W.
Robinson W.H.
Rodway W.J.
Rosser C.C.
Rossiter F.
Rothin W.L.
Ruck A.H.
Ruck T.W.
Rudelsheim L.
Rudge H.
Russell D.K.
Rymer F.A.

Saint H.
Sampson J.H.
Sargent E.G.
Saunders C.L.
Scott S.A.
Screen R.
Scrivens E.J.
Seaborne L.G.
Seabright H.A.
Selwyn E.F.
Selwyn J.
Shermer W.
Sheward A.G.
Shirley F.
Shirley W.H.
Simmonds J.
Smart A.L.
Smith A.
Smith E.A.
Smith E.W.
Smith F.
Smith F.G.
Smith G.
Smith H.H.
Smith H.S.
Smith K.C.
Smith R.W.
Smith S.
Smith W.C.
Sterrett J.
Sterry G.E.
Stevens H.F.
Strike W.E.
Stubbs H.R.

Tandy A.W.
Taylor W.J.
Terrett P.G.
Thomas A.H.
Thomas C.
Thomas C.M.
Thomas E.A.
Thomas S.
Thomas T.
Thomas T.
Thomas T.D.
Thorn A.W.
Thorne J.P.
Thorpe J.A.
Toomer A.J.
Townley R.V.
Townley W.H.
Trayhern R.
Trenchard G.
Trotman R.A.
Trotter A.W.
Truman J.J.
Tudor F.H.
Turley A.B.
Turley E.
Turley E.F.
Turley G.H.
Turley H.A.
Turley W.
Turley W.R.
Turner S.
Turner S.J.
Twynning W.A.

Vaisey F.W.
Vaughan R.
Vedmore H.G.
Vick W.C.
Vickerry A.J.
Vincent A.W.
Voyce A.

Wainwright R.
Wakefield S.G.
Wakefield T.
Walden J.W.
Walding T.
Walkley L.
Walkley W.D.
Wallis W.J.
Ward C.
Warren C.E.

Warren D.
Warren E.
Waters C.W.
Watkins E.V.
Watkins F.
Watkins M.S.
Wayman A.A.
Weaver C.
Weaving W.H.
Webb D.
Webb H.
Webb J.
Webb J.
Wellington R.
Weston H.R.
White T.
Whittington F.
Whittle W.G.
Wilce A.J.
Wilce G.T.
Wilce S.W.
Wilcox A.E.
Wilcox H.A.
Wild F.W.
Wildin E.R.
Wilkes F.W.
Willett R.E.
Williams A.C.
Williams A.H.
Williams A.J.
Williams A.W.
Williams C.
Williams C.
Williams E.

Williams H.P.
Williams J.
Williams J.E.
Williams R.A.
Williams R.M.
Williams R.S.
Williams S.L.
Williams V.G.
Williams W.F.
Wilson J.
Wilton E.T.
Windsor F.
Windsor J.
Wingfield H.
Winsper-
  Cooper E.
Witts T.
Wixen A.T.
Wood C.N.
Wood E.A.
Wood W.
Woodhouse A.J.
Woodhouse H.
Worgan A.E.
Wright E.C.
Wright W.B.
Wyman F. James
Wyman F. John
Wyman L.G.
Wynn W.J.

Yemm F.E.
Young L.R.
Young R.L.

Note: This list only includes those stations which were part of 'F' Division at this time, not all of the stations covered in this book. Thus men who served as Specials at Ashleworth, Dymock, Hartpury, Minsterworth, Newent, Staunton, Redmarley D'Abitot and Westbury-on-Severn are not listed.

Appendix B
Police Details from the 1881 Census

Dwelling: CHURCH STREET HOUSE OF REMAND, LITTLEDEAN

NAME	OCCUPATION	RELATION	AGE	PLACE OF BIRTH
Gilbert WHITE	Police Constable	Head	38	Gloucester, Glos
Annie WHITE		Wife	31	Minchinhampton, Glos
Annie Louisa WHITE	Scholar	Daughter	7	Cheltenham, Glos
Harry Gilbert WHITE	Scholar	Son	6	Cheltenham, Glos
Walter William WHITE	Scholar	Son	5	Cheltenham, Glos
Arthur Edward WHITE	Scholar	Son	4	Cheltenham, Glos
Helen Mary WHITE		Daughter	2	Cheltenham, Glos
Emily Mary WHITE		Daughter	8m	Cheltenham, Glos
Thomas TRUMP	Coal Miner	Prisoner	25	Ruardean, Glos

Comments: With an 8 months old daughter, born in Cheltenham, PC White and his large family had only transferred to Littledean shortly before the census was taken. Note also that the census was very precise in taking people's exact whereabouts, so the unfortunate Thomas Trump is forever recorded as being a prisoner at this date. The address refers to the police station at Littledean Jail, not the earlier one also in Church Street.

Dwelling: BROAD STREET, LITTLEDEAN

NAME	OCCUPATION	RELATION	AGE	PLACE OF BIRTH
Robert SAMPSON	Police Constable	Head	40	Winkleigh, Devon
Penelope SAMPSON		Wife	35	Winkleigh, Devon
Clara SAMPSON	Scholar	Daughter	12	Minchinhampton, Glos
Frank SAMPSON	Scholar	Son	8	Minchinhampton, Glos
Dora SAMPSON	Scholar	Daughter	4	Minchinhampton, Glos

Comments: Dwelling only. PC Sampson had obviously spent some years at Minchinhampton police station, prior to transferring to the Forest.

Dwelling: BLAKENEY STREET, AWRE

NAME	OCCUPATION	RELATION	AGE	PLACE OF BIRTH
Joseph WILLIAMS	Police Constable	Head	28	Coln St. Aldwins, Glos
Rachel WILLIAMS		Wife	28	Beckford, Glos
Albert H. WILLIAMS	Scholar	Son	7	Lidenham (Beckford), Glos
Walter E. WILLIAMS	Scholar	Son	4	Lidenham (Beckford), Glos
Alice B. WILLIAMS		Daughter	1	Beckford, Glos
Robert NEWPORT	Police Constable	Lodger	28	Southerop, Glos

Comments: Again with a very young daughter born elsewhere, PC Williams was a recent arrival to the Forest. The dwelling addresses on the census tend to be vague. Awre probably refers to the parish rather than the village. This may just have been a dwelling but, given that there were two PCs living there, it may indicate the existence of another police station in Blakeney, after the one mentioned in 1857 but prior to the one in The Square.

Dwelling: DRYBROOK				
NAME	OCCUPATION	RELATION	AGE	PLACE OF BIRTH
Walter CONDUST	Police Constable	Head	27	Somerset
Mary Maria CONDUST		Wife	21	St Briavels, Glos
Hubert Walter CONDUST		Son	1	Coleford, Glos
William PACKER	Police Constable	Lodger	21	Oxford, Oxon
Annie JAMES		Visitor	14	Newland, Glos

Comments: Walter and Mary had probably only been married a couple of years and the visitor, Annie James, may have been her sister helping out with her baby nephew.

Dwelling: BILSON ROAD POLICE STATION				
NAME	OCCUPATION	RELATION	AGE	PLACE OF BIRTH
Chas. H. HAWKINS	Police Sergeant	Head	34	Frampton, Glos
Maria HAWKINS		Wife	35	Tetbury, Glos
Clara HAWKINS	Scholar	Daughter	6	Purton, Glos
Oliver HAWKINS	Scholar	Son	4	Purton, Glos
Minnie HAWKINS		Daughter	1	Coleford, Glos
Thos. ROSEBLADE	Police Constable	Lodger	25	Ashton Keynes, Wiltshire
Isaac COOK	Police Constable	Lodger	23	Bishops Cleeve, Glos

Comments: This is Cinderford police station. When the new railway station for Cinderford opened in 1900, Bilson Road was renamed Station Street.

Dwelling: POLICE STATION, WEST DEAN				
NAME	OCCUPATION	RELATION	AGE	PLACE OF BIRTH
Joseph SMITH	Police Constable	Head	45	Minchinhampton, Glos
Eliza ROGERS	House Keeper	Sister in law	53	Wotton-under-Edge, Glos
Thomas A. SMITH	Scholar	Son	11	West Dean, Glos
Syndey SMITH	Scholar	Son	9	West Dean, Glos
Charles H. DAVIS	Police Constable	Lodger	26	Stroud, Glos

Comments: This is somewhere in West Dean, near Russels Lodge, Parkend, which would seem to indicate that the village had an earlier station than the one at 'Hazeldene'. The widowed PC Smith was being looked after by his sister-in-law – is there a story here?

Dwelling: HIGH STREET, MITCHELDEAN				
NAME	OCCUPATION	RELATION	AGE	PLACE OF BIRTH
William MALLETT	Police Sergeant	Head	57	Stinchcombe, Glos
Martha MALLETT		Wife	63	St. Warnolds, Herefords
Albert STINCHCOMBE	Police Constable	Lodger	28	Hawkesbury Upton, Glos

Comments: This may be a rented dwelling, unless the station moved from Plats Row to High St. before moving to Townsend, or unless Plats Row was considered part of the High St. However, where the dwelling is a police station the census usually says so. Did Sgt. Mallett appreciate the coincidence of his lodger PC having the same name as his own place of birth?

A Forest Beat

Dwelling: SAILORS SQUARE, NEWNHAM

NAME	OCCUPATION	RELATION	AGE	PLACE OF BIRTH
William CURRY	Police Constable	Head	27	Huntspill, Somerset
Alice CURRY		Wife	26	Almondsbury, Glos
William A. CURRY		Son	2	Bedminster, Bristol
Alice Maud CURRY		Daughter	11m	Almondsbury, Glos
Eliza JENNINGS	Annuitant	Lodger	47	Blakeney, Glos

Comments: Dwelling only. PC Curry and his family were further recent arrivals to the Forest.

Dwelling: POLICE STATION, NEWNHAM

NAME	OCCUPATION	RELATION	AGE	PLACE OF BIRTH
Nathaniel WESTAWAY	Police Sergeant	Head	36	Winkleigh, Devon
Sarah Jane WESTAWAY		Wife	31	Charlton Kings, Glos
Ernest N. WESTAWAY	Scholar	Son	9	Charlton Kings, Glos
Ann D. WESTAWAY	Scholar	Daughter	7	Churcham, Glos
William H. WESTAWAY	Scholar	Son	5	Churcham, Glos
Sidney John WESTAWAY		Son	1	Ashleworth, Glos
George WILKS	Police Constable	Lodger	26	Hill, Nr Berkeley, Glos
Hubert RUFFEE	Labourer	Prisoner	21	Sheffield, Yorks
Samuel JONES	Iron Moulder	Prisoner	22	Yardley, Worcs

Comments: Lots of information to be gleaned here. Sgt. Westaway had only recently transferred from Ashleworth and prior to that he had served at Churcham, receiving his promotion from PC somewhere along the way. It would appear his career had begun at Charlton Kings police station in Cheltenham. Both prisoners are from some distance away, so had presumably come to the Forest looking for work in the iron industry. The nearest ironworks to Newnham at this date was at Lower Soudley. Finally, it is likely that Sgt. Westaway knew PC Sampson at Littledean well, as they both hailed from the same little village in Devon. The address probably refers to the police station when it was in Passage Lane, Newnham.

Dwelling: POLICE STATION, NEW ROAD, HANGERBERRY

NAME	OCCUPATION	RELATION	AGE	PLACE OF BIRTH
Jesal CLARK	Police Constable	Head	29	Nettleton, Glos
Mary E. CLARK		Wife	28	Wotton-under-Edge, Glos
Annie M. CLARK	Scholar	Daughter	5	Cheltenham, Glos
Edith E.M. CLARK		Daughter	2	Lydbrook, Glos
George WILLIAMS	Police Constable	Lodger	22	Leominster, Herefords

Comments: The address refers to Lydbrook's second police station.

Dwelling: BREAM ROAD, LYDNEY

NAME	OCCUPATION	RELATION	AGE	PLACE OF BIRTH
Edward WHITE	Police Constable	Head	26	Slimbridge, Glos
Sophea WHITE		Wife	26	Newnham, Glos
Mabel Louise WHITE		Daughter	1	Lydney, Glos
Francis Edward WHITE		Son	12d	Lydney, Glos

Comments: Dwelling only. PC White was celebrating the very recent arrival of a son and heir.

Dwelling: POLICE STATION & PETTY SESSIONAL COURT, LYDNEY

NAME	OCCUPATION	RELATION	AGE	PLACE OF BIRTH
Charles Albert CLARK	Police Sergeant	Head	29	Fairford, Glos
Mary Ann CLARK		Wife	31	Aylburton, Glos
Annie CLARK		Daughter	3	Drybrook, Glos
William HOPKINS	Police Constable	Lodger	26	Temple Guiting, Glos

Comments: As noted in the text (p.107), PS Clark died on 21 Aug. 1881, aged 29 – shortly after this census was taken. The birthplace given for his young daughter may well indicate that he had previously served at Drybrook police station.

Dwelling: POLICE STATION, ST BRIAVELS

NAME	OCCUPATION	RELATION	AGE	PLACE OF BIRTH
Henry MARTIN	Police Constable	Head	53	Prestbury, Glos
Eliza MARTIN		Wife	49	Ashchurch, Glos
Harriett Emily WHITE		Grandaughter	6	Bream, Glos
Thomas HELSTONE	Police Constable	Lodger	27	Crediton, Devon

Comments: The presence of PC Martin's grandaughter may be as a result of a brief visit at the time of the census or they may have been looking after her due to a family problem. PC Helstone was another Devonian. It will be noted that few of the men serving as police officers in the Forest at this time were born there.

Dwelling: COMMON, ST BRIAVELS

NAME	OCCUPATION	RELATION	AGE	PLACE OF BIRTH
Frederick DONNERY	Superannuated Police Inspector	Head	58	Ireland
Jane DONNERY		Wife	63	Somerset
William DONNERY	Superannuated Mayors Officer	Lodger	63	Ireland

Comments: Retired – Donnery might have been one of Chief Constable Lefroy's imports from Ireland. On the other hand, he might not have served in Gloucestershire at all! His elder brother was lodging with them.

Dwelling: COALWAY ROAD POLICE STATION

NAME	OCCUPATION	RELATION	AGE	PLACE OF BIRTH
Donald MACRAE	Police Superintendent	Head	39	Scotland
Mima MACRAE		Wife	40	Scotland
Annie E. MACRAE	Scholar	Daughter	13	Cheltenham, Glos
Henry NEWMAN	Police Sergeant	Head	39	Pauntley, Glos
Mary Ann NEWMAN		Wife	28	Ampney Crucis, Glos
Ann L. NEWMAN	Scholar	Daughter	8	Leigh, Glos
Emily M.A. NEWMAN	Scholar	Daughter	3	Leigh, Glos
Thomas A. NEWMAN		Son	2	Lydney, Glos
Mabel A. NEWMAN		Daughter	10m	Coleford, Glos
William HALL	Police Constable	Lodger	24	Northleach, Glos

Comments: This is Lord's Hill police station in Coleford. It would appear from his daughter's birthplace that Superintendent Macrae had previously served in Cheltenham and no doubt elsewhere too. Leigh, the birthplace of two of PS Newman's children, is near Coombe Hill, between Gloucester and Tewkesbury, so it is likely he had served in the police station there. His 3 year old daughter was born there but his 2 year old son was born in Lydney, whilst his 10 month old daughter was born in Coleford, so the dates of his transfers can be worked out quite closely. Note also that there must have been two sets of accommodation at the police station – the Superintendent's family would have been separate from PS Newman and his family – and that the subordinate had the pleasure of a PC lodger.

Dwelling: 8 COALWAY ROAD

NAME	OCCUPATION	RELATION	AGE	PLACE OF BIRTH
James RUSSELL	Police Constable	Head	29	Shipton, Glos
Alice RUSSELL		Wife	28	Dunsbon, Glos
Arthur RUSSELL	Scholar	Son	7	Coln St Aldwins, Glos
Ellen RUSSELL	Scholar	Daughter	5	Cheltenham, Glos

Comments: Again this is in Coleford. It was possibly a police house but, more likely, rented accommodation. PC Russell also appears to have served previously in Cheltenham.

Bibliography & sources

The History of the Gloucestershire Constabulary 1839 to 1985. H. Thomas. Alan Sutton, 1987
Blood on Coal. Ralph Anstis. Black Dwarf Publications 1999
Newnham News in the Papers. A. Lloyd
A House of Correction. J.R.S. Whiting. Alan Sutton, 1979
Custom, Work and Market Capitalism. C. Fisher. Croom Helm, 1981
Wings Over Gloucestershire. John Rennison. Piccadilly Publishing, 1988
Life in a Gloucestershire Village. Ted Ball
Ashleworth West Gloucestershire. Collins D. and others. A Severnside Village Local History Group
Who Killed The Bears? L. Clark
Tales from Dunk's Carner. John Christian, 1998
The Gloucestershire Police in the Nineteenth Century. B. Jerrard, M. Lit. dissertation 1977, in GRO
Victoria County History of the County of Gloucester, Vol. V. The Forest of Dean. ed. N. Herbert. OUP, 1995
The War Record Book of the Gloucestershire Special Constabulary
The Murder of Parish Constable Henry Thompson. R. Hale. (*Police History Society Journal* 1997 pp 20-21).
Petition. Gloucestershire Record Office (GRO) Ref. P1 VE 2/1
Police Station Diary, Hewelsfield 1840-1843. GRO Ref. Q/Y/2/4/9
Report on Police Stations by the Chief Constable and County Surveyor 1857. GRO Ref. Q/AP25
The Police & Constabulary List (Almanac) 1844
National Census data 1841 to 1891
Gloucestershire Constabulary map 1933, GRO Ref. Q/Y 5/4/3
The Diary of Edward Thomas Chipp by kind permission of Rosemary Howells
Plans of Lydney police station 1878, 1900 and 1972
A Petition of Second Class Constables for the County of Gloucester Police Force, 1907
Dean Archaeology No. 11, 1998
Police Officers Killed in the line of Duty. Compiled by Sgt. Anthony Rae, Lancashire Constabulary
Kelly's Directory (various dates)
Home Office Circular 114/83
Lydney Observer 15 July 1955

Acknowledgements

We would like to thank all those who contributed personal histories and photographs, the householders of former police stations for their co-operation and all those who have assisted us with our enquiries including: Dr A.J.P. Butler CBE, QPM, Chief Constable of Gloucestershire; Gloucestershire Record Office; Gloucester City Library; The Archive Shop, Lydney; Ruth Proctor Hirst; Averil Kear; Aleric Isaac of Photowatch, Cheltenham; Marion Voyce; Lionel Voyce; Ron Davis; Reg Hale; Mrs Joan Rooum (nee James); Tony Davis; David Bick; Ken Parsons; John Powell; Gordon Clissold; Ann Lloyd; Henry Boughton; Joe Wilkes; Ray Allen; Alec Pope; Ian Pope; Mrs D Collins; Mrs W Coones; Bob Smyth; Win Morris; Linda Brooks; Reg Brown; Tony Fardon; Reg Duberley; Mabel Beech; Melville Watts; Margaret Wyatt; Andy and Cherryl Barrow; Mrs A. Gould; Rosemary Howells (nee Chipp); the late Raymond Raymond; Pat Bolter; Mr and Mrs R. Ellis; Brian Raymond; Dennis Freeman; Geoff Waygood; Ron Stephens; The Telecottage, Cinderford; Mrs E. Olivey; Mrs J. Brazier; Dora Gwilliam; John Bryant: Bob Berryman; Edgar Bowring; Derrick Adams; Nadia Wheatstone; Pat Hutchings; John Smith; Jim Ludlow; Jack Kite; Graham Murdock; Bob Parker; Pete Hood; Ralph Wilkins; Dave Thompson; Ray Morgan; Tony Cresick; Dyke Stephens; Jack Williams; Ron Martin; John Dougan; Mr and Mrs Graham Parker; Jim Taylor; Tom Heaps; Les Tuffley; Tetbury Police Museum; Brian Toney; Sheila Brown (nee Leakey); Bob Brown; Joanne Sindrey; Sue Sindrey; Dave Smith; Geoff Light; Bob Phelps; Dennis Gething; Pat Allen; Vicky Deakin (nee Gwynn); Francis Field; David Bleaken; Ron Savage; Fred Hudson; Len and Megan Perry; Lynne Cooke; Dave Peake; Pat Bolter; Neil Thomas; Brian Brazil; Frank Rooum; Mary Impet.

Index – General

Abenhall, 116
Almondsbury, 139
Angel Hotel, Coleford, 82
Armed Response Vehicle, 45
Army Apprentices College, 136
Ashleworth, 7, 14, 15, 45, 51, 52, 89, 148
ASP baton, 45
Aust Ferry, 136
Avon & Somerset Constabulary, 44, 139
Awre, 110, 160

Bala, 30
Bamfurlong, 43, 45
Basic Command Unit, 45
Beachley, 9, 129, 136, 138
Bears, 85
Bearse, 11
Berkeley, 41
Best Value, 146
Biggleswade, 145
Bigsweir, 79
Birdwood, 61
Blakeney Hill, 17, 53
Blakeney, 14, 17, 53-56, 148
Blitz, 35, 74
Bolshevik Revolution, 144
Bowlash, 11
Bowls Club, Coleford, 82
Bream, 11, 18, 24, 30, 43, 57-61, 125, 129, 149
Brewster Sessions, 71
Bristol, 35, 74
Brockweir, 129
Brooklands, 73
Butchers Arms, 69

Caroline Symes Memorial Bowl, 60
Castleford Bridge, 139
Cave Rescue, 40
CCTV, 45, 84, 114
Chartist Movement, 134
Chase, Tidenham, 11, 15
Cheltenham, 42
Chepstow, 15
Chief Constable's Cup, 40
Churcham, 14, 15, 24, 61-91
CID, 44, 46
Cinderford RFC, 67
Cinderford, 17, 18, 43, 45, 62-68, 111, 149, 161
Clearwell, 69, 77
Clements End, 74, 81
Coalway, 74
Cold War, 35
Coleford, 14, 15, 18, 32, 33, 40, 43, 45, 70-84, 150, 164
Command & Control System, 45
Conference points, 14, 22
Control Room (see also Information Room), 42
Coronation Street, 146
Corse, 149
Crime & Disorder Act, 46
Crime Management Unit, 45, 46
CS Spray, 45
Cutlass, 19, 63

D Day, 83
Divisional Conferences, 34
Drybrook, 17, 85-87, 150, 161
Duncan Cottage, 72
Dursley, 73
Dutch Royal Family, 107
Dymock, 14, 15, 17, 30, 88, 150

Ecclesiastical Courts Jurisdiction Act 1860, 119
Edge End, 79
English Bicknor, 113

Farriers Court, 73
Feathers Hotel, Lydney, 21, 105
First World War, 19, 24, 144
Forest & Gloucester Div., 47
Forest Combination Cup, 143
Forestry School, Parkend, 125
Free Wales Army, 82
Freeminers, 17, 69

General Strike 1926, 20, 34
Glamorgan Police, 34
Gwent Constabulary, 42

Harrow (Harry) Hill, 19
Hartpury, 7, 30, 45, 51, 52, 89
Haw Bridge Murder, 81
Helicopter, 45
Hewelsfield, 11, 90, 129
High Beech, 15, 90
HMS *Marlborough*, 144
HMS *Melbreak*, 83
Huntley, 24, 30, 44, 45, 91, 92, 151

Incident Response Vehicle, 45, 47
Information Room (see also Control Room), 30
Inner-City Riots, 35
Inspector Neighbourhood Areas, 46, 119
Internet, 146

Lancaut, 11, 138
Lancote (see Lancaut)
Lightmoor Colliery, 19
Lincoln, 95
Littledean, 14, 15, 17, 18, 33, 63, 93-98, 100, 160
Longhope, 17, 30, 98, 99, 151
Luftwaffe, 74
Lydbrook, 14, 15, 32, 77, 100-103, 162
Lydney Park, 30
Lydney RFC, 35, 144
Lydney, 11, 14, 17, 32, 43, 45, 105-114, 152, 163

Metropolitan Police, 9, 95
Mile End, 80, 115
Miners Strike 1911, 34
Miners Strike 1921, 19
Miners Strike 1926, 20, 34
Miners Strike 1984, 35, 59
Minsterworth, 24, 45, 152
Mitcheldean, 9, 14, 15, 17, 32, 79, 116, 117, 152, 161
Mobile Column, 35

Moseley Green, 82
Motor Patrol (see also Traffic), 22, 30, 32, 110
Mounted police, 20

Naas Court, 109
Nailbridge, 85
National Hunt Festival, 35
New Age Travellers, 59
Newent, 9, 14, 17, 22, 32, 33, 44, 45, 52, 118, 119, 153
Newland, 14, 77
Newnham, 9, 14, 15, 17, 32, 63, 120-123, 153, 162
Norfolk, 47, 82
Northern Division, 44

Operation Countryman, 113
Operation Gemini, 45, 46, 114
Ostrich Inn, 80

Parkend Cricket Club, 102
Parkend Football Club, 125
Parkend, 17, 32, 42, 59, 124, 125, 153, 161
Patrol Ticket, 11, 14, 56
Pay Parade, 34
Pillowell, 54, 59
Pneumoconiosis, 145
Poaching, 41, 42
Police & Magistrates Courts Act, 45
Police Authority, 27
Police Band, 125
Police Box, 95
Police Choir, 59
Police Club, 109
Police Federation, 33
Police Information Point (PIP), 46, 57, 103
Police War Reserve, 27, 108
Public Safety Radio Communications Project, 146
Pubwatch Scheme, 114

RAF, 29
Railway Inn, Lydney, 109
Rank Xerox, 117
Redbrook, 73, 77, 79
Redhill House, 108
Redmarley, 126
Ross Spur (M50), 118
Royal Family, 35
Royal Horse Artillery, 95
RSPCA, 80, 145
Ruardean, 24, 30, 126, 127, 154
Rural Beat Officers, 48, 89
Rural Policing Panel, 48
Rural Policing Strategy, 48
Rural Watch, 48
Ruspidge, 17, 30, 128, 129, 154

Scharnhorst, 80
Second World War, 24, 83, 86, 121, 143, 144
Sedbury Park, 138
Seven Stars Inn, 44
Severn & Wye Railway, 102
Severn Auxiliary Rescue Association (SARA), 40

Severn Bridge (rail), 41
Severn Bridge (road), 40, 82, 139
Severn Bridge Disaster 1939, 41, 142
Severn Bridge Disaster 1960, 40, 41, 110, 113, 138
Severn Trow, 136
Sex Discrimination Act 1975, 34
Sharpness, 40, 41
Silicosis, 145
Somme, Battle of, 95
Sparsity Factor, 48
Special Constabulary, 45, 147-158
Speech House, 17, 95
Spout, 80
St Briavels, 11, 14, 15, 30, 44, 79, 129-133, 154, 163
Standing Joint Committee, 27, 30, 86
Staple Hill, 2, 109
Staunton/Corse, 17, 30, 44, 45, 52, 134-135, 149
Steam Mills, 85
Step Aside Inn, 108
Stonehenge, 35
Stroud, 42
Summer Solstice, 35
Sunderland, 19
Sunny Bank House, 79, 80
Sword Beach, 83
Symonds Yat, 75, 81, 102

Tidenham, 14, 15, 130, 135
Tonypandy, 34
Trafalgar Colliery, 18, 19
Traffic (see also Motor Patrol), 45, 46, 47, 77, 122
Trowgreen, 11
Tuthill House, 24
Tutshill, 44, 130, 135-139

UHF Radio, 43, 68, 82
US Army, 29

VHF Radio, 43
Viney Hill, 18, 54

Welsh Water Authority, 41
West Mercia Constabulary, 42
Westbury Court, 140
Westbury, 17, 139, 140, 155
Western Division, 44, 113
Whitecroft RFC, 143
Whitecroft, 54, 59
Whitminster, 142
Wilsbury, 11
Wintles Hill, 140
Womens Auxilliary Police Corps, 27
Woodcroft, 11, 15, 140
Woolaston, 129, 141-143, 155
Worcestershire Police, 126

Yorkley, 32, 42, 59, 125, 144-146, 156
Ypres, 24, 95

Index – Names

Adams, Derrick, 128
Adams, Mr., 74
Adams, W.J., 145
Allen, Ray, 71
Alway, Bruce, 109
Anderson, Don, 37
Anstis, Ralph, 20
Antell, Tom, 26

Bailey, Cyril, 114
Bailey, PC, 25
Bailey, Simon, 117
Bailey, William, 129
Baker, John, 11
Baldwin, PC, 25
Ballard, Dave, 38
Ballinger, Alan, 32
Bancroft, Capt., 56
Bannister, Simon, 128
Barmby, Bill, 32
Barnes, Norman, 80
Barnes, PC, 25
Barrow, Andy, 59, 60, 61, 125, 146
Barrow, Cherryl, 60, 61
Batchelor, PC, 25
Bathurst, Charles, 105
Baud, Eddy, 67
Bayliss, Harold, 26, 141, 155
Beale, PS, 36
Beard, Samuel, 17, 18, 95, 100
Beard, Thomas, 135
Beasant, Insp., 43
Beasley, George, 11. 129
Beaufort, Duke of, 78
Beddis, Chris, 25, 26, 59, 141, 142,
Bent, Insp. Alan, BEM, 20, 72
Berry, Dick, 38
Berryman, Bob, 38, 39, 40, 41, 42, 113, 114
Berryman, Russell, 38
Berryman, Sheila, 39
Berryman, Tony, 42, 111
Best, Gerry, 113, 114
Betteridge, William, 27
Bevan, John, 84
Bick, David, 15, 118
Birch, Cecil, 26
Birch, Edward, 15, 93
Bird, Dickie, 32, 38
Blake, Peter, 81
Blanton, Reg, 28
Bleaken, Albert Henry, 72, 144
Bledisloe, Viscount, 30, 108
Blick, Dennis, 25, 100
Bliss, George, 27
Bolan, K., 39
Bolter, Pat, 84
Born, SC, 29
Boughton, Jim, 25, 126, 154
Bowels /Bowles, William, 11
Bowring, Edgar, 26, 56, 73, 74, 75, 110, 121, 144, 145
Box, Mr., 56
Box, Thomas, 11
Bricknell, Malcolm, 125
Broad, Ossie, 26, 32
Brokenshire, Mrs, 78
Brokenshire, PC, 78
Brown, Hugh, 120
Brown, Jock, 26, 59, 149

Brunsdon, Dave, 111
Bryant, John, 113
Buckland, Tom, 26, 117, 152
Bucknall, Keith, 133
Bull, PS, 24, 25, 66, 67
Bullock, Dave, 111
Bullock, Vic, 26, 72, 73
Bunning, Elizabeth, 130
Bunning, John, 130
Burke, Kevin, 43, 122
Burns, Mike, 78
Butt, Mr, 15, 70

Calver, Mark, 38
Calway, Brian, 118
Cameron, Malcolm, 38, 113
Cameron, WPC, 25
Cann, John, 68
Carter, Albert, 24, 26, 27, 67, 147
Carter, Bert, 26, 54
Carter, George, 125, 153
Carter, M.F., 56, 122
Chandler, Bill, 26, 140
Chantry, John, 51
Checkley, PC, 130
Chester-Master, Lt Col Richard, Chief Constable, 24, 139
Child, Liz, 119
Child, PS 97, 118
Chipp Edward Thomas, 18, 19, 63, 71
Chipp, Lucy, 63
Christian, Admiral Henry, Chief Constable, 17, 53
Christian, John, 86
Clark, Charles Albert, 107
Clarke, Nobby, 32
Clarke, PC, 109
Clarke, PS, 29, 152
Clarke, Victor, 38
Clissold, Gordon, 40
Coates, John, 24, 25, 26, 130
Cockings, Joseph, 116
Colchester-Wemyss, Lt. Col. J.M. OBE, JP, 140, 147
Colchester-Wemyss, M.W, 140
Coldicutt, PC, 36
Coldicutt, PS, 24, 25, 107
Cole, PC, 25
Constable, PC, 32
Cook, PC, 155
Cook, Shaun, 39
Cooke, George, 140
Cooke, John, 116
Coombes, Frank, QPM, 68
Cooper, Ernest Albert, 116
Cottle, PC, 130
Cox, PC, 25
Crawley, Fred, 95
Crawshay, Edwin, 63
Cresick, Tony, 132
Crewe, Jim, 86
Crocker, Trevor, 133
Cross, Stan, 32, 118
Crouch, Reg, 75
Crowther, PC, 25
Cullimore, Len, 111
Czaplinski, Unteroffizier, 74

Davies, Demon, 143

Davies, PC, 148
Davies, Pete, 122
Davies, Terry, 139
Davies, Tudor, 113
Davis, Ron, 76, 137
Davis Tony, 84
Day, Edgar, 25, 26, 32, 130, 131, 132, 154
Day, John, 131
Day, Lilian, 131
Day, Peter, 113
Daykin, John, 27
Deakin, Vicky, 79
Dibben, F.W., 124
Dibden, Cliff, 26, 107
Dix, Rob, 48
Dorothy, I., 39
Dougan, John, 130
Dowsell, George, 26, 74, 75, 153, 154
Drennan, Noel, 27
Drennan, PC, 130
Drew, Alan, 144, 145
Drinkwater, Harry, 81
Durn, Frank, 102
Duval, Doug, 111
Dyer, Malcolm, 84, 102

Eagger, Gary, 119
Eagles, PC, 141
Eley, Harold,b 134
Elliott, Gilbert, 32
Emerson, Frank, 26, 32, 38, 144, 156
Emery, Dennis, 77
Endy, Mike, 87, 130
Evans, Fred, 122
Evans, Hector 121
Evans, Ron, 125
Evans, Sam, 73

Fardon, Tony, 134, 144
Fardon, Wilf 'Joe', 25, 26, 134, 144, 156
Farmer, Brian, 143
Farmer, PC 130
Faulconer, Percy, 27, 29
Ferryman, PS, 24, 25, 107
Field, Francis, 32, 77, 109, 115
Finch, Arthur, 26
Finch, PC, 100
Finch, PS, 110
Fisher, Roy, 43
Foice, Paul, 26, 108
Francis, Leonard, 32
Francis, PC, 85
Freeman, Dennis R., 68, 137, 138
Freeman, Eugene, 24, 25, 107

Gale, Paul, 38, 39
Gardner, Insp., 36
Gardner, John, 140
Garston, PC, 130
Gay, PC, 25
Gething, Dennis, 69
Giles, Bernard, 43
Girdlestone, Terry,40
Gleed, Henry, 120
Glover, Fred, 32, 137
Godfrey, William, 120

Goode, John, 96
Gould, Capt. 63
Gould, Doris, 26
Gould, John, 52
Grayhurst, PC, 36
Green, Bill, 102
Green, German, 143
Green, Insp., 24, 25
Green, PC, 25
Griffin, John, 32, 110
Griffin, Supt., 71
Griffiths, Lawrence, 77
Gulliford, Nigel, 122
Gunter, Annette, 68
Gwilliam, Ben, 27, 31, 44, 83, 111, 112, 113
Gwilliam, Bob, 113
Gwilliam, Dora, 44, 83, 111
Gwynne, John, 125
Gwynne, Roger, 125

Hale, PC, 25
Halford, A., 39
Hall, Roger, 48
Hamblin, PS, 72
Harding, Cornelius, 54
Harding, Jack, 59
Harman, PC, 97
Hart, Andrew Jock, 127
Hart, Theo, 27
Harvey, F.W., 144
Hawkes, Doug, 27
Hawkins, John, 117
Hawkins, PS, 85
Heal, Rev. Harold, 132
Heath, Ted, 6, 39, 87, 110
Heffner, August, 74
Hemming, Jim, 111, 126
Henderson, PC, 130
Henn, Col. W.F., CBE, MVO, KPM, Chief Constable, 73
Hernamann, John, 120
Heselton, Colin, 68
Hewinson, Frank, 26
Hicks, PC, 36
Hicks, Walter, 41
Hills, Bert, 32, 110, 143, 145
Hobday, PS, 24, 25, 36
Holder, PC, 130
Holme,s George, 26
Holmes, Graham, 82
Holmes, PC, 130
Hood, Pete, 83
Hopson, Phil, 125
Horan, John, 47
Horton, W., 110
Houghton, I., 39
Houghton, Jim, 26
Howkins, John, 27
Hudson, Fred, 27, 29, 73, 74
Hughes, Des, 38
Hull, Albert, 57
Hunt, Doug, 67
Hutchinson, Paul, 39, 68
Hyatt, Mr & Mrs, 116
Hyett, John, 27, 128

Impett, Mary, 107
Ireland, Joe, 25, 26, 54, 100
Ireland, Kevin, 118

167

Isaacs, Nigel, 122
Isaacs, PC, 130

Jacobson, PC, 102
James, Edward George, 25, 26, 28, 85, 117, 121, 122, 123, 153
James, L.S., 151
James, Les, 117
James, Mrs, 117
James, Robin, 117
Jayne, Frank, 32, 41, 77, 142
Jefferies, Colin, 52
Jefferies, John, 52
Jefferies, PC, 52
Jeffries, PC, 25
Johnson, Andy, 68
Johnson, Bert, 85
Johnson, Jimmy, 77
Jones, Bob, 52, 89, 115
Jones, Dave, 38, 122
Jones, David Ch Supt., 79
Jones, George Edward, 100
Jones, Jennifer, 145
Jones, Mike, 38
Jones, PC, 85

Kear, Henry, 124
Kenny, Vic, 38
Kerrod, Paul, 39
Keyse, Terry, 38, 39, 103
Kingscott, Bert, 79, 81, 83, 145, 146
Kingscott, Joan, 79, 83, 146
Kirby, Samuel, 11
Kite, Jack, 80, 81, 82

Lambert, Kevin, 114
Lander, William H., 9, 120
Large, Charles Frederick, 24, 25, 74, 147, 152, 153
Large, PC, 148
Lark, Terry, 38, 39, 87
Lawrence, Pip, 111
Leakey, Bert, 32, 109, 110
Leakey, Sheila, 109
Lefroy, Anthony T., Chief Constable 1839 - 1865, 9, 11, 12, 13, 51, 90, 120
Light, Geoff, 39
Lipett, PC, 25
Lloyd, Bob, 134
Lloyd-Nash, Liz, 118
Lodge, Henry, 32, 111
Long, Walter, 79, 80
Lopes, Hon. Ethel, 56
Ludlow, Jim, 27, 54, 107, 122, 136, 141, 143
Ludlow, Mrs, 122, 136, 142, 143

Machin, Henry, 74
Maden, PC, 135
Manning, Stuart, 103
Mannion, Peter, 113
Markham, Eric, 32
Martin, Ken, 115
Martyn, SC, 29
Mary, Queen, 109
Masterson, Phil, 32
McCormick, Steve, 38
McGarr, Gerry, 52, 89
McKnight, Joe, 26, 67
McNeill, Ian, 38, 39
McWilmott, PS, 27
Meadows, Arthur, 27
Meadows, PC, 36
Meek, Roger, 125

Meredith, Denise, 103
Merrett, Arthur, 32
Merrett, PC, 102
Merrett, PS, 36
Merriman, Len, 26, 136
Midwinter, C., 26
Miles, Geoff, 67, 113
Miles, Roger, 38
Miller, Fred, 26
Millichip, Elizabeth, 32, 110
Mills, S., 39
Milton, John, 80
Minett, Fred, 25, 26, 38
Mock, Reg, 38
Monks, Frank, 111
Moore, Eric, 39
Morgan, Richard, 145
Morris, Frank, 25, 26, 35, 36, 37, 102, 136, 155
Morris, Joseph, 19
Morris, Simon, 102
Morris, William, 18, 54, 55, 107
Morris, Winston, 38, 102, 103
Morse, Dean, 68
Morse, Glen, 68
Moss, Ferdy, 38, 140
Moss, Ken, 32
Murdock, Graham, 45, 68, 113
Murdock, Wayne, 45
Mynett, Arthur, 74

Nash, William, 116
Newman, Alfred Frederick, 26, 30, 31, 38, 56, 107, 109
Newman, Bob, 77
Newport, PC, 17, 54
Nicholls, B., 26
Nicholls, Frank, 26, 32, 35, 77, 100, 102, 103
Norris, Joe, 146

Packer, Insp., 65, 66, 67
Paget, Cyril, 26, 32, 75, 153
Pagett, Gilbert, 25, 98, 121,
Park, Clifford, 109
Parker, Bob, 32, 38, 130, 131, 132
Parker, Mary, 68
Parnell, Justin, 68
Parris, Sid., 83
Parslow, Frank, 117
Parsons, Bob, 38
Parsons, Ken, 68, 75, 77, 78, 82, 83, 107
Parsons, Pearl, 83
Peake, David, 119
Pennington, Harry, 122
Perkins, Dick, 113
Perry, Len, 95
Perry, Les, 32, 141
Perry, Mike, 67, 111
Phelps, Bob, 68, 92
Phelps, PC, 25
Phelps, PS, 56
Phillips, Keith, 38
Philpott, Tony, 125
Pickering, PC, 130
Pitman, Reg, 32
Pole, PC, 22, 25
Pope, Alec, 64
Powell, Theo, 77, 110, 111, 112
Preest, Reg, 125
Price, Dave, 125
Price, PC, 85
Prisk, F, 72, 73
Prosser, Tom, 115
Pugsley, Tom, 26, 54, 75

Pursehouse, Paul, 110, 111

Radcliffe, Glyn, 143
Randell, PC, 25
Reed, Bruce, 59
Reed, C., 39
Reeks, Joe, 26
Reeve, Alf, 67
Reid, PC, 89
Roberts, Jack 'Cromp', 80
Roberts, William, 54
Robinson, Ron, 137
Roderick, P., 39
Rogers, Jack, 27, 128
Rogers, W.T., 21, 25, 86, 150
Rooum, Frank, 102
Rooum, Joan, 85, 117, 121
Rumbelow, Roy, 38
Russell, Brian, 20
Ryan, Cornelius, 83
Ryder, Dennis, 111

Sandells, Eric, 77
Sandells, John, 102
Sands, PC, 130
Sargent, Gordon, 38
Sarson, Rod, 38, 128, 129
Saunders, Gordon, 32, 38, 127
Savage, Ron, 31
Schmidt, Heinrich, 74
Schofield, Leanne, 133
Scudamore, Bill, 143
Sealbright, Joseph, 140
Sharpe, Pete, 38
Shelswell, John, MBE, 20, 24, 25, 35, 36, 37
Shergold, Denis, 59
Sherlls, John, 129
Shipton, James, 140
Short, Gary, 43
Simpson, R., 39
Sindrey, Geoff, 6, 113
Skinner, Clifford, 43
Sladen, Tom, 128
Smith, Alan, 32, 38
Smith, C.A.('Cas'), 22, 25, 108
Smith, Dave, 48
Smith, Deena, 119
Smith, Keith, 39
Smith, Mary, 109
Smith, Ron, 32, 38
Smith, Ronald W. C., 86
Smith, Terry, 52, 89, 115
Soper, Leonard, QPM, Chief Constable, 39
Stephens, Donald, 32
Stephens, Ron, 32, 78, 80, 108-9
Stoneham, Peter, 111
Straw, Jack, 48
Strawford, William, 121
Swatton, PS, 107
Swift, Fred, 26

Tanner, Charles, 105
Tapscott, Leo, 82
Taylor, A., 26
Taylor, A.W. 25, 154
Taylor, Alec, 128
Taylor, Arthur, 81
Taylor, Fitzroy Fred, 20, 25, 26, 35, 37, 72, 73, 74, 143, 144
Taylor, Jim, 74, 143
Thomas, Alf, 109
Thomas, Cyril, 32, 38, 125
Thomas, Harry, QPM, 125
Thomas, Herbie, 111

Thomas, M., 39
Thomas, Neil, 35, 38, 39, 43, 113, 128, 129, 143
Thomas, William, 140
Thompson, D., 39
Thompson, Henry, 100
Thorn, SC, 29
Tibbotts, Dick, 26
Townsend, Don, 77
Townsend, Paul, 135
Tracy, Bill, 133
Tredgett, Dave, 146
Trotman, Edward, 109
Truman, Terry, 145
Turley, Roger, 111
Turner, Dave, 38
Turner, Jack, 27
Turner, Ollie, 130
Tuttiett, Edwin, 25, 26
Twyford, Bob, 128

Underwood, Dereck, 113
Underwood, J., 39

Vaile, Dick, 113
Voyce, Frederick, 66, 67, 72
Voyce, Lionel, 72

Wadley, Alan, 111
Wakefield, PC, 26, 56
Wales, HRH Prince of, 60
Walker, Daniel, 11, 129
Walker, Dean, 114
Walkley, Chas, 32
Watkins, Barry, 87
Watkins, Graham, 111, 112
Watkins, Harry, 21, 26, 49, 95
Watkins, Lewis, 32
Watkins, Rex, 32
Watts, John, 108, 136
Waygood, Geoff, 125
Weaver, Lee, 38, 39, 103
Webb, Bill, 32, 38, 137
Weekes, Reg, 25, 26, 59, 124, 149
Weir, Andy, 109, 136
White, PC, 85
White, Peter, 111
Widdows, H., 150
Wilcox, John, 38, 113
Wilkins, Ralph, 102
Wilks, PS, 36
Willett, Campbell Jack, 33, 95, 96, 113
Willett, Edna, 96
Willetts, Dave, 83, 130, 133
Williams, John, 39
Williams, PC, 25
Williams, Sam, 119
Williams, SC, 29
Williams, Taff, 140
Williams, W., 72, 73
Wilson, Edmund, 52
Wilson, Elizabeth, 52
Wilson, George, 52
Winters, Ted, 145
Wintle, Ellen, 124
Witts, Don, 112
Wood, Arthur, 83, 115
Wood, Fred, 77
Woodward, Arthur, 24
Woodward, Cyril, 27
Workman, George, 32
Wyatt, Gerry, 110, 111
Wyatt, Margaret, 74

Rens van Loon

Creating Organizational Value through Dialogical Leadership

Boiling Rice in Still Water

Springer

Rens van Loon
School of Humanities, Dialogical Leadership
Tilburg University
Tilburg
The Netherlands

ISBN 978-3-319-58888-9   ISBN 978-3-319-58889-6 (eBook)
DOI 10.1007/978-3-319-58889-6

Library of Congress Control Number: 2017940612

© Springer International Publishing AG 2017
This work is subject to copyright. All rights are reserved by the Publisher, whether the whole or part of the material is concerned, specifically the rights of translation, reprinting, reuse of illustrations, recitation, broadcasting, reproduction on microfilms or in any other physical way, and transmission or information storage and retrieval, electronic adaptation, computer software, or by similar or dissimilar methodology now known or hereafter developed.
The use of general descriptive names, registered names, trademarks, service marks, etc. in this publication does not imply, even in the absence of a specific statement, that such names are exempt from the relevant protective laws and regulations and therefore free for general use.
The publisher, the authors and the editors are safe to assume that the advice and information in this book are believed to be true and accurate at the date of publication. Neither the publisher nor the authors or the editors give a warranty, express or implied, with respect to the material contained herein or for any errors or omissions that may have been made. The publisher remains neutral with regard to jurisdictional claims in published maps and institutional affiliations.

Printed on acid-free paper

This Springer imprint is published by Springer Nature
The registered company is Springer International Publishing AG
The registered company address is: Gewerbestrasse 11, 6330 Cham, Switzerland

*Dedicated to my dearly loved grandchildren Nora, Benjamin, Roos, and Marijn.
In our future world, they will give and receive leadership.*

Foreword I

I once asked my father how he gauged success. He offered two measures. First what your child thinks of you when he or she becomes an adult. And second the legacy you leave at work.

My son is young, and I hope someday he will regard me with something close to the love and admiration I feel toward my father. On a closer horizon, I have been thinking a lot about the legacy I will leave when I retire after more than 40 years at Deloitte, most recently serving as Deloitte Global CEO.

I dream of a legacy in which hundreds of thousands of Deloitte professionals around the world wake up every day with a passion to achieve our shared purpose: *to make an impact that matters.* In my leadership roles over the years, I have tried to make a meaningful impact by articulating and fostering a "culture of purpose," in which we work together to achieve amazing things for our clients, colleagues and communities. Therefore, I am excited, and proud, that my own Deloitte colleague, Prof. Dr. Rens van Loon, has outlined in *Dialogical Leadership* a fresh approach to how we can engage with each other to unlock solutions to the most "wicked" problems.

Dr. van Loon's premise begins with communication. Of course, the idea that effective communication is essential to leadership is not new. Communication—and especially the ability to influence rather than dictate direction—has become increasingly important as hierarchical management models go the way of the dinosaurs. However, Dr. van Loon argues that despite more emphasis in recent decades on softer leadership skills such as communications, the potential of *dialogue* is often overlooked.

Therefore, what's different about this book is that, rather than focusing on how to get *your* point across better, it helps the reader better receive *other* points of view. In the process, leaders create more authentic exchanges, build trust and free their teams to move off into new directions previously unthinkable to any single participant. Guided by a deep understanding of psychological and sociological principles, Dr. van Loon provides practical advice and case-studies showing how to use dialogue as an agent of transformation and innovation. It works at both the organizational and individual levels.

A couple years ago, I went from serving 70,000 professionals as chairman of the board for Deloitte in the US, to serving 244,000 professionals around the world as Deloitte Global CEO. My goal has remained consistent: to embed a shared purpose deep into the fabric of the organization's worldwide network. Yet when I made the transition, I was concerned whether I would be able to stay true to my leadership style—which involves frequent, personal touchpoints with colleagues at all levels of the organization. But how could I scale my communications to a much larger and diverse population?

Taking a page from *Dialogical Leadership*, I've learned not to *waste precious face time with lengthy prepared remarks espousing my point of view*. I allow plenty of time for dialogue. If I find the group is reticent, I challenge them to ask me the difficult, or inconvenient, questions. This usually gets people talking. That is step one. Step two is listening. That is a lot harder because it involves getting outside ourselves, and experiencing the discussion from the diverse perspectives of the participants.

In a global organization, the variety of thoseperspectives increases tenfold. Ironically, my own immigrant experience reminds me to appreciate the differences but then focus on the commonality— i.e., shared purpose. For example, I boarded a plane and left India for the first time to attend graduate school in the U.S. As I made the transition from an Indian citizen to an American citizen, I learned to not allow myself to be defined or constrained by labels—because those labels rarely had anything to do with the value of my ideas. However, the value of my ideas had a great deal to do with my own unique experiences and how they combined with others' to create something wholly new.

Several years back my son asked me what I "do". I gave him what I thought was a pretty good description of how I travel around meeting with clients, colleagues and other key stakeholders. When I finally paused, he asked one more question: *Are you changing the world?* That gave me a good indication of the expectations he will have of me once he grows up.

It is an expectation increasingly held by all stakeholders as well. It requires leaders who can effectively manage change in a world marked by technological disruption, political and economic turbulence, and rapidly evolving customers and employee needs. Our best leaders will not be heros with all the answers but those adept at listening and knowing when, and how, to follow the best thinking. *Creating Organizational Value through Dialogical Leadership* is written for anyone interested in becoming that leader. That parent. That person.

Punit Renjen
Deloitte Global CEO

Foreword II

Dialogical leadership helps people to give leadership to others by becoming better leaders of themselves. This is the beating heart of this book, in which Rens van Loon applies this kernel principle to leaders themselves. As being involved in dialogical relationships with others and with oneself at the same time, this kind of leadership blossoms on the fertile soil of mutuality. If leaders are involved in developing dialogical relationships with others, they are, *at the same time,* creating a more advanced and fertile contact with themselves. This highly dynamic two-way leadership, in which two kinds of relationship profit and learn from each other, signifies a definite farewell to any static conception that considers leaders as individuals in themselves and as having 'traits' or 'capacities' that are supposed to determine their behavior. This book teaches us that insight in the largely unknown mind of the other is inextricably bound to insight in the partly known workings of our own minds. Every new contact in a boundary-crossing world is, at the same time, a discovery of the unexpected potentials of our own self.

What do we mean by 'dialogue'? This term, if employed by politicians who want to demonstrate their 'good will' in media exposures, is not more than a buzz word for 'negotiations'. However, this language game has the disadvantage of covering the most precious potentials of dialogue as a highly fertile and even necessary form of interaction in our time. Why being so appreciative of dialogue? The main reason is that we live in a time in which there is no infallible individual who can rightly claim the final and exclusive solution for so-called 'tough' or 'wicked' problems like climate change, the existence of different and even clashing value systems, immigration, international terrorism, and leadership in organizations on their way towards highly discontinuous and largely unpredictable futures. Faced with such thorny problems, individuals, groups, and organizations can do no better job than bringing different people together who, in their combination and mutual complementation, create a dialogical space for the exploration of possibilities and alternatives which are potentially new to each of the participants. It is precisely this dialogical space that in this innovative book is of central concern, not only at the interface between different participants but also *within* the spaces of the mind of each participant.

However, the question of 'What is dialogue'? is still insufficiently answered if we do not take into account its most dynamic aspect. Dialogue is not to be understood as just an exchange of existing opinions or positions. When people share their cherished views and opinions, even if they express their respect and appreciation to each other, there is 'nice contact' but no dialogue. An essential feature of dialogue is that one's initial point of view changes by and during the process of interchange. One's initial position becomes changed and developed during the process itself. Dialogue is not a co-incidence of input and output. On the contrary, the input changes during the process of its formation. Dialogue is not easy, because it requires participants to *open* their initial position to mutual criticism, doubt, change, and, thanks to this openness, to further development. It requires you to give up, or at least, change your initial position to which you were emotionally attached! Therefore, innovation is associated with pain. However, at the end of a dialogue, you get to a point where you are different than before and have the feeling that you have learned something. The dynamic nature of dialogue can only fully be understood if one realizes that the *process* is more important than the *content* of the exchange. The feeling of moving into the right direction and the invention of the appropriate procedures as 'traveling tools' is more decisive for a 'good dialogue' than the content of any preconceived 'right answer.'

Precisely, at this point Rens van Loon introduces the fascinating concept of 'transpositioning'. Together with his clients, often leaders in large companies, he explores the nature of I-positions both in their professional situation (e.g., I as entrepreneur, I as manager, I as coach, I as professional) and in their private situation (e.g., I as a father, I as a sports fanatic, I as a volunteer, I as a hobby farmer). Each of such positions has their own specific energies and motivations. Rather than considering them in their splendid isolation, he brings them in active contact with each other in dialogical way, so that these positions can learn from each other. During the process itself, this results in new combinations of positions in which the positions profit from each other's energies and motivations. Like people with different positions in an organization can combine their energies and motivations to create something new, we find in this book surprising examples of the process in which different I-positions in the self are combined in the form of productive coalitions.

I'm particularly glad to write this foreword because Rens was at the cradle of the Dialogical Self Theory, when he co-authored with me and my late friend and colleague Harry Kempen, the first psychological article on this topic in the *American Psychologist* in 1992.[1] During the 25 years after this publication, several hundreds of books and articles have been published in this area of expertise. I consider this book as a pearl in the continuing stream of publications, a shining example of theoretical rigor and practical relevance to the development of dialogical leadership.

---

[1]Hermans, Kempen, and van Loon 1992.

What is my personal learning process during the dialogical exploration in my own self? As a young boy in primary school, I was seen as a 'dreamer' who was physically present but psychologically absent. I lived in my own internal world, isolated from the others around me. As a result I was continuously ridiculed by my teachers and bullied by my class mates. The dreamer in me was an unacceptable shadow position which had to be removed in the service of my adaptation to a pressing social environment. Only much later in my life, I gradually became aware of the fact that the dreamer was not my weakness but my strength. Actually, the Dialogical Self Theory emerged as a coalition between the dreamer and the scientist as originally separated positions in myself. Finally, I could admit to myself that I'm a 'dreaming scientist.' This coalition formed the basis of a productive cooperation with highly esteemed colleagues and Rens has been and still is a highly prominent one over the years. We both resonate with C.S. Lewis' statement "You are never too old to set another goal or to dream a new dream."

Hubert Hermans
President of the International Society for Dialogical Science,
Founder of the Dialogical Self Theory

Reference

Hermans, H.J.M., Kempen, H.J.G., & van Loon, E.(Rens)J.P. (1992). The dialogical self: Beyond individualism and rationalism. *American Psychologist, 47.*

Preface

I was in Atlanta a week before the 2016 Presidential election and you could sense the tension about what was going to happen. For many people unexpectedly, Donald Trump became President Elect. Barbara Kellerman[2] was one of the speakers during the Atlanta International Leadership Association (ILA) conference in that year, as she had won an award for her work. In her five-minute speech she gave the audience a wake-up call: our assumptions are wrong! It is about the followers. We have to change our perspectives from leader-centric to follower-driven views. And, even more important, technology has changed the relation between leader and followers. A week later, the outcome of the elections proved this to be true. After a Brexit, we had an unexpected winning of Trump for President. In our work as leader-follower researchers we have to pay attention to this change: stop thinking that being a leader is more important than being a follower. Stop thinking that context is not important. Stop thinking that leadership is static, it is a dynamic and unpredictable relation between people, which are not primarily rational. And we have to stop thinking that our (business) universities are capable of delivering good leaders, in the sense of effective, ethical and authentic leaders. We are not. We thoroughly have to rethink our view on leadership and followership, the role of technology and internet, and the context of a globalized world. We have to reconsider how we can teach leadership in a manner that it might contribute to better (in the triple sense as mentioned before: effective, ethical and authentic) followership and leadership.

It is my hope that this book contributes to this adaptive challenge, as our contemporary world seems not to be able to make this shift happen, although we know we should. *Change starts with us*, in leading ourselves, in—not—following others, in leading others in the right direction, in being authentic. We can contribute to the common good, however little and small our influence might be. If you are present in your daily working, with your colleagues, your superiors, with your partner(s), with your children, that might be the start of a transformation. As a follower and as a

---

[2]Kellerman 2012.

leader, act relationally effective, ethical and authentic. I hope this book can help you on that journey. It is not easy, but if you manage to live from the center of this triangle of effectiveness, integrity and authenticity, it will contribute to your reason of being, to the integral purpose in your private life, in your career, and in your professional life in society and organizations ('ikigai'[3]).

Although I tried to write this book accessible andreadable, the topic of dialogical leadership and transformation is an adaptive challenge. I am not giving easy answers, as this will not help you in the end. You have to work through the challenge yourself, you have to reflect, to think and to develop discipline. Since a book is not a living dialogue, and you—as reader—are free to determine your own sequence of reading and digesting the text, I offer a form of guidance. Those who want to read practical examples and cases, start reading Chaps. 6 and 7. Also without the depth of the theory, you are able toget an understanding what is intended here. Those who are primarily interested in how you set up a dialogical transformation process with leaders and followers in an organization, start reading Chaps. 4, and 5. Apart from general explanations, many details are described in these chapters, examples and practical guidelines given. Those who are more deeply interested in the theory of the self, dialogue as an epistemological, ethical and relational form of conversation start with Chaps. 2 and 3. The fundamental assumption in this book is that theself, including the self of leaders and followers, is relationally constructed, dynamic and open for continuous change. If you grasp the essence of what is described in Chap. 2, you understand the basic concepts of Dialogue and Dialogical Leadership. And you will be able to apply this in a natural and spontaneous way. Feel free to read as you wish. The book is a document that comes to live in relation with you. Write your comments in the text, agree, disagree, think and rethink, become more aware of your assumptions. If this happens, I feel we reach what I hope. Chapters 2–6, and 8 start with an overview of key points, and at the end of each chapter there are some questions for further reflection.

Tilburg, The Netherlands   Rens van Loon

---

[3]'Ikigai' is the Japanese concept, meaning a *reason for being* or a *life worth living,* all elements of life including: work, career, hobbies, relationships, friendships, spirituality, and so on. Nick van Dam used this concept in his inaugural address as a professor of Corporate Learning at Nyenrode University (The Netherlands), to illustrate the importance of the discovery of your purpose as bringing meaning to your life. This is important in the corporate world, where employees can be at risk as work-life gets out of balance. (van Dam 2016, p. 93).

Acknowledgements

I am grateful to clients who gave trust to work with them, to my teams and myself. If you talk about leadership development and coaching, it is primarily about *trust*. You don't get trust based on your title or reputation of your company. You receive it in conversations and collaboration as a result of mutual respect, a promise of impact and fulfillment. As a reflective practitioner, I work for more than 30 years with clients. Through this experience, I was able to develop a concept of *Dialogical Leadership*. I feel great respect for the people I have worked with, and I am particularly grateful to those who permitted me to write about our experiences, insights, good and bad results. Special gratitude I owe to the Océ team. We worked together for a long period, and I am honored that I could present our cooperation as a case-study. You can't do this work on your own; it is possible with professional colleagues. I want to mention Tina Strookappe, Jeroen Seegers, Arnold Roozendaal, Hebe Boonzaaijer, Naomi van Loon, Katrijn Knaapen, Angel Buster, and many others I have worked with.

This book has its origin with my teachers. Ad Peperzak, Professor Emeritus of Ethics, showed me how to think conceptually by conscientiously reading and analyzing texts. Ulrich Libbrecht, Professor Emeritus of Comparative Philosophy, Mathematics, and Sinology, demonstrated conceptually what *free energy* and *freedom* mean. Hubert Hermans, Professor Emeritus of Personality Psychology, introduced me to methodologies and how to apply nomothetic psychology to singular individual human beings. An important contribution in the realization of this book was provided by my teachers of Tai Chi. They let me experience how thinking and feeling are based in our bodies.

I started this book around 2010. I used my travel and waiting time in airplanes and airports to read articles and books on the subject for several years. In 2014, I took a sabbatical to think and write for several months in a row. The result was a rich, yet unstructured text. Thanks to my reviewers at the time, I suspended my view and delayed writing for two more years before completing the manuscript. I had the good fortune of meticulous reviewers who provided me with valuable feedback: Hubert Hermans, Ken Gergen, John Rijsman, Katrijn Knaapen, Ronald

Meijers, Gerda van Dijk, and Pom Somkabcharti. In particular, I owe much to Pom, as she supported me in designing the structure of the book. I deeply thank all these people for their time and focused energy in reading, reflecting and reviewing Dialogical Leadership.

Over the years, I had conversations with many people on the role and meaning of *dialogue and leadership* as the topic of this book. Hubert Hermans is my reliable partner in dialogue as we meet often, talking about all kind of topics, related to Dialogical Self Theory, the organization of the Dialogical Self Academy (DSA) and the biennial conferences of the International Society of Dialogical Science (ISDS). During the last conference in Lublin (Poland) we had extensive conversations on the topic. I owe much to my colleagues within this network, as ideas grow and mature into new concepts and methodologies in this context. Masayoshi Morioka and his Japanese colleagues vividly and naturally bring to life one of the central concepts of this book, '*ma*' (space). I also thank my colleague from Israel, Dina Nir, for our conversations over the years and the insight of what dialogue means when you are in ongoing hostilities. Ken Gergen's work is a rich source of inspiration for me, his feedback and core insights as expressed in *Relational Being* have influenced me profoundly. Our conversations at the dinner table with Mary joining us were very joyful. Jutta König stimulates our research by having developed a method to apply Dialogical Self Theory to cross-cultural leadership. The process has just begun and I hope the book contributes to this adaptive challenge.

I also thank my colleagues and board members of the International Leadership Association (ILA). Our meetings and yearly conferences are sources of inspiration for anybody who wants to think, discuss and write about leadership and followership. In particular I owe much to Jean Lipman Blumen, Ira Chaleff, and Jill Hickmann as they helped me to fundamentally rethink the essence of followership. Our chair Katherine Tyler Scott is a living example of deep listening, enabling dialogue and, leading of our board meetings inspired by the core values of ILA. Mansour Javidan's view is an eye-opener for reconsidering cross-cultural leadership and followership. Barbara Kellerman encouraged us to keep the feet on the ground and accurately assess the results of our efforts in leadership services. Georgia Sorenson made me aware of the value of invisible leadership. I appreciate collaborating with Rob Koonce, as we did in *Followership in Action: Cases and Commentaries*.

I owe my colleagues within Deloitte. Ardie van Berkel, Wim Scheper, Yves van Durme, and Miriam Tops who enabled my sabbatical in 2014. With Euan Isles, Fred Miller, Nick van Dam, Adam Canwell, Neil Neveras, and Marjory Knight, I had intense conversations and collaborations about the content of leadership frameworks and programs for clients. Specially, I thank Katrijn Knaapen, Karlijn Kouwenhoven, and Tessa van den Berg for being my co-authors in three published articles/chapters that paved the way for this book. Without these primary activities, intense thinking and rethinking of the materials this book would not have become reality. I appreciate the discussions in our leadership group with Katrijn Knaapen, Angel Buster, Heike Dekker-Schäch, and others.

Acknowledgements

Rijk van Kooy is the creator of the visuals in the book, and thanks to our co-operative process of *'visualizing the invisible'*, this book has become a piece of art. Martijn van Hal is my co-author in Chap. 7, and reviewed the entire book. With Wassili Bertoen, I had intense conversations on leadership and innovation. I am grateful to Fred Nijland for his cooperation and review of the sections on innovation. Angel Buster was my reliable reviewer and support over the last three months. Petra Tito, Human Capital Leader at Deloitte, supported the process of writing, mentally, and business-wise. Jorrit Volkers, Dean of Deloitte University EMEA, reviewed the text, and, he showed me in practice how to lead a large organization. I am grateful that Punit Renjen, Deloitte's global CEO, was willing to write a foreword for this book. If we talk about *'making an impact that matters'*, we have to be skillful in the art of dialogue, being present and opening our minds to other perspectives than those already known. After my conversation with Roger Dassen, who was CEO in Deloitte Netherlands in 2009, as part of my solicitation, I drove home and I felt I was willing to work for this man. His inspirational style and the way he appreciates a deep dialogue with his people (with me during that interview), gave me a sense that I had found a good home-base to work from.

At Tilburg University, I feel supported by the Dean Willem Drees, the Vice-Dean Paul Post, and by my colleague professors, Gerda van Dijk, John Goedee, and Freek Peters. Especially, I owe much to Arie de Ruijter, as he illuminated one of the most difficult topics in leadership: *power in relation to dialogue*. John Rijsman made me aware of the importance and possibility of doing reflective practitioner research in an unprejudiced and flexible manner. Jaap Denissen brought me in contact with the *'wisdom of the leader'*. Gerda van Dijk is an important source of inspiration, as we work together closely, and clearly know which direction we want to go with our research and teachings. Our article *'Dialogue as Condition Zero'* is the starting point of a fascinating quest to explore, describe, and teach 'good leadership'. At Tilburg University, I appreciate the conversations I have with the chancellor Emile Aarts, as these are a source and a reality check of our ideas about leadership and dialogue.

I thank the publisher Springer for the support during the process of producing this book. In particular, Stefan Einarson and Chris Wilby. A good relation with the publisher is a basic condition for quality. A book cannot come to life without people supporting the author in his daily activities, as almost nobody nowadays has the opportunity to solely focus on the process of writing. Hilda Koevoets is my trusted executive assistant in the complicated process of planning and organizing. Roos Bos edited the last version of the text in detail.

In 2016, I made a trip to Japan with our youngest daughter Iris. In that period, we hiked from temple to temple, and we enjoyed Japanese culture. We had conversations about life, about being father and daughter, about the mutuality in that relation, about leading and following. As a father, I followed my daughter in Japan, as she followed her parents during a trip to the US 13 years before. I learn a lot about the essence of leading and following through our children Mieke, Pieter,

Maarten, Meike, Iris, Max and our grandchildren Nora, Benjamin, Roos, and Marijn. Humans are born into a culture, and have to be initiated in the traditions and regulations, the culture of their future world. Educating children is to some extent closing the open minds of children, with a promise to re-open, consciously, and confirm their freedom to think, feel and act in an autonomous way. When the grandchildren are with us, we lead them with love and respect for the young life. They will be the leaders and followers of the future, but for now, we have to set the right example of what we want them to become: good human beings, authentic, and effective. That is why I dedicate this book to them. They open our hearts.

Without my wife Roos, I would not have written this book. I thank her for being an anchor in my life, physically, emotionally, rationally, and spiritually. We have loved each other since 1974 and have learned the *lessons of life* individually as a shared experience. I am grateful.

References

Kellerman, B. (2012). *The end of leadership*. NY: HarperCollins Publishers.
Van Dam, N.N.H., (2016). *Learn or Lose*. Inaugural Lecture. Nyenrode Business University.

Contents

1	Introduction	1
	References	4

Part I The Theory

2	Dialogical Self Theory	7
2.1	Self as a 'Society of Mind'	8
	2.1.1 Weaving Self and Dialogue Together	9
	2.1.2 Dynamic Positioning of the Self	14
2.2	Relationally Constructing Self in Language	16
	2.2.1 'Centering My High Note'	19
	2.2.2 Self as a Dynamic and Relational Verb	20
	2.2.3 Deriving Meaning from the Context	21
	2.2.4 Independency as Relationally Embedded	22
	2.2.5 "To Be Is to Be Relational"	23
2.3	Key Concepts in Dialogical Self Theory	24
	2.3.1 An Act of Self-Reflection (Meta-Position)	24
	2.3.2 Being (De-)Stabilized (Centering and De-Centering)	25
2.4	Information and Space in Positioning Self	26
	2.4.1 Energy and Information	27
	2.4.2 Free Energy	28
	2.4.3 Energy Space	29
	2.4.4 Creating Space in Dialogical Relations	32
	2.4.5 Space as 'Space Between'	34
2.5	Transposing Patterns of Behavior	35
	2.5.1 An Empty Self?	36
2.6	Reflections on My Personal Narrative 1	37
	2.6.1 Fragments of My Self-Narrative in 1987	38
	2.6.2 Becoming Aware of I-Positions	38
	2.6.3 Looking Back to My Earlier Self	39

	2.7	Questions for Further Reflection........................	39
	References...		41
3	**Dialogical Leadership**..		43
	3.1	Leadership as a Relational Process......................	44
		3.1.1 Good Leaders Deploy Different Styles	45
	3.2	The Myth of the Leader–Follower Dichotomy	46
		3.2.1 Good Leadership as Effective and Ethical...........	47
		3.2.2 Leadership Is 'By Definition' Relational............	50
		3.2.3 A Confrontation with Values......................	51
		3.2.4 A Dynamic Leadership Concept	52
	3.3	What Is Dialogical Leadership?........................	53
		3.3.1 Leading Self and Others	55
		3.3.2 When to Apply Dialogical Leadership?.............	56
		3.3.3 Four Pillars of Dialogical Leadership	58
	3.4	Reflections on My Personal Narrative 2	58
		3.4.1 My Secret Name	60
		3.4.2 A Distinctive Inner Voice	60
		3.4.3 Centering My Self.............................	61
	3.5	Questions for Further Reflection........................	61
	References...		63

Part II The Practice

4	**Creating Conditions for Generative Dialogue**...................		67
	4.1	From Thoughts to Thinking	68
		4.1.1 Dialogue as Meaning Flowing Through Us...........	69
		4.1.2 Dialogue as Face to Face Encounter	70
	4.2	The Art of Thinking Together	71
		4.2.1 Listening with an Open Mind	72
		4.2.2 Suspending Your Judgment.......................	72
		4.2.3 Respecting Other Views	73
		4.2.4 Voicing from the Heart	73
		4.2.5 Creating Conditions for Dialogue	74
		4.2.6 Conversation, Debate, and Dialogue: Crises in the Process.............................	74
		4.2.7 Switching Between Debate and Dialogue	78
	4.3	Generating New Meaning, Transforming Reality	80
		4.3.1 Mutual Understanding...........................	80
		4.3.2 Being a Multibeing	81
		4.3.3 Generative Dialogue	82
		4.3.4 The Power of Storytelling........................	83
		4.3.5 The Impact of Affirmation.......................	83
		4.3.6 Reflecting on Yourself..........................	84
		4.3.7 Third-Person Listening	84

4.4	Recognizing the Other		86
	4.4.1	Creating Space	87
	4.4.2	Recognizing Alterity	87
	4.4.3	Innovation as Opening the Mind	88
	4.4.4	Mutually Understanding	88
	4.4.5	Power Differences	89
	4.4.6	Being Fully Present	89
4.5	Dialogue and Transformation		90
	4.5.1	Emerged Accidentally, Defended Inflexibly	90
	4.5.2	Conditions for Change	91
	4.5.3	Changing the System	93
4.6	Creating Conditions for Generative Leadership Dialogue		94
	4.6.1	Generic Aspects for a Generative Dialogue	94
	4.6.2	Setting up an Individual Leadership Dialogue	99
	4.6.3	The Role of the Facilitator in Setting up a Dialogue for a Team	102
	4.6.4	Qualities of a Good Facilitator	103
	4.6.5	Categories of Interventions	103
4.7	Some Considerations		104
	4.7.1	This Kind of Facilitator Doesn't Exist	104
	4.7.2	Controlling the World	105
	4.7.3	Power as an Interfering Factor	105
4.8	Reflections on My Personal Narrative 3		107
	4.8.1	Developing a Habit	107
	4.8.2	A Moment of Crisis	107
	4.8.3	Out of My Comfort Zone	108
4.9	Questions for Further Reflection		110
References			111

5 Towards a Theory of Embodied Dialogue 113

5.1	A Dynamic Balance		114
	5.1.1	Physically Disconnected Words	115
	5.1.2	Being Born into a Culture	116
	5.1.3	Defining Ourselves	116
5.2	Dialogue as Generating New Meaning		122
	5.2.1	Dialogue as a Participative Mode of Interacting	125
	5.2.2	Applying Dialogue in a Leadership Context: A Methodology	129
5.3	Exploring I-Positions in Dialogue		131
5.4	Resistance in Dialogue		133
5.5	Creating Transformational Space		135
5.6	A Methodology of Connecting I-Positions		137
5.7	The Process of Reconciling I-Positions Illustrated		141
	5.7.1	"I Feel Frustrated"	141
	5.7.2	The Entrepreneur and the Hobby Farmer	142
	5.7.3	"The Gate of Frustration Is Closed"	145

5.8		Reflections on My Personal Narrative 4	147
	5.8.1	Moments of Transformation	147
	5.8.2	Shifting Dominance	148
	5.8.3	Suspending My Will Power	150
5.9		Questions for Further Reflection	150
References			151

Part III The Impact

6 Dialogical Leadership and Wicked Issues 155

6.1		Living in an Unpredictable World—the Implications for Leaders	156
	6.1.1	Studying Leadership Is not yet Being a Leader	157
	6.1.2	Creating Conditions for Dialogue	158
	6.1.3	Constructive Depolarizing	159
6.2		Leading Change Through Dialogue	161
	6.2.1	Change and Transformation	162
	6.2.2	Starting with 'Why'	163
	6.2.3	Visioning and Voicing	165
6.3		When to Apply the Dialogical Leadership Approach?	167
	6.3.1	Taking a Bird's Eye View	169
	6.3.2	From 'What' to 'Who'	169
6.4		Case-Studies	170
6.5		Case-Study *Darrell*: Sailor-Captain and General Manager	172
	6.5.1	"I Lost My I"	172
	6.5.2	Transposing Sailor-Captain into General Manager	174
6.6		Case-Study *Marc*: Engineer, Artist, and Karate-Teacher	176
	6.6.1	"I Have to Open Up"	177
	6.6.2	The Painter Balances the Engineer	177
6.7		Case-Study *Michelle*: HR-Director and Mother	180
	6.7.1	"I as Burned Out"	180
	6.7.2	"Being Overruled"	182
	6.7.3	Reconciling Control and Care	184
6.8		Case-Study *Ian*: Changing My/Our Destiny	186
	6.8.1	"I as Taking My Responsibility"	186
	6.8.2	"Improving the Quality of Life"	188
6.9		Case-Study *Nicholas*: Listening to My Inner Voice	190
	6.9.1	"I Want to Be Independent"	190
	6.9.2	"I Want to Be Heard"	191
6.10		Future Research	191
6.11		Reflections on My Personal Narrative 5	194
	6.11.1	Solving Wicked Issues for Myself	194
	6.11.2	I Am Not a Master of My Destiny	195
	6.11.3	My Magnetic Needle	195

	6.12 Questions for Further Reflection	197
	References	197

7 Case-Study. Dialogical Leadership and Teamwork 199
    7.1 Leadership and Innovation with Océ 199
    7.2 Creating a Mindset for Trust and Dialogue 201
    7.3 The Power of Sharing Personal Narratives 209
    7.4 Exploring Team Values and Team Purpose 218
    7.5 Taking a Pause 223
    7.6 Practicing New Ways of Interaction 225
    7.7 New Challenges and Old Habits 230
    7.8 Reflections 234
        7.8.1 Dealing with Misunderstanding 234
        7.8.2 Dealing with Paradoxes 236
        7.8.3 Paradoxes in Terms of I-Positions 237
        7.8.4 Working with Core-Values 238
        7.8.5 The Strength of Weak Ties 239
    References 239

Part IV The Implications

8 The Future of Leadership 243
    8.1 You Are *Always* Both 245
    8.2 Redefining Research into Leadership and Culture 250
        8.2.1 An Adaptive Challenge 252
    8.3 Leading Innovation 254
        8.3.1 Leading Exponential Organizations 258
    8.4 Leading on Big Data 259
        8.4.1 Reality Is Unpredictable 260
        8.4.2 Unstructured Data in a Box 260
        8.4.3 Going Forward 262
    8.5 Listening to Silence 264
    8.6 Reflection 264
    8.7 Questions for Further Reflection 266
    References 267

9 Boiling Rice in Still Water 269
    References 271

About the Author

Rens van Loon is a professor and a consultant specialized in leadership and organizational change and transformation. He graduated from Radboud University Nijmegen in the Netherlands with a degree in philosophy in 1986 and completed a Ph.D. in social sciences and psychology in 1996. In 2015 he was appointed the world's first Professor of Dialogical Leadership in the School of Humanities at Tilburg University, The Netherlands. A consultant for more than 25 years, he has developed worldwide leadership programs and worked closely with leaders in both the private and public sectors.

A trained psychologist, he began, over 15 years ago, to combine Dialogical Self Theory with his own practical experience as a consultant. The result was Dialogical Leadership, a new approach to leadership, teams, and organizations explored in this book.

Van Loon is the author of three previous books, published in Dutch, and of numerous academic papers on leadership, dialogue and change. He has been a director with Deloitte Consulting since 2009. He serves as a Board Member of the International Leadership Association (ILA), is active in the International Society for Dialogical Science (ISDS), and the Dialogical Self Academy (DSA).

List of Figures

Fig. 2.1	The spirit of the dialogical self	11
Fig. 2.2	Grayson Perry. A map of days	17
Fig. 2.3	Grayson Perry. A map of days—detail	18
Fig. 2.4	Sources of information	33
Fig. 2.5	Reflections on my personal narrative 1	40
Fig. 3.1	A contextual and relational leadership concept	49
Fig. 3.2	A dynamic leadership framework	54
Fig. 3.3	Four pillars of dialogical leadership	59
Fig. 3.4	Reflections on my personal narrative 2	62
Fig. 4.1	Creating conditions for dialogue	75
Fig. 4.2	Switching between debate and dialogue	79
Fig. 4.3	Creating conditions for generative leadership dialogue	97
Fig. 4.4	Setting up an individual leadership dialogue	100
Fig. 4.5	Reflections on my personal narrative 3	109
Fig. 5.1	Being born into a culture	117
Fig. 5.2	Defining ourselves	121
Fig. 5.3	Dialogue as generating new meaning	123
Fig. 5.4	Dialogue as a participative mode of interacting	127
Fig. 5.5	Applying dialogue in a leadership context: a methodology	128
Fig. 5.6	Exploring I-positions in dialogue	132
Fig. 5.7	A methodology of connecting I-positions	138
Fig. 5.8	Case-Study Peter 1	143
Fig. 5.9	Case-Study Peter 2	144
Fig. 5.10	Case-Study Peter 3	146
Fig. 5.11	Reflections on my personal narrative 4	149
Fig. 6.1	When to apply dialogical leadership	160
Fig. 6.2	Type of problems and approaches	168
Fig. 6.3	Case-Study Darrell 1	173
Fig. 6.4	Case-Study Darrell 2	175
Fig. 6.5	Case-Study Marc 1	178
Fig. 6.6	Case-Study Marc 2	179

Fig. 6.7	Case-Study Michelle 1.	181
Fig. 6.8	Case-Study Michelle 2.	183
Fig. 6.9	Case-Study Michelle 3.	185
Fig. 6.10	Case-Study Ian 1.	187
Fig. 6.11	Case-Study Ian 2.	189
Fig. 6.12	Case-Study Nicholas 1.	192
Fig. 6.13	Case-Study Nicholas 2.	193
Fig. 6.14	Reflections on my personal narrative 5.	196
Fig. 7.1	Journey overview: leading innovation to grow.	200
Fig. 7.2	Individual preparation: creating the mindset for trust and dialogue.	202
Fig. 7.3	Case-Study vice-president strategy.	204
Fig. 7.4	The power of sharing personal narratives.	210
Fig. 7.5	Lencioni's view on team development.	214
Fig. 7.6	Exploring team values and team purpose.	220
Fig. 7.7	Exploring team values and team purpose.	221
Fig. 7.8	New challenges and old habits.	231
Fig. 8.1	Emergent mindset: from hierarchical to dialogical.	247
Fig. 8.2	Overview of concepts.	257

Chapter 1
Introduction

> *So written words are like death. Texts belong in schoolbooks. Only the process of metamorphosis in speaking a lively language may reveal the truth and only spoken words can react fast enough to justify the eternal progress of active thinking.*
> Laurent Binet (Binet 2016, 173; translated by the author.)

In this book, we develop a new approach to leadership that draws on the work of Dutch psychologist Hubert Hermans, best known for Dialogical Self Theory. Dating from the 1990s, Dialogical Self Theory, which Clark University professor Jeffrey Arnett has called one of "the most important and original new theories in the social sciences in the past 20 years", sees the 'success' or psychological 'health' of the individual as partly dependent on his or her ability to integrate different roles or 'I-positions' through 'internal and external dialogue'. It holds that where integration is poor and dialogue defective, dysfunction and reduced wellbeing usually follow. The book extends these ideas to the psychology of leadership, arguing that 'generative' dialogue and reciprocal exchange are necessary for effective, authentic, and ethical leadership. And for the long-term health and wellbeing of an organization.

Despite more emphasis on leadership skills such as communication and talking and listening in recent decades, the true potential of dialogue is often overlooked. *Dialogical Leadership* re-defines dialogue as an agent for positive change at both corporate, team and individual levels, and as a 'creative force' in organizations.

What are the conditions for change and transformation in the way people think, feel and act and what is the role of dialogue in creating them? How does 'generative' dialogue differ from other forms of conversation? What is the role of dialogue in solving 'wicked problems'[1] and in high-performance teamwork and innovation? What are the implications of dialogue for daily working life, for the daily practices of leaders and followers? What is the impact of dialogue and a dialogic mindset on wider society?

In my view, generative dialogue is 'condition zero' for solving wicked problems and coping with the challenges of a volatile, uncertain, complex and ambiguous

---

[1] 'Wicked problems' are issues where no fixed answer is available. 'Complex issues', 'Adaptive challenges' are other terms used to indicate this type of problems leaders are confronted with.

world. I would like to redefine the leader—follower dichotomy in dialogue, where the balance of power might shift, and the good leader 'follows'. Over-all, I wish to illustrate that organizations are complex, organic and dynamic systems, whose future is shaped partly by relationships and interactions between people—by the quality of dialogue.

In my work as a professional consultant, I regularly have in-depth conversations with clients, mostly leaders in organizations. We often talk about change and transformation, and how you get things done in the company. The power of a good dialogue is a way to open up people for complexities, for the multileveled interaction with their context and for finding creative solutions for tough issues. What I would like to achieve with this book is to arrive at a deeper understanding of the transformative character of the dialogue, primarily in the context of organizations, teams and individuals. What differentiates dialogue from other forms of conversation, such as debate and discussion?

The book is written for r(l)eaders who want to understand this process of influencing. To deeply understand how a process of transformation can take place through dialogue. I will describe the conditions for transformation and describe these in a conceptual and practical manner. Based on my experience both as an academic and a business and leadership consultant, the book explains the core concepts of Dialogical Leadership and how it is applied in practice. I learned the process of dialogue, debate and discussion by a combination of experience, reflection and theory. I invite the reader to go through a similar process: reflect on your experience and apply theory to improve the way you act, think and feel. I feed you in this cycle by writing on different levels. My colleague Tessa van den Berg and I used this as the basic concept to master the skills of dialogue and dialogical leadership.[2] I owe Ken Gergen, who set an example for me to write in this way in his book *Relational Being*.[3]

The first level is the *academic* voice. Dialogical Leadership is based on *Dialogical Self Theory*. In the theory and practice of Dialogical Leadership we apply 'generative dialogue' as a key mechanism for transformation in organizations. This view rejects the idea that successful organizations are purely 'rational systems' that conform to scripts laid down by leaders, and it puts dialogue and co-creation—'reciprocal exchange'—at the heart of successful change and transformational journeys. The Dialogical Self Theory starts from the kinds of questions leaders ask themselves—their 'internal dialogue'—and the quality of their interactions with others—their 'external dialogues'. The main purpose of *Dialogical Leadership* is to achieve a deeper understanding of how to apply generative dialogue in circumstances in which it proves transformative. In my work as a professor of Dialogical Leadership, I have experienced that students appreciate the dialogical approach as an attractive one. They mention that the approach contributes to an

---

[2]Van Loon and Van den Berg 2016.
[3]Gergen 2009b.

increased awareness and development of ethical leadership.[4] The concept of Dialogical Leadership could be added to the academic discourse on leadership as a required approach for 'wicked issues'.

The second level is the voice of the *practitioner*. In my work as a consultant, I've seen individual people, teams and organizations make positive changes as a result of insights gained through individual, team and group dialogues. Sharing this experience is an important motive for this book. I hope the concept contributes to the professional education of current and future leaders and members of organizations. We have lots of examples that are illuminating for the reader. I have experienced in a period of more than thirty years working with leaders and members in organizations, as individuals, in teams and in large groups the vital role of dialogue in the process of change. Through these experiences, I have become fascinated by moments of transformation, moments that matter. I have witnessed people transforming deeply through insights in individual and group dialogues. My drive is to better understand and more precisely describe what happens in these moments of transformation. How can we create conditions to make this happen? Do we recognize it also when happening spontaneously? The importance of truly understanding lies in the role leaders and members have in processes of organizational and individual transformation. Too many leaders still think they can transform their organization without changing their way of acting, thinking and feeling themselves. If we can describe these moments of transformation more precisely, hopefully we can design educational and training programs to teach leaders and members of organizations in applying these lessons. We give examples of practice on individual level, on team level and illustrations derived from change in organizations as a whole. Cases are anonymized, unless permission was explicitly given to mention the name of the company or the individual.

The third level is my *personal experience*. In this book, I experiment with autoethnography.[5] I use my personal development as a case. At the end of a chapter, I reflect on my personal narrative related to the chapter, titled *Reflections on my Personal Narrative*. I describe and reflect the development of myself in terms of dialogical self-theory, change and transformation. I share with you as a reader some of my experiences and insights that transformed my way of thinking, feeling and acting, professionally and personally.

---

[4]Dialogue is an ethical theory, as it starts with respect for alterity as the moral feature of dialogue par excellence. Alterity implies discovery, acceptance and stimulation of the differences between self and other in dialogical relationships (Hermans and Konopka (2010, 183). Respect for alterity is one of the crucial characteristics of dialogue, and in that sense 'ethical'. Hickman combines in her leadership framework effectiveness and ethics (2016, xii–xiii). My longer term scientific ambition is to demonstrate and empirically validate the relation between effective, authentic, and ethical leadership conceptually and practically as one. I cannot succeed in that ambition in this book, as there is more scientific research and practitioner reflection needed.

[5]Gergen (2009b) uses this expression for describing your self-narrative.

Dialogical Leadership offers a new concept of I-positioning, drawing on Hubert Hermans'[6] Dialogical Self Theory, called *transpositioning or transposing*. This term will be coined in the text. *Dialogue as generating new meaning*—what Ken Gergen[7] refers to as 'generative dialogue'—is elaborated. And a *conceptual dialogue map*, a guide for conversations that combines works by William Isaacs[8] and Masayoshi Morioka[9] will be presented. I wish you as a reader an experience of reflecting *on, in* and *for action* as a leader and as a member of a larger community. I sincerely wish this reflection contributes to the quality of your leadership *and* your membership in the organizations and societies you live in.

References

Binet, L. (2015). *La septième fonction du language*. Editions Grasset & Fasquelle. [De Zevende Functie van Taal. (2016). Amsterdam: Meulenhoff Boekerij. Dutch translation].

Gergen, K. J. (2009a). *An invitation to social construction* (2nd ed.). London: Sage.

Gergen, K. J. (2009b). *Relational being: Beyond self and community*. New York: Oxford University Press.

Hermans, H. J. M. (Ed.). (2016). *Nine methods for stimulating a dialogical self: Applications in groups, cultures and organizations*. Switzerland: Springer.

Hermans, H. J. M., & Hermans-Konopka, A. (2010). *Dialogical self theory. Positioning and counter-positioning in a globalizing society*. Cambridge: University Press.

Hickman, G. R. (2016). *Leading organizations: Perspectives for a new era*. Thousand Oaks: Sage.

Isaacs, W. N. (1993). Taking flight: Dialogue, collective thinking and organizational learning. *Organizational Dynamics*, 24–39.

Isaacs, W. N. (1999). *Dialogue and the art of thinking together. A pioneering approach to communicating in business and in life*. New York, NY: Doubleday.

Morioka, M. (2008). Voices of the self in the therapeutic chronotype: *Utuschi* and *Ma*. *International Journal for Dialogical Science, 3*(1), 93–108.

Morioka, M. (2012). Creating dialogical space in psychotherapy: meaning-generating chronotype of *ma*. In H. J. M. Hermans, & T. Gieser (Eds.), *Handbook of Dialogical Self Theory* (pp. 390–404). Cambridge: University Press.

Van Loon, E. (Rens) J. P., & Van den Berg, T. (2016). Dialogical Leadership. The "Other" way to coach leaders. In H. J. M. Hermans (Ed.), *Nine Methods for stimulating a dialogical self: Applications in groups, cultures and organizations* (pp. 75–93).

---

[6]Hermans and Hermans-Konopka 2010; Hermans 2016.

[7]Gergen 2009a, b.

[8]Isaacs 1993, 1999.

[9]Morioka 2012, 2008.

Part I
The Theory

> *By three methods we may learn wisdom:*
> *First, by reflection, which is noblest;*
> *second, by imitation, which is easiest;*
> *and third by experience, which is the bitterest.*
> Confucius (Chinese Philospher 551–479 BC.)

We live in a world of increasing interconnectedness and continuous change. Our world has become extremely transparent (accounting reporting requirements included in regulations), perpetually uncertain and fragile (black swans like 9/11, tsunamis), instantly obsolete (speed of changes, e.g., information technology, genomic medicine and organic chemistry), and is deeply complex and unpredictable (e.g., energy renewal, environmental sustainability, terrorism and radicalization issues).[1] As society, we face significant challenges, including recurring financial and economic crises—which also represent a crises of leadership—and issues relating to the public sector: "how do we rethink and recalibrate security, healthcare and education?"[2] Some of these issues are global, like population growth, a growing chasm between rich and poor, food safety and the food supply, depletion of natural resources, etcetera. In such a complex world we are confronted with issues that have to be designated as complex and wicked.

The Dutch Prime Minister Rutte answered in an interview about Putin, when he was asked about the opinion the Russian President might have: "Then I have to look into Putin's head. That's technically difficult."[3] I quote this to make us think about the process of knowing: to identify what's going on in someone's mind we have to involve in a conversation with that person, and ask. We have to get access to his/her self. If somebody is not willing to share his or her thoughts with me, I have to guess or hypothesize, but I will not know for sure. Even if you tell me, I can't be sure. You might be afraid to tell me what you really think as I am your superior, or you admire me, or you never say what you really think, you don't want to disappoint me, etcetera. Answers are given in a relation between people. Even if I force by physical and/or psychological pressure you to open up your thoughts, you can remain silent and don't give me access to your thinking and feeling.

---

[1]Helt 2007; Ismail 2014; Hagel III, Brown, and Davison 2012; Johansen 2012.
[2]Van Dijk 2014.
[3]Buitenhof January 12, 2014. (Dutch TV program).

© Springer International Publishing AG 2017
R. van Loon, *Creating Organizational Value through Dialogical Leadership*,
DOI 10.1007/978-3-319-58889-6_1

Is it possible that our thoughts are somewhere *in* our brains *as substances*? That future amended research with MRI scans will enable us to read your process of thinking directly, without you declaring, and maybe even before effecting your thoughts? Antonio Damasio, the prominent neurobiological researcher: "The fact that no one sees the minds of others, conscious or not, is mysterious. We can observe their bodies and their actions, what they do or say or write, we can make informed guesses about what they think. But we cannot observe their minds, and only we ourselves can observe ours, from the inside, and through a rather narrow window."[4] Damasio's efforts to solve the mystery are focused on how the process of the conscious mind meshes with the other processes of physical cells living together in aggregates called tissues, how the mind and the body are relating. With all our psychological and neuroscientific experiments we don't know yet exactly how we *immediately* know that the man who just entered my room is 'Peter'. Going one step further than perceiving identity: Peter is Peter. How do we perceive that Peter is truly *Peter*, that he is authentic?[5]

References

Damasio, A. (2003). Mental self: The person within. *Nature, 423*(6937), 227–227.
Damasio, A. (2012). *Self comes to mind: Constructing the conscious brain*. Random House LLC.
Hagel III, J., Brown, J. S., & Davison, L. (2012). *The power of pull: How small moves, smartly made, can set big things in motion*. Basic Books.
Helt, G. (2007). *Beyond. Towards a new paradigm for leadership*. glh@moosewilson.com
Ismail, S., Malone, M.S. & Van Geest, Y. (2014). *Exponential Organizations: Why new organizations are ten times better, faster, and cheaper than yours (and what to do about it)*. Diversion Books.
Johansen, R. (2012). *Leaders make the future: Ten new leadership skills for an uncertain world*. Berrett-Koehler Publishers.
Kahneman, D. (2011). *Thinking, fast and slow*. New York: Farrar, Straus and Giroux.
Van Dijk, G. (2014). *Organizational Ecology: Simplicity in Complexity*. Tilburg University Press.

---

[4] Damasio 2012; 2003.
[5] Kahneman 2011.

Chapter 2
Dialogical Self Theory

> *'I' is a verb dressed as a noun*
> Julian Baggini (Baggini 2011, 126)

Abstract

- 'To be' is 'to be related'.
- Getting access to '*self*' is a *relational* process.
- Dialogical Self Theory conceptualizes self in terms of a dynamic *multiplicity of relatively autonomous I-positions* in the (extended) landscape of the mind.
- Core of Dialogical Self Theory and Social Constructionism are permanently changing *relations, internally and externally*. At the heart of both views is self as 'a continuously changing process of relational co-creating and relational positioning and counter/re-positioning in space and time'.
- *Free energy* is the human capacity to move away from immanent natural patterns.
  Without free energy, there is no self.
  Without free energy, there is no dialogue.
- The Japanese word '*ma*' combines in one concept: *physical space, temporal space, relationship and silence.*
- The concepts of *creating 'ma'*—as a living pause—and *freeing energy* enable us to understand the processes of change and transformation.
- '*Transposing*' or '*transpositioning*' is a mental act to bring I-positions from one domain in life/work to another in order to create transformation in the position repertoire. The 'energy' of one I-position is brought to another.
- I-positions can be described as 'empty' concepts, which you can apply on a variety of situations.

In this chapter, the theoretical background of the Dialogical Self is our subject. We describe self as a *society of mind* (Sect. 2.1), and explore the role of *language, relational, social constructionism* (Sect. 2.2). Some of the *key concepts* of Dialogical Self Theory are explained, which will be consistently applied throughout the text (Sect. 2.3). *Energy*, *information* and *space* are defined as basic conditions for a dialogical self (Sect. 2.4). The concept of *transpositioning* is explained as a technique to create transformational space through dialogue *in* the *self* and *in relation* with *others* (Sect. 2.5). This chapter is completed with a personal reflection, where I apply the concept of Dialogical Self to my own development through time.

2.1 Self as a 'Society of Mind'

In 1992, Hubert Hermans co-created the Dialogical Self Theory.[1] Dialogue is a central concept in his view. As we live "in a world society that is increasingly interconnected and intensely involved in historical changes, dialogical relationships are required, not only *between* individuals, groups and cultures, but also *within* the self of one and the same individual."[2] The leading message, and in my view the reason why the work was adopted well by scientists and practitioners, is the similarity between society at large and the individual mind. Hermans takes the self not as an entity in itself, but as emerging from social processes in relations and history. As a consequence our 'selves' are a constantly changing result of all kind of stimuli that influence us. He holds a view of self as a process of continuously changing internal and external relations.

Hermans considers the self as multivoiced and dialogical. Inspired by the original ideas of William James and Mikhail Bakhtin, Hubert Hermans, Harry Kempen and Rens van Loon wrote the first psychological publication on the "dialogical self" in which they conceptualized the self in terms of a dynamic multiplicity of relatively autonomous I-positions in the (extended) landscape of the mind. The self can be described as a microcosm of society—child, parent, partner, professional, worker—that has to relate to the wider society and network of others, to the context in which it must function. I-positions are both internal and external: a leader's sense of his/her professional self (as a professional leader), for example, extends from 'my role'—'I the leader'—to 'my reports', 'my organization' and 'my peers and colleagues'. As *positioned*, the self is localized in space and time, that is, part of a greater whole (global world, collective history), as *I* it has the potential to become part of a broader whole (as a *we*).[3] In this conception, the *I* has the possibility to move from one spatial position to another in accordance with changes in situation and time. The *I* fluctuates among different and even opposed positions, and has the capacity to give each position a voice so that dialogical relations between positions can be established. The voices function like interacting characters in a story, involved in processes of question and answer, agreement and disagreement. Each of them have a story to tell about their own experiences from their own position in time and space. As different voices, these characters exchange

---

[1]The concept Dialogical Self was coined in Hermans et al. 1992; Hermans and Kempen 1993.
[2]Hermans and Hermans-Konopka 2010; Hermans 2013.
[3]Hermans and Konopka 2010, 173. See also: Hermans and Gieser 2012.

information about their respective me's and mines, resulting in a complex, narratively structured self.

> Impact of Symbols in Self-narratives
> Hubert Hermans is emeritus professor of Personality Psychology at Radboud University and was chairman of the Supervisory Board of the Han Fortmann Center at the Radboud University of Nijmegen. We met in 1986 in the context of the Han Fortmann Center, where western and eastern philosophical, religious and meditation practices were combined in lectures, courses and trainings. One of these courses was a workshop in the allegory of the cave in Plato's Politeia. To explore the impact of symbolism and metaphors in self-narratives, we used the theory and method developed by Hermans and his group, Valuation Theory and Self-Confrontation Method.[4] How can you integrate an insight or message, which you get by reflecting on a metaphor or symbol in your self-narrative? Topic for further research was to create a better understanding of the transformative role of symbolism in self-narratives. In an experimental workshop with the symbolism of the cave, we observed that the method of connecting people with symbolism in a holistic way was very impactful. Here we combined experiencing and reflecting, with dancing, conversation, listening to music, sharing theory about history of religion and philosophy, meditation and silence. Although we heard from all participants that the impact of the workshop was immense, we did not understand how it worked exactly. That was the beginning of my Ph.D. research project.[5]

2.1.1 Weaving Self and Dialogue Together

Dialogical Self Theory weaves *self and dialogue* together in such a way that a more profound understanding of the interconnection of self *and society* is achieved. Usually, the concept of self refers to something 'internal', something that takes place within the mind of the individual person, while dialogue is typically

---

[4]Before Hermans created the Dialogical Self Theory, he designed the Valuation Theory and the Self-Confrontation Method from 1974. The most accurate summary of this theory and methodology is written by Hermans and Hermans-Jansen 1995. *Self-Narratives. The Construction of Meaning in Psychotherapy*. The spirit of this work (combining idiographic and nomothetic approaches within the narrative paradigm) prepared the concept of Dialogical Self. In practice we observed clients verbalizing their self-narratives from multiple perspectives and positions, sometimes opposed, sometimes complementary.

[5]Published as Van Loon 1996. *Symbols in Self-Narrative. Interpreting by means of Self-Confrontation Method* [book in Dutch].

associated with something 'external', that is, processes that take place between people involved in communication. The spirit of the Dialogical Self can be understood by understanding that we are living in a *space*. This is an *external* space and an *internal* space. In this space we can feel *low* (sad) and *high* (happy), *close* to yourself[6] (authentic) and *far* from yourself (inauthentic). Within our bodily boundaries, we continuously make *vertical* and *horizontal* movements. The space we live in is not only internal, it is also extended to the external world, it is beyond the boundaries of our bodily skin. Our mind is populated by many people about whom we are constantly thinking and feeling. That is the reason why Hermans uses the expression: 'we live in a *society of mind*'. The self is a society of mind and at the same time part of a larger society. The composite concept 'dialogical self' goes beyond the self-other dichotomy by infusing the *external to the internal* and, in reverse, to introduce the *internal into the external*. In the figure the two spaces and the dynamics between internal, external, close, far, low and high, are visualized (Fig. 2.1).

In that society of mind we position ourselves in basically two different modes of I-positioning: internal and external. The self does not only include internal positions, but also external positions. As functioning as a 'society of mind', the self is populated by a multiplicity of 'I-positions' that have the possibility to entertain dialogical/monological relationships with each other. Examples of *internal I-positions* are: 'I as the son of my mother', 'I as a dancing teacher', 'I as intuitive'; 'I as rational'; 'I as impatient'; 'I as relaxed'; etcetera. Examples of external I-positions are: my father, my mother, my Latin teacher, Peter (my best friend), George (my enemy), etcetera. What they have in common is that they all have a sense of meaning for you, and are loaded with affect. In a society of mind happens what also happens in the outer societal world: there is a form of conversation (dialogue/debate/discussion) between different I-positions. Examples. The intuitive I continuously criticizes the rational I. The relaxed I encourages the ambitious I to take it easy, etcetera. In internal dialogues you can listen to other voices in yourself (I-position repertoire). Internal and external I-positions are simultaneously present. There is not always a sharp separation between the inside of the self and the outside world, but rather a gradual transition. When some positions in the self silence or suppress other positions, monological relationships prevail with the risk of

---

[6]What exactly is meant here? Is there an essence assumed? No, the expressions 'close to yourself' or 'far from yourself' refer to how we relate to where we are in that moment of place and time, it is by definition contextual. 'I with my friend' refers to a different meaning of closeness than 'I during a lecture for psychologists'. For authenticity the same applies: it is relational, contextual, and internally and externally, dialogical. It is so difficult to express this accurately, as the daily use of expressions such as self have 'container'-connotations (true self, deeper self, etcetera). Hermans in his book *Democratic Self* (2017, in press, n.p.) uses the word 'elusive process' to characterize self. "The metaphoric use of society works as 'glasses' that offer a sometimes surprising perspective that will allow to go deeper into the workings of this elusive process that we try to demarcate by the simple word 'self.'".

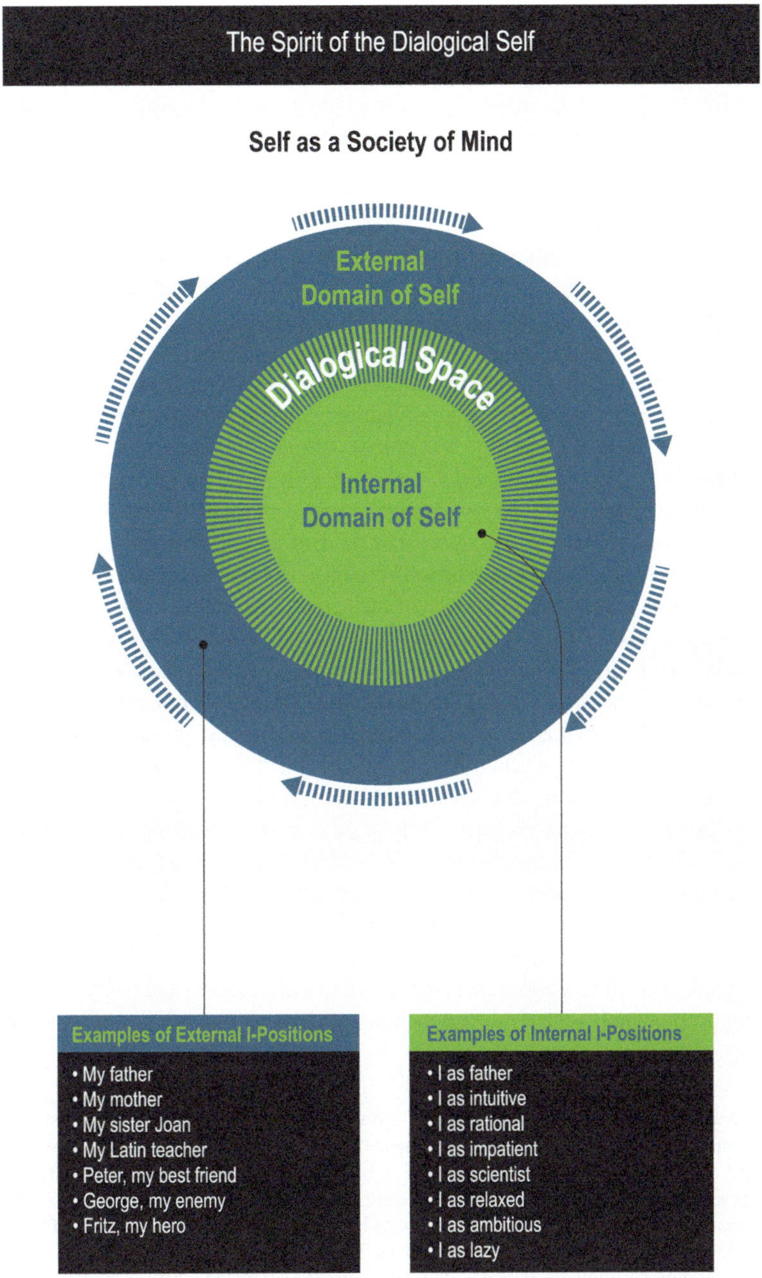

2.1 Self as a 'Society of Mind'

Fig. 2.1 The spirit of the dialogical self

radicalizing.[7] When positions are recognized and accepted in their differences and alterity (both within and between the internal and external domains of the self), dialogical relationships might emerge with the possibility to further develop and renew self and other. The theory of the dialogical self is designed to describe and stimulate these internal and external conversations.[8]

> Miranda's Story
>
> This case study illustrates how Dialogical Self Theory provides some useful insights into the value of applying these principles in executive coaching. Dialogical Self Theory is, perhaps, best understood by thinking about the process someone goes through when faced with an important decision. He or she will likely weigh up the implications for their personal and professional lives and be influenced by a predisposition either towards optimism or pessimism, and by the example of a parent, employer, teacher or some other (positive or negative) role model—even though these people are not physically present. Our brains are stores of multiple thoughts and experiences—ours and other people's. We remember, and to an extent are shaped by, the words and attitudes and behaviors of others, in our present and our past.
>
> Most of us manage this 'society of the mind' adequately, most of the time. We navigate between the I-positions fairly smoothly and fairly naturally—and we don't feel any strong sense of disintegration or that they're pulling us apart. At times, however, our ability to manage comes under threat—and with it our sense of security and identity. Some of the biggest threats occur in the workplace. People often find it hard to balance the demands placed on them by their employers with the demands placed on them in their domestic or private lives. The situation can be particularly serious where someone feels that their sense of identity has been compromised by the introduction of a new I-position —for example, I as leader or boss—and they're having to act in ways that aren't really 'them'. The challenge becomes how to integrate this new position successfully into the 'society of mind'. Dialogical Self Theory helps by encouraging someone to talk about their feelings and difficulties—and to try to open a dialogue in which apparently opposing positions are reconciled. One of the

---

[7]In his book *Celebrating the other* (2008), Edward Sampson suggests that we sustain our self-esteem through "self-celebratory monologues", stories about how good we are and how successful. To sustain these stories, we need other people who are less than good. We thus construct worlds in which others are irrational, unthinking, and sinful and so on. He spoke of these monological and self-celebratory constructions as being oriented around the notion of a singular and rational self, who is able to know the *other* as the other really (or probably) is, who can speak for and about others (followers, women, other ethnic groups). (Hosking 2011, 456). "Conventional wisdom tells us that each of us is like a small container, designed to prevent our "inner essence" from leaking out. We believe that in order to be a proper container, each individual must become a coherent, integrated, singular entity, whose clear-cut boundaries define its limits and separate it from similarly bounded entities" (Sampson 2008, 17).

[8]Inspired by a video of Hubert Hermans http://www.dialogical-self.nl/.

tenets of Dialogical Self Theory is that contradictions create opportunities for new meaning. A practitioner will, effectively, finds ways of helping a client turn the conflict they face to their advantage and make something positive out of it. The following example will help to explain how.

Miranda is a fully trained engineer in her early 40s who returned to full-time work five years ago following a 'career break' to bring up her three children. She balanced motherhood with a part-time job at a local further education college, teaching engineering and mechanical constructing, so did not find the return to full-time employment a huge wrench. The past five years have been happy ones, overall—and Miranda has enjoyed her job.

Things are changing, however. The finance director at the company she works for is leaving and, much to her surprise, Miranda has been given his job. It's the opportunity of a lifetime—the kind of job she dreamed of before she had children—and it couldn't have come at a better time. Miranda's husband was made redundant six months ago and is finding it hard to get a new job. It's been agreed that he'll stay at home and take over from the childminder so Miranda can pursue her career. On the face of it, things are perfect. Miranda is a feminist who always wanted a career, and the increase in salary, plus the savings in childcare, mean financially they're much more secure.

There's a catch, though. Miranda feels uncomfortable in her new role. All the other members of the board are male—and one, the operations director, appears to take a particularly hard-hitting approach to business. Something she once heard her first boss Frances say keeps circling in Miranda's head: "The hard fact is that to succeed in business as a woman you have to become more like a man". The first board meeting is a disaster. Miranda finds herself spouting facts and figures purely to prove she has the same kind of analytical brain as a man. She has some concerns about the proposed growth strategy— the markets are under-researched—but she's reluctant to express them for fear of seeming too risk-averse and negative. She's floundering—unsure of who she is—and she's losing her confidence. She wants to walk away but doesn't feel she can. The implications for her family would be too serious. Besides, she feels she has a responsibility to the founder and managing director and to the team below her. What can she do?

The company has arranged for Miranda, as a new director, to be 'coached' by an external consultant who happens to have a background in Dialogical Self Theory. The coach understands Miranda's problem partly as an identity crisis and begins to help her integrate her new role into the 'society' of her self. She encourages Miranda to acknowledge and embrace the many I-positions that make up her sense of self. It's clear to the coach that Miranda has become so stressed by her situation that she's been unable to think clearly and that internal dialogue has broken down. What does Miranda the feminist (internal I-position) have to say to Frances the role model (external

I-position)? What can Miranda the mother and the teacher tell the operations director? Where's the reciprocal exchange?

Miranda is helped to understand that denial of who she is, is dangerous—both for her own mental and emotional health and for her professional development. She has lessons and strengths she can bring to the business—and many of them spring from the I-positions she's trying to suppress. If she remembers her roles as mother/carer and teacher she will become part of the repertoire of external I-positions of other directors—and help the sum of the board be greater than its individual parts. Her peers, in other words, will benefit from the insight and wisdom of a new 'voice'.

At the next board meeting, Miranda applies some of the insights she's learned as a teacher to challenge the proposed growth strategy—and receives support from the non-executive director on the board. The sense of reconciliation and resolution she feels gives her more confidence and she begins to settle into her new role. Thanks to this approach, she is better able to 'direct the energy' of the team she leads—and make the optimal contribution to the company. More than this, she's more likely to search her personal repertoire of beliefs and experiences when faced with new and different challenges. Miranda, through the 'lessons' of reconciling her I-positions, blazes a trail for emotional intelligence and authentic leadership—and her organization is the stronger for it.

2.1.2 Dynamic Positioning of the Self

Positioning makes the concept of the dialogical self dynamic as it enables us to *position* the self in space. S*pace* is used in a double sense. On the one hand, it is the 'physical' space: *I* am standing *here*, *my father* is standing *there*. On the other hand, it is metaphorical: *my father's voice* resonates in my '*I-position as a lawyer*'. This is in line with observations that people often use metaphorical language to explain how I-positions take place in their life. To give an example. One of my clients—Helen—said she struggled with low self-confidence in working-situations. Although she was perceived in her organization as very skilled and senior, internally she felt very insecure. One of her I-positions was '*I as riding my horse*'. In that position she felt highly self-confident and was able to act effectively, even in unknown and dangerous situations. By bringing the energy of the *physical* I-position of the horse-rider *metaphorically* to that of the business world, her level of self-confidence raised increasingly.

Professionally, my first experience with the impact of the concept of the Dialogical Self was with one of the participants in the research project for my Ph.D.[9]

---

[9]I have described this case in an article in a Dutch magazine *Speling*, titled *Symbols as a way for personal integration* (Van Loon 1990), 13–18.

A woman—Diana—participated in the workshop on symbolism of the *tree*. She spontaneously felt attracted to this symbol. Later she told me she did not dare to participate in the workshop on the symbolism of the cave, as this symbol frightened her intuitively. In exploring the impact of the meaning of symbols in self-narratives, Diana told a negative emotional story about her life. One exception: when she was crafting wood, she felt well. It was remarkable for her to experience that by intentionally strengthening this I-position ("I as crafting wood"), she became able to function in society in a more adjusted manner. After a few years, she was active as a dancing teacher. What she did was metaphorically transposing a physical I-position ('I as crafting wood') into other domains of her life ('I as a dancing teacher'). My interest in this phenomenon was born.

"One of the basic tenets of the dialogical self-theory is that people are continuously involved in a process of positioning and repositioning, not only in relation to other people but also in relation to themselves."[10] The verb 'positioning' is a spatial, relating one, it refers to 'here' and 'there'. "When a person positions herself 'somewhere', there are always, explicitly or implicitly other positions involved that are located in the outer space around us or in the inner metaphorical space of the self."[11] Between different I-positions, there can be a dialogical or monological relation. "The voice of my mother in me shouts to not take life so seriously and take it easy". As I-positions result from relations in the past, they can be more or less internalized. The concept of positioning plays at several levels: in our 'self-reflection and self-talk', in our relations, in social order and in our cultural activities.

> "Tiny Man Walking in an Empty Space"
> In the artwork *A Map of Days,* Grayson Perry creates a self-portrait, which you can use to illustrate the basic concepts of the Dialogical Self Theory in a visual and creative way. Perry constructed his self-portrait like a town, a citadel, whereby the town walls can be interpreted as the skin. The 'self' is not a simple unchangeable thing, but a lifelong process of 'work in progress'. What is remarkable in his drawing of the self is that the picture is an open space. Not a central, container, static point. Our 'self' consists of continually changing layers of experience. Grayson Perry, whose female I-position frequently appears as 'Claire', himself says "My sense of self is a tiny man, kicking a can down the road."[12]
>
> Having a look at some of the details in the middle of the picture, you see a tiny man ('a sense of self') walking in an empty space. Around this space, creative side, spiritual side, dark side, bright side. On the right, a female portrait with 'the inner you' (referring to Claire). On the left, 'the real me' with words as 'the vast something', 'silent call'. On the right some additional

---

[10] Hermans and Konopka 2010, 7.
[11] Hermans and Konopka 2010, 8.
[12] Exposition at Bonnefanten Museum in Maastricht, the Netherlands, 2016.

> information: tinnitus, motorcycle license, Chelmsford 1960, bad back, kidney stones, ex-mountain bike racer, blonde hair, blue eyes, married, one child, grammar school, B.A. fine art, hyperopia, acid reflux.
>
> Perry uses quite interesting distinctions: thoughts, concepts, and theories; guesses, speculation, and hypothesis; patterns, declaration, texture, contrast, metaphors, and interpretations. He visualizes internal and external dialogues, and monologues, that continuously took and take place in a beautiful manner. Accessible and easy to understand, as we—each of us—might draw an etch like this to describe our 'self' (Figs. 2.2 and 2.3).

2.2 Relationally Constructing Self in Language

Dialogical Self is a relational concept of self. In Hermans' view, "the autonomy of the self is not constituted in an internal intra-individual negotiation made by one I-position with respect to another, but it is 'intensely interwoven with external dialogical relationships with actual others.'"[13] Moments of insight into my self and my actions are relational to others, nurtured or discouraged by them. The relational *self* can be positioned at the intersection of time and space lines: in the present between past and future; in the relation between self and other, 'I' is positioned in an internal and external spatial relation.

In the constructionist view, the self does not have an existence apart from its surrounding, it is co-created in relation with society. The external *dialogue* between person and other is *interiorized* in a *society of selves*. "Society, from its side, is not 'surrounding' the self, influencing it as an external 'determinant', but there is a 'society-of-selves'; that is, the self is in society and functions as an intrinsic part of it."[14] In the concept of the Dialogical Self, *internal self* and *external dialogue* are mutually inclusive: external conversations contribute to an inner sense of self.

The self is constructed in the context of internal relations, interpersonal relationships and large social systems: "We participate in multiple relationships—in the community, on the job, at leisure, vicariously with television figures—and we carry myriad traces of these relationships.[15] Gergen puts relationship at the heart of human being. His central thesis is that mental processes are in relationships, not so much in the head of individuals. There is no reality or beauty without humans constructing a reality together in language, actions, symbols and metaphors. In our culture, we have defined human being as physically and mentally separated from other selves. Gergen's attempt is to generate an account of human action that can

---

[13]Gallagher 2009.
[14]Hermans and Gieser 2012, 2.
[15]Gergen 2009; Gergen et al. 2001

2.2 Relationally Constructing Self in Language

Grayson Perry, A Map of Days

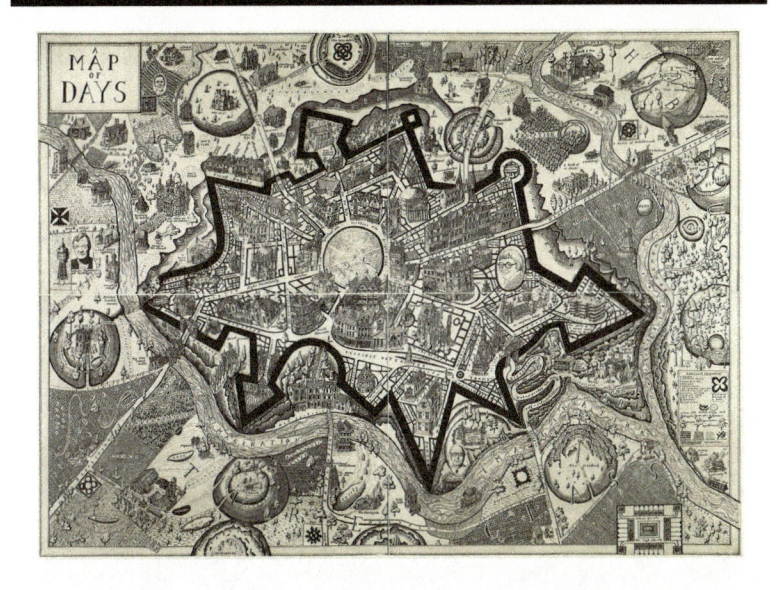

Grayson Perry
A Map of Days, 2013
Etching from four plates
Sheet size: 119,5 x 161 cm
© Grayson Perry
Courtesy the Artist, Paragon Press and Victoria Miro, London

Fig. 2.2 Grayson Perry. A map of days

Fig. 2.3 Grayson Perry. A map of days—detail

2.2 Relationally Constructing Self in Language

replace the assumption of separated selves[16] with a vision of relationship. He demonstrates that virtually all intelligible action is "born, sustained, and/or extinguished within the ongoing process of relationship."[17] Daniel Siegel describes our mind as constructing a linkage across time (past—present—future), and thus constructing '*our selves*' across time.[18]

We are no longer limited by geographies, the world is real time connected. The positive and optimistic view of the constructionist orientation is expressed in the valuation of the dialogue as a tool for creating a better world: "If collaborative relationships are the source of inspiration and action within a group, it is essential that such relationships be used to reduce conflict across groups."[19] "Whatever is essential about human nature is to be found between people in a social dialogue, talk, conversation, debate and so forth, and not in the inner recesses of an individual abstracted from these ongoing transactions."[20] This pre-supposes a level of *free space and free energy* in the relational conversation.

2.2.1 'Centering My High Note'

An example. In programs with leaders we stress the relational importance of verbal and non-verbal language. How do you express what you intend to say? 'Do we *under—stand* each other?' Are you aware of the words that you use? 'Reaching out to grasp something' 'reaching out to comprehend something with your mind.'[21] What kind of language is used here? It is a recurrent observation that people don't *recognize* the difference until they actually *sense* it. As they want to articulate a change they would like to make, people don't know how to find the right words. We recommend to use dynamic words, such as verbs, preferably in the gerund form ('willing', 'doing', 'changing', and so on) in combination with a noun. For one of our participants in a leadership program for IT professionals, it took a serious effort of several days to voice a core insight and action: '*centering my high note*'. The IT-leader explains what this means for her. She could only function at the highest level in the IT organization if she felt anchored, using the metaphor of the high note. She explained the metaphor. As a semi-professional singer, she knew that you can only sing a high note if you are well centered in your lower abdomen. She felt she was not centered enough in her working life. Once you discover the importance of expressing in a dynamic way, it makes people more precise in articulating what they want.

This example illustrates the importance of dynamic and accurate wordings *in relationships*. In two directions. For the IT-leader it was as important *for herself* to

---

[16]'Bound self' or 'bounded identity' implies being separated from other selves.
[17]Gergen 2009, xv.
[18]Siegel 2017, 18.
[19]Gergen 2009, 110.
[20]Sampson 2008, 21.
[21]Siegel (2017) frames this 'embodied language' (21).

find exactly the right words, as she was not clear about what went on in herself, why she was so hesitant (internal dialogue). But also *for people around* her to whom she had to communicate about her uncertainty to accept a new role in the organization (external dialogue). By creating more clarity and expressing this in a dynamic way, she was able to understand what was going on *in* herself, and she could also communicate this more clearly than ever before. The fragment illustrates how language and use of words is affecting our view on reality, in a dual sense: internally and externally.

2.2.2 Self as a Dynamic and Relational Verb

Gergen reflects on this process in a beautiful way. How you express in wordings determines so much. Do you use as a noun or a verb? When he was writing his book *Relational Being*, he had "a strong urge in writing this book to use the phrase *relational self,* as opposed to *relational being*. This would have placed the volume more clearly in the long and estimable tradition of writings on the self. However, the term "self" carries with it strong traces of the individualist tradition. It suggests again a bounded unit, one that *interacts* with other distinct units. Further the "self" is a noun, and thus suggests a static and enduring entity. However, the term "being", ambiguously poised as a participle, noun, and gerund, subverts the image of a bounded unit. In being, we are in motion, carrying with us a past as we move through the present into a becoming."[22] Gergen points out that we have to deal with language in its tendency to become static. This is also one of our most important roles in sessions where we work with leaders and transformation. To make people aware of the language they—often unconsciously—use, and the impact—often unintended—this language has on other people. If I say "*I* rely on *you*", language defines *me* as separate from *you.* We have to deal with this characteristic of our language. We live in a world where we are born *in a language that already exists.* If we want to work and live in this world we have to deal with languages as pre-existing, already co-constructed actions of our human ancestors. I recommend people to experiment with language, or to learn a new language. By doing so, you enter a new relationally co-constructed world, that might make you more aware of your static worldview. And open our mind. "What if there were no nouns?" Experimenting with language can be exciting. The moment you try to articulate reality in terms of relation and movement your experience of the world surrounding you will completely change. Just try for one day. Using as many as possible relational and dynamic verbs. Gergen makes the thought provoking comparison of describing the world in terms of dancing. The romantic movie *August Rush* (2007) illustrates this. An orphanage boy, looking for his father and mother, starts unravelling the mystery of who he is. The theme of the movie is '*follow the music*'.

---

[22]Gergen 2009, xxvi.

The heart of the story is that August Rush perceives everything in the world around him in terms of music, rhythm, beat, pulse. Every noise he hears, from rain to train, traffic and wind, he translates in terms of music and rhythm. The experiment to perceive reality through music is attractively visualized. This made me aware of how differently we experience the world we live in.

Sampson finishes his analysis of the self as social construction in a positive manner: "This dialogic construction of human nature will not reveal the essence of either party, but rather unfold an emerging, shifting and open horizon of human possibilities, which cannot be readily known in advance or outside the dialogue, but emerges as a property of the ongoing dialogue itself."[23] This is an essential element of dialogue, as we will see later: *creating new knowledge and insights*. Sampson clearly demonstrates how much effort it takes to make relations truly dialogical and equal. I illustrate the importance with an example.

We worked with a leader, Chris, and his team as part of a larger leadership development program. At the beginning of the program, as a way of introducing the 'open and equal' atmosphere we wanted to create during the days of the program, the manager of the team shared a story with his colleagues. He opened himself up and he told about his private life. He told about his girlfriend and how he tried to influence her to buy a new car. He proudly told how he influenced her to buy a car she did *not* really want, but was more his preference. The audience sensed how Chris manipulated his girlfriend. Even when people in his team made some remarks, he felt proud about his way of influencing his girlfriend. Chris was not aware of any negative impact of his personal power over her and how his story affected the entire session very negatively. Nobody felt equal power or openness as a starting point for a conversation in the team. Nobody really opened in the group, is was merely politeness towards the leader. Was it a waste of time and energy? The leader apparently did not learn anything from these experiences. The team mistrusted him now even more than before. This is a main reason to have in-depth conversations with each of the participants, and the leader in particular, before starting a leadership transformation program. You have to establish a safe and secure basis as a starting point.[24]

2.2.3 Deriving Meaning from the Context

This brings us to the point of context. Words we use derive their meaning in a context. The moment we isolate words from their contextual phrases, they might lose their meaning. "The meaning of a word is not contained within itself but derives from a process of coordinating words. Without this coordination the single words within a novel would mean very little."[25] The next step to understand the

---

[23]Sampson 2008, 24.
[24]See also Kohlrieser et al. 2012.
[25]Gergen 2009, 32.

implications of social constructionist view is that this also applies for acts. "…there is no action that has meaning in itself, that is, an action that can be isolated and identified for what it is. There are no acts of love, altruism, prejudice, or aggression as such."[26] It is impossible to define 'good' leadership, without knowing the context. Some people think good leadership is characterized by a specific set of personality traits and competencies. In my view this is impossible. You have to pay attention to the context. Words and actions derive meaning through reciprocity, and come to life or are destroyed in coordinated action. Let me illustrate this by an example. In one of the sessions with a team of leaders, a financial officer, Karl, stood up in the group and started telling a story about his way of working in a very precise rational and conscientious way. As a financial officer, he knew the importance of guidelines and following the rules, designed to bring the corporate values to life. At the same time, Karl described his way of working with his colleagues as very open for their feedback. His co-workers had the opposite feeling and harbored the perception that the CFO was *not* open for their opinion and continued on his own trail of thinking. While listening to questions and remarks of his colleagues in the meeting, Karl's non-verbal behavior changed. From using his hands openly in front of his body, he crossed his arms and raised his eyebrows. What his co-fellows observed was a closed non-verbal posture.

Without being consciously aware, the CFO in the example is impacted not only by the content of the words, but also by the 'atmosphere' around it. He was not aware of feeling resistance, but his bodily gestures changed unintentionally without him knowing consciously. In relational influencing, it is not about wording, but also about other elements such as the non-verbal behavior and the emotional atmosphere. Co-action is more than words alone. Speaking and writing are physical actions, as other bodily movements such as laughing, crying, and shuffling and so on. The distinction between verbal and non-verbal communication is false. They are mutually related. Experiment with listening to the verbal expressions without looking at the non-verbal behavior. Look at the non-verbal without listening to the words spoken. As in our example, it is one and the same and, if it is not congruent, it causes confusion. As "unified acts of coordination, with words, movements, facial expressions forming a seamless whole."[27]

2.2.4 Independency as Relationally Embedded

In developing a relational view of human action, Gergen makes one further step in terms of causality. He describes the issue as "On the one hand there is *causal* explanation, favored by most social scientists. People change because of external forces impinging on them. As commonly said, for example, people can be

---

[26]Gergen 2009, 33.
[27]Gergen 2009, 34.

2.2 Relationally Constructing Self in Language

'influenced', 'educated', 'rewarded', 'threatened', or 'forced' to change their behavior. On the other hand there are explanations lodged in the assumption of *voluntary agency,* favored in our daily relations and in courts of law. For example, we say that people are free to choose between right and wrong, or to decide what they want to do in life."[28] Both are not satisfactory. Gergen develops an alternative way of explaining human action: it is through collaborative action that meaning emerges. Causality and agency follow from relationship, historically determined and culturally specific.[29] What we traditionally identify as independent elements are mutually dependent for defining its meaning. Gergen gives the example of a man wearing a mitt, standing alone in the field. This does not define baseball. It is when we bring all the elements into a *mutually defining relationship* that we can speak about playing baseball. We can speak of the baseball game as "a form of life in this case that is constituted by an array of mutually defining "entities."[30] Let me illustrate this. I had an in-depth dialogue with a leader, Derek, who characterized himself as extremely independent. Basically, he kept some core values in his heart that he did not allow to be violated in whatever way. During his private and professional life, he took tough decisions, such as not accepting shares of the family company. His independence was the most important good in his life. In our conversation, there was a phase where Derek became aware of this fixed mindset in relation to his wish to be truly independent. Confronted with the question if he was born with a fixed set of values in his mindset, he became silent. Step by step his awareness grew that he developed that attitude over time in his youth at home. The conversation made Derek think about his independency, and what this meant for his flexibility. In the organization, people characterized him as 'inflexible'. He started looking at the relational field in his family and organization through different eyes and became aware that true independency is relationally embedded.

2.2.5 *"To Be Is to Be Relational"*

As a partner in dialogue, I bring the consequences of social constructionism to the table as a thinking exercise. I invite people to experiment with this dynamic way of looking at the world around them. In my own experience, this also caused a massive change in my worldview. I am educated and trained to believe in 'the truth'. As a student in philosophy and a doctor in social sciences, I was predetermined for the truth. Often I was even thinking that I was a gatekeeper of that form of truth. Regularly, I shouted internally, *"that's not true!"* Quite often, I express this verbally. And I observe many colleagues in business and academia doing the same. Since I deeply understand what it means to *be relational*, I have become more

---

[28]Gergen 2009, 49.

[29]Cf. *reticular causality* Libbrecht 2007, 96.

[30]Gergen 2009, 54. He uses the term 'confluence'.

prudent and careful. I would describe this process of change as a *paradigmatic transformation*. This way of using *theory in practice* is what Gergen wants to reach with his book *Relational Being*, using *it* as a living metaphor, as an open and unfinished, dynamic concept. "Thus, what is novel for us really is a novel *creation*, an *emergent*, something uniquely new that never has existed before and not just a re-arranging of already existing entities. Thus instead of patterns and repetitions, we must become oriented in our inquiries toward uniqueness, toward the noticing and describing of singularities."[31] "To be" is "to be related."[32]

What does this mean for our theory and practice? Core of Dialogical Self Theory and Social Constructionism are permanently changing relations, internally and externally. At the heart of both views is self as a *continuously changing process of relational co-creating and relational positioning in space and time*.

2.3 Key Concepts in Dialogical Self Theory

I-positioning can be external and/or internal positioning. As we have seen, positioning is relational, I-positions are—purposely, or by coincidence—'co-created' in the past and retained within the personal repertoire of I-positions. I-positions can be used to develop the self.

In the notion of *I-Position*, multiplicity and unity are combined in one and the same composite term: 'I as ambitious', 'I as anxious', 'my father as an optimist', 'my beloved children', 'my irritating colleagues' and so on. These examples[33] illustrate how by using *I, me or mine* unity and continuity are created in a multiplicity of different, even contrasting, aspects of the self as irritating versus beloved, and ambitious versus anxious. An example. A 45 year old sales director, Adam, uses the following words to describe the way he functions in the business and privately. 'I as very result-oriented'; 'I as thinking and acting very quickly' as opposed to 'I as impatient and restless'; 'I as having no sincere interest in other people'. In terms of discipline, he characterizes his way of acting as 'I as undisciplined in my thinking' (especially those aspects where I have my doubts and don't know the answer yet) versus 'I as very disciplined', where he refers to the performance he shows to other people.

2.3.1 An Act of Self-Reflection (Meta-Position)

In using I, we see there is a level of unity, and the expressions itself refer to a multiplicity. In the notion of *meta-position* "the *I* is able to leave a specific position,

---

[31]Shotter 2010, 3.

[32]Krishnamurti (1895–1986) was a speaker and writer on philosophical and spiritual subjects. Many of his lectures are about the self and developing the mind Bohm 1996, 47.

[33]Hermans and Konopka 2010, 9.

and even a variety of positions and observe them from the outside, as an act of self-reflection."[34] The self touches an overview from which different positions can be reflected in how they are interconnected as a superordinate position—a product of two or more positions."[35] To continue with Adam, in the conversation about this multiplicity of contrasting aspects of his self, he tries to comprehend and verbalize the unity, which he feels below his impatience. He expressed: "When I am driving my car, when I am jogging and when I have 'open time' (= no appointments in my calendar), I feel rest." Articulating this pattern meant for him taking a meta-position as regards to his hasty life. He formulated a kind of conclusion: "I pass these states of rest (driving, jogging and 'open time') over into my daily functioning".

In this example, meta-position refers to the moment and process of reflecting on his manner of thinking and acting. The notion of a *third position* refers to the process of reconciling two conflicting I-positions.[36] In creating a third position, the two original ones can be unified without removing their original differences and tension. Applying this on the example of Adam. If we follow him in the next step from the perspective of the *third position*, we observe primarily that there is a strong resemblance with the meta-position. But we make an essential addition. In the process of reflection, a *third position* was formed, as he understood how "I as deliberately disciplined in what I do *and* how I think" might bring more unity (rest and relaxation) to his functioning as a director and improve his performance.

By intentionally formulating an insight and an action, Adam combines discipline with his behavioral (sales) quality, added with discipline in his *behaving*, and, in his *thinking*. As Adam has both qualities, it is primarily about applying these, more than developing from scratch. What happened in the process is that space was created in the process of thinking and reflecting of Adam. In the conversation, his normal speed was *slowed down*, just by asking some questions that had a deeper reach than he was used to. And by not automatically reacting to his typical kind of 'sales' and 'speedy managers' behaviors and words. And by striving for answers that were real answers to the questions.

2.3.2 Being (De-)Stabilized (Centering and De-Centering)

Another important distinction is made between *centering and decentering* processes. *Decentering* processes are "centrifugal movements that differentiate or disorganize the existing position repertoire so that it becomes open to innovation."[37] As an example 'I as an engineer' can be decentered by 'I as a dancing teacher'. The rational engineer can be destabilized by allowing intuitive and

---

[34]Hermans and Konopka 2010, 9.
[35]Raggatt 2012, 31.
[36]Hermans and Konopka 2010.
[37]Raggatt 2012, 31. Innovation is here meant in the sense of 'renewal'.

emotional ways of working as a dancing teacher. *Centering* processes are described as "centripetal movements that contribute to the organization and integration of the position repertoire."[38] 'I as a mountaineering guide' integrates two opposing I-Positions ('I as autocratic leader' and 'I as motivated to develop people') and is an illustration of a centering process.

Most people are not aware of some of their I-positions as such, in relation to the issue/dilemma at hand. I-positions come to consciousness in relation. As an example: 'I as a horseman' is—of course—known as an I-position, but not in relation to 'I as a change leader'. Connecting these I-positions in a new way can be the source of a fundamental shift. This might transform the self, positioned differently within a newly organized position repertoire. The process of positioning and repositioning is enabled by a generative internal and/or external dialogue, where people feel safe to make new connections in the position repertoire. In Chap. 6, several cases are given to further explain and illustrate the key-concepts of the dialogical self theory, such as centering and decentering, core-, meta-, third-, and promoter-position. Summarized:

- *Core-position*: a position on which the functioning of other I-positions depends.
- *Meta-position*: a superordinate position, the product of two or more I-positions.
- *Promoter-position*: an I-position which gives order and direction in the development of the position repertoire as a whole.
- *Third-position*: a mediator between two conflicting positions.
- *Centering and decentering*: integrating and disintegrating an I-position repertoire.

2.4 Information and Space in Positioning Self

> We have to remember, that what we observe is not nature herself, but nature exposed to our method of questioning.
>
> W. Heisenberg[39]

This step in the process of thought developed in this book requires some extra attention and effort to understand what is meant. Normally in a conversation this can be explained related to the level of understanding and experience of the other person. We want to understand what '*relational co-creating and relational I-positioning*' means and how it works in practice, and how you can apply this yourself. Therefore we need to explore how human beings get information from the world they live in. Ulrich Libbrecht[40] designed a model that enables us to analyze and

---

[38]Raggatt 2012, 31.

[39]*Physics and Philosophy: The Revolution in Modern Science* (1958). Lectures delivered at University of St. Andrews, Scotland, Winter 1955–56.

[40]Libbrecht 2007.

understand the way we try to comprehend the world around us. We explore the concepts *energy, information, and space* as Libbrecht describes them. The concept is visualized and used to describe how I-positioning works and how we use different sources (experience, knowledge, action). The concepts of *creating space* and *free energy* are critical to understand and apply these processes.

I first met Professor Libbrecht as a keynote speaker in 1987 at a Physical Science conference at the Radboud University named *Tao: the Way of Nature*. He is a mathematician, a sinologist and a comparative philosopher. After the conference, we invited him to lecture for a small group of students at our university. Here he explained his comparative model of philosophy. What helped me was his distinction between bound and free energy. The main message I got from the lectures of Libbrecht was: there are different sources to get information from the world around us and in ourselves: from your body as being bound to nature, through your rationality as knowledge you get from objective science and logic, and through your experience you learn about subjectivity, e.g. through literature, art and religion. Accepting that one exclusive mode does not exist is an insight, which I apply on a daily base in my work with leaders and members of organizations. How to reconcile the sources of physical acting with rational thinking and emotional experiencing. In my own practice, it was tough to reconcile my emotional experiences with my professional rational life as a managing director of our company at that time.

2.4.1 Energy and Information

Let's explore how Libbrecht's view can help us in understanding these three sources of information. He builds his concept, starting from two basic axes, derived from Chinese thinking about the cosmos: *energy (ch'i)* and *information*. Both are chosen as—in his view—they are paradigm free and all-pervading. "Energy provides a dynamic universe that can be considered a phenomenological *space*, i.e. a space that consists of events. Information transforms it into an epistemological *space*, i.e. a space that can be known and described."[41] Information cannot exist without energy, as nothing can happen without energy. Energy without information has no epistemological meaning, as there is nothing more to say. It is as it is. Libbrecht suggests to use *energy* to describe every act, idea and feeling. Changes in the energy balances inform us about the worlds around and in us. These changes enable us to act instinctively (as bound to nature), to think more objectively (as in science) and to experience the *numen*, the mystery of life (as in religion and mystic). To give an example. You write or say 'Golden Gate Bridge' and "voila, energy has information—it stands for something other than the pure form of energy

---

[41]Libbrecht 2007, 93.

that manifested from a sea of possibilities to this one actuality."[42] Information expresses itself in the world by energy transformations, the unfolding of a potential into an actual something. Energy-as-information can be felt in your mental experience as it emerges moment by moment.

Libbrecht differentiates between bound and free energy. *Bound energy* designates "energy, which is confined to a fixed pattern."[43] We can think here about so-called dead matter, from quarks to organic molecules, where there is no freedom. The behavior of such dead matter is predictable. Although many of us want to return to the state of natural, ecological innocence and happiness, this has become impossible for humans, as we created a world that is not only ruled by nature and instincts. But also by consciousness, in Libbrecht's words *free energy*. Life is characterized by free energy in varying degrees: plants have a limited degree of freedom. They can turn to face light, which a stone can't, they can very slow and gradually move towards the most favorable environment. Animals have a higher degree of free energy: they can move within their ecological environment, adjusting it by building nests, webs, dens, etcetera. They have a certain freedom in terms of choosing their food, habitat, partner, etcetera. As far as we know now humans have the highest degree of free energy: "We know this from the cultural creations developed in the course of human evolution. Culture is actually a collection of new behavioral patterns produced by labor. It made humans very mobile creatures, drastically changing their environment and also adapting to it."[44] In this sense, humans have been able to create transformational space in history and change their lives fundamentally, from living in caves as hunters and farmers to living in cities, spending leisure time in shopping malls to working in global virtual teams on virtual tasks. Free energy expresses itself in increasing degrees of change. Free energy is conditional to develop a sense of self in the act of 'kicking a can down the road'. Free energy is condition zero for dialogue, as we will demonstrate later.

2.4.2 Free Energy

What do we mean by *free energy*? Libbrecht distinguishes between immanence and transcendence, two important terms in understanding this process. "Immanence is derived from in + manēre, 'staying in'; animals are nature's captives but humans also have a considerable immanent dimension. Transcendence means 'rising

---

[42]Siegel 2017, 31. Siegel, too, comes to the conclusion that *energy and information flow* is the central element of a system that is the origin of the self (and the mind). He gives a nice example of how energy as information works. I am writing this fragment here in my book, and my energy was transformed in my nervous system, activated my fingers to type these words to send meaning to you, the reader of this text. In the flow change is involved, between you and me, change in location, and, change in time. (56).

[43]Libbrecht 2007, 94.

[44]Libbrecht 2007, 94.

above': in their culture, humans rise above nature. This does not, however, mean that humans are transcendent beings; they are not gods or pure spirits elevated above earth, they remain rooted in the earth: they cannot escape the need to feed, sleep and reproduce."[45] For our understanding dialogue and self, 'being rooted in nature, in the natural body'—with its immanent, bound energy processes—is an important aspect. People tend to underestimate their dependency of human *nature*, as in the fast moving and changing world we tend to think that we are able to adapt to whatever we want. *Free energy is the human capacity to move away from immanent natural patterns.* Without this our boundary would have been the pattern in nature, which works as it works, reticular, ecologic and cyclic. We would be continuously living in the present, without mindful awareness.

Libbrecht introduces the term *information* as our informative relation to the universe. "All energy that transforms itself into informative phenomenality comes from the cosmos."[46] Following Chinese philosophical intuition, Libbrecht defines the universe as an *energy (ch'i) space*. By defining space in this way, it allows us to look at space from different angles: as *energetic* space, as *informative* space and also as *ethical* space. For our purpose this is important, as *space* is a central element in the process of dialogue. Libbrecht gives a more detailed definition of each.

2.4.3 Energy Space

Energetic space is a complex whole of force fields: space is energy. One could compare this with a magnetic field, filling the entire space, not directly perceptible, but by its effects. "In a *ch'i* space, phenomena can influence each other from a distance because they are linked to each other by a force field."[47] Energetic means moving, changing continuously. Causal relations are like network relations, reticular causalities, instead B bilaterally being caused by A. Siegel formulates this as energy and information flowing within and between a self and other people *in patterns of communication.* "We can say that energy and information flow occurs between our body and the non-body components of the world—the world of 'others' and our environment—as well as within us—within our body, including its brain."[48]

Informative space refers to how we acquire information from the world around us by getting in an epistemological relation with it as we are able to transcend nature, to deviate from natural predisposed patterns, to 'free energy'. In this relation we get information from and about the world, which we try to verbalize in language

---

[45] Libbrecht 2007, 95.
[46] Libbrecht 2007, 95.
[47] Libbrecht 2007, 96.
[48] Siegel 2017, 33.

and understand in concepts (science), translate in actions and interventions (technology, architecture, etcetera).

Ethical space means that not everything that is possible is also allowed. We can build a house, but we can also make a nuclear bomb, using our capability to move away from immanent natural patterns. So ethical and legal limits are placed on what man may achieve with his free energy. "Yet even with these ethical restrictions, the number of new patterns of order allowed remains extremely large, since I can always combine and recombine. This is expressed abundantly clearly in the number of cultural patterns, of which there are a great many varieties, and thereby also illustrates the wealth of human potential."[49]

2.4.3.1 Arrow and Field Energy

In this energetic-informative cosmos, the world in which we live, we are able to direct energy in different ways. In the process of 'changing the world around us' free energy can be *concentrated* and focused on a goal, like an *arrow* on a target. Cultural patterns—technological, architectural, artistic, and religious—are the result of *concentrated energy*. You deliberately try to reach something through focusing, and reaching a well-defined target needs a form of discipline. As an example, in sports we see that you need a strong will and hard discipline to become Olympic champion.

Free energy can also be *deconcentrated*, and released in a *field*. With field energy, you surrender to the effect of the field, which induces a particular experience in you, without knowing exactly 'how'.[50] When we eat we destroy patterns of order constructed by nature, but this is to protect our body against entropic breakdown. Libbrecht gives an illustration of the magnetic needle: "Imagine I am some kind of magnetic needle: I can point the needle at a particular goal by tightening a screw; but if I release the needle it will be influenced by the magnetic field and will be subject to its particular effect."[51] An example: if you consciously try to reach something through sensing the atmosphere during a conversation in the room, you reach this by *non*-focusing. In terms of concentration and discipline, I call this *soft discipline*, where you reach something through *de*concentrating. This quality of energy and will is important for understanding the transformational processes in dialogue. We will come back to this description in defining characteristics of dialogue in Chap. 4. A good dialogue can take both forms of free energy, concentrated and deconcentrated.

---

[49]Libbrecht 2007, 98. See also Hickman 2016. Hickman brings the concepts of effective and ethical leadership together in her view on *good* leadership.

[50]Siegel 2017, 33: "On the level of neuroscience, no one understands how neural firing might create the subjectively felt experience of a thought, memory or emotion. We just don't know." Brain scientists use the term *neural representation* to indicate a pattern of neural firing that stands for something other than itself.

[51]Libbrecht 2007, 99.

2.4 Information and Space in Positioning Self

Let us have a closer look at the two forms information can take, *arrow* and *field energy*, and apply that to *consciousness*. I can concentrate my energy on the patterns of order of a particular object, analyze them and learn to understand their structure. I do not create the structure of the object, e.g. the DNA structure of the genes is developed by nature itself, revealed by man. We do not create the structure of an object, but we form or construct it in our mind. What we call science is "nothing but reading out patterns of order in nature."[52] We call this *knowledge*, objectivity, science. In the course of evolution life evolves in complexity and finally produced man. "It is important to note that not only the material structure becomes increasingly complex, but at the same time energetic binding loosens: energy is freeing itself. In man, part of it becomes free in what we traditionally call: mind."[53] In *logos* (reason) the distance between the observer (subject) and the observed (object) is maximal. We use terms as objectivity, science, a statement is true or false (can't be both), controlling, following the laws of logic and mathematics. This way of freeing energy has led to brilliant innovative discoveries, we are able to lead our lives as we do in our globalized culture thanks to this human faculty. On the other hand the global crises that we are confronted with nowadays refer back to the fact that we are not able to organize and control our life without mistakes. Man-made disasters lead back directly to this failing capability.

I can also deconcentrate my energy as a field of *experience*. "However, experiences cannot be made accessible by insight—no one can find out by analysis what the scent of a rose is, or love, a musical experience or a mystical experience. The word 'experience' derives from the Latin verb *experiri,* to 'test or to try'."[54] We have to go through an experience to know what is being referred to. And to undergo an experience you have to open up and become receptive. In a mystical experience oneness of subject and object are maximal. Here expressions are used as experiencing and subjectivity, which applies to art, religion, and literature. We use concepts such as authenticity, drama, symbolism and storytelling. A narrative can have more meanings simultaneously, being genuine and not corresponding to objective reality. Most people never reach the highest stages of knowing and experiencing. That is the reason why eminent science takes so much training, time and effort. The same for art, literature and religion. In Libbrecht's comparative model he refers to the Buddhist tradition, where centuries were spent in perfecting the states of reaching mystic union. In meditation[55] the highest state is being mindful, without interfering, without 'doing'. Like *thinking* (objectivity, science,

---

[52]Libbrecht 2007, 101.

[53]Libbrecht 2007, 74.

[54]Libbrecht 2007, 101.

[55]Ricard refers to an ethical component in mindfulness. To be fully aware of what goes on in and outside of us and to understand what is the nature of our perceptions opens the ethical dimension "to discern whether or not it is beneficial to maintain this or that particular state of mind or to continue to pursue whatever we are doing at the present moment." (Ricard 2011, 67). In the act of slowing down in time and space, an ethical dimension of our being might emerge spontaneously. What we actively need to do is: slowing down.

logic), *experiencing* (subjectivity, religion, art, literature, dialogic) can be perfected in years of training with the right mixture of hard and soft discipline, concentrated and deconcentrated energy.

2.4.3.2 Nature, Knowledge, and Experience

In 'perfect' science, the relation between subject and object is independent from one another (S ≠ O), the observation/experiment is replicable by another scientist with the same outcome. In a 'perfect' mystical experience, subject is *one* with the object (S = O).[56] This description is an ideal, most of our 'scientific insights' and 'mystic experiences' are somewhere between the two extremes. The message is that *both* sources of getting information from the world around us are appropriate, depending on context and objective. This is important for leaders, as they have to use all three sources in the process of influencing, leading and following (Fig. 2.4).

2.4.4 Creating Space in Dialogical Relations

Now we are ready to apply what we know about 'space' in dialogical relations. Masayoshi Morioka is a professor of Psychology in Kyoto. He uses the Japanese word *ma* (間) to describe what happens in a conversation and applies this to the dialogical self concept. The Japanese word *ma* has multiple meanings. "It can imply a space between two things, or it can indicate a space between one moment and another moment."[57] So *ma* refers to both *space and time*. In Japanese culture, space is perceived "according to the dynamism inherent in the non-separation of space and time."[58] The word *ma* is also used to describe the *quality of interpersonal relations*. The process of talking and listening creates unique *ma* between persons. The character *ma* also indicates *the space between you and me*, and the *creative tension in between*. Without this lively tension, *ma* between individuals might be lost. The relational aspect of *you and me* is represented in one and the same Japanese character. *Ma* can refer to both external relationships with others, but also with other voices in an internal dialogue. Lastly, *ma* can also refer to a pause, a—significant—*silence* in the internal and/or external conversation. In this silence, a process of distancing oneself from oneself might start, and new meaning can be generated. "The quality of time experience of 'ma' is not linear, such as past—present—future, but a non-linear condensed one."[59]

---

[56]See also: Jaworsky 2012.
[57]Morioka 2012, 398.
[58]Morioka 2012, 398.
[59]Morioka 2008, 105.

2.4 Information and Space in Positioning Self

Sources of Information

Free energy
(transcendence)

Information

Knowledge ⟷ Experience

Energy

Nature

Bound energy
(immanence)

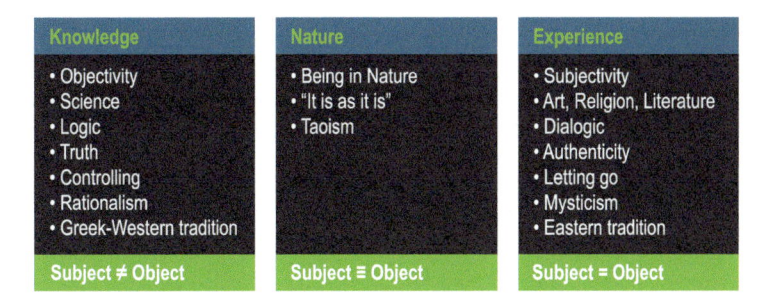

Knowledge	Nature	Experience
• Objectivity	• Being in Nature	• Subjectivity
• Science	• "It is as it is"	• Art, Religion, Literature
• Logic	• Taoism	• Dialogic
• Truth		• Authenticity
• Controlling		• Letting go
• Rationalism		• Mysticism
• Greek-Western tradition		• Eastern tradition
Subject ≠ Object	**Subject ≡ Object**	**Subject = Object**

Fig. 2.4 Sources of information

The Japanese word *ma* combines in one concept: *physical space, temporal space, relationship and silence*. *Ma* can be 'a living pause' in a dialogue, where two minds are connected.[60] The concepts of *creating* '*ma*'—as a living pause—and *freeing energy* enable us to understand the processes of change and transformation. Heifetz also mentions the power of silence in case you have to work with wicked issues (adaptive challenges) and to convince people emotionally, not only rationally. His advice is to 'allow for silence' as "silence gives people time to absorb what you just have said. When you encounter resistance to a proposed intervention, remind yourself how hard it is for your audience to take in your message because it may be about losses they have to sustain."[61] Crossing a boundary and engaging in a dialogical uncertainty is part of that process. You don't know the outcome beforehand. This applies to the levels of self, team and organizational and societal change, as we shall see later in the description of case-studies.

2.4.5 Space as 'Space Between'

Intentional change and transformation presuppose a level of free energy as a necessary condition. This does not imply that there cannot be change processes *without free energy*, as nature is characterized by continuous change: those who continuously adapt to these constantly changing natural conditions survive as the fittest. Human beings are born as bound energy, with the possibility of freeing energy. In two extremes. We can do this *rationally*, by trying to analyze, master and control the world around us as much isolated as possible from our individual subjectivity. And we can use our free energy to *experience* the world around us *relationally* and as co-actions of fabricating a world with other people. Actuality shows that *both* are active in our daily life. From materialist and reductionist perspectives and also based on neuroscientific studies and the results of psychological experiments, numerous theorists argue that self-agency is an illusion. Characteristic for this view is that intentional self-action is positioned *in* the individual system, *or* it does not exist. Our answer here is that action has to be relationally positioned.

"If we view the self as something that emerges from intercorporeal and intersubjective interactions, and develops in social interactions with others, then we are forced to face the question of autonomy in a different way."[62] Meaning and emotional significance are co-constituted in the interaction, not in the private

---

[60]Morioka 2015, 81.
[61]Heifetz et al. 2009, 267.
[62]Gallagher 2009, 492; Gallagher 2012.

2.4 Information and Space in Positioning Self

boundaries of your head. From the earliest point in our lives we are involved in interactions. Through all kind of embodied practices we build step by step an understanding of others, and also of our self. This allows us to think about the self-in-the-other and the other-in-the-self. This could help us in the process of reconciling independence and dependence. It enables us to relationally position ourselves in a space between me and the other, be it an individual, groups, a thing, etcetera. In this sense *space* is *space between*. We can describe space in conversation as *physical* (how is our non-verbal behavior?), as *logic* (how is our mode of arguing with one another?) and as numinous *field* space (how do we experience what is going on between us?). All three are inter-spaces on different levels, and as such important in being relational. For leaders all three levels of inter-spaces are important in the process of leading and following. You can't skip one of the three by saying that you exclusively work on the rational level, without being affected by the experiential and physical.

We assume there is an I that has the capability to free energy to transcend the immanent physical energy through reasoning and experiencing. A self, an *I,* that is able to consciously change natural patterns, that breaks through Nature as it is. This happens in dialogue, internally and externally (and of course in other type of human actions). Let us explore the concept of *transpositioning*, as the act of transposing an I-position from one domain of your life to another.

2.5 Transposing Patterns of Behavior

> Information can be seen simply as energy patterns with meaning beyond the energy flow itself.
>
> Daniel Siegel[63]

In a conversation with one of my clients, we were talking about contributing to the common good, as one of the drivers of my partner to do the work he does. While he was sharing his experience of using the art of telling narratives to empower his management team, he said: "We want to transpose the behavior from one domain in our work to another". I had an 'eureka-moment', a new term emerged: *transposing or transpositioning*. As transposing the mindset (thinking, feeling and acting) of one domain of your work/life to another via the act of I-positioning.

We describe *transpositioning* as *"bringing I-positions from one domain in life/work to another in order to create transformation in the position repertoire."*

- Transpositioning
  We speak of transpositioning of I-positions if someone transposes a state of mind of being a 'fowler' in her private life to being a 'coach' in the company.

---

[63]Siegel 2017, 319.

The 'energy' of one I-position is brought to the other. This might happen intentionally, and doesn't exclude that it can also happen spontaneously.
- Transforming
Transpositioning is aimed at creating a transformation in how you think, feel and act in one or more I-positions.
As a boxer a man felt very relaxed under the heaviest stress situation in the ring during a fight. As a general manager he was easily brought out of balance and would become emotional if he got instructions that he did not like at first sight.

Let me give an example to illustrate this mechanism. I gave a lecture on Dialogical Self Theory for a management team of an organization. During the coffee break, I spoke with a program manager. She reacted on what I had said about people taking different I-positions in life, without intentionally connecting these with one another. She said she was a beekeeper in her private life. She recognized how her way of acting as a beekeeper could be transposed to her role as a program manager. How she 'managed' a program was very much influenced by how she worked with a swarm of bees. In the act of becoming aware of the similarity of the two situations, the process of transpositioning takes place. From now on she will be conscious of the two I-positions. The 'state of mind' when working with bees is—by having a short conversation in a coffee-break—consciously transposed to her job with programs and their managers.

2.5.1 An Empty Self?

Looking back on the central concepts we developed in this chapter, we need some reflection. First a scientific one. What needs to be explored further and demonstrated more clearly is *how* the Dialogical Self Theory is related to the body. Although we started with a strong emphasis on the embodied mind (*the body in the mind*),[64] there is still a lot of research to do in this domain. With this book I contribute to this discussion by developing a research concept based on the scientific work of Libbrecht: Nature (body), Knowledge (rational thinking), and Experience (subjective feeling). I pay attention to the non-verbal aspects of leading and following in my work. We propose to videotape conversations to get a clearer view on how new meaning emerges differentially in a dialogical or debate relation. Non-verbal, physical presence of partners in conversations is important. The same

---

[64]Hermans et al. 1992. See also: Lakoff and Johnson 1999. See also Siegel 2017: "…our mental activities, such as emotions, thoughts, and memories, are directly shaped by, if not outright created by, our body's whole state….and that our relationships with others, the social environment in which we live, directly influence our mental life." (10–11). Siegel's concluding remark and starting point for the rest of his book is that the mind (the self) can be seen as *relational* and *embodied*. The contribution of Siegel's research is that he integrates brain research in his approach (which is out of scope for this book).

2.5 Transposing Patterns of Behavior

applies for the researcher. Can we develop a first-person research method, which we combine with objective data, gathered in the research process? And, in the terminology of Gergen, you cannot ask a question (on paper, on screen, face-to-face) without making a relational impact.[65] How to make this an integral part of our research methodology?

Secondly, reflecting on I-positions and the society of mind. What is the status of I-positions? Do they exist separately from being formulated in language? Are they constructs to make statements in narratives about myself and others? An I-position has no ontological status, i.e. an I-position does not have an objective reality, separately from the relation with 'me'. A tree or a mountain exists, independently from me, defining 'trees' and 'mountains' in words. An I-position has an epistemological meaning: it is a relational and dialogical construct (externally and/or internally) as part of a self-narrative. Theoretically, everything (word, object, metaphor, symbol, and etcetera) might get the function of an I-position in a self-narrative. You can describe I-positions as 'empty' concepts, which you can apply on a variety of situations. The meaning it gets, is dependent on the relational context in which it is co-constructed.

What we want to reach with the International Society for Dialogical Science and with the Dialogical Self Academy is to systematically train researchers and consultants/psychotherapists/leaders in applying the spirit of the Dialogical Self approach. With this book I hope to contribute to a more detailed description of how these internal and external dialogues take place. There is inherently a tension between a prescribed manual for an objectifying research project and this type of research, where the subject of the researcher is essential for relation with the other subject 'under research'.

2.6 Reflections on My Personal Narrative 1

In this chapter about the Dialogical Self Theory, I use—as a form of autoethnography[66]—the development of my 'self' as a case of description and analysis. The first moment of applying self-reflection and dialogue systematically in my life was in 1987. At that time, I did my first self-investigation as part of the certification process in the Self-Confrontation Method with my supervisor at the university. The first phase consists in constructing your self-narrative in terms of 'valuations'. These are 'units of meaning' where you express in your own wording aspects of your self-narrative. You formulate as accurately as possible. The second phase explores these valuations affectively by scoring with a list of affect-terms. The last phase

---

[65]By being present and asking a question (Presence) you cannot 'undo' your relational act as if it is an objective one (Absence). Ctrl-alt-delete doesn't exist in human interaction. You can forget. You can forgive. You can't delete.

[66]Gergen 2009, 237.

consists in having a conversation with the psychologist to talk about the results.[67] Then follows a process of change, validating and re-constructing your self-narrative.

2.6.1 Fragments of My Self-Narrative in 1987

To give an impression of my self-narrative at the time, some valuations that were important for me in terms of their affective profile are exemplified here. These were aspects of my life I felt very positive about in that period (max = 100[68]): "I recognized something of my essence in Tai Chi and Taoism that I further developed." (90); "As a child I felt really happy with my mother: drinking tea together, helping her in the household." (88); "As working principle in my life (inclusively work), I agree to take only *'what I truly understand'*."(81). At the other end of the affective spectrum, the emotionally negative part of my self-narrative. "My mother has an attitude to me: 'behave normal, don't shine out', 'maybe you are not able to do that!'"(2); "To empower myself surviving in the ruthless competitiveness at boarding school, I lost contact in these six years with whom I truly am." (10); "What I learned through negative experiences, is that you have to wear a 'coat' to not go down in society (as in the sphere of competitiveness at boarding school)". (15); "Leaving home for boarding school as a twelve year old boy felt for me like being separated, as becoming homeless from my secure family environment." (29).

In the analysis my supervisor and I made at the time, we concluded that for me 'playing' ("As a child I loved playing, losing myself in the play") was very important, it was positively correlated[69] to a lot of positive experiences in my life: primary school, my mother, my wife, practicing Tai Chi, spirituality. The opposite extreme was 'boarding school', where my trust and safety were severely shocked. I most frequently scored feelings as trust, freedom, self-esteem, energy, strength; least frequent were feelings such as guilt, tenderness, despondence, anger and self-alienation.

2.6.2 Becoming Aware of I-Positions

In this self-investigation, I also formulated an I-position in the form of 'my secret name'. I literally formulated: 'my secret name gives direction to my attitude in my

---

[67] Hermans and Hermans-Jansen 1995, 14–72.

[68] General well-being is measured with the following formula: $Q = P/P + N \times 100$. P = sum of positive feelings; N = sum of negative feelings; Q = general positive quality. The higher, the more positive. To give you a sense of reference, my general well-being at this period in time (1987) scored 60.

[69] A correlation (r) represents the extent of correspondence between the affective modality of two valuations, the profiles for any two rows in the affect matrix (for details: see Hermans and Hermans-Jansen 1995, 43).

personal and working life'. This name was affectively correlated with many aspects of my self-narrative, such as 'relying on my intuition', 'true understanding as my working principle in life'. It also correlated with a sentence that could have been a dialogical self-statement: "I put on many coats, they all fit me well". This name was the reason I wanted to do a Dialogical Self investigation later, when we were working on the article for the American Psychologist[70] on this topic. I was interested in getting more clarity about the impact on myself, from a personal and scientific perspective, as I felt this I-position had a positive influence on my life. I was curious how this worked (Fig. 2.5).

2.6.3 Looking Back to My Earlier Self

I make two observations here. The first one is that by means of the Self-Confrontation Method, you make an overview that is valuable as a 'photo', as a 'still' in time. A complete self-narrative, formulated in your own words and about topics that are relevant for you in a period of your life, is valuable as it gives you the opportunity to reflect (and look back) in a structured manner. The combination of words and feelings gives information you normally tend to filter out, as you are constantly moving in time.

The second observation is that the concept of dialogical self 'comes to life', once you make it part of your self-narrative. By bringing forward I-positions in the conversation with your partner in dialogue, it becomes an integrated part of the self-narrated story and can be connected with other parts of your self-narrative. There has to be a secure and safe basis of trust to bring your most private thoughts to the table. Your partner in conversation has to develop an intuition to hear I-positions in the narratives people tell. By asking a more specifying question about an—mostly unconsciously given—hint, you create the opportunity to share new information. By telling, by being listened to and thinking about questions, the first step in the process of relationally co-constructing meaning is made.

2.7 Questions for Further Reflection

- Describe your 'self' in terms of I-positions, using the two circle model.
  - Firstly do this exercise for yourself: what are the most important I-positions for you? You can read the examples given in the text as a source of inspiration, but remember that you can find these by yourself. Take the time and be patient.

---

[70]Hermans et al. 1992.

Reflections on My Personal Narrative 1

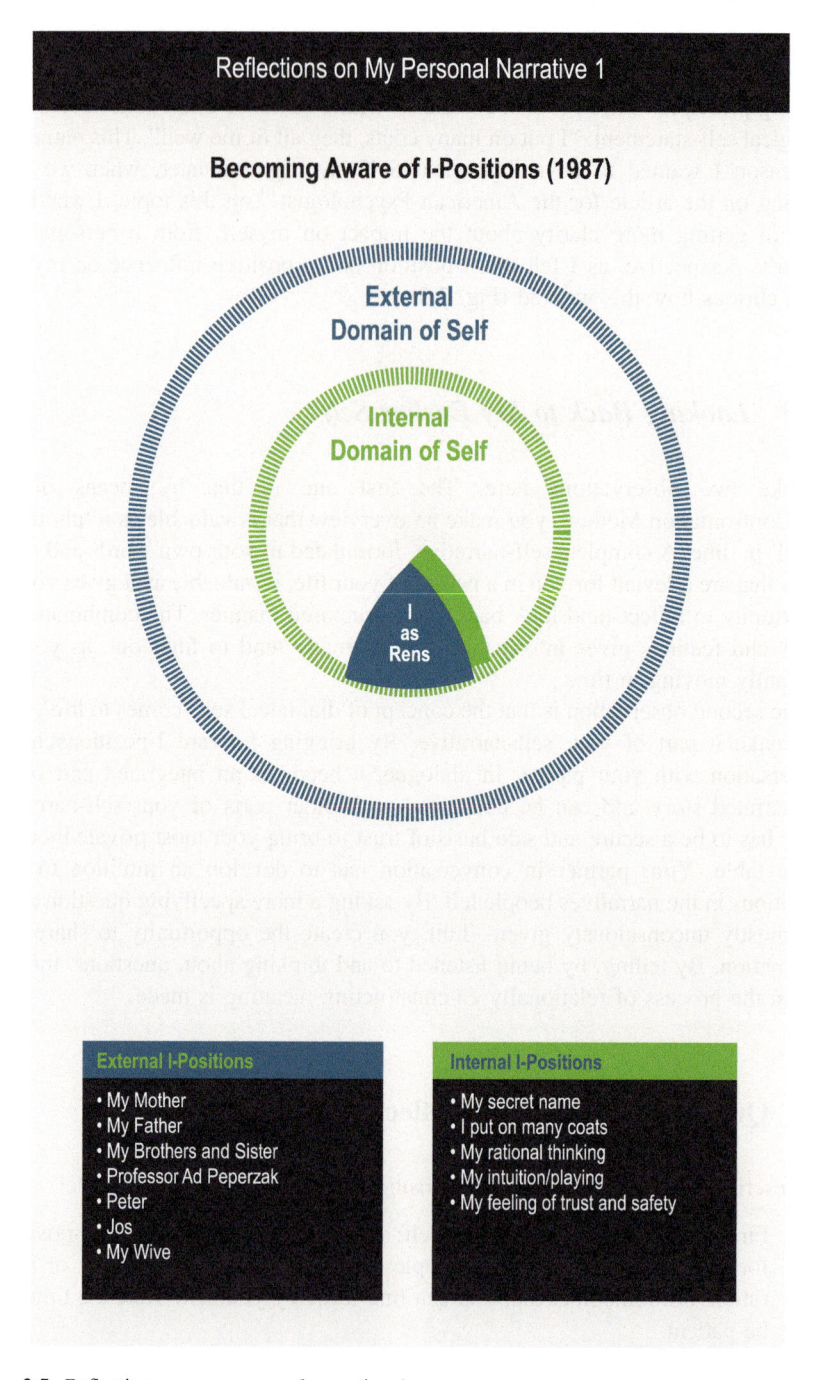

Becoming Aware of I-Positions (1987)

External Domain of Self

Internal Domain of Self

I as Rens

External I-Positions
- My Mother
- My Father
- My Brothers and Sister
- Professor Ad Peperzak
- Peter
- Jos
- My Wive

Internal I-Positions
- My secret name
- I put on many coats
- My rational thinking
- My intuition/playing
- My feeling of trust and safety

Fig. 2.5 Reflections on my personal narrative 1

- Secondly, have a conversation with a friend, do the same; help your friend to formulate his/her I-positions.
- Thirdly, have a similar conversation with a colleague in the workplace. Pay attention, in particular to I-positions in the workplace that are potentially conflicting and/or complementary.

Compare the outcomes. Think about the influence of your partner in conversation, while looking for personal aspects of yourself.

- Describe moments where you were able to 'create free energy' and intentionally changed a facet of your private/work life.
  - Did you reach something because you really did your utmost best, you used your will-power? What was/is the role of concentrated energy?
  - Did you reach something because it came naturally, without visible effort, it happened spontaneously? What was/is the role of deconcentrated energy?
  - Contemplate on how you keep these mechanisms active in your daily functioning, to concentrate, act as an arrow, and to deconcentrate, move in a field.

References

Baggini, J. (2011). *The ego trick. What does it mean to be you*? London: Granta Books.
Bakhtin, M. M. M. (1981). *The dialogic imagination: Four essays* (No. 1). Austin: University of Texas Press.
Bohm, D. (1996). *On dialogue*. New York: Routledge.
Gallagher, R. (2009). *How to tell anyone anything: Breakthrough techniques for handling difficult situations at work*. AMACOM.
Gallagher, S. (2012). *Epilogue. A philosophical epilogue on the question of autonomy*. In H. J. M. Hermans & T. Gieser. (Eds.), *Handbook of dialogical self theory* (pp. 488–496). Cambridge: University Press.
Gergen, K. J. (2009). *Relational being: Beyond self and community*. New York: Oxford University Press.
Gergen, K. J., McNamee, S., & Barrett, F. (2001). Toward transformative dialogue. *International Journal of Public Administration, 24*(7&8), 679–707.
Heifetz, R. A., Grashow, A., & Linsky, M. (2009). *The practice of adaptive leadership: Tools and tactics for changing your organization and the world*. Boston: Harvard Business Press.
Hermans, H. J. M. (2013). A multivoiced and dialogical self and the challenge of social power in a globalizing world. In: R.W. Tafarodi (Ed.), *Subjectivity in the twenty-first century. Psychological, sociological, and political perspectives*. Cambridge: University Press.
Hermans, H. J. M. (2017). *Democratic self*. NY: Oxford University Press. (in press).
Hermans, H. J. M. http://www.dialogical-self.nl/.
Hermans, H. J. M., & Gieser, Th (Eds.). (2012). *Handbook of dialogical self theory*. Cambridge: University Press.
Hermans, H. J. M., Kempen, H. J. G., & Van Loon, E. (Rens) J. P. (1992). The dialogical self: Beyond individualism and rationalism. *American Psychologist, 47*.
Hermans, H. J. M., & Hermans-Jansen, E. (1995). *Self-narratives: The construction of meaning in psychotherapy*. New York: Guilford Press.

Hermans, H. J. M., & Hermans-Konopka, A. (2010). *Dialogical self theory. Positioning and counter-positioning in a globalizing society*. Cambridge: University Press.

Hermans, H. J. M., & Kempen, H. (1993). *The dialogical self. Meaning as movement*. NY: Academic Press.

Hickman, G. R. (2016). *Leading organizations: perspectives for a new era*. Thousand Oaks: Sage.

Hosking, D. M. (2011). Moving relationality: Meditations on a relational approach to leadership. In A. Bryman, D. Collinson, K. Grint, B. Jackson, & M. Uhl-Bien (Eds.), *The SAGE handbook of leadership* (pp. 455–467). London, UK: Sage.

James, W. (1890). *The principles of psychology* (Vol. 1). London: MacMillan.

Jaworsky, J. (2012). *Source. The inner path of knowledge creation*. San Francisco, CA: Berrett-Koehler Publishers.

Kohlrieser, G., Goldsworthy, S., & Coombe, D. (2012). *Care to dare: unleashing astonishing potential through secure base leadership*. New York: Wiley.

Lakoff, G., & Johnson, M. (1999). *Philosophy in the flesh: the embodied mind and its challenge to Western thought*. New York, NY: Basic Books.

Libbrecht, U. (2007). *Within the four seas…: Introduction to comparative philosophy*. Belgium: Peeters Publishers.

Morioka, M. (2008). Voices of the self in the therapeutic chronotype: *Utuschi* and *Ma*. *International Journal for Dialogical Science, 3*(1), 93–108.

Morioka, M. (2012). Creating dialogical space in psychotherapy: meaning-generating chronotype of *ma*. In H. J. M. Hermans, & T. Gieser (Eds.), *Handbook of Dialogical Self Theory* (pp. 390–404). Cambridge: University Press.

Morioka, M. (2015). How to create *ma*—the living pause—in the landscape of the mind: the wisdom of the NOH Theater. *International Journal for Dialogical Science, 9*(1), 81–95.

Raggatt, P. T. F. (2012). Positioning the dialogical self: recent advances in theory construction. In H. J. M. Hermans, & T. Gieser (Eds.), *Handbook of dialogical self theory* (pp. 29–45). Cambridge: University Press.

Ricard, M. (2011). *The art of meditation*. London: Atlantic Books Ltd.

Sampson, E. (2008 reprint). *Celebrating the other: A dialogic account of human nature*. Chagrin Falls, Ohio: TAOS Institute Publications.

Shotter, J. (2010). *Social construction on the edge: 'Withness'—thinking and embodiment*. Chagrin Falls, Ohio: TAOS Institute Publications.

Siegel, D. J. (2017). *The mind. A journey to the heart of human being*. NY: W.W. Norton & Company.

Van Loon, E. (Rens) J. P. (1990). Symbols as a way for personal integration. *Speling*, 13–18. [Dutch].

Van Loon, E. (Rens) J. P. (1996). *Symbols in self-narrative. interpreting by means of self-confrontation method* [book in Dutch]. Assen: Van Gorcum.

Chapter 3
Dialogical Leadership

> *You know something, general, sometimes they can't tell when you are acting and when you are not.*
> *General Patton: "It isn't important for them to know. It is only important for me to know."*
>
> F. Schaffner (1970) Patton [Movie]

Abstract

- Dialogical Leadership is both a philosophy of leadership and a way of working and behaving.
- A Dialogical leader is able to manage both the *society of mind* and the *society of members* through the tool of reciprocal exchange.
- A dialogical leader is not caught in a single position as there is free energy ('ma') *to step out of the framework, the cage of your thoughts, reframing issues in a more appropriate manner.*
- *Organizations are relational*, rather than purely rational, systems, and are fundamentally reticular in nature, the products of multiple interactions and relationships between people.
- The dichotomy between *leader and follower* is unhelpful and false: the best, most robust, solutions are co-created by leaders and followers.
- Effective leaders are able to *adapt* their approach and style to reflect changing circumstances—without betraying their principles or losing their sense of personal identity.
- The future depends partly on leaders' ability to find intelligent and imaginative solutions to complex and difficult issues and *create the conditions for dialogue* in their context (organization, society, and team).

This chapter holds the 'heart of the vision'. It explains how Dialogical Self Theory relates to leadership and what it means for organizations today. It discusses the link between leaders and followers and the idea of reciprocal exchange. Inspired by the theory and practice of the Dialogical Self, I introduced the term *Dialogical Leader* in 2003,[1] where the concept of Dialogical Self was applied to leadership for the first time. The idea of Dialogical Leadership developed as we were confronted in our

---
[1]Van Loon and Wijsbek 2003.

practice with leaders that did not flexibly adjust to roles they have to fulfill in the workplace, although they showed these capabilities in other domains of their life. The concept of Dialogical Leadership enables leaders to reflect on and act in the different roles they have to fulfill by starting an internal dialogue between I-positions (as roles they play in life in general). The concept is internationally coined in 2015 in the article *Dialogical Leadership. Dialogue as Condition Zero*'.[2] At Tilburg University (the Netherlands) I did my inaugural speech as professor of Dialogical Leadership in 2015 on October 9th, titled: *Dialogical Leadership. Across Boundaries.*[3]

Starting from a definition of leadership as a relational process (Sect. 3.1), the myth of the leader-follower dichotomy is questioned (Sect. 3.2). After having defined Dialogical Leadership (Sect. 3.3) the approach is applied to practice. Before going to Part II—the Practice—a personal reflection is given (Sect. 3.4) and questions for the reader (Sect. 3.5).

3.1 Leadership as a Relational Process

Leaders nowadays have to deal with regulation, complexity, speed of continuous change, diversity and fragmentation, communication and transparency, changing expectations of the workforce, managing polarities and multiple time horizons, customer sophistication and value propositions, sustainability and corporate social responsibility. A long list of items that are simultaneously on their agenda. For leaders this means to feel comfortable with ambiguity, to show self-reflection and know themselves, to let people contribute, and to build trust. To have a compelling story, to inspire innovation and creativity, and to set a standard for adaptability and flexibility. It also means to not be afraid to fail and capable of facilitating the possible, to be skilled in building and managing networks, and to know how to use influencing capacities in a skillful manner. To collaborate across disciplines with experts in other areas, and also have in-depth expertise in a single field.[4] Becoming aware of the relational aspect of leading is fairly factual.

Expectations and requirements of leaders have changed significantly over the past 20 years. The 1970s concept of servant leadership, developed by Robert Greenleaf,[5] has been revived in newer models emphasizing followers and their needs. 'Authentic leadership', 'respectful leadership' and 'reflective leadership' now feature regularly in management writing and academic journals. The term

---

[2]Van Loon and Van Dijk 2015. Before 2015, the concept of Dialogical Leadership was explored in Van Loon, *The Secret of Being a Leader. Searching for the Essence* (2006), and summarized in a whitepaper, Van Loon, *Dialogical Leader. Developing Leaders for the Future* (2010). Other authors using the term *Dialogische Führung* are Dietz and Kracht (2011).

[3]The inaugural address was delivered in Dutch.

[4]Conference Board 2011. *Leadership Essentials for 2020 and beyond.*

[5]Greenleaf 1970.

3.1 Leadership as a Relational Process

emotional intelligence, popularized in the 1990s by Daniel Goleman and used to describe qualities such as self-awareness and social skill, has become part of the language.[6]

The good leader has been 're-imagined' as a 'community builder', able to connect with others and to create a strong sense of meaning and purpose. In research for their book on authentic leadership *Why Should Anyone Be Led By You?* in the early 2000s, Rob Goffee and Gareth Jones found that 'community' and sense of 'significance' topped the list of followers' needs. High scores for the competencies traditionally identified by consultants—for example, self-confidence and critical thinking—are no longer seen as wholly reliable markers of leadership potential. 'People' skills are seen as necessary for top performance. "Power in organizations is the capacity generated by relationships."[7] Management and leadership theories have advanced to the point where the vision is of a 'humane organization' in which employees are seen not as assets to work hard and wear out but as people to nurture and develop.[8] From a relational perspective leadership can be defined as an interactive process, where *'relating'* is the core concept: members in an organization are engaged in a process as collaborative partners.

3.1.1 Good Leaders Deploy Different Styles

At the same time, it's been acknowledged that a one-size-fits-all-approach to running an organization won't work. Good and effective leaders are flexible, capable of deploying different styles at different times in the history of their organizations. The concept of 'fluid leadership' co-exists with the new progressive models; the modern leader is perceived as someone able to change and adapt without any loss of integrity, authenticity and effectiveness. Daniel Goleman identified six distinct leadership styles "springing from different components of emotional intelligence" and highlighted the need for leaders or teams of leaders to move seamlessly between them.[9] "*Coercive leaders* demand immediate compliance. *Authoritative leaders* mobilize people toward a vision. *Affiliative leaders* create emotional bonds and harmony. *Democratic leaders* build consensus through participation. *Pacesetting leaders* expect excellence and self-direction. And *coaching leaders* develop people for the future. The research indicates that leaders who get the best results don't rely on just one leadership style; they use most of the styles in any given week." Jonathan Gosling and Henry Mintzberg,[10] meanwhile, have conceived of the manager as a 'weaver' who pulls together the threads of different

---

[6]Goleman 1995.
[7]Wheatley 1994.
[8]Hill 2013.
[9]Goleman 2000.
[10]Gosling and Mintzberg 2003.

'mindsets', weaving them 'over and under the others to create a fine, sturdy cloth'. Managing involves five tasks, each with its own mindset: *managing your self* presumes a reflective mindset; *managing organizations* means that you have to use your analytic mindset; *managing context* refers that you are able to contextualize within the worldly environment; *managing relationships* is about the collaborative mindset; and *managing change* is action. Leaders need to explore and integrate those five aspects.

So people running organizations are expected not only to conform to a progressive, people-centered model in which emotional intelligence, empathy and imagination count for as much as strategic vision and rationality but also to adapt this model according to the situations they find themselves in and to call on a repertoire of styles and skills. Goleman's coercive leadership can be seen as the right response in a crisis, his coaching leadership as the model in less turbulent times and his affiliative leadership as one of the bridges between them. If the skills set and profile for the leader are different, so, too, integration is the job.

3.2 The Myth of the Leader–Follower Dichotomy

As indicated previously, from a relational perspective, leadership is defined as an interactive process, where '*relating*' is the core concept: members are engaged in a process as collaborative partners. Leadership is the process of organizing and relating. Not as separate individuals in a *leader-follower* dyad, which is representing an entity perspective, but as relation-based leadership, leadership conditions in already organized situations. Kilburg and Donohue describe leadership as: "*complex multidimensional, emergent* process in which the leader(s), follower(s) and other stakeholders (formal and informal) in a human enterprise *use* their characteristics, capabilities, thoughts, feelings and behavior *to create mutually influencing relationships,* that enable to *co-evolve* strategies, tactics, structures, processes, directions and other methods of building and managing human enterprises with the goal of *producing* adaptive success in their chosen niches in the competitive evaluative and evolving ecology of organizations."[11] In this description authors try to capture all elements in one formula, which is precarious, but useful.

This definition encompasses the complexity of the subject and the lack of clear universal guidelines and principles. It emphasizes the essentials of leadership. A few observations.The first is that authors use the expression *emergent process*. Like dialogue leading is treated as a process, that emerges in a relation between leaders, members of an organization and other stakeholders. The second one is about *mutually influencing*. Similar to dialogue leading is a mutual process. Conceptually and in reality there is no leading without following. Theoretically leading and following are mutually implicated, you can't think about the one

---

[11]Kilburg and Donohue 2011.

3.2 The Myth of the Leader–Follower Dichotomy   47

without the other. In reality, you can't lead without people following you, and vice-versa. Last observation is about *producing*. The process of leading and following results in producing something, here defined as success. The result of the emerging process of mutually influencing results in products and services. Leads to a change in the environment.

3.2.1 Good Leadership as Effective and Ethical

In this context, a description of Gill Robinson Hickman's view on leadership is important. She designs a contextual and relational concept of leadership.[12] She combines in good leadership two implications, that mostly are separated. She refers to good leadership as *effective and ethical*. In this sense, leadership is the *ability to act good* and *to enable others to act good* (effective and ethical). The concept intends to promote good leadership in a double sense in organizations.[13] Hickman focuses on leadership as a process of shared responsibility among leaders and members[14] of an organization. She focuses less on leadership as a *person* or *position*. In her concept, she aligns the organization with changes in the external and the internal environment, based on common purpose and core values, leadership philosophy, ethics, and social responsibility. As we will demonstrate later in this book, core values and purpose are critically important to create a sense of direction for individuals, teams and the organization as a whole. This helps members of an organization to intentionally select and cultivate a leadership concept and culture to fit the common purpose and organizational processes and practices. We will illustrate this in the case description on team and organization-level in Chap. 7 on these three levels. Hickman starts from the assumption that a leadership concept is more than a style or framework, it is a deliberate choice and forms the essence of an organization's integrity. By acting in an authentic manner in this line, leaders demonstrate a leadership philosophy as a central guiding principle for their actions, feelings and ways of thinking in business and society.

In terms of leader-member relation this has important consequences as it implicates by definition fluid roles among leaders and members to accomplish the common purpose based on all members' capabilities, expertise, motivation, ideas and circumstances. Not simply based on formal roles and authority, it establishes an

---

[12]Hickman 2016.

[13]To demonstrate that good leadership has this double meaning of effective and ethical is a separate research project, that would be worthwhile to do for a Ph.D. student. As the two are separate, it is possible that we speak about good leadership in the sense of effectiveness, while not serving the common good (like in the financial crisis).

[14]Hickman uses five terms next to another for members of an organization: organizational participants, followers, team-members, employees or associates. We have experienced that choosing the right expression in the relation leader-follower is critically important to not evoke the wrong associations (i.e. passivity in this role). See also: Koonce et al. 2016.

ethical foundation to create a trustworthy and nimble organization that is concerned about the effect of its decisions and actions on its members, external stakeholders and society as a whole. Hickman's view is summarized in the Fig. 3.1.

What is challenging for the future is to change the mass media expression *leadership* into *relational leading*. The word leadership refers—linguistically and mentally—to a paradigm that *you* lead *other* people—as actors in a play—instead of reciprocally influencing human beings. One way to overcome the leadership crisis is to transform the vision of leading and following essentially in all our actions and phrasing. "From a constructionist standpoint, we are barely at the beginning. This is so because the vast bulk of leadership writing locates the source of leadership in the individual as opposed to collaborative relations."[15] A charismatic leader can only be charismatic by virtue of people around, who treat their leader in this manner. From a constructionist view, none of the qualities attributed to good leaders stands on itself. "To say anything about the leader as a single human being is to miss the process of relationship responsible for the very idea of 'the leader'".[16] Although business schools don't pay much attention to dialogue, because "as is traditionally held, it is reasoning and facts that count",[17] there is a growing awareness of an organization as more than a rational system. It is above all a *relational system*, a system of giving meaning and interpreting behavior, both economic and psychological behavior. In a globalized world, we need to become more aware how we *construct* our worlds. "This view of socially constructed worlds represents a major transformation in contemporary understanding. Traditionally, we have placed a premium on *the truth*, as if there is some set of words that is uniquely suited to represent the world as it is. This view continues to be shared in both science and society."[18] But if we take a closer look to what is going on in the world, we see the truth being manipulated (and also corrected) by science because of public goals. "From a constructionist perspective, however, the world comes to be what it is for us by virtue of its relationships. Whatever exists, simply exists. But the moment we begin to describe or explain, we are taking part in a cultural tradition—one tradition among many."[19] Much of the business is done in English, but it is only one of the many languages on earth, most people's worlds are defined in another language. Our words are the products of preceding conversations our ancestors had. With these words, that we inherited, we describe and construct our contemporary world, very much different from one thousand years ago, two or three, or five thousand years ago. And with our words, we also express what we think is rational, valuable and morally good. From a social constructionist view, dialogue about what is real, rational and good is essential in creating those common understandings by which

---

[15]Gergen 2009a, 148.

[16]Gergen 2009a, 149; Hersted and Gergen, 2013; Cunliffe and Eriksen 2011.

[17]Hersted and Gergen 2013, 17.

[18]Hersted and Gergen 2013, 20.

[19]Hersted and Gergen 2013, 20.

3.2 The Myth of the Leader–Follower Dichotomy

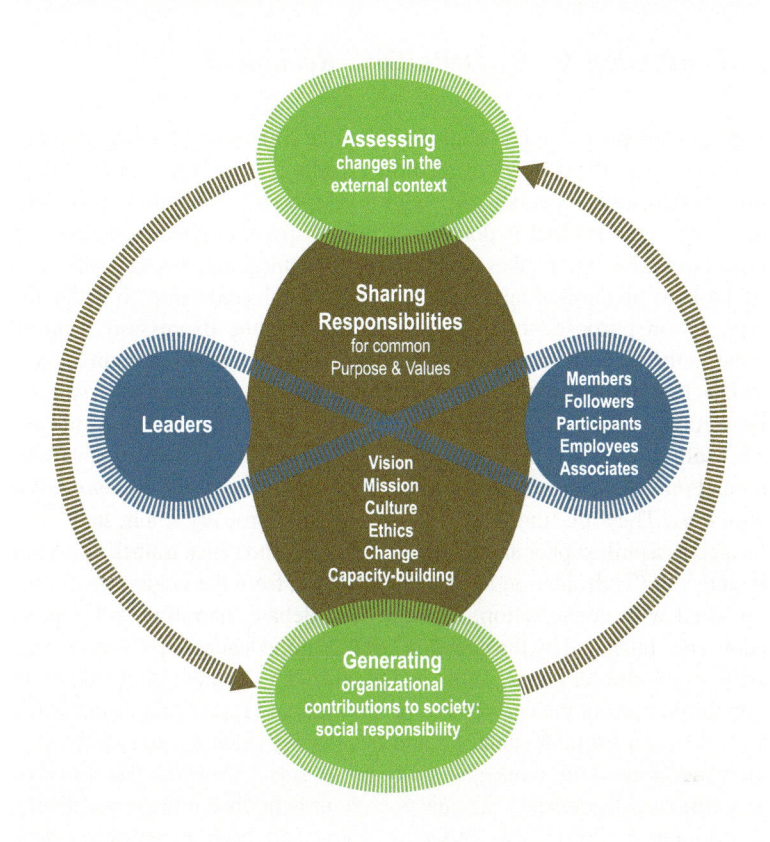

A Contextual and Relational Leadership Concept

- **Assessing** changes in the external context
- **Sharing Responsibilities** for common Purpose & Values
- **Leaders**
- **Members / Followers / Participants / Employees / Associates**
- Vision / Mission / Culture / Ethics / Change / Capacity-building
- **Generating** organizational contributions to society: social responsibility

Source: Hickman, 2016, 1

Fig. 3.1 A contextual and relational leadership concept

we lead our lives, our societies and our organizations. "To be organized at all depends on collectively coordinating words and actions."[20]

3.2.2 Leadership Is 'By Definition' Relational

A core insight and profound personal change since 2003 is that I deeply accepted and started to work with the concept of relational leading. A frequent confrontation with this subject occurs when people ask: "who is your boss?" What do you answer? In a culture in organizations that is dominated by trait-psychological and container-self approaches to leadership, it takes a while to change this paradigm. Organizations still tend to look to an individual leader and individual leadership, but the trend is changing. I—on purpose—often systematically use the expression *Leading and Following* in the text. The combination and using verbs instead of nouns. You could reformulate Baggini's quote "'I' is a verb dressed as a noun' as: '*Leadership* is a verb dressed as a noun'.[21] What applies to self, applies to leadership in the same manner. 'Self and other', 'leader and member', the two *cannot exist without one another* and *they theoretically and practically need each other to become self-aware and conscious*. They are 'mutually reflexive and reciprocally implicated.'[22]

Educated as a philosopher and as a personality psychologist, trained as a Valuation Theory and Self-Confrontation Method Consultant, from the beginning of our practice I worked with conversation, dialogue and debate, narrative and appreciative methodologies. Intrigued by the question 'what is good leadership?' I started to study this theme in my master thesis 'What is a good man?' At the time, I studied Plato's views on this subject in the early Western tradition and Lao-Tzu's vision in Chinese Taoism. The quest for understanding and developing *good leadership/good people* motivates me in my daily work and study up to today. Over the last thirty years, I worked with many leaders and the question about being/becoming a good, effective, ethical and authentic leader was frequently conversed, both in one to one dialogues and in sessions with leadership teams. *Effectiveness, authenticity,* and *ethics* are implied in leadership. Both in literature,[23] and in our practice, these concepts prove to be important. Authentic leaders are described as having the capabilities of self-awareness, balanced processing, self-regulation, and ethical, relational transparency. These are characteristics of an open and honest dialogue as well. Effective

---

[20]Hersted and Gergen 2013, 21.

[21]Baggini 2011, 126: "Thought and feeling are what matter *does*, when it is arranged in the remarkably complex way that brains are. Matter is all that is needed for them to exist, but they are not themselves lumps of matter. In this sense, "I is as verb dressed as a noun." We are—in Baggini's view—made up of nothing more than physical stuff, but to describe our true nature, you need more than just a physical vocabulary. "We are no more than, but more than just, matter." (123).

[22]Hawes 1999.

[23]George 2003, 2007; Grint 2005, 2010a; Litaer 1993; Luthans and Avolio 2003.

leaders have more impact if they are perceived by the others as effective *and* authentic, *and* ethical. Authentic leadership is described as a process "which results in both greater self-awareness and self-regulated positive behaviors on the part of leaders and associates, fostering positive self-development."[24] Kernis[25] defines authenticity as consisting of four components: *self-awareness* as accurate knowledge of one's strengths, weaknesses and idiosyncratic qualities. *Relational transparency*, involving genuine representation of the self to others. *Balanced processing* as the collection and use of relevant, objective information, particularly that which challenges one's prior beliefs. *Internalized moral perspective* as self-regulation and self-determination.If we speak about authenticity and inauthenticity in terms of the Dialogical Self Theory, we speak about 'being genuine, being 'your self', in a *relational and dialogical* manner'.

3.2.3 A Confrontation with Values

"Ethics is central to leadership because of the nature of the process of influence, the need to engage followers in accomplishing mutual goals, and the impact leaders have on the organization's values."[26] As a leader, you have to be aware of your own values, your leadership principles and the ethical boundaries. Once you get in a situation in which you are under pressure, you can test the strength of your values and ethical leadership in reality.[27] An example from my own career. One event is burned in my memory as an example of how to react when there is an attack on your core values. In the beginning of my career as consultant, we—my wife and I—had our two-person consulting practice. We had a big client. Our client was happy with the results and the way in which we had our conversations with the managers (sixty leaders in a public organization). We worked as a contractor and one day my 'boss'—who paid our invoices each month—said: "Rens, I want a copy of all personal files of the participants." I responded immediately and without hesitation: "No, Paul [not his real name], I am *not* going to give you the files. I feel bound to the ethical code of Dutch Psychologists (NIP-code), we are not allowed to give files to others without explicit, written consent." "Ok, Rens, if you refuse, this is our last project together," Paul answered. He is a tall man, and a powerful pusher. I kept my nerves and replied in a friendly manner: "I am sorry about that. I like to work with you. For me this doesn't need to be our last project together." I was surprised by myself that I did not react irritated and pushing back emotionally, as he was breaking our agreement, that the personal files would not be copied. After this incident, we did a few more projects together. He did not break up the working relation.

---

[24]Luthans and Avolio 2003, quoted in Parry 2011, 63.
[25]Kernis 2003.
[26]Northouse 2007, 347.
[27]George 2007.

Although I could have reacted by pushing back, I was able to stand by my ethical values while also managing to keep the business relationship. And I was mindful to say 'no' to an improper proposal as in the end clients prefer to work with people who stand by their principles because it generates trust.

3.2.4 A Dynamic Leadership Concept

Apart from leadership as effective, authentic and ethical, leadership frameworks need to be described in terms of relationality, co-construction and network causality. We talk about a network, where influencing is reticular, like in a complex system with multiple relations. In 2006, I designed a dynamic concept of leadership, which has been developed over the years and stems from a combination of practice and theory.[28] Good leading and good following—in the sense of its effectiveness—is being agile in applying elementary movements: giving direction, pushing and pulling, without identifying with one of these styles of influencing.[29] Three levels of energy (physical doing, intuitive experiencing, and rational knowing) are involved here. From a relational perspective, leadership is defined as an interactive process, where *'relating'* is the core concept: members are engaged in a process as collaborative partnership. Leadership as a process of organizing and relating from a shared purpose and shared values. Not as separate individuals in a *leader-follower* dyad, but as a mutually implicated relation.

This contains three parts:

1. Leading by *setting a vision, getting things done* (pushing) and *connecting other people in this process of realization* (pulling).
2. Influencing by using *rational capabilities* (rational knowing, thinking, head), by *sensing* what is going in yourself and your environment (intuitive experiencing, feeling, heart), by (intentionally and unintentionally) showing your *body-language* (physical doing, acting, hands).
3. Fulfilling the basic *leadership roles* in the context, as an *entrepreneur* (setting direction), as a *manager* (getting things done), as a *coach* (through developing people), as a *change-leader* (leading the process of change) and as a *professional* (leading in a profession).

---

[28]Van Loon 2006. Most important contributors are: Valuation Theory, Self-Confrontation Method, Hermans and Hermans-Jansen (1995) Dialogical Self Theory, Hermans and Gieser (2012); Hermans and Hermans-Konopka (2010), Institute of Dutch Quality, Van Loon and Roozendaal (2006) Leadership Theories and the epistemological theory of Ulrich Libbrecht (2007), and—of course—conversations with clients, individually, with their teams and the organization as a whole.

[29]You can switch between these styles if there is 'ma', as a pause, as a significant *silence* in the internal and external relation. Here a process of distancing oneself from oneself starts, and new meaning and action can be generated. Creating free energy, flexibly switching between concentrating and *deconcentrating*, in a *field* of relation.

3.2 The Myth of the Leader–Follower Dichotomy   53

Let us have a look at the elements of this basic model as a description of elements in a process. All aspects are in a dynamic interrelation, mutually influencing and continuously changing. We use this concept, when we have a conversation with leaders on how they lead, follow, think, feel and act. We create the formal and informal conditions for a safe and secure context for setting up a dialogue (Fig. 3.2).[30]

In a conversation, all elements are subject for further exploring, primarily in the form of questions and generating new insights about your style of leading and following. The concept indicates the basic elements:

1. Context: organization, team, culture, society, market.
2. Styles: giving direction, pushing, pulling.
3. Sources: rational knowing (rationality, head), intuitive experiencing (feeling, heart), physical doing (acting, hands).
4. Basic roles: entrepreneur, manager, coach.

Although it seems basic, many people I met never had a dialogue about their leadership without all kinds of input in the form of appraisals, assessments, and personality surveys. This empty[31] concept is also used to explore I-positions in the internal and external dialogue as a leader, as we will see later.

3.3 What Is Dialogical Leadership?

As the name implies, Dialogical Leadership centers on dialogue more precisely, the reciprocal exchange of knowledge, experience and ideas. This is what makes it so suited to an age of 'relational' models based on people's needs. What I say about leadership frameworks has to be understood in terms of relationality, co-construction and reticular causality. We talk about a network, where influencing is not linear, but reticular. As the previous chapter made clear, Dialogical Leadership has its roots in the fields of psychology and social science. It applies Dialogical Self Theory to leadership and organizations. The 'self' is seen as consisting of a number of different 'I-positions' (e.g. roles), and effective, authentic leadership as dependent on the individual's ability to navigate between or integrate them successfully. Dialogical Leadership focuses on external dialogue between people and on internal dialogue.[32] It is described as a dynamic *multiplicity* of *I-positions* in the *landscape* of the mind. As *voiced positions* they allow *dialogical*

---

[30]For the details, see Chap. 4. Creating Conditions for Generative Dialogue.

[31]I use the word 'empty' here, as the content is filled in the conversation in an unique and singular way. It enables people to construct their self-narrative in a conceptually complete manner, as they are invited to reflect on the core elements applied to their own life and work as a leader and as a follower. If the reader is convinced of an element that is missing in the conceptual framework, you are invited to send an email to the author, as we continuously want to improve the concept.

[32]See the illustrative case-studies in Chaps. 6 and 7.

54   3   Dialogical Leadership

A Dynamic Leadership Framework

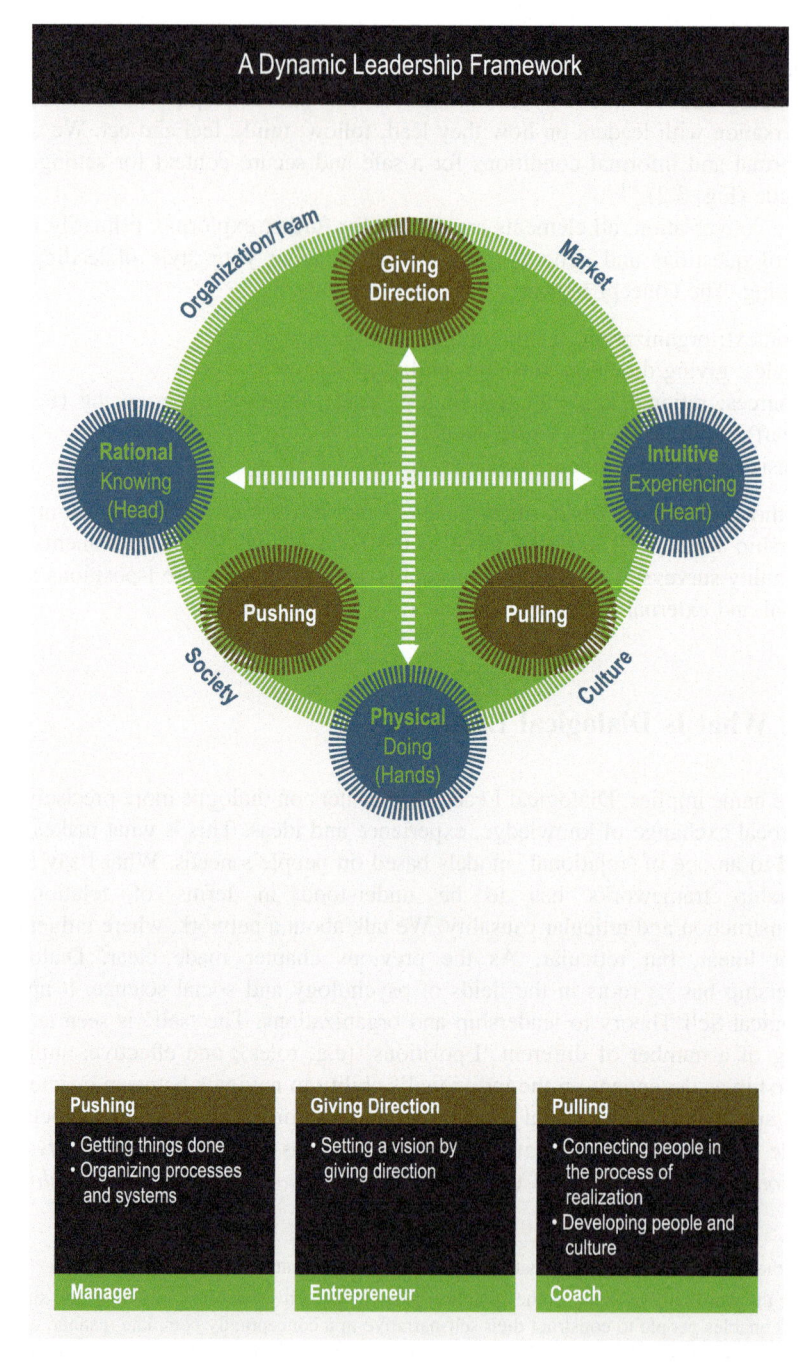

- Organization/Team
- Market
- Society
- Culture

- Giving Direction
- Rational Knowing (Head)
- Intuitive Experiencing (Heart)
- Pushing
- Pulling
- Physical Doing (Hands)

Pushing	Giving Direction	Pulling
• Getting things done • Organizing processes and systems	• Setting a vision by giving direction	• Connecting people in the process of realization • Developing people and culture
Manager	**Entrepreneur**	**Coach**

Fig. 3.2 A dynamic leadership framework

3.3 What Is Dialogical Leadership?

relationships both within and between people.[33] At the individual level, a dialogical leader is faced with the challenge to enable the dialogue between the various I-positions within the self. At the level of teams and organizations, a dialogical leader is faced with the challenge to transform the contradiction between the multi-voices of colleagues, stakeholders and competitors (etc.) between, e.g. local and global, unity and multiplicity, consistency and inconsistency and between self and the other.

3.3.1 Leading Self and Others

A Dialogical Leader is able to manage both the *society of mind* and the *society of members* through the means of reciprocal exchange. This description illustrates how you can meet the requirement not only for a more progressive, people-centered form of leadership but also for fluid and adaptive leadership. People who are able to integrate or move successfully between different I-positions through internal dialogue are more likely to be able to switch flexibly between different ways of working, e.g., as a coach, change-leader or entrepreneur and technical professional. One of the necessary skills of (current and future) leaders can be defined in Dialogical Self terms as showing "flexible movements between a diversity of I-positions that are relevant to the functioning of the organization as a whole."[34] Leaders faced with the challenge of dealing with tensions and multi-voices have to develop a 'compass' (with a 'North') in themselves for their thinking, feeling and acting. One of the challenges contemporary leaders face is how to act effectively and authentically in a fast-moving and permanently changing world seemingly without any stability and time to reflect. By consciously creating *awareness and free energy* ('*ma*' as a pause) they might become enablers to transform self and organization. Isaacs uses 'metalogue' for this highest stage of generative dialogue, referring to a process of creativity and innovation, 'meaning flowing'.[35] This is the point where effectiveness and authenticity come together. A dialogical leader is able to create an atmosphere for dialogue. Dialogical leadership is about creating space and *atmosphere*. "What happens lies beyond power or control of anyone singular I-position. Everything goes apparently 'spontaneously', without visible effort. It happens in a synchronic, coincidental way."[36] This reminds us to the description both

---

[33]Hermans et al. 1992.

[34]Hermans and Hermans-Konopka 2010, 326.

[35]"Metalogue reveals a conscious, intimate, and subtle relationship between the structure and content of an exchange and its meaning. The medium and the message are linked." Isaacs 1993, 38.

[36]Hermans 2006, 51. [Translated from the Dutch text].

Isaacs and Bohm give when they speak about 'meaning moving'[37] and 'meaning flowing'.[38] The expression 'atmosphere' is essential. Dialogical Self Theory and Dialogical Leadership techniques allow leaders to adapt without betraying their core principles or putting their sense of personal identity at risk. They are, therefore, consistent with the idea of authentic leadership—that the leaders who earn the trust and respect of employees are those who, to quote Gareth Jones, don't 'role play' their way through their working lives but behave as their real, relational selves.[39]

"The model of the dialogical leader transcends not only the notion of the container self, so typical of the modern model of the self, but also the notion of the container organization. In principal, all stakeholders who are part of an extended organization are dependent on the actuality and needs of the parties involved, and these parties are potential positions in the external domain of the self of the dialogical leader."[40] Issues are treated as things, they need a medicine for the illness. If we do some 'objective interventions' such as radical cost reduction and talent restructuring, accompanied by an attractive and visual communication program, and some zero and follow up measuring, the problem will be solved, before a specific date. Gergen explains that problems in organizations are traditionally treated as 'things', both by managers as by consultants. "Life in organizations is dynamic. Everywhere within the organization—from the mailroom to the boardroom—participants are continuously generating their local sense of the real and the good, who is doing what to whom, and whether it is good or bad. Realities and moralities will necessarily conflict, and with such conflicts often comes suspicion, animosity, a loss of morale, and more. These are the daily challenges of organizational life, and when the tensions are high they can deeply hinder organizational functioning."[41]

3.3.2 When to Apply Dialogical Leadership?

'Wicked problems'—for which there are few recent precedents and even fewer known solutions—increasingly feature on the agendas of businesses and government organizations. Ranging from oil and resource constraints to demographic and social change, these problems demand an innovative, imaginative approach—and the 'collective intelligence' of multiple shareholders and stakeholders. For 'wicked' issues, no fixed answer is available.[42] In an unpredictable and complex world, dialogue is 'condition zero' to find the answer in the process of asking the right questions. For many leaders setting up a good dialogue is not easy. Very often there

---

[37]Isaacs 1999.
[38]Bohm 1996.
[39]Goffee and Jones 2006.
[40]Hermans and Konopka 2010, 330.
[41]Gergen 2009a, 147.
[42]Grint 2005 distinguishes between crises, tame and wicked issues.

3.3 What Is Dialogical Leadership?

is no time, no awareness, and no willingness to slow down the process and to really listen and explore the issue at hand. "Conversation is an act of change, a (de-)construction of meaning".[43] The impact of dialogue can be great. A good dialogue might transform one's meaning system by opening up knowing, experiencing and doing in a way that is more appropriate to the *present, the now*. 'Re-setting' of our way of perceiving is one of the outcomes of a successful dialogue process. A leader has to create an atmosphere to make this happen. A good leader is aware of the atmosphere (s)he creates.[44]

Colin Price expresses this moment of 'creating space' in a beautiful way in a movie, titled *Beyond Performance*. He speaks of the space that is developed in thinking and the consequence of it. The moment you realize your thinking is captured, *that moment of realization*, is the moment that you have stepped out of it right here, 'ma' as a pause. You transform your thinking and your leadership as you step into a different place, where you are operating in a new world of endless possibilities. This is an illustration of the space that is crucial for transformation. This happens par excellence in a dialogic state of mind, where meaning is flowing freely, instead of being caught in *problems*, *puzzles* or *polarity*.[45] In his view, the highest level of leading and thinking is embracing *paradox*. This is an illustration of *transforming in a dialogic mind*. Although Price does not use the term dialogue in the movie, he explicitly applies dialogue for team to get better results. "As a rule of thumb, 80% of the time the team spends together should be devoted to dialogue, and just 20% to presentations."[46] He further recommends a well-structured agenda for an effective dialogue in three stages: personal reflection, discussion in pairs or small groups, and whole team discussion.

Characteristic for dialogical leadership is the ability to deal effectively with opposites and paradoxes. A dialogical leader is not caught in a single position as there is free energy *to step out of the framework, the cage of your thoughts, reframing issues in a more appropriate manner*. This applies to leading others and leading self, externally and internally. The notion of a *third position* refers to the process of reconciling two conflicting I-positions. In creating a third position, the two original ones can be unified without removing their original differences and tension. For example, '*I as a coach*' can be a third position, without losing the productive tension of the other I-positions '*I as willing to help other people*' and '*I as know-it-all*'.[47]

---

[43]Ford and Ford 1995.

[44]This refers to a mode of realizing activity in between active and passive, a *participative mode* (Bohm 1996, 96–109). A *participative mode* is crucial for describing the atmosphere in a dialogue in an appropriate way. Cf. what was mentioned before about field awareness and deconcentrated energy by Libbrecht (2007).

[45]*Problems: what* to do, either ↔ or? *Puzzles: how* to solve on a continuum of either ↔ or? *Polarity: how* to solve simultaneously in two opposing directions?

[46]Keller and Price 2011, 213.

[47]See Sect. 5.7 for an extensive description of this case.

3.3.3 Four Pillars of Dialogical Leadership

Dialogical Leadership applies the core concepts of the Dialogical Self Theory to the domain of leadership. Four main elements characterize Dialogical Leadership.

1. It is a flexible combination of an *internal and external dialogue* of the leader and the members of his/her community.
2. In an internal reflexive dialogue, Dialogical Leadership is about the ability to create space between the different roles you can play as a leader, so that you are able to choose what role is required in a specific situation. We distinguish five basic roles

    a. As *entrepreneur*, setting direction for the organization
    b. As *manager*, as organizing the processes to get things done
    c. As *coach*, as developing the people and the culture of the organization
    d. As *professional*, as referring to the content of what you deliver
    e. As *change leader*, as enabling processes of continuous learning and change in the company.[48]

3. In an external reflexive dialogue, Dialogical Leadership is about the ability to proactively switch between styles as related to the type of issues you are confronted with

    a. Using a push style in case of crisis and immediate action (giving an answer)
    b. Using a combination of a push and pull style in case of complicated (tamed) issues (providing an answer)
    c. Using a pull style in case of complex (wicked) issues, in case there is no answer known and you have to mobilize the thinking power of all stakeholders (asking the right questions).

4. It refers to the capability to create *conditions for a generative dialogue*, with your members and within yourself.

    In the Fig. 3.3 the core elements are summarized.

3.4 Reflections on My Personal Narrative 2

In June 1993, I did my second self-investigation, with the same supervisor. In the period in-between, I was working on my Ph.D. research and worked with individual clients and with groups of participants, both in the Self-Confrontation Method as

---

[48]In Sect. 4.6.2 the roles of *change leader*, and *professional* will be described and discussed more in detail.

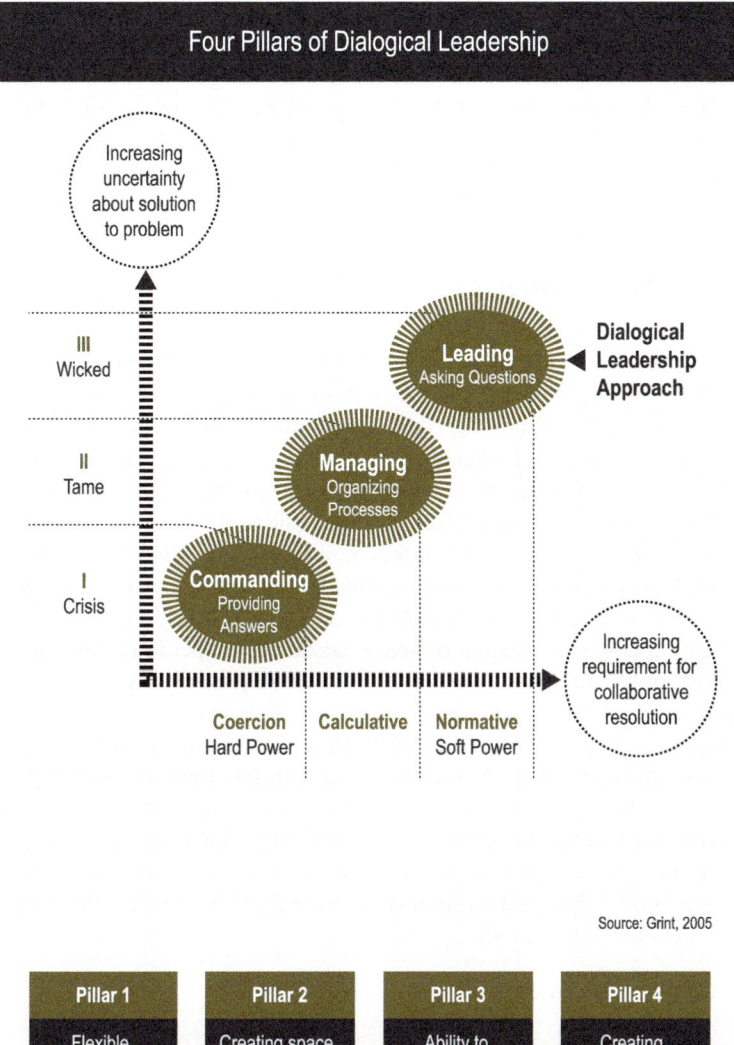

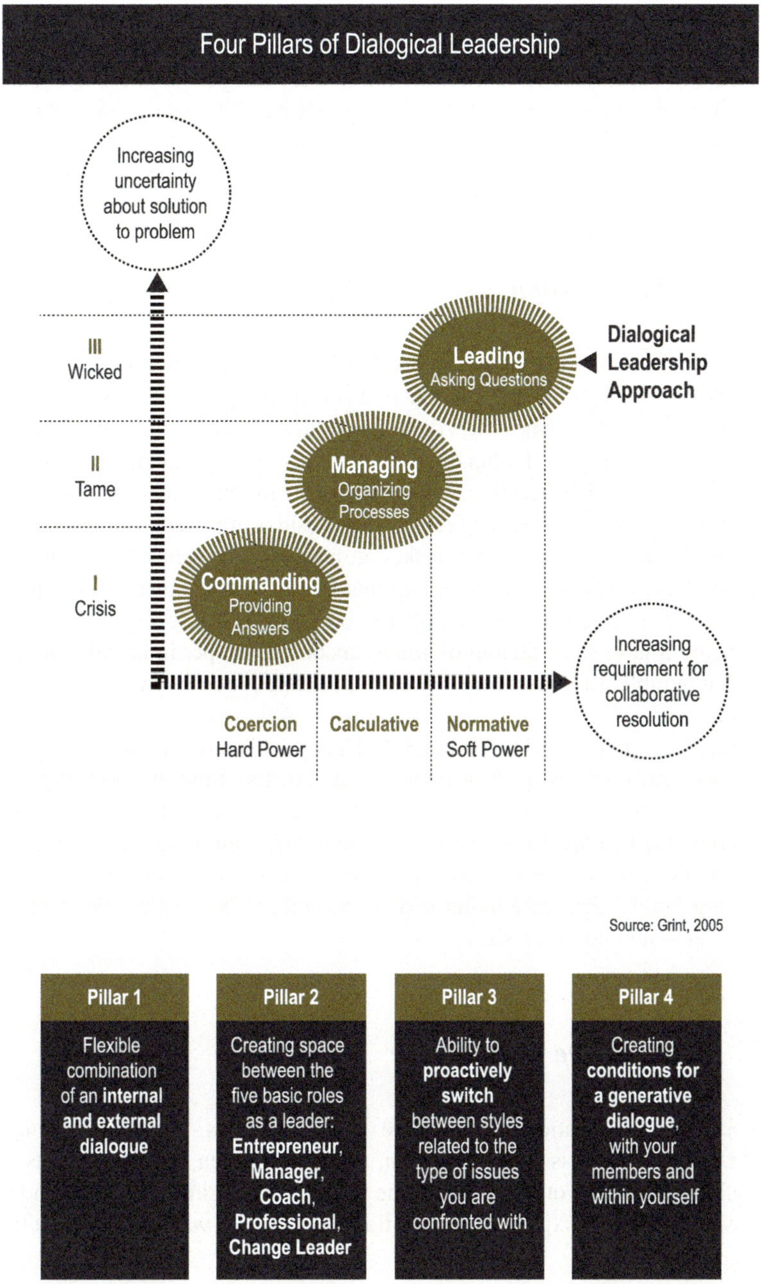

3.4 Reflections on My Personal Narrative 2

Four Pillars of Dialogical Leadership

- Increasing uncertainty about solution to problem
- III Wicked
- II Tame
- I Crisis

- **Leading** — Asking Questions ◄ **Dialogical Leadership Approach**
- **Managing** — Organizing Processes
- **Commanding** — Providing Answers

- Coercion / Hard Power
- Calculative
- Normative / Soft Power

- Increasing requirement for collaborative resolution

Source: Grint, 2005

Pillar 1	Pillar 2	Pillar 3	Pillar 4
Flexible combination of an **internal and external dialogue**	Creating space between the five basic roles as a leader: **Entrepreneur, Manager, Coach, Professional, Change Leader**	Ability to **proactively switch** between styles related to the type of issues you are confronted with	Creating **conditions for a generative dialogue**, with your members and within yourself

Fig. 3.3 Four pillars of dialogical leadership

well as workshops around symbolism. I was teaching students in Valuation Theory and Self-Confrontation Method at the Radboud University (Nijmegen). I explicitly requested my supervisor to work with the newest insights of the Dialogical Self Theory. I wished to analyze and discuss my self-narrative in this line of thinking and hoped to draw lessons from it for my personal life and for my professional practice.

3.4.1 My Secret Name

Without going into the details of the results, I will focus on two I-positions at that time: 'I as Rens' and 'I as Levi'. In my first self-investigation, one of the sentences was about my secret name, 'Levi', a name that emerged intuitively during a workshop on symbolism I attended. This name referred to my intuitively felt connection with Jewish tradition. "Somewhere in myself I feel the image of my mother: the Jewess." A sentence feeling very positive for me.[49] In my daily life at specific moments before a difficult task, e.g. a difficult conversation, I consciously applied the Levi I-position, by *imagining* that I acted in that situation from this Levi I-position. I discovered this as helpful to cope with difficult situations, as in my experiencing it gave me a feeling of being 'anchored' deeper in myself and it made me less vulnerable for stress. *It felt as if I had a safe place in myself*, from where I could act.

For me, as an expert in Dialogical Self Theory, it is a remarkable experience to analyze my material *as if it was a client*. At the time we did my second self-investigation, I was not able to look at it with the emotional distance I have now. I conclude that what I intuitively felt, and why I intuitively created 'Levi', is that this helped me to cope with a difficult situation in my physical life: taking care for a young family, earning a living in an economic crisis situation, building up my career, in new and complex situations.

3.4.2 A Distinctive Inner Voice

If we analyze the relation between the two I-positions, I make the following remarks.[50] 'I as Rens' is a core position, which is chosen, as it represents how I physically interact with other people in the world around, situated in time and place. The reason I wanted to explore this I-position more precise was because I felt tension

---

[49] $Q = P/P + N \times 100$. P = sum total of positive feelings; N = sum total of negative feelings; Q = general positive quality. The higher the number, the more positive the sentence is experienced (here 88).

[50] I use Raggatts ordering in the handbook of Dialogical Self Theory (2012, 31).

and uneasiness in my 'daily life'. 'I as Levi' is in the Dialogical Self Theory terminology an *I-position in the internal domain of self,* with a distinctive inner voice.

In terms of *dynamic* elements, Levi functions as a position that gives direction and order in the interplay between 'I as Rens' and 'I as Levi' (*promoter*-position). Although invisible for the outer world, for me, Levi was an important source to develop in my external life. I felt capable of doing things that I—as Rens—would never have done without Levi supporting me in the back. I was strongly influenced by my mother's statement to the little Rens: "Behave normal, don't shine out, maybe you are not able to do that!" Taking up the challenge to work with top leaders in organizations was possible—in Rens' view—thanks to the imaginary support of 'Levi'.

3.4.3 Centering My Self

In terms of *developmental* processes, the I-position of Levi centers the organization of the self-narrative of 'I as Rens'. 'I as Levi' affectively scored much higher positive on the same sentences than 'I as Rens'. The influence of 'I as Levi' on the self-narrative of 'I as Rens' is that of a *centripetal* movement, as it integrates elements in an emotional positive way, which were rated negatively from the perspective of 'I as Rens'.

Other I-positions that were implicitly present in the case were not explicitly mentioned in the self-investigation: such as 'I as Tai Chi practitioner', 'I as father', 'I as husband', 'I as management consultant'. These were I-positions within the external world I lived in in that period. Our analysis was limited to 'I as Rens' and 'I as Levi'. It was in the beginning period of applying the Dialogical Self Approach, we were not yet fully attentive to elaborating all implicit I-positions in self-narratives. Reacting in an appropriate way to these references and hints, can be a positive promoter and developmental tool to transform self into more wholeness and integrated I-positions (Fig. 3.4).

3.5 Questions for Further Reflection

- Describe your 'leadership' and 'followership' in terms of I-positions. In which I-position are you able to 'give leadership'? In which to 'receive leadership'?
    - Firstly do this exercise for yourself.
    - Secondly, have a conversation with a colleague, do the same.
    - Thirdly, have an imaginary conversation with your superior. If possible, start a real dialogue face to face.

Reflections on My Personal Narrative 2

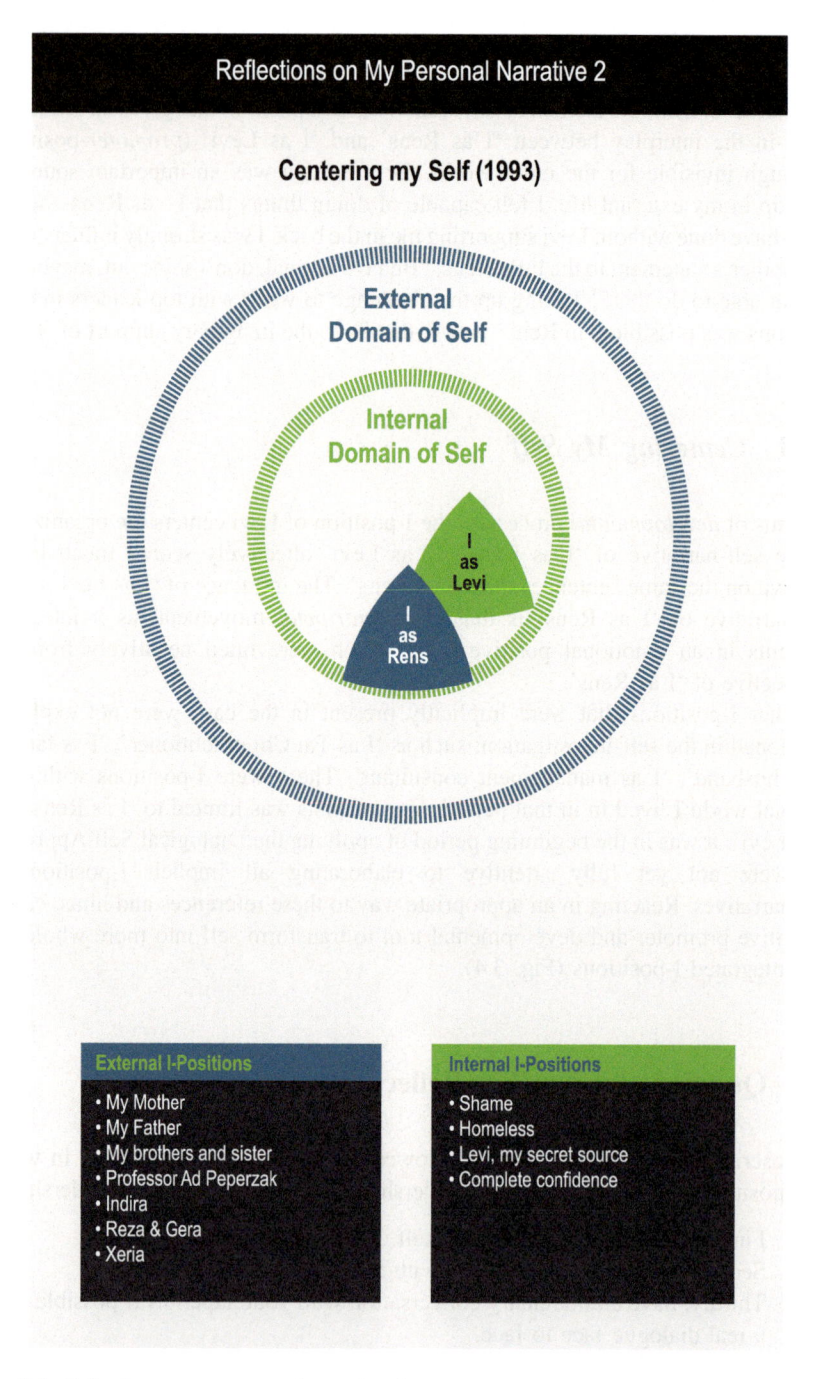

Centering my Self (1993)

- External Domain of Self
- Internal Domain of Self
- I as Levi
- I as Rens

External I-Positions
- My Mother
- My Father
- My brothers and sister
- Professor Ad Peperzak
- Indira
- Reza & Gera
- Xeria

Internal I-Positions
- Shame
- Homeless
- Levi, my secret source
- Complete confidence

Fig. 3.4 Reflections on my personal narrative 2

Compare the outcomes of 1, 2, and 3.

- Describe moments in your professional life, where you (intentionally) switch (ed) between:
  - Giving direction, pushing, pulling.
  - Influencing in a rational, intuitive, bodily (non-verbal) manner.
  - If applicable: between the roles of entrepreneur, manager, coach, change-leader, and professional.

Draw some conclusions based on these reflections.

What is the most important insight, which you can apply as an action in the future?

References

Baggini, J. (2011). *The ego trick. What does it mean to be you?* London: Granta Books.
Bohm, D. (1996). *On dialogue.* New York: Routledge.
Cunliffe, A. L., & Eriksen, M. (2011). Relational leadership. *Human Relations, 64*(11), 1425–1449.
Dietz, K.-M., & Kracht, T. (2011). *Dialogische Führung. Grundlagen—Praxis—Beispiel: dm Drogerie—Markt.* Frankfurt am Main: Campus-Verlag.
Ford, J.D., & Ford, L.W. (1995). The role of conversations in producing intentional change in organizations. *Academy of Management Review. 20,* 541–570.
George, B. (2003). *Authentic leadership: Rediscovering the secrets to creating lasting value.* New Jersey: Jossey-Bass.
George, B. (2007). *True north: Discover your authentic leadership.* New Jersey: Jossey-Bass.
Gergen, K. J. (2009a). *An invitation to social construction* (2nd ed.). London: Sage.
Gergen, K. J. (2009b). *Relational being: Beyond self and community.* New York: Oxford University Press.
Goffee, R., & Jones, G. (2006). *Why should anyone be led by you? What it takes to be an authentic leader.* Boston: Harvard Business School Press.
Goleman, D. (1995). *Emotional intelligence: Why it can matter more than IQ.* New York: Bantam Books.
Goleman, D. (2000). Leadership that gets results. *Harvard Business Review.*
Gosling, J., & Mintzberg, H. (2003). The five minds of a manager. *Harvard Business Review, 81*(11), 54–63.
Greenleaf, R.K. (1970). The Servant as Leader. Center for Servant Leadership.
Grint, K. (2005). Problems, problems, problems: the social construction of "leadership". *Human Relations, 58,* 1467–1494.
Grint, K. (2010a). Wicked problems and clumsy solutions: The role of leadership. In S. Brookes & K. Grint (Eds.), *The public new leadership challenge* (pp. 169–186). New York: Palgrave Macmillan.
Hawes, L. C. (1999). The dialogics of conversation: Power, control, vulnerability. *Communication Theory, 9*(3), 229–264.
Hermans, H. J. M. (2006). *Dialoog en Misverstand. Leven met de toenemende bevolking van onze innerlijke ruimte.* [*Dialogue and Misunderstanding*] Soest: Uitgeverij Nelissen.
Hermans, H. J. M., & Hermans-Konopka, A. (2010). *Dialogical self theory. positioning and counter-positioning in a globalizing society.* Cambridge: University Press.
Hermans, H. J. M., Kempen, H. J. G., & Van Loon, E. (Rens) J. P. (1992). The dialogical self: Beyond individualism and rationalism. *American Psychologist, 47.*

Hersted, L., & Gergen, K. J. (2013). *Relational leading. practices for dialogically based collaboration*. Chagrin Falls, Ohio: TAOS Institute Publications.

Hickman, G. R. (2016). *Leading organizations: Perspectives for a new era*. Thousand Oaks: Sage.

Hill, A. (2013). 'The monday interview' with charles handy, 'charles handy: Righting management wrongs'. *Financial Times, 14*.

Isaacs, W. N. (1993). Taking flight: Dialogue, collective thinking and organizational learning. *Organizational Dynamics, 24*–39.

Isaacs, W. N. (1999). *Dialogue and the art of thinking together. A pioneering approach to communicating in business and in life*. New York: Doubleday.

Keller, S., & Price, C. (2011). *Beyond performance: How great organizations build ultimate competitive advantage*. New Jersey: Wiley.

Kernis, M. H. (2003). Toward a conceptualization of optimal self-esteem. *Psychological Inquiry, 14*(1), 1–26.

Kilburg, R., & Donohue, M. (2011). Toward a "grand unifying theory' of leadership: Implications for consulting psychology. In *Consulting Psychology Journal: Practice and Research, 63*(1), 6–25. American Psychological Association.

Koonce, R. (2016). All in "The family": Leading and following through individual, relational, and collective mindsets. In R. Koonce, M. C. Bligh, M. K. Carsten & M. Hurwitz (Eds.), *Followership in action. cases and commentaries* (pp. 3–14). Emerald Books.

Libbrecht, U. (2007). *Within the four seas...: introduction to comparative philosophy*. Belgium: Peeters Publishers.

Litaer, G. (1993). Authenticity, congruence and transparency. In D. Brazier (Ed.), *Beyond carl rogers* (pp. 17–46). London: Constable.

Luthans, F., & Avolio, B. (2003). Authentic leadership development. In K. S. Cameron, J. E. Dutton, & R. E. Quinn (Eds.), *Positive organizational scholarship* (pp. 241–258). San Francisco: Berrett-Koehler.

Northouse, P. G. (2007). *Leadership: Theory and practice*. London: Sage.

Parry, K. W. (2011). Leadership and organization theory. In A. Bryman, D. Collinson, K. Grint, B. Jackson & M. Uhl-Bien (Eds.), *The SAGE handbook of leadership* (pp. 53–70). London, UK: Sage.

Raggatt, P. T. F. (2012). Positioning the dialogical self: recent advances in theory construction. In H. J. M. Hermans & Th. Gieser (Eds.), *Handbook of dialogical self theory* (pp. 29–45). Cambridge: University Press.

Schaffner, F., (1970). *Patton* [Movie]

Van Loon, E. (Rens) J. P. (2006). *Het geheim van de leider. Zoektocht naar essentie. (The secret of being a leader. Searching for the essence.)* Assen: Van Gorcum. [Available as pdf file in English translation].

Van Loon, E. (Rens) J. P. (2010). *Dialogical leader. Developing leaders for the future*. Deloitte University.

Van Loon, E. (Rens) J. P., & Van Dijk, G. (2015). Dialogical Leadership. Dialogue as Condition Zero. *Journal for Leadership Accountability and Ethics, 12*(3), 62–75.

Van Loon, E. (Rens) J. P., & Roozendaal, A. (2006). *Leiderschap als kunst. Moed om te veranderen. (The Art of Leadership. Courage to Change)*. Zaltbommel: INK.

Van Loon, E. (Rens) J. P., & Wijsbek, J. (2003). *De organisatie als verhaal. Dialoog en reflectie als uitgangspunt voor ontwikkeling van organisaties, leiders, teams en medewerkers. (The Organization as a Narrative. Dialogue and Reflection as a startingpoint for developing Organizations, Leaders, Teams and Employees)*. Assen: Van Gorcum.

Wheatley, M. J. (1994). *Leadership and the new science: Discovering order in a Chaotic world*. San Francisco, CA: Berrett-Koehler Publishers.

Part II
The Practice

Chapter 4
Creating Conditions for Generative Dialogue

> *Working amidst the cacophony of a multiple-band dancefloor, one needs a sanctuary to restore one's sense of purpose, put issues in perspective, and regain courage and heart.*
> Ron Heifetz (Heifetz 1994, 273)

Abstract

- *'From thoughts (patterns from the past) to thinking in the now'* is conditional for change in Bohm's view. Allowing thinking to flow freely between people in dialogue opens new insights into the world.
- *Debate* is primarily focused on converging, convincing others; *dialogue* on diverging, understanding others and self. Both approaches are equally valuable. Critical is using the right approach for the issue at hand.
- In Gergen's view, dialogue is a precious talent humans have as it incorporates our *relational being*. Relational understanding and showing yourself as a multibeing (showing more I-positions) are phases in creating a generative (transformative) dialogue.
- Dialogue incorporates and recognizes the alterity of other people and of other I-positions (*otherness*). In this sense dialogue is an ethical theory in Hermans's view.
- Successful transformation is in the right balance between *freedom* and *structure*. You need a solid structure to make a transformation process generative, and the freedom of people to be motivated.
- *Creating conditions for generative dialogue* is critical if they don't occur spontaneously. A *good* leader is able to deal with this, despite (formal) inequality in working relations.

In this chapter, dialogue is our core topic. In the next sections we will explore forms that conversations can take, namely dialogue and discussion, and apply these insights to the process of the emergence of new meaning in the concept of the Dialogical Self and Dialogical Leadership. As we have seen in the previous chapters, in relational interactions (as leading, following, co-constructing, conversation, etc.) *free energy*[1] is a crucial condition for creating space and emerging new

---
[1] Libbrecht 2007; Morioka 2008; 2015.

meaning. In this chapter, we describe how to create generative dialogue conditions with the goal of enabling the r(l)eader to put this into practice.

We start with Bohm's understanding of dialogue, summarized as 'from thoughts to thinking' (Sect. 4.1), followed by the views of Isaacs as 'the art of thinking together' (Sect. 4.2), Gergen's 'generating new meaning to transform reality' (Sect. 4.3), and Hermans', 'recognizing alterity in the other' (Sect. 4.4).[2] Our insights are applied on processes of transformation in Sect. 4.5, dialogue and transformation, and Sect. 4.6, creating conditions for dialogue, individually and for a group. This is illustrated with examples from our practice followed by sections with rational reflections (Sect. 4.7), personal reflections (Sect. 4.8), and questions for further reflection (Sect. 4.9).

4.1 From Thoughts to Thinking

David Bohm was an inspiring thinker on dialogue.[3] As a physicist, he made significant contributions to theoretical physics, particularly to quantum mechanics and relativistic theory. At the same time, Bohm is one of the most quoted people in the field of dialogue theory and methodology. Having deeply analyzed how human beings interpret reality. By assuming we can observe an objective truth via the scientific method, we co-construct reality in a specific way and educate people in our culture to perceive it similarly.

In reading Bohm's book *On Dialogue*, I was triggered by its *simplicity in complexity*. Bohm, Libbrecht, and Gergen, they all create an awareness in their readers that we cannot *directly* observe the world *as it is*. We construct our perception in language. Bohm offers a possibility to escape from the reductionist paradigm of truth as static. As in our bodily awareness, we can feel immediate feedback (proprioception), we have to explore how this works for our thinking. Can you, by suspending your judgment, get instantaneous feedback?

---

[2]We knowingly don't pay attention in this book to the philosophical dialogue tradition starting with Plato, Aristotle, Cicero, Seneca, Buber, Levinas, and others, although we recognize the continuing influence of these authors. The same for the African Dialogue (*kgotla*) tradition that is also influential in current organizational developments: a *kgotla* is a public meeting, community council or traditional law court of a Botswana village. De Liefde 2002. Describing and integrating these aspects of the dialogue tradition into the Dialogical Self Theory approach is out of scope here.
[3]Bohm 1990; 1992; 1996; Bohm and Factor 1995.

4.1.1 Dialogue as Meaning Flowing Through Us

Bohm assumes that *thought* shapes our reality, and that dialogue shapes thought and thinking processes consecutively. He interprets *dia-logos* as *'meaning flowing through us'*. Dialogue is in his view a process of direct face-to-face encounter by which people can participate in a common pool of meaning—a kind of 'shared mind' or 'collective intelligence'.[4] For Bohm dialogue is *the* form of conversation where people are allowed to retain a sense of self, *while simultaneously creating space for the voice of the other person(s)*.[5] He argues that past 'thoughts' stay on as a pervasive presence in our current thinking and sensing about what is going on around us. In his schema, 'thought' as fragments of past experience has an ever-present tendency to construct false coherence in interpreting the present. There is a representative barrier (*thought*) and a participative capability (*thinking*), where the former *conceals* and the latter *reveals* new knowledge.[6] Bohmian dialogue is a free-flowing group conversation in which participants attempt to reach a common understanding, experiencing everyone's point of view fully, equally and nonjudgmentally. This can lead to new and deeper understanding. The purpose is to solve communication crises that society faces, and the entire human nature and consciousness. Bohm's view utilizes a theoretical understanding of the way thoughts relate to universal reality. David Peat, Bohm's biographer, points out he "proposed that the reality we see about us (the explicate order) is no more than the surface appearance of something far deeper (the implicate order)[...] the ground of the cosmos is not elementary particles, but pure process, a flowing movement of the whole."[7] "There is no place in a relativistic theory for the idea that the world consists of fundamental 'building blocks'. Instead, the world should be conceived as a universal flow of events and processes."[8] Bohm compared the explicate order to the patterns in a river. The swirls in the river are distinct forms, and in some cases can have high degrees of stability. But these patterns emerged from and are an integral part of the totality of the system of the water. So there is separation without separateness.[9]

The issue, as Bohm describes, is that we do not know how to live together in a changing world. We only know how to live based on truths from the past, which today inevitably results in one group attempting to impose their truths on another. Bohm realized that defending core beliefs and the resulting incoherence is widespread in the world. Conversely, collective coherent ways of thinking and acting only emerge when there truly is a flow of meaning, which starts with openness for other views, an approach that defensiveness precludes. "Science has become the

---

[4] Bojer et al. 2008, 122.
[5] Tierney 2011, 85.
[6] Ballantyne 2004, 117.
[7] Isaacs 1999, 166.
[8] Bohm in Libbrecht 2007, 193.
[9] Isaacs 1999, 167–168.

religion of modern age. It plays the role that religion used to play of giving us truth."[10] Bohm refers in his work and life to understanding a participatory universe, where meaning is continuously unfolding and where we, as individuals, have to take a part in co-creating a true understanding of the universe. As in a genuine dialogue, where "each person is participating, is partaking of the whole meaning of the group and also taking part in it."[11] Dialogue explores the manner in which thought—viewed by Bohm as an inherently limited medium, rather than an objective representation of reality—is generated and sustained at the collective level. An inquiry like this necessarily calls into question deeply held assumptions regarding culture, meaning and identity. "In its deepest sense, dialogue is an invitation to test the viability of traditional definitions, of what it means to be human and to explore the prospect of an enhanced humanity."[12] In Bohm's view, dialogue aims to understand consciousness per se, as well as the problematic nature of day-to-day relationship and communication.

4.1.2 Dialogue as Face to Face Encounter

In Bohm's view, dialogue is a face to face, direct encounter, not an endless speculation and theorizing. "In a time of accelerating abstractions and seamless digital representations, it is this insistence on facing the inconvenient messiness of daily, corporeal experience that is perhaps the most radical of all."[13] The process of thought behind our individual and collective assumptions will be explored in a dialogue. The opinions we have are products of past thought, collectively as a culture and individually in your own life history. It is all programmed into your memory. Opinions tend to be experienced as truths, even though they may be created from your own personal and cultural background, learned from your father and mother, from family and teachers, through reading and partaking in the media. As assumptions, you have—often subconsciously—identified with them, and hold them to be true, not only for your life, but also for others. Individual thought is mostly the result of collective thought and of interaction with other people. Everybody makes his own 'unique' mix of the words in his thoughts and experiences, and contributes this to the interaction. Bohm attributes enormous power to people thinking together in a coherent way. In dialogue, such a process of collective thinking could become reality. In the process of dialogue, we give attention to the actual process of thinking, and the order in which it happens, through listening and observing where the process loses coherence and no longer works. *"We are not trying to change anything, but just being aware of it. And you can notice the*

---

[10]Bohm 1996, xi.
[11]Bohm 1996, xiii.
[12]Bohm 1996, xvi.
[13]Bohm 1996, xx.

similarity of the difficulties within a group to the conflicts and incoherent thoughts within an individual."[14]

Bohm distinguishes between the *Observer* and the *Observed* in his inquiry to understand the nature of our inner experience. He speaks of a 'self', which observes and acts upon itself. As an example: if 'I' have free energy to be aware of 'me being angry', an opportunity to change my anger, might be possible. This does not imply in Bohm's view that there is a separate entity, but there is a dynamic relation, as in Hermans' dialogical self, and James' distinction between 'I' and 'me'.[15] In terms of Libbrecht's concentrated and deconcentrated awareness, the relation between the Observer and the Observed is an example of field-awareness. The approach of Bohm is elaborated by Isaacs, our topic in the next section.

4.2 The Art of Thinking Together

William Isaacs[16] is the author of *Dialogue and the Art of Thinking Together* (1999) and the driving force behind the MIT Dialogue Project, which draws heavily on Bohm's view. In the context of this book, he is an important author on dialogue, in particular because he describes the *process* of conversation, debate/discussion and dialogue in detail.

Isaacs's guidelines for a good dialogue are to suspend your assumptions and certainties, observing the observer, listen to your listening, slowing down your inquiry, becoming aware of your 'thought'-patterns and being not afraid of polarization, even embracing it.[17] "Dialogue is about a shared inquiry, a way of thinking and reflecting together. It is not something you do to another person. Rather it is something you do with people. Indeed, a large part of learning has to do with learning to shift your attitudes about relationships with others, so that we gradually give up the effort to make them understand us, and come to a greater understanding of ourselves and each other."[18] In his book, he describes four capabilities we must develop to make a dialogue generative: *listening, suspending, respecting,* and *voicing*. We will have a short look at each characteristic.

---

[14]Bohm 1996, 24.

[15]James 1890.

[16]William Isaacs is Founder and President of Dialogos, a leadership consulting and strategy development firm based in Cambridge, MA. He co-founded the Organizational Learning Center at MIT and is a Senior Lecturer at MIT's Sloan School of Management. His focus is on raising the level of dialogue and collective leadership, reducing polarization and cross boundary conflict, and producing large scale transformative change. Brown et al. 2005.

[17]Isaacs 1999, 33.

[18]Isaacs 1999, 9.

4.2.1 Listening with an Open Mind

One of the most important characteristics of a good dialogue is that participants listen to each other. This implies that you become aware of how you listen. Listening in an open minded way implies being present in the here and now, being aware of the disturbances in yourself, and—if applicable—being aware of resistance in yourself to accept a view that differs from yours. "Perhaps the simplest and most potent practice for listening is simply to be still. By being still in ourselves, quieting the inner chatter of our minds, we can open up to a way of being present and listening that cuts through everything."[19] Being able to truly listen is a dynamic flow, where you are able to keep your equilibrium in thinking, feeling and acting. When we become aware of the quality of our listening, our listening changes spontaneously.

4.2.2 Suspending Your Judgment

The art of listening is closely related to suspending your judgment. Frequently we are not able to listen well, as our judgment continuously interferes internally. "We can learn to suspend our opinion and the certainty that lies behind it. Suspension means that we neither suppress what we think nor advocate it with unilateral conviction. Rather, we display our thinking in a way that lets us and others see and understand it. We simply acknowledge and observe our thoughts and feelings as they arise without being compelled to act on them."[20] We cannot just stay with the facts, as our internal voice shouts: "that is not true!" Instead of following your judgments, try to access and "to recognize and embrace things that you do not already know."[21] Once you are able to do this, a reservoir of energy is released which might be used for something other than advocating your own ideas. By asking a question, seeking clarification or offering support the moment you sense your judgment is getting in the way, you provide space for new thinking. By asking questions you direct your inner thinking outwardly, into the dynamic relation of the conversation, instead of into the internal dynamics of your thoughts, assumptions, emotions and conclusions. The process described here is a very difficult one to practice, as our automated thoughts, emotions and acts continue to proceed relentlessly. "Instead of good answers, we need good questions."[22] If we are able to ask good questions, we will be able to transform our conversations into a real dialogue. A good question can be defined as '*one that opens your mind, your way of thinking, feeling and acting for a new perspective*'.

---

[19] Isaacs 1999, 101.
[20] Isaacs 1999, 135.
[21] Isaacs 1999, 137.
[22] Isaacs 1999, 149.

4.2.3 Respecting Other Views

"To respect someone is to look for the springs that feed the pool of their experience."[23] It is as if you are looking again, observing the other person differently, looking from a different perspective. Respecting means honoring boundaries, not intruding. "Respect is looking for what is highest and best in a person and treating them as a mystery that you can never fully comprehend."[24] Respect has many levels: in dialogue we cultivate respect for self, for others, for differences, and particularly for those who oppose what I have to say. Respect is an active deed. Visibly showing respect is very important for leaders (and parents) when they meet resistance. If somebody opposes you, show respect and try to truly understand (by listening and suspending your judgment) what the other is declaring.[25]

4.2.4 Voicing from the Heart

To speak your voice is perhaps one of the most challenging aspects of a genuine dialogue. "Speaking your voice has to do with revealing what is true for you regardless of other influences that might be brought to bear."[26] "To discover what *we* think and feel, independent of these circumstances, requires courage."[27] Apart from courage you also have to be able to feel fear, and to explore what that is. Babiak and Hare describe the issue with psychopaths in business is they don't feel fear.[28] It takes willpower to speak your voice, to concentrate energy to make your view known. You need to have a feeling of self-trust to be able to speak up if you want to, and to be silent if you don't want to express what is on your mind. One of the fragments in Isaacs' book I have seen in our work with leaders, is how important and difficult it is to accept silence: "Finding and speaking one's voice requires a willingness to be still. Daring to be quiet can seem like an enormous risk in a world that valuates articulate speech. But to speak our voice, we may need to refrain from speaking, and instead, listen. *Not every word that comes to us needs to be spoken.* In fact, learning to choose consciously what we do and do not say can establish a great level of control and stability in our lives."[29] Actively being aware of the atmosphere in the team as deconcentrated energy, might cause you to remain

---

[23]Isaacs 1999, 110.

[24]Isaacs 1999, 117.

[25]George Kohlrieser describes the impact of respect in hostage situations, where there is physical intimidation. Kohlrieser 2006.

[26]Isaacs 1999, 159.

[27]Isaacs 1999, 160.

[28]Babiak and Hare 2006.

[29]Isaacs 1999, 163.

silent and not to act. The ability to choose: voicing *and* being silent. Both are significant qualities in a dialogue.[30]

4.2.5 Creating Conditions for Dialogue

Important in Isaacs' thinking about dialogue is how to create the conditions for a dialogic atmosphere. What are the conditions you produce to make a free exchange of ideas in dialogue possible? Isaacs' contribution to the development of dialogue as a tool is his dynamic description of the processes of conversation, debate and dialogue. Critical interventions are made at the junctions. Isaacs introduces the term 'container'. "A container is a vessel, a setting in which the intensities of human activity can safely emerge."[31] The function of a container is to create a condition which allow a certain amount of pressure for an openness to new ways of thinking which are outside your comfort zone. There must be enough energy. People need to feel a substantial level of safety.[32] Figure 4.1 demonstrates four phases in the process, with moments of crisis in the process of dialogue.[33] Having a look at the figure, the arrows refer to the moments of change as 'tipping points' in the conversation. What starts as an ordinary conversation might turn spontaneously into a dialogue or discussion. Although Isaacs describes this process in a sequence in time, these phases can take place synchronously and move forwards and backwards several times is possible. 'Tipping points' in the conversation are crucial.

4.2.6 Conversation, Debate, and Dialogue: Crises in the Process

In the first phase, you bring people together with the aim of enabling a conversation between them. In Latin, the word 'converse' means 'to bring together'. When people in one room start to give their views and opinions, the first 'crisis' moment takes place. To turn the conversation into a discussion implies that the participants defend their own views. The result is a discussion or a debate. A good discussion has great value but differs completely from a dialogue. Isaacs uses the word *degenerate* if the conversation turns into a discussion or debate, where there are winners and losers, victory and loss. Isaacs speaks articulately of the need to build a

---

[30]Heifetz devotes a section to speaking from the heart, as "inspiring people calls for you to *speak* from the heart (expressing what you are feeling) .....Requires being in touch with your own values, beliefs and emotions." Heifetz et al. 2009, 269–270.
[31]Isaacs 1999, 242.
[32]How this works in detail and its impact is illustrated in the case-studies in Chaps. 6 and 7.
[33]Isaacs 1993.

4.2 The Art of Thinking Together

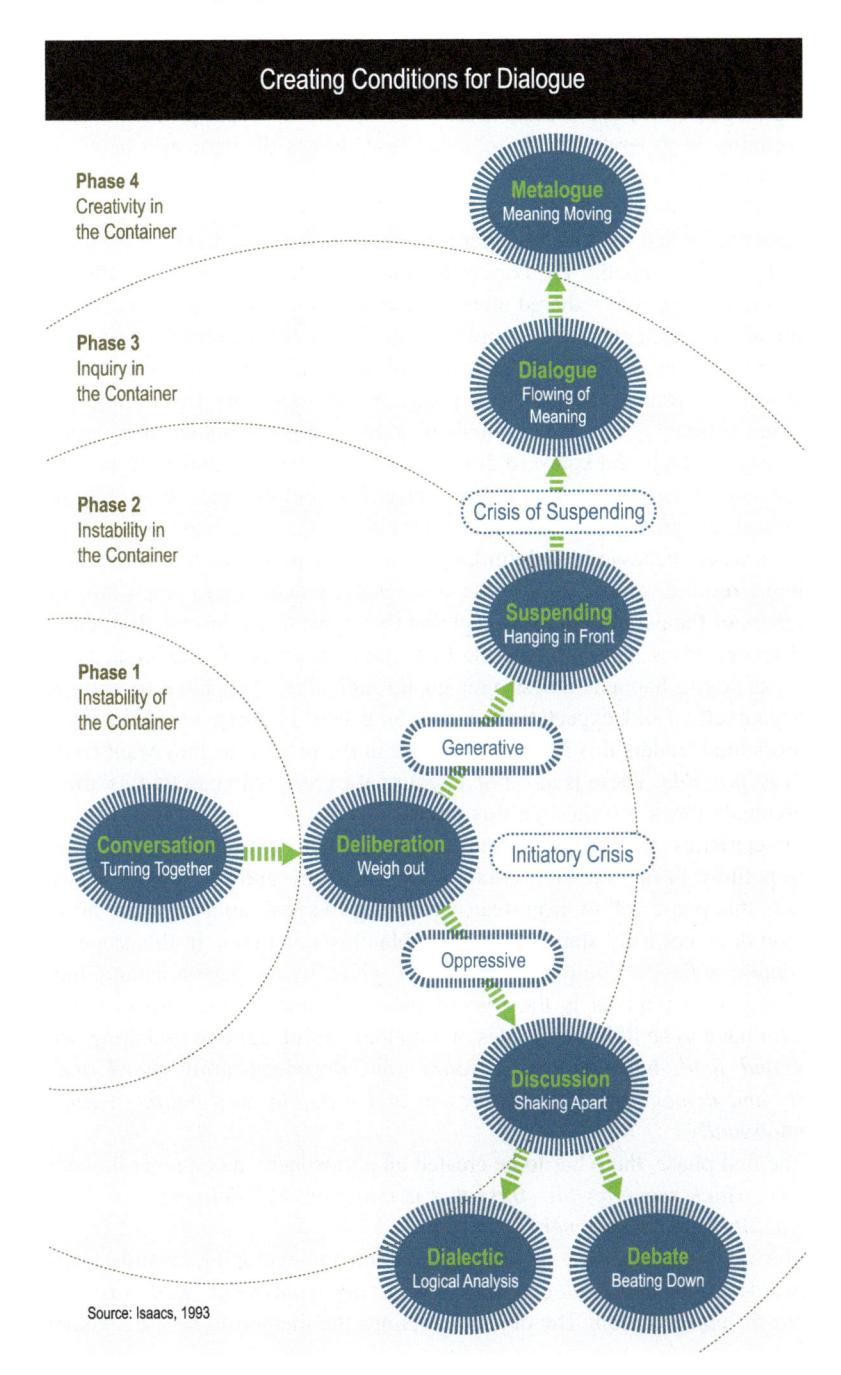

Fig. 4.1 Creating conditions for dialogue

container for dialogue, to create a climate and a set of explicit or implicit norms that permit people to handle 'hot issues' without getting burned.[34] A conversation turns into a dialogue—here we use the word *generative*—as in the process of dialogue new meaning is generated in the conversation. Isaacs distinguishes between four phases in this process.

Instability of the Container

People are invited to come together for a meeting, a session, where the dialogical approach will be applied. "The core of the theory of dialogue builds on the premise that the effect of people's shared attention can alter the quality and level of inquiry possible at any particular time. People can gradually learn to refine their modes of collective awareness to promote increasingly more subtle and intelligent modes of interaction. The process is very demanding, and at times very frustrating; it is also deeply rewarding."[35] When individuals of a group come together, they bring with them a range of tacit, unexpressed differences in perspectives and expectations. The first challenge for participants is to recognize this, and to create the willingness to explore and recognize these differences. To make a dialogue happen people need a safe place where behavioral and thinking patterns are permitted to change. To begin a dialogue requires clarity about how you set the guidelines to reach this and the willingness of the participants to accept that they have to go through different points of resistance, crises. Isaacs labels the first one as a crisis of *emptiness*, you can't make a dialogue happen, unless you go through this. You have to endure, and empty yourself of old expectations if anything new is going to occur. For many action-oriented leaders this is a terrible phase in the process as they want results, *as quickly as possible*. There is also not an external expert, who can fix this, the group of individuals has to go through this phase.

Characteristics of phase 1 are politeness, people continue their old habits of talking politely to one another; courtesy, followership and fear. We regularly see people in this phase follow from fear, not daring to speak up as they are afraid. As reflection does not truly start, a culture of blaming continues. In this stage, *'being the example of the change we want to reach'* given by the person leading the team is critically important as is the role of the facilitator. The chairperson and the facilitator have to be living examples of a dialogic mind, agile in switching between *arrow and field*, between *concentrating and deconcentrating, hard and soft, friendly and demanding, strongly present and invisible, well-balanced rationally and emotionally*.

In the first phase, there has to be created an atmosphere, a container in the words of Isaacs, *which regulates the stress that is inherent to a dialogue*.

Instability in the Container

In the second phase, there are critical moments in developing towards a dialogue or towards a debate. *Dialogue and debate are equivalent, both are effective methods for conversation.* The objective defines the method to be used, sometimes

---

[34]Schein 1993, 35.
[35]Isaacs 1993, 35.

4.2 The Art of Thinking Together

debate, occasionally dialogue, at times mere instruction. It depends on the topic, the problem you want to solve.[36]

Sometimes you have a rational debate, with the emotional tensions accompanying the process of defending your point of view. In Fig. 4.1 we see a *downward arrow* with the word '*oppressive*'. If it takes this direction, the conversation turns into a discussion or debate. It is important for a chairperson to make people aware of these moments. To not let it happen unintentionally, but intentionally, by making people aware of the moment of change. The *upward arrow*, with the word '*generative*' points to the phase where the participants have signed on to practice suspending their judgments. "We deliberately seek to make observable and accessible these general patterns of thought and feeling, and more critically, the tacit influences that sustain them."[37] Often this causes a general feeling in the group that is not pleasant, it feels like being frustrated and ambiguous. It feels like 'heat'. "All of this 'heat' and instability is exactly what should be occurring".[38] The role of the chairperson/facilitator is crucial in this phase of *instability in the container*. He/she is not explicitly correcting or imposing order on what is happening, but *models* 'how' to suspend what is happening to allow greater insight into the order that is present. Often participants struggle with polarization and conflict, with the clash of personally held beliefs and assumptions. This is a difficult stage in the process, in particular if the members in a (potentially generative) dialogue are leaders with 'swollen egos' that are not used to admit that it could also be different and that they don't have the (right) answers themselves. Many leaders are not used to holding back their own views, verbally and non-verbally. As a result of this crisis, and to move to the next phase, *inquiry in the container*, participants need to intentionally 'sign on' to open up for each other's ideas and views. Let's have a look at the next phase in the process of reaching a true dialogue: *inquiring*.

Inquiry in the Container

The two preceding phases are the most difficult and challenging ones as we have to adjust habitual behavioral and thought patterns with its inherent resistance. Now we enter a zone, where participants are more used to open up for ideas and views that are different from their own opinion. People stop speaking and thinking *for* others or for the group. There is a shift here from 'third person data'—stories about other people—to 'first person data', inquiries into how things look from where I stand, the spirit of curiosity awakens. "People here can become sensitive to the cultural 'programs' for thinking and acting that they have unwittingly accepted as true."[39] By opening up for others, by suspending your standpoint and listening on a deeper level to the group as a whole, participants might be able to explicate and formulate what was implicit and not-being-said until then. This leads to positive

---

[36]See Chap. 6: Keith Grints' leadership framework (crises, tame and wicked issues). This will be elaborated later in the text.

[37]Isaacs 1993, 35.

[38]Isaacs 1993, 36.

[39]Isaacs 1993, 37.

insights, sometimes groups become aware of going the wrong direction or acting erroneously. The group begins to sense more collectively, pleasure and pain. In what we have described so far, the mixture of *arrow and field energy* begins to reach a more dynamic balance. The secret of a good dialogue is in the dynamic balance between structure (process) and freedom (content).

Creativity in the Container

In this phase, participants in the group begin to think 'together', to sense more than individual views and words. Based on new understandings creativity might emerge, new meanings, that were not visibly present before, pop up in the collective conversation. This is *'The Art of Thinking Together.'* *It is an art, you get it for free, but you have to work for it (arrow energy) and you have 'to let loose' (field energy).* This is the junction where old thought patterns might vanish and new thinking patterns arise. "At this point, the distinction between memory and thinking becomes apparent".[40] Isaacs calls this experience *'metalogue'*, or 'meaning flowing with it', like Bohm. "Metalogue reveals a conscious, intimate, and subtle relationship between the structure and content of an exchange and its meaning. The medium and the message are linked: information from the process conveys as much meaning as the content of the words exchanged. The group does not *have* meaning, in other words, it *is* its meaning."[41] This is the state that is perceived as absolutely authentic. The experience itself is 'healing' for its participants, as there is no separation between your authentic 'self' and the way you position your 'I's in the external world.

4.2.7 Switching Between Debate and Dialogue

At the end of this section about Isaacs' view on dialogue, Fig. 4.2 gives an overview of differences between debate and dialogue.[42] *Debate* is primarily focused on converging, convincing others; *dialogue* on diverging, understanding others and self. Both approaches are equally valuable. Critical is using the right approach for the issue at hand.

Before we continue with Gergen's view on dialogue, a remark about a significant difference between my view on facilitating a dialogue process and Bohm's and Isaacs' views. Both authors primarily work with self-reflection to suspend ones thoughts and emotions. I add feedback by making the implicit *explicit* in reflecting it *in the moment*, by using the technique of time-outs. In building the container, a facilitator has this demanding task in the first phases of dialogue. Mostly, in the last

---

[40]Isaacs 1993, 38.

[41]Isaacs 1993, 38.

[42]Based on the model of Isaacs, inspired by the work of Bohm, Gergen and Hermans on dialogue, complemented with our experiences, I constructed a figure, differentiating between Debate and Dialogue. By using verbs instead of nouns I want to articulate the dynamic character of both ways of conversing. See Chap. 6.3 When to apply the Dialogical Leadership Approach?

4.2 The Art of Thinking Together

Switching between Debate and Dialogue

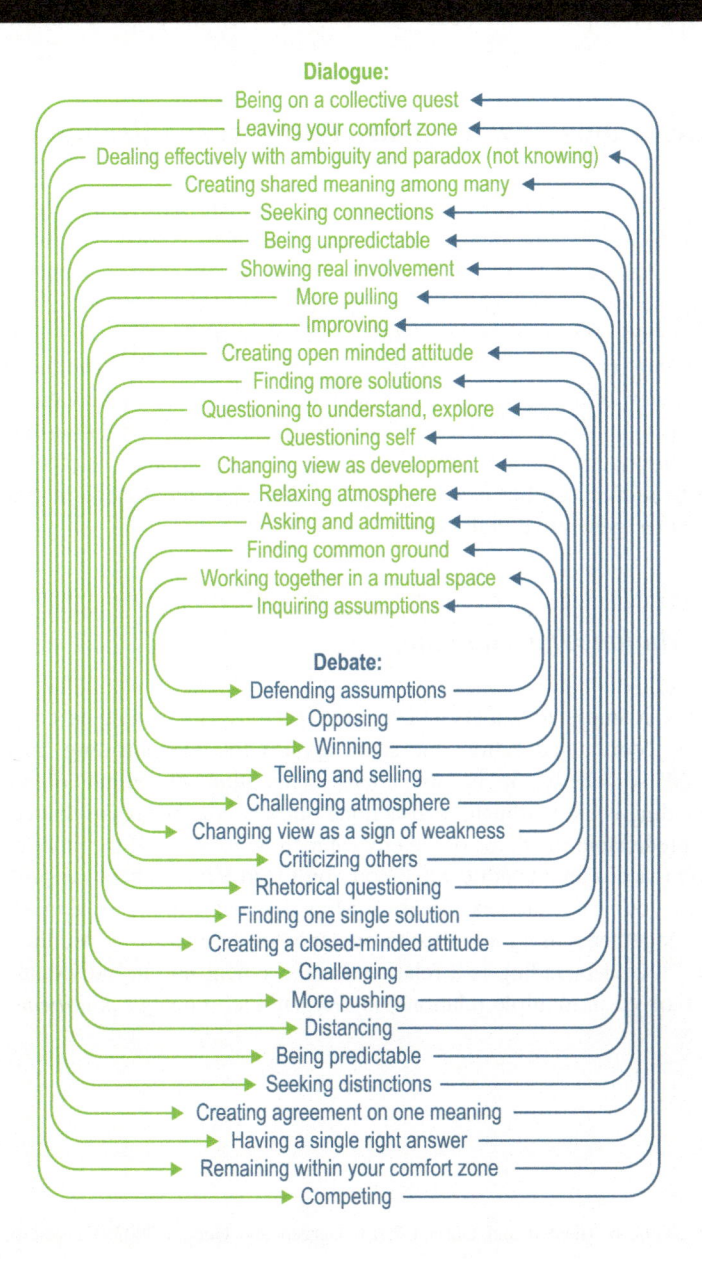

Dialogue:
- Being on a collective quest
- Leaving your comfort zone
- Dealing effectively with ambiguity and paradox (not knowing)
- Creating shared meaning among many
- Seeking connections
- Being unpredictable
- Showing real involvement
- More pulling
- Improving
- Creating open minded attitude
- Finding more solutions
- Questioning to understand, explore
- Questioning self
- Changing view as development
- Relaxing atmosphere
- Asking and admitting
- Finding common ground
- Working together in a mutual space
- Inquiring assumptions

Debate:
- Defending assumptions
- Opposing
- Winning
- Telling and selling
- Challenging atmosphere
- Changing view as a sign of weakness
- Criticizing others
- Rhetorical questioning
- Finding one single solution
- Creating a closed-minded attitude
- Challenging
- More pushing
- Distancing
- Being predictable
- Seeking distinctions
- Creating agreement on one meaning
- Having a single right answer
- Remaining within your comfort zone
- Competing

Fig. 4.2 Switching between debate and dialogue

two phases, feedback as a facility tool is not needed anymore as the participants in dialogue apply the principles by themselves. In my experience, a group tends to stick to the principles of dialogue once they have felt the positive impact of it.

4.3 Generating New Meaning, Transforming Reality

In Gergen's view,[43] dialogue is a precious talent humans have as it incorporates our *relational being*. A core concept explained throughout these works is *generative dialogue*. Dialogue is an appropriate technique to describe dynamic relations: "Dialogic methods often enable participants to escape the limitations of the realities that they enter, and enable them, working collaboratively, to formulate modes of understanding or action that incorporate multiple inputs."[44] The positive and optimistic view of the constructionist orientation is expressed in the valuation of the dialogue as a tool for creating a better world: "If collaborative relationships are the source of inspiration and action within a group, it is essential that such relationships be used to reduce conflict across groups."[45] He takes three steps in creating the conditions for generative dialogue.

4.3.1 Mutual Understanding

What does it imply to understand another person? If meaning is co-created in relation as coordinated action, the same applies for understanding. In trying to understand somebody, it is not about penetrating the mind of the other. Understanding is to coordinate your actions, showing the behaviors that correspond with the predictable standards of the environment you live in. If the other bursts into tears, you react in an empathic way. You don't start talking about the problem you foresee in your calendar next weeks. "Mutual understanding is akin to dancing smoothly together, sailing a frisbee to one another, or effectively peddling a canoe together."[46] Understanding is a relational achievement not an individual one. We are all involved in multiple relations, in Gergen's terminology *multibeing*.

---

[43] Gergen 2009a, b; Hersted and Gergen 2013; Gergen and Gergen 2003; Gergen and Gergen 2004; Gergen and Thatchenkery 1996; Gergen et al. 2004.
[44] Gergen and Thatchenkery 1996, 368.
[45] Gergen 2009b, 110.
[46] Gergen 2009b, 112.

4.3.2 Being a Multibeing

Who are participating in dialogue? Together, we have created many different realities among values, rationalities, and practices of relating. We have ongoing relationships with family members, neighbors, teachers, colleagues, and clients, along with members of our company, religious and political groups. We also carry with us traces of past relationships, a childhood friendship, a first tyrant boss, an inspiring teacher, etcetera. We have developed several unique patterns of understanding and the capacity to live in multiple worlds. So we talk and act differently if we are with our children and family, with clients in formal meetings, or in political or religious environments. "One might say, that we are *multibeings*, capable of being many persons."[47] Some examples of—in Dialogical Self terminology—I-positions you could take: 'I as a mother', 'I as a son', 'I as a director', 'I as a husband', 'I as a scientist', 'I as a street fighter', 'I as a co-worker', 'I as a dancer', and so on. I as a multibeing can be seamlessly associated with Hermans' dialogical self and the I-positions you take in life.

If we want to participate in a dialogue we have to find a common reality. If I respond to my colleague from a totally different perspective, we will not be able to understand one another. We have to agree about a shared reality. Although we have the capability to adapt and develop an unlimited number of different positions, we have to reduce our potential to a narrow range that is (more or less) in line with our direct environment to make mutual understanding happen. Gergen calls this *bounded identity*. If you are a professor, there must be a certain continuity in your verbal and non-verbal behavior, you are expected to react intelligently and in a reflective mode. If you are a king, you are not expected to noisily drink beer in a pub, as this behavior is not expected from a man in that position. Through life, one builds a few of these 'bounded identities' (as I-positions). The most important characteristic to keep in mind is that your identity is *relationally* bounded, externally with the context, and internally with the I-position-repertoire you developed over time. If you change something in your identity, the relation with others and with you changes too. If the other is not involved in the process of change, misunderstanding or conflict could easily be the consequence. "If we define dialogue as a relationship between separate, autonomous individuals, each with private interests, perceptions and reasons, we create a gap. We imply that, in spite of temporary agreements, the other will always be alien, unknown and fundamentally untrustworthy. We construct a world in which it is "all against all". In contrast, if we define meaning as a relational achievement, we open doors to new and possibly more useful forms of dialogue."[48] This is what Gergen defines a generative, transformative dialogue.

---

[47]Gergen 2009b, 113.
[48]Gergen 2009b, 118.

4.3.3 Generative Dialogue

Gergen invites us to "approach dialogue as a joint creation of meaning, one in which the parties draw from tradition, but in which they can also create new realities and ways of relating. When we have antagonistic traditions, then we may search for or create forms of dialogue that we call *generative or transformative*. That is, participation in these dialogues would specifically bring the participants into a new form of coordination".[49] Its core purpose is to create more understanding, even to describe the conditions and skills, which enable the process of generating new meaning and of transforming reality based on the past—and in the present, to break with old patterns of thinking, feeling and behaving in order to change one's behavior, emotions and habits from now on in the future. Instead of being confined to traditions that are delivered to us, we wish to *consciously create new realities*. The role of intention is crucial here. If people don't want to change their convictions and constructs, old beliefs will be defended, with words, with weapons, in wars.

Gergen distinguishes aspects, which are relevant for a good understanding of generative dialogue. Some of these relate to channeling blame in a positive way. "If all that we take to be true and good has its origin in relationships, and specifically to the process of jointly constructing meaning, then there is reason for us to honor—to be responsible to—relationships of meaning making themselves. There is value, then, in sustaining processes of communication in which meaning is never frozen, but remains in a continuous state of becoming."[50] If we want to participate in a transformative dialogue, and start the conversation with an attack straight into the face of the partner in conversation, failure will be a serious risk. Gergen mentions some techniques and insights to change this pattern. My observation is that the level of awareness or consciousness of at least one pole in the relation is critical to make this happen. If there is no *free energy* in the relation, the dialogue will turn into a debate, or degenerate into a conflict, or even worse, a fight. The real challenge in conflicts is to not fall back in individual blaming. Reacting with free unfocused energy to a focused attack could be the challenge. If a push is followed by a push-back, we have resistance and competition. If a push is followed by a pull action, there is no more focus, and the action will transform into a field of deconcentrated energy. This is possible if there is free energy, awareness in at least one of the poles of the relation. Being able to free energy during a conflict, to not identify with a 'construct as the one and only truth' can be possibly an opening to solutions in conflict situations.

---

[49] Gergen 2009b, 119.

[50] Gergen 2009b, 120–121. Exactly this happened when we worked with the team described in Chap. 7. In the process of defining core values and (positive and negative) behavioral indicators, they decided to replace "blaming *the other*" with "taking *your own* responsibility".

4.3 Generating New Meaning, Transforming Reality

Some more aspects that are relevant in Gergen's view to make a dialogue generative and transformative are mentioned here: storytelling, affirming, self-reflecting, and third person listening. I will describe each briefly.

4.3.4 The Power of Storytelling

Once you start using narrative language, people listen better. Overall, we observe that abstract arguments tend to come less to life in an audience, except when you are with professional experts in the same field of science, art. If you start with "I once met a CEO, a woman, whose first question to me—as an advisor of the board—was: why should I trust you?", you immediately catch attention, to continue with your story about gaining trust as a dynamic relational process between individuals with different histories in 'trusting others'. Even if there is resistance in the other person to start listening to you, you neutralize this by pulling the other person to a situation that is familiar for almost all humans: somebody does not actually give you the trust you think you deserve based on your experience and knowledge. Sharing a personal story generally generates more acceptance than abstract and rational reasons why you are so trustworthy.[51]

4.3.5 The Impact of Affirmation

"Because meaning is born in relationship, an individual's expression alone stands empty. To come into meaning, someone else's affirmation is a required supplement."[52] The power of relational meaning making is so strong, you often observe in the body language if somebody agrees or disagrees with your point of view. Experienced speakers, salesmen and negotiators are experts in using these signals to their benefit. The impact of *affirming* is strong. People need to be affirmed to become successful and to learn from experience. The impact of *neglecting* is enormous. *Co-reflecting* is one of the skills that you could develop to affirm. Partners in dialogue are comparable to mirrors, they reflect each other, in words, in feeling, in non-verbal behavior. If somebody tells you a miserable message, you don't laugh. You try to react fittingly verbal and non-verbal.

---

[51] This technique is used in the first phases of working with teams and organizations. By creating the context that people start sharing narratives and answer questions posed by their colleagues there is—almost—automatically an opening of the mind relationally; see Chap. 7: the power of sharing narratives.
[52] Gergen 2009b, 123.

4.3.6 Reflecting on Yourself

The challenge in a transformative dialogue is to shift the conversation in the direction of self-reflecting, towards questioning one's own assumptions and I-positions. "If one's grounding realities are heard and affirmed, and the conversation becomes increasingly coordinated, the stage is set for another significant move towards transformative dialogue: self-reflection."[53] In our tradition of strong ego's we are not trained in that skill, especially not in leadership teams. We have developed singular, coherent selves, unified and static, frequently even inflated personalities as an outcome of the individualist tradition. This makes us more fit for discussing, debating, challenging and fighting than it does for starting a transformative dialogue. In reflecting on ourselves, we can find more than one voice, we start to listen to other voices, and to manage our *society of mind*.

4.3.7 Third-Person Listening

"When two groups are battling over their differences, a member of one of the groups may be asked to step out of the conversation, and to observe the interchange. By moving from the first position, in which one is arguing for his or her standpoint, to a third person stance, the individual can observe the conflict with other criteria at hand."[54] We use this technique and instruct one of the group to observe the interaction, without interfering. Sometimes we extend the instruction to try not to show any non-verbal reaction while observing. This technique frees energy in the observer, as normally you identify with the role and position you have taken in the conversation. As a third-person observer you are free to watch. This is in my experience a very powerful technique as it impacts the self of the observer, and the observed, the group. The fact that somebody is *visibly* watching changes the situation: it adds a higher level of awareness in the interaction and stimulates people to show example behavior. It is comparable with a meta-position in your own repertoire of internal and external I-positions.[55]

Reading Gergen's work is challenging and inspiring, particularly for the insight that you have to leave the idea of 'one truth' behind, as I am educated with an all ingraining sense of 'truth'. Although of course I knew it rationally, it was extremely difficult for me to really accept it (and sometimes still is!). In my study of philosophy, even in reading Nietzsche, there was always a glimmer of truth which opened my mind in a challenging way, bringing me 'out of my comfort zone'. At the same time, I like to explore what happens when I allow the basic belief about truth to change, listening to the words spoken around me in a different way, watching

---

[53] Gergen 2009b, 125.
[54] Gergen 2009b, 126.
[55] All these aspects mentioned here, are illustrated in Chaps. 6 and 7 in the case-studies.

television and reading books, through new, unobstructed eyes. Although it felt as a paradigm shift for me personally, one of my reviewers observed that I still tend to preach. Apparently that pattern of behaving and thinking is marked in me. It also demonstrates how difficult fundamental transformation is, even when it is your daily job to work with leaders and their teams in this domain.

- Generative Dialogue and Appreciative Inquiry

How can leaders ensure they create the conditions for 'generative' or 'transformational' dialogue? One answer is Appreciative Inquiry. Developed in the 1980s by David Cooperrider, a specialist in organizational behavior, it aims to transform the capacity for change by focusing on positive experiences and positive 'futures'. Its relationship to productive dialogue is described in a paper by Ken Gergen: "Appreciative Inquiry practitioners begin with the belief that topic choice and question formation are the most important moves in shaping dialogue. Much effort is made toward creating questions around positive topics that guide attention toward peak experiences and strengths ... Questions are designed to encourage participants to search for stories that embody these affirmative topics."[56]

An Appreciative Inquiry approach can be particularly valuable when the psychological barriers to change are stronger than normal and when 'history' obstructs co-operation as is illustrated in the following case of Medic Inn: Transformational dialogue in a system under siege.

Appreciative Inquiry practices are particularly applicable to cases in which groups are locked in spirals of negation and vengeance. One case study in particular conveys the value of Appreciative Inquiry as a mode of creating transformative dialogue in a system under siege. In the early 1980s, The Medic Inn, a one-star hotel facility, was taken over by a larger enterprise and given the mandate to transform itself into a first-class, four-star facility. The parent company invested in the property and upgraded the physical facilities. However, the quality of service was slow to change. Managers were locked in cycles of interpersonal conflict and interdepartmental turf wars. Interpersonal tension and competition were seemingly insurmountable obstacles to overcome. It was clear to consultants that the managers needed to engage in a different kind of dialogue in order to overcome conflict and move toward a new standard of excellence.

The consultants in this case created a task force of managers to take a collective journey to Chicago's famous Tremont Hotel, one of the premier four-star properties in the county. Here, they interviewed managers about the factors they felt contributed to excellence. A typical question was: What were the peak moments in the life of the hotel—the times when people felt most energized, most committed, and most fulfilled in their involvement? Later, the

---

[56]Gergen, Gergen and Barrett 2004.

participants interviewed one another about their own peak experiences in their hotel, and then began to articulate aspirations for a possible future. In these discussions, there were no traces of the cycles of blame and turf protection. The group returned to their hotel with a new cooperative spirit and a renewed capacity to generate consensus. They continued the dialogue that had begun with the Appreciative Inquiry at the Tremont and within a few months developed a collective strategic plan for excellence. Within a few years they had achieved a four-star rating from the Michelin rating service.

The story of The Medic Inn is about the co-creation of 'new worlds', in the 'reciprocal exchange' between parties, a shared vision of the future emerges. When applying the principles of Dialogical Leadership, the balance of power shifts, the power dynamics change. Followers don't just take part—they co-create. Commentators such as Daniel H. Pink have, in recent years, emphasized the importance of 'intrinsic rewards' such as sense of autonomy in effective problem solving.[57]

Dialogical Leadership is linked to personal change and personal development and growth and, in turn, the development and growth of the organization. Focusing on relationships in organizations, it is a progressive approach that supplements, rather than supplants, established models such as emotional intelligence and authentic leadership. It sees generative dialogue as the medium for positive change and transformation and encourages leaders to open dialogue at both the 'local' and corporate levels. Dialogical leaders embrace the multiple influences that make up their identities and find bridges between apparently opposing or contradictory positions. And they see the 'involved participation' of followers as the *sine qua non* of leadership.

4.4 Recognizing the Other

Dialogue takes a central role in the thinking of Hermans, as we have seen. Here, I describe Hermans' view on external dialogue. He refers to it as a 'way of being'. In the Handbook of Dialogical Self Theory: "….from the perspective of the Dialogical Self Theory, dialogue is something 'precious'. It is the social expression of a human capacity that is not only valuable in itself but also must be fostered and developed in the service of self and in a society in which people are willing and able to create new and innovative meanings, solve problems in productive cooperation, and take the alterity of other people and their own selves into account for the welfare of themselves and society."[58] In a presentation for the Dialogical Self Academy he

---

[57]Pink 2011.
[58]Hermans and Gieser 2012, 13.

4.4 Recognizing the Other

summarized dialogue as embracing "contradiction as a fertile soil for the emergence of meaning."[59] Let us have a closer look at how Hermans defines dialogue. A good dialogue consists of the following basic elements[60]: It contributes to a minimal *coherence* in an otherwise fragmenting world, *without falling back* on the self-contained unity typical of the modern self. It represents a *moral* purpose, and a *developmental* purpose. *Coherence* provides us with a sense of meaning and gives us the ability to live our lives. But we have to take in consideration that dialogue does not get the status of something that gives us stability for the sake of stability. A good dialogue also breaks through the coherence of personal experience, breaks through the coherence of *my* world, as I construed it over time in past experiences and relationships. Here it relates strongly to the fourth aspect, the *developmental* purpose.

In Hermans' view on dialogue, which is a mix of moral/ethical meaning and efficiency, we can distinguish a number of aspects.

4.4.1 Creating Space

"When two or more people are increasingly involved in a dialogue, they feel the emergence of an invisible common space in which they feel accepted as dialogical partners and feel the freedom to express their experiences from their own point of view."[61] If we are able to create conditions for a good dialogue to grow, this experience of being in a common space is recognizable. In this state, it is easier to listen to and accept views different from your own ideas. The emotional dimension is important. People have to be sensitive for the different levels in a dialogue: content and relation. Emotion and non-verbal behavior are critical for creating space, as we have seen before with Bohm, Isaacs and Gergen.

4.4.2 Recognizing Alterity

A good dialogue incorporates and recognizes the *otherness* of other people and of other I-positions. Here Hermans and Konopka introduce a moral aspect of dialogue. "In its most general sense, alterity refers to the otherness of the other and its recognition as intrinsically valuable."[62] By recognizing the other *as otherness*, dialogue comes to life; it enables you to break out of your own—by definition— limited view on the world and yourself. The other *as being different from you* might open your eyes to look at yourself and the world with new eyes. This can only happen if you are willing to accept this otherness in your life. As it might change

---

[59]A presentation Hermans did for the Dialogical Self Academy on 25.2.2014.
[60]Hermans and Hermans-Konopka 2010, 174–192.
[61]Hermans and Konopka 2010, 181.
[62]Hermans and Konopka 2010, 183.

your worldview, and thus has consequences for your life in general. Of course this has a moral dimension. It is not because of morality or ethical laws that I accept the otherness of the other, but by deeply knowing that my vision is not the only true vision. It is because of learning and developing that I am willing to open up. The other person opens my worldview, just by 'being another'.

4.4.3 Innovation as Opening the Mind

In a good dialogue, you learn about yourself and you can use this for your further development. This is one of the most convincing reasons why a dialogic mindset and attitude is valuable for contemporary globalized culture with its crises. The dialogic mindset has to be learned and developed systematically. People are born with an open mind and the ability of freeing energy[63] in multiple directions and developing an information relation with the world. We saw two extremes: objectivity and science versus subjectivity, art, religion, and literature. Most minds close more and more during education into a limited set of views and cultural rules. To keep our mind open, we have to break with routines in thinking, feeling and acting. Dialogue is par excellence a 'technique' to open our mind. We have to learn this and systematically train ourselves to listen, suspend our judgments and show respect. "Dialogue in itself is a developmental process and an active learning-via-interchange that gives an impetus to the self. That is, it introduces elements to the self that were not there before the dialogue took place, and, once introduced, are experienced by the participants as valuable."[64] There has to grow a willingness in the partner in dialogue to open up for an*other* vision, be it in the form of a statement or a question.

4.4.4 Mutually Understanding

As part of the process of a good dialogue, misunderstanding is not avoided. It is even recognized as such and made productive in mutually understanding. Essential for a dialogue is that participants don't claim to have an ultimate truth. "Dialogue becomes possible only when parties involved in interchange acknowledge that there are more possible perspectives from which a particular topic can be considered. Any absolute truth claim denies the existence of multi-perspectivity and therefore blocks the innovative potentials of dialogical activity."[65] Here we refer to the first notion about creating space in the conversation. A good dialogue can only take

---

[63]Libbrecht 2007. The assumption here is, that learned responses can be unlearned, i.e. they can change.
[64]Hermans and Konopka 2010, 175.
[65]Hermans and Konopka 2010, 180.

4.4 Recognizing the Other

place if space can be created for other views and standpoints. Libbrecht's insight encourages us to free energy to respond through use of a strong pull as opposed to a concentrated push, as will-power impacts the process of mutual understanding. As a participant in a dialogical process you switch between an *active controlling mode* (focused energy), and a *receptive listening mode* (field energy).

4.4.5 Power Differences

In a good dialogue *power differences* are recognized in relations (conversation, discussion and dialogue between partners).[66] There are differences in power that might block dialogue. Nowadays in organizations it is popular to rename performance appraisals as performance dialogue because of the inherent risk of inequality due to the presence of hierarchy and various power relationships. Normally, if people sense this inequality, they hold back in how they behave and what they share. In a generative dialogue equality is an important factor for creating the conditions for a conversation that is generative and transformative. If leader and member are engaged in a conversation, hierarchy is always present, in a formal and informal (body language, tone of voice) way. In the end, a formal leader has the right to take a decision that will have an impact.

4.4.6 Being Fully Present

Dialogue is deepened by participating in a broader field of awareness: *broadening awareness*. This refers to what Libbrecht means by *deconcentrated field energy*, the needle of the compass. In a good dialogue there can be silence: *speaking silence*. I have experienced that this is one of the most impressive characteristics of dialogue: becoming aware of the impact of *speaking* and *silence*. "In this state the self is neither fixed nor imprisoned in one particular position nor overly attached to it. There is an experience of free space in which the *I* can move flexibly from one position to the other without losing contact with any of them."[67] The self becomes

---

[66] And also in the self between I-positions. What applies for individuals, applies also for aspects of the self. Some I-positions are more dominant present than others and sometimes they take over.

[67] Hermans and Konopka (2010) quote Krishnamurti, 189. In September 1981, I attended a lecture of Krishnamurti in Amsterdam. I was 26-years old and impressed by the thousands of people in the meeting hall. Some of his words I remember: "two man sitting on a bank..." What impressed me more than his words, was the *silence* before Krishnamurti entered stage. Some minutes before he entered on stage, a deep quietness came in the huge hall, people stopped talking spontaneously without a visible sign. This is what Hermans and Konopka describe as a 'broader field of awareness'. Senge et al. (2004) refer to the same phenomenon. Heifetz et al. (2009) mention four functions of silence: tension, relief, peace and curiosity. You can sense the quality of the silence by watching others' body language and eye contact and by simply feeling the mood in the room (267).

open and willing to accept alterity with an open mind and heart. This aspect of generative and transformative dialogue is one of the most remarkable to describe. "Silence can have a very different meaning: being fully present in the actual situation without any distraction from interfering thoughts or verbalizations."[68] In a dialogical process you switch between *active controlling* and *receptive listening*. Becoming able to flexibly switch between them is crucial to creating relational space. You become aware of what happens in the here and now and act upon that. *Understanding* in an experiential *and* theoretical manner how this impacts a field of awareness is a central aspect in generative dialogue.

In the next section the insights of Bohm, Isaacs, Gergen and Hermans are recombined with my own thinking and experiences in the domain of creating the conditions for generative dialogue.

4.5 Dialogue and Transformation

As we have seen before in terms of social constructionism, we relationally co-create different/new meanings, and inevitably this leads to new actions. If there is a clear urgency, it might be easier to break a routine. If there are quick wins to the process of change, this makes it more comfortable, as you immediately sense some positive effects. If you deeply comprehend what we think and do is a result of a long culturally determined process of relationally co-constructing reality, you feel yourself free to play with this given and allow yourself to innovate and think out of the box. Transformation can be described as a dynamic, dialogical process, as a re- or deconstruction of *meaning and acting* systems, which occurs in and through conversations on several levels, such as verbal, non-verbal, and metaphorical language.[69] A certain openness of mind is crucial for change and transformation.

4.5.1 Emerged Accidentally, Defended Inflexibly

To start with a question: a*re you familiar with phenomenon 34C?* Let me explain it. I was on a flight from Amsterdam to Montreal. Before take-off in Amsterdam a

---

[68]Hermans and Konopka 2010, 189.

[69]Tierney 2011, 100. Glaser (2013) distinguishes between three levels of conversation: transactional, positional, and transformational. In *transactional* conversations information is exchanged and 'informing' as giving and taking information is the most important goal of the interaction, space is closed. In *positional* conversations 'power' is exchanged, the goal of the conversation is to persuade. In *transformational* conversations 'energy' is exchanged, you share to discover and to mutually create space. This type of high trust conversations are most like generative dialogues: you have the ability to ask questions for which you have no answers. Remarkably the term 'dialogue' doesn't occur in the index.

4.5 Dialogue and Transformation

flight attendant came to the passengers asking if somebody was willing to change seats, as there was a mother and a young child who would like to sit next to one another during the long flight. *Nobody wanted to change seats.* Of course you have a choice to pick a seat during check-in, but in general the seat you get is a coincidence. Nevertheless, people don't want to change (same seat, aisle or window, with one or two rows in between). This incident made me clearly aware of the basic structure of a conviction: co-constructed *accidentally*, defended *inflexibly*. Many of our habits in thinking, feeling and acting are created in the '34C' way. You get attached to something you got by coincidence. I name this form of resistance *phenomenon 34C*.

A young project manager in my audience during a lecture on transformation and leadership said to his colleagues: *"The first step outside starts on the inside."* If you don't make a step internally, if you are not motivated, if you are not willing, change might not occur and you might get stuck in resistance. Successful change depends on the willingness of individuals to change their mindset, to start thinking, feeling and acting in a different way about topics such as their job, their way of doing things etcetera.[70] In a process of transformation it is important to convince people, and in doing so to make them think themselves, to enable the process of emerging new opportunities, new meaning and new motivation. That is why dialogue is important in a process of transformation. In dialogue, change emerges from both individuals and the group as a whole. This type of change is more sustainable because it is internally motivated. Hermans and Hermans-Jansen[71] suggest that people do not change without having some element of stability. People need a degree of stability and safety in a process of change. Dialogue can be an important tool in creating conditions for a process like this. Thanks to our ability to create space and free energy, we can intervene in the natural course of events happening in the world. Mankind continuously causes all kinds of intentional changes (innovations), often with unintended, ambiguous consequences.

4.5.2 Conditions for Change

Four factors are important when we talk about change[72]: people have to *agree* in *willing* the point of change; the *conditions* for change must be in line with the expected new thinking and behavior; people must be *able* to make the change happen; and, the new behavior and thinking should be *modeled* actively by people in the organization. It has to do with *willingness* and *being able* to experiment with a new way of thinking about yourself, feeling and acting. Positively, this implies that you can start doing new things, innovating, exploring and discovering. On the other

---

[70]Lawson and Price 2003.
[71]Hermans and Hermans-Jansen 1995, 100.
[72]Lawson and Price 2003.

hand, and this might be experienced by some people as negative, it means disruption and breaking away from a familiar planning of the world. Phenomenon 34C was an example of accidental resistance. In the following example, resistance from within the system is illustrated.

A 40-year old manager was previously owner of a family-owned company that was sold to a larger enterprise. He had become member of the management team in the new organization. In our dialogue, he learned more about himself, in particular how he developed a narrow focus on his life as purely working. How he worked with only one criterion: results. He got overworked, drove too fast in his car, slipped, and got heavily injured in a life threatening accident. While he was in hospital, his eyes opened for his old habits, but the insight appeared not to be sustainable. After a few years, he was in exactly the same old mold: working, working, and working. In our leadership dialogue, he became deeply aware of the feeling being stuck in a fixed frame in his life. He discovered that he—unconsciously—allowed his family to use him for their own goals, as he was cognitively the most intelligent and dedicated worker in the family. The process of becoming aware of this feeling and the way he expressed this to his family caused a tremendous clash in the *system* of the family. He disrupted continuity in the company and in this sense had a negative effect. He resigned and left the company, chose for his wife and children, deciding to free himself from the financial bonds with his larger family.

This example illustrates that a self-reflective insight can be beneficial for yourself but works out differently for the world around. I have also experienced that the result of a good dialogue can be counter-productive for the organization. When people become more self-conscious and develop a stronger sense of awareness in the process of transformation through dialogue, they can take decisions that break away from old patterns, which are imperative for a company, a society, a partnership. I have seen many people (leaders themselves) who went to their superiors to have a conversation about a topic they avoided for a long time. The most extreme I ever experienced was a young manager who resigned immediately after the dialogue by giving his boss a call from the car during the way back to the office.

Huczinsky and Buchanan describe different aspects of organizational change. Change programs in organizations often aim to transform business performance by delivering new processes, new systems and new structures. But most change programs fail.[73] Transformation will take place, when individuals in their roles as leaders and members of an organization start thinking, feeling and acting differently. This requires leading by example at all levels, and putting the conditions in place to make the transformation happen. Transformational change is defined as

---

[73]The success rate of planned change programs is less than 40% (Meaney and Wilson 2009). Major corporate transformations have an even higher rate of failure to achieve their goals (Gardini et al. 2011.

"large-scale change, involving radical, frame-breaking and fundamentally new ways of thinking, solving problems and doing business."[74]

A distinction can be made between change leaders that are more collaborative and consultative (high on pulling and connecting) such as *coaches* (people-centered, inspirational and participative) and *charismatics* (visioning in a charismatic and challenging manner). Styles that are more coercive and directive (high on push) are *captains* (directing in a systematic and task-oriented manner) and *commanders* (transforming in a decisive, tough-minded and forceful manner).[75] Organizations are confronted, as individuals are, with different moments of transformation. So it depends on the issue at hand and the change that you want to realize, which style of change-leader is most appropriate for the situation.

4.5.3 Changing the System

Change emerges from within the system.[76] In terms of consciously transforming yourself, this implies being ready to reflect on your own thinking, feeling and acting, on your motives and limits by self-reflection and feedback; acquiring more insight into the patterns underlying your behavior and personality. Showing the courage to draw conclusions, develop the hard and soft discipline to make change happen. You have to be willing and able to put through the transformation process on several levels. What can I *do*? What do I truly *want*? What do I *expect* from the world? Who am I *truly*? These are difficult questions to answer. If you don't have a sense of who you really are, in the depth of your being, how can you determine what Life expects from you? If you truly know what you want in your life and work, it might be easier to make that happen. Intentionally transforming self assumes free energy. Directing 'the arrow to a purpose' and simultaneously 'being aware of a deconcentrated field of energy'. Do you have a sense of direction in terms of a purpose and a sense of what is important for you in terms of values that you want to live? This will be illustrated later in the cases, individually, as a team and as an organization.

If willingness to change is limited to expressing good intentions, this is not enough to make it happen. Back in everyday life, especially in cases of high stress, many people fall back in old routines, although you can use apps and technical support to remind you. The secret of successful transformation is in the right balance between *freedom* and *structure*. In terms of process you need a solid structure to make a transformation process generative, and in terms of being motivated freedom is vital. 'Creating safety, by applying the ground principles of dialogue' is unconditionally important to reach a stage of change. The way you

---

[74]Huczynski and Buchanan 2013, 624.
[75]Stace and Dunphy 2001.
[76]Holzmer 2013, 47.

apply the rule is not by controlling, but by 'being the model of not judging, accepting and being patient'. We mentioned the importance of creating 'a safe place' to make a change process happen.[77] This brings a big dilemma too, as we are often forced to change in a situation that is not safe and secure at all! This makes individual and collective transformation challenging.

Dialogue is not morally superior to debate. Critical is *when* you apply what method? It is about the free energy, the willingness and ability to consciously choose for a way of working. As you can read in Fig. 4. 2 comparing debate and dialogue, debate is more about making your point, advocating a known insight as the right one, while dialogue is about co-creating new insights to generate new meaning. Dialogue is an approach that might help us in specific domains—wicked problems—to impactfully solve these. "Once people rediscover the art of talking together, they do not go back, this rediscovery seems to have awakened something deep within us, some recognition of what we have lost as our societies have drifted away from the core practices that can make them healthy. Once awakened, people do not go back to sleep."[78] Once you have sensed the depth of what happens in a good dialogue, you don't forget this and would like to apply it regularly. In the next section, we have a look at the conditions we have to create to make a process of generative dialogue happen.

4.6 Creating Conditions for Generative Leadership Dialogue

Apart from building the container for a generative dialogue and going through some crises, you can mention some aspects that are important when you set up a dialogical transformation journey. We distinguish here between *generic aspects* for a generative dialogue (Sect. 4.6.1), setting up an *individual leadership dialogue* (Sect. 4.6.2), and setting up a *dialogical leadership journey for a team* (Sect. 4.6.3).

4.6.1 Generic Aspects for a Generative Dialogue

The process of dialogue involves becoming aware of a pattern of thinking, feeling and acting that lies beneath a group's culture or way of interacting with each other. In organizing the conditions, there are some aspects, you take into account to make the process of generative dialogue successful. Following aspects are important.

---

[77]Simmons 1999.

[78]Peter Senge wrote a preface in Isaacs' book *Dialogue and the art of thinking together*. These are his remarks about the impact on people in organizations. Isaacs 1999, xx.

An important tool in the process of successful transformation is that of the facilitator. "The tools, the design, and the process: it is easy to let concerns around these issues preoccupy us, and yet the most important tool that we have at our disposal as facilitators *is ourselves and our presence*. That is of course not to say that the others don't count. It is simply to state that the importance of the preparation, presence and the state of mind of the facilitator is crucial."[79] Apart from the material preparation, the mindset and presence of the facilitator is very important for the process. As a facilitator, you influence what happens in a group to a great extent, by what you say and do, and also in the way you are present in the room. You are the example of presence. You are the one who uses *arrow* concentration by example, and the group also looks at you in the deconcentrated *field* awareness. If there is any incoherence in your behavior and wordings, this will have an impact on the group process. Train yourself as a facilitator to at all times have a level of free energy, space, enabling you to break with a pattern of fixed habits in the way you do the conversation. A good facilitator is able to deal with the *unexpected and unplanned*. A skilled facilitator stays present to what shows up in the moment, having an open eye and mind for what is going on in the group and the individuals. If you get caught in a structure that you prepared, or a result that you must reach, you cannot be in the moment, and observe what is really needed in the process. Kohlrieser developed for this characteristic the expression 'the mind's eye', Isaacs, 'the third position'. As a facilitator, it is important to permanently have free energy *to be not identified* with the process, the content, the participants, but nevertheless *being present in the here and now*.

- *Clarity of Purpose*

Why are you bringing this group of people together? What is it that you want to reach with this selection of people? Clarity of purpose is important, as it enables people to accept the rules, as the process of dialogue is not easy. In determining the purpose of the dialogue, it is also important to have an idea about the needs, what is it that the group needs to develop in order to go into the process of dialogue?

- *Asking Good Questions*

Good questions *open* the mind of people, and *redirect* thinking energy into a new direction. Good questions enable you to develop a broader view on reality, what you have come to define as your/our reality so far. Good questions *create space*, they open possibilities to think differently. "The power of good questions cannot be underestimated. Good questions are catalytic. They open a new learning field. They stimulate thought processes, curiosity, and the desire to engage with a group, and they are central to what defines and distinguishes a dialogue."[80] People that ask good questions let you time to look for the answer instead of pushing you to give an answer immediately. Good questions are those where you don't have an immediate answer. Good questions activate your thinking and feeling abilities and

---

[79]Bojer et al. 2008, 23.
[80]Bojer et al. 2008, 19.

open new ways of thinking, feeling and acting. Good questions are at the heart of a generative dialogue.

- *Participating and Participants*

Inclusiveness is essential for a dialogue. To reach this, we have to look for ways of connecting with people and including different voices in the group to speak up. All participants in a dialogue setting have a contribution, they are in the room because they give something to the group and get something out of the situation. In management teams, we explicitly expect people to contribute, and we invite them to do so. If they tend to withdraw from the process, we use this as an important part of the dialogical process. In a solid dialogue process *each* of the participants is *present* and *contributes* to the process in their own style. Of course the way people contribute is different, some speak more than others. The risk of damaging a dialogue process comes—amongst other reasons—because participants are distracted by mobile devices, emails and so on. We see people are mentally absent, having difficulty to be mentally *and* physically present. Connecting, creating conditions to make true relating possible, for yourself and the team, is an important factor for successful dialogues (*and* for successful leadership). You reach this also by setting specific and practical ground rules for interacting. And by training the participants in how to apply these principles and rules of discipline, hard and soft, focused and unfocused: deep listening, suspending your judgment, visibly showing respect, and voicing.

- *Principles*

Before the dialogue starts, the group agrees about the principles that will be followed during the sessions. Some of them are *showing respect, being here, you are allowed to bring everything to the table, if you need a break ask for a break, switch off your mobile devices, and everybody is responsible for the principles.* You could add to these some more specific principles or rules in certain situations such as *rotating leadership, sitting in a circle, with or without tables.* The reason for defining and practicing principles in a clear way is that they create a condition for people to feel *safe*. Opening up in a dialogue, suspending your assumptions and changing your view on what you thought so far as being true, is *an intense and confrontational process, where resistance is inherent.* If you feel safe in the context, you can start experimenting with new thinking, feeling and acting.

- *Diverging and Converging*

As a facilitator, you flexibly switch between diverging and converging.[81] The *divergent* phase of process is a time of opening up possibilities, issues or themes. It is about generating alternatives, gathering diverse points of view, allowing disagreement in and suspending judgment. The *convergent* phase is about arriving at, and making explicit, conclusions, insights and next steps of the process towards acting and implementing. In Fig. 4.3 you see 'Dialogue' and 'Diverge' as the first

---

[81]Cf. Libbrechts (2007) view on field and arrow, deconcentrated and concentrated energy.

4.6 Creating Conditions for Generative Leadership Dialogue 97

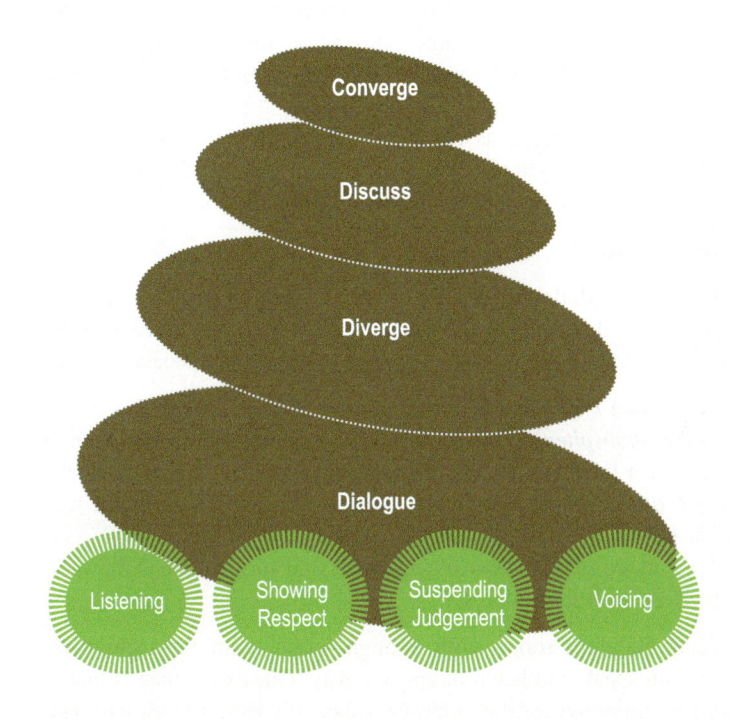

Fig. 4.3 Creating conditions for generative leadership dialogue

two phases, followed by 'Discuss' and Converge'. Here you understand that dialogue and discussion are equally valuable, used in different phases of the process and with different goals. "Transformative dialogue processes that truly allow for divergence often include a 'groan zone' or 'grey fog' situation in the middle. The groan zone is that somewhat painful place, where everything is a little too chaotic, unclear and unstructured. Sometimes this is a time of conflict and storming, sometimes it is characterized more by confusion and feeling overwhelmed by complexity or even despairing."[82] In this phase, the role of the chairperson or facilitator is very important, as participants look at you how you deal with this frenzy situation, primarily non-verbally. By experience we know that this phase is not easy, both for members and for leaders (facilitators or chairpersons).

- *The Right Space*

If you organize a dialogue it is important to find the right location. The physical environment is co-determining the outcome of a dialogue process. This aspect is often underestimated. Some questions you ask yourself in selecting a room:

- Is there enough *physical space* to interact with one another?
- How is the *atmosphere* in the room? Is it a relaxing room? Will there be enough fresh air for a long session? Is there enough light, how does it smell?
- Are there *distractions* in or nearby the room that might interfere with the dialogue process?
- Is coffee and tea served? Any other snacks and food? How is the service? Does this interfere with the process?

You need the right room, with enough space, with the right acoustics, the participants can speak and listen in an easy way. Our experience is that finding the right venue is important for the outcome, especially if you work with leaders, who are used to five star hotel-accommodations, with lots of food and alcohol. These factors are mostly *not* endorsing success.

Showing your flexibility in adapting the structure once the dialogue process has started, is the most critical competency of a good facilitator/chairperson. Every process is different from what you expected. So you have to be willing and able to adapt smoothly, without losing sight of your purpose, the reason of being together. My experience is that you have to prepare accurately: concentrating in a rational mode with focused discipline. Once everything is ready for the session: deconcentrate, empty yourself as a facilitator and *become* an example of the mix of the arrow and the field, of hard and soft discipline. This is not easy. Neither for the participants, nor the facilitators/chairpersons/leaders. The reason why I spend so much text on this subject is exactly this: leader = chairperson = facilitator. In all these I-positions you have to develop a discipline (soft and hard) to consistently show a way of thinking, feeling and acting like this. Practicing is a lifelong journey for leaders and members.

---

[82]Bojer et al. 2008, 19.

4.6.2 Setting up an Individual Leadership Dialogue

Having individual conversations with people about their leadership can be a goal in itself, or as preparation for a journey with a group. We provide members in dialogue with a framework for reflecting on their thinking, feeling and acting as leaders (Fig. 4.4).

In this dialogue, we use all elements mentioned in the figure: organization, team, culture, market, and society; giving direction, pushing and pulling; knowing by rational analysis (rationality, head), experiencing by intuition (feeling, heart), and doing by physical presence (acting, hands); entrepreneur, manager, coach, change leader, and professional. We invite people to reflect on each aspect, and apply it in their own situation. We work with flipchart or whiteboard, the framework is step-by-step built in a distinctive way during the dialogue. Let's go through it step by step.

Exploring your being a leader

The first phase is exploring, trying to find where to begin. "Thinking about your being a leader, could you tell me: what does leadership mean for you?" "What does it mean for you to be a leader in this organization?" "Could you give an example where you consciously switch between leading and following?" These are examples. By listening carefully, you ask follow up questions, especially examples, like: "When you were younger, did you have the idea/plan becoming a leader in your professional career?" "Are you a leader in informal situations?" "How is your leadership expressed at home, with your partner, with the children?"

Before you go to a next phase, ask: "What is the most important insight you take away from the last part of our conversation?" By listening carefully you get an indication of the level of understanding and it prepares you for the next steps.

Exploring your leadership styles

In the second phase, questions that you can ask, after having explained the first part of the framework, are: "Could you give an example, where you were high on vision/push/pull?" By asking exploring, non-judgmental questions we want to get a clear picture—as a photo. During the process, you can go deeper, by asking questions, which are adding a new direction, as "If you are normally more pushing, could you give me an example of the *opposite*? Where are you high on pulling, although you normally don't pull so much?" If people find an example, elaborate it: "What caused you to make this choice of behaving, as it is not your preferred style?" "Was it effective?" "How did you feel, when acting like this?" Here we normally find starting points for a process of increased awareness and change, as people start to become conscious of behavior that is not representative for their way of acting.

Exploring your leadership sources

In the third phase, after having illustrated how you influence people (rationality, rational analysis, head—intuition, experiencing, heart—body, doing, hands[83]), you

---

[83]See also Fig. 3.2.

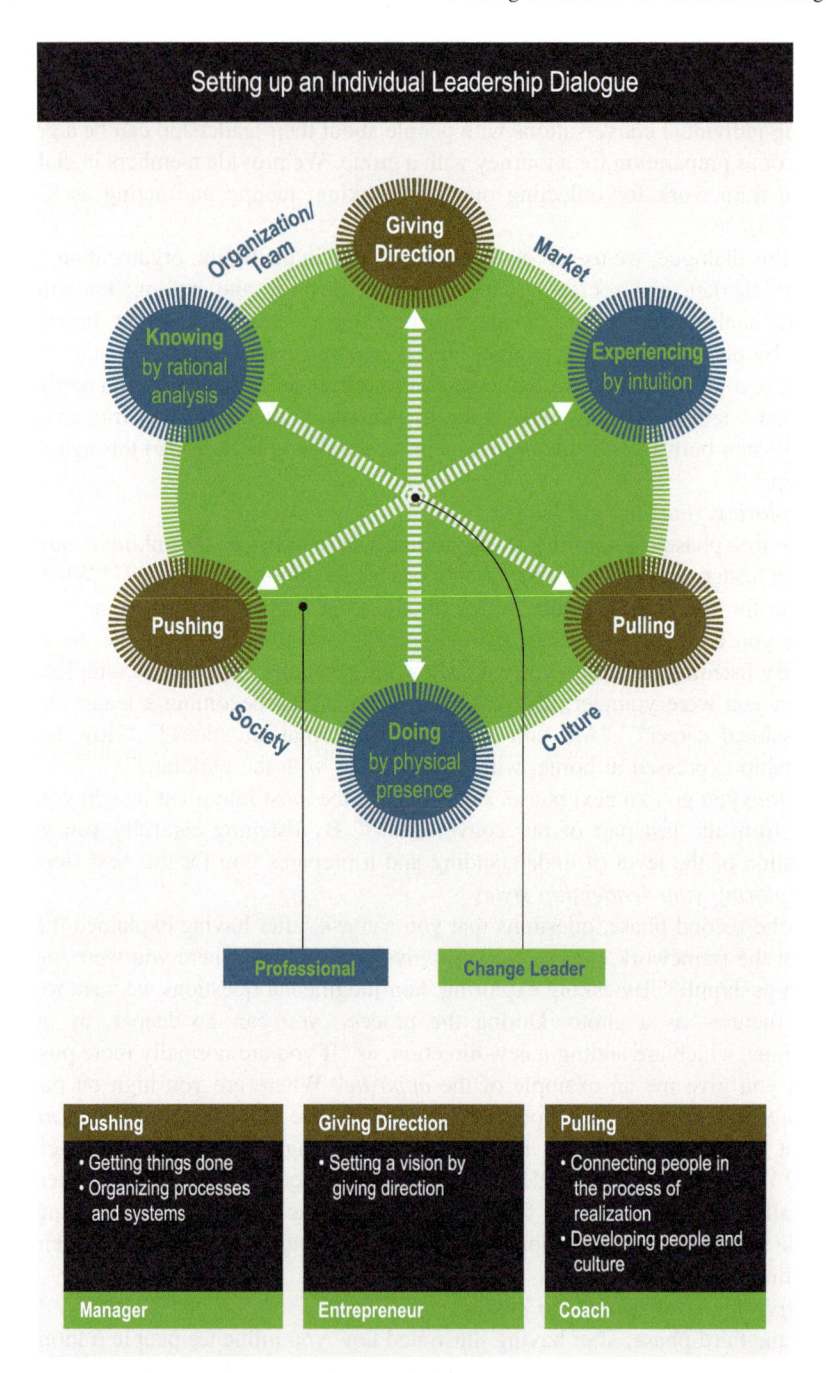

Fig. 4.4 Setting up an individual leadership dialogue

ask questions as: "Could you give an example where you were high on knowing by rational analysis/intuitive experiencing/physical presence?" "If you are normally more intuitive, could you find an example of the opposite?" "Let's elaborate this example: what made you effective?" What is described here in a few lines, normally takes hours. If you listen carefully, and a trust relation is established, you will discover mutual reflection reaches a deep level quickly. I use mutual, as dialoguing in this way is intense for all parties, both for the participant and for the facilitator.

Exploring your leadership roles

In the fourth phase, after having explained different leadership roles (entrepreneur—manager—coach—change leader—professional), the conversation continues with questions like these. "What is your preferred role? When do you feel at your best?" "Could you give an example where you were high on the change leader role?" "If you are normally more like a manager (getting things done, structure, processes), could you find an example of the opposite role (coach/entrepreneur)?" "Let's elaborate an example: were you effective, what made you not effective?" "How about your being a professional?" "How is that related to your leadership?" "Can you describe situations where you have been a leader in change? How did this work for you?" "How did you cope with resistance?" "With whom and when, successfully?" "And with whom not successfully?"

Exploring the context

In the fifth phase, you turn to explicitly exploring the context. Think about questions such as, "Having a look at your team, how would you describe your role within the team?" "In what circumstances are you most effective within your team? Give an example". "In what circumstances/with whom are you less effective or not effective at all?" "Let's have a closer look at this example." "Thinking about your superior, how do you influence him/her? What role does (s)he have in your view?" "How would (s)he describe you in terms of styles/sources/roles?"

Although five phases are indicated here, as a facilitator you are able to intentionally improvise, move to another level, and open up another perspective. Each conversation is unique and like others. The leadership concept and the five phases in the conversation support you as a facilitator in this process, be aware of not applying it mechanically. If people get the feeling that you are doing an 'interview' and ticking off boxes on your list, it isn't a generative dialogue anymore.

At the end a dialogue is concluded by formulating overall themes, lessons learned, gathering important insights, looking forward to actions. You ask questions, such as "What is the recurring theme in what we have said so far?" "What lesson did you learn today, that you can apply tomorrow?" "What could be a slogan for your current and future development?" In terms of success these individual dialogues are crucial. Here the participants are prepared to open their mind in a meeting with the rest of their team. Learning agility, the willingness to continuously learn, is crucial for those who lead (and those who participate). In a formal leadership role, you have no choice: learning is an integral part of your function. Immersive and continuous—first person—learning.[84]

4.6.3 The Role of the Facilitator in Setting up a Dialogue for a Team

Here our focus is on generic elements, which can be explained separately from illustrative cases.[85] We distinguish between the role of the facilitator in doing interventions, the qualities of a good facilitator (Sect. 4.6.4) and the different types of interventions that can be done (Sect. 4.6.5).

As a facilitator you are—par excellence—the one who shows that you are able to apply the principles of dialogue—respect, suspending judgments, listening, asking questions and voicing—*and to break the pattern*. You have the courage *'to put the fish on the table.'*[86] This implies you have the power to break through a pattern of actions and words that sometimes seems unstoppable. You also have the skill to listen, without any action or reaction, keeping silent, not interfering at any level, trusting that the group will give the accurate response. So *courage and humility meet in a good facilitator. Credibility, reliability and intimacy* are described as important factors to build trust.[87] A too high relation to your own self-orientation is critical. If you are predominantly self-oriented, your credibility will not lead to high trust. A visible orientation to the other person(s) is your authentic attitude.

---

[84]Of course you can use tools for feedback such as intake surveys, 360°-surveys, personality questionnaires, but these are not necessary in this phase. Your partner is the source for information. You don't want to be engaged in a discussion on the outcome of a tool, you try to open up a leader's mind for sincere and deep self-reflection. In this sense you can use everything that has relevance for the individual as input. My lesson learned in the past is that I suggest people to bring insights (reports) from earlier conversations/tests/ sessions, if they want. Use outcomes of previous tools and sessions as input for reflection here and now. Integrate insights from past sessions into the dialogue, so you don't waste energy, or start over again.

[85]In Chap. 7, an entire process is worked out in detail as a case-study.

[86]Kohlrieser describes fishermen in Sicily, cleaning fish for the market. "Suddenly, I realized this was what good conflict management is all about: "putting the fish on the table" and going through the bloody mess of cleaning the fish to prepare for the great fish dinner at the end of the day." Kohlrieser 2006, 108.

[87]Maister et al. 2000, 69.

4.6.4 Qualities of a Good Facilitator

- *Listening* very well on different levels, verbally and non-verbally, not jumping to any conclusion or interpretation; not being concerned with your own agenda or ego, but following the team's atmosphere, without being identified with it.[88]
- Closely connected, a facilitator has developed a strong sense of *personal awareness and authenticity*. A good facilitator has developed the meta-skill of being aware what happens in the group *and* in him/herself. Not being bound too much to one's ego is a very important aspect, especially in working with leaders, who are used to competing on that level. And, last but not least, knowing your limitations. As a facilitator you are not perfect, know when to stop and hand over to somebody else in the group (or in/outside your organization).
- A good facilitator has *mastered the art of asking questions*. The most powerful tool of the facilitator is asking questions, making space for the answer to come from the person to whom the question is asked. A good question opens the mind.
- *Seeing the big picture*, being able to be aware of the broader field in a group (in a deconcentrated way), recognizing patterns. You have an eye for the 'whole'. "Taking a holistic approach is also about being able to see patterns, helping the group make connections as they work, and recognizing that multiple intelligences are at work."[89]

4.6.5 Categories of Interventions

When we start a process of a leadership journey with a team, the first intervention is to have in-depth conversations with all participants before the group dialogue sessions take place. The same person as the one who will take later on the role of the facilitator has face to face dialogues. These conversations are meant to build trust, mutual trust. The participant gets used to the facilitator, and vice versa. For these conversations, you need at least two hours, sometimes it takes a day and a half. The facilitator needs to establish a basis of trust, safety and respect. Once you are in the full dynamic of your thinking, feeling and acting with your team, there is inherently a level of resistance to an external power that 'stops' you in the full flow, in the midst of a process. Establishing trust and respect before the meetings take place, are important goals of these conversations before the dialogue-sessions.

A second set of interventions takes place during the dialogue-sessions. From the very beginning of the dialogue, all irregularities in relation to listening, respecting,

---

[88]Lao Tzu expresses this 'being full of emptiness' 'The sage has no mind of his own, he takes as his own the mind of the people.' Lau 1963, 110.

[89]Bojer et al. 2008, 25.

suspending and voicing, are addressed *immediately*. We do real time interventions by means of time-outs to set the right example immediately. In the time-outs we tell stories about past experiences where we have seen similar events happen. We ask questions to the group, to individuals, about what they have perceived. And we give direct feedback, on the content level, the non-verbal level, and the process-level. Generally this phase creates a strong pressure in the group, implicit behavioral and thought patterns are made explicit. This refers to what we before indicated as the 'groan zone' or 'grey fog' situation. In these interventions the real power of a facilitator is experienced.

A third kind of intervention you can do during dialogue sessions is related to giving specific feedback to an individual. This can be at different levels: content, process, behavioral, non-verbal, rational, and emotional. The impact is greater if this is combined with illustrative stories and examples from previous sessions and dialogues. Sometimes related to literature and research. These interventions can be done in the plenary group, but also one-to-one in the coffee and tea breaks or during breakfast, lunch and dinner.

There will be flesh on the bones in part III where we give several examples of how this works. At the same time this is a critical stage in building the theoretical and practical foundation for the Dialogical Leadership approach. Before we continue some critical reflections.

4.7 Some Considerations

4.7.1 This Kind of Facilitator Doesn't Exist

In reflecting on the last two sections, creating the conditions for transformation and the role of the facilitator/leader in this process, you can ask yourself if this is realistic. Is such a leader profile not too idealistic? Jaworski emphasizes that the level of the '*intervener*' is determining the level of the outcome of the process.[90] If this is correct, it implies that we have to work in the broadest sense on the *level* of *being* of a leader.

My first conclusion is that it is not easy to respond to the criteria mentioned above. I have worked with leaders and facilitators who are able to meet these criteria, but many don't. What is crucial in my view is that these people are aware of this process as a continuously learning process, and that they dare to 'not know' an answer. Here we speak about the condition of a leader as the one who has the status and the right of doing these kind of interventions. Somebody who is able to contribute to transformation in other people.[91] Later we will explore the role of a leader

---

[90] "The role of the facilitator—and the state of the facilitator's consciousness—is critically important to enabling creative discovery..." Jaworski 2012, 49.

[91] See also: Van de Kerkhof 2013; Senge et al. 2004; Kahane 2007; 2010.

as being able to take the I-position of a promoter. That you as a leader are able to promote the development (as a re-organizing of the I-position repertoire) of members of your team. That is what we call transforming par excellence.

4.7.2 Controlling the World

That the world which we live in is constantly changing in different speeds is a fact. In the process of constant change, levels of stability exist. The self is continuously changing although there are some stabilities on the physical and the mental level. It seems as if humans tend to look for and invent stabilities in the changing world by holding transitional objects, by using metaphors and rites-of-passage in periods of change, by resisting change and clamping to the accustomed ordering of the world. Most scientists nowadays agree with this epistemological principle that the world is permanently changing and that we, humans, try to regulate those changes by developing knowledge, with the aim to have influence and control. We have collectively developed free energies to explore, describe the world around us in *cause-and-effect* laws and to control—successfully and sometimes unsuccessfully—these laws for increasing our comfort and prosperity. Nevertheless we know we will never be able to 'dominate' the world, that there will always be 'black swans', 'tipping-points', and 'singularities'.[92] Sense making, relationality and dialogicality can be important aspects in dealing with these phenomena.

4.7.3 Power as an Interfering Factor

The theoretical issue you might have with dialogical leadership is that formal leadership is *by definition* hierarchical in organizations, while dialogue—*by definition*—presupposes free space and equality. One of the basic paradoxes in this sense is related to *power*: although it is present, try to think, feel and act independently (with respect!) *within* a relation, where formal power is present. In your *internal dialogue* power inequality is not a formal one, you are able to break through, once you become aware and can create space ('ma'). This is exactly what happens when there is an internal dialogue between unequally powered I-positions. In your *external dialogues*, power can be a real issue. While having a conversation with peers and colleagues is normally on equal ground, dialogue with superiors or direct reports are formally unequal. Having a dialogue with your superior is formally imbalanced, as is a dialogue with your own reports. Formally, both relations are unequal in terms of formal power and so—by definition—possibly problematic

---

[92]'Black swans' (Taleb 2010), 'Tipping-points' (Gladwell 2005), and 'Singularities' (Diamandis and Kotler 2012).

in a generative dialogue. I refer here to a dancing partner with a thin line between leading and following.[93] On the physical level it is difficult to determine who exactly is leading. The comparison with the dance makes you aware that you can't lead if you don't follow! Ultimately, this is also valid for every situation in daily life. A difference is that because of material consequences and fear people give in. *Philosophically speaking, there is no leading without willingness to follow*. In this sense, ultimately, power does not necessarily have influence.

Another level is the dialogue with your environment, externally with the system. Here, we have the same issue as above. Essentially there can be no system without people willing to follow. In reality systems have a huge impact on relationships. "When participating in social contexts, individual voices and their dialogical relationships are to a great extent expressions of institutional and historically bound collective voices and, at the same time, limited by them. As a consequence, power differences structure and constrain, overtly or covertly, both the process and the content of dialogical relationships."[94]

Judith Glaser distinguishes between three levels of power in conversations. The first level is *transactional influence:* tell and ask, you influence through information sharing and you tell what is on your mind (I-centric). The second level is *positional influence*: advocate and inquire, you influence others to move towards your position by using your personal and/or positional power. The third level is that of *transformational influence:* share and discover: you release energy to co-create, and to influence through energy shifting.[95] Life consists of all three levels of conversations, it is about developing the art of flexibly switching between the levels, related to the issue at hand.

To gain a better understanding of how these mechanisms actually work in daily practice we have to do more action-based and practical research. For instance by doing 'in-depth probes' into leadership, individually, as teams and in the organisation as a whole through 'describing narratives' from more than one I-position could give more clarity about how power and dialogue can co-exist in organizational life. In many organizations dialogue is used in different variations to deal with change, organizational and societal developments and with performance and appraisal. Leadership implies that you have to deal with formal power in a way that allows you—if you are in a formal leadership position—to apply a dialogical approach. This means, to create conditions, where your team is mobilized (i.e. is bestowed with the informal authority) to co-create a solution for a wicked issue.

---

[93] Van Loon and Kouwenhoven 2016.
[94] Hermans and Gieser 2012, 11.
[95] Glaser 2013.

4.8 Reflections on My Personal Narrative 3

Change has played an important role in my life. In this chapter creating the conditions for dialogue and transformation processes have been described. I reflect on some moments of transformation in my own life, related to the former scheme of I-positions.

4.8.1 Developing a Habit

Since as long as I can remember, I was setting myself targets for change. Restlessness, worrying, feeling rushed and impatient were familiar moods for me. Apart from the job to earn a living for the family, I felt a serious *search for meaning*. Let me give some examples of the change actions I did to break routines or to focus attention and energy on new domains. As a student, I planned to sit in another seat in the auditorium for each lecture. During working groups, often taking many hours, I set myself a target to ask at least two or three questions, I did not park my car twice at the same place. These were all actions to activate my mind, to move out of my comfort zone and train myself to become more aware. I went through barriers for myself and others. I would—looking back—characterize my discipline as 'hard' having used primarily focused and concentrated energy. Since my mid-twenties I work in my journals with '*reflection and/or action slogans*' that change per period of a few months to half a year. I worked with these reminders to consciously create more awareness and presence and to break through routines. During a period of my life (2003–2008) I travelled around the world for clients and visited many countries. Continuous change, and simultaneously I had my 'habit of breaking through routines'. There was a kind of paradox active in me. Apparently willingness to change and being attached to routine are two aspects in my life. Externally quite stable, people assess me mostly as quiet, thoughtful, not taking risks, and not being emotional and passionate. Internally I was very emotional and not quiet at all. I was permanently looking for new horizons. I felt—as I formulated in my first self-investigation in 1987—like homeless, longing for my home.

4.8.2 A Moment of Crisis

A remarkable moment in my professional and personal development was a group dialogue session with colleagues in 2005. It felt as a moment of 'crisis'. We used to discuss client-cases and listen to each other's way of working with clients and teams. We asked questions, made professional remarks and gave each other feedback on how we professionally and personally worked. I brought in a case in which I worked with a city manager. He had stress-issues and was thinking about changing his career. He wanted to explore new directions in his professional and personal life with me as his coach. We did a technically perfect self-investigation and I made a clear analysis, which we discussed for further action. But without any success! Nothing happened. The client did not come back. I went through all steps as indicated in the working procedures. I asked the group for feedback. One of my colleagues made me tremble on my feet with her remark: "maybe he did not feel safe with you, did you think about that?" I was worried as I knew the answer immediately: 'No, he did not feel safe at all, as I used my rational razor blade to analyze his situation without providing the safe and secure basis'. But I was afraid for the answer. I understood that a technically correct and accurate analysis is not a sufficient starting point for change. I realized the context within which the analysis was discussed was not the right one for my client. He was brought out of his comfort zone by my analysis, conveyed without compassion. My colleagues recommended me to not only use my rational analysis, but also to integrate a more intuitive and sensitive aspect of myself during the interaction with the client. As I was trained to primarily start from the factual analysis, this was not easy for me. On the other hand, in workshops I facilitated in symbolism and in my Tai Chi lessons, I functioned primarily on my intuition. As a lyricist I wrote a lot of texts, purely intuitive. But the I-positions '*I as a rational thinker*' versus '*I as an intuitive Tai Chi practitioner*', '*I as an intuitive lyricist*', felt disconnected. The core question for the coming years for me was: how can I integrate the rational thinker I-position with the intuitive Tai Chi practitioner and lyricist? Basically this was a process that took many years. How to facilitate the internal dialogue between these two opposites? How to reconcile the polarity? How to transpose the intuitive energy of the lyricist to the rational thinker? As the internal power of the rational thinker was much stronger than the intuitive practitioner.

4.8.3 Out of My Comfort Zone

There seemed to be no I-position that could play an intermediate role between the rational thinking I-position and the more intuitive one. The dilemma I had was finding a third position where I could connect rational analysis with intuition. 'I as Levi' was secreted for my colleagues, and for me it was present as a kind of invisible support from the back, as a 'promoter position'. But not as an external 'third position', as a mediator between the two 'conflicting' positions. 'I as an intuitive lyricist' was an internal I-position too, which I could not bring forward to reconcile the opposites.

In terms of *developmental* processes, what happened was a *decentering* process, I was brought into a zone of discomfort. I felt myself as seriously disorganized. I was urgently looking for an answer. In this period in my career around 2005, I had no conversations with my supervising psychologist. In my internal reflections, though, 'I as Levi' supported me as an anchor-point in myself, comparable to the role it took in the beginning of my career. But 'I as Levi' was not effective anymore in my external dialogues and process of reflections with others.

To summarize: at this point in my life, my position repertoire consisted of the following I-positions: (Fig. 4.5)

4.8 Reflections on My Personal Narrative 3

Reflections on My Personal Narrative 3

Out of my Comfort Zone (2005)

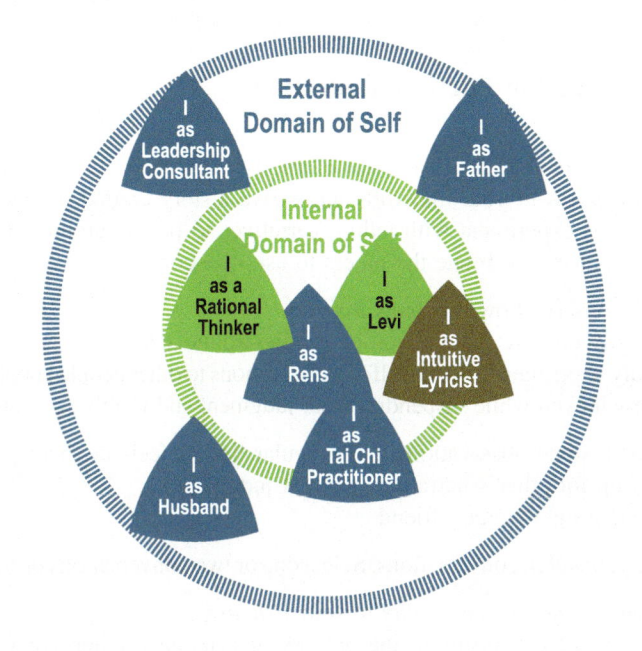

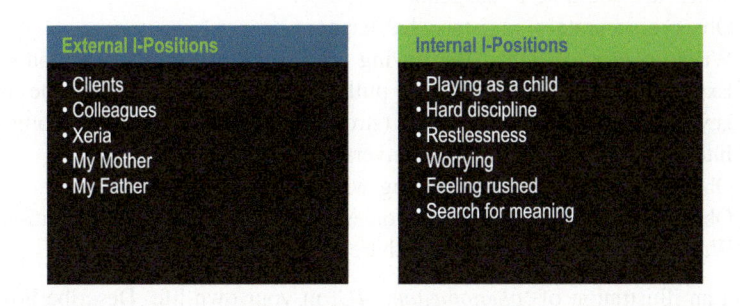

External Domain of Self
- I as Leadership Consultant
- I as Father

Internal Domain of Self
- I as a Rational Thinker
- I as Levi
- I as Rens
- I as Intuitive Lyricist
- I as Tai Chi Practitioner
- I as Husband

External I-Positions
- Clients
- Colleagues
- Xeria
- My Mother
- My Father

Internal I-Positions
- Playing as a child
- Hard discipline
- Restlessness
- Worrying
- Feeling rushed
- Search for meaning

Fig. 4.5 Reflections on my personal narrative 3

The period was a transformation from 'I as a rational thinker' to 'I as an intuitive lyricist'. I was looking for a more intuitive and direct way to express myself verbally and non-verbally with clients. Looking at it from a distance, it seems a *paradox. I primarily rely on my rational thinking in my professional working with clients, secretly supported from the I-position 'I as Levi'. Simultaneously this hidden position hindered me to actively use my intuition in 'I as Rens'.* How to reconcile this paradox?

4.9 Questions for Further Reflection

- Contemplate about your life in terms of a self-narrative. Write down for yourself seven key words in your life/work and weave a story around it. In the coming seven weeks, experiment with telling narratives to people around you (family, colleagues, etcetera). Invite the others to ask questions.
    - Firstly observe how this feels for you.
    - Secondly observe the reaction of people around you.
    - Thirdly experiment for yourself to ask questions to other people about what they share with you while suspending your judgment and visibly showing respect.

  Write down some observations, in particular how it feels to share your stories and to open up for other's narratives without judgment?
  Share your insights with a friend.

- Observe yourself in conversations. Select one or two conversations during a week.
    - Become aware of the *quality of your listening.*
      Describe what happens in the process of listening? When are you able to keep your attention to what is said by your partner? When not?
      Describe the process of focused listening as accurately as possible.
    - Become aware of *assumptions.*
      Try to suspend your assumptions, popping up automatically.
      When are you able to suspend, when not?
      Observe accurately, register what happens.
      Write down an insight, after having practiced 'suspending judgments.'
    - Experiment with pushing and pulling in conversations, as one of the key-differences between debate (strong push), and dialogue (strong pull). Intentionally push while in a conversation, intentionally pull.
      Observe how this flexible playing with pushing and pulling feels.
      Observe the differences in reaction with your partners in conversation.
      Write down some insights and share this with a friend.

- Find an illustration of '*phenomenon 34C*' in your own life. Describe how you deal/dealt with the situation. Describe yourself (thinking, feeling, and acting) in terms of flexibility and inflexibility. What conclusions do you draw from your observations?

References

Babiak, P., & Hare, R. D. (2006). *Snakes in suits: When psychopaths go to work*. New York: Regan Books/Harper Collins Publishers.

Ballantyne, D. (2004). Dialogue and its role in the development of relationship specific knowledge. *Journal of Business & Industrial Marketing, 19*(2), 114–123.

Bohm, D. (1990). A new theory of the relationship of mind and matter. *Philosophical psychology, 3*(2–3), 271–286.

Bohm, D. (1992). Thought as a System. (Transcript of seminar held in Ojai, California, from 30 November to 2 December, 1990).

Bohm, D. (1996). *On dialogue*. New York: Routledge.

Bohm, D., & Factor, D. (1995). *Unfolding meaning: a weekend of dialogue with David Bohm*. New York, NY: Routledge.

Bojer, M., Roehl, H., Knuth-Holesen, M., & Magner, C. (2008). *Mapping dialogue. Essential tools for social change*. Chagrin Falls, Ohio: TAOS Institute Publications.

Brown, J., Isaacs, D., & World Café Community. (2005). *World Café: Shaping Our Futures Through Conversations That Matter*. San Francisco: Berrett-Koehler.

De Liefde, W. H. (2002). *African tribal leadership: voor managers: van dialoog tot besluit*. [For managers: from Dialogue to Decision] Kluwer.

Diamandis, P. H., & Kotler, S. (2012). *Abundance: The future is better than you think*. New York: Simon and Schuster.

Gardini, M., Giuliani, G., & Marricchi, M. (2011). Finding the right place to start change. *McKinsey Quarterly, November (Source: Organization Practice downloaded, 11)*.

Gergen, K. J. (2009a). *An invitation to social construction* (2nd ed.). London: Sage.

Gergen, K. J. (2009b). *Relational being: Beyond self and community*. New York: Oxford University Press.

Gergen, K. J., & Gergen, M. (2003). *Social construction. A reader*. Thousand Oaks, CA: Sage.

Gergen, K. J., & Gergen, M. (2004). *Social construction. Entering the dialogue*. Chagrin Falls, Ohio: TAOS Institute Publications.

Gergen, K. J., & Thatchenkery, T. J. (1996). Organization science as social construction: Postmodern potentials. *Journal of Applied Behavioral Science, 40*(2), 228–249.

Gergen, K. J., Gergen, M., & Barrett, F. (2004). Dialogue: Life and death of the organization. In D. Grant, C. Hardy, C. Oswick, & L. Putnam (Eds.), *Handbook of Organizational discourse* (pp. 39–60). London: Sage.

Gladwell, M. (2005). *Blink. The power of thinking without thinking*. New York: Black Bay Books.

Glaser, J. E. (2013). *Conversational Intelligence: How Great Leaders Build Trust and Get Extraordinary Results*. New York: Bibliomotion, Inc.

Heifetz, R.A. (1994). *Leadership without easy answers* (Vol. 465). Cambridge: Harvard University Press.

Heifetz, R. A., Grashow, A., & Linsky, M. (2009). *The practice of adaptive leadership: Tools and tactics for changing your organization and the world*. Boston: Harvard Business Press.

Hermans, H. J. M., & Gieser, Th (Eds.). (2012). *Handbook of dialogical self theory*. Cambridge: University Press.

Hermans, H. J. M., & Hermans-Jansen, E. (1995). *Self-narratives: the construction of meaning in psychotherapy*. New York: Guilford Press.

Hermans, H. J. M., & Hermans-Konopka, A. (2010). *Dialogical self theory. Positioning and counter-positioning in a globalizing society*. Cambridge: University Press.

Hersted, L., & Gergen, K. J. (2013). *Relational leading. Practices for dialogically based collaboration*. Chagrin Falls, Ohio: TAOS Institute Publications.

Holzmer, D. (2013). Leadership in the time of liminality. *The Embodiment of Leadership: A Volume in the International Leadership Series, Building Leadership Bridges, 43*.

Huczynski, A., & Buchanan, D. (2013). *Organizational behaviour* (8th ed.). Edinburg: Pearson Education Limited.

Isaacs, W.N. (1993). Taking flight: Dialogue, collective thinking and organizational learning. *Organizational Dynamics,* 24–39.

Isaacs, W. N. (1999). *Dialogue and the art of thinking together. A pioneering approach to communicating in business and in life.* New York, NY: Doubleday.

James, W. (1890). *The principles of psychology* (Vol. 1). London: MacMillan.

Kahane, A. (2007). *Solving tough problems. An open way of talking, listening and creating new realities.* San Francisco: Berrett-Koehler Publishers, Inc.

Kahane, A. (2010). *Power and Love. A theory and practice of social change.* San Francisco: Berrett-Koehler Publishers Inc.

Kohlrieser, G. (2006). *Hostage at the table. How leaders can overcome conflict, influence others, and raise performance.* San Francisco, CA: Jossey-Bass.

Lau, D.C. (1963). *Lao Tzu. Tao Te Ching.* Translated with an introduction. London: Penguin Books.

Lawson, E., & Price, C. (2003). The psychology of change management. *McKinsey Quarterly,* 30–41.

Libbrecht, U. (2007). *Within the Four Seas…: Introduction to comparative philosophy.* Belgium: Peeters Publishers.

Maister, D. H., Green, C. H., & Galford, R. M. (2000). *The trusted advisor.* New York: Simon and Schuster.

Meaney, M., & Wilson, S. (2009). Change in recession. *People Management,* 15(10).

Morioka, M. (2008). Voices of the self in the therapeutic chronotype: *Utuschi* and *Ma. International Journal for Dialogical Science, 3*(1), 93–108.

Morioka, M. (2015). How to create *ma*—the living pause—in the landscape of the mind: the wisdom of the NOH theater. *International Journal for Dialogical Science, 9*(1), 81–95.

Pink, D. H. (2011). *Drive: The surprising truth about what motivates us.* Baltimore: Penguin.

Schein, E. H. (1993). On dialogue, culture and organizational learning. *Organizational Dynamics,* 22, 27–37.

Senge, P. Scharmer, C., Jaworski, J., & Flowers, B. (2004). *Presence. An exploration of profound change in people, organizations and society.* NY: Random House.

Simmons, A. (1999). *A safe place for dangerous truths. Using dialogue to overcome fear and distrust at work.* New York: Amacom.

Stace, D., & Dunphy, D. (2001). *Beyond the boundaries. Leading and re-creating the successful entreprise.* Sydney: MacGraw-Hill.

Taleb, N. N. (2010). *The black swan: The impact of the highly improbable fragility.* New York: Random House LLC.

Tierney, A. (2011). *Dialogue: A connection of roots and branches. An enquiry into labeling discourses through the use of multi-stakeholder Dialogue in Dis-ability Services.* Dissertation, Tilburg University, Netherlands.

Van de Kerkhof, T., (2013). *The you of leadership: An intuitive approach to effective business leadership* (Vol. 1). LID Editorial.

Van Loon, E. (Rens) J. P., & Kouwenhoven, K. (2016). Dancing leader. Leading and following. In: R. Koonce, M. C. Bligh, M. K. Carsten, & M. Hurwitz (Eds.), *Followership in action. Cases and commentaries.* Emerald Books.

Chapter 5
Towards a Theory of Embodied Dialogue

> ....*a clumsy combination of reluctant leaders and autonomous followers.*
> Laura Empson (Empson 2013)

Abstract

- Culture is incorporated in the body and the body is incorporated into culture.
- The self is embodied, relational, and dialogical, positioned in time and space.
- Dialogue can be defined as a 'participative' mode of interacting, physically, rationally, and intuitively.
- Dialogue is an ethical and epistemological theory, as it starts from the fact that both parties in conversation don't know the answer, and decide to explore possible answers by researching their own and other's values and assumptions.

If all we do has no meaning at all, this could cause people to choose for death. Bohm suggests, that the human process of freeing energy in thinking and consciously acting establishes *distinctions*, but that there is *participation* between those distinctions, between people, between thought and feeling, between anything. "Ultimately the nature of all the world is that it is all mutual participation—everything is in everything."[1] This is where Libbrecht refers to if he speaks about *my nature, being anchored in Nature*. The individual body is discrete from others—although not totally, because it merges with air, light and food. There is no place where the energy of body really ends—its boundary is relative, even after death. Baerveldt and Voestermans describe functional electro-chemical processes as conditional for the production of meaning. If certain body parts are damaged, this might have impact on your behavior and meaning making. The emphasis of Social Constructionism is: "The states and functions of the body become a cluster of cultural instead of natural, biological constructions. The formative and rhetorical aspects of language have a strong bearing on these cultural constructions."[2] The authors summarize the role of the body in the process of meaning making as "the structure and meaning of bodily conduct originate from discursively constructed cultural resources that provide the

---

[1]Bohm 1996, 102.
[2]Baerveldt and Voestermans 1998, 163.

scripts carried out by bodily gestures and postures."[3] These words refer to the same mechanism as Libbrecht describes. By culturally freeing energy, the body partly transcends basically bound energy processes.

5.1 A Dynamic Balance

Adam Kahane applies in his book *Solving Tough Problems* the body as a metaphor on how you might deal with dilemmas and with tough issues. He uses his experiences from working with John Milton, a martial arts and meditation teacher. John made a movement with his hands, which surprised Adam, as he had never seen this before. "His right hand was curled into a fist and it was cupped by his left hand."[4] The meaning of this 'mudra' was explained as the right hand representing the *yang*, the *masculine*, the *creative*. The left hand, which softly holds the right, represents the *yin*, the *feminine*, the *receptive*. What is exciting here, and an excellent project for further experimenting, is how we combine literal and metaphorical meaning. Experiment in listening while your hands are closed into fists, and listening with open hands. Observe the differences, make it object of playing. "The right hand represents open talking. The fist is not clenched tightly: you should be able to pull a pencil through it. It represents talking with, not talking at. And the left hand represents open listening."[5] Open listening (listening from the heart) and open talking (speaking from the heart) are two movements in the same generative dialogue. Or, to use the metaphor of the body, literally, two movements in the same generative dance. Later Kahane applies the same principle to dealing with dilemmas, a universal experience for leaders and followers.[6] He refers to dilemmas such as pluralism versus centralism, technical excellence versus customer focus, competition versus cooperation. His answer lies in finding a *dynamic balance* of the two components of a dilemma. Kahane links this with how you walk. The same mechanism of using a metaphorical expression and applying this literally on how you physically walk. Learning to apply contrasting values is like learning to walk on two legs. "We can't walk on only one leg, just as we can't address our toughest social challenges only with power or only with love. Walking means moving first one leg and then the other and always being *out* of balance—or more precise, always being in dynamic balance."[7] Here, Kahane makes a reference to the yin-yang symbolism, in which the black yin part contains a small white yang dot and vice versa. We see how verbs tend to enlighten this dynamic aspect of dealing with dilemma's more than nouns. Nouns tend to position themselves at the

---

[3]Baerveldt and Voestermans 1998, 163.
[4]Kahane 2007, 112.
[5]Kahane 2007, 112.
[6]Kahane 2010.
[7]Kahane 2010, 54.

extremes, while the verb can be positioned in a dynamic manner in between. Learning to deal in this way with opposites and resistance on the physical level, helps you in practicing agility at the mental level. By deeply experiencing how the dynamic balance works in the process of your walking, enables us to develop a more precise insight how it works at a mental level.

5.1.1 Physically Disconnected Words

Here, I connect with Hermans and Kempen who wrote that imagination "is a basic image-schematic capacity for ordering our experience. The concept of imagination can only be properly understood if one realizes that the body is *in* the mind."[8] One of the outcomes of my Ph.D. research *Symbols in Self-Narratives* is an increase in creativity and sensitivity in the participants, both in writing as in imagining, when being more consciously aware of the associations coming from the body, while moving, dancing or standing still.[9] Our body is vital, as we identify our self, we separate us from others, we want to feel how we are like others and different from others, setting boundaries in relations. By our body, we can sense our uniqueness? I give an example from my own experience, where as a young student my self-image was profoundly confused by a discrepancy that I felt was shown between the bodily presence and the mental presentation of one of my teachers at the time. As a student, I attended lectures of excellent professors. I remember one,[10] who was at that time one of the most famous Dutch professors in Modern Philosophy. In front of the lecture hall, he walked with his head high, his eyes directed to heaven, pitching complicated verbal constructions and wordings to us, young students, who were abundantly admiring him. It was as if his head (mind) was disconnected from his body. In my examination, I got a high score. After the oral examination, I stood outside the room and asked myself: do I understand what I have verbalized in my examination with the professor? Answering this question honestly, *no*, I did not understand what he was talking about. What I did seemingly very well, is repeating the language and wordings he wanted to hear. I also asked myself if the professor himself knew what his words meant, if his words were based on experiential insight. I started to doubt his knowledge. I thought he was repeating what he had heard and read, without deeply understanding and in a creative way constructed new phrases, to impress others, us, young students. This insight was a moment of serious crisis for me. I fundamentally asked myself: "What is the basis for real knowledge?" This formed the starting point for my quest. At that time, I promised myself not to be a believer of complicated words, but to ask for evidence and to experience.

---

[8]Hermans and Kempen 1993, 10. Here the authors follow Johnson (1987).

[9]Lengelle 2016.

[10]J.H.A. (Jan) Hollak (1915–2003) was a famous Dutch philosopher, an expert in the philosophy of Hegel. His lectures were famous, described by a Dutch novelist A.F.Th van der Heijden as a man who was not a philosopher, but a philosophic medium. Philosophy spoke through him.

5.1.2 Being Born into a Culture

In my search for understanding, I was much helped by an article of one of the co-authors in the first Dialogical Self article,[11] Harry Kempen. He was fascinated by the role of the body in general and in different cultures specifically. Kempen returns to 'wholly corporeal imagination' as the starting point of social constructions.[12] He starts from the human body as universal and the process of 'selfing' as an evolutionary need. In all cultures, the human body has the same basic structure: feet versus head; left versus right; belly/lower abdomen versus back. And a center, in the middle, visualized beautifully in a representation of Leonardo da Vinci's Vitruvian Man (Fig. 5.1).[13]

Kempen concludes that the biological system from which and for which culture is produced is not empty. It is filled with universal variables. We are born in a culture, the set of alternatives is reduced dramatically by norm formation in the culture we are educated. "Self-options are biologically given. A culture can—and must—restrict the potential combinatorial explosion which they entail. We live in one (maybe two or three) cultures that are present on the globe. And in doing so, *culture enters the body*. The body is not only the place where culture takes off, it is also its *landing* place. Our self is not something that hovers around our skin."[14] Gergen illustrates this with an example of a doctor. We construct the concepts of our physical bodies in a variety of ways. "In medicine, a doctor may approach a patient's body as simply 'an object to be repaired'. From the patient's point of view, he or she is effectively reduced to a piece of meat. The result of this difference may be an insensitivity on the doctor's part to the full and important life situation of the patient."[15]

5.1.3 Defining Ourselves

Kempen's ambition was to show how within different cultures *selves* develop with more or less stabilized preferences for one or more task-options based on the bodily structure:

- Defining a *boundary* for the self: how are you relating to bodies around you? You have to delineate your body as to how it is related with bodies around you. You define a kind of *boundary,* which is to contrast yourself to the non-self, with objects and other selves. This is something you learn in your education, in the process of acculturation. There are cultures where the boundaries between bodies and selves are fluent and those where we see the opposite. In the US, you

---

[11]Hermans et al. 1992.
[12]Kempen 1998.
[13]This figure is based on the Vitruvian Man (1490) by Leonardo da Vinci.
[14]Kempen 1998, 65.
[15]Gergen 2009, 47.

5.1 A Dynamic Balance

Fig. 5.1 Being born into a culture

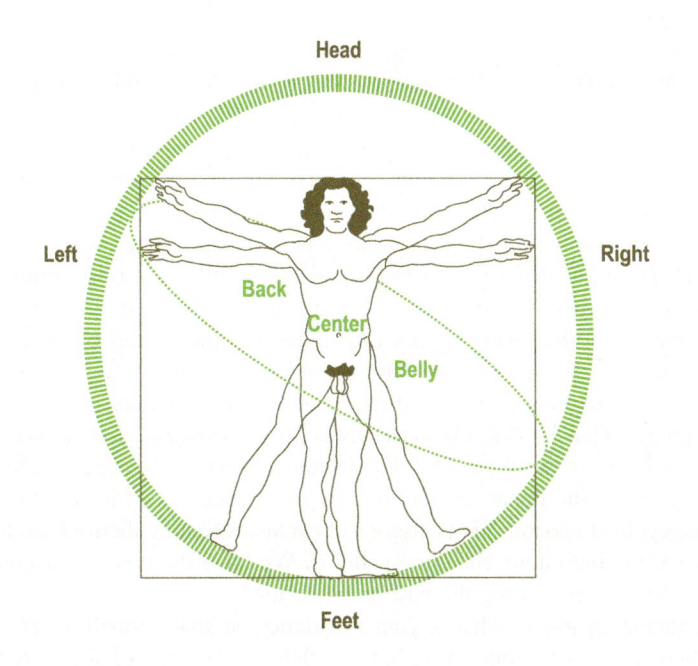

are not allowed to touch your colleague, as this might be sexual harassment, in France and Italy bodily contact is part of the daily interaction. In our office in Paris, colleagues kiss each other when entering the office in the morning.

- Evaluating a *situation*: how do you evaluate a situation: good, bad, good *and* bad, neutral?

  As a subjectifying body you *evaluate* the situation. You assess it, depending on the culture you live in, and you give it a value: is it good (+), is it bad (−), or good and bad (+/−), or neutral, not good, nor bad (=)? In the process of getting acculturated, we learn to assess quickly and act on the basis of the outcome of that evaluation. In the beginning of our education, we form a judgment, as the little baby only assesses the situation in terms of pleasure and pain, attract and avoid, not in moral terms. Later in our lives, we need to free energy to not have a quick and automated assessment of a situation and consciously think if this is good, neutral, bad, or even more difficult to deal with, good *and* bad, a paradox.

- Orientating in *time*: what is your orientation in time: linear, cyclical?

  You have to preserve successful activities from the past and to abandon non-successful ones in order to perform effectively in the present, with a view to the future. That is, the self must develop a *time orientation*. Kempen distinguishes between two types of time orientation: time can be experienced as *linear* and *cyclic*. In the linear version, time is experienced as an irreversible process. In the cyclical version, life is a series of events, repeating themselves. It is about survival in continuous changing patterns. We have *the now*, as distinguishable from *the not-now*, being the past or the future.

- Orientating in *space*: what is your orientation in space: small, large, ecologic, mathematical, numinous? You have to define the range of the activity-*space*. "Where do situations begin which I may overlook, which I may judge as lying beyond my scope?"[16] As regards to space, Kempen comes to two options, if we think about how a self might position in relation to space: *small* and *large*. In my view, this is not discriminating enough as space might take different forms. I would add here in Libbrecht's terminology: let's distinguish between *ecologic space* in Nature (bound energy), *mathematical space* in Science (free energy) and *numinous field space* in Mysticity (free energy).[17] This distinction helps us to better understand what happens in the different phases of a process such as a conversation, where different levels of space and time are active.

- Understanding the nature of *your actions*: do you react, act, receive, or, participate?

  You have to decide upon *activity* or *non-activity*. If you are confronted with a situation as a subjectifying body, you *evaluate* this and decide (unconsciously or

---

[16]Kempen 1998, 61.
[17]Libbrecht 2007, 290.

5.1 A Dynamic Balance

deliberately) to take action, do something or, the other possibility to refrain from action. You can react on what happens around you by an *active* mode, trying to influence and change the situation, by intentionally taking specific measures to that end. You can also react to what happens in your environment by being *receptive*, by just watching and observing what is going on, without acting yourself. Without intentionally changing the situation.

In line with what I described about realizing activity (active and receptive), a third mode is *participative mode*.[18] Although we create free energy in our thinking and acting to establish *distinctions*, there is also *participation* between those distinctions, between people, between thought and feeling, between anything. *For our argumentation, this observation is important, as in my view the participative mode, and the role of your body in it, is crucial for describing dialogue in an appropriate way.* I point out the relation between setting boundaries and the way of acting. If you combine a fluent boundary with the participative mode of acting, this absolutely makes sense. If you try to combine a fluent boundary-setting with the active mode of realizing activity, you intuitively sense a form of tension between these two. In Libbrecht's terminology, we see parallels between active mode and concentrated, focused energy; and passive mode and deconcentrated, field energy. The participative mode mostly resembles a mystic experience, where there is mindfulness and freedom to act, but no immediate action, just awareness. In the process of acculturation, people get used to a specific way of dealing with these tasks, and after a period of time, claim that this is the '*only* right' approach. The body and its primary tasks can be common as basic structure for how we develop in the world: how we *define* ourselves, how we *act*, how we *assess*, how we deal with *time and space*. Based on the body, with its bound energy defining limits to what we can influence, we in general distinguish—based on Libbrecht's model—between freeing energy in concentrated or/and deconcentrated form. Libbrecht considers 'reason' as a *function* of the human body: "Man is not an animal with added intelligence (as is written in Genesis), but a *specific human body* capable of freeing energy and transforming it into deeds."[19]

> "There is no Body without Cultural Meaning"
>
> What I explore is the importance of the physical basis in all we know and experience. The physical structure is shaping what and how we know and experience. Libbrecht's analysis of the three domains, *nature* with its immanent bound energy, *science* with its transcendent free energy in the form of objectivity, and *art, religion and literature* with its transcendent free energy in subjectivity. All is rooted in the body, in corporeal nature. I had a conversation

---

[18]Bohm 1996, 96–109.
[19]Libbrecht 2007, 109.

> with a Dutch professor in Anthropology, Toon van Meijl, and we were discussing about the role of the body in different cultures, and if there are universal structures. He said "there is no body without cultural meaning". I agreed by referring to Kempen's research and his attempt to formulate universal structures. In my view the body is such a structure. *You aren't able to get something done, unless you are a body.* The physical body is the starting point from where you might develop towards a scientist, artist, mystic or novelist, you must have been born as a physical body, otherwise you don't exist. In this sense, I work towards an embodied theory of knowledge, dialogue and leadership.

Kempen tries to demonstrate body as starting point for each of us. We are born in a culture, and have to be educated and brought into a value-system of the particular culture. When you travel over the world, you see a lot of differences. But everywhere on earth, a complete human body has the same structure and characteristics, despite cultural differences you might see. "We are—notwithstanding all cultural differences—akin to each other because there are body-bound self-universals which produce commonality alongside specifics."[20] How culture is incorporated into the body, or how the body is incorporated into culture, differs. The bodily base is everywhere visible. For Kempen, the subjectified body is the objective stance that psychology looks for to escape inherent cultural relativism, seemingly inherent to social constructionism.[21] Lakoff and Johnson share this view. They take as their central concept *the body in the mind*.[22] Mental ideas come from corporeal positions, properties of categories (e.g. in, on, across) are mediated by the body, rather than being determined directly by a mind-independent reality.[23] The body projects its schemes in the mind. I apply the bodily structure to understand what happens in dialogue. The concepts of self, leadership, dialogue, change and transformation are combined. We are at the heart of my vision of developing a theory of embodied self and dialogue: *the embodied, dialogical, and relational self is positioned on the junction of time (past, present, future) and space (internal, external) with the potential of generating new meaning and new selves, formulated as I-positions* (Fig. 5.2).

- Embodied: your *body* provides a ground structure.
- Dialogical: you reflect on yourself *internally*.
- Relational: you reflect on yourself *externally*, in relation with other(s).
- The process of generating new meaning is created by freeing energy: *transformational space*, containing physical, temporal, relational aspects as designated in Japanese concept 'ma'.

---

[20] Kempen 1998, 66.
[21] Kempen 1998, 67.
[22] Lakoff and Johnson 1999.
[23] Lakoff and Johnson 1999, 28.

5.1 A Dynamic Balance

Defining Ourselves

Self as Embodied, Relational and Dialogical

Formulating new I-positions

Transforming

Generating new meaning

間
Self
Physical Space
Temporal Space
Relationship
Silence

Reflecting

Acting

Past — Present — Future

Embodied	Dialogical	Relational
Ground structure: • Feet ⟷ Head • Left ⟷ Right • Front ⟷ Back	Internally, reflexive, positioned in time (past, present, future) and space (internal, external)	Externally present between Self and Other

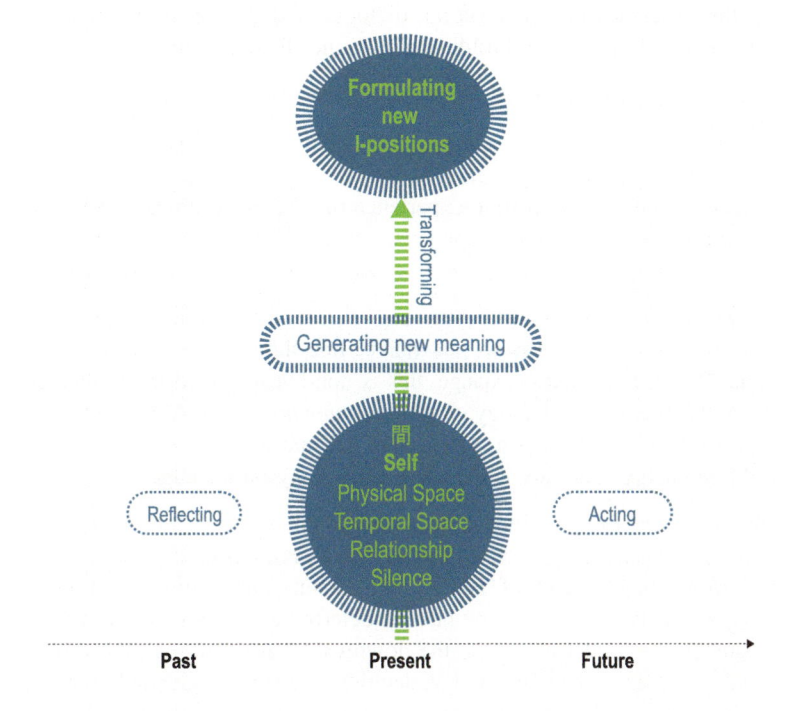

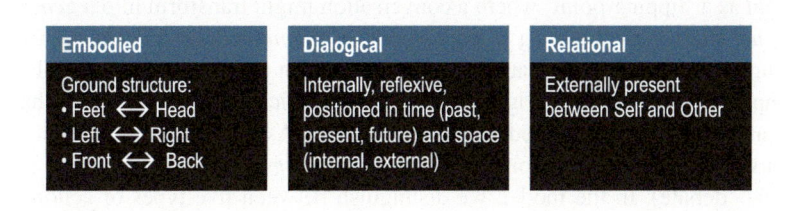

Fig. 5.2 Defining ourselves

5.2 Dialogue as Generating New Meaning

Dialogue is described as a process that takes place in time. The aim of dialogue is to collectively think in the present, based on experiences and insights from the past and looking forward into the future in terms of actions. Figure 5.3 distinguishes between the processes of conversation, dialogue and debate, in a similar way as Isaacs describes the phases in building a container for dialogue.

→ the *horizontal axis* represents *linear time*: past—present—future.

| the *vertical axis* represents the *present* ↕. This is where *freeing energy* takes place. Here is the act of *suspending judgment*. This is the point where *creating space* occurs. "The quality of time experience of 'ma' is not linear, such as past—present—future, but a non-linear condensed one."[24] The Japanese word *ma* combines in one concept: *physical space, temporal space, relationship and silence.*

↑ the *upward arrow* refers to the phase a conversation transforms into a dialogue. In the model of Isaacs, this refers to innovating, free thinking, creating new meaning (metalogue). As *transformative* change, this is non-linear, pulled in an unpredictable direction. In Libbrechts terminology, *timeless as numinous field*. Although you prepare all conditions to make it happen, you cannot be sure it takes place, as it is deconcentrated free energy, causality is reticular, 'serendipity on the edge'.

↓ the *downward arrow* refers to the phase a conversation transforms into *generating logical meaning, pushing in the rational, predictable direction.* Here I use the term *dialecting* instead of Isaacs' expression *oppressing*, as in my view, depending on the issue at hand, you have to determine what kind of conversation is appropriate. In the model of Isaacs, the downward arrow are the phases of identifying and discussing, debating and dialecting (repeating, bounded thinking and re-creating). This is characterized as *dialecting*, predictable, logical. In terms of Libbrecht, linear, causal energy, obeying the laws of cause and effect. *Debate and discussion generate logical meaning.*

We use the term conversation as the middle point. At this point, a conversation might take different forms. Looking back to what has been in the past as *reflecting on action*, for example telling your story. Looking forward into the future by talking about what you are willing to do, *reflecting for action*. In the present, a critical moment as a 'tipping point' where a conversation might transform into a *generative dialogue*, when new meaning is generating '*in the now*'. The conversation might also turn into a *debate*, generating logical meaning in a dialectic process. All forms are important and can be the right answer for a specific situation. This might happen spontaneously or in an enabled way by facilitation. As we have seen the first phase of conversing and deliberation is that of *suspending* (→ dialogue) and/or *identifying* (→ debate). In the model, we distinguish between five types of action

---

[24]Morioka 2008, 105.

5.2 Dialogue as Generating New Meaning

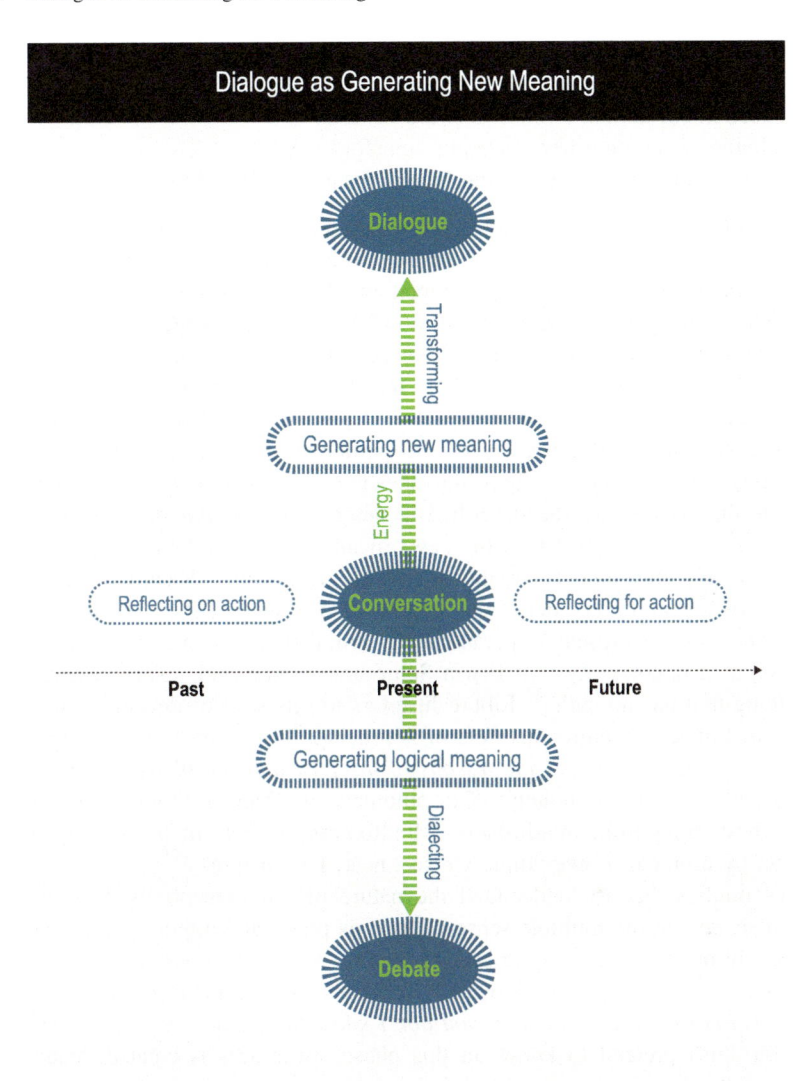

Fig. 5.3 Dialogue as generating new meaning

- Conversation: chatting, communicating
- Reflection on action: looking backward in time
- Reflection for action: looking forward in time
- Dialogue: generating new meaning, transforming
- Debate or discussion: generating logical meaning, dialecting

Are participants in dialogue able to suspend their physical, rational, and intuitive reactions? This is where we support people in the process by making them aware from *a bird's eye view* of what is happening. By slowing down the process real time: what is happening in the present, now? What do you hear, what do you see, and what do you think, what is the difference between what you see and what you hear? Here the implicit is made explicit, the 'I' of the participants, their eyes and ears, opened for more than one perspective. Creating a validation of the thinking, feeling and non-verbal processes of the participants in the *present*—that's the ultimate goal of the dialogue. This illustrates the experience of how in a generative dialogue the process can be described as '*reciprocally implicated and mutually reflexive*'.[25] The construction of new meaning is a relational process of co-constructing meaning and reality in a dialogic action.[26] Ricard describes the moment of the *now* very detailed: "The past no longer exists, the future hasn't arisen yet and the present is paradoxically simultaneously still and unchanging because, as a famous physicist Erwin Schrödinger once said, "The present is the only thing that has no end."[27] Libbrecht refers to this state of deconcentrated free energy as timeless, a numinous field of non-being.[28] In a generative dialogue, we are *in the present including the lessons of the past and the plans for the future.* Ricard describes this accurately: "Our automatic mechanical thought patterns are the furthest thing from mindfulness. Mindfulness consists in being fully aware moment by moment of everything we see, hear, feel or think."[29]

This implies that we understand the nature of our perceptions, that there is created *space*—in the multiple sense of '*ma*' as physical, temporal, relational and silence—in our thinking, feeling and (re-)acting. Suspending assumptions leads to inquiring and reflecting. Not knowing is for many of us difficult to tolerate. In this phase, *you consciously know that you don't know the answer,* you recognize that and you don't pretend to know. In this phase, awareness is created, leading to realistic reflection. *In the process of dialogue, you truly touch the fundamentals of your values and your knowing.* Realizing something is not valid or a wrong belief can be a shocking experience. This leads to asking new questions, to find new answers on different levels. In this sense, dialogical leadership is an ethical and an epistemological theory and practice.

---

[25]Hawes 1999, 252.
[26]Gergen 2009, 147.
[27]Erwin Schrödinger 1922. My view on the World. Quoted in Ricard 2011, 67.
[28]Libbrecht 2007, 290.
[29]Ricard 2011, 66.

5.2 Dialogue as Generating New Meaning

The Art of Tai Chi

I have been attracted by the potential power of the body all my life. Around 1975, I saw a movie with the Chinese Master Chungliang 'Al' Huang. He showed in this short movie a Tai Chi form, a series of movements, performed slowly, with a combination of suppleness and concentration that fascinated me from the very first time. I wanted to learn that. We looked for a teacher in our university town Nijmegen and, within a few years, I was enjoying to practice the art of Tai Chi. Since that time, these exercises give me a moment of dynamic rest in a rushed world. I travelled around the world during a period of my life, and wherever I was, I found a moment of dynamic stability in these simple exercises. And it is a recurring theme. During the 2013 International Leadership Association conference in Montreal, Lew Yung-Chien, a Canadian Tai Chi teacher, did a workshop where soft transformation from yin to yang was practiced with a group of interested people. Here we *experienced* physically what it means to dynamically balance. The softness and the stillness of practicing these simple exercises felt great, even for people who were not used to this way of using the body. Tai Chi gives me a greater awareness of my body and bodies around me, where the boundaries are less hard and more open than we normally expect in our daily experiencing and speaking. This experience particularly was of great importance for me in applying this in leading and following. Not only in the safe place of the dojo, where you always start with showing respect, by making a bow for each other, but also in the open arena space of competitive society and organizations. The physical basis of relational meaning in dialogue and leadership is deeply embedded in my life through these experiences with Tai Chi.

5.2.1 Dialogue as a Participative Mode of Interacting

Dialogue can be defined as a participative mode of interacting. Basically, I learned dialogue by technical trainings in conversation techniques, but the real impact I experienced through practicing and experiencing Tai Chi and dance. I became familiar with techniques of applying push and pull on the physical level in partner exercises named 'pushing hands'. Pushing hands is an exercise, where two people are connected with their hands, so lightly that they lose contact the moment you are not mindfully present. Once you are connected you start moving with your entire body, while the back of the hands keep connected. In a process of joint movement, while keeping connected, a process of leading and following starts. This exercise is intended to intensify awareness and mindfulness.[30] You can't simultaneously think or do something else, you have to be *in the moment*, or you lose connection. By doing these kind of exercises, you can sense how to create real connection with somebody else by following in a deconcentrated participative manner. You experience a thin line between following and leading. Sometimes you don't even know if you are leading or following. Another lesson you learn from this exercise is that if you start thinking, you immediately lose contact. If you are too much focused concentrated, you lose connection. Closing your eyes while doing the exercise helps to become more completely aware and mindful without being distracted by what the eyes perceive.

In analyzing different types of movement, we categorize three: pushing as an *outgoing* movement, pulling as *following*, and where to go as *giving direction*. You can set direction by pushing and by pulling. At that time, I was a researcher at the university and my task was to teach students the principles of conversation. I intuitively made the connection between these physical exercises and the art of having a conversation. The same principles as applied in the physical exercise, are working—metaphorically—in a conversation: subtle contact, who leads, who follows, when you lose contact. Since that time, I teach and practice dialogues as a 'participative mode of interacting'.[31] *Giving direction, pushing and pulling* can take the form of a physical movement, and we can project this to how we influence by rational knowing, by convincing in a rational manner. We might do that in a *setting direction* mode, or in a *push* or *pull* mode. Same for intuition, experiencing, feeling. Six constituents (giving direction, pushing, pulling, knowing by rational analysis, experiencing by intuition, and doing by hands) are needed to comprehend (and change) processes such as leading, influencing and having a conversation. It describes a ground structure in conversation. It contains the basic elements of a mutually influencing relation on different levels: physical, rational, and intuitive. Applying this concept in conversations has proven to be helpful to enable clients to get more clarity in their processes of leadership, influencing and reflecting. Especially when applied in the context of their own natural environment, supported by tools such as video and assessments for validation (Fig. 5.4).

---

[30]Kabat-Zinn defines mindfulness as intentional cultivation of non-judgmental moment-to-moment awareness. Kabat-Zinn 1996. For an application of mindfulness and Dialogical Self, see also: Van Loon 2016.

[31]The same principles apply in dancing as we described in a chapter in Van Loon and Kouwenhoven 2016. With my colleague Karlijn Kouwenhoven we explore leading and following in Salsa dancing.

5.2 Dialogue as Generating New Meaning

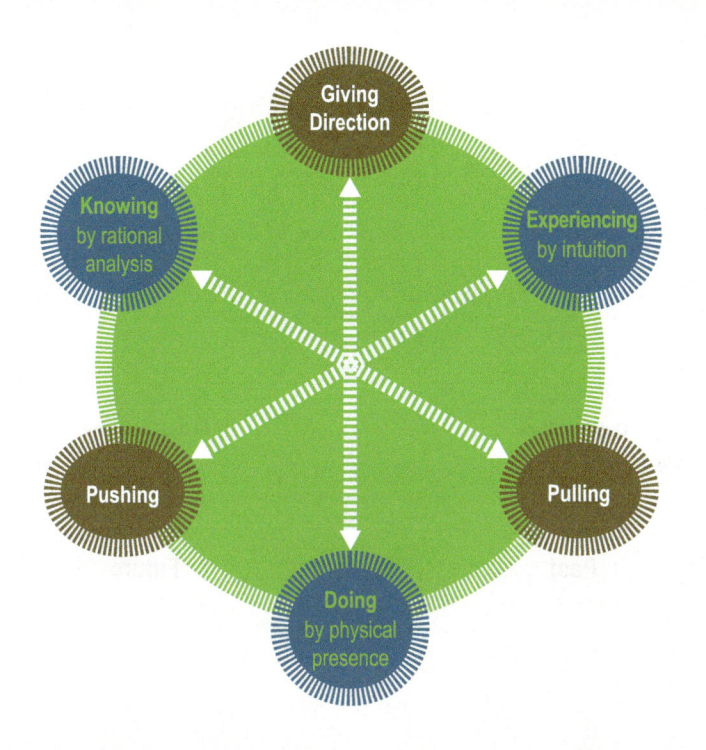

Fig. 5.4 Dialogue as a participative mode of interacting

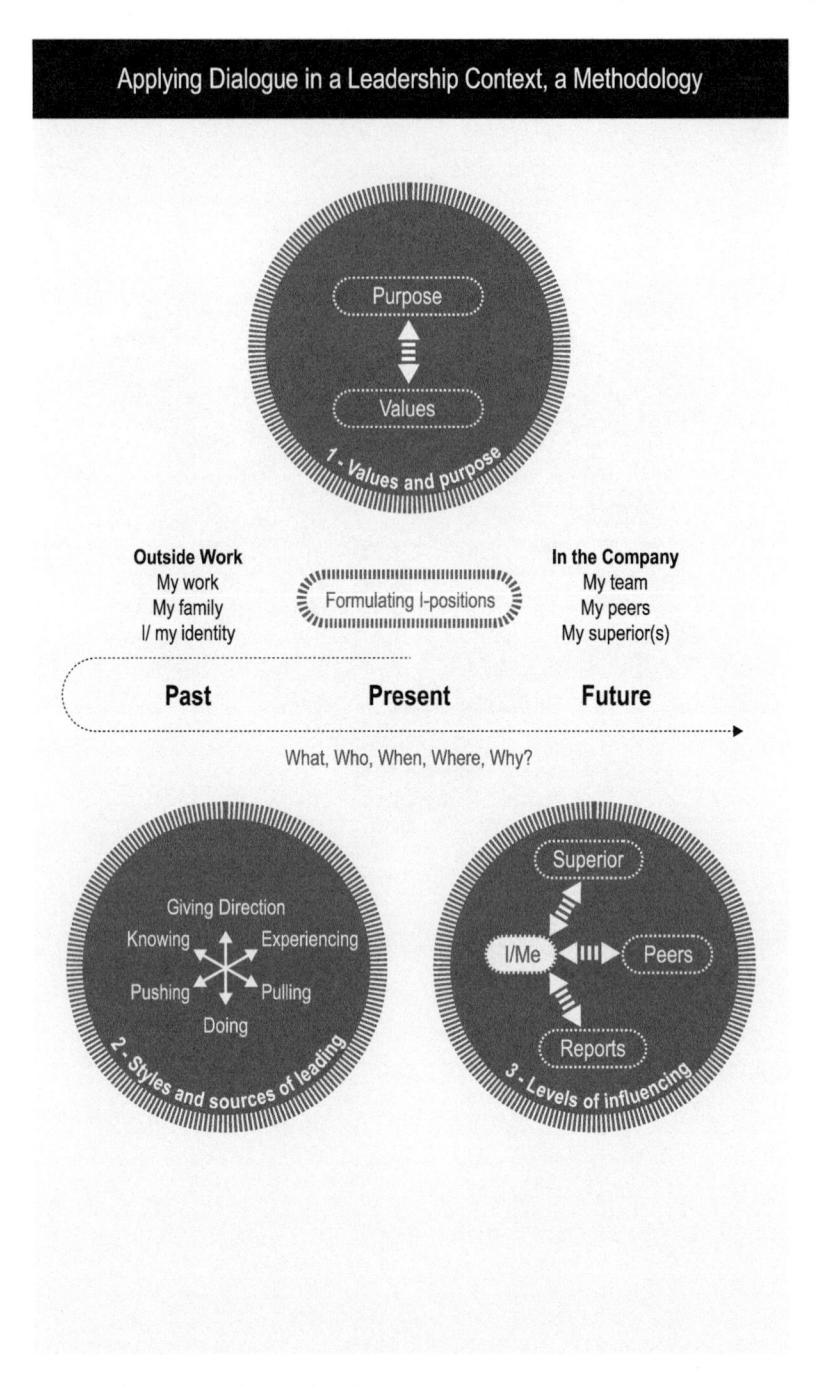

Fig. 5.5 Applying dialogue in a leadership context: a methodology

5.2.2 Applying Dialogue in a Leadership Context: A Methodology

Looking back at our analysis of dialogue and debate elements in the containers of Isaacs, we conclude that the same elements are important: creating a container for dialogue, building a structure where people feel safe and secure, showing role model leadership, being transparent in your expressions. What follows are two conceptual frameworks, the first one for a dialogue (Fig. 5.5), the second one for exploring I-positions in dialogue (Fig. 5.6, Sect. 5.3,). You can uses these figures as a *map for your dialogues.*

In the middle is the time dimension. We are familiar with that axis from previous figures. On the *horizontal* dimension, you find past, present and future. You invite your partner in dialogue to express what he/she thinks, sees, hears, and feels in the present, while in dialogue with you. This is *reflection in action.* The dimension of the *past* is where you reflect about your thoughts, feelings and actions in terms of describing, expressing the essence of an experience, evaluating and—quite often— also judging. This is *reflection on action.* In the dimension of the *future,* you look forward to what you want to do, to your future actions, to your wishes and worries. This is *reflection for action.* A generative dialogue flexibly moves on this axis.

The *present* is where you start and where you return. As a general rule, a generative dialogue consists in asking questions to elaborate positive and negative behavioral examples. This might be in a rational manner, of might be described experientially and intuitively. Technically, this can be summarized with the classical five W's: *what, who, when, where* and *why*? You need all of them to get a clear picture of the situation.

In the *vertical* dimension, you can go into different directions. Which one you choose, depends on the situation and the individual you converse with: in the company, in the private dimension of life. Here you follow in a deconcentrated way.

The *workplace/company* dimension can be part of the dialogue on several levels. What follows are typical questions (not a list).

- Can you describe *yourself* in the workplace? How do you introduce yourself? In a leadership dialogue, you can ask "*what makes you a leader* in this context of your organization?" In my experience this is a powerful question as it brings the experience of leadership at the heart of the organizational context. "Why should anyone be led by you?"[32]
- Can you tell me something about your *work*? What is it that you normally do on a day? What motivates you, in terms of purpose and values? Can you describe your purpose in your work? What is it that you want to create/realize/make happen in your work? Can you describe some values that are important for you in your work? What happens when one of these values is violated?

---

[32]Goffee and Jones 2006.

- What does your *team* look like? Describe members of the team in terms of positive and negative behavioral experiences? Who is easy for you to influence? Who is complicated? Are you recognized as a leader? Normally we ask people to sketch their team structure (with names) on a flip chart and we chat about every member of the team, preferably through the lenses of vision, push, pull, rationality, intuition and non-verbal presence.
- Who are your *peers*? Describe colleagues in terms of positive and negative behavioral experiences? Who is easy for you to influence? Who is complicated? Are you seen as a leader by your peers? Give examples (positive and negative).
- Tell me about your *superior*? Can you describe him/her for me? How is it for you to influence him/her? When is it complicated? What makes him/her a leader that you voluntarily want to follow? What makes your boss follow you? (Give examples).

The separating professional and private lives is artificial from a Dialogical Self Theory point of view, as I-positions don't recognize boundaries between these domains. Culture is important where to start in a dialogue. In some cultures, people start talking about how their private and business life are fused, in other cultures people don't want to explicitly talk about their private experiences. Listening carefully, without pushing is—in most cases—sufficient to build conditions for dialogue and openness. *Respect resistance*. If your partner declares a domain as not allowed to enter, respect it. By truly showing respect, you might create conditions for opening that domain too.

In the figure, the *private* dimension outside your organization/work is represented in the upward direction. This can be described on different levels:

- Can you tell me something about how you describe *yourself*? What do you tell, when you introduce yourself somewhere?
- What does your *family* look like? Your mother? Your father? Your partner? Your children? Do you have brothers and sisters? The domain of the family sometimes takes a long time to talk about.
- Can you tell me about your life *outside work*, your hobbies, and sports? Religion, politics and personal beliefs can also be subject for conversation.

As a general rule: listen carefully to what is said in the 'in between sentences'. Our experience is that often I-positions are communicated implicitly or between the lines. We recommend to work with a whiteboard and flip chart, jotting down keywords. In the case-studies examples are given of how you can summarize these conversations.

Dialogue is a *reciprocal process*. If you—as a leader, professional counsellor, or coach—are closed in your non-verbal behavior, in your emotions and in what you express verbally, this will strongly impact the interaction. My advice is to open up yourself, share experiences, while keeping focus primarily on your partner in dialogue. Sharing a story about how you dealt with values that were violated encourages to think and talk about one's own experiences.

5.2 Dialogue as Generating New Meaning

In the figure, you additionally find *Sources* and *Styles* of leading, levels of influencing and formal *Power*, and *Values* and *Purpose*. In the back of your mind these themes and levels are continuously present and together they take the form of a conceptual map for your dialogue. You can freely switch between the dimensions and levels, how this works in practice depends on the dialogical process, where you are in the process of building the container of trust (stability, inquiry and creativity) to have a generative dialogue.

Last of all, some relevant topics you might want to talk about:

- Can you tell me about your core values and beliefs?
- What were moments of change in your life/career?
- How do you set direction in strategy work? Can you give an example of success? One of failure?
- Can you give an example of how you make choices?
- If you apply change and transformation to your life? What does it look like?
- How do you deal with risk?
- Can you describe a conflict you are in? How do you deal with confrontations?
- How do you cope with stress? Can you give an example of high stress and effective acting? When are you at risk?
- What happens if you are confronted with ambiguity and paradox? Can you give an example? When do you react effectively? When not?
- What happens with you when somebody does not trust you? Can you give an example?

5.3 Exploring I-Positions in Dialogue

The conceptual framework for dialogue functions as a mind map while having dialogues. If necessary explain it, the primary purpose is to support you as a facilitator during long conversations and assuring to have covered relevant topics. The second framework in this section gives you an insight in how a repertoire of I-positions might be explored and co-constructed in dialogue. (Fig. 5.6)

On the left of the figure, you find examples of external I-positions. 'SVP' and 'chairman of the BoD' are formal roles in the organization. These examples might be important as they represent different aspects that can become part of a repertoire of I-positions. When you know the formal roles people have in an organization, you can check if these are also part of their internal I-positions. If you look on the right of the figure you find examples of internal I-positions. These refer to mindsets and emotional states, which are verbalized by the individual, often in an idiosyncratic manner. As an example: 'I as an odd beekeeper' refers to how this person feels if he is trying to manage a chaotic project. As a rule of thumb, here you only mention I-positions that are truly relevant. Following are some generic questions to help

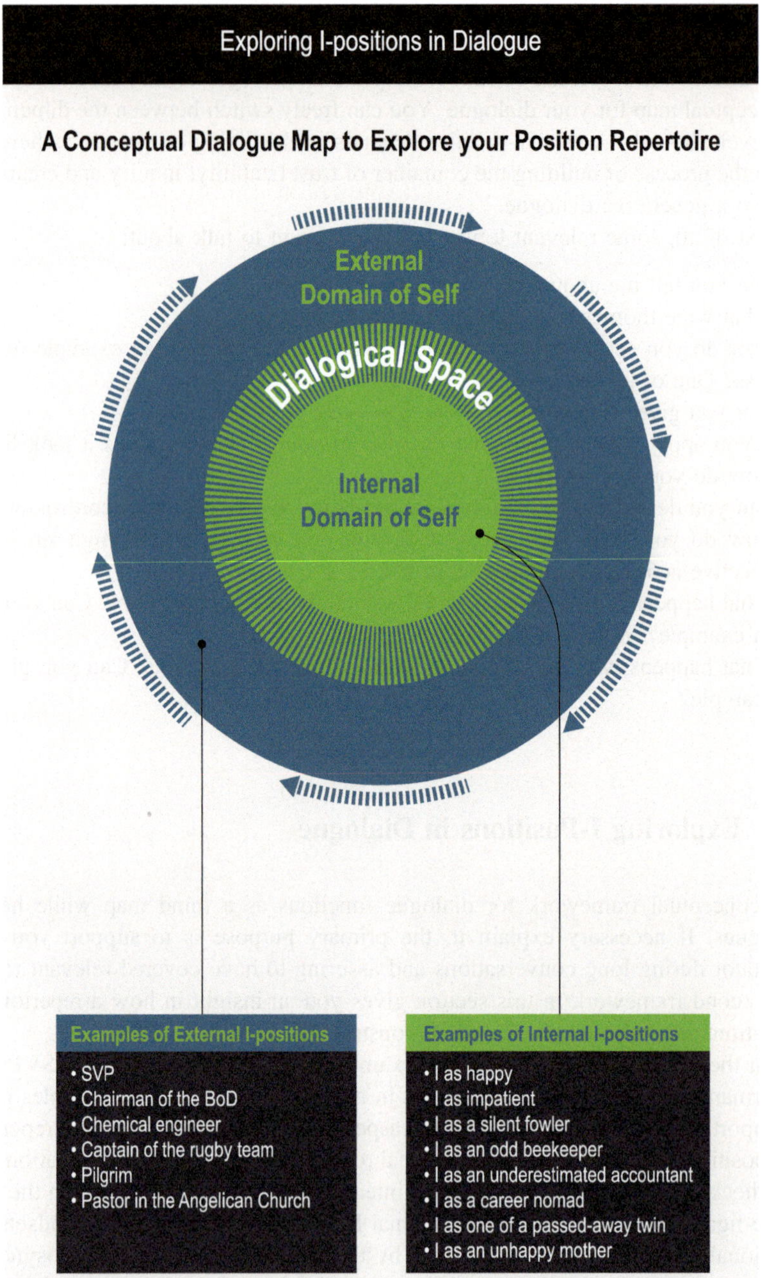

Exploring I-positions in Dialogue

A Conceptual Dialogue Map to Explore your Position Repertoire

External Domain of Self

Dialogical Space

Internal Domain of Self

Examples of External I-positions
- SVP
- Chairman of the BoD
- Chemical engineer
- Captain of the rugby team
- Pilgrim
- Pastor in the Angelican Church

Examples of Internal I-positions
- I as happy
- I as impatient
- I as a silent fowler
- I as an odd beekeeper
- I as an underestimated accountant
- I as a career nomad
- I as one of a passed-away twin
- I as an unhappy mother

Fig. 5.6 Exploring I-positions in dialogue

people formulating their idiosyncratic I-positions: "If I formulate '…', how is that for you?" 'I as a dog trainer'. By giving the example, you can open a domain for somebody, where he/she did not think about spontaneously.

5.4 Resistance in Dialogue

Resistance is a frequently occurring phenomenon in debate and dialogue. Often we see that people don't want to change their thinking, feeling and acting. That might have different reasons. Sometimes because people are happy with how it is, sometimes as they are afraid of the unknown. In general, resistance is "an unwillingness or inability to accept or to discuss changes that are perceived to be damaging or threatening to the individual."[33] Hermans and Hermans-Jansen describe the phenomenon that once a person has constructed a story in which life events are ordered, "he or she develops a tendency to consolidate the story and a concomitant resistance to change it."[34] People might protect the ordering, the structure they made for their life, and this gives a degree of stability over time and space. People might be happy with 'as it is' and not willing to be brought out of balance, out of their comfort zone. Or don't understand the 'why' of changing. Many people are afraid of change. They like what they have and they don't know what they will get if they change the situation. Each individual is different in this perspective. Don't think what might be easy for you to change is the same for somebody else. You have to be aware of possible resistance if you work with conversations, dialogue and debate. *Resistance is inherent*, even if people are willing and able to make the change happen.

Sharing an example of resistance from my professional life. In my work, I often have to deal with resistance. An example par excellence is an experience I had in a leadership program in the US. I arrived on Sunday and Monday morning at 8 a.m. we started our leadership dialogue in the boardroom of the company. My partner in conversation was not willing to cooperate. He was polite, kept distance, saying the process of leadership development was useless if his superior—the chairman of the global board—did not fulfill the agreements. He did not receive feedback as part of an agreed process, so what could be the use of this conversation? I tried to convince him, that even without formal feedback he could start the process of self-reflection in our conversation. As a strong character, he was convinced that he was wasting his valuable time. Later that morning, I called my assistant and said, "I am not sure, maybe he will send me home before the end of the day!"

Then the atmosphere changed. I apologized for the omissions, as the feedback forms were not properly filled out. I specified how we could do some good work in terms of self-reflection on his leadership thinking and behavior, without the detailed

---

[33]Huczynski and Buchanan 2013, 628.

[34]Hermans and Hermans-Jansen 1995, 47–48.

feedback of his people. I asked questions that made him think seriously, such as: "Can you describe, what makes you a leader in the company?" "How does your leadership look like?" "Can you give examples of moments where you were able to flexibly switch between different styles of influencing?" "If you look at your career, where are you now in terms of what you want to leave as a legacy in the firm?" What changed the atmosphere was that my partner in dialogue sensed that I was 'in the moment' asking questions that were really important for our mutual reflective process. I was not doing a 'formal interview', ticking off the boxes. I truly tried to connect with him. Important was that I openly and honestly respected his resistance. I did not disagree with what he said. The real turning point came when we chatted about his career and he expressed that he wanted to become a teacher after retiring from business. I asked him the question: "*How is the teacher present in your current role as CEO of the firm?*" Here his view on career and performance opened up, as he never thought about the two I-positions connected, but always separated from each other in time. He always thought about retiring from business and then taking a teacher role at university. Here his mind truly opened for thinking in a new way. His resistance disappeared and changed into a real wish to reflect and even change his view on the process of leadership development. From an *active resister*, he changed into an *active supporter* and promoter of the leadership development process, starting with himself. In the process of dialogue, a question was asked to him, and he did not know an answer. That made him think. That opened his mind and made the resistance disappear. He started to trust me. He felt safe in dealing with wicked issues. 'Ma' was created in our conversational relation.

An important lesson I learned is 'embracing resistance to change without judgment'. If you work with people that are not willing, a first reaction could be a 'pull-one', trying to understand what the real reason for resisting is. By doing this, you consciously connect with your partner in conversation. Don't ignore resistance, don't push back as an automatic mechanism. Connect with resistance and redirect the energy of a resisting person/group of individuals. Of course you can anticipate on resistance by analyzing the group you are going to work with in a change process. Positive reinforcing and feedforward work better than negative feedback. Look for moments of change that you want to realize in the present and support people to project that into the future. Recombine different views and I-positions. As illustrated, by asking questions that open the mind of your conversation partner, you redirect the resistance energy in a new, collective direction, instead of opposing. This is how you apply dialogue as a participative mode of interacting.

To accept another person non-judgmentally as he/she is/was (and sometimes is still) difficult for me. In my supervision, and peer-dialogues I discovered that suspending judgment is easily said, but very difficult to do. As I described in former parts of my personal experiences, I had strong opinions, already as a young boy. I learned the basic attitude in the Tai Chi partner exercises, as described above. If you resist to what is done to you in a physical way, it becomes more difficult to keep yourself intact and to not be pushed away. I experienced how it complicated my exercises, if I had mental resistance to the person I worked with. I experienced that if I am free from expectations and thoughts, my body is more flexible and my

5.4 Resistance in Dialogue

mind more at rest. I was able to be more agile in a way I never thought would be possible for me, physically and mentally. By not judging, by accepting what happened 'as it is'.

Rational understanding is one, when we talk about resistance. Accepting emotionally and physically is even more complicated. By transposing the Tai Chi experiences to the situation of communicating, it became easier for me to accept whatever came on my 'path' in the conversation. Even when I thought to have mastered it to a high level, in peer to peer feedback from my colleagues, I realize there is still a lot to do. Especially as verbal and non-verbal behavior are so strongly interconnected. Often my judgment is expressed non-verbally, subconsciously.

In processes of change and transformation, you can't deny resistance. First of all, *be aware of possible resistance*, analyze and look at the situation in a realistic way. Don't start from assumptions, look with a sharp eye what kind of resistance you might expect, what is your real position? "Are you trusted?" "How urgent is the situation?" Secondly, point out the *importance of the time frame*. If you have more time, your approach will be different from when you don't have time at all. If you think you can go quickly, the risk might be that you get disconnected and lose trust completely. Think carefully about the time frame. Thirdly, deal with resistance in an *adaptive manner*. Sometimes you need to *educate/communicate,* which is high on pulling and connecting. At other times, you can work in the continuum from *participation, involvement, facilitation and support, negotiation* to *coercing implicitly and explicitly,* which *is* high on pushing and power. We have to be aware that each approach has its advantage and drawback. If you pull too much in a crisis situation, you will be too late. If you push too much in a transformational change for the entire organization and overrule resistance, the drawback will be serious.[35] What is the type of issue we have to solve? Is it a crisis? Is it a known and defined technical problem? Is it a complex and unknown adaptive issue? Each type of issue has its own approach.

5.5 Creating Transformational Space

Thirty spokes share one hub.

Adapt the nothing therein to the purpose in hand.

Lao Tzu[36]

Dialogue and reflection are essential in the process of opening up to new ideas and possibilities. In dialogue research, this is described in different manners. In the *space between,*[37] in *tension as creative power for meaning making ('ma'),*[38] in the

---

[35]Kotter and Schlesinger 1979.
[36]Lau 1963, 67.
[37]Hickman and Sorenson 2014.
[38]Morioka 2008.

space between words, the unknown emerges and becomes visible, a new collective reality may emerge. Dialogue and conversation are described in connection with transformative change work, such as the appreciative inquiry approach and other projects such as MIT Dialogue Project.[39] In line with Hickman's[40] view on leadership, I affirm that generative dialogue leads to a greater level of authentic, effective, and ethical leadership. You could say dialogue is an ethical and epistemological theory, as we start from the fact that both of us don't know the answer. So there can be plural moralities and realities. Voices can express different ideas.

Recently, I did a presentation for members of supervisory and non-executives boards. Topic for us on the agenda was to discuss leadership, culture and behavioral change.

Three topics emerged in the discussion. The first one is the *importance of explaining the 'why'*. If people don't get exactly what is the reason why we are going to, for example, increase our risk management, they probably will not really open their mind. Changing mindset to truly understand requires the 'why' to be fully clear. Otherwise there might be the risk that people comply, follow the rules, but don't understand the reason behind it. And leave it, as soon as the external reinforcement is absent.

The second one is about *influencing somebody's mindset*. The audience—as they are on a distance of the organization and daily operations—wondered how they could more effectively influence the mindset of leaders in the organization they supervised. I put forward the assertion that you have to use a dialogical approach, to really open up mutually, if your ambition is to influence the mindset of the executive board in the company. Especially in political and power ruled environments this is very complex. I recommended the audience to experiment with asking questions and listening precisely to the answers. You might recognize quality of people by the way they react and are present in a dialogue like this. Too often unclear answers are given. And—last but not least—be the example of an open mindset yourself.

The third topic is about *recognizing quality in leaders*. How do you recognize quality in the people that report to you? Of course we have results, facts and figures. They are important. Also important, and from a leadership perspective in a complex organization, maybe even more important, is how you are present in the conversation, in the meeting. Are you able to respond to a question in a differentiated way? Are you consistent in verbal and non-verbal behavior? Are you able to real time integrate new information in your knowledge database? Is this visible and sensible in the meeting? Keep all the senses open. We sometimes rely on sources of information that don't correspond with the reality in front of us. Sharpening your faculties.

Talking about risk management. Each day, we can be a witness of examples that 'life is unpredictable', despite all efforts we take to control and manage risks. That's why there is so much power in dialogue as a leadership technique. Preparing your mind for the unexpected—continuously.

---

[39]Hosking 2011; Isaacs 1999.
[40]Hickman 2016.

A thought-provoking description of opening the mind for new learnings is that of Miyamoto Musashi. He describes learning in terms of Japanese martial arts. "Learning is the gate to acquiring the Way. That is why learning is the gate and not the house. When you see the gate, you must not think you have arrived at the house. You have to go through the gate to get to the house that is beyond and behind the gate. If what you have studied and practiced goes completely out of your mind, you can easily make the techniques of any art at all your own, without being held back by thoughts of what you have already learned and without deviating from what you already know. This is the spontaneous absorption of knowledge without being conscious that you are doing it. To stop thinking about learning, to let go your thoughts and harmonize them without being conscious of it, is the *final goal* of the Way."[41] My Tai Chi teacher Al-Huang formulated it as "True knowledge is like boiling water, with steam and energy rising up. True knowledge is like snowflakes that fall into the pan of water. They melt and disappear when they reach the surface. *You do not see what you are actually learning—it dissolves into you and becomes you, and changes you.*"[42] Through years of practicing Tai Chi and contrasting it with my academic training, I had the opportunity of experiencing this tension for myself—a tension between knowledge from the outside (reasoning) and knowing from the inside (experiencing). And how it can be reconciled if you reconcile reasoning and experiencing within your body. That is one of the most important things I learned through practicing Tai Chi.

5.6 A Methodology of Connecting I-Positions

At this point, the dynamics of Gergen's *relational co-constructing*, Libbrecht's *freeing energy,* and Morioka's *creating space* converge in *creating transformational space*. In my view, this is a core concept for better understanding dialogue as condition zero for change: *space*. The intermediate 'space' in dialogue creates potential for transformation. With this core insight in mind, I describe the process of dialogue between I-positions, internal and external in the following section. There are three phases:

1. *Formulating* (opposing) I-positions
2. *Connecting* I-positions in a dialogue (external and/or internal)
3. *Transpositioning:* as a result of the generative dialogue new meaning might emerge resulting in new intentionally formulated I-positions (as third, meta or promoter position).

We will use these schema's in Chap. 6 to explore and explain processes of transformation in the self. Figure 5.7 shows the dynamics of such a dialogical process: formulating I-positions; connecting I-positions, and transpositioning.

---

[41]Musashi 1993, 21.
[42]Huang 1973.

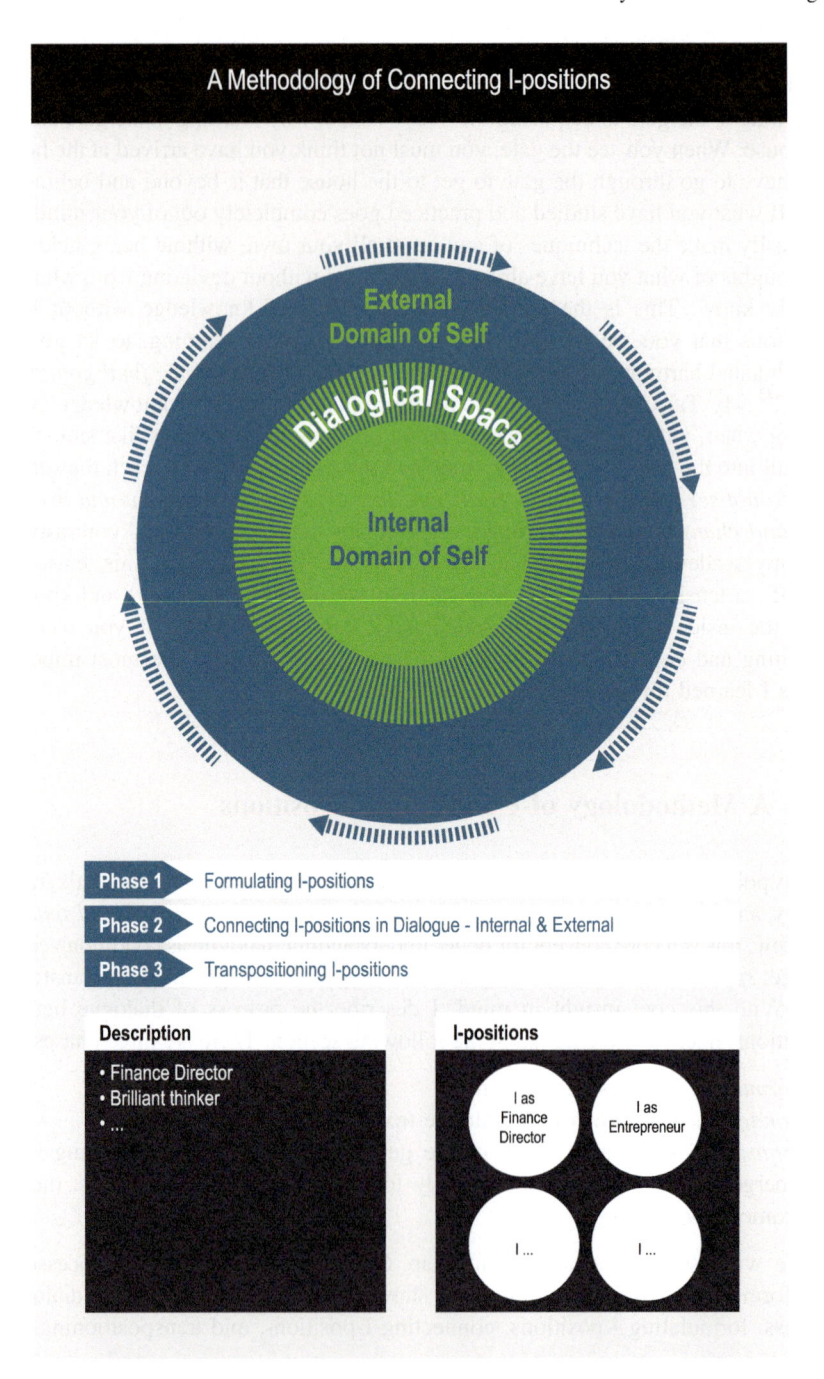

Fig. 5.7 A methodology of connecting I-positions

5.6 A Methodology of Connecting I-Positions

Gerda van Dijk and I wrote "that current and future leaders need to develop an effective interpersonal and intrapersonal capacity to become aware of their own emotional dilemmas and thinking silos, to open up and to reconcile dilemmas rationally and emotionally.[43] In our view, the dialogical self-theory, in particular the methodology of formulating, combining and recombining I-positions, is a helpful concept. Some examples: 'I as SVP'; 'I as chairman of the BoD'; 'I as a chemical engineer'; 'I as captain of the rugby team'; 'I as a pilgrim'; 'I as a pastor in the Anglican Church'. This way of positioning yourself in different external and internal manners is relationally co-constructed in the context of interpersonal relationships and social systems. Let us have a look at the variety of I-positions we encounter in daily practice. Verheijen described five generic I-positions. Based on his view, I come to the following list:

- The physical dimension, the body (*homo corporealis*): 'I as a physical being'.
- The motivating, the willing dimension (*homo volens*): 'I as a willing man/woman'.
- The playful dimension (*homo ludens*); 'I as a playing human'.
- Man constructing and marketing all kind of things (*homo faber et economicus*); 'I as a craftsman'.
- The dimension of sense making (*homo significans*). 'I as looking for meaning'.[44]

Figure 5.7 shows how you could use this as a starting point for a conversation with yourself or with other people to explore your I-position repertoire. Heifetz describes the self as a system. So you have to understand the full complexity, multiplicity and inconsistency of your own system. This refers to what we call in this book I-positions, many and potentially conflicting. They show a figure with the basic roles a person can play: manager, technician, mediator, advocate, sibling, parent, spouse, and friend. Of course this list is not extensive.[45]

During my meetings with clients, I collected I-positions that were communicated during our conversations. This list originates from my working with clients in about two years. Let us have a look at this list of I-positions. People often mention I-positions unintentionally, when telling their self-narrative in dialogue. An example. When we talk about his role as a managing director, my conversation partner tells: "Normally I react quite balanced, even when the pressure is heavy, or even very heavy. That's something I developed in one of my hobbies. Even when the stress is very high in the project, I stay calm and keep the overview." Here you ask a follow up question: "Can you tell me about your hobby?" My observation is that many people are not proactively open about other than formal roles they take in life. *Establishing trust* in dialogue is important to get this information. Establishing

---

[43]Van Loon and Van Dijk 2015, 63.

[44]Verheijen 2012.

[45]When dealing with wicked issues (adaptive leadership) you—as an individual system—make interventions in a social system of which you are a member. Heifetz et al. 2009, 212.

trust implies following guidelines for dialogue: truthfully connecting in conversation, suspending your assumptions, slowing down the process of inquiry, no jumping to conclusions and consciously following. I worked with many people who for the first time intuitively related different aspects of their life. As illustrated, it is often an opening *question* of the other person that makes you think about elements you normally don't think about intentionally. A list of I-positions can—by definition—never be complete. The transformational impact of intentionally thinking and talking about I-positions is in the act of *'dialogically positioning and re-positioning'*. This can be a *formal* role (e.g., 'I as chairman of the BoD'), an expression that you use *metaphorically* (e.g., 'I as a silent fowler'), or a *psychological* state (e.g., 'I as impatient'; internal I-position).

In the next list, you find examples of 'formal' roles that leaders can have in a company, as external I-positions. These I-positions you can define, just by looking at somebody's resume or at the organizational chart.

- I as an operational leader
- I as a matrix leader
- I as a business leader
- I as an entreprise leader
- I as a business analyst
- I as a (senior) consultant
- I as a (senior) manager
- I as a director
- I as a (senior) partner
- I as a crisis manager
- I as a strategic HR-leader
- I as the chairman of the Board
- I as a technology leader
- I as a member of the supervisory Board
- I as a strategy director
- I as a scientist-entrepreneur

In the following list, examples are given of singular internal I-positions. These idiosyncratic I-positions are formulated during conversations, and you cannot know what is meant, unless you know something of the context in the dialogue. To find out what is the meaning, you have to explore somebody's self-narrative in more detail. An example: 'Uncle Fred' refers to somebody who was train machinist, and also a philosopher, being an idol for the person who formulated this I-position.

- I as a boxer with an open hand
- I as autonomous
- I as Uncle Fred
- I as eagle
- I as Don Quichote
- I as religious
- I as a rebel

5.6 A Methodology of Connecting I-Positions

- I as a dog trainer
- I before/after my severe car-accident
- I as open-minded
- I as competitive
- I as a bird watcher
- I as a pianist
- I as tough
- I as meditating
- I as thinking out of the box
- I as dancer
- I as a joker
- I as insecure
- I as passionate

The scope of a categorization like this is limited, it cannot be complete, it gives an impression of the richness of possible I-positions. *Every 'word or utterance' can take a transformative role by being positioned or repositioned in the repertoire of I-positions*. The function of this list is exemplary: if you register a series of conversations, these type of I-positions will naturally come forward.

5.7 The Process of Reconciling I-Positions Illustrated

We illustrate the process of reconciling with a case study,[46] where the schema of transpositioning I-positions is applied.

5.7.1 "I Feel Frustrated"

Peter is in his mid-forties when we meet. He is a successful finance director with a strong track record in business development. He pre-selected and bought many companies all over Europe. He describes himself as being impatient and sometimes impulsive. Over a period of two-and-a-half years, we had seven one-on-one conversations[47] plus two team sessions with his team at peer level. His colleagues describe Peter as confident and sometimes arrogant as they often get the impression that he always knows better. He has a habit of overruling others, instead of

---

[46] Van Loon and Van den Berg 2016. This case is originally published in Hermans 2016. *Nine Methods for stimulating a dialogical self: Applications in groups, cultures and organizations*, 75–93.

[47] The first one was a one-and-a-half day leadership dialogue, supported by additional tools such as 360° behavioral feedback and personality assessment based on Big5 theory. This is not described here. Follow-up conversations were two hour dialogues.

developing them to a higher level of performance. We describe four core I-positions, which were formulated in our conversations: *I as an entrepreneur, I as a hobby farmer, I as finance director* and *I as willing to help other people*. When Peter sensed that his *willingness to help other people* was destabilized, he felt his entire repertoire was being disorganized. He used the expression '*I feel frustrated*' (Fig. 5.8).

5.7.2 The Entrepreneur and the Hobby Farmer

The process of Peter's development is characterized by phases, the first reconciling the tension between the I-positions of the finance director and his willingness to help other people. The second phase in reconciling the I-position of the entrepreneur with that of the hobby farmer. Let's have a more detailed look.

In next figure, Peter's I-positions are represented. We describe the following I-positions (internal versus external). *I as entrepreneur* versus *I as a hobby-farmer; I as a finance-director* versus *I as willing to help other people; I as an expert* versus *I as working as a mentor with young people; I feel stressed* versus *I need space; I want to be connected with nature*. In this phase of the process we connect the I-positions in external dialogue while stimulating the internal dialogue in Peter (Fig. 5.9).

Peter is a brilliant thinker; he knows this is one of his truest talents. In his role as a finance director, he is able to use his rationality to the utmost. His successes in the organization are mainly dependent on this strongly developed I-position. Many of his technical competencies are interrelated. In this I-position, Peter is described by his peers as a 'know-it-all', indicating that he tends to over-articulate that competency. He is inclined to overrule people as they do not describe reality 'as it is': the truth. In that case, this I-position is dominant and sometimes with a strong negative impact.

The *I as willing to help other people* I-position is described as "I as reliable and supportive". Peter feels happy in helping people, supporting them in understanding the case at hand. For him this is a vital I-position, primarily present in his private life, but also in the workplace, be it in a lesser degree. He loves working as a mentor with young people, looking for professional support.

In the conversations, Peter expressed that he likes to teach young people, to use his knowledge and experience to support others in developing their business insights and skills. Occasionally, he is invited to teach financial courses at a business university. He became aware that his tendency to act as a wiseacre hindered him from being perceived as a true supportive boss/colleague. Sometimes he felt as if these I-positions of 'the finance director' and 'his willingness to help other people' were unrelated and conflicting. It felt for him as a "confusing cacophony of voices, lacking any insightful organization."[48] Peter wanted to align his core competencies—being rational and being supportive—in a more consistent way.

---

[48]Hermans and Hermans-Konopka 2010, 228.

5.7 The Process of Reconciling I-Positions Illustrated

Case-Study Peter 1

"I feel Frustrated"

- Finance Director
- Brilliant thinker
- "Know-it-all"
- Entrepreneur
- Stressed
- Impatient and impulsive
- Arrogant
- Overruling others

I as Finance Director
I as Entrepreneur
I as willing to help other people
I as a Hobby Farmer

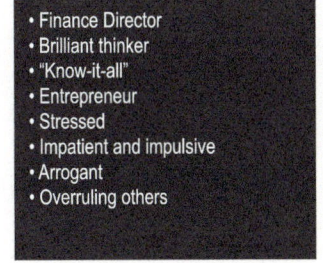

Fig. 5.8 Case-Study Peter 1

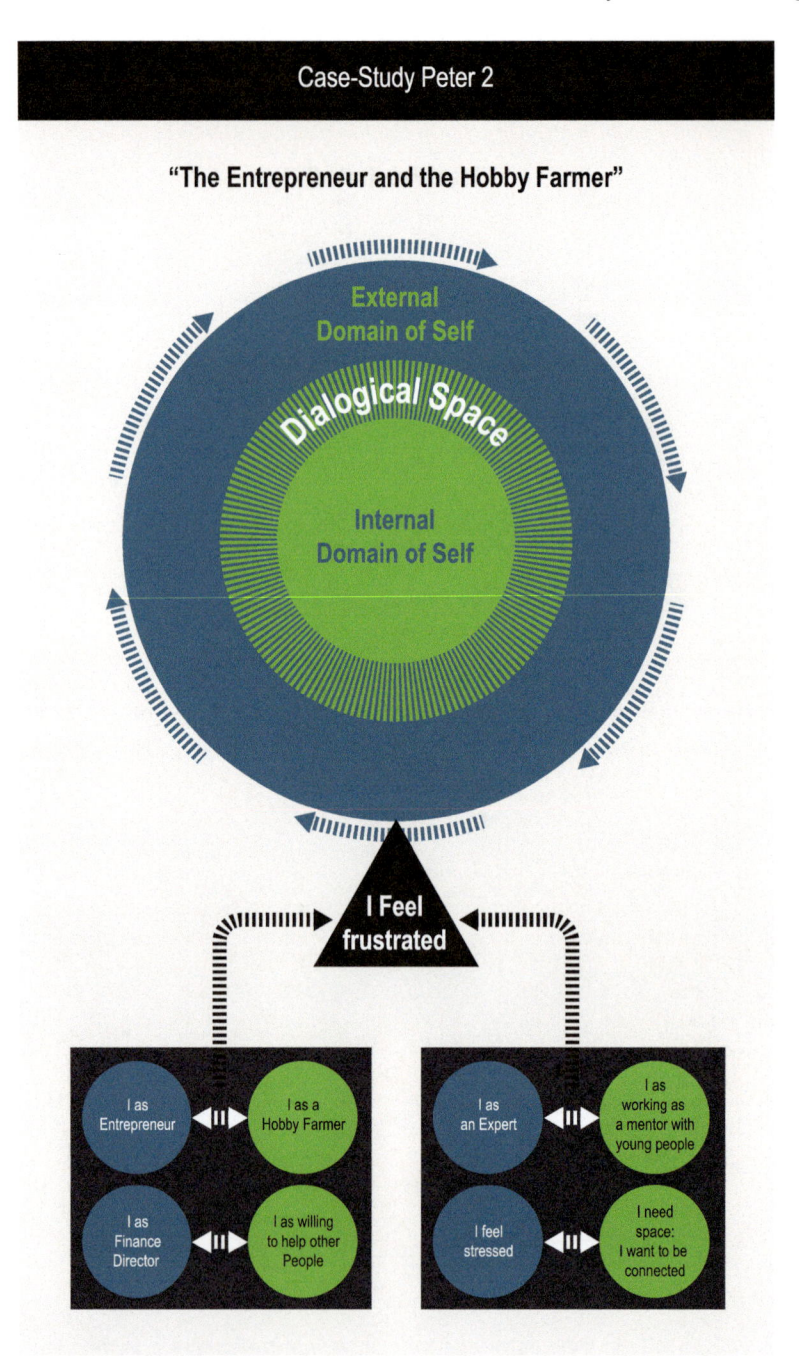

Fig. 5.9 Case-Study Peter 2

While talking about this tension, he also reflected about situations where these two I-positions were *not* conflicting. First, he spoke about a situation where he acted as a *coach*. Thinking about himself as a coach he used the expression "sharing knowledge by asking questions", instead of knowing better and correcting. A second situation was related to being a *teacher*. In front of students, he was open and willing to support them in developing their insights themselves, instead of rectifying them. Consciously thinking about acting as a teacher and/or coach, he deliberately choose for the coach. He felt he wanted to develop his capabilities as a coach. This could create more order and give direction. He explored what he needed to do (in terms of training and courses) to become a professional coach.

'*I as a coach*' creates the openness to integrate different aspects of Peter's self. "By integration, we mean that positions are reorganized in such a way that they result in a more adaptive self."[49] Peter felt that this newly voiced I-position had the potential to bring him to a higher level of performance in his working and private life.

5.7.3 *"The Gate of Frustration Is Closed"*

Peter describes a significant part of his working life in terms of expanding businesses. He truly acts as an entrepreneur, by pre-selecting, analyzing and buying companies in the market to create a stronger portfolio of businesses for the company. Viewed from this I-position, his rational and dominant behaviors are described as strengths (both by himself, his boss, his peers and the people he leads). Peter is a strong entrepreneur with well-developed commercial and analytical skills. Shadow-side of this strength is that he is stressed, unable to find relaxation, almost always travelling (Fig. 5.10).

'*I as a hobby farmer*' reinforces for Peter his need for freedom and space (physical and mental), his feeling of being connected with his family and the animals on the farm. This is a strong counterweight for his I-position as an entrepreneur. In his own words: "I need space and I want to be connected with nature". When he is at home he strongly recognizes what he misses when he is traveling and what he needs to be more healthy and happy. These two I-positions were tense opposites for him. He often felt frustrated as he seemed unable to solve this tension.

In our conversations, we spent much time talking about the two I-positions. In this process Peter was asked to think about a possible connection between the entrepreneur and the hobby farmer, sketched on a sheet of paper. Looking at the two I-positions, generated an association immediately: '*I as an entrepreneur who is a hobby farmer*'. Through voicing in this manner, he re-organized and centered his position repertoire by reconciling two elements conceptually in one I-position.

---

[49]Hermans and Hermans-Konopka 2010, 228.

Fig. 5.10 Case-Study Peter 3

5.7 The Process of Reconciling I-Positions Illustrated

The two positions are formulated in a dynamic balance, instead of being experienced as opposites, as Peter felt before the conversation.[50]

Peter repositioned '*I as an entrepreneur who is a hobby farmer*' in his personal repertoire. He got the feeling that this way of viewing himself integrated the entrepreneur with his strong personal wish to be "in nature" and to develop more towards a coach. The series of dialogues had a deep transforming impact on his professional functioning and personal life.

Summarizing the two aspects of his personal repertoire, at the end of our conversations he formulated: "*the gate of frustration is closed*".

5.8 Reflections on My Personal Narrative 4

The period in my life after 2005 can be described as a search to reconcile rationality and intuition. For me this was a tough issue, I sincerely did not know how to solve it. It made me desperate. My desire for continuous change was present in my inner life as a quest for real understanding and experiencing in combination with a level of tenseness, restlessness, feeling rushed and worrying in my outer life.

5.8.1 Moments of Transformation

Looking back, I summarized for myself moments of transformation and the concurring crises.

- When I was around 20 years old, I wanted to obtain true knowledge. My teachers were not giving me what I needed. In this crisis, I left university and started to practice Tai Chi intensively. Step by step, I became more used to and self-confident in relying on my body as source for information. Tai Chi teaches me to listen to the wisdom of my body and to rely on its agility to adapt to new, unknown situations. By not taking immediate action. By following, by pulling, by suspending my thoughts.
- When I was around 30, I was at university again and starting to work at different locations. I left the world of the Tai Chi 'dojo', as a safe place where you practice meditation and the art of Tai Chi with other students. I had a family and I worked in the outer, material world. I felt unsure about my capabilities how to take care for a young family, earning a living in an economic crisis situation, building up my career. I came in new, complex situations, I became a management consultant. In this crisis, 'I as Rens' intuitively created 'I as Levi' as an

---

[50]Technically speaking: it is through *repositioning*—visually, linguistically—that a new insight and I-position emerges. Here two different aspects of his reality are placed close to one-another visually and the 'iuxta-positioning' works by itself.

internal I-position to support me from the back in performing my job. In me developed an invisible (and imaginary) power, 'I as Levi'. I felt supported continuously in my material life by this I-position. This happened intuitively.

- When I was around 40, I worked successfully as a management consultant, completed my Ph.D. as a scientist, and became partner in a psychological consultancy firm. We did thousands of assessment centers, worked for large global organizations and I was confronted with the limits of rational knowledge at work. In that crisis, I asked myself: how can I use my intuition in my work? I developed a skill to write personal letters as a summary of leadership development projects, instead of formal reports. After sessions with teams and individuals I tried to capture my experiences and insights in poetry, in metaphorical language, and I started to consciously use metaphors and storytelling in my working with leaders.
- When I was around 50, using metaphorical language and my intuition had become a more natural part of my way of working and living. I experienced combining rational analysis, metaphorical language and special attention for the role of the body in non-verbal language and presence is powerful.
- When I was 54, I started to work with another psychologist as my mentor. *He demonstrated me how to suspend my willpower.* Until that moment, my will was one of my most important tools. We started a deep reflecting process, where he extremely tested my 'ego', my 'assumed self'. In our conversations I became aware how 'I as Levi' not only supported me, but simultaneously blocked me in my development as 'Rens'.

Softening my will was one of the first phases, and instead of living with two separate I-positions, I now learned to rely on 'I as Rens' as a core-position, without support in the back from 'Levi'. My I-position as *Tai Chi practitioner* lost its influence and became neutral, as did 'I as thinker'. On the contrary, the influence of 'I as intuitive' was growing increasingly stronger. I relied more on my intuition. In my conversations with clients, I intentionally used this aspect more. I became aware of the fact that you can act successfully without explicitly mobilizing your willpower. I realized what it means to truly suspend your view. If you are trained as a 'gatekeeper of truth', it is not easy to open your mind for the 'non-being of truth'. What I learned is how to truly suspend your opinion, simply verbalizing what is going on in the moment itself during the conversation. It made me aware of how you can move beyond self. A new field of experiencing for me, an unknown domain. For me, this was an intriguing period in my life, as I changed jobs, in that period, I joined Deloitte.

5.8.2 Shifting Dominance

Analyzing this phase of my process in terms of Dialogical Self Theory, the position repertoire is profoundly changed. After the modification in meaning of 'I as Levi' and 'I as Tai Chi practitioner', 'I as thinker' and 'I as Rens' are also shifting in meaningfulness and dominance in the I-position repertoire (Fig. 5.11).

5.8 Reflections on My Personal Narrative 4

Reflections on My Personal Narrative 4

Shifting Dominance (2010)

External Domain of Self
- I as Leadership Consultant
- I as Father
- I as Scientist
- I as Intuitive
- I as a Rational Thinker
- I as Rens
- I as Lyricist
- I as Director Deloitte
- I as Grandfather
- I as Husband
- I as Tai Chi Practitioner

External I-Positions
- Leadership Consultant
- Scientist
- Director Deloitte
- Father
- Grandfather
- Husband
- My supervisor

Internal I-Positions
- Immediate knowing
- Soft discipline
- Relying on my intuition
- Suspending my opinion
- Opening my mind for the non-being of truth
- Simply verbalizing
- Moving beyond self

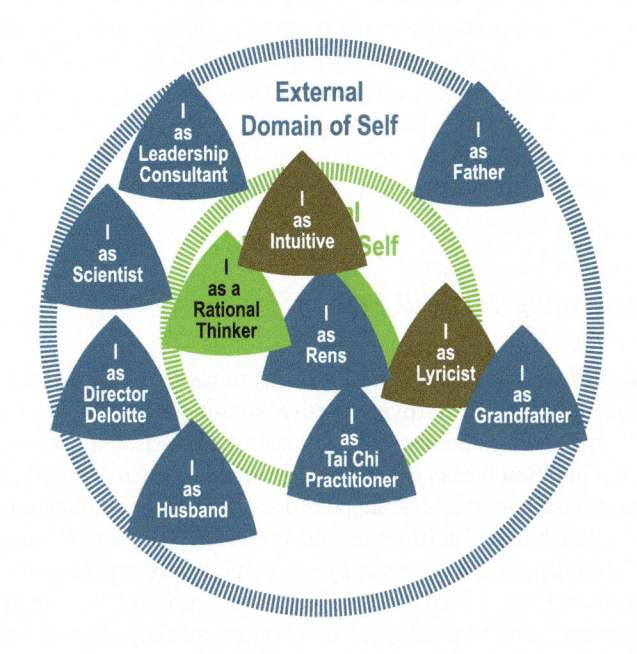

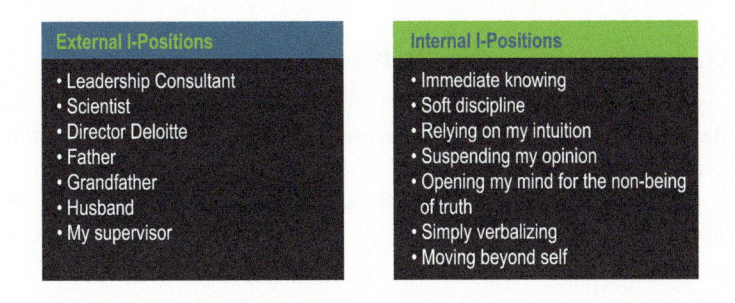

Fig. 5.11 Reflections on my personal narrative 4

The most dominant I-position in this phase is that of 'I as lyricist' referring to intuition as the most important source of information. 'I as Tai Chi practitioner' has lost its position as counter-position. It has become a promoter-position, since the role of the body as source for information is critical for the new central I-position: '*I as lyricist/intuitive*'.

The two core positions 'I as Rens' and 'I as a thinker' take a more decentered position, they still have influence in the position repertoire, but not as dominant as before. 'I as Levi' is now a purely internal position, which has lost its meaning. It has become a reminiscence. As external I-positions we see 'I as Scientist', 'I as director Deloitte', 'I as Leadership consultant', 'I as Husband', 'I as Father', and 'I as Grandfather'. A new external position that was added to the repertoire since I became a grandfather of three granddaughters and a grandson.

5.8.3 Suspending My Will Power

Experiencing without consciously willing seems to be the next step in my process. I seem to have moved from an (over-) 'active' to a more 'participative mode'. My body is no longer setting boundaries of rationality and reasoning between self and non-self, as my intuition breaks through this artificial boundary. In this phase, I feel more deconcentrated energy; what happens does so without an intentional effort of my willpower. In Chinese Taoist terms, this is called 'wei-wu-wei', acting through not acting. "Experiences dissipate energy. One can deduce this from the change in the psychosomatic state, which we often name 'enthusiasm': we are enthused by love, aesthetic emotion, national pride or religious stirrings. It puts me in a particular mood, as I am tuned by environmental factors (e.g. nature), or the 'human condition' or the Great Cosmic Wonder....my state of consciousness is altered and this influences my physicality, my social relations (e.g. sympathy) and my dealings in the world."[51] This was more or less how I felt in that period, happy.

5.9 Questions for Further Reflection

- While speaking and listening, experiment with different bodily postures and write down your insights.
  Also pay attention to what impact specific bodily postures have on your thinking, feeling and acting.

---

[51]Libbrecht 2007, 101.

- Do you have experiences of deep understanding, hearing words and concepts in conversations? Try to explain verbally or by writing down your process and content of understanding.
  Do you have an opposite experience that you don't understand a clue of what is meant? How do you react? What kind of action do you take to start a process of understanding?
  Analyze what causes deep understanding in you.
- With a good friend, make a walk. Connect with each other with the back of your hands; lead him/her, with his/her eyes closed, through the wood. Change roles after a while. Don't speak, be silent, and observe what happens, both while leading and when being led. Make some notes.

References

Baerveldt, C., & Voestermans, P. (1998). The body as a selfing device. In H. J. Stam (Ed.) *The body and psychology* (161–181).

Bohm, D. (1996). *On dialogue*. New York: Routledge.

Empson, L. (2013). Who is in charge? Exploring leadership dynamics in professional service firms.

Gergen, K. J. (2009). *Relational being: Beyond self and community*. New York: Oxford University Press.

Goffee, R., & Jones, G. (2006). *Why should anyone be led by you? What it takes to be an Authentic Leader*. Boston: Harvard Business School Press.

Hawes, L. C. (1999). The dialogics of conversation: Power, control, vulnerability. *Communication Theory, 9*(3), 229–264.

Heifetz, R.A., Grashow, A., & Linsky, M. (2009). *The practice of adaptive leadership: Tools and tactics for changing your organization and the world*. Harvard Business Press.

Hermans, H.J.M. (Ed.). (2016). *Nine methods for stimulating a dialogical self: Applications in groups, cultures and organizations*. Switzerland: Springer.

Hermans, H. J. M., & Hermans-Jansen, E. (1995). *Self-narratives: The Construction of meaning in psychotherapy*. New York: Guilford Press.

Hermans, H. J. M., & Hermans-Konopka, A. (2010). *Dialogical self theory. Positioning and counter-positioning in a globalizing society*. Cambridge: University Press.

Hermans, H. J. M., & Kempen, H. (1993). *The dialogical self*. Meaning as movement. NY: Academic Press.

Hermans, H. J. M., Kempen, H. J. G., & Van Loon, E. (Rens) J. P. (1992). The dialogical self: Beyond individualism and rationalism. *American Psychologist, 47*.

Hickman, G. R. (2016). *Leading organizations: Perspectives for a new era*. Thousand Oaks: Sage.

Hickman, G. R., & Sorenson, G. J. (2014). *The power of invisible leadership: How a Compelling common purpose inspires exceptional leadership*. Los Angeles: SAGE.

Hosking, D. M. (2011). Moving relationality: Meditations on a relational approach to leadership. In A. Bryman, D. Collinson, K. Grint, B. Jackson, & M. Uhl-Bien (Eds.), *The SAGE handbook of leadership* (pp. 455–467). London, UK: Sage.

Huang, A. C. L. (1973). *Embrace tiger, return to mountain: the essence of t'ai chi*. U.S.: Real People Press.

Huczynski, A., & Buchanan, D. (2013). *Organizational behaviour* (8th ed.). Edinburg: Pearson Education Limited.

Isaacs, W. N. (1999). *Dialogue and the art of thinking together. A pioneering approach to communicating in business and in life*. New York, NY: Doubleday.

Johnson, M. (1987/2013). *The body in the mind: The bodily basis of meaning, imagination, and reason*. Chicago: University of Chicago Press.

Kabat-Zinn, J. (1996). Mindfulness meditation: What it is, what it isn't, and its role in health care and medicine. *Comparative and psychological study on meditation*, 161–170.

Kahane, A. (2007). *Solving tough problems. An open way of talking, listening and creating new realities*. San Francisco: Berrett-Koehler Publishers, Inc.

Kahane, A. (2010). *Power and Love. A theory and practice of social change*. San Francisco: Berrett-Koehler Publishers Inc.

Kempen, H. J. G. (1998). *Mind as body moving in space. Bringing the body back in self-psychology*. In H. J. Stam (Ed.), *The body and psychology* (pp. 54–70). New York: Sage Publications.

Kotter, J. P., & Schlesinger, L. A. (1979). *Choosing strategies for change*. Cambridge: Harvard Business Review.

Lakoff, G., & Johnson, M. (1999). *Philosophy in the flesh: the embodied mind and its challenge to Western thought*. New York, NY: Basic Books.

Lau, D.C. (1963). *Lao Tzu. Tao Te Ching*. Translated with an introduction. London: Penguin Books.

Lengelle, R. (2016). What a career coach can learn from a playwright: Expressive dialogues for identity development. In H. J. M. Hermans (Ed.) *Nine methods for stimulating a dialogical self: Applications in groups, cultures and organizations* (pp. 37–53). Springer, Switzerland.

Libbrecht, U. (2007). *Within the four seas…: Introduction to comparative philosophy*. Belgium: Peeters Publishers.

Morioka, M. (2008). Voices of the self in the therapeutic chronotype: *Utuschi* and *Ma*. *International Journal for Dialogical Science*, 3(1), 93–108.

Musashi, M. (1993). The book of five rings. *The Warrior Series Book, 2*, 21.

Ricard, M. (2011). *The art of meditation*. London: Atlantic Books Ltd.

Van Loon, E. (Rens) J. P. (2016). Review of the article "Dialogical and eastern perspectives on the self in practice: Teaching mindfulness-based stress reduction in Philadelphia and Seoul". *International Journal of Dialogical Science*.

Van Loon, E. (Rens) J. P., & Kouwenhoven, K. (2016). Dancing leader. Leading and following. In R. Koonce, M. C. Bligh, M. K. Carsten & M. Hurwitz (Ed.), *Followership in action. Cases and commentaries*. Emerald Books.

Van Loon, E. (Rens) J. P., & Van den Berg, T. (2016). Dialogical leadership. The "Other" way to coach leaders. In H. J. M. Hermans (Ed.) *Nine methods for stimulating a dialogical self: Applications in groups, cultures and organizations* (75–93).

Van Loon, E. (Rens) J.P., & Van Dijk, G. (2015). Dialogical Leadership. Dialogue as Condition Zero. *Journal for Leadership Accountability and Ethics* Vol. 12(3), 62–75.

Verheijen, D. J. C. (2012). *De roep om de menselijke maat* (Doctoral dissertation).

Part III
The Impact

Chapter 6
Dialogical Leadership and Wicked Issues

Abstract

- Living in an unpredictable world (VUCA as volatility, uncertainty, complexity and ambiguity) implies that leaders have to learn skills in dealing with wicked, adaptive challenges: how to create conditions for generative dialogue as a mindset and a method to deal with wicked issues.
- Dialogue is a powerful tool to open a person's mind for change and transformation and to redirect resistance in an effective and constructive manner.
- Leaders should be trained to flexibly differentiate their approaches if confronted with crises, tame and wicked issues. Crises require control and immediate response; tame issues routine and rational proper management; wicked issues need normative, soft power, and asking the right questions to open new perspectives on the issue to collectively find normative answers. Here Dialogical Leadership is condition zero.
- In the case-studies is illustrated how dialogically working with I-positions changes a leader's effectiveness. Some core mechanisms are illustrated such as centering and de-centering.
- *Transpositioning or transposing* is added to the Dialogical Self Theory terminology, defined as "(intentionally) bringing I-positions from one domain in life/work to another in order to create change in the position repertoire."

Before we look in detail to the individual case-studies in this chapter and to a team-case in the next chapter, I make a short side-step to the meaning of living in an unpredictable world, how to lead change through dialogue, and when to apply a dialogical approach.

6.1 Living in an Unpredictable World—the Implications for Leaders

Technology fundamentally changed the relation between leaders and followers, as is illustrated by the recent outcome of elections in several countries. In such a complex world we are confronted with issues that have to be designated as complex, wicked, and adaptive. VUCA is an acronym—volatility, uncertainty, complexity and ambiguity—used to describe and reflect on conditions and situations we are in. Originally used in the context of the U.S. Army, the term is now used to describe strategic leadership and development in organizations.

- *Volatility* refers to the nature and dynamics of change, change forces and change catalysts.
- *Uncertainty* relates to a lack of predictability and the sense of awareness and understanding of events and issues.
- *Complexity* is the multiplex of forces, the confounding of issues, lack of clear cause-and-effect chains and confusion.
- *Ambiguity* refers to the haziness of reality, the potential for misreads, and the mixed meanings of conditions, no clear cause-and-effect chains.[1]

For most contemporary organizations—business, military, education, government and others—VUCA is a practical code for awareness and readiness. Beyond the simple acronym is a body of knowledge that deals with learning models for VUCA preparedness, anticipation, evolution and intervention. Bob Johansen describes ten skills for dealing with an uncertain world. The world is experiencing great uncertainty and perplexity accompanying the global recession, high unemployment, industrial production stained by ongoing pollution of the environment, and the consequent issues of global climate change. These challenges are accompanied by a wave of political and social unrest (terrorism, diaspora of migrants over the world, radicalization, and so on). Johansen's view is that leaders need to develop new skills to guide their organizations and communities into the future. Leaders have to immerse themselves in continuous, *first person*, learning to create foresight, insight and action in a VUCA world. "In order to increase their readiness and ability to make the future, leaders must immerse themselves in the future and return to the present ready to make a better future."[2] He describes ten leadership skills:

1. *The maker instinct*: the ability to exploit your inner drive to build and grow things, as well as connect with others in the making.
2. *Clarity*: the ability to see through messes and contradictions to a future that others cannot yet see. Leaders must be clear about what they are making, but flexible about how it gets made.

---

[1]Source: Wikipedia.
[2]Johansen 2012, 3.

3. *Dilemma flipping*: the ability to turn dilemmas—which, unlike (rational) problems, cannot be solved—into advantages and opportunities.
4. *Immersive learning*: the ability to immerse yourself in unfamiliar environments, to learn from them, to experience in a first person manner.
5. *Bio-empathy*: the ability to see things from nature's point of view; to understand, respect and learn from its patterns.
6. *Constructive depolarizing*: the ability to calm tense situations where differences dominate and communication is broken down—and bring people from divergent cultures toward positive engagement.
7. *Quiet transparency*: the ability to be open and authentic about what matters, without being overly self-promoting.
8. *Rapid prototyping*: the ability to create quick, early versions of innovations, with the expectation that later success will require early failures.
9. *Smart-mob organizing*: the ability to create, engage with, and nurture purposeful business or social change networks through intelligent use of electronic and other networks.
10. *Commons creating:* the ability to seed, nurture and grow shared assets that can benefit all players—and allow competition at a higher level.[3]

6.1.1 Studying Leadership Is not yet Being a Leader

Some reflections on the work of Johansen. In his work, there is great similarity with what we described in the sense of being able to switch between concentration and *de*concentration, between what he names 'foresee', deeply 'understand' and 'act'. You can't deal with a VUCA world if you don't have the ability to switch between the levels of taking a distance view (as deconcentrated, field energy) and taking action (as concentrated, arrow energy). There must be a strong presence in the here and now, but at the same time you have to move up towards an eagle view, overviewing the situation from a different perspective, to a third position. You can learn this in the form of what Johansen names *immersive learning*, as first person learning. In Libbrecht's model this is *experiencing*. Siegel's approach in his research of the mind is being present for the reader *personally* and *intellectually*.[4] Remarkable honestly Johansen declares: "Being the president (of the Institute for the Future) was much tougher than I expected. I realize now that many of the challenges were inside my head and I was not ready for them. I was frequently frustrated and occasionally downright discouraged. I had physical reactions such as headaches, almost every afternoon. I had emotional reactions, such as unexpected

---

[3]Manders 2014.

[4]"Being scientific about the mind requires that we not only respect empirical findings, but also honor the subjective and interpersonal." Siegel 2017, 17.

tears at awkward times."[5] This made him aware that *being a leader* is much harder than *studying leadership*. "Being president during a very difficult time gave me firsthand experience that added greatly to my understanding of leadership and where it needs to go in the future."[6] Here we see the immediate value of experience. It is difficult to write down the right things if you don't have been in leadership (or comparable) situations yourself. I share Johansen's conclusion: "We don't just live in the present. We are rooted in the past and we have chances to make the future."[7] If we would just live in the present as bounded energy, there would be no culture, no art and poetry, no technical innovations, no wicked issues, no VUCA world. Nature does not need humanity for its existence. The external world is not dependent on mankind. A natural world that exists already for millions of years without us, human beings. A world that does not need our world-view to perpetuate itself. It is *because we humans are able to free energy to make our future,* that we have created culture, art and poetry, technical innovations, wicked issues in a VUCA world. "The most striking characteristic of this world of phenomena is its changeability: seasons, life, evolution, etc. all express its impermanence. The world is not a collection of things, but a playing field of events."[8] Libbrecht uses *permanent change* as the term to describe the world. A world with problems and with possibilities. I share Johansen's conclusion that our VUCA world, with all its threats, is at the same time loaded with opportunities. As *volatility* can yield to *true vision*, *uncertainty* can lead to *deep understanding*, *complexity* can yield to *genuine clarity* and *ambiguity* can yield to *authentic nimbleness*. But this will not happen spontaneously, therefore an individual and collective intentional act is needed. The challenges and issues have to be transformed *through a process of internal and external dialogue*. That's what the second reflection is about.

6.1.2 Creating Conditions for Dialogue

A second reflection is that I don't see the skill of *creating conditions for a generative dialogue* as required for future leadership in Johansen's list of ten skills. Although it might be present if you read between the lines, I am surprised that Johansen did not add this skill explicitly. He mentions 'Making the future begins with listening', 'active attention as the ability to filter out noise and distraction, combined with a strong ability to stay centered—even when overwhelmed with stimuli', 'showing urgent patience as being both urgent and patient, depending on what is needed at the time', and 'being able to find meaning is coincidence, by sensing synchronicity in patterns of events and actions'. Although he did hundreds

---

[5]Johansen 2012, 20.
[6]Johansen 2012, 21.
[7]Johansen 2012, 3.
[8]Libbrecht 2007, 91.

of workshops all over the world, and "there were no obvious additional future leadership skills that were suggested to me",[9] I would add this explicitly and prominently as a skill to the list. As a leader, you have to be able to create the conditions that people dare to deeply understand and act differently, one-to-one, in your team, in the organization, in society, dependent on your role in the context. So pro-actively creating conditions for a generative dialogue is number eleven.

6.1.3 Constructive Depolarizing

A third reflection is about *constructive depolarizing*. Johansen describes this as the ability to calm tense situations where differences dominate and communication has broken down—and bring people form divergent cultures toward positive engagement. There is a similarity with the dynamic process in the Dialogical Self Theory: bringing I-positions, that are in a polarized relation, into a dialogical one, and possibly transform, reposition or re-center. The mechanism in the internal domain of the self and the external dynamics in a relation are mediated by the skill of creating conditions for a dialogue between these opposed (internal and/or external) positions. This happens primarily by creating space, by intentionally moving to a higher level of reflection, to enable you to see a pattern.[10] And to intentionally act on the pattern you see by transforming this to a higher level.

Faced with a specific type of issues, wicked issues, dialogue is not a nice to have, but a requirement for good leadership. As there is no fixed solution to wicked issues, dialogue can provide a way out of being stuck. "Dialoging can help to bring forth and support appreciation (rather than judgment and critique), discussion of what can be done (rather than what cannot), and a sense of relational responsibility (rather than blaming others). Dialoging makes space for ongoing emergence, for improvisation."[11] As most of our leaders are trained to give answers, often even quick answers, for many of them this approach is a challenge, that brings them out of their comfort zone. The Dialogical Leadership approach is not a panacea, you have to find out when to apply, and to apply it properly. What I underpin here is that leaders need to learn to flexibly switch between different styles of leading, where the dialogical is an appropriate one for wicked issues. Figure 6.1 summarizes this. We will describe this later in a more extensive way.[12]

---

[9]Johansen 2012, 3. See also: Jaworsky 1998.

[10]Reineke Lengelle expresses this in a beautiful manner "Writing is dialogical in nature: the moment words are committed to paper, the 'I' who is writing, connects to the 'Me', who is expressed here." Lengelle 2016, 51.

[11]Hosking 2011, 461.

[12]Heifetz uses the term 'adaptive problems' for wicked problems: these require learning, the solution and implementation are not clear. The responsibility for the solution is in the relation between leader and follower. It is remarkable that Heifetz does not use the term 'dialogue' to characterize this relation. Heifetz 1994.

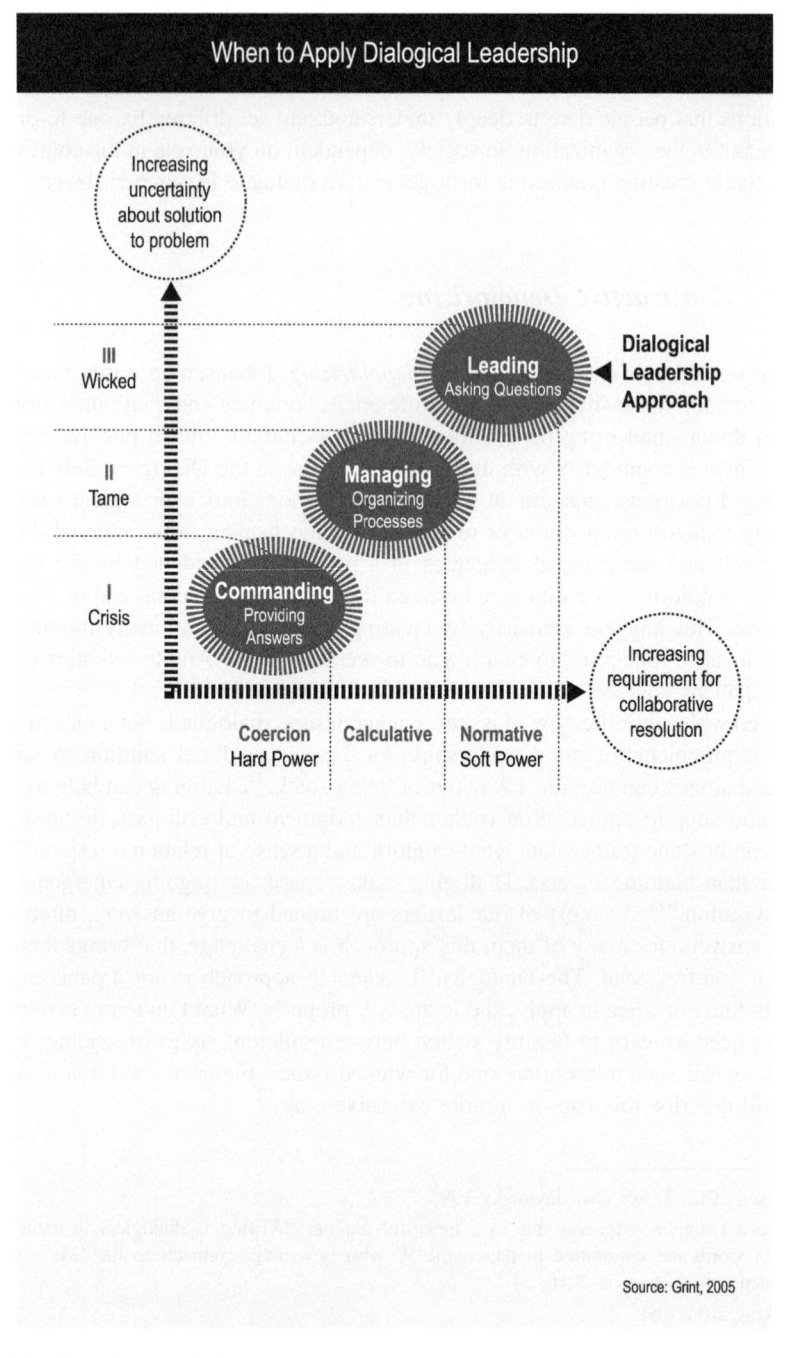

Fig. 6.1 When to apply dialogical leadership

6.2 Leading Change Through Dialogue

Before we go in-depth into describing crisis, tame and wicked issues, I focus your attention for a while on the process of change and transformation in general. If you want change, a process of dialogue seems to be inefficient in the beginning as it takes you much time. Setting up the conditions for dialogue takes time and you need to slow down first. You need to create *space* for reflecting, individually and as a group, space in the sense as we have seen it before: taking the time, sitting down somewhere, building the relation with self and other. This is the opposite of how the business world works today. Profit is measured by narrow economic criteria like quarterly returns. Fast, faster, as fast as possible. Self-reflection needs time in the beginning. Building a relation needs time in the beginning—later it—hopefully—pays back. Once you have a solid foundation, you can continue on that promptly, without losing time.

It is difficult to *free time, to create space to transform.* Dialogue might be experienced as a long way around or a slowing down of the problem solving. "But real change does not happen until people feel psychologically safe, and the implicit or explicit norms that are articulated in a dialogue session provide that safety by giving people a sense of direction and a sense that the dangerous aspects of interaction will be contained."[13] This stipulates the importance of the facilitator/chair: he/she must be able to do real time interventions to make it safe and secure. In the set-up phase of a change and transformation journey, a facilitator has this role of functioning as 'the third person' awareness, as from a meta-position guiding the process and building a container for dialogue. Changing habitual beliefs, assumptions, emotions and behaviors is a tough issue. There is a lot of heat and stress involved, and that has to be guided in the right direction.

On a practical level, we live in a world that is changing fast. The connection between individuals and entities is becoming stronger and stronger in technology developments as nanotechnology, home health monitoring, new business models, asset sharing, quantified self (developing self-knowledge through numbers), and so on. These developments result in new professions such as *urban farming, digital death management* (making stories out of your life-logged material), *big data analyst, 3-D printing handyman.*[14] Crises and threats are crucial change moments, as we saw in Isaacs' crises in the process of conversation. Crises might engender degenerative processes and/or generative processes, depending on how you deal with them. If you define it as feeding, nourishing your opportunities to transform and change for the better, it creates new chances. If you define it as loosing what you had, that you can't deal with your life as you did until then, it turns out to be a huge threat and a great risk.

---

[13]Schein 1993, 35.
[14]Van Dam 2016.

6.2.1 Change and Transformation

'*Changing*' refers to 'thinking, feeling, acting *differently*' while '*transforming*' as 'thinking, feeling, doing *different things*'. In change the object is the same, in transformation the object is essentially different. Change and transformation refer to different levels of changing. Leading change means creating a context, an environment, where people can change their thinking, feeling and acting in a safe and secure way, to reach a common purpose.[15] So it is also neutralizing fear for change, as many people become anxious to leave behind what they are used to. People generally want to belong to a greater community, but at the same time can be anxious to be rejected and not recognized by the group. If you want to express yourself in a different manner, there is always a risk of being rejected. In leading, you can show the ability to connect people with one another in a shared vision, a common purpose that the community wants to realize. Goffee and Jones insist on sharply being aware that leadership is about doing a task and reaching a purpose. "In this sense, leadership is instrumental. It is a relationship designed to achieve something. This distinguishes it from other types of relationship—friends or family for example—that might be regarded as intrinsically good or desirable."[16] The 'why' of changing is important for people to go for it. The 'why' becomes even more important if we think about fundamental change: why would anyone be led by you in a process of fundamental change? This is a crucial question leaders have to reflect if they request others to change, or to follow them in a change process.[17]

In a survey with over 2.500 responses from across a range of regions, industries, specialties, and seniorities, Keller[18] identified four common factors for success in change projects that were shared among the executives participating. I structure these four factors, using a vision-push-pull framework: exercising strong *leadership*

---

[15] *Change oriented behavior* is a dimension of leadership behavior separate from task-oriented and relations-oriented behavior. Some of these behaviors: Monitoring the external environment, interpreting external threats and opportunities for the team or the organization, finding innovative ways to adapt to changing external conditions, encouraging innovative thinking by followers, facilitating collective learning by a team or organization, articulating an inspiring vision for the team or organization, and implementing major changes in strategies. Yukl 2011, 294. Melina et al. 2013, give a lot of references to change: arts-based learning potential for transformational change, weakness of will as barrier to change, dialogue as social process of change, learning required for change, learning through process of change. In *Culture, Leadership and Organizations. The GLOBE study of 62 societies,* there is a relevant reference to change. "A central feature of charismatic leadership is the envisioning of change and an innovative vision to which followers should aspire." House et al. 2004, 65.

[16] Goffee and Jones 2006, 231.

[17] For the interested reader, I recommend to take knowledge of *Mapping Dialogue. Essential Tools for Social Change* (2008) by Bojer, Roehl, Knuth & Magner. Authors describe dialogue methods designed to meet collective social challenges, such as Appreciative Inquiry (David Cooperrider), Change Lab (Otto Scharmer), The Circle (Christina Baldwin), Open Space Technology (Harrison Owen). A detailed exploration of these methods is out of scope for this book.

[18] Keller et al. 2010, 624–625.

6.2 Leading Change Through Dialogue

as the core element, setting clear *goals* as visioning, using logical program *structures* as pushing, and creating ownership and *involvement* as pulling.

- *Exercising strong leadership*: "It helps if leaders 'role model' the desired changes, focusing on organization cultures (or 'mindsets'), and developing capacity for continuous improvement".
- *Setting goals*: "One of the main themes of this study concerned the need to focus on strengths and achievements, and not just on problems." They also found that *progressive transformations* succeeded 50% more often than *defensive transformations*. So going for growth, improved performance and expansion seem to be more successful than reactive, seeking cost reduction.
- *Working with a logical program structure*: "Success was linked to breaking the change process down into specific, clearly defined initiatives with a logical program, which those who were involved were allowed to shape or 'co-create'". This also refers to what we have seen before, that the level of relational co-constructing is important to get people committed.
- *Ownership and involvement*: "Success was also associated with high levels of employee engagement and collaboration." This illustrates how important elements of connecting with people are if organizations are going through change.

Keller et al. indicate that change programs are likely to be more successful if you pay attention to all four factors in their mutual relations. "Of the organizations which used all of these tactics, 80% met their approaches, compared with only 10% of those organizations which had used none of these approaches." This indicates that in change programs, one might say *integrating leading* with *setting clear directions*, *providing clear structures* and *clearly connecting with all stakeholders* are criteria for success.

6.2.2 Starting with 'Why'

Kotter explicitly stresses the importance of clarifying the direction of change in a clear vision. If people truly understand the 'why', they will be more motivated to implement it. Kotter describes some crucial techniques in communicating that vision.[19] Hereunder these are looked over and commented with a few words.

- *Keeping it simple*
  Jargon must be eliminated. One of the hick-ups in communication is that we refer to our own jargon and forget that what is familiar for ourselves is not necessarily known by others. Speaking simple is important to communicate clearly.

---

[19]Kotter 1996.

- *Using metaphors and examples*
  Images is worth a thousand words. We already have seen the importance of using metaphors as they create space in your mind. A metaphor leaves a message, which the mind cannot translate unambiguously.
- *Being on multiple forums*
  You have to be in big meetings but also in the one-to-ones in the corridor. Many leaders think that the vision is clear if it is written down in a memo and presented in a plenary meeting at the beginning of the project. You have to be present on the communication channels where people presently get their information (Twitter, YouTube, Yammer, Facebook).
- *Repetition*
  Ideas sink in deeply only after they have been heard many times. An advice leaders might take as a rule of thumb: "Speak about our vision at least three times a day". And preferably in situations where it is not formally on the agenda, but in typical day-to-day conversations.
- *Leading by example*
  Be the change that you want to realize. If your behavior is inconsistent with what you preach as a vision, people will get confused and resist. Be consistent in your behavior, verbally and non-verbally.
- *Explaining of seeming inconsistencies*
  As reality is not consistent, if there are inconsistencies blocking a deep understanding of what you want to communicate, bring them to the table. Use dialogue as a method to explain and if somebody asks a question, give an answer, and check if the question is *fully answered*. Many presenters of a vision don't really answer the questions that were asked. Very often, I see people repeating their message, again. Try to really understand the question, and then answer. If you don't have an answer, be open and try to find the answer. Indicate that you will send an email or other message to communicate what you have found. Daring to face inconsistencies visibly and relationally strengthens you and increases your impact enormously.
- *Give-and-take*
  Use dialogue, not monologue. The importance of dialogue as a means of creating reciprocal understanding in the process of mutual reflection. Visibly using the dialogical technique of listening and respecting. If you are able to make it a truly reciprocal process of listening and being listened to, the chance that the change will be successful increases significantly.

As a change leader and as a coach, you have to be able to help others to cross a boundary which they will not easily cross on their own. A transformation leader needs vision and energy. He is also able to give others what they *need*, and not just what they like. Goffee and Jones call this *'tough empathy'*. "It means leaders never lose sight of what they are here to do. They give people what they *need* rather than what they *want*. They never forget the task and the purpose as well as the people."[20]

---

[20]Goffee and Jones 2006, 63.

This capability is not easy to develop, as it requires all the characteristics described before as necessary to build the conditions for a dialogue: listening, respecting, suspending, and voicing. In my experience, voicing (of tough empathy) is difficult for many leaders, as it presupposes that you have the courage and the ability to verbalize what the other person(s) need. That is—at all levels—a precarious task.

6.2.3 Visioning and Voicing

"Visioning and voicing—thought and implicate order: what if our thinking at a certain point in time, that we ourselves perceive as independent from what is going on in the environment, is 'an explicate version of some more implicate order?'"[21] Bohm thinks of what we observe and take for reality as surface phenomena—explicate order—, unfolding and emerging from an underlying—implicate—order. He characterizes consciousness as a process in which at each moment, content that was previously implicate is presently explicate, and content which was previously explicate has become implicate. The word vision could mean that you are able to look at what is being said in the group/in the organization/in society from these perspectives, to see the larger creative cycles, the implicate order. "The application in dialogue of this principle begins with the practice of voicing, of listening for and speaking my authentic voice, which ultimately flows from the implicate order."[22] Ask yourself and listen: "What is expressed here as a common theme—expressing an implicate order message—through the wording of the participants in a dialogue?

In our sessions with leaders, we pay explicit attention to articulating individual and collective insights accurately in the different phases of the dialogue. What we practice is formulating insights, based on experiences during the meeting. It is practicing verbalizing what goes on in and between you in the team. Sometimes we are surprised, as insights emerge that were marginal in the conversation or never mentioned before. What we also practice is unfocused listening. After each participant has verbalized new insights, we ask the group to voice the 'story of the team', the implicit themes and topics in the group as a whole. Often these insights and collective observations are remarkable, as they open up a new dimension in the group. Some people are capable of verbalizing new insights immediately, others need time for digesting what happened. We don't push anybody in this process, we only recommend to be aware of upcoming insights, feelings and actions, and to write it down.

---

[21] Isaacs 1999.
[22] Isaacs 1999.

- Using the Word 'I'

Many people, even if they assert something very important about their view on the company or their private life, don't use 'I'. Instead they say 'you'. An important condition for a good dialogue is that it is not only about your 'ego' or your fixed views in life and organizations. To use 'I' in the right way is not so simple. Using the power of 'I', in combination with your name, is a very influential way of pronouncing what you want to say. Being humble and modest on the other hand, how do you reconcile these two? Getting used to be silent if you don't have to speak, voice softly, quietly, consciously choosing the right words to express your message, being careful in how you say it. Consistently expressing yourself on the verbal and the non-verbal level, being ONE. Using in a supple way I/Me, You, We, It, 'to the point', as intended. Once you are aware of the impact of how you speak, you start choosing your words more carefully.

Edgar Schein made the following statement about dialogue in the process of change in organizations: "I will also argue that dialogue is necessary as a vehicle for understanding cultures and subcultures, and that organizational learning will ultimately depend on such cultural understanding."[23] In his view, dialogue takes a central element of any model of organizational transformation. Schein is convinced of the importance of dialogue in changing cultures in organization. The role of the executive level is important, although they are very often reluctant in engaging in this kind of collective self-reflective analysis. For leaders to reveal to others and to themselves that they do not understand all of the assumptions on which they base action, and that they make mistakes in their thinking can be profoundly threatening, and elevating if they get across that block. Organizations do learn with a set of assumptions that characterizes their present culture and subcultures. But if any new organizational responses are needed that involve changes in cultural assumptions or learning across subcultural boundaries, dialogue must be viewed as an essential component of that learning. "Dialogue lies at the core of organizational learning. Without dialogue, individuals and groups cannot effectively exchange ideas or develop shared understanding. Although dialogue has been addressed in organizational learning literature it has not been examined explicitly as the core mechanism by which strategic leaders influence the learning process at and between individual, group and organizational level."[24] We aim to contribute to a better understanding of dialogue at the heart of the process of leading and learning. Participants learn to suspend their assumptions, judgments, reactions, impulses, emotions in this process. Attending, noticing and becoming aware of what is going on in yourself and the group. It implies setting energy free to observe the processes in you and others, rationally, emotionally, and physically. Observing without

---

[23]Schein 1993, 27.

[24]Parry 2011, 63.

judging right or wrong. Your thoughts, physical sensations and emotions are exposed so they can be seen by yourself and sometimes by others in the meeting. Your colleagues/peers become a mirror, reflecting the content of your thoughts and the underlying structures. A most remarkable phenomenon is *that in the process of being observed, the process changes.*[25] Once you developed the capability of real time attending your thoughts, feelings/emotions and actions (= reflection *in* action), they will *spontaneously* transform. In modern complex organizations, we need leaders that are able to "detect emergent, unintended dynamics and create dialogue between corporate objectives and these autonomous forces."[26] Leading complexity involves negotiating a company's way forward through the tensions between leaders' plan and self-organized emergence. "These tensions, themselves, become a valued vehicle for questioning and revising leadership strategies that fail to appropriately reflect the complexities of the organization seeking to achieve them."[27]

6.3 When to Apply the Dialogical Leadership Approach?

Scharmer and Kaufer[28] emphasize that complex problems require complex solutions. You cannot apply a single-focus approach. You have to be multilingual and show an approach whereby you broaden and deepen the definition of the issue at hand in order to get all the relevant parties committed to participate—to create participative power. In line with Grint, Kahane, Scharmer and Kaufer, and Heifetz, Grashow and Linsky[29] we explore this dialogical approach. *Wicked issues must be approached with dialogue as leadership skill.* By using *generative dialogue* and *dialogical self-approach*, we refer to recent innovative trends in human and organizational development to demonstrate that dialogue in this sense is condition zero for change and transformation.

Keith Grint distinguishes between different types of issues leaders in business and politics or society are faced with. Each of these issues requires a different form of leadership. *Tame issues* can be handled with routine and proper management, we know how to tackle them. *Crises* require forceful action, control and an immediate response. *Wicked problems* are in a category where the solution is shrouded in mystery (Fig. 6.2).

---

[25]Bojer et al. 2008, 124.
[26]Buckle-Henning and Dugan 2007, 411.
[27]Henning and Dugan 2007, 411.
[28]Scharmer and Kaufer 2013.
[29]Grint 2005, 2010a; Kahane 2007; Heifetz et al. 2009.

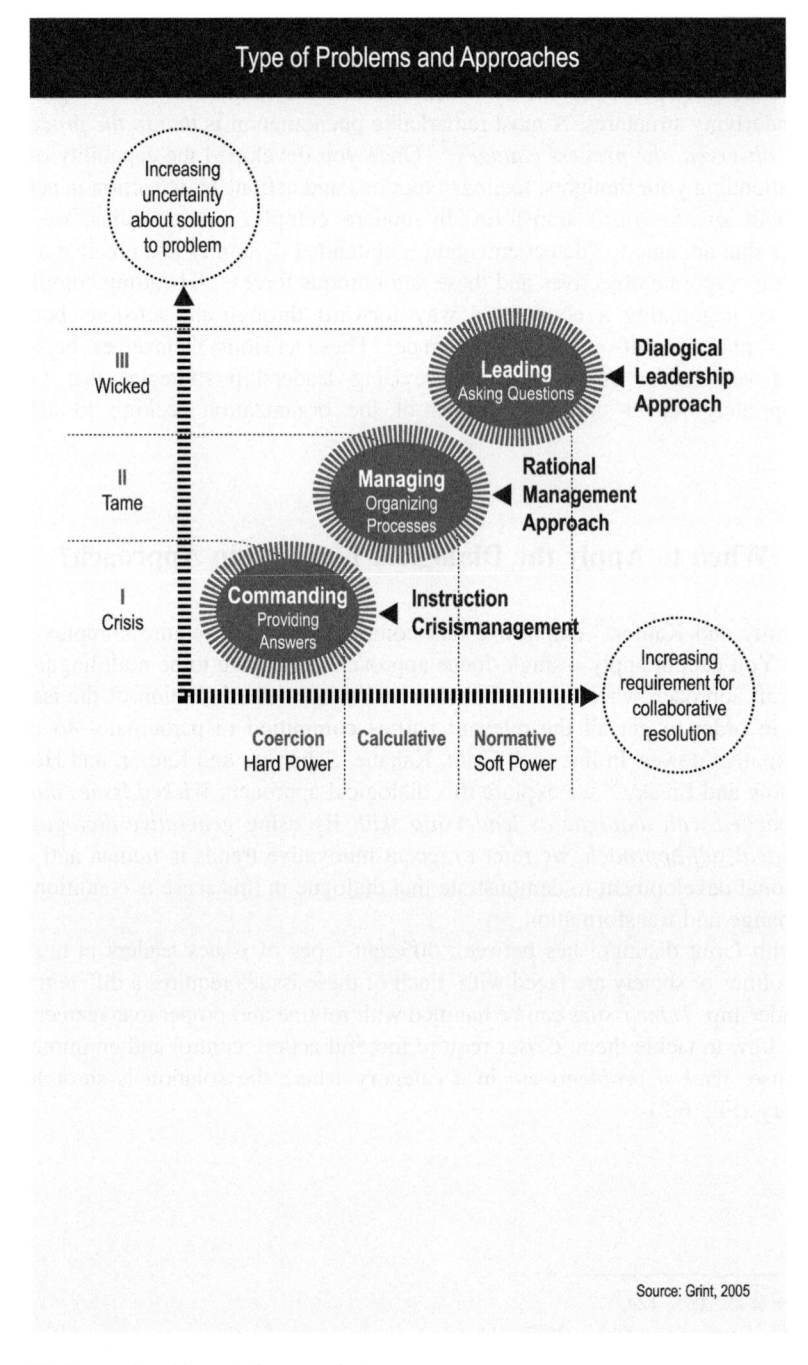

Fig. 6.2 Type of problems and approaches

6.3.1 Taking a Bird's Eye View

Taking a bird's eye view, we see many modern managers behaving as if crisis is universal and omnipresent. The time and calmness required to reflect are ignored, opinions and insights of others—or one's own intuition—only half heard. I argue for training leaders to intentionally choose their style dependent on the definition of the issue at hand and the context of organizational, cultural and societal development: decisive action as instruction, disciplined management as rational discussion, or leadership in the form of dialogue. Good leadership means being capable of considering an issue from the outside while still being involved enough to take decisions and act—rising above and beyond your own economic, cultural and scientific thought pattern and letting in a new 'paradigm'. Taking a new perspective, for yourself and in conversation with your team and organization. The rapidly changing world we live in offers us a necessity and an option, because the financial, ecological and ethical crises are congesting the prosperity machine. Consumers no longer trust their governments, banks and companies. We may have achieved progress, the by-product has been increasing depression and fear among people. The quality of leadership in the future requires a distinction between different styles, deliberately using your potential to know rationally and to experience intuitively. Not falling back into the usual crisis-like state! Leaders will have to be able to switch their connectivity with the Internet world on and off at will, depending on the issues they are faced with.

6.3.2 From 'What' to 'Who'

Grint's issues can be classified as *critical*, *tame* or *wicked* based on two criteria: *knowledge of the solution*, and *the leadership style required to tackle them*. In a *crisis* (e.g. fire in the city) as leader(-shipteam), you have to take control of the situation, commandeering, hard power and coercion are effective answers to solve the problem. If we are faced with a *tame* problem, something we have seen before, where a solution is known (e.g. heart surgery), a calculative and management approach of the leader(-shipteam) will be effective. *Wicked* issues are those for which no known solution exists (e.g. hunger versus obesity on global scale; global leadership crisis); and for which leaders must not assume that they have the answers. They must empower their team to deliver, and should accept the continual review and refinement of 'clumsy' solutions as a valid way of tackling wicked issues. Many options and opinions are possible. So true leadership is needed in the sense of soft power to collectively find normative answers. In the last category of issues a dialogical leadership approach might be effective. Although CEO's are paid to have answers, their greatest contributions to organizations may be—in this line of thinking—asking the right questions and by doing so, directing the collective energy of the organization into the right direction.

Van Dijk refers to this type of issues. In her view, the most important tool of the leader is his/her 'self': "In leadership, the focus must then shift from the results achieved by leaders (the 'what') and the processes used by leaders (the 'how') to the sources from which leaders (the 'who') operate. The main leadership tool is the 'self': the state of mind of the leader as the source from which all action originates. This requires for the full human repertoire to be called on and employed: the intellect of the mind, the empathy of the heart and the spirit of the will—the driving force behind all action for both individuals and groups."[30] This is in line with Isaacs, who refers to the important role of dialogue for developing leadership. "As a leadership method, the dialogue approach differs from other methods because you must develop it within yourself, and model it for others, before you seek to apply it in the teams you lead or the problems you face. In this sense, dialogue invites you into greater balance as a leader."[31] Whether you as a leader are able to do this "depends on the ability to reconstruct and manipulate memory records in a working brain space parallel to the perceptual space, an offline holding area, where time can be suspended during a delay and decisions freed from the tyranny of immediate responses."[32] Our memory is programmed to react automatically, only if there is free space between input and output, there can be a phase of suspending your immediate responses, you automatically having a judgment. Here we see again the importance of what we described in the inner dialogue, creating free energy in terms of Libbrecht, 'ma' in terms of Morioka, to intentionally act (or not-act). In the following sections, we will take a deep dive into some case-studies to illustrate and better understand the dynamism of transformation of an individual self expressed in terms of I-positions.

6.4 Case-Studies

Society as a methaphor for the self is sensitive for both dialogue and power.

Hubert Hermans[33]

I-positioning takes place in the external and internal domain of the self, and is relational. I-positions are—purposely or by coincidence—'co-created' in the past and retained within the personal repertoire. I-positions can take a developmental influence in the repertoire of the self. Raggatt[34] distinguishes between decentering and centering processes. *Decentering* processes are "centrifugal movements that

---

[30]Van Dijk 2014.
[31]Isaacs 1999, 11.
[32]Damasio 2012, 290.
[33]A quote Hermans made during the Global Conference on Dialogical Self, Lublin, Poland, 2016.
[34]Raggatt 2012, 31.

differentiate or disorganize the existing position repertoire so that it becomes open to innovation". As an example 'I as an engineer' can be decentered by 'I as a dancing teacher', when you—suddenly—comprehend that technical rationality is not effective as a dancing teacher, but that you could apply dancing teacher skills in your role as a technical manager. *Centering* processes are described as "centripetal movements that contribute to the organization and integration of the position repertoire." As an example here 'I as a mountaineering guide' integrates two opposing I-Positions: 'I as autocratic leader' and 'I as motivated to develop people'. In this example, the man is able to reconcile his dominant push style with his wish to develop and support people in an I-position as 'mountaineer-guide'.

In my reflective-practice, I added a new process, entitled as *transpositioning* or *transposing*. I define this as "*intentionally bringing I-positions from one domain in life/work to another in order to create change in the position repertoire.*" For example, 'I as a runner' reflects on my life as 'I as a business-leader' and by this process of reflecting a new perspective emerges. The state of mind of being a 'fowler' in your private life is transpositioned to your being a 'coach' in the company. The 'energy' of one I-position is brought naturally to the other. In my view and experience, the broad applicability of the Dialogical Self Theory and Dialogical Leadership on change and transformation is exactly here. Most people use I-positions they are not aware of as such, in relation to the issue/dilemma at hand. As an example: 'I as a horseman' is—of course—known as an I-position, but not in relation to 'I as a change leader'. By connecting these I-positions in a new way is the source of change. This shift might transform the repertoire of the self, when positioned differently within the whole. This process of positioning and repositioning is enabled by a generative internal and external dialogue, where people think outside of their usual patterns and are asked to make new connections, either by somebody else (the other person) or by themselves (another I-position within the repertoire). I will describe the following cases.[35]

Case-Study *Darrell*: Sailor-Captain and General Manager

A process of centering is illustrated where we explain how a general manager shows two completely different manners of reacting on stressful events. We demonstrate how a question opens the mind and thoroughly changes a fixed mindset and how he is able to connect the mindset of the sailor-captain with that of the general manager as an example of transposing I-positions. Sect. 6.5.

Case-Study *Marc*: Engineer, Artist, and Karate-Teacher

In this section is illustrated how a position and behavioral repertoire of a leader can be expanded by connecting different I-positions with each other. Three different influencing styles of an engineer-manager, a painter-artist and a karate-teacher *within one person* are brought together into the space of internal dialogical reflection. Sect. 6.6.

---

[35]All cases are anonymized and are given a name randomly.

Case-Study *Michelle*: HR-Director and Mother
A process of getting out of balance and burned *down by stress* is illustrated as an example of de-centering. Here I illustrate how the system of an HR Leader is destabilized and the impact on her personal (burn out) and professional life as a consequence of a haunting conflict with her superior. Sect. 6.7.

Case-Study *Ian*: Changing my/our Destiny
The process of *listening to an internal voice* and promoting that voice into a central motivation in life is described in the next section. I *as changing my/our destiny*. Here is demonstrated how external voices of a father, friend and mother can be integrated in a position repertoire and have a strong influence on someone's life. Sect. 6.8.

Case-Study *Nicholas*: Listening to my Inner Voice
In the last section, I explain how one of my partners in dialogue starts looking for what brings different—opposing—voices together into one direction. How do you reconcile being stubborn and open? Sect. 6.9.

Let us have a look in detail. In all cases, it might be useful to also reflect about your own I-positions, as the topics that are described and illustrated are unique, and simultaneously examples of universal patterns in human behavior and personality.

6.5 Case-Study *Darrell*: Sailor-Captain and General Manager

A 45 year-old male engineer—Darrell—works for a multinational where he is responsible for medical instruments across Europe.[36] His hope is: *"how can I recover my 'I'"*? Although he is very successful as a leader in his local companies, he does not feel happy in his role. Darrell thinks about taking a sabbatical to sail around the world, to make the trip of his life. As an engineer, he tends to solve issues in a rational way, but he is often confronted with emotional issues in his daily leading practices.

6.5.1 "I Lost My I"

The dialogue revealed a basic stress in his functioning to involve the roles of *general manager* and *sailor-captain* (Fig. 6.3).

As *general manager*, Darrell feels stressed. In this I-position, he feels generally negative stress. His emotions become even more stressed if hierarchically higher leaders give instructions out of sync with what he thinks is good for the company.

---

[36] Van Loon and Van Dijk 2015. This case was originally published in the *Journal for Leadership Accountability and Ethics* Vol. 12(3), 69–70. The study is expanded with additional data and interpretation.

6.5 Case-Study *Darrell*: Sailor-Captain and General Manager 173

Case-Study Darrell 1

"I lost my I"

- Rational engineer
- Unhappy in his current role
- Reacting emotionally
- Wanting to take a sabbatical
- How can I recover my I?

I as a Sailor Captain | I as a General Manager

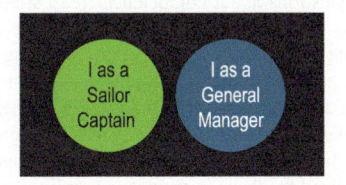

Fig. 6.3 Case-Study Darrell 1

He expresses: "I don't accept corporate directions, which are not aligned with my strategy." He does not accept this type of influence and his stress becomes ineffective as he vents his emotions on his environment. In his I-position as *sailor-captain* his stress is positive. Darrell feels relaxed, stays calm even in stormy weather and dangerous situations over which he has no influence.

6.5.2 Transposing Sailor-Captain into General Manager

A process of transpositioning could start as soon as Darrell understood how he exposed two completely different reactions to situations out of his control: hierarchical higher instructions and the weather. We asked him the question: "how can a man who stays calm and relaxed in physically dangerous and complex situations, be so emotionally unhinged by his superiors giving him conflicting assignments?" By creating the awareness during the dialogue and allowing the process of thinking and feeling to slow down, Darrell—as in a shock—became aware of this discrepancy between the different I-positions. It likewise revealed the ineffectiveness of his beliefs, feelings, and emotions of *the general manager*-position and their potential in the "I as the *sailor-captain*"-position when transposed to the role "I as *general manager*". Reconciliation of these two I-positions led to the leader's mindset being more complete. By metaphorically transposing the mindset of the *sailor-captain* to the *general manager-position,* a positive impact became sensible and visible. These I-positions equally represent him, but they were acting in different, not connected domains of the self (internal and external) (Fig. 6.4).

Observations of his team and superiors confirmed a robust behavioral change. Darrell said *the question* completely transformed his emotional state. In the process of his development as a leader, he also gathered feedback in a systematic way through a 360° degree questionnaire.[37] The profile on the scorings was strong on the operational and strategic competences. His lower scores were on personal leadership and leading and developing people. This was illustrated by feedback

---

[37] A 360° questionnaire gathers information about your performance in a systematic way, based on specific questions about competences (e.g. strategic leadership, people leadership, result oriented leadership, personal leadership) and observable leadership behaviors (e.g. 'Uses financial analysis to evaluate strategic choices', 'creates a feeling of energy, excitement and personal investment', 'coaches people in the development of their skills', etcetera). People rate themselves on a five-point scale, and are subject to rating of their superior, their peers and their direct reports, as well as clients or other people outside the organization that are able to give feedback based on observed behaviors. In a 360 feedback respondents also have the opportunity to give specific individualized feedback in their own wordings. (e.g. 'you are a good team-player', 'you could take decisions faster, and you hesitate in taking difficult decisions about people'). A 360 tool is a valuable tool to validate changes of people, in particular as it compares the self-rating with how you are perceived by your environment. The feedback must be part of a dialogue, not just a report to read. The conversation (dialogue/discussion) is the most important part of the tool, as this determines the impact.

6.5 Case-Study *Darrell*: Sailor-Captain and General Manager

Case-Study Darrell 2

Transposing Sailor Captain into General Manager

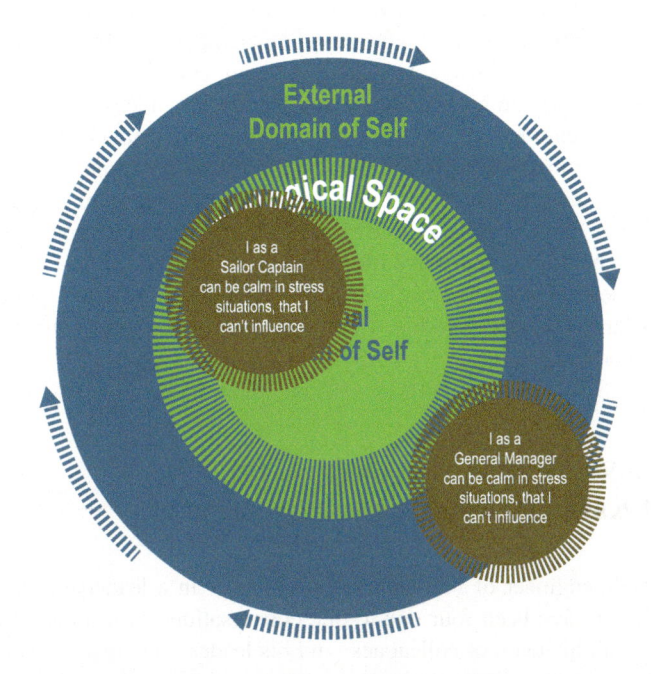

External Domain of Self

...nical Space

I as a Sailor Captain can be calm in stress situations, that I can't influence

...al ...of Self

I as a General Manager can be calm in stress situations, that I can't influence

Golden Question:
"How can a man who stays calm and relaxed in physically dangerous and complex situations be so emotionally unhinged by his superiors giving him conflicting assignments?"

Positive Stress

I as a Sailor Captain

I accept the weather although I don't have Influence

Negative Stress

I as a General Manager

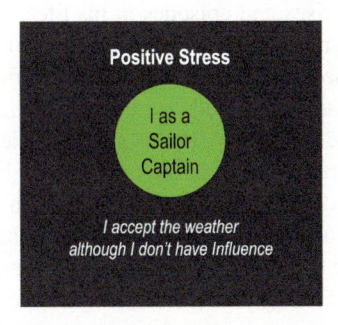

I don't accept Corporate Directions, that are not aligned with my Strategy

Fig. 6.4 Case-Study Darrell 2

comments, such as "You excel, when you are acting close to the business"; "Operationally, you are very strong, you have great business knowledge and experience"; "You demonstrate a clear understanding of the strategy of the company"; "You have a strong drive for success"; "Be careful with showing your level of frustration with 'corporate' (HQ) and the message you send to your people, as they 'read' your frustration and get worried"; "Build in some space/rest/patience in the way you perform, to make you more efficient; think about your work-life balance"; "React less impulsive and less emotional, even when you are right!"

Later, his superior and his peers gave him feedback in a leadership development session with the entire team, that he had become more patient. They reported a significant change in his behavior, in the sense that he—confronted with guidelines from corporate—reacted more controlled, less emotional and more efficient. He also got the feedback that his presence during the meetings was more open and friendly. From his team members, he received feedback that he had become calmer, and that his ceaseless determination to work was tempered. He himself also reported that his work-life balance was more stable. Darrell decided to take the sabbatical to sail around the world.

6.6 Case-Study *Marc*: Engineer, Artist, and Karate-Teacher

Marc is a male engineer of 55, when he participates in a leadership development project.[38] There have been four one-to-one conversations over a period of a year, one session with his team of colleagues (and his leader), one team session with his team-members in the European countries (where he was the leader). He is responsible for a large part of an engineering organization's European business. He describes himself as "enjoy[ing] life. Without passion, color and fun, I can't live. I am the main actor in my life, as you are 'playing' your life as a human being. Life is not easy." He went through a series of crises and episodes in his life/career. His father died when he was 16 years old. He married early, from this first marriage a son was born. Later he got divorced, married twice more. There is a daughter from his second marriage. Marc describes himself as impulsive. In his youth, he was aggressive and tried to find a way to release his energy. He became a karate-fighter, won several awards as black belt karate practitioner. He started his own business, became very successful. He likes 'the good life'. He is impulsive; he—in his own words—cannot accept stupidity. In the dialogue about his leadership, he has several statements about him being a leader: "I like to lead/coach." "As an *engineer*, I don't like grey. I am direct. It's black or white." During the conversation, he spoke about

---

[38]Van Loon and Van Dijk 2015. This case was originally published in the *Journal for Leadership Accountability and Ethics* Vol. 12(3), 70–72. The study is expanded with additional data and interpretation.

his passion for painting and that he had been a karate teacher. He was not used to reflect about his leadership career and his life in this 'dialogical way'. Marc realized during conversations that 'he has to open up more for his colleagues in the process of collaborating'.

6.6.1 "I Have to Open Up"

He formulated three I-positions:

- "I as an *engineer/Managing Director*: black/white, I don't like the grey, I am direct."
- "I as a karate teacher: respect, protocol is important; I have my feet always on the ground, stability."
- "I as an artist (painter): I like passion, color, expression; this is my 'crazy part'"(Fig. 6.5).

Marc expresses that he wants to open up more for his colleagues in the process of collaborating. We see how these three I-positions result in a different profile of leading. His I-positions are represented in terms of his leadership styles. In our meetings with leaders, we invite them to think about their styles (vision, push, and pull) in terms of how much energy they spend in each of them. The outcome of this process of self-assessment is a series of percentages.[39] Leaders become more aware of the complementarity of their styles, especially when applied to more than one I-position and in the context of the team, and when this is validated in the context of their team/organization by conversations and feedback.

6.6.2 The Painter Balances the Engineer

As an *engineer*, Marc is primarily rational and visionary (60% vision); as an artist and *painter*, he is more intuitive and open to all impressions (60% pull); as *karate teacher*, he is dominant and physically strongly present (60% push) (Fig. 6.6).

By developing a meta-position and combining the three I-positions, Marc realized the necessity of becoming more complementary and how the three could

---

[39]Van Loon 2006. Here a method to (self-)assess leadership styles and sources is described, by dividing 100% amongst 'giving direction'—'pushing'—'pulling'. And 100% for 'rationality'(knowing by rational analysis, head, thinking)—'intuition' (experiencing by intuition, heart, feeling) —'non-verbal' (doing by physical presence, hands, acting). By assessing yourself (and others) in different I-positions (roles), people develop an increased awareness of patterns in their knowing, experiencing and doing, which they can validate in conversations with themselves, with superiors, peers, employees, and other stakeholders. In a leadership development session with a team, this conversation is a fixed part of the agenda. In Marc's case-study this procedure is illustrated.

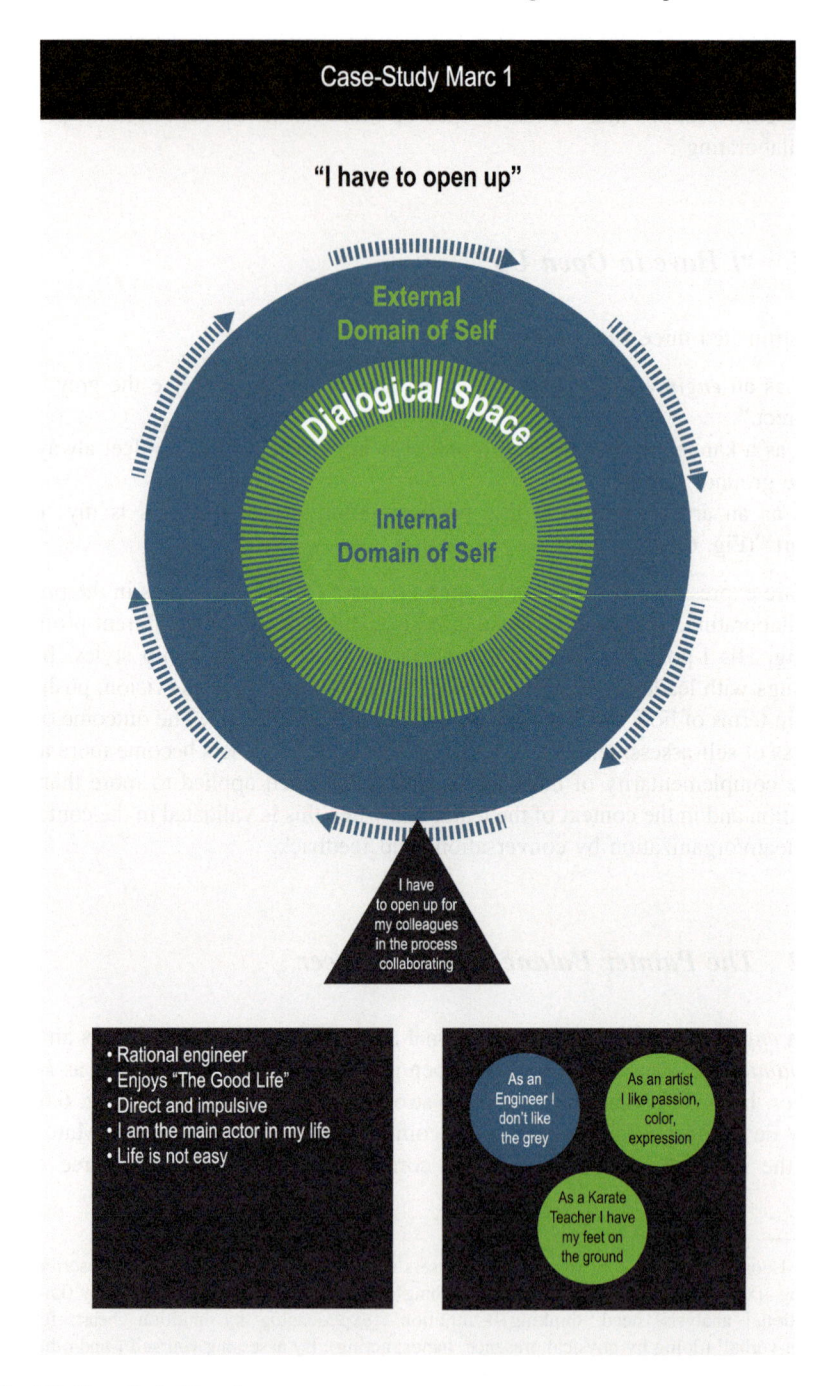

Fig. 6.5 Case-Study Marc 1

6.6 Case-Study *Marc*: Engineer, Artist, and Karate-Teacher

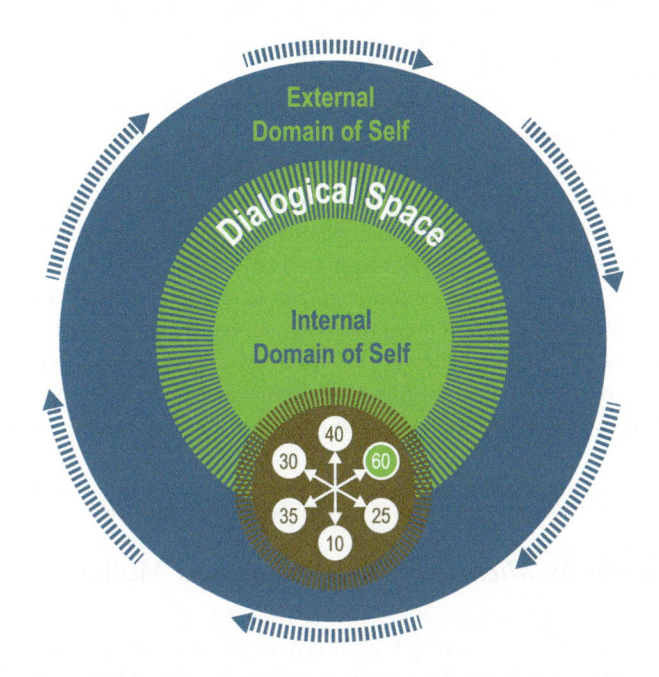

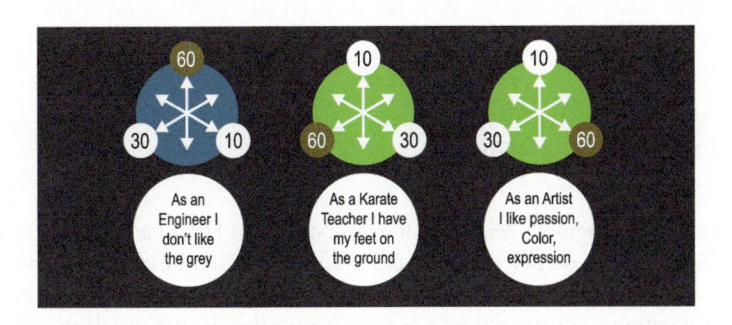

Fig. 6.6 Case-Study Marc 2

reinforce each other and become one. In terms of percentages, he made the following scores. Leadership *styles*: vision 40%, push 35% and pull 25%. S*ources* of influencing: rationality 30%, intuition 60% and non-verbal 10%. He applied this intensified awareness immediately. In his management team meetings, he opened up more about his artistic side—he showed some of his canvases and spoke about his passion. Marc became more aware of the—unintended—impact of his non-verbal behavior—he wears the posture and directive style of the karate teacher on his sleeve.

There were still some tough challenges awaiting him, as his impulsiveness, strong non-verbal presence, and tendency to push often ruled primarily his impact. His boss recommended him to ask for more feedback and experiment with asking more open questions, instead of the more pushing way of instructing his people.

Using the internal and external dialogue to integrate the three I-positions initiated Marc to feel more 'as one'. His team and colleagues now regard him as more holistic, as the *painter* balances the *engineer* in a more natural way. His team specifically said they liked him more this way, although his being—too—dominant permanently lurked in the shadows—the non-verbal part of human influencing is difficult to change. The basic insights Marc immediately started to practice were to open up more when collaborating and to adapt more effective and attuned leadership styles.

6.7 Case-Study *Michelle*: HR-Director and Mother

Michelle is 34 as we meet, and a high potential HR-director by growing into the role step by step internally in the organization. She is a psychologist with a passion for personal development and coaching. In the context of an international organization, she is responsible for Switzerland for HR in four regions. Over a period of three years, we had several bilateral conversations plus team sessions with the local management team, one session with her own HR-team. Michelle is very eager to learn and develop.

6.7.1 "I as Burned Out"

Here how 'I as a mother' decenters the system of the HR Leader is demonstrated and has deep impact on her personal and professional life: burn out, catalyzed by a conflict with her superior. In the leadership dialogue, she formulated two contrasting I-positions. Her formal role in the organization is that of HR-director: '*I as an HR-director*'. She also formulated an I-position about her being a mother: '*I as a mother*'. The difference between these two I-positions led to an internal and external conflict, resulting in a decentering of the position repertoire, ending in a

6.7 Case-Study *Michelle*: HR-Director and Mother

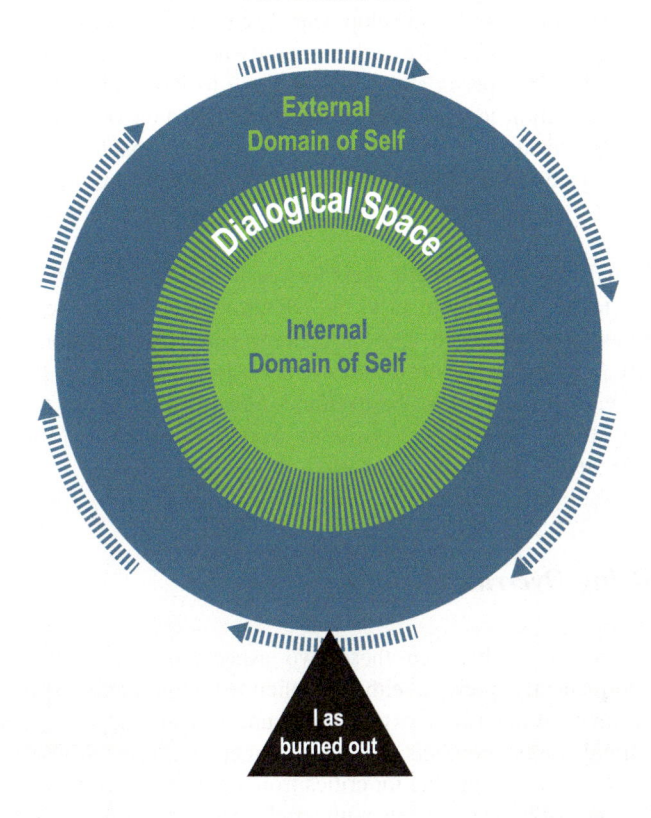

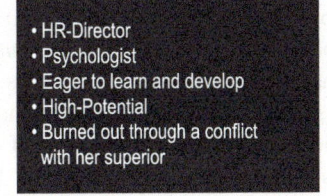

Fig. 6.7 Case-Study Michelle 1

burn out situation. In the following section, we will analyze this aspect of her narrative (Fig. 6.7).

Let's have a closer look at Michelle's repertoire of I-positions, in particular two aspects of a *decentering* process in her development, a conflict between *dependency and independency*. Although the case is more comprehensive, we focus here only on the *decentering* aspect of her development. The most important I-position is '*I as a mother*'. Here she refers to her role in the family being quite important. She takes this role seriously. She speaks about her ambition to move up the organizational ladder and her ambition to become a professional HR director and a professional coach in the organization. At home, she is extravert, capable of managing the family in an effective way. She formulated as characteristic I-positions: '*I as independent*', '*I as extravert and ambitious*', '*I as a coach*' and '*I as a professional*'.

In her formal HR-role, Michelle feels less assured and self-confident. This primarily refers to her managerial tasks as HR-director, such as the more formal rulings she has to get arranged, like introducing new HR-regulations and negotiating with HQ. In these responsibilities, she feels dependent on the Managing Director of the local company in Switzerland. She is aware of her emotional vulnerability for stress. Two more I-positions were formulated as '*I as emotional vulnerable for stress*' and '*I as dependent*'.

6.7.2 "Being Overruled"

Over time, the tension between these two aspects of her position repertoire developed permanently present, either implicit or in a more explicit manner. Especially in times of intensified external pressure, as with budgeting, performance appraisals, fraud cases, conflicts in the management team, Michelle felt less self-confident and was susceptible for critics from her boss. At one moment in time, he overruled some of her agreements with employees without having informed her. He also did not ask her for her view on the case. This was filling the bucket over the edge. She could not come to work for a longer period: she felt burned out by stress (Fig. 6.8).

Analyzing this process in terms of dialogical self terminology. '*I as a mother*' and '*I as an HR-director*' are opposing I-positions. '*I as extravert and ambitious*' and '*I as independent*' are I-positions in the internal domain of self. Observe that her independency was not clearly visible at work, unless in her professional role as a coach and trainer. These are driving and highly energetic aspects of her life, expressed in two core-positions '*I as a coach*' and '*I as a professional*'. Much of what she does in and how she feels about her professional life depends on these qualities. Hidden behind '*I as an HR-director*' are two I-positions, destabilizing her effectiveness: '*I as dependent*' and '*I as emotional vulnerable for stress*'. In the figure is symbolized how this negative results in a burn out. Her position repertoire is *decentered* in such a manner that it broke down. Michelle was not able to start a

6.7 Case-Study *Michelle*: HR-Director and Mother

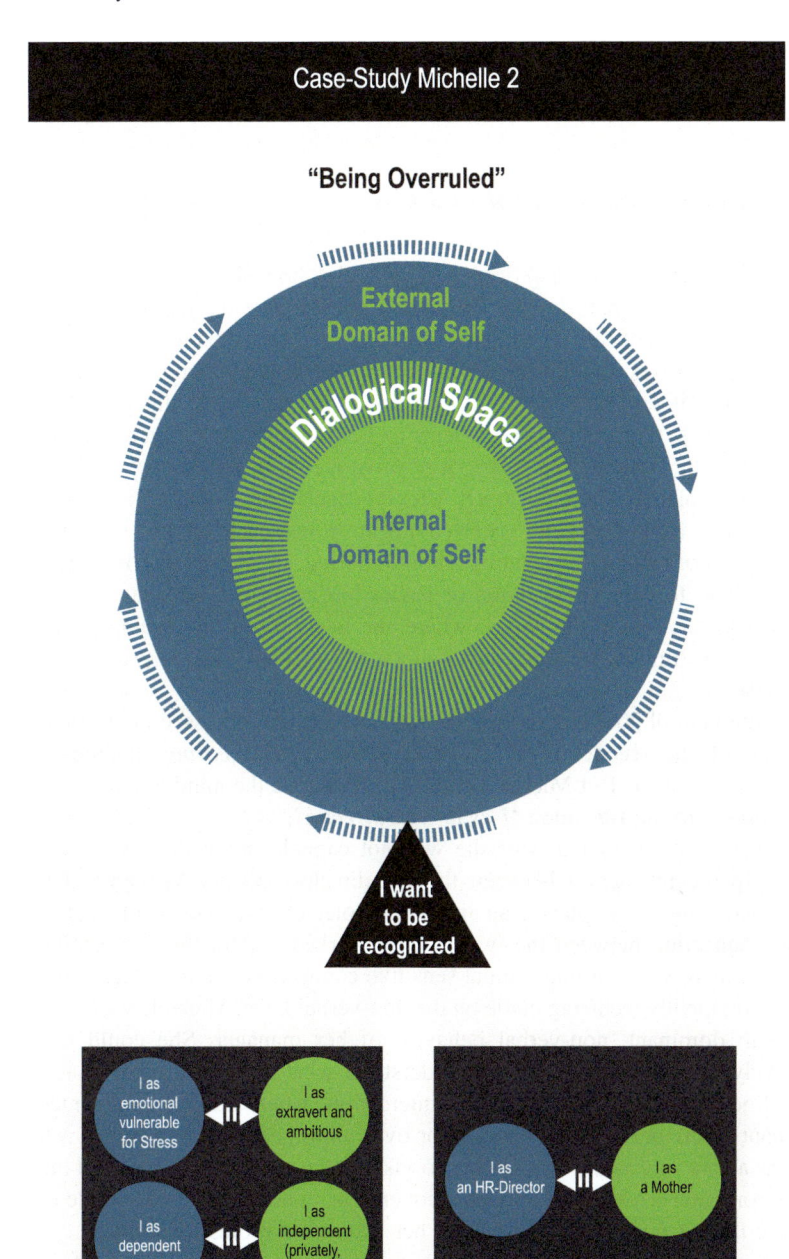

Fig. 6.8 Case-Study Michelle 2

reconciliation of I-positions alone. Her system was severely disorganized and she needed counselling support to get back on track.

6.7.3 Reconciling Control and Care

We analyze this case one step deeper to get a clue how she decentered as a strong and independent woman, as Michelle could not stabilize the tensions in the outer and inner domains of self. The most important one is that she felt *not recognized by her manager*. It was difficult for her to cope with this emotional pressure, as in her HR-role she felt dependent on his assessment and judgment. In this period, she got a 360° feedback, with negative comments on her formal functioning as HR-director. In the figure this is indicated. She got positive feedback for competencies such as analyzing problems, communicating, listening, sensitivity, sociability and integrity. On the other hand, Michelle received negative feedback on her capabilities in planning and organizing, delegating and monitoring. In her role as HR-director, she primarily had to *control*. In terms of leadership roles, she is mostly a *manager*. Opposed to this role is the *coach*, where she is strong in developing people, she feels as an instrument for their development. In this role, she is primarily *caring* (Fig. 6.9).

The moment of potential transpositioning, which we addressed in our dialogues, was that of the reconciliation of her *controlling* and *caring* qualities in her I-position as *mother*. But Michelle could not transpose the mind-and-heart-set of 'I *as a mother*' to the I-position '*I as an HR-director*'.

If we try to understand why she was not capable doing this, we have to go deeper. In the interaction between the HR-director and her Managing Director, *power* and *connection* played an important role. On the one hand, there was a strong connection between the two as they worked together very intensively for years and there was a strong mutual sensitive connection. On the other hand, there was a permanently recurring battle on the non-verbal level. Michelle was not able to deal with dominant, non-verbal behavior of her manager. She could not react effectively, although she rationally understood what she could have done differently. She withdraw herself from an interaction, when she was confronted with dominant behavior, such as offending or overruling people in a meeting. Although she was aware, it was difficult for her to visibly and effectively cope with this kind of confrontations. After having been recovered from her burn out, Michelle decided to leave the organization and focus on her skills as a professional coach.

Here we come to the conclusion that in a dialogue a moment of transformation can be touched, and that the partner in conversation deeply understands the insight, but is not capable of implementing it in daily functioning. Taking a look at this case from a distance and formulate a conclusion or recommendation two come to mind. The first is realizing that insight in itself is not enough to make a process of transformation happening. Sometimes counselling or psychotherapeutic support is necessary to translate insights into actions. This is closely related to the second

6.7 Case-Study *Michelle*: HR-Director and Mother

Case-Study Michelle 3

Reconciling Control and Care

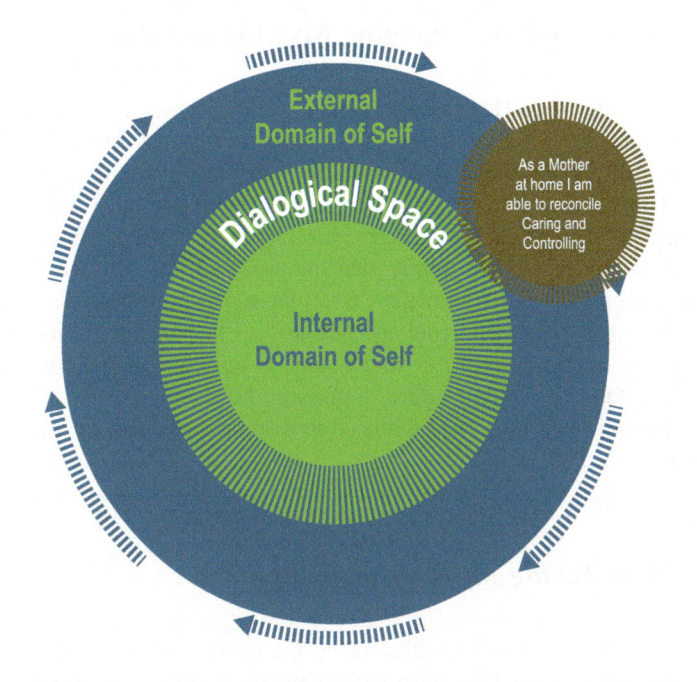

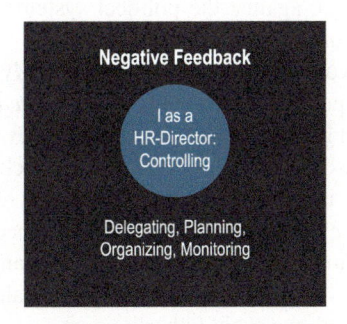

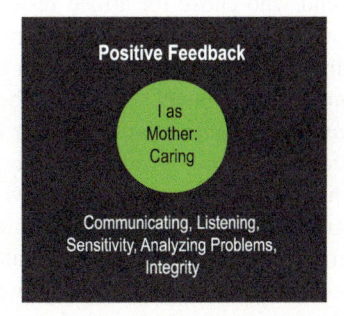

External Domain of Self

Dialogical Space

Internal Domain of Self

As a Mother at home I am able to reconcile Caring and Controlling

Negative Feedback

I as a HR-Director: Controlling

Delegating, Planning, Organizing, Monitoring

Positive Feedback

I as Mother: Caring

Communicating, Listening, Sensitivity, Analyzing Problems, Integrity

Fig. 6.9 Case-Study Michelle 3

conclusion. We have to be aware of the—often unintended—impact of non-verbal behavior. As leaders and followers, we can make a strong unintended non-verbal impact, which can destabilize the relation with other people.

6.8 Case-Study *Ian*: Changing My/Our Destiny

Ian is 45 when we meet. He is an entrepreneur, very successful in international jobs. He was promoted to a business unit responsibility in a global firm. He is Irish, lived in Dublin in a period of political instability and was as a child confronted with violence. His parents got divorced when he was a child. His father was an alcoholic. In his view as a child and adolescent, his father wasted his life with pleasure, instead of taking his responsibility. His mother took care of the family. As a relatively young man, Ian left for the US to play sports professionally, but changed after the first year into engineering and business, as he realized his added value for society would be higher in a role as a leader of an international company. He is married and has two children. Here, I illustrate how *others-in-the-self* promote a series of I-positions, which can be related to external positions, he was confronted with in the past. I focus on two.

6.8.1 "I as Taking My Responsibility"

The core of Ian's personal I-position repertoire consists of '*I as changing my/our destiny*'. He intensely had the wish and ambition—from very early in his life—to transform the situation in which he and his family lived into a better one. This central theme in his life originated from two people who were very influential in his life: his mother who took up her life after being divorced taking care for the family and a friend who chose for armed resistance against the political system. Around this theme, different aspects emerged in our dialogues (Fig. 6.10).

The first 'other-in-the-self' is split in two, a positive and a negative. '*My mother who created her/our own life again*' is the positive aspect, '*My father wasted his life with pleasure*' is the negative influencer in his life. Ian wanted to be *as his mother*, internalized her attitude to life, that was extremely difficult, and can be characterized as highly disciplined, collaborative, taking all opportunities and creating a good chance in her own life and that of her beloved. He did not want to become as his father, who was an alcoholic, and although he was very talented in an artistic way, he did not develop this in any way. In the same way, he internalized his mother's voice in a positive way, he pushed away his father's voice.

The second 'other-in-the-self' is negative in the sense that Ian was absolutely not willing to follow this path in his life: '*My friend who chose for armed resistance*'. Dynamically, this example had a strong influence on him, as his friend really made a decisive choice in his life, but he could not agree on the content. Ethically, he was

6.8 Case-Study *Ian*: Changing My/Our Destiny

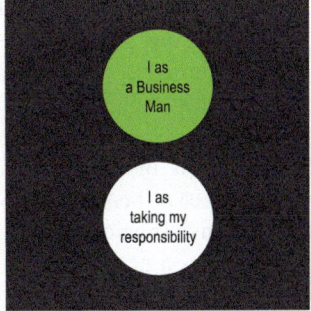

Fig. 6.10 Case-Study Ian 1

opposing armed resistance, as he had felt as a child the negative impact of physically violent and intimidating actions. Based on these three people (mother, father, and friend), he intentionally designed his own life and consciously took decisions to make that happen. As an example, he left his country at a young age, a huge step. Ian intuitively knew that he had to go overseas to develop his skills, physically as a basketball player, and intellectually as an engineer and as a business man. '*I as taking my responsibility*', '*I as a business man*' and '*I as an engineer*' are three I-positions that express this.

6.8.2 "Improving the Quality of Life"

Additionally some I-positions can be grouped around the core: '*I as changing my/our destiny*' and '*improving the quality of life/supporting people*'. The first one is '*I am seen as a leader*'. From his early youth, others in the village looked at Ian as their leader, in sports, in conflicts children have, in solving issues at hand. He was seen as somebody who was able to bring people together. In his own words, he was not so much motivated to present himself as a leader, he was pulled into that role by others around him. In the position repertoire these aspects are visible in '*I as bringing people together*', *I as reconciling different views*' (Fig. 6.11).

Motivating for his quest in life are two more aspects: '*I as continuous learning*' and '*I as exploring cultures*'. Ian's attitude is to be continuously open for new experiences, emotionally and intellectually.

Reflecting on this case, some observations come to mind.

Negative external experiences in his life functioned as external promotor-positions, which were transformed into a positive purpose setting direction for himself. A strong ethical consciousness is present from his early youth, both in terms of supporting his mother and the family as in rejecting the violence as a way to change the future. We talked about this in our dialogues, he said that the ethical conscience simply is present in him, when I asked him about the origin. "It is naturally present in me, a sense of justice and unfairness, and I oppose against it by doing good, by bringing people together, by reconciling opposites."

The case illustrates that "the child is initially oriented towards the other, is shaped by the other's speech and actions. But soon the child starts to disregard the other for the sake of an 'internal' world, in which the other may be reconstructed or imagined."[40] In this case, his mother's voice was internalized and could function as a promotor for transformation in his life, his father's and friend's voices were rejected and served as a negative point of reference for Ian's future development.

As a last observation, evaluating your life narrative and reconstructing this in terms of I-positions gives people an insight in their lives that normally is not present. By bringing more core-influences together and expressing a general theme

---

[40]Raggatt 2012, 34.

6.8 Case-Study *Ian*: Changing My/Our Destiny

Case-Study Ian 2

"Improving the Quality of Life"

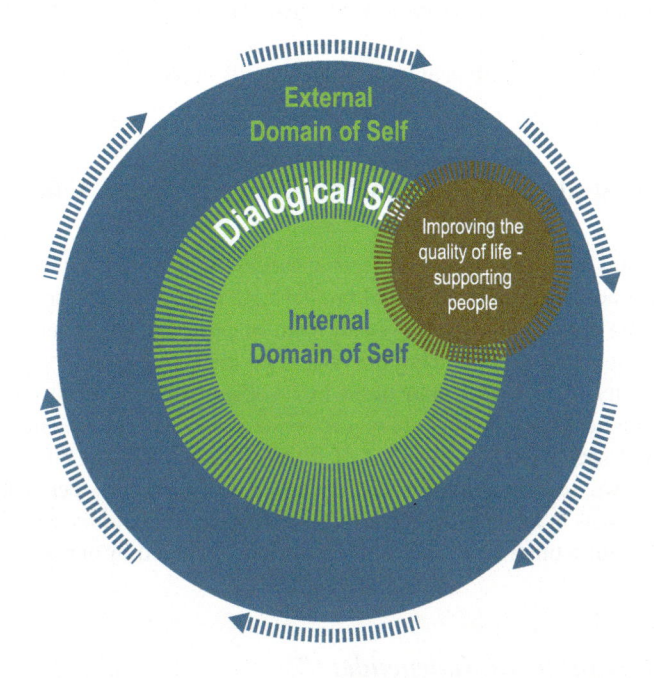

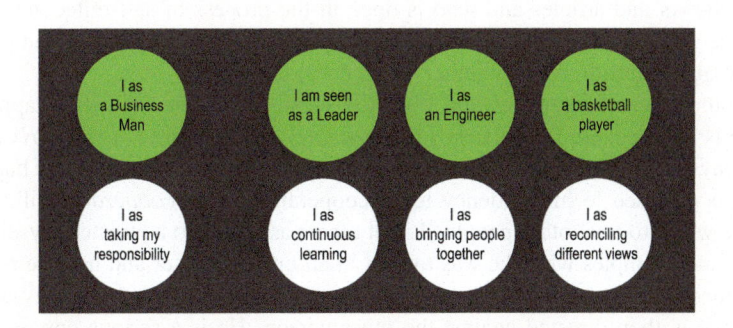

- External Domain of Self
- Dialogical Sr...
- Internal Domain of Self
- Improving the quality of life - supporting people

- I as a Business Man
- I am seen as a Leader
- I as an Engineer
- I as a basketball player
- I as taking my responsibility
- I as continuous learning
- I as bringing people together
- I as reconciling different views

Fig. 6.11 Case-Study Ian 2

for your life in a slogan is a real challenge. You can experience this if you try to do this for your own life. In the phase of a dialogue, where 'meaning flows between partners in conversation' such a life slogan 'emerges', comes to voicing spontaneously, without effort, within a dialogic atmosphere. Here the concept of 'ma' comes to life: space is created *in* time, the process is *slowed* down, and partners in dialogue are able to listen to the flow of meaning being expressed. That is 'new meaning flowing' in terms of Bohm and Isaacs. Giving expression to the 'field awareness', in terms of Libbrecht, to activate what Bohm calls a participative mode.

6.9 Case-Study *Nicholas*: Listening to My Inner Voice

Nicholas is mid-fifty when we meet. He is a successful engineer with a strong track record in technological innovation and projects. He is responsible for innovation in Europe for the company. He has a small team of professionals around him. Most important assignment is convincing the board and managing directors on peer level of the necessity of technical innovation in a conservative technical environment, where people tend to do what they did yesterday in terms of entrepreneurial visioning and strategy. Over a period of a year, we had several bilateral conversations plus two sessions with his team. The core of Nicholas' personal position repertoire consists in the tension between '*I as listening to my inner voice*' and '*I as a fighter*'. Around this theme, different I-positions emerged in our dialogue.

6.9.1 "I Want to Be Independent"

One theme in his self-narrative is '*I as careful*' as opposed to '*I as willing to be independent*'. In our conversations, he appears to be an in-depth thinker who reads lots of books and articles and who is open in the process of self-reflecting. In the dialogue, he is a careful, lively conversation partner and visibly enjoys the process of dialoguing and thinking together. (Fig. 6.12)

Another pair of opposites and potential tension is related to what happens if justice is violated. He formulates '*I as obstinate*' as opposed to '*I regularly reflect about myself*'. Nicholas describes himself as impatient and irritated if this happens, which is opposed to his tendency to be cooperative. '*I as cooperative*' illustrates how he wants to treat other people "I treat others as I want to be treated myself". He gave some examples when he was treated in an unfair manner and how he reacted. From these stories, you could sense that the extraverted energy he usually used to cooperate is then directed against the other person. He is a serious opponent. He formulates: "I am not strong in dealing with unfairness". If that happens he transforms into a 'fighter'. This is in line with how he describes his core values: freedom to choose, trust, ethics and justice. He is convinced that it is not allowed to violate these values, for nobody. When he is however confronted with a violation of his core values, his cooperative attitude changes instantly in the opposite: he becomes a fighter and obstinate.

So, although Nicholas is characterized by "I am very open, I can have chats with everybody," and, "Once people have given trust, you can't shame that," he can be very impatient and stubborn. He describes himself as a fighter, with positive and negative aspects. In his view this refers to his willingness to be independent. His career was developed in this way, he always wanted to be as independent as possible, mentally and materially. He always was looking for new challenges, in the sense of developing *self* and developing *things*. Nicholas formulates: "I am always trying to make the world a bit better, which is my Purpose".

Then I asked him: "What connects these I-positions? What could be in the middle as an I-position that binds all these elements together and makes you 'one'?" At this moment in time, mind space was created to emerge new meaning in his system. He formulated immediately and intuitively: "*I want to be heard.*"

6.9.2 "I Want to Be Heard"

In this phase, he added the sentence that he always listened to his inner voice, as we saw before. He thinks about himself as purpose-oriented, as being able to speak from a deeper anchored source in himself. The issue for him is that regularly people did not listen to him, that he was not heard at all. In these cases—we spoke about a lot of examples—he radically switched from high on *pull* (careful cooperative) to high on *push* (inflexibly fighting) (Fig. 6.13).

What struck me in our conversations was his open mind, he was like an encyclopedia, he gathered as much information and knowledge as possible. At the same time, it was not easy for him to be silent and truly listen to what was said. A moment of transformation in this dialogue was the facilitator creating temporal and mental space to enable the emerging of '*I want to be heard*'. What I as partner in dialogue had to do is slowing down the tempi of talking, as his outgoing high energy did not stop spontaneously. Creating 'ma' enabled him to find an inner positioning.

6.10 Future Research

Systematically and experimentally exploring the role of dialogue in strategic organizational change and transformation projects might be an important object for future research on how to develop (position/re-position) external and internal I-positions, necessary for the process of transformation, against the background of

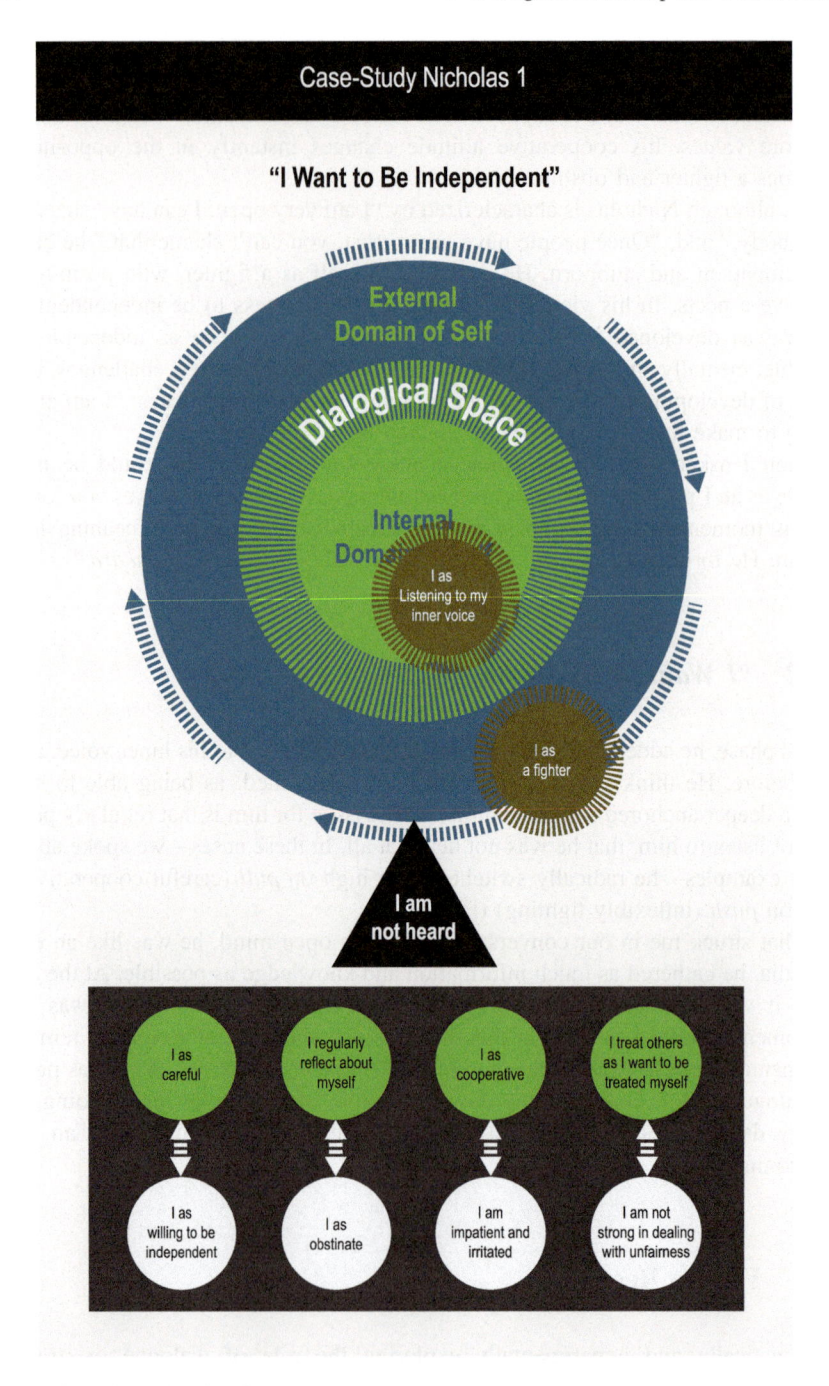

Fig. 6.12 Case-Study Nicholas 1

6.10 Future Research

Case-Study Nicholas 2

"I want to be Heard"

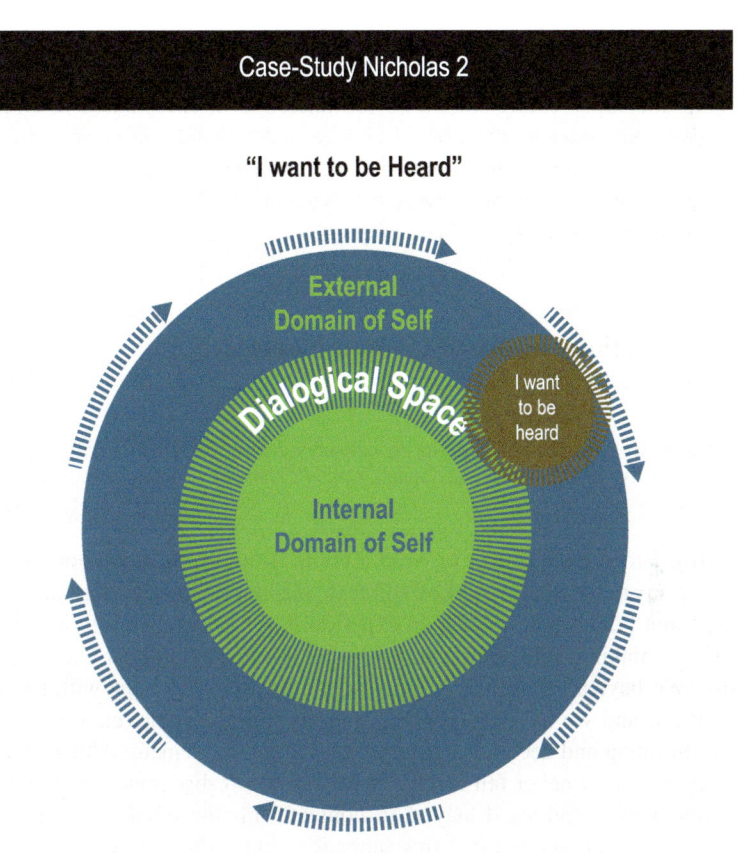

- External Domain of Self
- Dialogical Space
- I want to be heard
- Internal Domain of Self

- Once people have given trust you can't shame that
- I am very open; I have chats with everybody
- I am trying to make the world a bit better

Fig. 6.13 Case-Study Nicholas 2

the dialogical leadership approach. We have to look systematically at both sides of change: process, systems and structure as technical and tame problems, while leadership and followership should be formulated as wicked, adaptive challenges. Such a dynamic conceptualization of change and transformation processes might help to do more fundamental research into organizational change programs and make them more effective, inclusively the dynamics of leadership and followership with the inherent resistance in these projects.

6.11 Reflections on My Personal Narrative 5

> We comprehend so much, and we try to rationally control our life as much as possible. Simultaneously we know there is so much we can't know at all. Lyrics cherishes this.
>
> Marja Pruis[41]

In 2014, I took a sabbatical to write a book. Actually the book you are reading now was prepared in that period of stillness, meditation, and writing and walking. I realized that I did not have such an experience of free creative activity since I left university. Thinking, reflecting and writing, it felt during months like a holiday in paradise. We have a beautiful garden, I have a private workplace with lots of light and fresh air, and we have woods and rivers in the immediate environment. Each day concentrating and deconcentrating in one natural movement. Although I did my writing every day, I never felt forced. It was as if soft discipline came naturally to life in my daily activities. I stayed in contact with the office, I even did some sessions with clients while I had this sabbatical, but it did not bring me out of my quiet concentration. Each Saturday, I sat down and wrote a new strophe in a poem. Each week, I added a new phase in poetic words about what I had worked out over the week. I felt as if my rational thinking, my intuitive sensing and my Tai Chi meditation were completely integrated. I felt true happiness.

6.11.1 Solving Wicked Issues for Myself

If I look back in my life, I describe my quest as a wicked issue. I never formulated it in this way, as I had the conviction that I was able to solve it by myself and that I did not need anything apart from intelligence and discipline. Intuitively, I created an imagined aspect of myself in the I-position of Levi. That helped me, but at the same time disintegrated who I am as *one* living human being. What I now realize better than ever before is that—faced with wicked issues—silence and listening to voices

---

[41]Pruis 2016.

in and around you is critically important. I experienced that the answer is not there in my mind or will-power, but that it can be *given* in dialogue. In the original sense: listening, suspending judgments, accepting 'what is'. Through external and internal conversation an answer might emerge. You cannot guarantee success. It is not a trick. In this sense, I follow Ricard and practice *the art of meditation* "Automatic thought patterns only strengthen our dependence on causes of suffering, while regular meditation, far from bringing about any kind of stupor or destroying spontaneity, leads to the freedom that comes with mastery of the mind and inner peace."[42]

6.11.2 I Am Not a Master of My Destiny

I experienced that since I am aware and accepted that I am *not* a master of my destiny, my life opened up in a more natural way. I learned to listen what life expects from me, instead of dictating what I expect from life. That transformational turn-around took many years. I realize I could not have gone a shorter way.

In the figure below, we summarize the I-positions that are working in myself at the present time. As internal I-positions we find 'intuitive sensing' (lyrics), 'mystic moving' (Tai Chi) and 'rational thinking' (scientist), working in shifting synchronizations. All three are present in 'who I am', free from situational context. In the figure, this is represented by the inner circle. In the outer circle, the I-positions are indicated: I as a 'grandfather', a 'father' and a 'husband'. My family life is very important for me. It is my home. I as a 'professor', a 'director' and a 'leadership coach'. In my work, I can express these roles in a satisfying manner. At the top of my position repertoire I wrote 'I as a lyricist'. I experienced that this is most satisfying way of working. Sketching life and living in symbols, metaphors and images, which enables to understand life, without creating the illusion of fully mastering or grasping.

6.11.3 My Magnetic Needle

For me, the journey of change and transformation is exciting and has just begun. I feel more equipped and confident. I hope that we—as leaders, teachers and parents —reach out to people around us to enable them to find their way in an unpredictable mysterious world (Fig. 6.14).

Only if I can become silent, *my magnetic needle* might be directed by the field that I experience, and this refers to a reflective attitude. I have to open myself, to become receptive, unfocused and silent. Once that emerges, it seems as if many different I-positions naturally find their true North.

---

[42]Ricard 2011, 104.

Reflections on My Personal Narrative 5

My Magnetic Needle (2014)

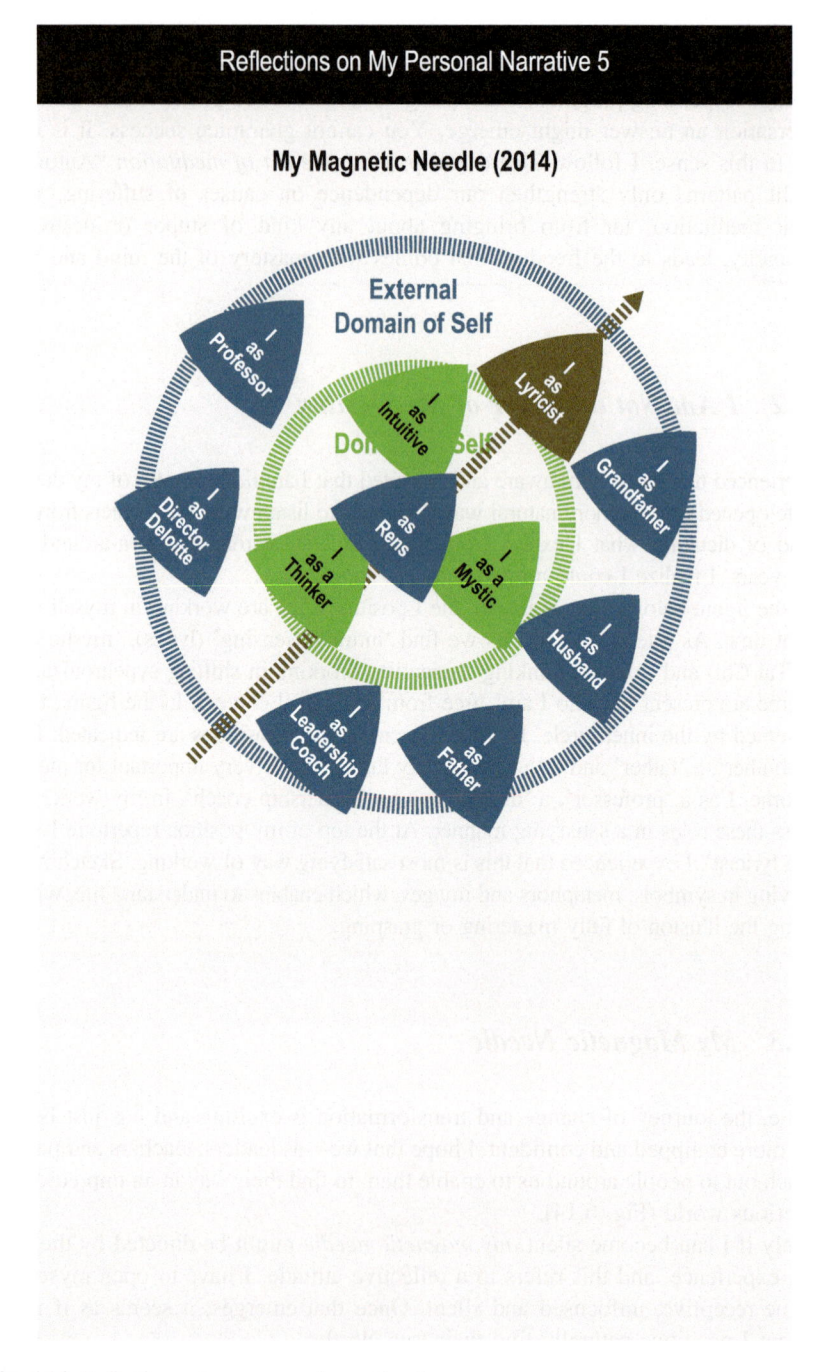

- I as Professor
- I as Lyricist
- I as Intuitive
- I as Grandfather
- I as Director Deloitte
- I as Rens
- I as a Thinker
- I as a Mystic
- I as Husband
- I as Leadership Coach
- I as Father

External Domain of Self

Domain of Self

Fig. 6.14 Reflections on my personal narrative 5

6.12 Questions for Further Reflection

- Contemplate about your work and life career in terms of *openness* for change and transformation
    - Can you give examples *when, where* and *with whom* in your life/career you were able to naturally adopt a change in your way of thinking, feeling and acting?
    - Write down examples from different periods of your life. Spend some time having a conversation about your findings with a colleague or a family member.
- Ponder about your work and life career in terms of resistance for change:
    - Can you give two examples of tough resistance against change? W*hen, where* and *with whom* in your life/career? Try to deeply understand what the source of resistance was. Look at your 'self' as if it was a good friend asking for advice.
    - Write down some insights and actions.
- Start a conversation with a friend and a colleague about '*willingness and resistance' to change*
    - Look for moments of change in your life, and divide your life in episodes, marked by these moments.
    - Try to find a title for each period.
    - Give each period a score of happiness (between 1 and 10).
    - Give each period a score in terms of effectiveness (between 1 and 10).
    - Write down some insights based on this view on your life.

References

Bojer, M., Roehl, H., Knuth-Holesen, M., & Magner, C. (2008). *Mapping dialogue: Essential tools for social change*. Chagrin Falls, Ohio: TAOS Institute Publications.
Buckle-Henning, P., & Dugan, S. (2007). Leader's detection of problematic self-organized patterns in the workplace. In *Complex systems leadership theory* (pp. 386–412). Mansfield, MA: ISCE Publishing Company.
Damasio, A. (2012). *Self comes to mind: Constructing the conscious brain*. Random House LLC.
Goffee, R., & Jones, G. (2006). *Why should anyone be led by you? what it takes to be an authentic leader*. Boston: Harvard Business School Press.
Grint, K. (2005). Problems, problems, problems: The social construction of "leadership". *Human Relations, 58,* 1467–1494.
Grint, K. (2010a). Wicked problems and clumsy solutions: The role of leadership. In: Brookes, S. & Grint, K. (Eds.). (2010). *The public new leadership challenge*. New York: Palgrave Macmillan, 169–186.

Heifetz, R. A. (1994). *Leadership without easy answers* (Vol. 465). Cambridge: Harvard University Press.

Heifetz, R. A., Grashow, A., & Linsky, M. (2009). *The practice of adaptive leadership: Tools and tactics for changing your organization and the world*. Cambridge: Harvard Business Press.

Hosking, D. M. (2011). Moving relationality: Meditations on a relational approach to leadership. In A. Bryman, D. Collinson, K. Grint, B. Jackson & M. Uhl-Bien (Eds.), *The SAGE handbook of leadership* (pp. 455–467). London, UK: Sage.

House, R. J., Hanges, P., Javidan, M., Dorfman, P., & Gupta, V. (2004). *Culture, leadership and organizations: The GLOBE study of 62 societies*. Thousand Oaks California: Sage Publications, Inc.

Isaacs, W. N. (1999). *Dialogue and the art of thinking together: A pioneering approach to communicating in business and in life*. New York: Doubleday.

Jaworsky, J. (1998). *Synchronicity: The inner path of leadership*. San Francisco, CA: Berrett-Koehler Publishers.

Johansen, R. (2012). *Leaders make the future: Ten new leadership skills for an uncertain world*. California: Berrett-Koehler Publishers.

Kahane, A. (2007). *Solving tough problems: An open way of talking, listening and creating new realities*. San Francisco: Berrett-Koehler Publishers, Inc.

Keller, S., Meaney, M., & Pung, C. (2010). *What successful transformations share*. Chicago and London: McKinsey Quarterly Publishing.

Kotter, J. P. (1996). *Leading change*. Cambridge: Harvard Business Press.

Lengelle, R. (2016). What a career coach can learn from a playwright: Expressive dialogues for identity development. In H. J. M Hermans (Ed.), *Nine methods for stimulating a dialogical self: Applications in groups, cultures and organizations* (pp. 37–53). Springer, Switzerland.

Libbrecht, U. (2007). *Within the four Seas…: Introduction to comparative philosophy*. Belgium: Peeters Publishers.

Manders, K. (2014). Leaders make the future: Ten new leadership skills for an uncertain world [review]. *Johansen, B Journal of Applied Christian Leadership, 8*(1), 113–116.

Melina, L. R., Burgess, G. J., Falkman, L. L., & Marturano, A. (Eds.). (2013). *The embodiment of leadership*. San Francisco: Jossey Bass.

Parry, K. W. (2011). Leadership and organization theory. In A. Bryman, D. Collinson, K. Grint, B. Jackson & M. Uhl-Bien (Eds.), *The SAGE handbook of leadership* (pp. 53–70). London, UK: Sage.

Pruis, M. (2016). *Zachte riten [Soft rites]*. Amsterdam: Prometheus.

Raggatt, P. T. F. (2012). Positioning the dialogical self: recent advances in theory construction. In H. J. M. Hermans & Th. Gieser (Eds.), *Handbook of dialogical self theory* (pp. 29–45). Cambridge: University Press.

Ricard, M. (2011). *The art of meditation*. Atlantic Books Ltd.

Scharmer, C. O., & Kaufer, K. (2013). *Leading from the emerging future: From ego-system to eco-system economies*. California: Berrett-Koehler Publishers.

Schein, E. H. (1993). On dialogue, culture and organizational learning. *Organizational Dynamics, 22*, 27–37.

Siegel, D. J. (2017). *Mind. A journey to the heart of human being*. NY: W.W. Norton & Company.

Van Dam, N. N. H. (2016). *Learn or lose*. Inaugural Lecture: Nyenrode Business University.

Van Dijk, G. (2014). *Organizational ecology: Simplicity in complexity*. Tilburg University Press.

Van Loon, E. (Rens) J. P. (2006). *Het geheim van de leider. Zoektocht naar essentie. (The secret of being a leader. Searching for the essence.)* Assen: Van Gorcum. [Available as pdf file in English translation].

Van Loon, E. (Rens) J.P., & Van Dijk, G. (2015). Dialogical Leadership. Dialogue as Condition Zero. *Journal for Leadership Accountability and Ethics* Vol. 12(3), 62–75.

Yukl, G. (2011). Contingency theories of effective leadership. In A. Bryman, D. Collinson, K. Grint, B. Jackson & M. Uhl-Bien (Eds.), *The SAGE handbook of leadership* (pp. 286–298). London, UK: Sage.

Chapter 7
Case-Study. Dialogical Leadership and Teamwork

Leadership is the ability to act and to enable others to act
M. Asscher (De Gids 2016/3, 5)

7.1 Leadership and Innovation with Océ

In 2015 and 2016, we conducted a leadership and innovation project with Océ,[1] entitled '*Leading Innovation to Grow*' with a team of two Boardmembers (CEO and CFO) and 11 (Senior) Vice Presidents (SVP). Océ competes in a hypercompetitive market. Its leadership team wanted to be more aligned on strategic issues by creating more awareness and effectiveness in *how* they work together. In this chapter, this case leads us in the text on three levels: the individual leader and the process of transformation; the team of the Board, EVP's, and SVP's and their collective narrative; the organization as such. In Fig. 7.1, the steps of the journey are visualized.

Four leaders explicitly reflect on the process as a whole. After we had gone through the whole process, they were invited to share their thinking on their own process, the journey as a team, and the overall impact on the organization. These stories are interjected in this chapter as separate text boxes. There are two more sections, one about trust and one describes a reflective conversation of the adviser with the CEO.

---

[1]Océ is part of the Canon group. Océ is a global leader in digital imaging, industrial printing and collaborative business services. The organization operates as a global network of R&D centers to connect emerging digital print technologies to future markets. Océ is headquartered in the Netherlands and has locations throughout Europe, the Americas and Asia, employing about 12.000 people.

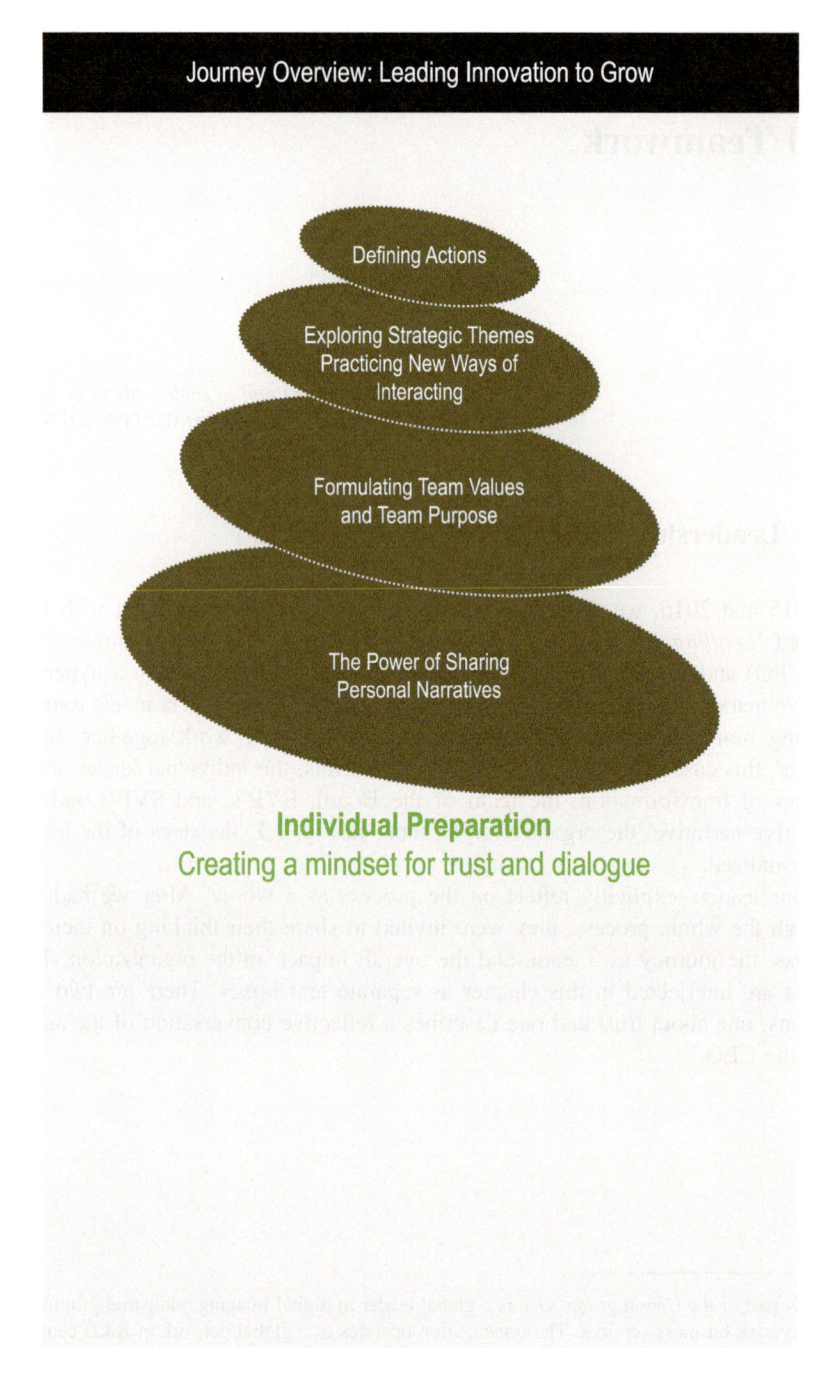

Fig. 7.1 Journey overview: leading innovation to grow

7.2 Creating a Mindset for Trust and Dialogue

Before a leadership team journey begins, it is critical for all leaders to have individual dialogues about topics such as: exploring individual values and purpose, exploring individual leadership positions from a past, present and future point of view. A dialogue about individual leadership styles includes push versus pull behavior, influencing behavior (rational versus intuitive) and the role of non-verbal communication, and also specific themes based on individual leaders' needs. With a carefully facilitated process, leaders become more aware of their purpose, values, motives and impact.

The individual dialogues with the members of the team consisted of a one-and-half-day conversation. The structure of the process was as previously described in the text, along the time axis of present—past—future, in combination with the values—purpose axis. Special detailed attention was given to individual leadership styles. These were explored in line with the leadership concept as explained in the foregoing chapters: vision—pushing—pulling; thinking—feeling —(non-verbally) acting. Participants were invited to bring other materials to the conversation (such as 360° surveys, personality scans and assessment reports—if they felt it would add value). All thirteen conversations were done with the author of this book in a period of about two years.[2] It was an explicit pre-condition that everybody would go through this process of *relational self*-reflection to prepare every individual leader for the sessions with the team. Like you cannot love another person before you love yourself, one cannot reflect in interpersonal relationships before you have reflected on yourself. If this pre-condition is not met, group dialogue risks to become superficial and, hence, not add true value. These conversations were also used to establish a level of trust and safety that enabled participants to start the journey of shared reflection and conversation (Fig. 7.2).

In preparing the conversations, the following main themes were derived.

First: reaching a *reciprocal process of co-creation*, where each member of the team is invited and stimulated to voice his vision with as common goal to reach a shared vision for the entire team of Board and SVP's. In this process, members spoke about the importance of being stimulated to truly express their thoughts and worries in a dialogue to find common ground. Exploring what connects the individual members of the team was described as important. There was a wish to balance push and pull-behaviors, as there was at that moment too much pushing and not enough pulling behavior. As predominantly rationally trained professionals (e.g. engineering, finance), they tend to primarily work from rationality, with a lack of balance between thinking and feeling. Sometimes intuition is the actual source for an idea/vision but disguised as a rational insight in the communication. Intuition should be recognized in the daily interaction as an effective source of influencing, next to rational argumentation, especially as the company has to think about innovation and experiments.

---

[2]The interviews with the participants about their experiences and the impact of the process are done by Martijn van Hal, who co-authored this chapter.

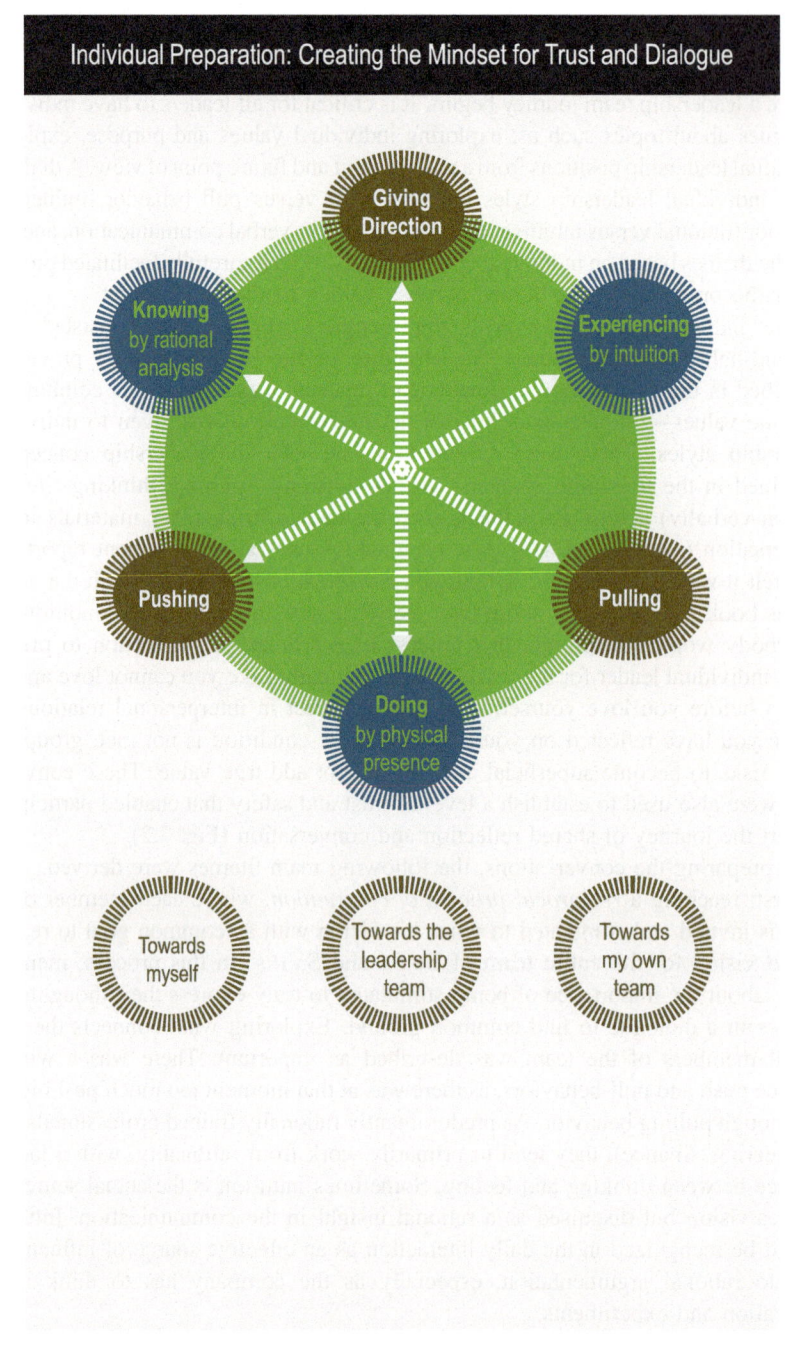

Fig. 7.2 Individual preparation: creating the mindset for trust and dialogue

7.2 Creating a Mindset for Trust and Dialogue

The second theme was formulated as building a basis for *shared reflection in the group* (it was not yet one team), more self-confidence and independent communicating amongst the group. The wish—and necessity—to become and act as one team was explicitly expressed. Until then, most interactions were bilateral meetings about specific business issues.

The last topic for further exploration was building an explicit *relation of openness, dialogue,* and *interpersonal trust relationships* between participants. As there was no sense of a safe and open atmosphere in the collective meetings the level of trust and voicing—opposing—opinions had to be developed further. What is necessary to build a trust relation?

We illustrate the individual process with an example. The VP Strategy characterized himself with the following sentences:

- My purpose: Through working in several dimensions, I feel more freedom.
- My autonomy protects my integrity; that is my core.
- I have an insight that life can be over instantaneously, feels redemptive for me.
- I never lie.
- I am able to express myself in a wide variety of ways.
- I want to continuously learn and see new things.
- I am a stable person; I am an independent thinker.
- My core values are integrity, directness, independence, and fixing issues.

Here you find the result of such a leadership deep dive dialogue. Five I-positions are given with their scores[3] on the leadership concept (Fig. 7.3).

You see how the VP Strategy experiences great differences between his roles within and outside the company:

- As a *strategist,* he is high on vision, giving direction, and rationality, knowing by rational analysis.
- As a *director of communication,* his highest score is on pushing.
- As *sparring partner* of the Chairman of the Board, the CEO, he is high on vision, rationality and experiencing by intuition.
- As a *'fixer'* of problems, he scores himself high on pushing.
- In his *family,* he feels high on giving direction, experiencing by intuition, pulling, and non-verbal. In a later session however, after having validated his scores, he indicated pull and push are more balanced.

---

[3]This is a self-score, given during the conversation. We invite our partner in dialogue to validate the score (as an intuitive assessment) after the session by asking for feedback and discuss it with colleagues. The highest scores in the I-position are marked. This is an illustration of a method to (self-)assess leadership styles and sources, by dividing 100% amongst 'vision'—'push'—'pull'. And 100% for 'rationality'—'intuition'—'non-verbal'. By exploring your styles and sources in different I-positions, you develop an increased awareness of patterns in thinking, feeling, and acting. In this leadership journey a conversation about these insights is part of the agenda in the preparation. For details: Van Loon 2006.

Case-Study Vice-President Strategy

Giving Direction
Knowing — Experiencing
Pushing — Pulling
Doing

I as Strategist
- Giving Direction: 50
- Knowing: 50
- Experiencing: 30
- Pushing: 10
- Pulling: 40
- Doing: 20

I as a Director of Communication
- Giving Direction: 10
- Knowing: 30
- Experiencing: 40
- Pushing: 70
- Pulling: 20
- Doing: 30

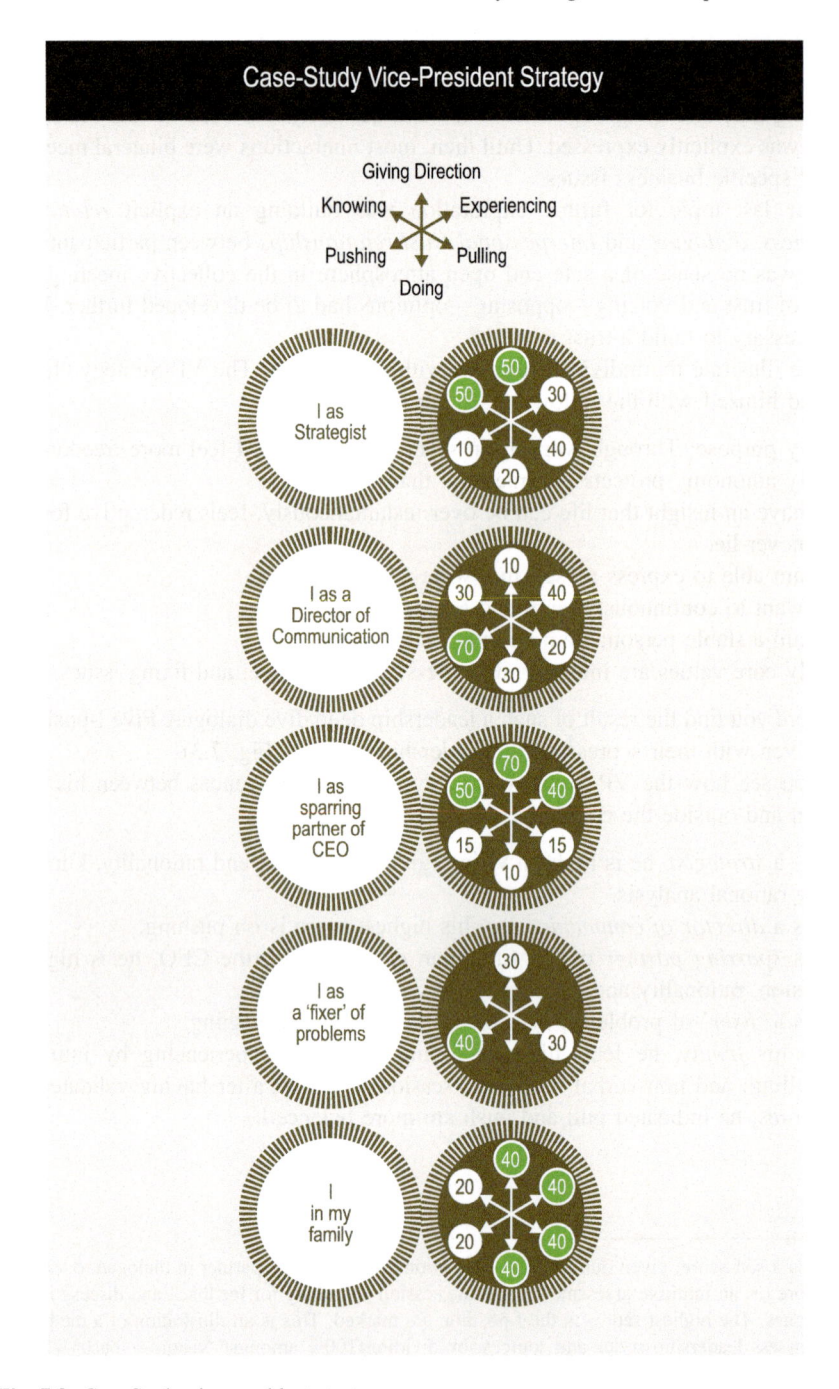

I as sparring partner of CEO
- Giving Direction: 70
- Knowing: 50
- Experiencing: 40
- Pushing: 15
- Pulling: 15
- Doing: 10

I as a 'fixer' of problems
- Giving Direction: 30
- Pushing: 40
- Pulling: 30

I in my family
- Giving Direction: 40
- Knowing: 20
- Experiencing: 40
- Pushing: 20
- Pulling: 40
- Doing: 40

Fig. 7.3 Case-Study vice-president strategy

7.2 Creating a Mindset for Trust and Dialogue

With these I-positions, he covered the complete scale of the leadership concept. He immediately realized, by looking at the scores, that he applied different styles and sources in different situations, and that his performance could have more impact when he uses a mode of influencing intentionally and more aligned with the context and the issue at hand. You could conclude that *transpositioning* of I-positions is applied spontaneously here.

Some of his personal thoughts on purpose and core values are illustrated here with some quotes. Based on the conversation, he formulated some insights and actions:

- "I want to enrich myself by using more levels of influencing (visioning, interacting, time-outs)".
- "Just don't do anything for a while".
- "Die Lage ist mein Lehrer". To express that he learns from every situation he gets in; this is a quote he remembered (without source).
- Using the metaphor: 'the apple in the pocket'. This refers to leading a horse into a trailer, by having an apple in your trousers pocket and walking yourself in front of the horse. A horse will spontaneously follow.
- "Bringing more strategy into fixing problems".

We followed the process of the VP Strategy during the leadership journey. Several times insights/actions in his process are described.

- "I feel like a pilot. I jump from one ship to the other." "I have a small department but I have an immense responsibility for the whole. I feel it my duty to pilot." "My job will remain or even become more critical with increasing complexity. We need distance and not get caught up by day-to-day operations."
- "I have learned that I am beginning to learn to trust the team." "The team is getting and communicating clearer. It speaks out and shares thought and concerns more honestly."
- "The values and purpose as defined fit very well to me and the team." "For me personally, this was the best session especially with the blindfold.[4] As you noticed I did not like that at all but I appreciate the conversation afterwards. I deliberately did something I knew I didn't like. Thank you for showing respect."
- "We had a quite large communication by the CFO on the financial situation. It was the first time we did this. The team worked really well. Response from the organization was overwhelming. Openness and transparency is something that is really appreciated by employees. They were very happy. There was a lot of

---

[4]After they had worked in sub teams on specific topics, the assignment was to report back to a blindfolded group. Aim of the exercise is to practice listening, without being distracted by what you see (non-verbal behavior) in the audience. For the presenter (not blindfolded) the challenge was to make an impact without getting non-verbal (and verbal) feedback from the group. The impact of a simple exercise like this can be massive, supposed the level on trust is well set. We could not have done this in one of the first two/three phases of the journey.

unrest. This was picked up by communication and others. Disappointing sales and financial figures led to rumors and uncertainty. With the information of our CFO, everybody was on the same page. The fact that we were transparent was appreciated and also the content."

- Reflecting the entire process:
    - For myself: "InterVision. I have something on my mind and reflect it with you. I did that for one of my colleagues on new business and it worked very well. Makes work richer. Continue private coaching. Is one on one coaching something for me?"
    - For the Board and Senior Vice Presidents team: "I would definitely continue with some form of these leadership sessions. I would consciously and proactively look for themes for sessions like this."
    - For my own teams: "I want to lead by example. I want my teams to embody the values and purpose. This is easy for the strategy team as it has this mindset already and is small. Mindset is different in the Communication Team where I would need to do more explaining and sending. With my Strategy Team it will be more reciprocal."
    - For the entire organization: "Derivatives of values and purpose we need to use in communication (perhaps indirectly, not necessarily direct)."

This illustrates the individual ongoing change process of this leader. In the beginning, he was hesitant and not visibly experimenting within the context of the team of the Board and the SVP's. At the end, he explicitly brought himself out of comfort zone by experimenting with new behavior (the blindfold exercise). His remarks illustrate the process of increasing trust.

We could describe this for all participants, but for the sake of brevity and illustration, we limit here to one member of the team.

> . Individual Reflection of the Vice President Strategy
> *A New Sense of Self Generates New Ambitions and Challenges.*
>
> The VP Strategy had few expectations when the *Leading Innovation to Grow* journey was launched. The group consisted of 'Senior Management' which the VP Strategy is not, so the invite came as a surprise. He was curious as to what the journey would mean to him: "I work a lot with the CEO and via him my work is shared with others normally, but I never worked together with this group in its entirety before, only when it concerns strategy".
>
> Looking back over time, he confirmed that he became part of the team and his sense of belonging increased. In journeys like these, there is the pitfall of losing the team feeling after off-site team sessions have not occurred for a while: "Although we made good steps in the Mid Term Planning (MTP) process where a lot of *suspending your judgments* was practiced, the team feeling is less strong lately. I see people fall back in old behavior, including myself perhaps." A feeling like this can be disappointing after you became part of a team: "with my *Personal Narrative* I communicated my role

to the team and how I felt it. Now I don't know whether my role is accepted by the other leaders or not." This point illustrates the challenge of sharing *Personal Narratives*. One leader voices (one-way interaction), but the extent to which others understand, or adhere to, what one says remains unexplored. To explore leaders need to engage in dialogue with each other (two-way interaction). The VP Strategy indicates this by saying the following: "Maybe it is not a fallback from the team but maybe my expectations were misaligned. It is in the interplay between me and the other leaders where I need to clarify this."

The process made the VP Strategy aware of his position in the leadership team and his informal power: "I think it was really good that I articulated to both the group and myself that I see myself as the pilot." At the same time, more self-awareness generates new ambitions and challenges, also for the VP Strategy. He explains this in the following way: "before I had the role of the free keeper. I could kick a bit, help a bit, and move on. Now, I feel more important for the company results. I belong to the team but also share the responsibility. Not just my own department. So it brings me awareness, it is growth for me as a leader and as a person. But now I want more." Additionally, the VP Strategy highlights the improved decision making capability: "during the Mid-Term Plan (MTP) sessions we got the feedback that the discussion was more open, questions were asked, and we listened to each other. There was mutual respect for dialogue."

Within his own team, the VP Strategy operates on a much more personal level. A shift was made from a task-oriented management style to a people-oriented management style. Or how he puts it: "sometimes it is really easy to just execute tasks. But I am more aware now. I am the pilot so now I articulate what I think. So before I would say to my people: "We made a strategy plan, it looks good and the boss is happy." Today, I say: "we have a really good strategic plan and now we have an obligation as an organization to live up to the expectations". So I share my feelings on what needs to happen with the team, instead of focusing in tasks." Voicing your concerns and ambitions as a leader leads to higher engagement levels due to the fact that challenges are relationally articulated, and if they are articulated they are more likely to be dealt with.

Becoming a more connected leadership team makes individual leaders more aware of their shared ambition and context. This helps the VP Strategy in communicating with partners to know what he stands for and what the organization stands for: "I am more aware of the impact I have and can have and I keep that in mind when interacting with partners, whether it is a university or a potential joint venture partner. The feedback I get from partners is that it is clear who I am and what I want for my organization when I am at the table." Thus, becoming one leadership team has an impact on how this leader positions himself more effectively toward the outside world.

> For the VP Strategy, the values trust and openness are extremely important. He indicates this by saying: "I think the only way I can and will work is by being transparent, and by trusting people. In my position, I cannot act differently." Experiencing joy is sometimes forgotten or (temporarily) not possible for leaders: "Joy I sometimes forget as a result of the intensive process of exploring my role within the leadership team." The purpose gives the VP Strategy guidance: "the purpose looks like a no-brainer, but the fact that we spend a day on it to articulate it indicates it isn't. I believe in the purpose, and when things are not being picked up by the business units I feel responsible. And I make a proposal on how to organize for things that are currently not in our scope but do fit our purpose. So in that perspective the purpose really helps."
>
> The *Leading Innovation to Grow* journey made the VP Strategy much more aware of himself and initiated a personal growth journey. This individual reflection can be best described by the following quote: "I thought I had a stable balance. Now I am in the midst of a personal journey and looking for a new stable balance. I am learning a lot and not done yet."

Creating conditions for change

After the individual conversations were completed, the CEO and Senior Vice President HR mobilized the rest of the leadership team to join sessions with the entire group to explore opportunities for team development and strengthening the leadership for the organization as a whole. Often CEOs, CFOs and COOs are change makers within organizations. When transformation involves the actual leadership of an organization it is key for the CEO and SVP HR to collaborate and set the right example for change. In our observation, a relationship and initiative like described here is frequently lacking. In this process, the organization showed a strong initiative to create conditions for a successful transformative journey.

Designing the journey

The team journey was carefully designed and consisted of five one and a half day offsite sessions at an external location over a period of six months. Multi-day sessions allow for bonding and trust building in a group. For example, having dinner together allows for informal knowledge sharing, shared reflection. More importantly, multi-day sessions enable flexible agenda setting. There is no need to rush. The external location stimulated leaders to take a pause from everyday business and focus on their individual and leadership team development. Agendas were co-created and co-facilitated by the leaders themselves but moderated by external facilitators. In a process like this, it is important for external facilitators not to push agendas and content, but let leaders discuss what they want to discuss while reflecting on dialogical behavior. The moderators made sure everybody joined sessions prepared (e.g. by asking to prepare content on a certain topic). Every session started with a group check-in, and ended with a group check-out, stimulating leaders to engage in reflective and listening mode of presence. Important quotes and actions were reported as detailed as possible in order for leaders to trace back their learnings. Obviously, a leadership team transformation cannot be finished within five sessions, but it is a suitable time frame to develop essential foundations.

7.3 The Power of Sharing Personal Narratives

In a project like this, you have to prepare the individual minds separately, but also set the rules for the group as a whole. If you want to create an atmosphere for dialogue and open reciprocal thinking, people have to feel safe and secure. We used a technique in line with Isaacs' description of building the container to create an atmosphere for dialogue, training participants systematically to listen, visibly showing respect to one another and suspending their judgment, with the aim to create a better understanding. At the same time, we trained people to voice their thinking, and to express their intentions as accurately as possible. In Fig. 7.4, the four phases of this process are described. Starting with dialogue to open minds and diverge, skims into a process of converging and discussing the results. In step three (exploring strategic themes) and step four (making the approach action-based for one strategic topic) this is illustrated.

Participants started using these conditions for dialogue and discussion in their daily functioning. Most of us are trained to respond in a resistance-mode during day-to-day activities. Instead of trying to really understand what is meant, we tend to continue in our own line of thinking, resisting others' view. Often this process is unconscious and without negative intentions. A typical expression is "Yes, but I ...." In a team that has the intention to collaborate and innovate we stimulate the dialogue mode. Truly explore the ideas of your colleagues to inspire a shared process of innovation.[5] In the first phases of a journey like this, discipline is needed, first of all represented by the facilitators, to decrease the habit of sticking to your own thinking, feeling and acting. In a group of highly educated and specialized engineers, finance, sales, IT, and strategy leaders, this is not an easy task. To transform it into a new group habit takes perseverance. Once the positive effects are felt in the communication within and outside the team, people begin to enjoy practicing this approach.

In the first session the WHY, 'the reason why we are here', was explained, by the CEO. In the preparation conversations, the wish for co-creating the process (inclusively its content) was expressed explicitly. We name this process: relational co-creating of the journey. To keep in close contact in each step, preparing each next session is crucial. It is vital to apply the principles of dialogue, in the sense of suspending what you think you know is good for the group and to keep your sensitivity open as much as possible. This is summarized as:

---

[5]To inspire literally means to take breathe in, to fill with spirit. Inspiring is the capacity to move people by reaching into their hearts from deeper sources of meaning. Heifetz et al. 2009.

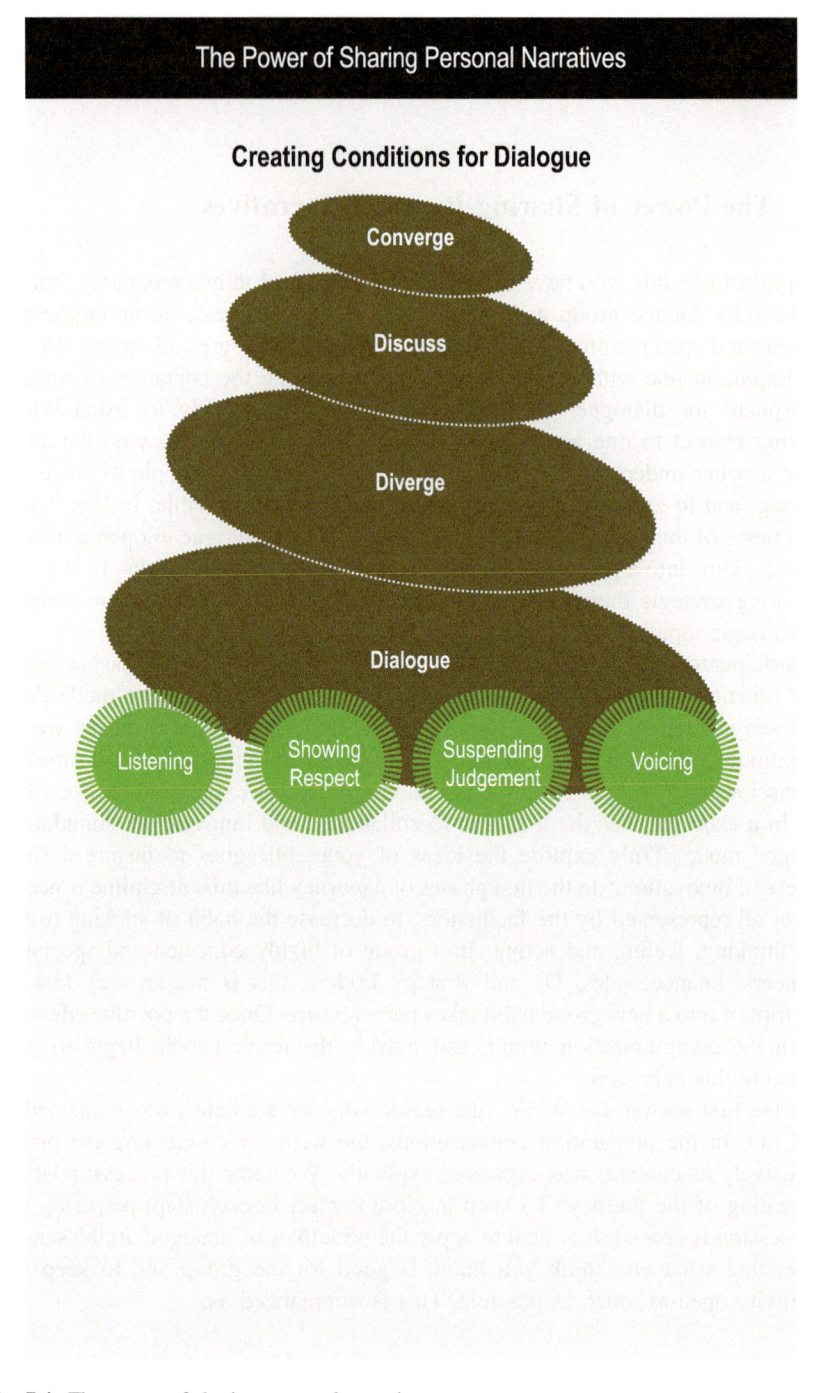

Fig. 7.4 The power of sharing personal narratives

7.3 The Power of Sharing Personal Narratives

- *Relational co-creation*: creating the next steps of our journey together through dialogue. As a consequence of this decision, we each developed a step of the journey together, the SVP HR, the CEO and our team. To plan a process like this without a fixed plan that you already have in mind was challenging as participants wanted to know the steps and the end of the journey. For us, it was also a practice in suspending our own judgments, as you automatically tend to propose as a next step what you did in previous projects and from experience know it is effective. Forming a strong team that dares to feedback directly was critically important to make a process like this successful.
- *Balancing push and pull*: knowing when to pull, when to push. As we have seen in the previous chapters, effective leadership has to do with using push and pull in the right proportion, at the right moment. During the sessions, we supported participants in recognizing different styles, becoming more flexible in adapting to the context, the people involved and the topic of influence, and in experimenting with new combinations. Once people truly understand the styles and the sources experimenting becomes joyful and satisfying.
- *Exploring new ways of interacting*: experiencing how we can interact differently by real-time interventions. As explained, we did this type of interventions to make participants immediately aware of the impact and intention of their words and actions. In daily interactions, this often is not done and in most situations it is difficult as it sometimes feels awkward and inappropriate. Here, we intentionally created and sustained the sense of safety in the group.

In his welcome, the CEO said how important it is to find the right moment to start a journey like this. You have to be patient, as you need to have the right conditions in the team (who is in the team?) and the organization (what is it that the company needs?). In an organization that is making its money with innovative products and services (the 'what'), you might forget how you cooperate to make the 'what' happen (the 'how').

In the first session, each of the participants shared their personal narrative with the rest of the group. In advance, they were asked to prepare their view on leadership and innovation, based on three questions:

- How do you envision the future of Océ over the coming 5 + years?
- What are the organizational implications?
- What are the implications for you as a leader?

The role of a narrative is to attract, engage, motivate and call people to more fully achieve their potential. Narratives represent a powerful pull mechanism that can shape the world around us.[6] A narrative is open ended, it does not have to be a perfect story. That's why we asked people to speak without presenting slides. Based on their preparation, standing in front of the group, all shared their narratives. After telling their narrative, there was a phase of asking questions to better understand

---

[6]John Hagel—Deloitte Center for The Edge. http://edgeperspectives.typepad.com/edge_perspectives/2014/04/personal-narratives-insight-and-impact.html.

what was meant. Assumptions and leading questions were intervened with a time-out, with the request to reformulate in a more open, exploring way, trying to leave out implicit assumptions. For many people, this phase is a difficult one, as we —human beings—tend to immediately form a judgment in our mind, often visible in our non-verbal behavior. We encountered impatience, resistance, not knowing how to ask a question, frustration. Time we invested here, would be received back later. Here we illustrate this part of the process with two personal narratives: the first of the CEO. The second is of the VP Strategy we followed in the preparation conversation. We end by giving some remarkable quotes from the narratives.

The CEO:

> Océ Vision 2020+: "I experience an ever increasing complexity on both a societal and organizational level." "As a result, the interdependencies increase and therefore it becomes even more important how we interact with each other."
>
> Organizational implications: "I call it a network organization. If you have a problem at home, you Google it and solve it. We should do that internally too." "I think we have a good structure, but we need to have a better interaction. It is more about how we do things together."
>
> Personal Implications: "It was a very difficult topic to discuss, but from the feedback I get, it was easier to understand than I thought. It was a good feeling." "Give me feedback on where I can influence more."

VP Strategy:

> Océ Vision 2020+: "Our organization is a float of ships. They all should go into the same direction." "I see the world becoming more complex, as a result we will have more ships." "We need to do more to control the complexity of the future."
>
> Organizational implications: "Some ships we will keep, other will perhaps stay in the harbor." "We need big ships and small ships at the same time (ambidexterity)." "We need not only responsibility, but a sense of responsibility."
>
> Personal Implications: "I feel like a pilot. I jump from one ship to the other." "I have a small department, but I have an immense responsibility for the whole. I feel it my duty to pilot." "My job will remain or even become more critical with increasing complexity. We need distance and not get caught up by day-to-day operations."

Other Quotes—without mentioning roles—to get an impression of what was said:

> *Océ Vision 2020 +:*
>
> I think we should recognize that we are in a continuous process of taking care of old men (products and services that exist already for a long time) and growing babies (innovative products and services).
>
> I think we should structurally connect, that it is about us. I am moving from me to us.
>
> I strongly believe that to survive as a company, you must evolve and create, harvest and abandon your own technology which differentiates you from the mediocre and you should always strive to be among the best.
>
> *Organizational implications:*
>
> I have defined five themes under social innovation translated to HR: a faster and more efficient organization, standardization of processes, agility to change and to learn

7.3 The Power of Sharing Personal Narratives

determines success of the company, bridge differences in work capacity between generations and populations.

Run the company more like a standalone enterprise and tackle the administrative burden where it doesn't add value.

We need trust, opening each other's minds.

Personal Implications:

When I was young, I always asked why and how. I think the reason why I ask these questions was because I was curious. Deep in my heart, I was already looking for improvements.

I want to challenge the bureaucracy that I'm part of: Why are we doing this; do we decide and change fast enough; does it generate cash?

We want to look at the future, but first we need to look inside.

The urge for control and structure is a threat for innovation competence. Everywhere, even also in me.

Some comments and observations. Reason for quoting these fragments of the narratives is to illustrate the richness of the material. As indicated, in creating the conditions for dialogue, you need to be disciplined and motivated. But once you have reached a state of heightened awareness in the group, new energy is generated. In this group, we listened to the narratives of all participants (13). The level of attention was continuously high, as you have to be aware how you react and how you are present in the group. Normally, we are not prepared to listen in a mode where you ask questions and deeply try to understand what is said by the other person. Bohm[7] would describe this as moving from 'thoughts' (based on old patterns) to 'thinking together' (based on being relationally present in the here and now).

By introducing personal narratives, people opened up for one another in a new manner. People in organizations are often not used to taking a different route to cooperation: listening to each other and exploring what is said, trying to truly understand your colleague. By listening to many narratives, you hear views that are new for you. By encountering a broader reservoir of possible views, people might be opened in a new direction.

The first part of the journey[8] is maybe the most difficult. It takes a long time, and, you don't see results immediately. You have to be patient, but normally participants are impatient. It is tough, mentally, and physically. In modern organizations, people are used to multitasking and quickly moving from one activity to the next. The mechanism of multitasking and speeding up is disturbed systematically. Frustration was visible on faces and sensed in the room. This is what we mean by going 'out of your comfort zone'. To change your way of thinking, feeling and acting is confronting, breaking habits is not easy to do.

---

[7]Bohm 1996.

[8]One of the participants made the acronym: PROCESS. Propose, Reformulate/Reposition, Observe, Communicate, Enhance/Enrich, Solve, and Suspend—starting a new cycle.

Lencioni's View on Team Development

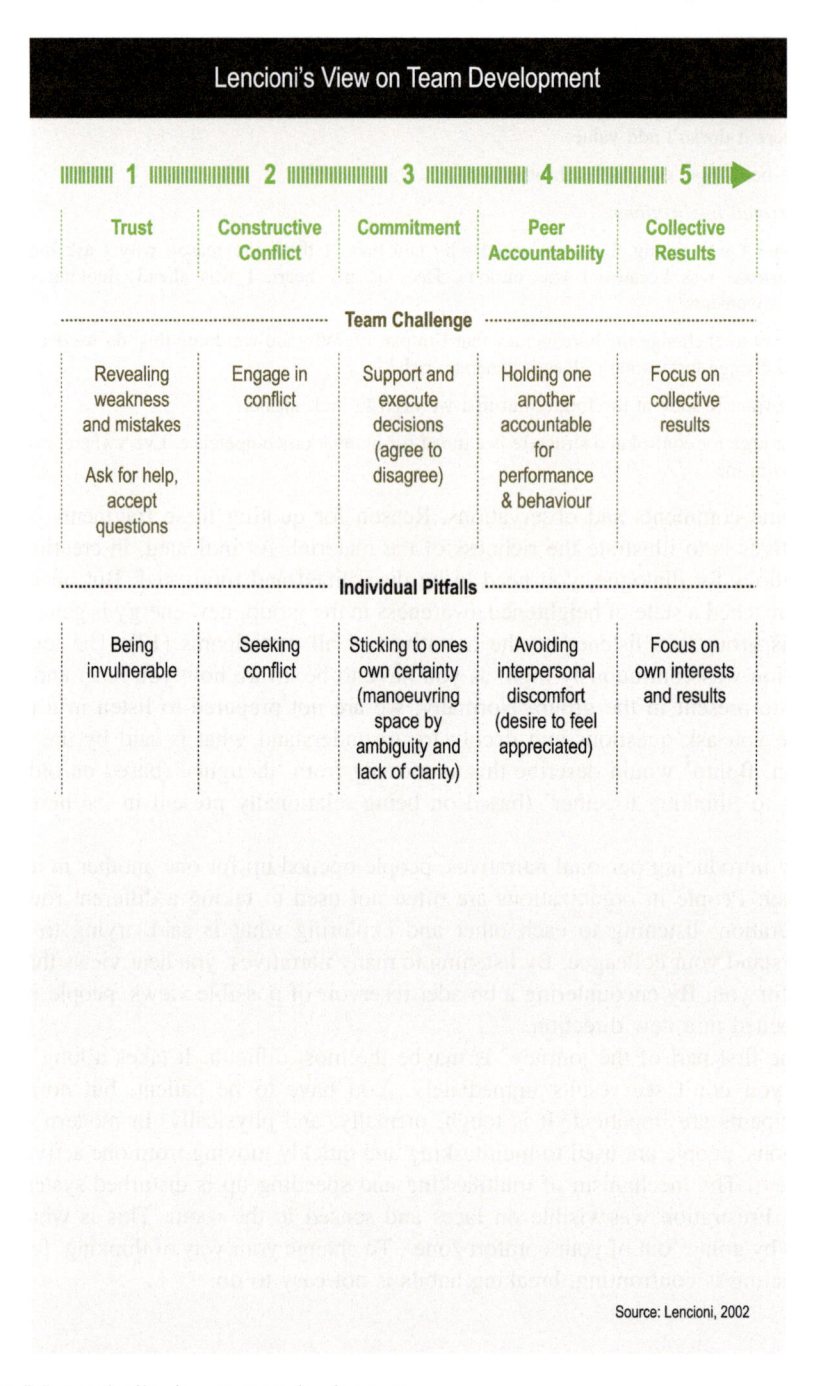

1 Trust	2 Constructive Conflict	3 Commitment	4 Peer Accountability	5 Collective Results

Team Challenge

Revealing weakness and mistakes. Ask for help, accept questions	Engage in conflict	Support and execute decisions (agree to disagree)	Holding one another accountable for performance & behaviour	Focus on collective results

Individual Pitfalls

Being invulnerable	Seeking conflict	Sticking to ones own certainty (manoeuvring space by ambiguity and lack of clarity)	Avoiding interpersonal discomfort (desire to feel appreciated)	Focus on own interests and results

Source: Lencioni, 2002

Fig. 7.5 Lencioni's view on team development

7.3 The Power of Sharing Personal Narratives

Lencioni's designed a model[9] for becoming a team in five phases, where he indicates building trust as step one, in which phase you start opening yourself (Fig. 7.5).

An indication of openness is accepting that people ask questions you might not be able to answer. Trust is expressed by not showing yourself as invulnerable, but allowing others to correct you. We have seen that phase clearly in this team. It took about three 24-hour sessions to build a solid foundation of trust. Members of trust teams give one another the benefit of the doubt, formulated in the list of behavioral indicators as "Relying on the non-proven potential of partners".[10] Here trust is defined as appreciating and tapping into another's skills and experiences, and look forward to meeting and other opportunities to work as a group. In the course of the journey we completed this phase. In my view, the most important indicator was that the team members explicitly wanted to have a session on 'wicked issues' (such as core technology, dealing with complexity and software strategy). Before we started this journey, nobody would have asked for these issues to be discussed in the plenary team. We just touched the other four phases of becoming a team in Lencioni's view. In terms of creating the container for dialogue as described by Isaacs[11] previously, you have to be permanently aware where you are in the process. Although the phases are described separately, they take place simultaneously, and quickly move up or down. It takes time to build trust, one incident is enough to destroy a feeling of trust.

Starting a journey as a process where you relationally co-create the direction and the content of the meetings implies that in each step you try to concentrate on what is next. Based on the many narratives of all participants, the following themes were formulated for further exploration. These were described as:

- *Defining us*: what kind of company are we and do we want to be? What is our joint agenda? How do we become an 'us'?
- *Connecting with each other*: we need more and a different kind of interaction, connect with respect.
- *Becoming one team*: we need to become more of a team and act as one team. Need for clear goals.
- *Developing talent*: we have to develop our people.
- *Improving speed*: we need to develop speed. Too much time is lost by speed bumps. We need a faster delivery process.
- *Being transparent*: by creating transparency, we may be able to create trust, so people believe and can be willing to change. An important topic is also transparency on financials.
- *Determining focus*: we need more focus, how do we make decisions and choices, based on which values. We need to develop a joint vision on the future.

---

[9]Lencioni 2002.

[10]See figure: overview of Team Values, Team Purpose, and Behavioral Indicators (Figs. 7.6 and 7.7).

[11]Isaacs 1993; Isaacs 1999.

- *Finding core*: we have to define what our core technology is and what our core competences are as an organization.
- *Dealing with complexity*: we need to think how we deal with an increasingly complex world, higher speed and lower costs.
- *Combining old men and babies*: we need to develop ambidexterity, setting up processes for new products while nurturing the old ones.

These ten topics were the starting point for the next sessions. The group decided to continue with the topic, highest on the agenda: *defining us*.

Before we go to the next phase, a few comments. If you collect thirteen narratives, you have the material that you need for a comprehensive transformation in your hands. It is remarkable that by telling and listening—in a regulated manner—you get information collected you need to bring a team and an organization further in a process of collective change and transformation. One observation is about the completeness of the information. If you analyze the material in terms of the conceptual leadership model as represented by Hickman,[12] we find all aspects addressed:

- *Sharing responsibility* between leaders and members of the organization: this is strongly expressed as an *intention* and as a *need*. In becoming a team and connecting with each other, determining focus as an organization within a changed context and as a responsible team.
- *Assessing changes in the context*: by explicitly listening to the divergent voices in the team, multiple perspectives on the context emerge in the process. Some people want to continue what was in the past, some realize that gaining a new identity implies leaving the old one behind. In terms of the Dialogical Self Theory, we see conflicting I-positions at work at an organizational level. What could be a merged/hybrid identity? In defining us, this is expressed for example in the question "are we a Rhineland[13] company?" And "are we doing what is good for us as a former organization or what is good for the new constellation?" This process of change has to be made step by step. Transforming your former identity into a new one is a wicked issue, an adaptive challenge.
- *Generating organizational contributions to society*: there is a strong connection with the people working for the company. Developing talent, retaining employees is a strong cultural characteristic of Océ. A Rhineland company or a typical Anglo-Saxon organization? This aspect has been elaborated later more explicitly in the purpose and the values.

We see that elements of Hickman's concept emerge in a natural manner, when you enable multiple voices in an organization to speak up. The concept society of

---

[12]Hickman 2016.

[13]Some authors use the term social capitalism with roughly the same meaning as social market economy, Rhine capitalism, typically when contrasting it with the Anglo-Saxon model of capitalism. Rather than seeing it as an antithesis, some authors describe Rhine capitalism as successful synthesis of the Anglo-American model with social democracy. (source: Wikipedia).

mind applies to individuals and to organizational processes.[14] Common purpose and shared values constitute a *compass* and a *map*, you need to determine *where* you are, and what your sense of direction is, individually and as an organization or society. Those are the next steps in the journey of this team. In this phase, the awareness of the urgency to change is present.

Another observation is based on a conversation I had with the CEO on the topic of *self*. As in physics, there is a fundamental uncertainty and relational influence when you interact with nature or with other selves. In our conversation, he stipulated that a person has many possible ways to act or to be in a relation to another person.

. A Conversation of the CEO and the Advisor[15]

The CEO made a comparison with the wave-function in physics. In quantum theory 'certainty' is lost. Here the aspect is uncertainty and/or stochastic effects at the smallest dimensions, here it seems that complete determinism is by principle impossible. Einstein did not like this aspect of quantum physics. This is the origin of his famous remark, "God doesn't play dice with the world." This is visible in the Schrödinger Wave-function: a formula which describes the probability of where a particle will be located. It holds for all things but the smaller the object, the bigger the possible uncertainties become. Nowadays, it is generally agreed that the wave function is very useful and that the math is right and that we can predict very well. Where many don't agree is how to interpret the uncertainty aspect. Einstein was sure it was because we do not understand nature well enough and have to wait for the next theory. Others like Heisenberg saw this uncertainty as fundamental to nature. Then you have the difference in opinion of whether the wave function collapses or not? The collapse is thought to happen when an observer does a measurement on the subject, a small particle, the uncertainty arises in the things you don't measure. For example, when you very accurately measure the position of a particle its momentum (velocity) becomes very uncertain.

"There is a wave-function which gives the probability that you will engage with a certain self in an external dialogue, or with a virtual self in an internal dialogue. If you can modify your wave-function in such a way that many selves have similar probability and you can influence when and how the collapse takes place, you can "optimize" your self towards the person with which you have started a dialogue". This resembles what is previously described as 'ma', taking a pause. By creating space, you enable yourself to adapt to (one of the many) possible self (selves) of the other person, in relation with you and the issue at hand. If you are willing and able to do this, you are more impactful as a leader because your pattern of acting and reacting is more adaptive to the single moment.

---

[14]How this works exactly in detail is out of scope for this book. It could be a topic for further (Ph. D.) research.
[15]Conversation August 24 2016.

> The 'self' in this sense is by definition relational (as opposed to static) and dialogical (as opposed to monological). What I liked in our conversation between CEO and advisor is that we concluded certainty does not exist. There is no *one* way of looking at what happens in organizations. There are always many ways to interact with a person. And—this is for a leader at each level important—you have many possible 'selves'. You can relate to others in different ways.

There is no *one* self, you can and should choose, depending on the context and the person with whom you are interacting. The parallel between psychology and physics is noteworthy, and a reflective conversation about this topic is valuable for both partners in conversation. It illustrates the possibility of looking from different perspectives and the 'art of thinking together'. You can't prepare a conversation like this, as new meaning emerges while interacting, as in a generative dialogue.

7.4 Exploring Team Values and Team Purpose

The second session in the journey was about 'defining us' as a team and exploring the purpose of the team and their shared values. The process of formulating purpose and values was a process of dialogue and diverging in the beginning, discussing and converging in the next phase, where the final wording emerged step by step. We observed that people wanted to move too quickly, by referring to what already was there. To align a group of individuals takes time and patience. We refer to values as the essential and enduring tenets of a community of people. A small set of timeless guiding principles which have intrinsic value and importance to those inside the community. Purpose as the community's reason for being, reflect people's idealistic motivations for doing their work, capturing the soul of the community. Please note that a purpose is different from a vision, since a vision is centered on what a community is giving to the world (e.g. your products, services and your actions).[16] Here a selection of associations on the values and the purpose in the first round is cited. Compare this with the full list of agreed values and purpose in the end.

- "Honesty towards each other"; "Respect for each other."
- "Fight competition and not each other."
- "Be an example for our direct reports."
- "The most critical value is to understand that we are different and to make that into a strength."
- "We need to step over our own shadow. If we all think we are the best then we will not achieve anything."

---

[16]Collings 1996. Remember Hickman's view on purpose as directing the process of relational responsibility in the organization. (Hickman 2016).

7.4 Exploring Team Values and Team Purpose

- "We need to have a way of working together to have something superior to individual interest."
- "We have to talk with each other and not about each other."
- "Alignment (common goals)." "Understanding a common target." "One common goal."
- "Innovation."
- "Togetherness, how we achieve that:
  - Trust and openness: support and learning from each other;
  - Dialogue: two way communication—willingness to understand each other;
  - Autonomy: empower people;
  - Passion: energy;
  - Imagination: we need imagination for new things;
  - Fun: making music;
  - Creativity: no innovation without creativity".
- "Everyone has his role:
  - One as coach/manager;
  - One as a team member/a player."
- "To stand shoulder to shoulder with trust and comradeship."
- "Trying to understand each other by respecting, trusting, willing to listen to each other."
- "Our first value is the first sentence of the process manual: working together for the common good."
- "Trust based on transparency and acceptance of different roles." "Trust in confidence."
- "Shared responsibilities and overlapping mandates. Everybody has his role and we have to accept each other's roles."

In subgroups, the results of the session were further discussed, elaborated and presented to the entire team. This process resulted in the following two figures of the purpose and the values. In this phase, it was a blend of dialogue and discussion, of diverging and converging. The important difference with the beginning of the process was that team members knew when and how to change their mode of conversation. Often the group did an adjustment itself, and sometimes there was a time-out by one of the facilitators. Once a team is familiarized with this mechanism, it starts working autonomously. Figures 7.6 and 7.7 illustrate the team values and team purpose.

We brought structure into the associations from all over the team. In the purpose "Together we create sustainable value by leading in production printing and services through innovation", we distinguished five categories, which are described by behaviors/characteristics. By formulating this level, there can be a conversation on the floor with employees: what does this purpose mean for you? For me? For our relation in the company? Participants said to be content with this outcome, and they were eager to start sharing with their own departments, in a reaching mode, as a start of a conversation with employees and colleagues.

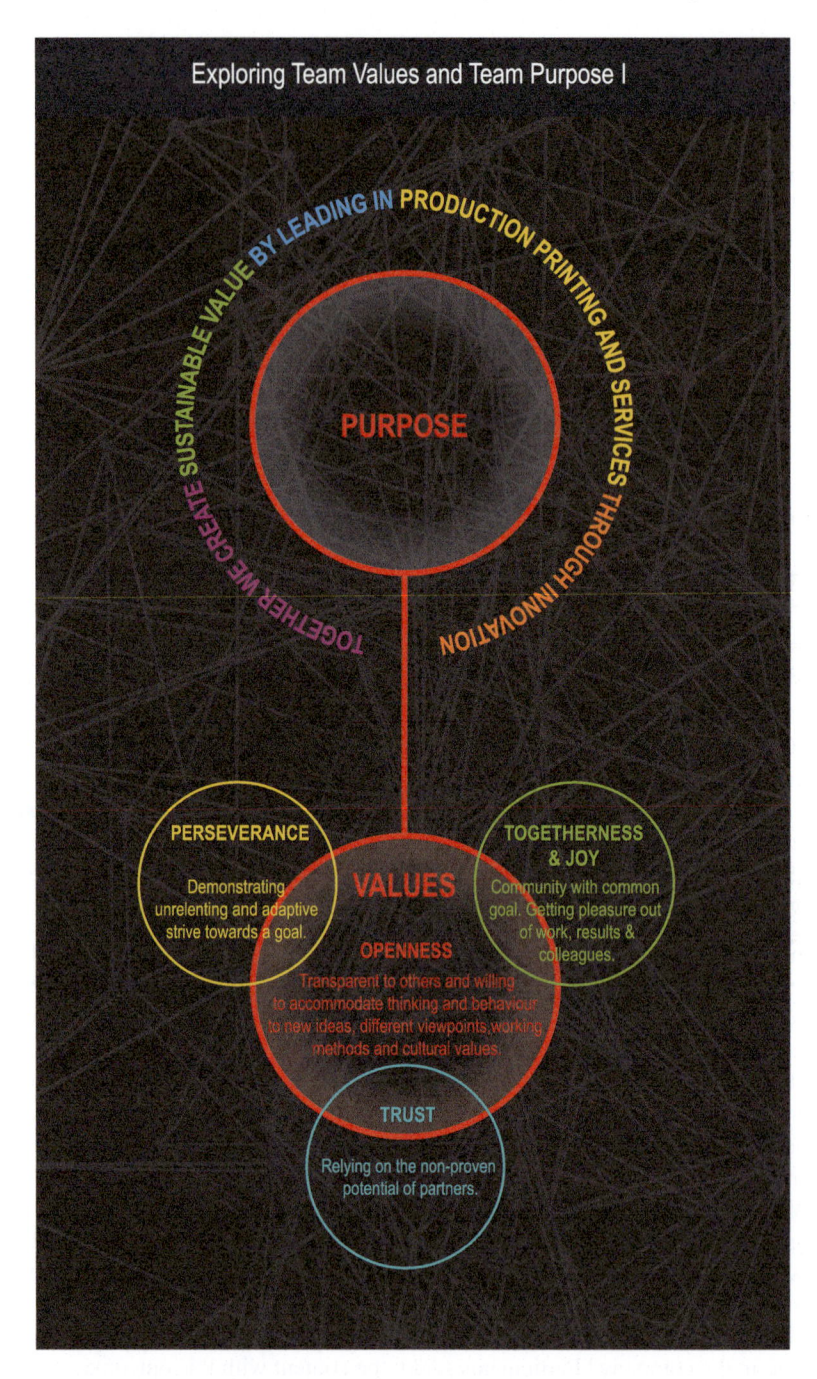

Fig. 7.6 Exploring team values and team purpose

7.4 Exploring Team Values and Team Purpose

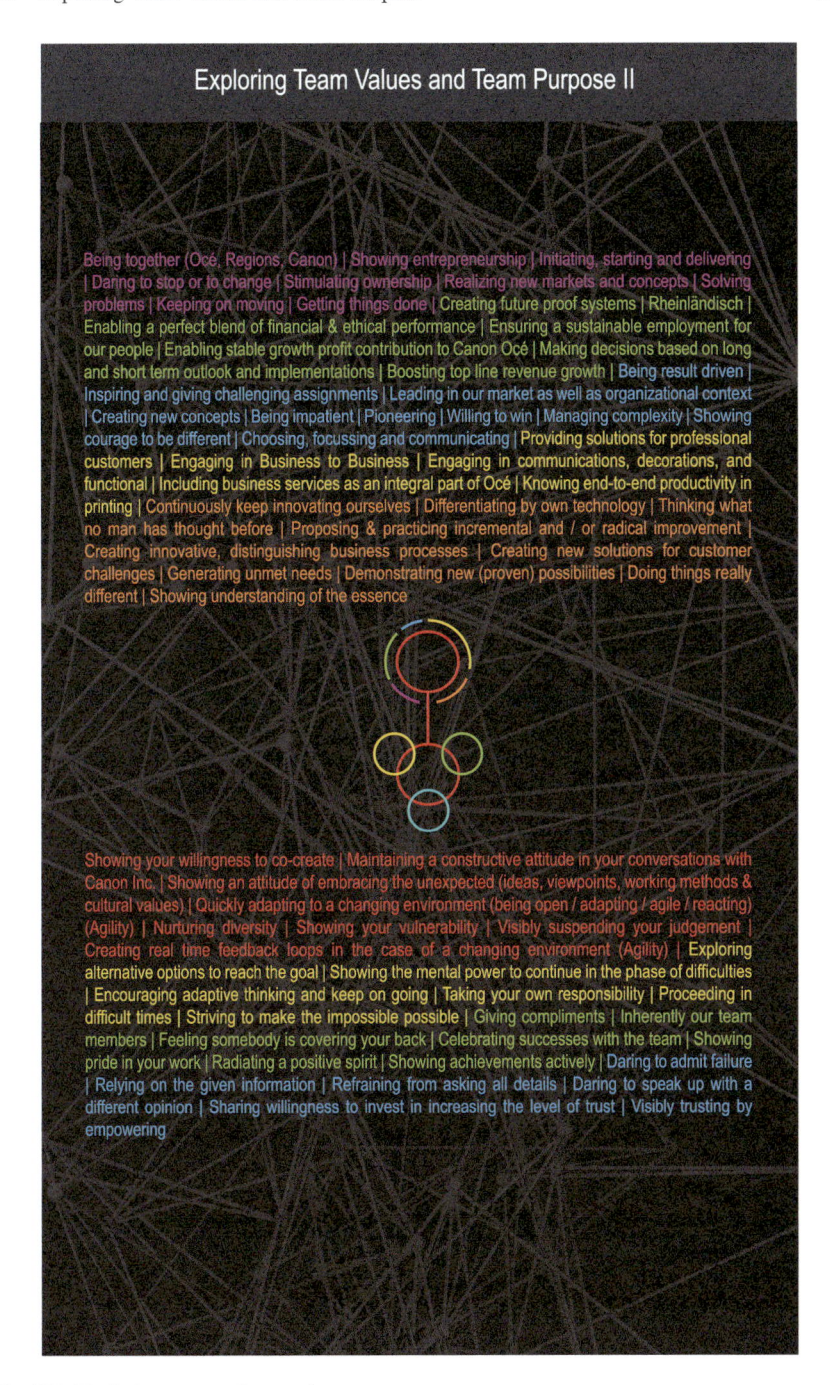

Fig. 7.7 Exploring team values and team purpose

To quote some of the comments made after having completed the purpose and the values:

- "If there is a misalignment between individual values and the purpose, then we need to voice that. It needs to be authentic."
- "The values and purpose as defined fit very well to me and the team."
- "I learned that the essence of a joint purpose and values creates compass."
- "We need more discussion on technology and regions to show our purpose and values."
- "Outcome of deepening our purpose is in parallel with the results of our engagement survey."
- "Sharing your personal purpose: what makes you tick?" "I would like to discuss our purpose in my MT."
- "Next time I would like to share my personal purpose with you during dinner."
- "I want to structure values and purpose in a story for the R&D organization. Part of the trainings and all kinds of things."

We co-created a structure that related the values in a meaningful way, where we kept the relation with the leadership view intact. There was a strong awareness, how to verbalize your thinking. Every word was carefully chosen and placed in the figure, in three or four iterations.

- *Openness*:
  "Being transparent to others and willing to accommodate your thinking and behavior to new ideas, different viewpoints, working methods and cultural values".
  Around this core value in the middle, three other values were clustered:
- *Trust*:
  "Relying on the non-proven potential of partners". Trust is fundamental for everything. The definition is challenging, especially because of the word 'non-proven'.
- *Perseverance*:
  "Demonstrating unrelenting and adaptive strive towards a goal".
- *Togetherness and Joy*:
  "Feeling part of a community, pursuing a common goal; getting pleasure out of work, its results and colleagues—and get energized by it."

All core values were illustrated by behavioral indicators. In a conversation, you can use these indicators to talk about specific examples, instead of the generic values. You can validate trust by asking yourself and others if you dare to admit failures. 'Openness' can be a topic for a conversation, where you check if you visibly show an attitude of embracing the unexpected. Ask for examples where you did this and where you didn't, in the eyes of your colleague. This process of validating in terms of behavioral examples on a daily basis in the workplace is very impactful. 'Togetherness and joy' can be explored in terms of your radiating a positive spirit and giving compliments. Here too, the conversation is critically important. You can't confirm on your own, behind your desk, that you are showing these behaviors. You have to engage in relation with members of the community. Exploring other views on your way of acting, not so much defending and confirming what you already know about yourself.

7.5 Taking a Pause

Some reflections on the second phase of the journey. It is about the importance of taking the time to have a dialogue on what brings you together as a team in this particular organization. Finding out and formulating precisely with the right words, in a relational co-creative process is critically important for the success of all following phases. Good leadership is about effective and ethical leading, not losing sight of your own and the organization's purpose and values, which serve as a road-map for your thinking, feeling and acting. By having explored this explicitly in the individual dialogues, shared in the personal narratives, conversed in the sessions, and in detail discussed in the small working-groups on the final description, content and intention are deeply anchored. They intentionally created 'ma'—as described previously in terms of Morioka[17]—and felt more deeply connected with their own values and purpose. Once thinking, feeling and acting based on an awareness of your value system has become a habit it helps leaders in periods of crisis in their presence, and their authentic effectiveness. "This idea is at the heart of *dialogical leadership*: dialogue and reflection *in* the self and *between* other selves are essential to developing effective and authentic leadership in organizations and society; they are the key to developing a deeper level of awareness and action."[18]

A second reflection is a more critical one. How to deal with the circumstances that in most modern organizations time is not available to work on the purpose and values in this manner? How often have you engaged in off-site sessions not leading to sustainable value in terms of improved relationships and collaborations? The CEO consciously decided to give every leader in the group individual dialogue sessions before the team sessions started. This in order for leaders to get to know themselves better before trying to understand others, and how they relate to others. Additionally, off-site team sessions were planned periodically (every three months) in order to understand, build and reflect, and create sustainable value. By doing this, you create discipline and motivation to work on how you cooperate, which is sometimes missing in organizations.

---

[17]Morioka 2012; Morioka 2008; Morioka 2015.

[18]Van Loon and Van Dijk 2015, 73.

Are you able as a leader to share your thoughts and worries, even when they are not crystallized in clear views and standpoints? We were able to observe in this journey that the CEO shared his personal narrative at a deeper level during one of the dinners. For the team, this was a remarkable experience, which was followed immediately by others also sharing their views at a deeper level than in the first session. In the context of this section, one quote is important: "If there is a misalignment between individual values and the purpose, then we need to voice that. It needs to be authentic." This illustrates what trust can do. Where cultures meet, differences become clearer in the process of collaboration. Western culture compared to Eastern cultures, such as Japanese, have a different view on feedback. Where in western cultures this might strengthen your position as a leader, in Japan it is culturally not acceptable. Traditionally, the Japanese language had no word for feedback because it just wasn't something that anybody did. So they had to make up a word, *fidobakku*.[19] Yet, it's still simply not something that's done. "If you don't hear from your Japanese manager, you're doing well," Schweitzer says. "If your manager asks for an update on your project that means you're not doing well." This illustrates how reconciling different cultures in your 'self', in your organization can be a 'wicked' issue. An adaptive challenge, where a simple answer is not possible.

Last reflection is about trust. Can people really rely on the unproven potential of others? Interdependence grows together with uncertainty (how to deal with 'wicked issues'?) and so does the need for trust.[20]

> . Generating Trust Relations
>
> The phenomenon of trust among teams is called interpersonal trust, the extent to which a person is confident in, and willing to act on the basis of the words, actions, knowledge, and decisions of another. Interpersonal trust consists of a cognitive and an affective dimension, with both dimensions having been recognized as determinants of successful problem solving.
>
> Cognitive interdependence is the extent to which the interest of a person cannot be achieved without rationally relying upon another. In affect-based trust, emotional ties linking individuals provide the basis for trust.[21] People are likely to rely on the benevolence of others in determining the extent to which they are forthcoming about their lack of knowledge (about the other person). Antecedents for affect-based trust are the level of citizenship behavior (the extent to which you engage in activities and behavior not being

---

[19]Sharon Schweitzer, CEO of Protocol and Etiquette Worldwide, and an expert on how managers can assimilate in foreign countries. Eric Barton in an online article: In Japanese workplaces, positive feedback is rarely given—accolades can cause you to lose face: http://www.bbc.com/capital/story/20160822-why-you-dont-give-praise-in-japan. (2016).
[20]Lavie 2006.
[21]Schaubroeck et al. 2011.

rewarded by the organizational system) and the frequency of informal interaction between the persons involved. Affect-based trust, with frequent social interactions and citizenship behavior, allows people to trust others with sensitive personal information, ideas and knowledge. The resulting social intimacy helps them to develop shared values, perceptions, and mental models.

Interpersonal relationships dominated by cognition-based trust might not always develop affect-based trust and therefore not have the shared values, perceptions and mental models which are important for complex knowledge sharing and, hence, resolve 'wicked issues'.[22]

Whereas one can look at a colleague's resume and remember his internal track record in deciding whether to trust one another, the development of affect-based trust and emotional ties takes time and investment. As in all relationships, the ability to trust one another at face value is an illusion. It needs work on both the cognitive and affectionate level and, hence, takes time to develop.

7.6 Practicing New Ways of Interaction

The third session in the journey was about exploring strategic themes. After having synchronized the minds and hearts in the opening of the session, we started exploring two strategic themes: interacting with the regions and defining core technology. The topics are coming from the first rounds of inventory what is on the agenda for the team and the organization. After having practiced the principles of dialogue and discussion, diverge and converge, the time had come to apply this on real topics, defined as wicked issues. There is no simple technical answer in the handbook of the manager! The answers have to emerge in the process of exploring and conversing the issues. Important here is that—content wise—the members had a sense of direction, derived from the values and the purpose. In the discussions the values and purpose were practiced. For confidentiality reasons, we can't illustrate the concrete discussions in more detail.

Here some reflections on the process are given.[23] The team observed that something had changed in the way of discussing the issues. "The intention is different now in our conversations. Instead of preaching, we start asking questions. By asking the right questions you can understand each other much better." Of course, this was not always and permanently the case. Sometimes we had to do

---

[22]Swift and Hwang 2013.

[23]The quotes were taken during the sessions by Martijn van Hal, who observed and described the entire process.

interventions, but what we also observed is the increased self-adjusting behavior in the sub teams. The moment a team member observed an assumption or ineffective (disturbing) push, this was put on the table. Illustrated by another quote: "We used to communicate in one direction. Now we listen, make decisions and take action. That is really different." This is exactly what we wanted to reach: making people aware how to relationally communicate, instead of sending a message, without relationally checking the feedback loops.

A second observation was caused by the CEO, who explicitly shared his view on the issues and said: "I can't get this fixed on my own. We need to do this together." In the context of sessions like these, this was very impactful for the team. They truly felt recognized as partners in the process of solving adaptive challenges. Our observation as facilitators was that also during breakfast, lunches and dinner, a high level of respect and presence was shown. The mechanism of 'opening yourself' to enable others to open up is demonstrated here.

- Individual Reflection of the Senior Vice President HR

    We learned how to create fundamental understanding by exploring relationships.

    The SVP HR expected the journey would initiate strategic changes which could benefit the company: "I expected new insights in terms of leadership and strategy within the boundaries of our mother company."

    The importance of a shared language regarding values and purpose has proven to be effective. Additionally, the first team session allowed for the identification of key strategic issues which also led to an initial concern with the SVP HR: "we so far only looked at two or three of these, but there are many more important topics. However, I can conclude that by now we talk differently with each other on issues we have to solve. It is clearly more of a dialogue looking for answers. You think more about another person's considerations, barriers, and the things that are on his mind. And then you talk about it."

    Reflecting on how this journey changed the way the leadership works, the SVP HR mentions an improved decision making capability: "I think it is going better, because we come to better decisions and better understanding. For example in the Mid Term Planning (MTP) cycle. I used to be partly involved in this. Now I am fully involved, which enables a better understanding of the whole context. This allows me to translate strategy into my own planning and thus my own MTP gives more answers and results than before. And since I am more aware of the context, I can ask better and more relevant questions." On a more personal level, he tries to withhold his opinion even more: "I try to understand what somebody is saying. For example, I made joint decisions on the staffing of my team to serve the business in a better way. We co-decide in the selection of new people in order to improve the HR practice. This was highly appreciated, and you get shared

7.6 Practicing New Ways of Interaction

responsibility as a result." The extent to which a decision making process such as a MTP is successful or not is a great way of evaluating leadership and team effectiveness due to the fact that multiple domains (incl. interests) need to come together for the common good. Decision making capabilities in itself have the potential to become *dynamic capabilities*[24] and create competitive advantage (e.g. when leadership teams of competitors do not practice and improve).

In his own team, the SVP HR learned to be more careful with his opinion, beliefs, assumptions and facts because it narrows thinking and openness to new thought and insights. "I challenge people to be more precise. People notice there are higher requirements now, work gets more intense and effective." He also mentions that he tries to switch roles from push to pull when needed: "Sometimes you need to decide due to time pressure. But for an initial discussion, using dialogue as such is an improvement. It allows me to challenge people to think further. It's a powerful tool."

The Labor Unions articulated after even tough negotiations on a new Collective Labor Agreement that discussions on difficult matters feel more like a cooperation now. The SVP HR explains: "even though the content was very tough, we had dialogue in a very constructive way. I most of the times operate in a different way now, and I think the Leading Innovation to Grow process accelerated my personal change in being more patient and open."

In the reflection on team values, the SVP HR states that the leadership team is not perfectly living up to its values yet, and that it needs time in order to also involve other colleagues in the process: "we are coming from a tightly compartimentalized organization, based on knowledge areas and decentralized local responsibilities. That is visibly changing but needs time. Within the leadership team, it is eminent but in the layer below colleagues are becoming a bit confused. We need to voice it more." Additionally, formulating a purpose is different from actually feeling alignment between organizational activities and the purpose. "It has to do with what we do and even more important what we don't do so we are able to focus more. We can address more strategic issues and the brutal facts to live up to our purpose." Reflecting on the practical translation of values on the work floor, the SVP HR indicates that on the value of togetherness an initiative is being developed to consolidate different department gatherings and parties into one big joint celebration in order to create a sense of unity and belonging among employees. Moreover, he tries to live the values in working with his HR team by translating the values into daily practice.

Making contact and exploring the relationship for the common good is his key learning. "You do not need to be best friends with your colleagues, but you do need to invest in each other. There is a lot to learn from each other,

---

[24]Eisenhardt and Martin 2000.

and this brings better decisions. And it is also in the small things: the tone in your e-mails, more respect and equality, the ability to address the most sensitive topics. To me, there is more fundamental understanding. And we've learned how to create that. Exploring the relationship". The SVP HR mentions that *dialogical leadership* was stronger than he initially thought it would be: "I am positively surprised. We started very open conversations in our team sessions. Also with the idea to broaden horizons with the team. But very fast, we came to the conclusion that we need to converge instead of diverge. Back to the core, making our organization more effective, more transparent, and as simple as possible. That is also a form of renewal, to achieve more with less, thus enabling us to focus more on the outside world, where our customers and competitors are."

The third observation originates from the environment. After these sessions, the team went back to their daily activities in the company. They are continuously perceived by others, changes in manners of interacting and behaving are noticed immediately is our experience. One comment made illustrates this: "Our controller mentioned that he saw a significant change in how we as a team interact." Apparently, it had become visible that there was more interaction in the team, before it was primarily sending and one-way communication, defending your own point of view. Another observation came from the organizational business planning process: "We now engage more relevant stakeholders, look beyond our own problems and help each other out. To me, it feels like this process is improved and even enriched."

During this session, we deepened the experience of communicating—verbally and non-verbally—by doing parts of the session blindfolded. It is remarkable what happens if you change a 'detail' in the interaction. Instead of using your eyes as a source of information, you have to rely on your ears. We have seen before the experiences of the VP strategy in more detail, what happened in his view. Our observation as facilitators was that respect and trust were deepened in the team. Although they were visibly inhibited, there was no resistance. Everybody accepted the intervention. I want to conclude here with one of the insights, formulated at the end of this session: "Now the most important thing is that our actions speak louder than words. We need to show the people what we stand for (in dealing with wicked issues). We need to incorporate the values into our daily activities and show our perseverance." I like to use the expression that the off-site sessions are like laboratory situations where you practice new ways of thinking, acting and feeling. Success is measured in daily practice.

. Individual Reflection of the Senior Vice President R&D
Before we were individual pieces of pie, today we are one pie with shared responsibility.

The SVP R&D expected to get to know each other better during the *Leading Innovation to Grow* journey. Or as he puts it: "Getting to know each other's drivers and what we find important. And that we would collaborate better as a result".

Looking back, a number of tools have proven to be very helpful in his day-to-day work activities. During the team sessions, the acronym of *Rain and Sun* was used to stimulate dialogue. Rain stands for React, Assume, Insist and Neglect. Sun stands for Suspend, Understand and Nurture. Adopting a 'Sunny' attitude stimulates dialogue and divergent thinking, whereas a 'Rainy' attitude stimulates debate and convergent thinking. He explains: "This Rain/Sun tool gave me insights on myself. Now, I take initiative to check my first reaction with my assumptions".

Reflection of the SVP R&D shows that he also adopts new tooling in working with the leadership team: "in our leadership team we have strong personalities. Previously, you would interpret the statements of your colleague for yourself and then judge based on that, or formulate your own (sometimes wrong) conclusions. Now, I check my assumptions, and that works based on when you talk about it with others. It sounds very trivial but it's really difficult." His articulation of this difficulty is of course no surprise, him being active in a fast-paced environment where flexible and fast switching between a dialogical self—dealing with adaptive challenges—and a decisive self—dealing with technical issues – is an art. It takes time to change and learn, for individuals as well as the leadership team. The R&D SVP indicates this by saying: "I sense that the [leadership] group became more sensitive on whether a conversation is Rainy or Sunny, but I can't say a big change has occurred yet."

Reflecting on his role within the R&D management team, he states that also in this context he is more aware of dialogical roles versus debate roles: "My default is Rainy, so I need to be aware that sometimes you don't get the desired effect. So sometimes during or after meetings I learn that I was in the wrong mode." The impact of the *Leading Innovation to Grow Journey* on the team is too early to evaluate, since the learnings were not discussed with the R&D management team thus far: "People come in and see the values and purpose on the wall, and they want to be involved. I also really want to deploy them in the team and I am thinking on how to do that. If I don't, this way of working will not spread to my team. It is very natural that some people are not aware of how they need to behave, but we will work on that."

The purpose is seen as something very important because "it is something we want together, and to me this is our binding factor. If you make a purpose together, it helps you to find the right direction and to compromise when needed. To balance your own interest with the interest of the other." Looking at the values he points out that perseverance is in the core DNA of the R&D organization, "but that the fact that others in the leadership team also articulated this value really helps to get things done". The value of trust was pointed out by the SVP R&D as being the most important value of all: "with trust, you need to build it. You can say to someone you can trust me, but nobody will ever say you can't trust me. Trust in the other is something which needs to grow within yourself. It needs time and interaction. Experience with others. If we did one thing in the leadership team it is that we had quality time together what we normally don't do during our work. Some years ago we were different pieces of pie, if I go to the board now I have the feeling I go to a team, where we have something to discuss, before this was not the case. Before I felt being controlled, and you would come to a meeting to report". Stressing this he mentions too how the value of trust already manifests itself in day-to-day operational R&D activities: "I always tell my people to assume positive intentions. The value of trust determines how we deal with each other and how we can achieve more together than on our own. For example, in our interaction with international colleagues we sometimes send something over and get questions accordingly. We feel that we did not do our job right. But they really want to understand! They simply do not understand. Our side feels like being judged. But a research question is being posed. We need to assume positive intentions at all times in order to collaborate effectively." The leadership team sessions reinforced this feeling: "it confirmed to me that all the individuals have positive intentions. We all have our own experience, considerations, goals etc. but we are all positive and that gives a good foundation to look for dialogue in difficult situations. Before you retreated to your own fortress and defended it, and didn't really care what others wanted."

When asking him about his important learning coming from the *Leading Innovation to Grow* journey the SVP R&D states that his long-lasting desire to work towards a real team has been fulfilled. "We went from individual pieces of a pie to a team with a shared purpose and individual responsibilities, *one pie*. And we are aware of the interaction between the different parts."

7.7 New Challenges and Old Habits

The fourth session in the journey was about translating insights into actions. After having synchronized, two issues were on the agenda. To be discussed, concluded and, if possible, translated into actions. As mentioned before in the text, we can't describe details here because of confidentiality.

Through working in this manner, discussions and meetings were held on two levels: content and processes of behavior and emotion. As we are able to simultaneously reflect on the content and the process, we are able to formulate actions, and principles of actions. In this case, one of the issues is related to communication. The team developed a new methodology for looking at and dealing with these issues and themes. Figure 7.8 represents a methodology for the process of communication.

Fig. 7.8 New challenges and old habits

- **Individual Reflection of the Chief Executive Officer**
  From Preaching to Reaching.

The most important goal with this journey was to form a team. "That was my goal, and I wanted to be a part of it. In this function, you sometimes experience a little distance between you and the rest, that's a given. It is an art to become a team, and I wanted to be part of it." This was the reason why the CEO chose to include external moderation in team sessions. This would give him during the sessions the opportunity to be part of the team instead of taking the role of the chairman.

"People understand me better because I spoke out. During the team kick-off session, at the dinner table, I mentioned what I find important and what I do not find important. This helps." He explains that in his observations the distance between individuals in the leadership team is much less, and that group behavior has improved. "The way we interact is more easy. For example, last weekend someone e-mailed me that he was going to 'radiate' something. Then I could refer to our saying *from preaching to reaching*, which we came up with during our team sessions, and I asked him to choose different wording in order to be effective. And everyone included in the e-mail understood." A shared experience in another context (read: not your own office) makes it possible to refer to these insights: "Soccer players need to practice in order to win games, we need to practice to align on ideas. You need to practice."

During the sessions, we talked extensively on how to improve openness, trust, togetherness and joy, and perseverance within the organization. Together with the communication team, the CEO decided to take affirmative action and be more open towards employees. Q&A sessions were organized for all sites including a process in which employees could articulate their questions up front in smaller teams to make it comfortable to ask all questions they wanted. All sorts of questions were posed (e.g. on the organization and on the CEO as a person) and were answered in an informal way. The answers were captured via video and put on the intranet. "It is the most visited internal website we ever had, so it had an impact. All internal employees can see it. It was a lot of fun as well. This was not about sending, this was about listening. And I could show a free way of interacting because I was not on stage." This illustrates how values can be operationalized on the work floor. Although a start, the traction in the organization also indicates that many employees have a desire for more openness within the organization.

The relationship with the international mother company is a very important one. The CEO explains how he adopts the mantra *from preaching to reaching* in his alignment meetings: "I spend a week there, my message was full with reaching. Literally. Even though it costs us a lot of effort. I mentioned to them that we would provide them with all the resources they need to support them. As opposed to last year where we said that you need to do something different. Last year, we were preaching. Today, if something does not work well, we send a team to help. It charges resources (time and people), and it is not our formal task. But we do it as we think we need to."

When answering the question to what extent the team values are embedded in the leadership team he explains: "By trial and error". I've been abroad to the mother company and when I debrief to the leadership team here, it is different from how I used to do it. A feeling of togetherness increases with that. And when being abroad I do not hold back, I am open". But there is still a challenge to improve interpersonal relationships: "we are pretty rational people, but you also need to understand each other's emotions and drivers. Understanding in the leadership team has improved, but will still need more effort. The value of trust manifests itself in interacting with customers, as the CEO explains: "The systems business is not a hit and run business. I sell something you will need my support for, for years. And I need a customer because there are not so many customers in this business. We are in a trust-based business".

The key learning for the CEO is that working together is very difficult and that it needs time to become good at it. One of our observations during the *Leading Innovation to Grow* journey was that leaders sometimes wanted to get too quick to a content level. But the content was not the point. "We worked very hard on how we cooperate, whereas normally you work on the content. We wanted to make sure that while being at work, we are effective". Off-site team sessions are appropriate for this purpose. The CEO stressed the importance of getting to know yourself before trying to understand others. "We gave everybody in the leadership team a year of coaching because we are very rational in our cooperation [...], because you cannot understand others if you do not understand yourself." This reflection illustrates how important individualized preparation for team leadership meetings is, since a realistic sense of who you are is key in accelerating mutual understanding.

Some insights people shared at the end of the last meeting. "I experience more voicing. Preaching versus reaching I practiced." Based on the experiences people have in dialogue (listening, respecting, suspending judgment), they started to practice this in their daily communication. Remarkable here is the sentence that one participant heard more voicing and less preaching. The mode of communicating is —in the view of this member—significantly changed. In general, it is important to know that voicing and preaching are two completely different modes of communicating. Preaching is like monologue, pushing a message; voicing is relationally verbalizing what can/needs to be said in the relation, it is the right (relational) balance between vision, pulling and pushing.

"Openness and transparency is something that is really appreciated by employees. They were very happy. There was a lot of unrest. This was picked up by communication and others. Financial figures led to rumors and uncertainty. With the information of the CFO, everybody was on the same page. The fact that we were transparent was appreciated and also the content." This is an example of actions, visible in the context of the entire organization. Thanks to the improved bonding in the team, actions were not solitary, but agreed and executed in a consistent manner. Although it seems simple, realizing and applying in the right mode and time is not easy. As the team felt a stronger connection with one another, their way of acting internally and externally became more consistent and impactful. And the behavior of the leaders has changed, as is demonstrated in this quote (shared with the entire team): "I've been on the road a lot for townhall meetings at our different geographical locations. At a specific location people expected me to deliver a message. I could use the CFO's message to do preaching and reaching. It was an eye opener, and the impact is huge. We invest to grow and tighten the balance. In terms of mindset, I said we have to go from preaching to reaching. Try to create pull. It came across well I think." The last quote I want to give here is about the process. "We do Inter Vision in the team. I was triggered by the openness. We ask each other to question and provide courageous feedback. It gives great insights."

They learned to listen, to visibly show respect, to suspend their judgment, before voicing. They learned to reflect on their own thinking, feeling and acting. They learned to trust each other. They learned the ineffectiveness of impatience. They have improved in their leadership styles by creating more pull than push. The team is ready for the next step: "This team with the right state of mind can achieve its target. We wanted to define ourselves, give us common purpose and become a team. We did it. We are ready for a next step." These were the concluding words of the CEO. Of course the journey is not over. Tomorrow is another day, with *new* challenges and *old* habits. But the level of relational connection, of behavioral and mental awareness has significantly increased. And, as we have seen in the reflections on time and space, presence has to be shown every single moment. Having been present in the past is not a guarantee for being present in the NOW.

Our critical reflections will follow at the end of the chapter, here we celebrate success for a while.

7.8 Reflections

Let's give some reflections and comments on the cases in the last four sections.

7.8.1 Dealing with Misunderstanding

The first is that you have to be able to deal with misunderstanding, with being misunderstood. As misunderstanding between people is inherent in relations, there is a task for people in a leading position to effectively deal with this phenomenon. In each form of communication (conversation, debate/discussion, dialogue), you recognize that misunderstanding is inherent to each and that your task as a

7.8 Reflections

dialogical leader is to create connection points where internal and external (I-) positions converge. Respecting alterity, as being different from your own view or feeling is crucial in enabling the process of transformation for yourself and for others (team, organization).[25]

A group passes through several phases in a journey as described above. Mostly people start being polite. In the phase that behavioral routines are broken, people experience chaos and are 'moved out of their comfortzone'. Resistance and anger are part of this phase, symptoms we have perceived and felt in our cases. Taking responsibility to *not* take responsibility is difficult for participants and for facilitators and chairpersons. Often they tend to solve the issue *for* a group or an individual. What you really need to develop as a facilitator is the ability to endure the stage of chaos without interfering or intervening. By not-acting, not interfering, you enable the group to go through this phase of chaos. Emotions are part of this process of changing mindset, where I perceive people becoming really irritated and demonstratively disconnecting. In Isaacs'model, this refers to the crisis *in* the container. Once the group has passed that stage, the atmosphere changes, the way of conversation, listening and showing respect to each other is transformed and the way to change might be embedded in the group and more solidly anchored in each of the individuals.

One of the most challenging misunderstandings is 'making jokes'. The first example is, where a facilitator opens with making some kind of joke, with the intention to release the atmosphere. I recommend to not act like this. If you start with jokes, the risk that the participants in the group will not take you seriously increases significantly, and you might set a wrong example. A second example is how to deal with jokes in a group. I have often perceived, that someone makes a serious remark or asks a thoughtful question, and as an immediate response somebody else makes a joke, about the person or what is said. As a facilitator, I immediately act upon this, to clarify that in a dialogue atmosphere, where we want to think together, these actions are not acceptable. Suspend your reaction, endure the tension. In particular, when we work with high level leaders, I refer to being able to endure stress as important for leaders and followers. If you make a joke, try to be clearly aware of the possible impact. If humor makes the container more stable and relaxes the atmosphere in the group, it is a welcome support in the process.

I remember clearly that we had a dialogue session with European leaders of a multinational in a beautiful venue. I had individual conversations before the meeting, everybody was prepared for a meeting of the minds. The first phase of building the container went rather smoothly. Participants were concerned with safety and trust, they respectfully listened to each other. They opened up more or less and told their stories about what in their view could be the vision for the company. Questions were asked and answers were given. In the afternoon, we wanted to go one level deeper going through the instability of the container towards proper inquiry. Suddenly, one of the participants became very irritated. He spoke up

---

[25]Hermans 2006, 53.

and said this was all waste of time. Why didn't the chairman of the session conclude and take a decision on the subject. This young leader was one of the most promising high potentials in the team, but he could not endure the stress of not getting an answer—immediately. By explicitly and visibly connecting with his irritation (= deconcentrating) we could quiet him down and open his eyes for how a group manages chaos to find each other in a deeper shared view on purpose and values for the company instead of one chairman formulating answers for the rest of the team. The intervention had two goals: calming down the emotions of the frustrated young leader and consciously directing the clashing energies into the direction of a generative dialogue, and not degenerate in a rational debate or discussion. Interventions at this level are not purely techniques, but a result of personal experience and strong presence in a dynamic balance of deconcentrated—letting things go—and concentrated—deliberately directing—interventions.

7.8.2 Dealing with Paradoxes

A second reflection concerns how you deal with paradoxes. Trompenaars developed a methodology to deal with paradoxes across cultures.[26] This process of reconciling is a striving towards and/and thinking, instead of either/or; win/win instead of win/loose. Characteristic for dialogical leadership is that it strives towards win/win. This *organizational ambidexterity* is essential for effective leadership and successful innovation.[27] Although in reality we are often caught in problems, puzzles and polarities, I emphasize that embracing paradoxes and dealing with the unknown, is typical for a dialogical leader, *if possible and appropriate.* Paradoxes can be defined as "opposite demands placed on leaders that *seem* to be contradictory, but can be combined in innovative ways."[28] If a leadership paradox is viewed as an opportunity to find a way to get the best of both worlds, a polarity is reconciled in a third position, in a *synthesis.* Meyer and Meijers distinguish five categories of paradoxes for leaders. They are summarized here in line with the categorization in this book in three basic roles, entrepreneur, manager, and coach.

In the role as *strategist/entrepreneur,* a leader has to deal with strategy issues, which relate to goal-setting. If we formulate this in terms of a paradox, it is that of *idealism and realism.* You can lead in a visionary style, emphasizing idealism and long-term ambitioning ('I have a dream!') versus leading in a pragmatic style, emphasizing realism and setting practical and realistic targets. A second paradox for the strategist/entrepreneur is that of *exploiting and exploring.* Leading in an executive style of exploiting and optimizing the existing organization can be

---

[26]Trompenaars and Hampden-Turner 2004.
[27]March 1991; Duncan 1976; Tushman and O'Reilly 1996.
[28]Meyer and Meijers 2010, 4.

7.8 Reflections	237

opposed to leading in an entrepreneurial way, focusing on creating the future organization.

In the *manager* role, you have to deal with the paradox of *unity and diversity*. This is about organizational issues. One option is leading in an integrative style, where you focus on unity, like-minded people in a cohesive team. The other extreme of the paradox is leading in a federative style, where you focus on diversity, a variety of people in a complementary team. Remember there is no predefined answer, dialogical leadership is about intentionally creating space between them. The second one for the manager is that between decision-making as the paradox of *directing and participating*. One manner is leading in an autocratic, top-down direction setting style as opposed to leading in a democratic, bottom-up participating and decision-making style.

In the *coach* role, a leader has to deal with people issues. Controlling can be described as a paradox of *giving tasks and creating conditions*. You can lead in a supervisory style, where you emphasize tasks and control performance in a direct manner. In a facilitative style, you create the conditions for monitoring performance indirectly, where accountability is directly with the workers. The two extremes of feedback can be described as challenging and appreciating. Leading in a demanding style implies challenging and confronting people, while an encouraging style appreciates and expresses confidence.

7.8.3 *Paradoxes in Terms of I-Positions*

A third reflection is about self and purpose in terms of the paradoxes as Meyer and Meijers describe these. Their ways of looking at the self of a leader fits perfectly in a dialogical self-perspective. You can formulate the poles in the paradoxes as well defined possible I-positions:

- I as *reflective*, emphasizing thinking, developing the best path forward in an analytical and disciplined manner;
- I as *proactive*, emphasizing acting, taking measures in a direct and intuitive manner; 'Just do it!';
- I as *authentic*, as leading in a consistent style, emphasizing predictability and remaining to your default approach;
- I as *adaptive*, as leading in a responsive style, where you emphasize flexible adjusting.

An open and empty self implies that you are able to develop several of these different aspects, as we have seen in the described cases. Depending on the I-position people can show completely different styles.

In this book the importance of values and purpose is stipulated. In the terminology of these paradoxes the differences between people and approaches can be described clearly. In dealing with purpose, you talk about core values where we have the paradox of being wealthy and being healthy. Leading in a *value*[29]*-driven style* implies emphasizing wealth, focusing on working in an economically sound way and making money. Leading in a *virtue-driven style* is about emphasizing health, working in a physically, mentally and spiritually sound way. If we look back at the Océ case and the individual cases, we can clearly see people struggling between these two poles of the paradox. In terms of sense making the last paradox is that of *self-actualizing and serving*. Do you lead in a *sovereign style*, emphasizing your self-actualization, and focusing on your self-interest? The other pole is about leading in a *servant style,* where service is central and the focus is on the common good of the organization.

If we characterize the servant and the sovereign in the vision—push—pull scheme, *I as a sovereign leader* is plotted as predominantly push, while *I as a servant leader* is generally pull. In the manager and the coach paradoxes, both push and pull styles might be appropriate, depending on the situation at hand. Embracing a paradox means transforming by 'opening up' in the space *between* the two poles, and creating the condition in yourself or the team for new meaning to emerge. Solving a paradox rationally is difficult. In terms of Libbrecht, you have to move into a level of field awareness. By defining paradoxes as I-positions, the possibility emerges to reconcile opposites as we have demonstrated in the cases. A dialogical mindset is condition zero to reach this level of reframing your thinking, feeling and acting. Applying the concept of Dialogical Self and Dialogical Leadership might be a step forward.

7.8.4 Working with Core-Values

A fourth reflection is about how we work with our core values as a firm. As a global company, we have formulated core values: Integrity, Outstanding Value, Commitment to each other, and Strength from Diversity. The added value of these values comes to life if they are embodied in the leadership and embedded in the firm's organizational culture. As a team of leaders, we intentionally worked on the art of being a good leader. Through dialogue at the table with your peers, we developed straight talk, how to engender trust, to show true collegiality.

What I learned from these exercises is that setting up a real dialogue is critically important in building trust and safety among each other. And that the role of the leader of the team is of utmost importance, showing genuine interest and setting the example of the leadership style that we want to show. Be aware of the difference of making a statement or asking a question. Become more aware of multiple levels of language, verbal and non-verbal. And, simple but crucial for true understanding each other, checking whether a question is satisfactorily answered. If not, asking

---

[29]Remind the confusion between value as financial and moral. Our language uses the same word with two completely different connoted meanings.

what part of the question is still unclear, and try again to answer. If the mechanism of checking has become habitual in the team, we have won an important battle. Simple agreements such as mobiles switched off, laptops closed, being non-verbally visibly present in the meeting and only speak if you have to say something. All this contributes significantly to presence in the meeting, prevents people to waste each other's time and makes meetings to become more enjoyable, efficient and worthy to attend.

7.8.5 The Strength of Weak Ties

What we have seen in the cases is that you have to look closely to the repertoire of I-positions. If you find I-positions with a weak tie, you might have found an opening for future transformation. That is also why I mentioned that the facilitator of the dialogue has to be experienced in hearing these connections. Remember as an example the 'sailor-captain' in one of our cases. If the other person in the conversation does not make the I-position explicit and asks questions about how it is connected with the rest of the system, it will disappear unnoticed. *Weak ties* are valuable in terms of change as they give new and so far unknown, implicit information, either about the network or about the self-narrative. Whelan and others[30] elaborated this in a convincing way for networks in organizations. The power of weak ties in a transformational project in an organization can be illustrated by an individual team member, which is on the edge of your team, but connected with other networks outside of the team. If you are able to activate this internally weak 'tie', it might become essential for creating transformation. With this in mind, we go to the last section, where I describe some implications of Dialogical Leadership.

References

Asscher, M. (2016). De rol van Leider. [The Role of a Leader]. *De Gids, 3,* 3–7.
Barton, E. (2016) http://www.bbc.com/capital/story/20160822-why-you-dont-give-praise-in-japan
Bohm, D. (1996). On Dialogue. New York: Routledge.
Collings, J. (1996). Building your company's vision. Harvard Business Review. September–October issue.
Duncan, R. (1976). The ambidextrous organization: Designing dual structures for innovation. In R. H. Killman, L. R. Pondy & D. Sleven (Eds.), *The management of organization* (pp. 167–188). New York: North Holland.
Eisenhardt, K. M., & Martin, J. M. (2000). Dynamic capabilities: What are they? *Strategic Management Journal, 21,* 1105–1121.
Heifetz, R. A., Grashow, A., & Linsky, M. (2009). *The practice of adaptive leadership: Tools and tactics for changing your organization and the world.* Boston: Harvard Business Press.

---

[30]Whelan et al. 2011.

Hermans, H. J. M. (2006). *Dialoog en misverstand. Leven met de toenemende bevolking van onze innerlijke ruimte.* [*Dialogue and Misunderstanding*]. Soest: Uitgeverij Nelissen.
Hickman, G. R. (2016). *Leading organizations: Perspectives for a new era.* Thousand Oaks: Sage.
Isaacs, W.N. (1993). Taking Flight: Dialogue, Collective Thinking and Organizational Learning. *Organizational Dynamics,* 24–39.
Isaacs, W.N. (1999). *Dialogue and the art of thinking together. A pioneering approach to communicating in business and in life.* New York, NY: Doubleday.
Lavie, D. (2006). Capability reconfiguration: An analysis of incumbent responses to technological change. *The Academy of Management Review, 31*(1), 153–174.
Lencioni, P. M. (2002). *The five dysfunctions of a team: A leadership fable* (Vol. 13). New Jersey: Wiley.
March, J. G. (1991). Exploration and exploitation in organizational learning. *Organization Science, 2,* 71–87.
Meyer, R., & Meijers, R. (2010). *Souvereign or servant? Cross fertilizing 20 approaches to develop a robust leadership style.* Center For Strategy and Leadership and Krauthammer. (3th revised edition).
Morioka, M. (2008). Voices of the self in the therapeutic chronotype: Utuschi and Ma. *International Journal for Dialogical Science, 3*(1), 93–108.
Morioka, M. (2012). Creating dialogical space in psychotherapy: Meaning-generating chronotype of ma. In H. J. M. Hermans & Th. Gieser (Eds.), *Handbook of dialogical self theory* (pp. 390–404). Cambridge: University Press.
Morioka, M. (2015). How to create ma—the living pause—in the landscape of the mind: The wisdom of the NOH theater. *International Journal for Dialogical Science, 9*(1), 81–95.
Schaubroeck, J., Lam, S. S., & Peng, A. C. (2011). Cognition-based and affect-based trust as mediators of leader behavior influences on team performance. *Journal of Applied Psychology, 96*(4), 863–871.
Swift, P. E., & Hwang, A. (2013). The impact of affective and cognitive trust on knowledge sharing and organizational learning. *The Learning Organization, 20*(1), 20–37.
Trompenaars, F., & Hampden-Turner, Ch. (2004). *Managing people across cultures.* Chichester, West Sussex: Capstone Publishing Ltd.
Tushman, M. L., & O'Reilly, C. A. (1996). Ambidextrous organizations: Managing evolutionary and revolutionary change. *California Management Review, 38,* 8–30.
Van Loon, E. (Rens) J. P. (2006). *Het geheim van de leider. Zoektocht naar essentie.* (*The secret of being a leader. Searching for the essence.*) Assen: Van Gorcum. [Available as pdf file in English translation].
Van Loon, E. (Rens) J. P., & Van Dijk, G. (2015). Dialogical leadership: Dialogue as condition zero. *Journal for Leadership Accountability and Ethics 12*(3), 62–75.
Whelan, E., Parise, S., De Valk, J., & Aalbers, R. (2011). Creating employee networks that deliver open innovation. *MIT Sloan Management Review, 53*(1), 37–44.

Part IV
The Implications

Chapter 8
The Future of Leadership

> *Time present and time past (…) What might have been and what has been Point to one end, which is always present.*
> T.S. Eliot (Eliot 1968. *Four Quartets*. Harcourt, U.S.)

Abstract

- The future of leadership is related to topics as leading and following, hybrid leadership, leading innovation, and leading on big data.
- Leaders and followers are by definition members of more than one context. Dialogical Leadership is a holistic approach for the person and the organization.
- Leadership and cultural research have to be redefined in the sense that research is an intervention in itself, influencing the relation with the object. Hybrid identity is an object for further investigation.
- Current organizations work worldwide with global, multicultural teams. The Kofi Annan Foundation mobilizes young leaders to fight against extremism. Mankind as one global world has to reconcile the agnostic, rational way of living with the mystery of live as experienced in singularity.
- Dialogue is part of an innovation process and needs to be organized carefully. A mindset of innovation and dialogue have the same characteristics.
- Reality is unpredictable. Confronted with *big data,* a mindset of scrutiny is a better indicator for accuracy than a too high level of confidence. Data don't have the same ontological status as physical objects.
- If a team reaches a level of collective silence, it is joyful to be present in that space. Soft discipline is needed to make this into a sustainable habit.
- Everything is relationship. *Ice is frozen water* and *water is melted ice*, so is our perception of the external and internal world.

In an article *Leadership in the Future,* Timothy Mack[1] mentions loss of dialogue in organizations as one of the critical aspects for current and future leadership. As a consequence of twenty-first century technology, all kind of new issues occur: too much information, all voices can have equal authority and authenticity, rise of

---

[1] Mack 2015.

buzzwords and secret professional languages. A loss of dialogue is observed in many leadership settings, while on the other hand internet (digital) communications overload ('din of white noise'). Mack gives the example that teams don't take the time to work on their team-building. And as we have seen in our case, it takes time to listen to one another and share stories about what motivates you in your work/life. Mack concludes that loss of dialogue likely leads to an increasing loss of mutual trust across the organization and society. He puts the question: 'how a leader can be heard against a din of white noise?' And he gives a direction for an answer, "One strategy is to enhance the dialogic nature of leadership communications by enhancing the value, relevance and uniqueness of the information being offered, thereby increasing the likelihood of it being noticed, considered, and acted upon."[2] As demonstrated in the previous sections of this book, if you create the conditions for dialogue, you have to be present, in your role as a leader and as a follower, so the quality of the interaction will rise instantaneously. The dynamics of listening, suspending judgment, respecting and voicing require a mindful presence, and by the act itself, awareness in the participants is improved. How we can make this happen is primarily up to us. We, ourselves, have to give the right example ourselves, *although the system isn't yet completely prepared,* and be mindfully present. Mack continues, that dialogue between leaders and followers "is now technologically possible almost everywhere around the world, thereby performing a number of useful tasks..."[3] He mentions building potential channels of connectivity, building new attitudes, providing both positive and negative feedback and creating special interest groups focusing on personal interests. In my view, all these might contribute to a better communication.

There will be a lot of management and leadership skills, which will be influenced, and maybe replaced, by technological developments and artificial intelligence, such as communication, science, thinking and reasoning, problem solving, and discipline. The role of technology in these aspects will become more and more important, maybe so dominant that we can speak of *e*-leadership, digital leadership. What we don't expect to be substituted by technology are the more creative and collaborative skills "...the ability to identify, understand, interpret, and communicate relevant new knowledge."[4]

Let us have a look forward and rethink some issues described and discussed in this book. First of all that leadership is by definition impossible without followership. In 'You are *always* both' (Sect. 8.1). I will illustrate a possible direction in leadership and culture research, as these two are also—by definition—linked and reciprocally implicated. We can't talk about leadership without referring to the cultural context (Sect. 8.2). Leadership and innovation is an important topic for the future. As demonstrated in the book, the mindset for dialogue and innovation are much alike (Sect. 8.3). Leading on Big Data will be a growing challenge

---

[2] Mack 2015, 11.
[3] Mack 2015, 16.
[4] Mack 2015, 16.

for our world (Sect. 8.4). A few previews, and a description of four possible scenarios. The role of taking a pause and listening to silence (Sect. 8.5) and some reflections (Sect. 8.6) conclude Part IV on the implications.

8.1 You Are *Always* Both

The central line of thinking in this book is that you are by definition a member of more than one context or world, and in this sense you are *always* both leading *and* following. In the foregoing, I illustrated how this works in the internal network of I-positions, an internal dialogue with yourself, who you are and what you want to do is demonstrated by this. An external dialogue with your team, your clients, your organization, your society and markets is also necessary. Network analysis methods confirm this reciprocally connectedness, other than hierarchical. It clearly shows dynamically the mechanism of being mutually connected. Networks can be vizualized, and clearly illustrate how we are relationally co-constructing relations in networks, that are not defined by well-defined and closed hierarchical structures.[5] Leaders will have to transform into 'new' relational leading: developing greater personal capacity to reconcile paradoxes, sensemaking by understanding who you are and where you are in terms of experiencing, expecting and feeling, and telling personal stories, deeply engaging people by crafting truthful stories.[6] We are only at the beginning of a radical paradigm shift. Dialogical Leadership as condition zero for effectively, authentically and ethically dealing with adaptive challenges is a positive change both at the level of the senior leader and his/her team and the corporate level of the organization. It will support current and future leaders in their capability and confidence to face these type of issues, when they are prepared in their mindset and skillset. They are skilled in applying a dialogical approach with its two main elements: using the Dialogical Self Theory as a professional development tool for integrating and reconciling opposing I-positions in the self; knowing when and how to apply the method for creating conditions for an external dialogue between members, teams, and stakeholders in the context. The former affects transformation at an individual level, the latter at the team and (inter-)corporate level, but the distinction between them is unclear, as they can be seen as part of the same continuum. Dialogical Self Theory provides tools to make a real impact and thereby strengthens their leadership capabilities and leadership 'range'—for the long-term good of themselves and the organization. If you want to change something successfully, you have to transform yourself in relation with your environment. Dialogical Leadership is a holistic approach: it envisions the 'whole' person of the leader and the 'whole' of the organization and the way they're connected.

---

[5]Whelan et al. 2011.
[6]Helt 2007.

Lessons in Following Leaders—A Conversation

I had long email conversations with my friend and colleague Rob Koonce about leading-following and the possible tension between the different relations that exist between people in organizations: contractual, collegial, collaborative, and cohesive.

Rob "As you look at the graphics,[7] imagine where you would place the dialogical self in what you see (Fig. 8.1).

Imagine the Dialogical Self as an emergent process in which a leader and a follower initially communicate via a hierarchical mindset. Using this mindset, tasks are commonly approached using an *either/or*, but not *both/and*, social orientation. In a business context, this approach leads to the pursuit of tasks being about me as a leader and you as a follower, but it is not about both of us. Under these conditions, I as a leader issue commands, which you as a follower are expected to passively carry out. (As we imagine this scenario, let us also acknowledge the potential influence of various cultural contexts).

In this emergent process, a hierarchical mindset places the leader and the follower in the lower half (contractual and collegial social orientations) of the figure shown. Here, we could think of the leader and the follower as a bit self-consumed with a lack of awareness of self and those around them as they go about performing tasks. As self-awareness and other awareness emerge, they independently have the opportunity to shift their mindset through self-reflection, training, learning (from trainings and the iterative process itself), and performance feedback. Consider the recent article on Reinventing Performance Management by Buckingham and Goodall[8]—from self-consumption/lack of awareness of self and others to being more fully aware of self and others. This is an independent process through which an individual leader or follower much travel over time to arrive at more collaborative and cohesive social orientations. As this awareness of self and others is perfected, a dialogical self emerges. This is true for a leader and a follower.

Now shift mental gears for a moment and assume that people (as CEOs, SVPs, VPs, Directors, etc.) lead and follow other people every day. Think of them in terms of the relational roles that they play both internal and external to the firm. Here, when we talk about a leader and a follower, we may be talking about one and the same person. The CEO leads and follows SVPs and others all day long as they carry out organizational processes. A VP leads and follows SVPs and directors all day long as they carry out organizational processes.

---

[7]Koonce 2016, 10.

[8]Buckingham and Goodall 2015. Here the importance of conversations is stipulated, be it discussions or—preferably—dialogues "…a better understanding comes from conversations—with your team leader about how you're doing, or between leaders as they consider your compensation or your career." (50). Core of the reinvented performance management system is that people are *recognized, seen,* and *fueled* by these conversations with their leaders.

8.1 You Are *Always* Both

Fig. 8.1 Emergent mindset: from hierarchical to dialogical

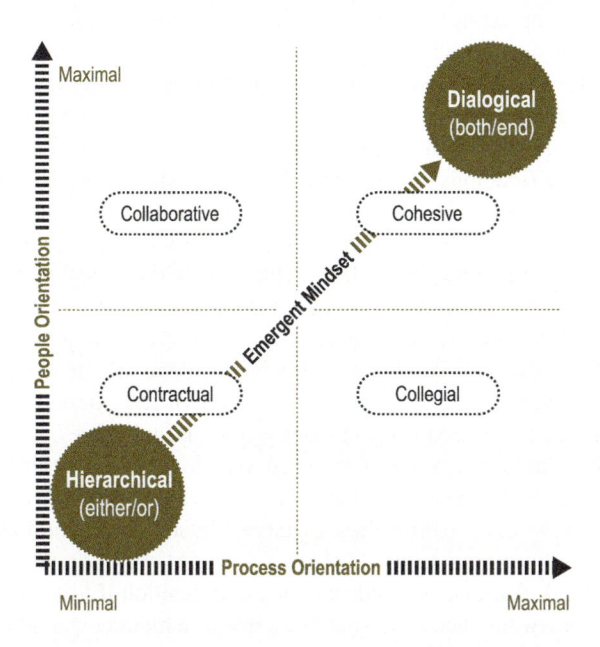

Now, think back to what I state about the hierarchical (either/or) vs. dialogical (both/and) mindset. As the Dialogical Self emerges, we shift from either/or (i.e, being *either* a SVP *or* aVP/Director) to both/and (i.e., we acknowledge and learn to better appreciate that whether we are a SVP or a VP/Director, SVPs and VPs/Directors are in this together…and the more that the SVPs and VPs/Directors become cognizant of this truth through self-reflection, training, learning (from trainings and the iterative process itself), and performance feedback, the more likely that we are to produce cohesive outcomes for the sake of self, others (relationships…teams, departments), and the collective (the organization, the greater community, etc.). If we choose to operate individually, relationally, and collectively through a hierarchical mindset, we lose individually, relationally, and collectively. That is not to say that more contractual or collegial orientations are never required in organizational life, but it is to say that without our full understanding of what is required to operate collaboratively and cohesively, we will never achieve our greater potential as individuals in relationships with others both internal and external to the firm in our pursuit of intertwining organizational goals and initiatives."

Rens "You use hierarchical as opposed to dialogical. In our article,[9] Gerda van Dijk and I use dialogue and debate/discussion. Thinking about these pairs of concepts, how would you bring these together: hierarchy—discussion/debate—dialogue?"

Rob "I think that discussion/debate is a mid-position if you will. I believe that it lies somewhere between what I describe as a hierarchical mindset in the truest sense of the word and a dialogical mindset. If a hierarchical mindset is representative of an *either/or* position and a dialogical mindset is representative of a *both/and* position, I believe that discussion/debate represents an imperfect blending of either/or and both/and. I believe that a person who leads and follows through a dialogical mindset is in a better position to truly understand all positions. They are able to better position self in the context of others as a result of their own understanding of self in relation to others. This is a crucial consideration that is too often forgotten in today's organizations. I also relate to what you write when you cite Hersted and Gergen[10]'…suspending judgment and instead being an observer'. Only one who leads and follows through a dialogical mindset can truly appreciate, and operate from, this stance."

Rens "Reading your case[11] is challenging and invites one to start a process of self-reflection. What could be the reason for two intelligent people to

---

[9]Van Loon and Van Dijk 2015.

[10]Van Loon and Van Dijk 2015, 67.

[11]The case describes how a business relationship between franchisor and franchisee ends up in a disappointing manner. "The more that we examined the series of events that had occurred, the more that we and other franchise owners felt like we had all become part of a system that was closed, one-sided, and uninterested in receiving feedback from the rest of the system." Koonce 2016, 7.

wholeheartedly *follow* (without any self-reflection) an offer that you—rationally—know you can't trust?"

Rob "We must begin by appreciating the fact that individuals in organizations are impacted by the past and present. If we assume that the Dialogical Self is an emergent process involving a shift in mindset (from hierarchical (either/or) to dialogical (both/and)), it seems reasonable to assume that as the individual comes to understand self in relation to others, the individual will also come to understand that following is either worthy of one's consideration or not so, at which time, they will exit or voice (which takes us back to the research of Hirschman[12] and other more recent authors). It is all tied together. Throw in a dose of Lipman-Blumen's The Allure of Toxic Leaders[13] and more recent research, and you enter a whole new realm of understanding the self to include the important distinctions between a hierarchical and dialogical mindset, as well as the orientations that accompany them."

Rens "What I don't read in the case is *what* deeply motivated these people to do what they did? They were promised independence, by becoming dependent. They never worked as hard as they did for the organization, but the reader does not get a sense of *why*?"

Rob "The two people mentioned in the case are very passionate people. One of them spent many years reflecting on self. Over time and through a lot of self-reflection, the person was forced to consider the importance of building and maintaining personal and professional relationships. Together, they built a relationship that outlasted an organization of hierarchical mindsets in which they no longer fit."

Rens "What could these people have done differently?"

Rob "Unfortunately, the individual mindset is tied to the relationships that it develops and of which it is a part in teams, departments, and organizations. This is why it is so important, in my humble opinion, for people to understand the importance of leading and following through individual, relational, and collective mindsets."

Rens "Have there been moments of 'insight', that (intentionally? subconsciously?) were neglected?"

Rob "To the degree that insights derive from being a part of a process to which we are tied, yes. We stuff memories away in hopes of arriving at something greater, while also remaining a part of systems that both fulfill and deplete what we have to offer."

Rens "For the reader, this level of reflection is as important as the rational analysis. At a higher level, my most important take-away from the case involves reflecting on the following question: How do intelligent people get lost as blind followers? In my view, this is an important topic for our time,

---

[12] Hirschman 1970.
[13] Lipman-Blumen 2004.

> where we assume people to be able to rationally become aware of what they do and think and, at the same time, seem to be following a path that will lead to emotional and financial impoverishment. The case described in your article might be illustrative for this purpose. Maybe this could be a topic for another article, where we analyze moments of insight, overlooked by followers, disregarded by leaders. Perhaps this could be a stepping stone to the *dialogical follower*."
>
> Rob "I look forward to continuing our dialogue."

8.2 Redefining Research into Leadership and Culture

"From a constructionist standpoint, it is useful to view organizations as a *field of conversation*. Wherever people are conversing, they are co-constructing meaning."[14] The Dialogical Self could be applied to working in and across cultures, to find out how we can promote a hybrid 'self' and 'organization'. Therefore we have to go in depth and use the external and internal dialogical capacity in people and organizations to create a greater insight in how this works.

Jutta König did an excellent research project,[15] where she makes use of the Dialogical Self Theory to create a greater insight in how cultural identities are formed. The research explores inner dialogues and interaction of people with different cultural backgrounds. Results show implications of globalization processes on individual development, how environmental discourses resonate in the emotional layers of personal cultural I-positions, and the innovative potential of dialogue in safe places. In using a methodology based on the Theory of the Dialogical Self, we will be able to delve deeper in the cultural diversity and polarity to define ways for dealing with the tensions. König designed a methodology, Personal Emotional Account of Cultural Experience, to understand the complexity of hybrid identity. One of her conclusions that has to be explored further is: "It would seem that dialogues in the social domain are mirrored in the Dialogical Self of migrants, and that we can recognize an internal power structure between personal cultural positions that is related to dominant discourses in society."[16] In her analysis of the role of 'ma' in dialogue and transformation, König's reflections are illustrative. "*Ma* can be defined as experiential place understood with emphasis on interval. There is no equivalent single term of *ma* in the English language, although I feel that perhaps liminality, interstitial and transition are closely related to the concept. Perhaps the essence of hybrids (....) is not their differing cultural positions but the

---

[14]Gergen 2009a, 145.
[15]König 2012.
[16]König 2012, 340.

8.2 Redefining Research into Leadership and Culture

space they occupy in the in between."[17] Here König comes close to the core view of this book: in dialogue, transformation is created in 'ma', *the space between*, where free energy is flowing and new meaning emerging. Cultural hybrid identity and hybrid leading and following might emerge from the same process.

A view like this helps us to set up research that reconciles rational and experiential approaches, bringing nomothetic and idiographic research methodology together. Dialogue is a way to do research. Gergen[18] makes a distinction between several methods of qualitative research, dialogue being one of them. You cannot exclusively research as an external, third person (it), but also as a first (I) and second person (You). König gives an example of how first and third person research might be combined. In my view, dialogue and dialogical research will be important for future leadership research and innovation. The science of physics pays attention to the role of the researcher/observer. What is the impact of the act of looking at an object? Is psychology a science of brain functions? Is psychology the study of a process of constructing meaning and the function of the brains in that process? If science wants to take the subject and subjectivism as an object for scientific study we logically come to the conditions and characteristics of the dialogue. You make an intervention if you do research. The sole act of asking a question, giving a form to fill out, and every conversation have their traces. In all social sciences, the very act of researching in itself inevitably changes (re-constructs) the relations you have with the object/subject of study. It is impossible *not* to intervene, once you enter into a relation. I refer to Libbrecht's analysis of Science, Religion and Nature, as described. We have to be clear in what we pursue and remember that the languages of Nature, Science (logicity) and Religion (mysticity) are *by definition* incompatible.[19] We have to find—in dialogical self-terms—a third, or meta-position. In terms of paradoxes: we must reconcile the opposites in the paradox.

What we would like to do is a *global cultural transformational research*, where we use philosophies as described in the Dialogical Self Theory, Dialogical Leadership, PEACE-methodology (Personal Emotional Account of Cultural Experience[20]) and other views that have to be determined. Applying this research in developing a globalized cultural approach to get a more refined and in-depth view of '*hybrid*' *identity*, not only as an object of scientific research and curiosity, also as a view on how to promote developing '*hybrid globalizing identities*'. As it is a wicked issue, we have to develop the courage to ask the right questions and create the right collaborative effort.

---

[17]König 2012, 197.
[18]Gergen 2014.
[19]Libbrecht 2007.
[20]König 2012, 255–266.

8.2.1 An Adaptive Challenge

Diversity of cultures is an important topic today for many current organizations as they work worldwide and have to mobilize global, multicultural teams. In this type of teams, you have to deal with a diversity of leadership styles, different cultural aspects and reacting effectively on verbal and non-verbal communication. Several researchers worked in this domain, such as Hofstede,[21] Trompenaars and Hampden-Turner,[22] and House et al.[23] These researchers did excellent work, primarily using quantitative questionnaires and a notion of container self and organization. In line with what is developed in this book and with what is described by Gergen,[24] I would like to expand this with qualitative research methods. My plea is for reconciling quantitative and qualitative research. Libbrecht's conceptual framework is a strong starting point for a global approach as it tries to reconcile Nature, Science, and Religion. Nature is an adaptive challenge as we are globally confronted with pollution and climate changes. Religious dogmatism is a wicked issue as this is the root for terrorist activities and social unrest. Science is not providing fundamental answers, as it is by definition more technical than fundamental about the core values of global society. Here is a true challenge for current and next generation of leaders and followers, be it in nature movements, in science paradigms or in religious groups. Let's have a look at one of these initiatives: the Kofi Annan Foundation.

The Kofi Annan Foundation fosters dialogue and leadership among young people by offering a platform where they can express their ideas and propose solutions to major public issues. More than half the world's population is under the age of 30.[25] These young people tend to be hardest hit by the world's inequalities and injustices. Their voices often go unheard even though they will inherit the consequences of decisions made today. For example, in recent attacks in Brussels, Lahore, Paris and Mali, the ongoing foreign fighter phenomenon, the thousands of young people who continue to join radical groups such as ISIS and Al Qaeda, and the emergence of far right extremist groups in many countries across the world, remind us that the threat from violent extremism is a global and generational struggle. On 12 April 2016, the Kofi Annan Foundation, with the support of the European Commission and One Young World, brought together ten young leaders. In the months to come, they will steer the way in countering and preventing violent extremism. Ten exceptional leaders with proven track-records in preventing and countering violent extremism in their communities were selected from 72 countries. Under the banner "Extremely Together", they will pool ideas, share experiences and produce a toolkit enabling them, their peers and thousands of young people

---

[21]Hofstede 1991.
[22]Trompenaars and Hampden-Turner 2004; Hampden-Turner and Trompenaars 2000.
[23]House et al. 2004.
[24]Gergen 2014.
[25]www.Kofiannanfoundation.org.

around the world, to turn the tide in the fight against extremism. "We are ten young people from diverse backgrounds who have, in our own ways, sought to find positive responses to violent extremism" Hajer Sharief from Libya said. "Now we have joined forces to learn from each other's experiences.""We will show that no matter where we are from, what faith we believe in, ethnicity we have or belief system we hold dear, we will not be silenced by the destructive, divisive and simplistic narratives told by a minority of extremists", Ilwad Elman from Somalia said. "Our vision for the future carries more hope, is more compelling and we aim to demonstrate that in the months to come."

Extremely Together will equip young people in communities around the world with tools and methods and inspire their peers with perspective where there is hopelessness, trust where there are misgivings, and unity where there is division. At the meeting in Geneva, the group vowed to tell the world a better story, to counter extremist narratives and encourage likeminded efforts globally. "We will bring those experiences back into our communities to support others driven into extremism by hopelessness, rage and false promises".

With extremist groups exploiting the grievances and identity crises shared by many young people, using social media platforms to radicalize and recruit peers, the next generation is perfectly placed to lead counter-extremism and build a peaceful and more stable world. "Nobody can do this alone", Neven Mimica, European Commissioner for International Cooperation and Development said. "We particularly need the support of our young people, their energy and passion, their innovation, insight and knowledge", he added. "This is why I am thrilled about our partnership with the Kofi Annan Foundation, which is aiming to empower young people to harness their creativity and take a leading role in the fight against violent extremism by using the most effective communication and educational tools". "I have great faith in the next generation" said Kofi Annan who joined the young advocates in Geneva, "It is time they take the lead now and start shaping the world that they will inherit." "We vow to be extremely constructive, extremely engaged", Björn Ihler from Norway said. "We come from diverse backgrounds and want our name to express the unity we all felt when first meeting one another. We truly are extremely together in this cause".

. Extremely Together's Young Leaders

- Ilwad Elman, from Somalia, who works to deradicalise members of Al Shabaab and promote gender equality in Africa.
- Bjorn Ihler, from Norway and survivor of the Anders Breivik terrorist attack, who uses art to counter extreme right wing narratives.
- Arizza Nocum, from the Philippines, whose initiative builds libraries to promote education and interfaith as a preventative solution to extremism.
- Syed Ali Abbas Zaidi, from Pakistan, who founded three non-profits focusing on counter extremism, social innovation, and interventions at different intersections between society and state.

- Hajer Sharief, from Libya, working to engage women and young people in peace building.
- Ndugwa Hassan, from Uganda, who works to train teachers, Imams and young people in countering violent extremism.
- Mimoun Berrissoun, from Germany, and co-founder of 180° Wende, a Cologne-based organization engaging with young people affected by extremism.
- Fatima Zaman, from the United Kingdom, who works to research and advice on counter-extremism policy.
- Jonah Obajeun, from Nigeria, whose work advocates education-based solutions to prevent radicalisation and extremism.
- Zaid Al Rayes, from Syria, who aims to create economic opportunities for the young to show alternatives violent extremism.

Some reflections on this initiative. I was struck by this initiative of the Kofi Annan Foundation. In terms of the core message of this book, fighting against extremism is fighting against radicalization of one I-position in your self. It is about creating space in your self and allowing the polarities in your self to start a dialogical relation. I heard a strong example during one of my lectures at Free University in Amsterdam. When asked for examples of conflicting I-positions, a young female student voiced two: how can I reconcile the *atheist* in me with the *Christian*? This is a strong example; and it will take her some time to bring these aspects in her self together. Humankind as one global world has to reconcile the agnostic and rational way of living with the mystery of life that we experience daily. Each day we can see this in beauty and in ugliness, in the birth of a child and the open eyes of a loving couple, in the unpredictability of a violent attack on innocent people because a voice in the self dominates as a dictator. Our challenge will be to apply the groundrules of dialogue to our selves and to others. This group of young people wants to set the example. I support that wholeheartedly.

8.3 Leading Innovation

Leaders of innovation should be aware that 'good voices' can sometimes be drowned out in the 'noise' of the debate and that participants need to be given time to collect their thoughts. The best ideas and solutions can come in the 'transformational space' between talking and listening and 'settling' on a solution and deciding. Eureka moments and epiphanies do not just happen in baths and under trees: they can happen in a room full of people. Dialogue as part of that process of innovation needs to be effectively organized.

.When Suspending Group Debate Enables Innovation

How can new product development teams best generate ideas and develop them into viable concepts? The 'obvious' answer—through interaction and working together—is not necessarily the right or best one. While some studies suggest group debate and group brainstorming offer significant benefits—for example, the ability to combine and integrate differing perspectives and motivate individuals through competition—others are much more skeptical.

Group interactions are associated with two particular—and related—risks when it comes to ideas generation: 'production blocking' and 'evaluation apprehension'. They can interrupt participants' thought processes, restrict their 'mental searches' and cause them to abort ideas prematurely. They can also intimidate more introverted members of the team, making them less likely to 'share ideas' for fear of being evaluated negatively by others.

These kinds of problems threaten the productivity of new product development teams and, by extension, the future of businesses. Several solutions have been proposed—including the use of skilled and trained facilitators and computer-mediated idea generation—but they tend to be costly and difficult to implement. What's more, their true value is uncertain. We don't know which of them work and under what circumstances—and there is no theory or empirical evidence about how successful they are at turning initial ideas into concepts.

A study from Rotterdam School of Management and Amsterdam University has come up with an alternative intervention: suspending group debate.[26] A method that reduces group 'noise', consists of allowing group discussion, then taking a short (five-minute) break for individual 'brainstorming' (during which participants can put their ideas down on paper) and, finally, re-opening the debate to allow ideas to be integrated into a concept. The authors, Daan Stam et al., tested their method in research involving a sample of more than 200 people and an experiment that simulated new product development teamwork. Participants were split into groups and asked to work on a real-life problem over the course of two months. They found that suspending group debate generated 53% more ideas and 47% more categories of ideas—and a higher number of original ideas.

They also found that these effects were more pronounced for groups with one member or more low on extraversion. This second result is in line with earlier research showing that introverts are less able than extraverts to multi-task and develop their own ideas while listening to others—perhaps because they seek out and are exposed to fewer social situations—but outperform them in solitude and silence.[27]

---

[26]Stam et al. 2013.

[27]Idea #388, Ideas for Leaders, IEDP, https://www.ideasforleaders.com, 2014.

What we have seen so far in exploring dialogue is that a mindset for innovation, as *free energy flowing and new meaning emerging in the art of thinking together*, is essential for dialogue. It is an important condition for finding *new answers* to the questions that are related with wicked issues as described. The conditions for a generative dialogue seem to be valid and conditional for an innovational process. The same principles are fundamental for innovating as they are for dialoguing: being able to suspend your view, instead of reacting immediately and primary, truly understanding what is going on, instead of assuming, and nourishing ideas and thoughts, instead of insisting on your own ideas and shooting off new ideas. These are basic rules applied in innovation workshops, where people learn how to relationally re-construct their worldview, opening their minds and co-create new visions and ideas. The domain of innovation points to a greater awareness of uniqueness and towards noticing and describing singularities. This is a paradigm shift, as we are trained to disregard the unique case in our research and primarily spend time, energy and money on the general pattern. Being immersed in an "ongoing confluence of relating" demands of us a radical change in attitude and behavior.[28] "We now need to explore what our thinking must be like if it has to take place in a 'fluid space', a space in which there are no finished 'things' in terms of which to conduct it, but only strands of *flowing* movement within already flowing surroundings, with occasional *dynamic stabilities* here and there, dependent for their nature upon their relational embedding within the larger flow of activity constituting our overall surroundings."[29]

Dialogical interaction and knowledge renewal are seen as processes that might co-evolve *within* and *between* companies, societies and cultures.[30] David Ballantyne applies dialogical thinking on business knowledge development. "Dialogical interaction helps trust develop between participants, and this facilitates learning and the generation of knowledge in the form of solutions to marketing and supply problems."[31] Ballantyne defines dialogue specifically as an interactive process of learning together.

I plea to set up a global research project, where principles of dialogue are used to explore the process of innovation, both in business, scientific and cultural environments. One of the challenging research projects would be to apply fMRI research on 'moments of transformation', 'the moment you get an innovative idea', 'the moment new meaning emerges in your system'. I-positions might be used to set up this in a 'workshop environment'. My hypothesis is that innovation and transformation happen *in the moment of connecting external ideas and internal I-positions*. I am curious what can be monitored physically in the brains.

---

[28] Gergen 2009b, 304.
[29] Shotter 2012.
[30] To give the reader an idea about the many links between Dialogue and Innovation: http://www.dialogueshouse.nl/the-mystery-of-innovation-dialogue/, http://www.ipma2014.com/28th-ipma-world-congress-linkedin-group-launched-innovation-through-dialogue-starts-here/, http://iese.edu/research/pdfs/DI-0633-E.pdf Using stakeholder dialogue as a source for new ideas.
[31] Ballantyne 2004, 114.

8.3 Leading Innovation

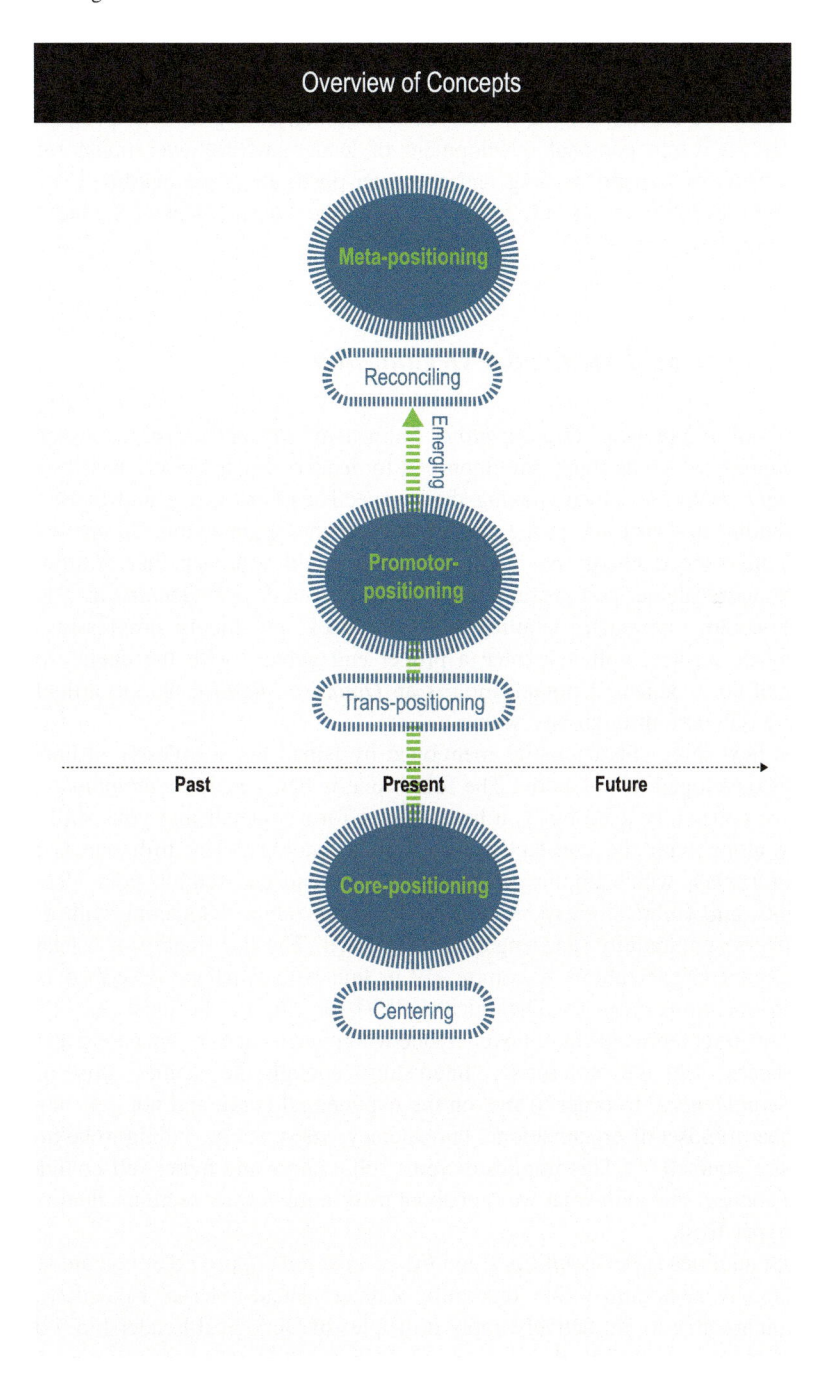

Fig. 8.2 Overview of concepts

In Fig. 8.2 I bring the different aspects of Dialogical Self Theory and Dialogical Leadership together in one overview. In terms of innovation meta-positioning and reconciling are crucial. This is where you intentionally bring in other perspectives. In terms of future personal development of leader and follower transformation mechanisms of transpositioning and promoter-positioning are helpful. Centering and core-positioning contribute to strengthening the current status of the individual leader and follower.

8.3.1 Leading Exponential Organizations

In his book *Exponential Organizations,* Salim Ismail makes a distinction between six qualities, which he thinks are important for leaders. Such a leader is a *Visionary Customer Advocate*, always taking the perspective of the client and consistently representing the customer at the highest level of the organization. To create order out of high-speed chaos requires a process-oriented approach that is ultimately nimble and scalable, and presupposes a *Data Driven Experimentalist* as a leader. A data-centric approach, entailing rapid feedback and timely progression of a product or service, will guarantee a proper engagement with the client. And, a leader of an exponential organization is an *Optimistic Realist,* able to articulate a positive outcome through any scenario.

The next three characteristics mentioned by Ismail are seamlessly in line with what is developed in this book. The fourth one is being *extreme adaptable* in the sense of constantly learning, you have to transform yourself and your skills constantly along with the constantly disrupting technology. The fifth one is being *radically open,* which implies being able to suspend and rethink your ideas and thoughts, and embracing experts outside the organization, interacting with a large and diverse community, and engaging the crowd. The last quality of a leader in Exponential Organizations is completely in line with what we described in this book forthcoming from the Dialogical Self Theory: he or she must be 'selfless'. Ismail even recommends to remove anyone who puts his or her own career ahead of the success of the enterprise. Interesting enough he names this quality *hyper-confidence.* "In order to live on the exponential curve and not get caught in the linear mindset of organizational bureaucracy, you must be willing to be fired or even fire yourself."[32] This implies extreme selflessness and hyper self-confidence. If you connect this with what we said about trust in the former sections, it correlates with hyper-trust.

Both qualities *hyper-confidence* and *hyper-trust* pre-suppose that you are able to intentionally re-organize your repertoire of internal and external I-positions, and that you are able to pro-actively apply principles of Dialogical Leadership. I didn't meet many people visibly showing these qualities, not in corporate companies, and

---

[32]Ismail et al. 2014, 212.

not in start-up or scale-up organizations. In 2016, we were in Amsterdam with some famous leaders, as Chris Anderson (3D Robots/Wired), Travis Kalanick (Uber) and Nathan Blecharczyk (Air BnB), and others. They were invited to think with the audience, leaders in corporate organizations, how to ignite innovation within large organizations with systems and rules of engagement. I was surprised that the tone of voice of some of these leaders was pre-dominantly autocratic and high on push. One of them described his organization as 'externally democratic, internally autocratic'. I would have expected that in a sustainable and ecosystem-oriented organization the sense of collaboration would be more visible in their way of acting.

If I compare this with the preferred leadership style developed in this book faced with wicked issues and adaptive challenges, it is considerably different. Maybe we have to rethink our view on leadership in exponential (start-up, scale-up) organizations, but that is not the topic of this book. I would like to invite you, the reader—in case you are a leader in this type of organization—, to reflect on the issue, and make your own observations to validate or invalidate this statement.

8.4 Leading on Big Data

Leaders of the future have to think about 'big data', you can't ignore this source of information and rely predominantly on your 'market or organizational intuition'. Recently, Michael Lynch published a fascinating book on this topic with a challenging title *The Internet of Us: Knowing More and Understanding Less in the Age of Big Data*.[33] In times where we get our information from internet and develop 'knowledge by search engine', we also need to think about developing 'wisdom', as a combination of knowledge, will and feeling. In terms of what we demonstrated in this book as an approach for dealing with 'wicked' issues, a dialogical approach might contribute to developing this type of wisdom. In generative dialogue, dimensions of ethics and epistemology are simultaneously present in relation with your partners in conversation. In our experience with clients, we have observed that *more understanding* emerged during dialogues. As an example I remember a conversation with a specialist in big data.[34] I was preparing this book, so I was keen to speak with him, as I hoped to get some answers on how leaders can deal effectively with the phenomenon of big data. *But he did not*. Instead of providing me with answers, he asked me questions that I could not answer. He more or less provoked me to find another road to reliable knowledge and wisdom. A few outlooks, just a touch, as it goes beyond the scope of this book.

---

[33]Lynch 2016.

[34]Pascal Occean is a colleague in Montreal (Canada).

8.4.1 Reality Is Unpredictable

He expressed that—although we want to predict as much as possible—reality is non-linear and unpredictable. Nassim Taleb[35] introduced the notion of a *natural fallacy* to describe how imperfect stories of the past shape our views of the world and our expectations for the future. Language implies that the world is more knowable than it is. Kahneman too, warns us that errors of predicting are inevitable, *as the world is unpredictable*. "The core of the illusion is that we believe we understand the past, which implies that the future should also be knowable, but in fact we understand the past less than we believe we do. *Know* is not only the word that fosters this illusion. In common usage, the words *intuition* and *premonition* also are reserved for past thoughts that turned out to be true."[36] For further clarification, I like to go back to Libbrecht, whose view I explained in this book.[37] He formulates this very accurately, as linear causality is only applicable in the domain of logical science, where Subject and Object are separate ($S \neq O$). Taleb, Kahneman and Libbrecht all recommend us to be more doubtful about what we know for sure. Less confidence is a better indicator for accuracy than showing off a high level of self-confidence in stating that something *is true*. Although we know this, leaders and followers tend to rely on predictions, given by leaders and analysts, and ignore this insight.

This applies to *big data*, 'the solution for all our problems'. In the media 'big data' has become a 'frame' to influence the world. Without context of language and knowledge, we don't know what is meant. You have to ask questions to the data to really understand its added value. Data are like 'wicked problems' for leaders: to truly understand its impact and meaning, you have to ask investigative questions, showing a high level of cooperative power and an even higher level of courage in recognizing your own ignorance. To transform data from information to knowledge and as a support for wise decisions, you have to go through this process. Although we gather as much data as possible, and although we can forecast a lot of situations, fundamentally, we cannot predict the world.[38]

8.4.2 Unstructured Data in a Box

The next topic the data specialist gave me was to think about what will happen if we put 'unstructured data in a box', what will be the impact? Although we have great advantage of the data we can use and interpret via our computers, we have to keep

---

[35]Taleb 2010.
[36]Kahneman 2011, 201–202.
[37]Libbrecht 2007.
[38]The human mind is characterized by bounded rationality, and human beings are by nature cognitively limited. March and Simon 1958.

in mind that *data* ontologically *don't exist* in the same way as the Rocky Mountains. *We relationally co-constructed them.* The last difficult question I was asked is how to define '*safe*?' I wanted to check with him if I could rely on the discretion of the data transmitted. I could not give a clear answer, in the same token, as you ask about 'trust'. When can you really trust somebody? How do you know for sure?

So, I expected to get answers, and I was sent home with even more difficult questions. This conversation took place more than two years ago, I am still reflecting on it, against the background that I think that big data should be explicitly connected in our daily practice and thinking with the possibility of a dialogical instead of a purely technical and managerial approach. One of the most critical phases in getting the information right is that we know how to interpret the data. "As we become more reflective, we begin to realize how much our initial perceptions can be colored by expectations based on our cultural learning and our past experiences."[39] We have to develop a sense of proprioception that the data we get projected and produced are accurate. So we have to check the assumptions, what are the basic assumptions upon which the data are built. In dialogue, you ask these questions to (in-)validate and (dis-)confirm. In my view we have to spend much more time and energy in researching—in an objectifying and subjectifying manner —what exactly happens in this global process of datafication. How are people in organizations trained to rightly interpret the data? What makes that a human eye (I) is able to see something, that the system doesn't see, cannot see, and vice versa. What makes the system far more effective than the human perception and assessment? We should pay more attention to these phenomena. In designing data analytic models, we ask series of questions to explore the world. In the process of modelling, *reality checking* is ultimately important as this can provide us with the trust that we measure what we want to measure. In constructing data and the process of measuring, we continuously have to check reality. Working with data analysis in a reliable manner implies at least the two following approaches:

- *Asking questions,* exploring: modelling; constructing data; measuring.
- *Reality* checking: asking the *right* questions; reporting the data *right*.

We remind the reader once again that data in itself is nothing, data must be *related* and *interpreted*. Mayer-Schönberger, one of the big data experts in Oxford, advises using this powerful method in the right way. "New principles are needed for the age of big data (…). Although they build upon the values that were developed and enshrined for the world of small data, it's not simply a matter of refreshing old rules for new circumstances, but recognizing the need for new principles altogether."[40] In finding these new principles, we have to think how dialogical techniques and a Dialogical Leadership approach might be helpful in solving the category of issues that we defined as complex, wicked and adaptive.

---

[39]Schein 1993, 33. See also: Schein 2010.
[40]Mayer-Schönberger and Cukier 2013, 17.

8.4.3 Going Forward

I realize that this section in the book is absolutely not enough to provide you with answers, but hopefully it provides you with new questions and a more critical attitude when you get a big data report tomorrow.

One suggestion for further developments. A Ph.D. student could set up a research project, where big data analysis is integrated with systematic reflection on a process of interpretation, while using the blend of rational analysis techniques and dialogical research methods. We could start with traditional management issues, such as assessing people, decision making and training future leaders, where we integrate big data analysis with dialogical approaches. In the end our goal is to explore how this works out with adaptive challenges. I realize this is not an easy topic for scientific research.

I end this section with a preview of some possible scenarios for future leadership.

> Four Future Leadership Scenarios
> *"Prediction is very difficult, especially about the future"*
> Niels Bohr
> Suderman and Foster[41] undertake a fascinating experiment by designing four extremely different scenarios for future leadership, based on an extensive study of trends and articles on strategic foresight. Based on two axes: the form of leadership: is there a focus on the role of the individual leader (*me*) versus a focus on the group/team (*we*)? The impact of technology in the workplace: is there a focus on dehumanizing versus humanizing the workplace? Based on these you can distinguish between four quadrants:
>
> - *Bio-circuitry Leadership*
>   - Dehumanizing—Me;
>   - 'Knowledge is Power';
>   - Leader typology: Coordinator, Controller, Organizer, Synthesizer, and Monitor;
>   - Team orientation: Performance; Teaming with Technology; Efficiency; and Individualistic Specialists;
>   - Characteristics: emphasis on technology over people; merging biology and technology; emphasis on the management of processes and systematization; rise of specialized knowledge; increased emphasis on silo strategy.

---

[41] Suderman and Foster 2015.

- *High-Pod Leadership*
  - Humanizing—Me;
  - 'Power to the People';
  - Leader typology: Innovator, Entrepreneur, Synthesizer, and Specialist;
  - Team orientation: Coupling Innovators with Altruistic Goals; Human Development; Transformation; and Multidisciplinary Collaboration;
  - Characteristics: the mindset that more is better; emphasis on technology to re-humanize the world; the paradoxical blending of specialists and generalists; networking of people and systems for greater efficiencies; emphasis on transformation, agility and innovation.
- *Murmuration[42] Leadership*
  - Humanizing—We;
  - 'People-Powered Projects';
  - Leader typology: Innovator, Entrepreneur, Visionary, Mentor, Team-Builder;
  - Team orientation: Empowering; Self-Leadership; Transparency;
  - Characteristics: flattening of organizational hierarchies; emergence of temporary organizations; cloud based workers; blending of human capital and robotics; people-centric approach to human capital.
- *Automaton Leadership*
  - Dehumanizing—We;
  - 'Processing People';
  - Leader typology: Driver, Competitor, Producer, and Micro-Manager;
  - Team orientation: Competing; High-Structure; Top-Down; Groupthink;
  - Characteristics: a new emphasis on the great man theory; integration of technology into humanity; internet of everything and everyone; organizations reside in a virtual holographic context; emphasis on results and efficiencies.

Although we can't predict the future of leadership by reflecting on these scenarios, they might help us to prepare for the radically different directions the world of leaders and followers might follow. And remember in 2050 what you thought in 2017 that might happen. Making notes and reflecting is useful in this, it might validate your perceptions and strengthen you to face a principally unpredictable world, a world you live in once you are born in a culture.

---

[42]Murmuration is the phenomenon we observe when a flock of thousands of starlings fly together as one. As they weave and dance through the air, they form changes and evolves, but remain visible as one identity. This leadership scenario mimics murmuration by blending many unique and complex parts into an overarching whole.

8.5 Listening to Silence

With one of my very experienced colleagues, we had a two week program for a global company in Australia. After a few days of individual conversations, we were for three days with a team of senior leaders. After having gone through all the phases described before, we reached a point that I still remember. This session was in 1998. *There was silence in the room.* We were sitting at a large table in the boardroom of the office and it felt quiet. Nobody spoke up loudly, people were chatting with one another with a level of concentration and connectedness that was remarkable. The leader, normally hyper-active, was quieted down. We enjoyed being together. Openness soared through the group. Most impressive was the sensation of real silence. Not the silence where you can hear the unspoken words of the people in the room. I keep this memory as a precious one in my heart.[43]

On purpose, I don't describe the content level in the example above. What I want to convey here is the message of silence, of quietness in the noisy minds of the people around the table. In this atmosphere, a group is more than the sum of the individuals. The collective power of thinking is much larger than the sum of the individual intellectual capacity in the room. In this phase, the way people are present in the room physically, emotionally and rationally, is in tune with the content of the collective thinking, feeling and acting process of the group as a whole. Being one of the people in the room and sensing this experience is a positive energy, enjoyable to be aware of. Is this lasting and sustainable? We have to be realistic. A year later, we had to start again, but we were at the level of the year before in less than a few hours. To make it sustainable, the dialogic process needs to be nourished regularly, as humans tend to fall back to old habits very easily. The soft discipline in sustaining a dialogic mind comes from everybody: those who lead, those who follow, those who facilitate.

8.6 Reflection

Whoever saves a life, it is considered as if he saved an entire world.[44]

Talmud

"He had dreamed a kind of integrity, a kind of purity that was entire; he had found compromise and the assaulting diversion of triviality. *He had conceived wisdom, and at the end of the long years, he had found ignorance.*"[45] This fragment in John Williams's novel *Stoner* struck me. We have to deal with reality of

---

[43]Grint 2010.
[44]Mishnah Sanhedrin 4:5; Yerushalmi Talmud 4:9.
[45]Williams 2012.

8.6 Reflection

leadership in organizations, which is often far from wisdom. "Once you are used to understanding each other in a different and silent manner, you discover how often words just distract from what is essential. The more essential the message, the better it is transferred in silence."[46] In Buddhism reality is described as "empty of independently existing animate or inanimate phenomena. Everything is relationship; nothing exists in and of itself".[47] Although Western action-oriented culture doesn't like these relativizing statements, we have to face them, as we can reach these insights from completely different perspectives. Once we have understood and assimilated this essential idea, we can start working on an accurate view of the world, our ego, and the nature of things and beings. "Wisdom is not a simple intellectual construction or a compilation of information. It arises from a precise methodology that allows us progressively to eliminate mental blindness and the affective emotions that derive from it and, in a way, free us from the principal cause of suffering."[48] Both dialogue and meditation use the effective and healing power of silence.

As being externally *and* internally silent, as ice is frozen water and water melted ice, so it is with our perceptions of the external world. To be attached to the reality of phenomena, tormented by attraction and repulsion, obsessed by gain and loss, pleasure and pain, praise and blame, fame and obscurity, is what causes the mind to freeze. Melting the ice of your judgments and concepts, so the fluid water of free perception can flow.[49] Essentially this state is that of a dialogical mind, internally and externally aware of these phenomena, capable to suspend what pops up in your thinking, feeling and acting.

Developing this practice is important for leaders, for parents, for teachers, for everybody who does not want to be caught in the net of the past or the future. In wordings, used by a neuroscientist: "Memory, tempered by personal feeling, is what allows humans to imagine, both individual well-being and the compounded well-being of a whole society, and to invent the ways and means of achieving and magnifying that well-being. Memory is responsible for ceaselessly placing the self in an evanescent here and now, between a thoroughly lived past and an anticipated future, perpetually buffeted the spent yesterdays and the tomorrows that are nothing but possibilities."[50] That is why every singular word and action are essential: it might bring an individual to insight, and save a world.

---

[46]Japin 2010. Fragment is translated by the author.
[47]Ricard 2011, 138.
[48]Ricard 2011, 138.
[49]Ricard 2011, 141.
[50]Damasio 2012, 297.

"Everything We Come Across Is to the Point"

John Cage[51]

Once a client of mine asked me—as part of an interview to acquire an assignment for his organization, where I had to counsel their executives—what my core beliefs are. Of course, I knew some immediately, but such a pervading question needs also time and reflection. When I came home I summarized. For you as a reader this might help you to do this exercise for yourself and it might support you in the process of understanding what I tried to do in this book.

- My body transforms energy in processes of understanding and experiencing by receiving and transmitting information from internal and external.
- We have to work to survive until we (possibly) reach a phase where living and working coincide.
- My thinking, our ability to analyze in a rational manner, enables us to analyze ourselves and the world around us: articulating life conceptually.
- My sensitivity enables me to intuitively understand people/material directly: intuitively understanding life.
- My existence as human being cannot be explained purely rationally; our existence is a mystery that we can experience genuinely and describe in narrative terms.
- Life is unpredictable, we don't know what will happen tomorrow. 'Everything we come across is to the point' (John Cage). Living the mystery.
- Be careful what you voice as it transforms reality.
- Be carefool. Play.
- "All things of value are defenseless".[52]

8.7 Questions for Further Reflection

- Make a list of your basic beliefs. Write them on a piece of paper, put that away and have a look at your writings ten years later. Notice the similarities and the changes.

---

[51]I heard this quote on the radio in 1988, when our youngest daughter was born. We used the quote on her birthday card.

[52]A poem by Lucebert, often quoted in Dutch.

- Do you remember moments of collective silence? Describe how you felt at such moments. Do you intentionally use moments of silence when you are in a conversation with people?
- How would you describe the future of leadership for yourself, for your organization, and for society? Try to formulate your thoughts in the tension of what is *ideal* and what is *realistic*.

References

Ballantyne, D. (2004). Dialogue and its role in the development of relationship specific knowledge. *Journal of Business & Industrial Marketing, 19*(2), 114–123.
Buckingham, M., & Goodall, A. (2015). Reinventing performance management. *Harvard Business Review, 93*(4), 40–50.
Damasio, A. (2012). *Self comes to mind: Constructing the conscious brain*. Random House LLC.
Eliot, T. S. (1968). *Four quartets*. Boston: Houghton Mifflin Harcourt.
Gergen, K. J. (2009a). *An invitation to social construction* (2nd ed.). London: Sage.
Gergen, K. J. (2009b). *Relational being: Beyond self and community*. New York: Oxford University Press.
Gergen, K. J. (2014). Pursuing excellence in qualitative inquiry. *Qualitative Psychology, 1*(1), 49.
Grint, K. (2010). The sacred in leadership: Separation, sacrifice and silence. *Organization Studies, 319*(1), 89–107.
Hampden-Turner, Ch., & Trompenaars, F. (2000). *Building cross-cultural competence: How to create wealth from conflicting values*. Chichester, West Sussex: Wiley.
Helt, G. (2007). *Beyond: Towards a new paradigm for leadership*. glh@moosewilson.com.
Hirschman, A. (1970). *Exit, voice, and loyalty* (Vol. 1, p. 970). Cambridge, MA: Harvard University Press.
House, R. J., Hanges, P., Javidan, M., Dorfman, P., & Gupta, V. (2004). *Culture, leadership and organizations: The GLOBE study of 62 societies*. Thousand Oaks California: Sage Publications, Inc.
Ismail, S., Malone, M. S., & Van Geest, Y. (2014). *Exponential Organizations: Why new organizations are ten times better, faster, and cheaper than yours (and what to do about it)*. Diversion Books.
Japin, A. (2010). *Vaslav*. Amsterdam: Arbeiderspers.
Kahneman, D. (2011). *Thinking, fast and slow*. New York: Farrar, Straus and Giroux.
König, J. (2012). *Moving experience: Complexities of acculturation*. Amsterdam: VU University Press.
Koonce, R. (2016). All in "The Family": Leading and following through individual, relational, and collective mindsets. Koonce, R., Bligh, M. C., Carsten, M. K., & Hurwitz, M. (Ed.), *Followership in action. cases and commentaries* (PP. 3–14). Emerald Books.
Libbrecht, U. (2007). *Within the Four Seas…: Introduction to Comparative Philosophy*. Belgium: Peeters Publishers.
Lipman-Blumen, J. (2004). *The allure of toxic leadership*. NY: Oxford University Press.
Lynch, M. P. (2016). *The internet of Us: Knowing more and understanding less in the age of big data*. New York: WW Norton & Company.
Mack, T. M. (2015). Leadership in the future. In M. Sowcik, A. C. Andenoro, M. McNutt & Murphy, S. E. (Eds.), *Leadership 2050: Critical challenges, key contexts, and emerging trends* (pp. 9–22). UK: Emerald Group Publishing.
March, J. G., & Simon, H. (1958). *Organizations*. New Jersey: Wiley.

Mayer-Schönberger, V., & Cukier, K. (2013). *Big data: A revolution that will transform how we live, work, and think*. Boston: Houghton Mifflin Harcourt.
Ricard, M. (2011). *The art of meditation*. Atlantic Books Ltd.
Schein, E. H. (1993). On dialogue, culture and organizational learning. *Organizational Dynamics, 22*, 27–37.
Schein, E. H. (2010). *Organizational culture and leadership* (4th ed.). San Francisco: Jossey Bass.
Shotter, J. (2012). Gergen, confluence, and his turbulent, relational ontology: The constitution of our forms of life within ceaseless, unrepeatable intermingling movements. *Psychological Studies, 57*(2), 134–141.
Stam, D., Vet, A., Barkema, H. G., & De Dreu, C. K. (2013). Suspending group debate and developing concepts. *Journal of Product Innovation Management, 30*(S1), 48–61.
Suderman, J. L., & Foster, P. A. (2015). Envisioning leadership in 2050: Four future scenarios: A case for relevant 2050 leadership—preparing for change. In M. Sowcik, A. C. Andenoro, M. McNutt & S. E. Murphy (Eds.), *Leadership 2050: Critical challenges, key contexts, and emerging trends* (pp. 23–38). UK: Emerald Group Publishing.
Taleb, N. N. (2010). *The black swan: The impact of the highly improbable fragility*. New York: Random House LLC.
Trompenaars, F., & Hampden-Turner, Ch. (2004). *Managing people across cultures*. Chichester, West Sussex: Capstone Publishing Ltd.
Van Loon, E. (Rens) J. P., & Van Dijk, G. (2015). Dialogical leadership: Dialogue as condition zero. *Journal for Leadership Accountability and Ethics 12*(3), 62–75.
Whelan, E., Parise, S., De Valk, J., & Aalbers, R. (2011). Creating employee networks that deliver open innovation. *MIT Sloan Management Review, 53*(1), 37–44.
Williams, J. (2012). *Stoner*. Amsterdam: Lebowski.

Chapter 9
Boiling Rice in Still Water

The core message of my book is *keeping your mind open for meaning emerging through all our interactions, on rational, intuitive, and physical level.* If you as a leader open your mind for what is going on in your followers, you can be more effective. You will be able to act in a more adapted way to what is wanted by the people around you, and hopefully that contributes to the world as a better place to live. I have experienced the healing power of generative dialogue. My work in organizational and leadership development and change makes me more aware daily. People love to be engaged in generative dialogues, opening their minds relationally.

This book is intended to make followers and leaders more aware of the world we continuously co-create. This book is envisioned to make you more conscious of other possible selves and worlds that we could create as *better*. I am a strong believer in the saying that change starts with me, with you.

If I change my thinking, my experiencing, and my acting, this will have an immediate impact on my environment.

If we as followers and leaders consciously reflect on who we are and who we would like to become. If you start to act as the one that you would like to become, that will have an immediate impact on your environment.

I do my best to understand and value the world and culture I live in. I am born in the Netherlands, baptized as a Roman Catholic, I live with that historical meaning given to me by my parents and grandparents. In my life, I started to build a strong love for the old Chinese Taoist culture. I became aware of another way of living and thinking. I love Japanese culture. I love Western culture. I came to realize that there are multiple worlds to live in. That I live in a world of multiple meaning.

I had to find a way of acting, to earn my money to buy food and materials for my living. In that world of meaning, I did my best to act realistically, to do well. I became aware of the possibilities of multiple actions. I became aware through a process of relational self-reflection that worlds of meaning are co-constructed within relationships. It makes me conscious of contingency. In another culture and society with different relationships my sense of meaning would have been different, but I live where I live, here and now, with other people around me. I convincingly learned from Viktor Frankl,[1] psychiatrist and creator of logotherapy, that accepting where you are and what the situation requests from you in the here and now, gives a great sense of inner peace.

I became aware that I am not fully determined by the past, that I can change my way of living and giving meaning. To realize this positive message of possible change gave me solid energy to look for new futures, beginning with my own future. By creating 'space', by meditating and by listening to other people, I can consciously take a decision to do something different, to confirm my freedom.

When worlds of meaning conflict, they may lead to alienation and aggression, thus undermining relations and their creative potential. Here we have the task to transform conflicts into chances, adaptive challenges into opportunities. I experienced that increasing your awareness and not identifying with your current position, might give support. My Tai Chi teacher Chee Soo taught me: "If you sense a fight is in the air, choose another route". If you can't escape the fight, keep in touch with your opponent, respect your opponent, and don't show disrespect. George Kohlrieser demonstrated this principle in negotiating in hostage situations.[2] These are the principles of dialogue. By being completely in the *present*, destructive energy might be transformed. Simple statement, not easily done.

Our greatest challenge is to not identify with our little ego…..being just one meaning out of infinite other possible meanings. Remember how we started this book with a quote of Grayson Perry: "My sense of self is a tiny man, kicking a can down the road."[3]

To conclude.

Dialogue exists when you are here and now in a generative relation, where meaning is exchanged and emerges. Hopefully, you realize after having read this book, that we cannot give you a script or a list to be successful in this art. I hope you have received some insights related to the mindset and the manner in which you can create conditions for dialogue, with people around you, within yourself and with the companies, societies, and cultures that surround you.

When you are in a *leadership* position you can apply this in every action you take in your company. When you are in a *follower* position, it applies in exactly the same way. *Relational Leading* implicates that leaders and followers/members of an organization, are reciprocally implicated, they exist because of each other. You are in both positions at the same time. Once you are aware of this phenomenon, you become more conscious in leading and following.

---

[1]Frankl 1985.
[2]Kohlrieser 2006.
[3]Exposition at Bonnefanten Museum in Maastricht, the Netherlands, 2016.

I conclude with an insight that I got while writing this book: like *self*, *dialogue* is a verb, which comes to life in relation, internally and externally. Dialogue is a living relational activity. Are you willing and able to transform at all levels of head, heart, and hands, *while* simultaneously *being space*, in the sense of 'ma', and creating value for your organization, your community, and your family?

Boiling Rice in Still Water.

Rens van Loon,
e.j.p.vanloon@tilburguniversity.edu

References

Frankl, V. E. (1985). *Man's search for meaning*. New York: Simon and Schuster.
Kohlrieser, G. (2006). *Hostage at the table: How leaders can overcome conflict, influence others, and raise performance*. San Francisco: Jossey-Bass.